The Definitive
Israel-Palestine Reader

Table of Contents

MAPS

Mandatory Palestine:

Mandate of Palestine

North Frontier est. by Franco-British Convention of Dec. 23, 1920 (CMD. 1195)

Eastern Frontier: Trans-Jordan separated from Palestine Mandate Sept. 1922

Area: c. 10,000 sq. miles (The size of Maryland)

Source: Central Intelligence Agency. Memorandum: Proposals for Resolving the Status of Jordan's West Bank (Nov. 1, 1973).

i

UN Partition Plan & UN Armistice Lines:

Source: UNITED NATIONS April 1983, Map No. 3067 Rev. 1

Territory Occupied by Israel in 1967:

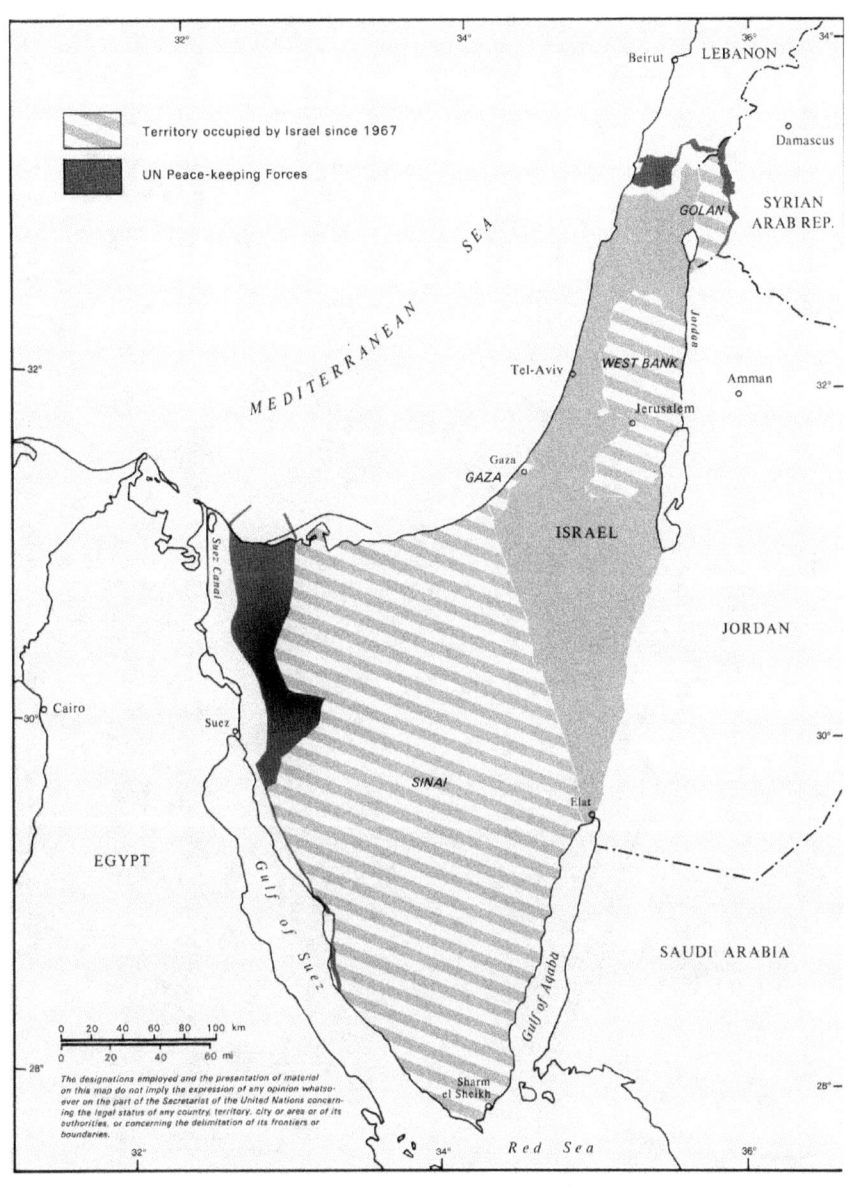

Territory Occupied by Israel Since June 1967:

TERRITORIES OCCUPIED
BY ISRAEL
SINCE JUNE 1967

LEBANON
Quneitra
Nahariyya
GOLAN
Nawa
Haifa
Tiberias
SYRIAN ARAB
REPUBLIC
Nazareth

MEDITERRANEAN
SEA
Netanya
Jenin
Tulkarm
Nablus
Qalqilya
Tel Aviv
WEST BANK
Jordan
Ramle
Jericho
Amman
Jerusalem
Bethlehem
Hebron
Dead
Sea
Gaza
GAZA
Rafah
Bersheeba
JORDAN

ISRAEL

EGYPT

SINAI

The designations employed and the
presentation of material on this map do
not imply the expression of any opinion
whatsoever on the part of the Secretariat of
the United Nations concerning the legal status
of any country, territory, city or area or of its
authorities or concerning the delimitation of its
frontiers or boundaries.

Élat

- - - - Armistice Demarcation
Line, 1949
- · - · - Boundary of Former
Palestine Mandate
- · · - · International Boundary

0   10   20   30   40 km
0   10   20   30 mi

West Bank & Gaza Following Oslo Agreements:

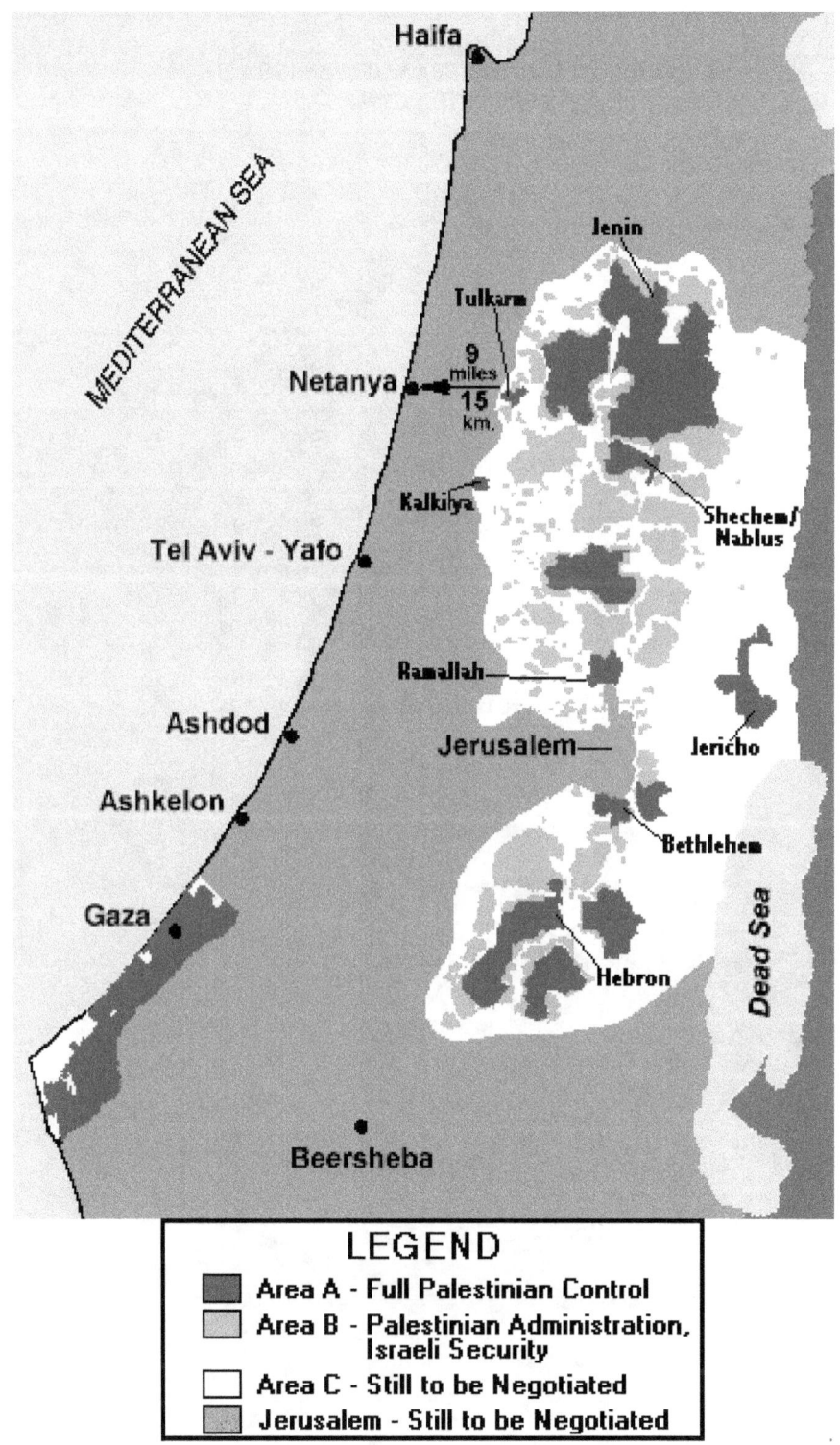

LEGEND

■ Area A - Full Palestinian Control
▨ Area B - Palestinian Administration, Israeli Security
□ Area C - Still to be Negotiated
▤ Jerusalem - Still to be Negotiated

Source: Arafat's Island's, INFORMATION REGARDING ISRAEL'S SECURITY   v
(IRIS) (https://iris.org.il/Arafats-Islands/)

Jerusalem Occupied and Expanded by Israel Since June 1967:

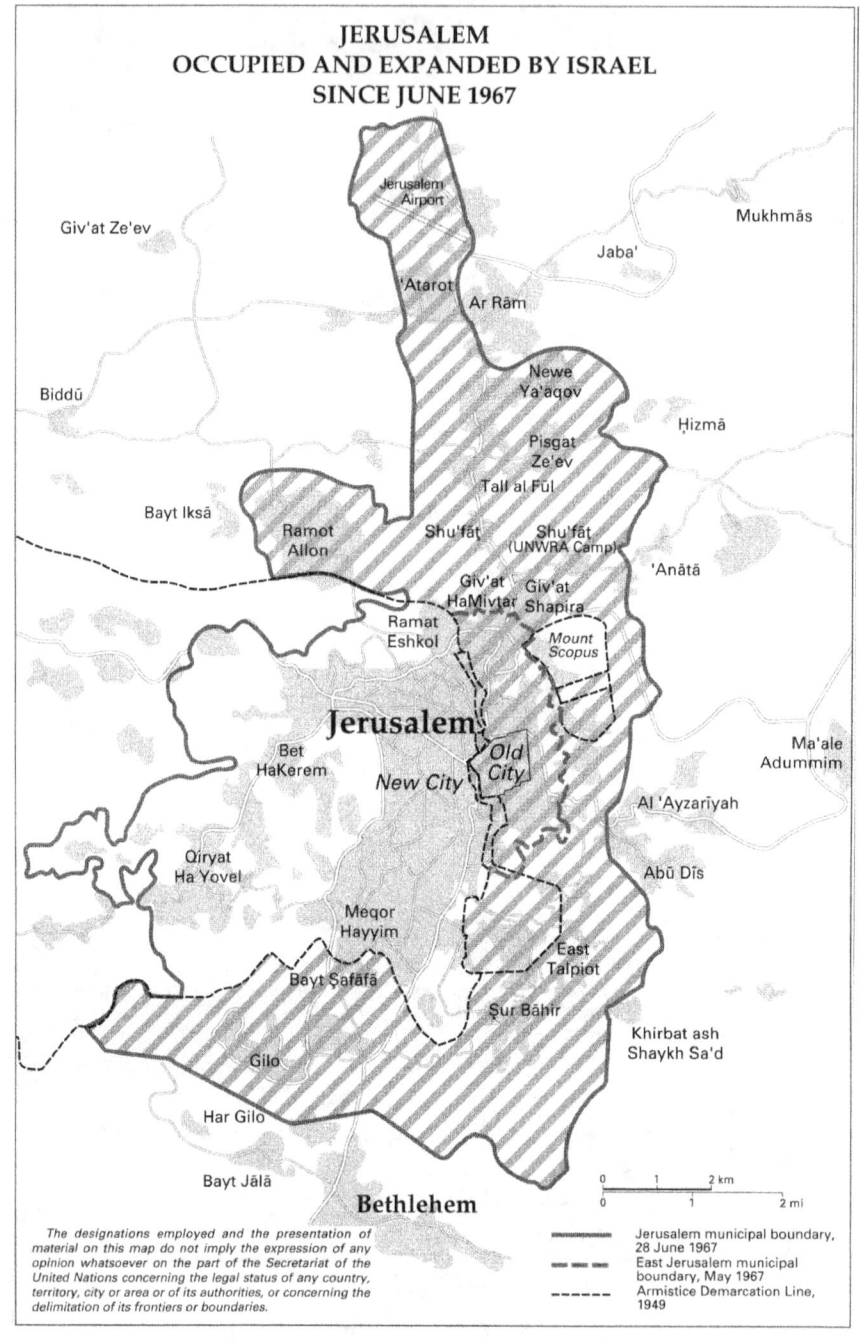

JERUSALEM
OCCUPIED AND EXPANDED BY ISRAEL
SINCE JUNE 1967

Jerusalem
Airport

Giv'at Ze'ev

Mukhmās

Jaba'

'Atarot

Ar Rām

Biddū

Newe
Ya'aqov

Hizmā

Pisgat
Ze'ev

Tall al Fūl

Bayt Iksā

Ramot
Allon

Shu'fāt

Shu'fāt
(UNWRA Camp)

'Anātā

Giv'at
HaMivtar

Giv'at
Shapira

Ramat
Eshkol

Mount
Scopus

Jerusalem

Bet
HaKerem

Old
City

Ma'ale
Adummim

New City

Al 'Ayzarīyah

Qiryat
Ha Yovel

Abū Dīs

Meqor
Hayyim

Bayt Ṣafāfā

East
Talpiot

Ṣur Bāhir

Khirbat ash
Shaykh Sa'd

Gilo

Har Gilo

Bayt Jālā

Bethlehem

0   1   2 km
0   1   2 mi

The designations employed and the presentation of
material on this map do not imply the expression of any
opinion whatsoever on the part of the Secretariat of the
United Nations concerning the legal status of any country,
territory, city or area or of its authorities, or concerning the
delimitation of its frontiers or boundaries.

——————— Jerusalem municipal boundary,
28 June 1967
— — — East Jerusalem municipal
boundary, May 1967
- - - - - Armistice Demarcation Line,
1949

Source: UNITED NATIONS September 1991, Map No. 3640 Rev. 1

Proposed Israeli Annexation of the West Bank:

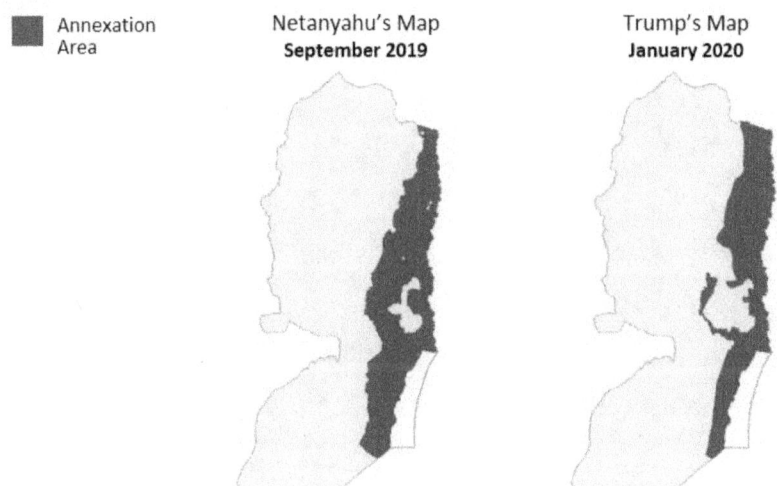

Annexation Area

Netanyahu's Map
September 2019

Trump's Map
January 2020

Source: Israel's Possible Annexation of West Bank Areas: Frequently Asked Questions, Jim Zanotti. CONGRESSIONAL RESEARCH SERVICE (CRS Report No. R46443) (July 14, 2020).

INTRODUCTION

The conflict between Israel and Palestine is complicated—in part because neither side is entirely wrong and thus the issue is largely a matter of perspective. A particularly salient example of this phenomenon is the creation of Israel in 1948. The facts surrounding this event are not in dispute, but Israelis and Palestinians perceive this event very differently. For Israelis it was cathartic—Jewish people overcoming centuries of persecution and oppression to collectively seize control of their own destiny and establish a refuge for global Jewry in their ancestral homeland. For Palestinians it was tragic—a foreign state imposed on their land and resulting in a mass exodus of peoples who have since been subjected to penury and political purgatory. These are two powerful narratives resulting from the same event. Compound this divergence over decades and you get the complex modern conflict.

This book seeks to help clarify this conflict by providing the underlying facts and a multitude of relevant perspectives. The book is structured into four parts, which in turn are broken down into sections. The first part is an overview of Zionism, both as a philosophy and as a movement. This is important background material that informs the rest of the book.

The second part is the historical narrative of the conflict—the story of how we got here. The narrative is broken down into discrete sections corresponding to distinct periods within this history. This history is not linear—different issues evolve at different speeds and events sometimes occur contemporaneously. The content in this section is organized so as to coherently tell the story, and thus content is not necessarily chronological and there is subject-matter overflow between sections. Background information is provided for documents when context is necessary and cannot be inferred from the document itself.

Part three concerns the dynamic aspects to the conflict. These are things continuously happening in the background throughout the history of the conflict. This book seeks to explain why these issues are important and how they continue to influence the conflict. Many of these issues correspond to the unresolved aspects of the conflict (i.e. refugees and settlements).

Part four overviews what the future holds and what a resolution to the conflict might look like. The individuals who authored works within this book are also overviewed at the end. This section briefly summarizes their professional credentials, and for government officials it provides their position at the time they authored the work(s) incorporated in this book. These are not full biographies, and many of the contributors have important accomplishments and accolades beyond what is provided here.

A few notes about the book. First, the scope of the book is limited to the conflict between Palestine and Israel. For this reason, there is minimal discussion of the Golan Heights (which concerns Syrian and Israel). Likewise, there is no discussion of historical events outside this scope, such as the 1956 Suez Canal crisis and the Gulf War (both of which tangentially influenced the Israel-Palestine conflict but were primarily about Western oil interests).

Aside from this Introduction nothing in the book is original—everything is reprinted from another source. Due to space constraints, very few of these works are provided in their entirety, and edits have been made for space. These edits consist of redactions and omissions, which are clearly indicated (except when omitted text occurred prior to text constituting the beginning of the work provided herein). Internal citations from the original works have also not been included. The documents generally share the same title as the original document. In certain instances, the document provided is titled with a subheading from within the document (the subsequent language is from that subsection). A citation is provided to the full document in all such instances.

This book contains both factual reports and personal commentaries, and many works are a blend of the two. Some of the viewpoints provided through these commentaries are contradictory—this is a function of the subjectivity of perception and the aforementioned divergence. Moreover, some of the viewpoints utilize "facts" that are not entirely true. Some of this is propaganda, and some it is mistaken. Regardless of intent, incorrect information sometimes becomes part of the conflict simply because enough people believe that it is true. Certain perspectives included in the book are prejudiced—these range from antiquated colonialist perspectives to outright modern bigotry. The former are necessary to provide a wholistic rendering of the relevant history, and the latter are an inescapable component of the modern conflict.

Both Israel and Palestine are dynamic societies containing a multitude of perspectives—there is no single "Israeli" side or "Palestinian" side. This book attempts to provide an array of these perspectives and illustrate the relevant intra-societal dynamics. However, this book is not an exhaustive account of the Israel-Palestine conflict, and some viewpoints are necessarily excluded.

PHILOSOPHY

The Jewish State (1896)
Theodor Herzl

No one can deny the gravity of the situation of the Jews. Wherever they live in perceptible numbers, they are more or less persecuted. Their equality before the law, granted by statute, has become practically a dead letter. They are debarred from filling even moderately high positions, either in the army, or in any public or private capacity. And attempts are made to thrust them out of business also: "Don't buy from Jews!"

Attacks in Parliaments, in assemblies, in the press, in the pulpit, in the street, on journeys --for example, their exclusion from certain hotels--even in places of recreation, become daily more numerous. The forms of persecution varying according to the countries and social circles in which they occur. In Russia, imposts are levied on Jewish villages; in Rumania, a few persons are put to death; in Germany, they get a good beating occasionally; in Austria, Anti-Semites exercise terrorism over all public life; in Algeria, there are traveling agitators; in Paris, the Jews are shut out of the so-called best social circles and excluded from clubs. Shades of anti-Jewish feeling are innumerable. But this is not to be an attempt to make out a doleful category of Jewish hardships.

I do not intend to arouse sympathetic emotions on our behalf. That would be foolish, futile, and undignified proceeding. I shall content myself with putting the following questions to the Jews: Is it not true that, in countries where we live in perceptible numbers, the position of Jewish lawyers, doctors, technicians, teachers, and employees of all descriptions becomes daily more intolerable? Is it not true, that the Jewish middle classes are seriously threatened? Is it not true, that the passions of the mob are incited against our wealthy people? Is it not true, that our poor endure greater sufferings than any other proletariat? I think that this external pressure makes itself felt everywhere. In our economically upper classes it causes discomfort, in our middle classes continual and grave anxieties, in our lower classes absolute despair.

Everything tends, in fact, to one and the same conclusion, which is clearly enunciated in that classic Berlin phrase: "Juden Raus" (Out with the Jews!)

I shall now put the Question in the briefest possible form: Are we to "get out" now and where to?

Or, may we yet remain? And, how long?

Let us first settle the point of staying where we are. Can we hope for better days, can we possess our souls in patience, can we wait in pious resignation till the princes and peoples of this earth are more mercifully disposed towards us? I say that we cannot hope for a change in the current of feeling. And why not? Even if we were as near to the hearts of princes as are their other subjects, they could not protect us. They would only feel popular hatred by showing us too much favor. By "too much," I really mean less than is claimed as a right by every ordinary citizen, or every race. The nations in whose midst Jews live are all either covertly or openly Anti-Semitic.

The common people have not, and indeed cannot have, any historic comprehension. They do not know that the sins of the Middle Ages are now being visited on the nations of Europe. We are what the Ghetto made us. We have attained pre-eminence in finance, because mediaeval conditions drove us to it. The same process is now being repeated. We are again being forced into finance, now it is the stock exchange, by being kept out of other branches of economic activity. Being on the stock exchange, we are consequently exposed afresh to contempt. At the same time we continue to produce an abundance of mediocre intellects who find no outlet, and this endangers our social position as much as does our increasing wealth. Educated Jews without means are now rapidly becoming Socialists. Hence we are certain to suffer very severely in the struggle between classes, because we stand in the most exposed position in the camps of both Socialists and capitalists.

PREVIOUS ATTEMPTS AT A SOLUTION

The artificial means heretofore employed to overcome the troubles of Jews have been either too petty -- such as attempts at colonization -- or attempts to convert the Jews into peasants in their present homes. What is achieved by transporting a few thousand Jews to another country? Either they come to grief at once, or prosper, and then their prosperity creates Anti-Semitism. We have already discussed these attempts to divert poor Jews to fresh districts. This diversion is clearly inadequate and futile, if it does not actually defeat its own ends; for it merely protracts and postpones a solution, and perhaps even aggravates difficulties.

Whoever would attempt to convert the Jew into a husbandman would be making an extraordinary mistake. For a peasant is in a historical category, as proved by his costume which in some countries he has worn for centuries; and by his tools, which are identical with those used by his earliest forefathers. His plough is unchanged; he carries the seed in his apron; mows with the historical scythe, and threshes with the time-honored flail. But we know that all this can be done by machinery. The agrarian question is only a question of machinery. America must conquer Europe, in the same way as large landed possessions absorb small ones. The

2

peasant is consequently a type which is in course of extinction. Whenever he is artificially preserved, it is done on account of the political interests which he is intended to serve. It is absurd, and indeed impossible, to make modern peasants on the old pattern. No one is wealthy or powerful enough to make civilization take a single retrograde step. The mere preservation of obsolete institutions is a task severe enough to require the enforcement of all the despotic measures of an autocratically governed State.

Are we, therefore, to credit Jews who are intelligent with a desire to become peasants of the old type? One might just as well say to them: "Here is a cross-bow: now go to war!" What? With a cross-bow, while the others have rifles and long range guns? Under these circumstances the Jews' are perfectly justified in refusing to stir when people try to make peasants of them. A cross-bow is a beautiful weapon, which inspires me with mournful feelings when I have time to devote to them. But it belongs by rights to a museum. Now, there certainly are districts to which desperate Jews go out, or at any rate, are willing to go out and till the soil. And a little observation shows that these districts -- such as the enclave of Hesse in Germany, and some provinces in Russia -- these very districts are the principal seats of Anti-Semitism.

For the world's reformers, who send the Jews to the plough, forget a very important person, who has a great deal to say on the matter. This person is the agriculturist, and the agriculturist is also perfectly justified. For the tax on land, the risks attached to crops, the pressure of large proprietors who cheapen labor, and American competition in particular, combine to make his life hard enough. Besides, the duties on corn cannot go on increasing indefinitely. Nor can the manufacturer be allowed to starve; his political influence is, in fact, in the ascendant, and he must therefore be treated with additional consideration.

All these difficulties are well known, therefore I refer to them only cursorily. I merely wanted to indicate clearly how futile had been past attempts -- most of them well intentioned -- to solve the Jewish Question. Neither a diversion of the stream, nor an artificial depression of the intellectual level of our proletariat, will overcome the difficulty. The supposed infallible expedient of assimilation has already been dealt with. We cannot get the better of Anti-Semitism by any of these methods. It cannot die out so long as its causes are not removed. Are they removable?

CAUSES OF ANTI-SEMITISM

We shall not again touch on those causes which are a result of temperament, prejudice and narrow views, but shall here restrict ourselves to political and economical causes alone. Modern Anti-Semitism is not to be confounded with the religious persecution of the Jews of former times. It does occasionally take a religious bias in some countries, but the main

3

current of the aggressive movement has now changed. In the principal countries where Anti-Semitism prevails, it does so as a result of the emancipation of the Jews. When civilized nations awoke to the inhumanity of discriminatory legislation and enfranchised us, our enfranchisement came too late. It was no longer possible to remove our disabilities in our old homes. For we had, curiously enough, developed while in the Ghetto into a bourgeois people, and we stepped out of it only to enter into fierce competition with the middle classes. Hence, our emancipation set us suddenly within this middle-class circle, where we have a double pressure to sustain, from within and from without. The Christian bourgeoisie would not be unwilling to cast us as a sacrifice to Socialism, though that would not greatly improve matters.

At the same time, the equal rights of Jews before the law cannot be withdrawn where they have once been conceded. Not only because their withdrawal would be opposed to the spirit of our age, but also because it would immediately drive all Jews, rich and poor alike, into the ranks of subversive parties. Nothing effectual can really be done to our injury. In olden days our jewels were seized. How is our movable property to be got hold of now? It consists of printed papers which are locked up somewhere or other in the world, perhaps in the coffers of Christians. It is, of course, possible to get at shares and debentures in railways, banks and industrial undertakings of all descriptions by taxation, and where the progressive income-tax is in force all our movable property can eventually be laid hold of. But all these efforts cannot be directed against Jews alone, and wherever they might nevertheless be made, severe economic crises would be their immediate consequences, which would be by no means confined to the Jews who would be the first affected. The very impossibility of getting at the Jews nourishes and embitters hatred of them. Anti- Semitism increases day by day and hour by hour among the nations; indeed, it is bound to increase, because the causes of its growth continue to exist and cannot be removed. Its remote cause is our loss of the power of assimilation during the Middle Ages; its immediate cause is our excessive production of mediocre intellects, who cannot find an outlet downwards or upwards -- that is to say, no wholesome outlet in either direction. When we sink, we become a revolutionary proletariat, the subordinate officers of all revolutionary parties; and at the same time, when we rise, there rises also our terrible power of the purse.

EFFECTS OF ANTI-SEMITISM

The oppression we endure does not improve us, for we are not a whit better than ordinary people. It is true that we do not love our enemies; but he alone who can conquer himself dare reproach us with that fault. Oppression naturally creates hostility against oppressors, and our hostility aggravates the pressure. It is impossible to escape from this eternal circle.

4

"No!" Some soft-hearted visionaries will say: "No, it is possible! Possible by means of the ultimate perfection of humanity."

Is it necessary to point to the sentimental folly of this view? He who would found his hope for improved conditions on the ultimate perfection of humanity would indeed be relying upon a Utopia! I referred previously to our "assimilation". I do not for a moment wish to imply that I desire such an end. Our national character is too historically famous, and, in spite of every degradation, too fine to make its annihilation desirable. We might perhaps be able to merge ourselves entirely into surrounding races, if these were to leave us in peace for a period of two generations. But they will not leave us in peace. For a little period they manage to tolerate us, and then their hostility breaks out again and again. The world is provoked somehow by our prosperity, because it has for many centuries been accustomed to consider us as the most contemptible among the poverty-stricken. In its ignorance and narrowness of heart, it fails to observe that prosperity weakens our Judaism and extinguishes our peculiarities. It is only pressure that forces us back to the parent stem; it is only hatred encompassing us that makes us strangers once more. Thus, whether we like it or not, we are now, and shall henceforth remain, a historic group with unmistakable characteristics common to us all.

We are one people--our enemies have made us one without our consent, as repeatedly happens in history. Distress binds us together, and, thus united, we suddenly discover our strength. Yes, we are strong enough to form a State, and, indeed, a model State. We possess all human and material resources necessary for the purpose.

This is therefore the appropriate place to give an account of what has been somewhat roughly termed our "human material." But it would not be appreciated till the broad lines of the plan, on which everything depends, has first been marked out.

THE PLAN

The whole plan is in its essence perfectly simple, as it must necessarily be if it is to come within the comprehension of all.

Let the sovereignty be granted us over a portion of the globe large enough to satisfy the rightful requirements of a nation; the rest we shall manage for ourselves.

The creation of a new State is neither ridiculous nor impossible. We have in our day witnessed the process in connection with nations which were not largely members of the middle class, but poorer, less educated, and consequently weaker than ourselves. The Governments of all countries scourged by Anti-Semitism will be keenly interested in assisting us to obtain the sovereignty we want.

The plan, simple in design, but complicated in execution, will be carried out by two agencies: The Society of Jews and the Jewish Company.

The Society of Jews will do the preparatory work in the domains of science and politics, which the Jewish Company will afterwards apply practically.

The Jewish Company will be the liquidating agent of the business interests of departing Jews, and will organize commerce and trade in the new country.

We must not imagine the departure of the Jews to be a sudden one. It will be gradual, continuous, and will cover many decades. The poorest will go first to cultivate the soil. In accordance with a preconceived plan, they will construct roads, bridges, railways and telegraph installations; regulate rivers; and build their own dwellings; their labor will create trade, trade will create markets and markets will attract new settlers, for every man will go voluntarily, at his own expense and his own risk. The labor expended on the land will enhance its value, and the Jews will soon perceive that a new and permanent sphere of operation is opening here for that spirit of enterprise which has heretofore met only with hatred and obloquy.

If we wish to found a State today, we shall not do it in the way which would have been the only possible one a thousand years ago. It is foolish to revert to old stages of civilization, as many Zionists would like to do. Supposing, for example, we were obliged to clear a country of wild beasts, we should not set about the task in the fashion of Europeans of the fifth century. We should not take spear and lance and go out singly in pursuit of bears; we would organize a large and active hunting party, drive the animals together, and throw a gelignite bomb into their midst.

If we wish to conduct building operations, we shall not plant a mass of stakes and piles on the shore of a lake, but we shall build as men build now. Indeed, we shall build in a bolder and more stately style than was ever adopted before, for we now possess means which men never yet possessed.

The emigrants standing lowest in the economic scale will be slowly followed by those of a higher grade. Those who at this moment are living in despair will go first. They will be led by the mediocre intellects which we produce so superabundantly and which are persecuted everywhere.

This pamphlet will open a general discussion on the Jewish Question, but that does not mean that there will be any voting on it. Such a result would ruin the cause from the outset, and dissidents must remember that allegiance or opposition is entirely voluntary. He who will not come with
6

us should remain behind.

Let all who are willing to join us, fall in behind our banner and fight for our cause with voice and pen and deed.

Those Jews who agree with our idea of a State will attach themselves to the Society, which will thereby be authorized to confer and treat with Governments in the name of our people. The Society will thus be acknowledged in its relations with Governments as a State-creating power. This acknowledgment will practically create the State.

Should the Powers declare themselves willing to admit our sovereignty over a neutral piece of land, then the Society will enter into negotiations for the possession of this land. Here two territories come under consideration, Palestine and Argentine. In both countries important experiments in colonization have been made, though on the mistaken principle of a gradual infiltration of Jews. An infiltration is bound to end badly. It continues till the inevitable moment when the native population feels itself threatened, and forces the Government to stop a further influx of Jews. Immigration is consequently futile unless we have the sovereign right to continue such immigration.

The Society of Jews will treat with the present masters of the land, putting itself under the protectorate of the European Powers, if they prove friendly to the plan. We could offer the present possessors of the land enormous advantages, assume part of the public debt, build new roads for traffic, which our presence in the country would render necessary, and do many other things. The creation of our State would be beneficial to adjacent countries, because the cultivation of a strip of land increases the value of its surrounding districts in innumerable ways.
[…]

The Anti-Semitism of the Present (British) Government (1917)
Lord Edwin Montagu

[…] I wish to place on record my view that the policy of His Majesty's Government is anti-Semitic in result and will prove a rallying ground for Anti-Semites in every country in the world.

This view is prompted by the receipt yesterday of a correspondence between Lord Rothschild and Mr. Balfour.

Lord Rothschild's letter is dated the 18th July and Mr. Balfour's answer is to be dated August 1917. I fear that my protest comes too late, and it may well be that the Government were practically committed when Lord Rothschild wrote and before I became a member of the Government, for there has obviously been some correspondence or conversation before this letter. But I do feel that as the one Jewish Minister in the Government I may be allowed by my colleagues an opportunity of expressing views which may be peculiar to myself, but which I hold very strongly and which I must ask permission to express when opportunity affords.

I believe most firmly that this war has been a death-blow to Internationalism, and that it has proved an opportunity for a renewal of the slackening sense of Nationality, for it has not only been tacitly agreed by most statesmen in most countries that the redistribution of territory resulting from the war should be more or less on national grounds, but we have learned to realise that our country stands for principles, for aims, for civilisation which no other country stands for in the same degree, and that in the future, whatever may have been the case in the past, we must live and fight in peace and in war for those aims and aspirations, and so equip and regulate our lives and industries as to be ready whenever and if ever we are challenged. […]

The war has indeed justified patriotism as the prime motive of political thought.

It is in this atmosphere that the Government proposes to endorse the formation of a new nation with a new home in Palestine. This nation will presumably be formed of Jewish Russians, Jewish Englishmen, Jewish Roumanians, Jewish Bulgarians, and Jewish citizens of all nations— survivors or relations of those who have fought or laid down their lives for the different countries which I have mentioned, at a time when the three years that they have lived through have united their outlook and thought more closely than ever with the countries of which they are citizens.

Zionism has always seemed to me to be a mischievous political creed, untenable by any patriotic citizen of the United Kingdom. If a Jewish Englishman sets his eyes on the Mount of Olives and longs for the day when he will shake British soil from his shoes and go back to agricultural

8

pursuits in Palestine, he has always seemed to me to have acknowledged aims inconsistent with British citizenship and to have admitted that he is unfit for a share in public life in Great Britain, or to be treated as an Englishman. I have always understood that those who indulged in this creed were largely animated by the restrictions upon and refusal of liberty to Jews in Russia. But at the very time when these Jews have been acknowledged as Jewish Russians and given all liberties, it seems to be inconceivable that Zionism should be officially recognised by the British Government, and that Mr. Balfour should be authorised to say that Palestine was to be reconstituted as the "national home of the Jewish people." I do not know what this involves, but I assume that it means that Mahommedans and Christians are to make way for the Jews and that the Jews should be put in all positions of preference and should be peculiarly associated with Palestine in the same way that England is with the English or France with the French, that Turks and other Mahommedans in Palestine will be regarded as foreigners, just in the same way as Jews will hereafter be treated as foreigners in every country but Palestine. Perhaps also citizenship must be granted only as a result of a religious test.

I lay down with emphasis four principles:

1. I assert that there is not a Jewish nation. The members of my family, for instance, who have been in this country for generations, have no sort or kind of community of view or of desire with any Jewish family in any other country beyond the fact that they profess to a greater or less degree the same religion. It is no more true to say that a Jewish Englishman and a Jewish Moor are of the same nation than it is to say that a Christian Englishman and a Christian Frenchman are of the same nation: of the same race, perhaps, traced back through the centuries—through centuries of the history of a peculiarly adaptable race. The Prime Minister and M. Briand are, I suppose, related through the ages, one as a Welshman and the other as a Breton, but they certainly do not belong to the same nation.

2. When the Jews are told that Palestine is their national home, every country will immediately desire to get rid of its Jewish citizens, and you will find a population in Palestine driving out its present inhabitants, taking all the best in the country, drawn from all quarters of the globe, speaking every language on the face of the earth, and incapable of communicating with one another except by means of an interpreter. I have always understood that this was the consequence of the building of the Tower of Babel, if ever it was built, and I certainly do not dissent from the view, commonly held, as I have always understood, by the Jews before Zionism was invented, that to bring the Jews back to form a nation in the country from which they were dispersed would require Divine leadership. I have never heard it suggested, even by their most fervent admirers, that either Mr. Balfour or Lord Rothschild would prove to be the Messiah.

I claim that the lives that British Jews have led, that the aims that they have had before them, that the part that they have played in our public life and our public institutions, have entitled them to be regarded, not as British Jews, but as Jewish Britons. I would willingly disfranchise every Zionist. I would be almost tempted to proscribe the Zionist organisation as illegal and against the national interest. But I would ask of a British Government sufficient tolerance to refuse to endorse a conclusion which makes aliens and foreigners by implication, if not at once by law, of all their Jewish fellow-citizens.

3.   I deny that Palestine is to-day associated with the Jews or properly to be regarded as a fit place for them to live in. The Ten Commandments were delivered to the Jews on Sinai. It is quite true that Palestine plays a large part in Jewish history, but so it does in modern Mahommedan history, and, after the time of the Jews, surely it plays a larger part than any other country in Christian history. The Temple may have been in Palestine, but so was the Sermon on the Mount and the Crucifixion. I would not deny to Jews in Palestine equal rights to colonisation with those who profess other religions, but a religious test of citizenship seems to me to be the only admitted by those who take a bigoted and narrow view of one particular epoch of the history of Palestine, and claim for the Jews a position to which they are not entitled.

If my memory serves me right, there are three times as many Jews in the world as could possibly get into Palestine if you drove out all the population that remains there now. *So that only one-third will get back at the most, and what will happen to the remainder?*

4.   I can easily understand the editors of the *Morning Post* and of the *New Witness* being Zionists, and I am not in the least surprised that the non-Jews of England may welcome this policy. I have always recognised the unpopularity, much greater than some people think, of my community. We have obtained a far greater share of this country's goods and opportunities than we are numerically entitled to. We reach on the whole maturity earlier, and therefore with people of our own age we compete unfairly. Many of us have been exclusive in our friendships and intolerant in our attitude, and I can easily understand that many a non-Jew in England wants to get rid of us. But just as there is no community of thought and mode of life among Christian Englishmen, so there is not among Jewish Englishmen. More and more we are educated in public schools and at the Universities, and take our part in the politics, in the Army, in the Civil Service, of our country. And I am glad to think that the prejudices against inter-marriage are breaking down. But when the Jew has a national home, surely it follows that the impetus to deprive us of the rights of British citizenship must be enormously increased. Palestine will become the world's Ghetto. Why should the Russian give the Jew equal rights? His national home is Palestine. Why does Lord Rothschild attach so much

importance to the difference between British and foreign Jews? All Jews will be foreign Jews, inhabitants of the great country of Palestine.

I do not know how the fortunate third will be chosen, but the Jew will have the choice, whatever country he belongs to, whatever country he loves, whatever country he regards himself as an integral part of, between going to live with people who are foreigners to him, but to whom his Christian fellow-country men have told him he shall belong, and of remaining as an unwelcome guest in the country that he thought he belonged to.

I am not surprised that the Government should take this step after the formation of a Jewish Regiment, and I am waiting to learn that my brother, who has been wounded in the Naval Division, or my nephew, who is in the Grenadier Guards, will be forced by public opinion or by Army regulations to become an officer in a regiment which will mainly be composed of people who will not understand the only language which he speaks— English. I can well understand that when it was decided, and quite rightly, to force foreign Jews in this country to serve in the Army, it was difficult to put them in British regiments because of the language difficulty, but that was because they were foreigners, and not because they were Jews, and a Foreign Legion would seem to me to have been the right thing to establish. A Jewish Legion makes the position of Jews in other regiments more difficult and forces a nationality upon people who have nothing in common.

I feel that the Government are asked to be the instrument for carrying out the wishes of a Zionist organisation largely run, as my information goes, at any rate in the past, by men of enemy descent or birth, and by this means have dealt a severe blow to the liberties, position and opportunities of service of their Jewish fellow-countrymen.

I would say to Lord Rothschild that the Government will be prepared to do everything in their power to obtain for Jews in Palestine complete liberty of settlement and life on an equality with the inhabitants of that country who profess other religious beliefs. I would ask that the Government should go no further.

ORGANIZATION

The Basel Program (1897)
THE FIRST ZIONIST CONGRESS

Zionism seeks to establish a home for the Jewish people in Palestine secured under public law. The Congress contemplates the following means to the attainment of this end:

1. The promotion by appropriate means of the settlement in Palestine of Jewish farmers, artisans, and manufacturers.

2. The organization and uniting of the whole of Jewry by means of appropriate institutions, both local and international, in accordance with the laws of each country.

3. The strengthening and fostering of Jewish national sentiment and national consciousness.

4. Preparatory steps toward obtaining the consent of governments, where necessary, in order to reach the goals of Zionism.

The Zionist Movement (1899)
Richard Gottheil

The May Laws of Count Ignatieff mark the beginning of the new Zionism. Instinctively, the Jew turned to his old home. Equipped with nothing but hope and an undaunted courage, many journeyed thither. Colonization societies were formed in Russia and Roumania—*Chovei-Zion* (Lovers of Zion) they called themselves for the most part. Similar efforts at colonizing Jews in Palestine had been made in the fifties by Sir Moses Montefiore, by Lord Shaftesbury, by Laurence Oliphant and by Dr. Friedman. In 1870, the first real colony (*Mihiveh Israel*) was founded by Charles Netter, under the auspices of the *Alliance Israelite Universelle*, an organization which has nobly pleaded the cause of the Jews wherever they were unable to do it themselves, and whose leaders were such men as Adolph Cremiaux and Albert Cohn. This, however, was a purely agricultural school. Here colonies soon grouped themselves near to it and spread out in other parts of the land. There are now as many as sixteen mother colonies, with other settlements attached which may bring up their number to twenty-five; around Jerusalem, near Haifa and Jaffa, in Galilee and now even beyond the Jordan. Their success is due to the splendid interest taken in them by Baron Edmond de Rothschild, who has spared neither expense nor trouble to help them through the experimental stage in which they were bound to remain for some years. Wine of various kinds is produced in the colonies, cognac, scent and soap. As soon as a proper market is found for these products, the colonies will all be self-supporting. […]

When the Jewish traveller, Benjamin of Tudela, visited, the holy places in Palestine in the twelfth century, he could find there no more than a few hundred of his people. Now there are about sixty thousand Jews in Palestine. Schools have been founded there by the Alliance, there is a high-school in the City of Jaffa, and a national Hebrew library in Jerusalem. This Abarbanel Library, as it is called, has been founded almost wholly through the exertions of Dr. Casanowitz of Bialoistock (Russia), who spent all his own fortune in so doing, and often takes his fees in books, which he then forwards to Jerusalem.

This indiscriminate colonization, and what was worse, the massing of poverty-stricken Jews in Jerusalem, had been going on for some years when, in 1896, a pamphlet called "Der Juden Staat" appeared in Vienna. The writer of it, Dr. Theodore Herzl, was a brilliant member of the editorial staff of the "Neue Freie Presse" of Vienna. He was by no means the first to preach the ideas for which he now stands. In Russia men like Binsher, in Germany men like Euelf, had done this before his time. But it is his merit to have definitely laid down the lines upon which any movement of this kind must run. His merit is even greater than this. As a refuge from Anti-Semitism merely, Zionism would have only a negative value. Herzl has supplied the ideal, or rather has formulated it in a definite manner: the ideal of a certain home and of a renewed life in common for the Jews. At the inspiration of his word and through his unflagging energy, assisted by such men as Max Nordau, what was but the individual effort of a few societies has become a goal towards which the Jewish people may walk. He has brought the question before the forum of European thought and to the ears of those who have in their hands the making of history. Before the first Congress at Basle in 1897, there were in various parts of the world one hundred and seventeen societies whose aims were more or less Zionistic. At the second Basle Congress in 1898, their number had risen to more than eight hundred. Before 1897, there were merely a handful of societies in the United States. The American Federation of Zionists now counts as many as one hundred and twenty-five societies; and there are quite a number of other Zionist societies not yet affiliated with the Federation.

The success of the Zionist movement presupposes the presence of such an ideal. [...]

[...] It has been a subject of reproach to us that in our ranks the great financiers, the men of great fortunes, are seldom to be found. The reproach touches them, not us. And in the end it matters little. Our strength lies in an idea: and in the long run ideas shape themselves out into history. At the last Congress it was resolved to found a company, which, working side by side with the Congress, should enable it to carry out whatever ideas it should from time to time adopt. During the present year, the Jewish Colonial Trust was brought into existence under the English Banking Laws and with its chief office in London. The necessary working capital has already been subscribed largely by the Jewish Proletariate. From every place into which Jewry is dispersed, the money has come, a free-will offering to the great work we have in view.

Nearly all the older *Chovei-Zion* societies have joined the movement of which the Basle Congress is the exponent. Some, however, have not. A large society in Lemberg, the English Zionist tents, and a few societies in Germany, still believe that simple colonization in Palestine is the only thing for which the Jews should strive. In this they show little insight into the changed economic conditions under which we now live. To make of the Jewish people simply an agricultural people, would be an attempt to turn back the hands of the clock; and to bring a large number of Jews into Palestine without at the same time assuring the stability of the new settlements, is to run a risk which the tremendous interests at stake do not permit. Yet, there are lines upon which the smaller force can work with no detriment to the greater, but rather as a help in bringing about the end which both have in view.
[...]

Aids Jews in Holy Land: National Fund's Report Tells of Wide Colonization Work (1926)

THE NEW YORK TIMES

Encouraging reports of reclamation and colonization of land in Palestine with the aid of the Jewish National Fund, the oldest agency of its kind, were made yesterday at the twenty-fifth annual conference of its members .... Bernard A. Rosenblatt, Chairman, reviewed the work in his annual report. Other speakers were Judge William B. Lewis of Philadelphian, Chairman of the United Palestine Appeal, and Louis Lipsky, President of the Zionist organization in America.

Jews now own 250,000 acres in the Holy Land, of which 50,000 acres were purchased by the Jewish National Fund, largely through pennies collected from Ghetto Jews all over the world, Mr. Rosenblatt said. Through improvements the land is now valued at $10,000,000, and is held by the fund for the Jewish people. Thirty-four Jewish agricultural communities have been established, he said, and to these the victims of war and of pogroms have been sent to start life anew.

Mr. Rosenblatt said that in the last year Americans contributed $498,176.69 to the National Fund, most of this being in small sums.

THE BEGINNING

The Changing East (1920)
T.E. Lawrence ("Lawrence of Arabia")

A picture writer once coined a phrase, "The unchanging East," and Time has turned round and taken revenge upon him. The East is today the place of change—of changes so great and swift that in comparison with it our Europe is standing still. [...]

We see the strain we have put on Asia soonest in the domain of matter. We evolved our own machinery in long centuries of struggle and invention, years in which the face of Europe gradually changed, without any too violent misery, to suit the new ideas: we had pack-horses, solid wheels, springless wagons, coaches, railways, motor cars, aeroplanes: we found the progress indecently fast at times, and put men with red flags to walk before the machines while we breathed—but what of Asia, which has stepped in a lifetime of thirty years from saddle-donkeys to Rolls-Royce cars, from blood-mares to aeroplanes? We grew by slow stages of muskets from bows to automatic guns: it took us five hundred years. The marauder of the desert laid away his spear just before the war, and to-day goes out on his raids with a Maxim. We invented the printing press four hundred years ago, and served a long apprenticeship by way of wooden types, screw and lever presses, steam presses, electric presses, to the cheap speed of the modern newspaper. The East has side by side the old-fashioned scribe, making each year a poorer living, and the linotype. The vernacular press came to them full-born. These are the material sides. Asia has in thirty years leaped across a stage which took us hundreds. She has not done it very well, perhaps, no better than parts of Russia, parts of the Balkans, parts of South America: the important part is that she has done it, and the Asia of Kinglake and Lamartine is wholly gone. [...]

This mental and moral growth is so hard to measure. The material changes prepare our heads to note great change in other ways, but their apprehension stays uncertain. There has been a change in ideas: we hear the people of Asia talking about representative government and parliaments. In our fathers' days they were governed by theocrats and autocrats. We think how long it took England to conceive and bring forth a House of Commons, and we begin to be astonished at this headlong Asia, There are labour troubles in Cairo and Bombay, a general strike in Mecca, trades union congresses in Constantinople. [...] Self-determination—yes, they have adopted that: League of Nations—they care more for it than we do. Things must be moving. Before the war we saw their politics changing, as the old springs of action became exhausted, and new motives came into play. In our fathers' days the East, and especially the Middle East, this side of Afghanistan, was logical, similar and simple. These countries, Persia, Turkey, Egypt and the rest, were old-established governments, of sultans and princes ruling by right, often by divine right, basing their regulations on the dictates of the state religion. The men were Moslems first, or Christians, or infidels of some sort. Later on, if there was any reason for it, they might be Turks or Arabs, but about this they were not too certain: the important thing was the faith. We cannot sneer at them. Only too recently, in the manuscript and crossbow days, we were like them. About 1870, though, we began to see stirrings of a new idea, the sense of nationality, which had been invented in Western Europe, and had moved slowly south and east, causing turmoil and wars in the separate countries as it passed. Nationality is a turbulent principle, and has cost probably as many lives as religion, in its much briefer reign. [...]

Its first symptoms of nationality were shown in Turkey, when Midhat Pasha began to use French words in government; and in Egypt when Arabi Pasha rose up in arms, and began to drive out the Khedive and his Turkish entourage. Both ideas were sternly discouraged. The English bolstered up the foreign dynasty in Egypt, and Abd el Hamid took up Pan-Islam, a hierarchic conception of Islam, as a corrective to the Midhat notions. He got it from a German book, which had been confusing the Caliphate and the medieval Papacy. However, the idea had a temporary success, and still holds some ground in India and Africa. For a few years there was peace in Asia [....] The new ideas were not dead—indeed, they could not be, with the Balkans offering such a lively breeding ground of nationality-microbes at the gate of Asia: and some twenty or thirty years later they were patent once more, this time not as agitations, but as conspiracies. Persia was full of them: in the end she broke out into disorder and obtained a constitution, whose precise use afterwards puzzled her. She knew that a constitution was the fashionable thing—everybody who was anybody in states had one— but it did not seem to be able to work, itself, and no one in Persia had learnt its habits. However, they still have it, and have had it for ten years.

Turkey then came out strongly, after the British had made some little adjustments in Egypt, as safety-valves for political vapours. Abd el Hamid was stiffer than our Lord Cromer or Sir Eldon Gorst, and so Turkey's nationalism got so pent up that at last it blew him quite off his seat. This was a short end to Pan-Islam: the spiritual and temporal master of Islam was put in prison, and then deposed in favour of a mental degenerate. The old cry would no longer work, as they all in one week took up the new one. Turkey announced the brotherhood of peoples. The young Turks had forgotten their statistics when they made this statement, but events soon showed them their mistake. The Turks were a minority—perhaps only thirty or thirty-five per cent, in the Ottoman Empire. The subject races, Greeks, Armenians, Albanians, Kurds, Arabs, who formed the rest, could understand the idea of brotherhood, for they had been reading Herbert Spencer and his like for years, and saw at once that they were equal to the

Turks, and that it was a sacred duty to go out and help them to establish this new era. So in their millions they began to join together, and think how best to carry on the common government.

Enver and his colleagues struck back in self-defence. They evolved a doctrine of Pan-Turanianism (a doctrine of mixed pedigree, out of a French book and a German book), which taught that the Ottoman Empire must become really Ottoman [....] [F[irst they would make these alien races inside the Empire one. It must be done quickly, for Europe was not looking kindly on them: so they took steps to lop the Greeks and Armenians to the proportions of their bedstead, and began to work upon the Arabs, to teach them Turkish as a first step, and to make them good Ottomans the second. They invented a sharp saying: "A Turkish ass is better than an alien prophet," to teach the people the relative worth of Islam and nationality. The subject races found Enver's little finger very heavy, and began to whisper to one another, in the strictest secrecy, that such things were contrary to the very principles of nationality in whose name they were done. These whisperings increased and became organised, till by 1914 there were healthy conspiracies, aiming to take local autonomy by force from Constantinople, afoot in Armenia, in Kurdistan, in Syria, and in Mesopotamia. Then the war came.
[…]
Then, when things were in this flux, thus came the war, and Asia, which had been moving fast for twenty years, put on a dizzy spurt, and left our expectations straining far behind. During the war Europe came bodily to Western Asia. On one side of the fence were the armies of the Germans, on this side the armies of the Allies. Each set great departments, fortified with all their resources, to work on the senses of the Orientals. We talked for and against Holy Wars, as finely as any Moslem dialectician. We preached of the rights of civilisation, of the laws of humanity, of international law, Geneva conventions, Hague conferences. We poured out leaflets, and picture papers, newspapers, films, all to convey an impression which should make the East understand us, and help us with conviction. Like other artists, the character we most illustrated in these productions was our own. The astonished peoples of Western Asia could not choose but hear us, and began, willingly or unwillingly, to see what we were like, and comprehend our least notions. They did not always like them, but they learned a lot. In particular they learned what each of us was fighting for (they heard it from all our mouths, and we all said much the same thing), and a thing sworn to by so many witnesses must surely be true. This liberty, this humanity, this culture, this self-determination, must be very valuable.

[…] In the nineteenth century they had had religion, a creed with a body as well as a spirit, one which showed them their road by day as well as by night. They regulated their manners, their meals, their trades, their families, their politics, by its light. The attempt of Abd el Hamid to rationalise this, to make it logical as well as theological, smashed it. When he fell, so did the rule of faith in works. The East remained Moslem, but its public life turned national. People called themselves Egyptians, or Arabs, or Turks, and their newspapers, directed by men emancipated from formal Islam by the influence of western ideas, carried this difference of motive, this new outlook, into the smallest points of life. The abstract standard by which politics and conduct were now judged was this new one of nationality. The nation became the rule of life, the modern creed—and as the war drew on Moslem learnt to go out and fight Moslem, and accept death gladly in battle for the new ideal. When England was at her greatest straits to defend her straggled holdings in the East, these feelings reached their height—and the best measure of their height is not that Indian Moslem fought Turkish Moslem to vindicate the place of India as a partner in our Empire, but that the people of Mecca, the centre of Islam, under its Emir, the Sherif of Mecca, the senior descendant of the Prophet, rose in rebellion against the Caliph, the Sultan of Constantinople, and that this rebellion carried everyone of Arabic speech in Asia at least sympathetically to its side. This was the final triumph, the highest expression there can ever be in Western Asia of the principle of nationality as the foundation of political action, opposed to the principle of a world-religion, a supra-national creed. Not the Galilean but the politician had conquered.

The armistice came, but did not check this movement; it made adherence to it more safe and more rational. The original stalwarts who marched north under Feisal side by side with Allenby had staked their heads on their fervent belief in an Arab Movement. Their victory made them fashionable, and removed the drawback of campaigning from their programme. Two months after the armistice Syria was nationalist in sentiment from south to north, Egypt was in arms against the British under a like banner, and the young officers of Turkey were banding together against the Sultan (thought to be out of date, silly, and too fond of Europe) to make a new Turkey out of the ruins of the old. […]

The question of a unity of the Arabic peoples in Asia is yet clouded. In the past it has never been a successful experiment, and the least reflection will show that there are large areas, especially of Arabia, which it would be unprofitable ever to administer. The deserts will probably remain, in the future as in the past, the preserves of inarticulate philosophers. The cultivated districts, Mesopotamia and Syria, have, however, language, race, and interests in common. Till today they have always been too vast to form a single country: they are divided, except for a narrow gangway in the north, by an irredeemable waste of flint and gravel: but petrol makes light of deserts, and space is shrinking today, when we travel one hundred miles an hour instead of five. […]

Two new elements of some interest have just set foot in Asia, coming rather as adventurers by sea—the Greeks in Smyrna, and the Jews in

Palestine. Of the two efforts the Greek is frankly an armed occupation—a desire to hold a tit-bit of Asiatic Turkey, for reasons of trade and population, and from it to influence affairs in the interior. [...] The Jewish experiment is in another class. It is a conscious effort, on the part of the least European people in Europe, to make head against the drift of the ages, and return once more to the Orient from which they came. The colonists will take back with them to the land which they occupied for some centuries before the Christian era samples of all the knowledge and technique of Europe. They propose to settle down amongst the existing Arabic-speaking population of the country, a people of kindred origin, but far different social condition. They hope to adjust their mode of life to the climate of Palestine, and by the exercise of their skill and capital to make it as highly organised as a European state. The success of their scheme will involve inevitably the raising of the present Arab population to their own material level, only a little after themselves in point of time, and the consequences might be of the highest importance for the future of the Arab world. [...]

This new condition, of a conscious and logical political nationalism, now the dominant factor of every indigenous movement in Western Asia, is too universal to be extinguished, too widespread to be temporary. We must prepare ourselves for its continuance, and for a continuance of the unrest produced by it in every contested district, until such time as it has succeeded and passed into a more advanced phase. [...]

This new Imperialism is not just withdrawal and neglect on our part. It involves an active side of imposing responsibility on the local peoples. It is what they clamour for, but an unpopular gift when given. We have to demand from them provision for their own defence. This is the first stage towards self-respect in peoples. They must find their own troops to replace our armies of occupation which we are going to withdraw. For this they must be armed, and must learn by having arms not to misuse them. We can only teach them how by forcing them to try, while we stand by and give advice. [...] We have to be prepared to see them doing things by methods quite unlike our own, and less well: but on principle it is better that they half-do it then that we do it perfectly for them. In pursuing such courses we will find our best helpers not in our former most obedient subjects, but among those now most active in agitating against us, for it will be the intellectual leaders of the people who will serve the purpose, and these are not the philosophers nor the rich, but the demagogues and the politicians. [...] They will not wish to take charge, but we can force their hand by preparing to go. [...] The alternative is to hold on to them with ever-lessening force, till the anarchy is too expensive, and we let go.

The Evolution of Palestine (1996)
Dr. Mahdi Abdul Hadi

The Arab countries were under Ottoman rule for a period of four centuries, and the Arab National Movement was an inevitable result of the Ottoman oppression, persecution and domination of the Arab people. The roots of the movement can be traced back to the Arab heritage, language and history: this is what made it genuine and gave it its originality and continuity.

[...]

On 5 November 1914, when the Ottoman state entered the war at the side of Germany against the allies, the Arabs stood at a junction. Either their link with the Ottoman state would continue, or they were to drop the connection and turn their attention to their national liberation movement, in which case their aim would be to unify its leadership, adhere to its independence goals, carry it to a new phase, and seize the opportunity to look for allies to help them achieve their goals.

The concept of the 'nation state' reached maturity and became the moving force behind Arab political thought and action. The Arab struggle shifted from demands for Arab autonomy to the call for a nation state and the struggle for its translation into a legal political reality.

The Arab search for allies to support their movement manifested itself in the following actions:

(1) A delegation of Syrian notables paid a visit to Lord Kitchener, the British High Commissioner in Cairo, requesting that Britain annex Syria and Egypt on condition that Syria enjoy independent administration.

(2) Talib An-Naqib, the representative of Basra in Iraq, made a similar offer to British envoys in Egypt and India.

(3) A number of Arab officers in Istanbul paid a visit to the British Ambassador to inquire about the position Britain would take in case certain conditions emerged. (Aziz Ali Al-Masri had been imprisoned for resisting the Ottoman authority and was awaiting sentencing.)

(4) The British government was fully informed about Sharif Hussein's (the Prince of Mecca) resentment towards the Turks. The resentment drove Sharif Hussein to seek independence using all possible means.

(5) Sharif Abdallah paid two visits to Cairo where he had secret talks with Jerusalem Governor Ronald Storrs about the possibility of taking action against the Turks to gain independence.

From The PASSIA Seminar On The Foreign Policies of Arab States. 21

The mutual interest of the Arabs and Britain in working against the Turks was their motive for an alliance, despite the differences in their final goals. The Arab National Movement entered a new phase in which it moved in two parallel directions to achieve its independence goals. The two directions were as follows:

1) formulating and legalizing its relations with the allies (Hussein-McMahon Correspondence);

2) unifying its ranks under one leadership. (The secret societies in Syria and Iraq, Fateh and Al-Ahd,[1] presented to Sharif Hussein a detailed proposal, the 'Damascus Protocol,' for a military revolt against the Turks and looked to him to assume leadership of the Arab National Movement.) [...]

---

[1] "*The Arab Fateh Society, founded in Paris in 1911*: The society moved to Beirut in 1913, and then moved again, in 1914, to Damascus. It was the first pro-independence group of Arabs and was responsible for planning the first general Arab conference in Paris, in 1913. The conference included delegations from various societies in and outside the Arab countries, and the topics discussed included national life, the struggle against occupation, Arab rights in the Ottoman state, the necessity for reform regarding centralization, and immigration from and to Syria.
"*The founding of the secret Al-Ahd Society in Istanbul in 1913*: Al-Ahd was founded by a number of Arab officers preparing plans for independence through revolt.

The Condition of Palestine After the War (1921)
Herbert Samuel

It is obvious to every passing traveller, and well-known to every European resident, that the country was before the War, and is now, undeveloped and under-populated. The methods of agriculture are, for the most part, primitive; the area of land now cultivated could yield a far greater product. There are in addition large cultivable areas that are left untilled. The summits and slopes of the hills are admirably suited to the growth of trees, but there are no forests. Miles of sand dunes that could be redeemed, are untouched, a danger, by their encroachment, to the neighbouring tillage. The Jordan and the Yarmuk offer an abundance of water-power; but it is unused. Some industries–fishing and the culture and manufacture of tobacco are examples–have been killed by Turkish laws; none have been encouraged; the markets of Palestine and of the neighbouring countries are supplied almost wholly from Europe. The seaborne commerce, such as it is, is loaded and discharged in the open roadsteads of Jaffa and Haifa: there are no harbours. The religious and historical associations that offer most powerful attractions to the whole of the Western, and to a large part of the Eastern world, have hitherto brought to Palestine but a fraction of the pilgrims and travellers, who, under better conditions, would flock to her sacred shrines and famous sites.

The country is under-populated because of this lack of development. There are now in the whole of Palestine hardly 700,000 people, a population much less than that of the province of Gallilee alone in the time of Christ. Of these 235,000 live in the larger towns, 465,000 in the smaller towns and villages. Four-fifths of the whole population are Moslems. A small proportion of these are Bedouin Arabs; the remainder, although they speak Arabic and are termed Arabs, are largely of mixed race. Some 77,000 of the population are Christians, in large majority belonging to the Orthodox Church, and speaking Arabic. The minority are members of the Latin or of the Uniate Greek Catholic Church, or–a small number–are Protestants.

The Jewish element of the population numbers 76,000. Almost all have entered Palestine during the last 40 years. Prior to 1850 there were in the country only a handful of Jews. In the following 30 years a few hundreds came to Palestine. Most of them were animated by religious motives; they came to pray and to die in the Holy Land, and to be buried in its soil. After the persecutions in Russia forty years ago, the movement of the Jews to Palestine assumed larger proportions. Jewish agricultural colonies were founded. They developed the culture of oranges and gave importance to the Jaffa orange trade. They cultivated the vine, and manufactured and exported wine. They drained swamps. They planted eucalyptus trees. They practised, with modern methods, all the processes of agriculture. There are at the present time 64 of these settlements, large and small, with a

From An Interim Report on the Civil Administration of Palestine, United Kingdom Colonial Office (1921). London: His Majesty's Stationery Office.

population of some 15,000. Every traveller in Palestine who visits them is impressed by the contrast between these pleasant villages, with the beautiful stretches of prosperous cultivation about them and the primitive conditions of life and work by which they are surrounded.

The success of these agricultural colonies attracted the eager interest of the masses of the Jewish people scattered throughout the world. In many countries they were living under the pressure of laws or customs which cramped their capacities and thwarted their energies; they saw in Palestine the prospect of a home in which they might live at ease. Profoundly discontented, as numbers of them were, with a life of petty trade in crowded cities, they listened with ready ears to the call of a healthier and finer life as producers on the land. Some among them, agriculturists already, saw in Palestine the prospect of a soil not less fertile, and an environment far more free, than those to which they were accustomed. Everywhere great numbers of Jews, whose religion causes them to live, spiritually, largely in the past, began to take an active interest in those passages of their ritual, that dwelt, with constant emphasis, upon the connection of their race with Palestine; passages which they had hitherto read day by day and week by week, with the lax attention that is given to contingency that is possible but remote. Among a great proportion, at least, of the fourteen millions of Jews, who are dispersed in all the countries of the globe, the Zionist idea took hold. They found in it that larger and higher interest, outside and beyond the cares and concerns of daily life, which every man, who is not wholly materialist, must seek somewhere.

Societies were formed which purchased areas of land in Palestine for further Jewish colonization. The Hebrew language, which, except for purposes of ritual, had been dead for many centuries, was revived as a vernacular. A new vocabulary, to meet the needs of modern life, was welded into it. Hebrew is now the language spoken by almost all the younger generation of the Jews of Palestine and by a large proportion of their elders. The Jewish newspapers are published in it. It is the language of instruction in the schools and colleges, the language used for sermons in the synagogues, for political speeches and for scientific lectures.

Large sums of money were collected in Europe and America, and spent in Palestine, for forwarding the movement. Many looked forward to a steady process of Jewish immigration, of Jewish land colonization and industrial development, until at last the Jews throughout the world would be able to see one country in which their race had a political and a spiritual home, in which, perhaps, the Jewish genius might repeat the services it had rendered to mankind from the same soil long ago.
[...]

THE PEACE CONVENTION

Conversation Held Prior to Paris Peace Conference (1919)
U.S. STATE DEPT.
[This conversation involved leaders from the U.S., British Empire, France, Italy, Japan, and the Hedjaz Kingdom (the WWI victors)].

Emir Feisal said that

In his memorandum of January 29th to the Peace Conference, he had asked for the independence of all the Arabic speaking peoples in Asia, from the line Alexandretta-Diarbekir southward.

He based his request on the following points:—

(i) This area was once the home of important civilisations, and its people still have the capacity to play their part in the world.

(ii) All its inhabitants speak one language—Arabic.

(iii) The area has natural frontiers which ensure its unity and its future.

(iv) Its inhabitants are of one stock—the Semitic. Foreigners do not number 1% among them.

(v) Socially and economically it forms a unit. With each improvement of the means of communication its unity becomes more evident. There are few nations in the world as homogeneous as this.

(vi) The Arabic speaking peoples fought on the side of the Allies in their time of greatest stress, and fulfilled their promises.

(vii) At the end of the war the Allies promised them independence. The Allies had now won the war, and the Arabic speaking peoples thought themselves entitled to independence and worthy of it. It was in accord with the principles laid down by President Wilson and accepted by all the Allies.

(viii) The Arab army fought to win its freedom. It lost heavily: some 20,000 men were killed. Allenby acknowledged its services in his despatches. The army was representative of Arab ideals and was composed of young Syrians, Lebanese, Hejazis, Mesopotamians, Palestinians, and Yemenis.

(ix) The blood of Arab soldiers, the massacres among the civil populations, the economic ruin of the country in the war, deserved recognition.

(x) In Damascus, Beyrout, Tripoli, Aleppo, Latakia, and the other districts of Syria, the civil population declared their independence and hoisted the Arab flag before the Allied troops arrived. The Allied Commander in Chief afterwards insisted that the flag be lowered to install temporary Military Governors. This he explained to the Arabs was provisional, till the Peace Conference settled the future of the country. Had the Arabs known it was in compliance with a secret treaty they would not have permitted it.

(xi) The Syrians who joined the Northern Army were recognised by the Allies as Belligerents. They demand through this delegation their independence.

His Father did not risk his life and his Kingdom by joining in the war at its most critical time to further any personal ambitions. He was not looking for an Empire. He rose up to free all the Arabic provinces from their Turkish Masters. He did not wish to extend the boundaries of the Hedjaz Kingdom a single inch.

His ideal was the ideal of all Arabic patriots. He could not believe that the Allies would run counter to their wishes. If they did so the consequences would be grave. The Arabs were most grateful to England and France for the help given them to free their country. The Arabs now asked them to fulfil their promises of November 1918. It was a momentous decision the Conference had to take, since on it depended the life of a nation inhabiting a country of great strategic importance between Europe and Asia.

(b) Syria The greatest difficulty would be over Syria. Syria claimed her unity and her independence, and the rest of the Arabic liberated areas wished Syria to take her natural place in the future confederation of liberated Arabic speaking Asia, the object of all Arab hopes and fears.

(c) Lebanon Some of the people of the present province of Lebanon were asking for French guarantees. Some of them did not wish to sever their connection with Syria. He was willing to admit their independence, but thought it essential to maintain some form of economic union in the interest of mutual development. He hoped nothing would be done now to render the admission of the Lebanon to the future confederation impossible, if it desired admission.

For the moment also the inhabitants of the rest of Syria hoped that the Lebanon people would of their own accord decide for federal union with themselves in Syria.

(d) Economic Interests The Arabs realised how much their country lacked development. They wanted it to be the link between the East and West, to hand on Western civilisation to Asia. They did not wish to close their doors to civilised people; on the contrary, as rulers of their own country, in their zeal for their country's betterment, they wanted to seek help from everyone who wished them well; but they could not sacrifice for this help any of the independence for which they had fought, since they regard it as a necessary basis of future prosperity. They must also guard their economic interests, as part of their duty as Governors. He hoped no Power imagined that it had the right to limit the independence of a people because it had material interests in their country.

(e) Religions Differences Arab religious differences were being exploited. These had been triumphed over in the Hedjaz army, in which all creeds co-operated to free their country. The first efforts of the Arab Government would be to maintain this welding of the faiths, in their common service of the principle of nationality.

(f) Palestine Palestine, for its universal character, he left on one side for the mutual consideration of all parties interested. With this exception he asked for the independence of the Arabic areas enumerated in his memorandum.

(g) International Enquiry as to Desires of the People When this principle was admitted, he asked that the various Provinces, on the principle of self-determination, should be allowed to indicate to the League of Nations the nature of the assistance they required. If the indications before the Conference in any one case were not conclusive as to their wishes for their complete independence or for their mandatory power, he suggested that an international inquiry, made in the area concerned, might be a quick, easy, sure and just way of determining their wishes.
[…]
4. Question of Mandatory **President Wilson** asked the Emir whether, seeing that the plan of mandatories on behalf of the League of Nations had been adopted, he would prefer for his people a single mandatory, or several.

Emir Feisal said that he would not like to assume towards his people the responsibility of giving an answer to this question. It must be for the Arab people to declare their wishes in respect to a mandatory authority. Neither he, nor his father, nor, he thought, any person now living, would be ready to assume the responsibility of deciding this question on behalf of the people. He was here to ask for the independence of his people and for their right to choose their own mandatory.

President Wilson said that he understood this perfectly, but would like to know the Emir's personal opinion.

Emir Feisal said that personally he was afraid of partition. His principle was Arab unity. It was for this that the Arabs had fought. Any other solution would be regarded by the Arabs in the light of a division of spoils after a battle. The Arabs had fought a hard fight to achieve unity. He hoped the Conference would regard them as an oppressed nation which had risen against its masters. The Arabs asked for freedom only and would take nothing less. He thought the Conference would be of the opinion that the Arab revolt had been as well conducted as any rebellion of an oppressed people in recent memory. The Arabs were an ancient people, civilized and organised at a time when the nations represented in this room were unformed. They had suffered centuries of slavery and had now seized the chance of emancipation. He hoped that the Conference would not thrust them back into the condition from which they had now emerged. The Arabs had tasted slavery: none of the nations gathered in the room knew what that meant. For 400 years the Arabs had suffered under a violent military oppression, and as long as life remained in them, they meant never to return to it.

Agreement for Arab-Jewish Cooperation (1919)
Dr. Chaim Weizmann and Feisal bin Al-Hussein

His Royal Highness the Emir Feisal, representing and acting on behalf of the Arab Kingdom of Hedjaz, and Dr. Chaim Weizmann, representing and acting on behalf of the Zionist Organization, mindful of the racial kinship and ancient bonds existing between the Arabs and the Jewish people, and realizing that the surest means of working out the consummation of their national aspirations is through the closest possible collaboration in the development of the Arab State and Palestine, and being desirous further of confirming the good understanding which exists between them have agreed upon the following Articles:

Article I

The Arab State and Palestine in all their relations and undertakings shall be controlled by the most cordial goodwill and understanding, and to this end Arab and Jewish duly accredited agents shall be established and maintained in the respective territories.

Article II

Immediately following the completion of the deliberations of the Peace Conference, the definite boundaries between the Arab State and Palestine shall be determined by a Commission to be agreed upon by the parties hereto.

Article III

In the establishment of the Constitution and Administration of Palestine all such measures shall be adopted as will afford the fullest guarantees for carrying into effect the British Government's Declaration of the 2nd of November 1917.

Article IV

All necessary measures shall be taken to encourage and stimulate immigration of Jews into Palestine on a large scale, and as quickly as possible to settle Jewish immigrants upon the land through closer settlement and intensive cultivation of the soil. In taking such measures the Arab peasant and tenant farmers shall be protected in their rights, and shall be assisted in forwarding their economic development.

Article V

No regulation nor law shall be made prohibiting or interfering in any way with the free exercise of religion; and further the free exercise and enjoyment of religious profession and worship without discrimination or preference shall forever be allowed. No religious test shall ever be required for the exercise of civil or political rights.

Article VI

The Mohammedan Holy Places shall be under Mohammedan control.

Article VII

The Zionist Organization proposes to send to Palestine a Commission of experts to make a survey of the economic possibilities of the country, and to report upon the best means for its development. The Zionist Organization will place the aforementioned Commission at the disposal of the Arab State for the purpose of a survey of the economic possibilities of the Arab State and to report upon the best means for its development. The Zionist Organization will use its best efforts to assist the Arab State in providing the means for developing the natural resources and economic possibilities thereof.

Article VIII

The parties hereto agree to act in complete accord and harmony on all matters embraced herein before the Peace Congress.

Article IX

Any matters of dispute which may arise between the contracting parties shall be referred to the British Government for arbitration.

Given Under Our Hand At London, England, The Third Day of January, One Thousand Nine Hundred and Nineteen.

Chaim Weizmann
Feisal Ibn Hussein

Reservation by the Emir Feisal

If the Arabs are established as I have asked in my manifesto of January 4th addressed to the British Secretary of State for Foreign Affairs, I will carry out what is written in this agreement. If changes are made, I cannot be answerable for failing to carry out this agreement.

Letter Correspondence Concerning Arab-Zionist Relations (1919)

Feisal bin Al-Hussein and Felix Frankfurter

Dear Mr. Frankfurter:

I want to take this opportunity of my first contact with American Zionists to tell you what I have often been able to say to Dr. Weizmann in Arabia and Europe.

We feel that the Arabs and Jews are cousins in having suffered similar oppressions at the hands of powers stronger than themselves, and by a happy coincidence have been able to take the first step towards the attainment of their national ideals together.

The Arabs, especially the educated among us, look with the deepest sympathy on the Zionist movement. Our deputation here in Paris is fully acquainted with the proposals submitted yesterday by the Zionist Organisation to the Peace Conference, and we regard them as moderate and proper. We will do our best, in so far as we are concerned, to help them through: we will wish the Jews a most hearty welcome home.

With the chiefs of your movement, especially with Dr. Weizmann, we have had and continue to have the closest relations. He has been a great helper of our cause, and I hope the Arabs may soon be in a position to make the Jews some return for their kindness. We are working together for a reformed and revived Near East, and our two movements complete one another. The Jewish movement is national and not imperialist. Our movement is national and not imperialist, and there is room in Syria for us both. Indeed I think that neither can be a real success without the other.

People less informed and less responsible than our leaders and yours, ignoring the need for cooperation of the Arabs and Zionists, have been trying to exploit the local difficulties that must necessarily arise in Palestine in the early stages of our movements. Some of them have, I am afraid, misrepresented your aims to the Arab peasantry, and our aims to the Jewish peasantry, with the result that interested parties have been able to make capital out of what they call our differences.

I wish to give you my firm conviction that these differences are not on questions of principle, but on matters of detail such as must inevitably occur in every contact of neighbouring peoples, and as are easily adjusted by mutual good will. Indeed nearly all of them will disappear with fuller knowledge.

I look forward, and my people with me look forward, to a future in which we will help you and you will help us, so that the countries in which we are mutually interested may once again take their places in the community of civilised peoples of the world.

Believe me,

Yours sincerely,
Feisal

* * *

Royal Highness,

Allow me, on behalf of the Zionist Organisation, to acknowledge your
recent letter with deep appreciation.

Those of us who come from the United States have already been gratified
by the friendly relations and the active cooperation maintained between
you and the Zionist leaders, particularly Dr. Weizmann. We knew it could
not be otherwise; we knew that the aspirations of the Arab and the Jewish
peoples were parallel, that each aspired to re-establish its nationality in its
own homeland, each making its own distinctive contribution to civilisation,
each seeking its own peaceful mode of life.

The Zionist leaders and the Jewish people for whom they speak have
watched with satisfaction the spiritual vigour of the Arab movement.
Themselves seeking justice, they are anxious that the just national aims of
the Arab people be confirmed and safeguarded by the Peace Conference.

We knew from your acts and your past utterances that the Zionist
movement -- in other words the national aim of the Jewish people -- had
your support and the support of the Arab people for whom you speak.
These aims are now before the Peace Conference as definite proposals by
the Zionist Organisation. We are happy indeed that you consider these
proposals "moderate and proper," and that we have in you a staunch
supporter for their realisation.

For both the Arab and the Jewish peoples there are difficulties ahead --
difficulties that challenge the united statesmanship of Arab and Jewish
leaders. For it is no easy task to rebuild two great civilisations that have
been suffering oppression and misrule for centuries. We each have our
difficulties we shall work out as friends, friends who are animated by
similar purposes, seeking a free and full development for the two
neighbouring peoples. The Arabs and Jews are neighbours in territory; we
cannot but live side by side as friends.

Very respectfully,
Felix Frankfurter

Article 22

To those colonies and territories which as a consequence of the late war have ceased to be under the sovereignty of the States which formerly governed them and which are inhabited by peoples not yet able to stand by themselves under the strenuous conditions of the modem world, there should be applied the principle that the well-being and development of such peoples form a sacred trust of civilisation and that securities for the performance of this trust should be embodied in this Covenant.

The best method of giving practical effect to this principle is that the tutelage of such peoples should be entrusted to advanced nations who by reason of their resources, their experience or their geographical position can best undertake this responsibility, and who are willing to accept it, and that this tutelage should be exercised by them as Mandatories on behalf of the League.

The character of the mandate must differ according to the stage of the development of the people, the geographical situation of the territory, its economic conditions and other similar circumstances.

Certain communities formerly belonging to the Turkish Empire have reached a stage of development where their existence as independent nations can be provisionally recognised subject to the rendering of administrative advice and assistance by a Mandatory until such time as they are able to stand alone. The wishes of these communities must be a principal consideration in the selection of the Mandatory.
[…]
The degree of authority, control, or administration to be exercised by the Mandatory shall, if not previously agreed upon by the Members of the League, be explicitly defined in each case by the Council.

A permanent Commission shall be constituted to receive and examine the annual reports of the Mandatories and to advise the Council on all matters relating to the observance of the mandates.
[…]

The King-Crane Commission Report (1919)

AMERICAN SECTION OF INTER-ALLIED COMMISSION ON MANDATES IN TURKEY

[This was a fact-finding mission concerning the "condition, relations, and desires" of peoples in the former Ottoman Empire].

E. We recommend, in the fifth place, serious modification of the extreme Zionist program for Palestine of unlimited immigration of Jews, looking finally to making Palestine distinctly a Jewish State.

1.   The Commissioners began their study of Zionism with minds predisposed in its favor, but the actual facts in Palestine, coupled with the force of the general principles proclaimed by the Allies and accepted by the Syrians have driven them to the recommendation here made.

2.   The commission was abundantly supplied with literature on the Zionist program by the Zionist Commission to Palestine; heard in conferences much concerning the Zionist colonies and their claims; and personally saw something of what had been accomplished. They found much to approve in the aspirations and plans of the Zionists, and had warm appreciation for the devotion of many of the colonists and for their success, by modern methods, in overcoming natural obstacles.

3.   The Commission recognized also that definite encouragement had been given to the Zionists by the Allies in Mr. Balfour's often quoted statement in its approval by other representatives of the Allies. If, however, the strict terms of the Balfour Statement are adhered to— favoring "the establishment in Palestine of a national home for the Jewish people," "it being clearly understood that nothing shall be done which may prejudice the civil and religious rights existing in non-Jewish communities in Palestine"—it can hardly be doubted that the extreme Zionist Program must be greatly modified.

For "a national home for the Jewish people" is not equivalent to making Palestine into a Jewish State; nor can the erection of such a Jewish State be accomplished without the gravest trespass upon the "civil and religious rights of existing non-Jewish communities in Palestine." The fact came out repeatedly in the Commission's conference with Jewish representatives, that the Zionists looked forward to a practically complete dispossession of the present non-Jewish inhabitants of Palestine, by various forms of purchase.

In his address of July 4, 1918, President Wilson laid down the following principle as one of the four great "ends for which the associated peoples of the world were fighting"; "The settlement of every question, whether of territory, of sovereignty, of economic arrangement, or of political relationship upon the basis of the free acceptance of that settlement by the people immediately concerned and not upon the basis of the material interest or advantage of any other nation or people which may desire a different settlement for the sake of its own exterior influence or mastery." If that principle is to rule, and so the wishes of the Palestine's population are to be decisive as to what is to be done with Palestine, then it is to be remembered that the non-Jewish population of Palestine-nearly nine tenths of the whole-are upon which the population of Palestine were more agreed than upon this. To subject a people so minded to unlimited Jewish immigration, and to steady financial and social pressure to surrender the land, would be a gross violation of the principle just quoted, and of the people's rights, though it kept within the forms of law.

It is to be noted also that the feeling against the Zionist program is not confined to Palestine, but shared very generally by the people throughout Syria as our conferences clearly showed. More than 72 percent—1,350 in all—of all the petitions in the whole of Syria were directed against the Zionist program. Only two requests—those for a united Syria and for independence—had a larger support. This general feeling was only voiced by the "General Syrian Congress," in the seventh, eighth and tenth resolutions of the statement. (Already quoted in the report.)[2]

The Peace Conference should not shut its eyes to the fact that the anti-Zionist feeling in Palestine and Syria is intense and not lightly to be flouted. No British officer, consulted by the Commissioners, believed that the Zionist program could be carried out except by force of arms. The officers generally thought that a force of not less than 50,000 soldiers would be required even to initiate the program. That of itself is evidence of a strong sense of the injustice of the Zionist program, on the

---

[2] "7. We oppose the pretentions of the Zionists to create a Jewish commonwealth in the southern part of Syria, known as Palestine, and oppose Zionist migration to any part of our country; for we do not acknowledge their title, but consider them a grave peril to our people from the national, economical, and political points of view. Our Jewish compatriots shall enjoy our common rights and assume the common responsibilities.

"8. We ask that there should be no separation of the southern part of Syria, known as Palestine, nor of the littoral western zone which includes Lebanon, from the Syrian country. We desire that the unity of the country should be guaranteed against partition under whatever circumstances.

"9. We ask complete independence for emancipated Mesopotamia and that there should be no economical barriers between the two countries.

"10. The fundamental principles laid down by President Wilson in condemnation of secret treaties impel us to protest most emphatically against any treaty that stipulates the partition of our Syrian country and against any private engagement aiming at the establishment of Zionism in the southern part of Syria, therefore we ask the complete annulment of these conventions and agreements.

part of the non-Jewish populations of Palestine and Syria. Decisions, requiring armies to carry out, are sometimes necessary, but they are surely not gratuitously to be taken in the interests of a serious injustice. For the initial claim, often submitted by Zionist representatives, that they have a "right" to Palestine, based on an occupation of 2,000 years ago, can hardly be seriously considered.

There is a further consideration that cannot justly be ignored, if the world is to look forward to Palestine becoming a definitely Jewish state [....] That consideration grows out of the fact that Palestine is "the Holy Land" for Jews, Christians, and Moslems alike. [...] With the best possible intentions, it may be doubted whether the Jews could possibly seem to either Christians or Moslems proper guardians of the holy places, or custodians of the Holy Land as a whole.

The reason is this: The places which are most sacred to Christians— those having to do with Jesus—and which are also sacred to Moslems, are not only not sacred to Jews, but abhorrent to them. It is simply impossible, under those circumstances, for Moslems and Christians to feel satisfied to have these places in Jewish hands, or under the custody of Jews. [...] In fact, from this point of view, the Moslems, just because the sacred places of all three religions are sacred to them have made very naturally much more satisfactory custodians of the holy places than the Jews could be. It must be believed that the precise meaning, in this respect, of the complete Jewish occupation of Palestine has not been fully sensed by those who urge the extreme Zionist program. For it would intensify, with a certainty like fate, the anti-Jewish feeling both in Palestine and in all other portions of the world which look to Palestine as "the Holy Land."

In view of all these considerations, and with a deep sense of sympathy for the Jewish cause, the Commissioners feel bound to recommend that only a greatly reduced Zionist program be attempted by the Peace Conference, and even that, only very gradually initiated. This would have to mean that Jewish immigration should be definitely limited, and that the project for making Palestine distinctly a Jewish commonwealth should be given up.

There would then be no reason why Palestine could not be included in a united Syrian State, just as other portions of the country, the holy places being cared for by an International and Inter-religious Commission, somewhat as at present under the oversight and approval of the Mandatary and of the League of Nations. The Jews, of course, would have representation upon this Commission.
[...]

36

The Sykes-Picot agreement is the foremost example of Western double-dealing in the Middle East since the discovery of oil. The agreement, formalized in an exchange of notes between the British Foreign Secretary and the French Ambassador to the United Kingdom in London, is named after its principal negotiators Sir Mark Sykes (1879-1919) and Georges-Picot (1870-1951). As one of several overlapping arrangements affecting the postwar settlement in West Asia secretly negotiated during the First World War, the agreement provided for the division of the region into spheres of influence comprised of nominally independent Arab states under the "tutelage" of British and French advisers.

The Husayn-McMahon Correspondence

The Sykes-Picot agreement is viewed as the foremost example of Western double-dealing in the Middle East because it appears to be inconsistent with the earlier Husayn-McMahon correspondence (1915). In this correspondence, the British Government had already reached an understanding with the Sharif of Mecca—custodian of Islam's holiest shrines—to recognize the independence of the Arab countries throughout the Levant and Arabia at the end of the war under the advice and guidance of Great Britain, in exchange for Arab support in expelling the Turks from Arabia. The British Government had conditioned this recognition on the exclusion of the "two districts of Mersina and Alexandretta and portions of Syria lying to the west of the districts of Damascus, Homs, Hama and Aleppo" where France had claims. A map illustrating the territory that had been set aside by the British Government for the Sharif of Mecca in 1915 was subsequently drawn up by mapmakers in the British Foreign Office. The map and the key confirmed that Palestine was to be "Arab" and "independent."

The Sykes-Picot Agreement

As compensation for French acquiescence to the British Government's decision to grant parts of southern Syria to the Sharifian Arab state in the Husayn-McMahon correspondence, the French Government requested access to Mosul in northern Mesopotamia, and specifically its oil-rich southern portion during the Sykes-Picot negotiations. Petroleum was first discovered in Mosul in 1899 in a British geological survey. In 1901, a German technical commission from Deutsche Bank described Mosul as a veritable "lake of petroleum." The Ottoman government gave a concession to Deutsche Bank to build a railway connecting Mesopotamia to Europe in 1903, and in 1904, an exclusive right to exploit the oil of Mosul and the neighboring province of Baghdad.

Victor Kattan, <u>Palestine and the Secret Treaties</u>, AJIL Unbound, Vol. 110, pp. 109-114, 2016 © Cambridge University Press, reproduced with permission.

The outbreak of war in 1914 would irrevocably alter the balance of power in the Middle East, where Turkey's concessions to Germany would no longer be recognized by Britain and France in the new world order. On 15 November 1915, Sir Charles Greenway, one of the founders of the Anglo-Persian oil company, requested confirmation from the British Foreign Office that the company would be given complete oil rights over any portion of the Turkish Empire which came under British influence. Confident of victory, Britain and France were determined to mould the region in its image, and to prevent any other state from competing with them for the acquisition of the region's resources. Even though the Levant was still part of the Ottoman Empire, and even though British troops had yet to occupy Turkey, the Sykes-Picot agreement began by declaring "[t]hat France and Great Britain are prepared to recognise and protect an independent Arab State or a Confederation of Arab States in the areas (A) and (B) marked on the annexed map, under the suzerainty of an Arab chief."

The Sykes-Picot agreement was viewed with concern by the Sharif when it became public knowledge because it sought to partition the Levant without his knowledge and consent into spheres of influence seemingly in contradiction to the Husayn–McMahon correspondence. In Palestine, this concern was aggravated because the Balfour Declaration—published by the British government two years after the conclusion of the Husyan-McMahon correspondence—created a further conflict of interest, this time between Arabs and Jews over Palestine's political destiny.

The Balfour Declaration

Britain decided to support Zionist aspirations to establish a Jewish national home in Palestine in the Balfour Declaration for a variety of reasons, both domestic and international. Not only was Palestine world-famous for its Christian, Muslim, and Jewish holy places, but Palestine was also home to Haifa, where Britain wanted to establish a free port to export oil to Europe. Promising Palestine to the Zionist Federation was a clever tactic to block French claims to Palestine after the war, but the Declaration was jarring to the Arabs of Palestine, not only because their interests appeared to be considered secondary, but because the Balfour Declaration contradicted the earlier Husayn-McMahon correspondence, and even the Sykes-Picot agreement, where Palestine was to be placed under international administration, "after consultation with Russia, and subsequently in consultation with the other Allies, *and the representatives of the Shereef of Mecca*." But the Sharif of Mecca was not consulted about the Balfour Declaration. Nor was the Zionist Federation specified as an interested party.

The population of Palestine was not consulted about the Balfour Declaration either. While self-determination was not a principle of universal legal applicability in November 1917, the Balfour Declaration conflicted with the Hogarth Message (January 1918) and the Anglo-French Declaration (November 1918) that promised the Arabs a nation of their own in Palestine. As the British Government expressed in the Hogarth Message, named after the director of the Arab Bureau (a unit of the Foreign Office) in Cairo, "the Entente Powers are determined that the Arab race shall be given the full opportunity of once again forming a nation in the world." This message was specifically applicable to Palestine: "So far as Palestine is concerned we are determined that no people shall be subject to another." In an attempt to reconcile this policy with the Balfour Declaration, the message referenced the return of Jews to Palestine but explained that the British Government was determined that Zionism had to be "compatible with the freedom of the existing population both economic and political."

In the Anglo-French Declaration, the Entente went further:

> The object aimed at by France and Great Britain in prosecuting in the East the War let loose by the ambition of Germany is the complete and definite emancipation of the peoples so long oppressed by the Turks and the establishment of national governments and administrations deriving their authority from the initiative and free choice of the indigenous populations.

The aim of the Anglo-French Declaration would later find expression in Article 22 of the Covenant of the League of Nations (1919), which recognized that "communities formerly belonging to the Turkish Empire have reached a stage of development where their existence as independent nations can be provisionally recognized." This independence, being provisional, was subject to the rendering of administrative advice and assistance "by a Mandatory until such time as they are able to stand alone."

A Twice Promised Land

These inconsistent pledges earned Palestine the reputation for being "twice promised" having been first promised to the Sharif of Mecca, only to have Britain contravene this pledge by concluding a secret agreement with France that would qualify that independence, and then by promising Palestine—home to the third holiest shrine in Islam—to the Zionist Federation despite opposition from the Arab population that had fought on the side of Britain in the war against Turkey. [...]

Despite these conflicting pledges, and despite opposition from the House of Lords, the Balfour Declaration was incorporated into the mandate for Palestine, which entered into force in 1923 [....]

The Settlement of the Middle Eastern Question (1989)
David Fromkin

The Middle East became what it is today both because the European
powers undertook to re-shape it and because Britain and France failed to
ensure that the dynasties, the states, and the political systems that they
established would permanently endure. During and after the First World
War, Britain and her allies destroyed the old order in the region
irrevocably; they smashed Turkish rule of the Arabic-speaking Middle East
beyond repair. To take its place, they created countries, nominated rulers,
delineated frontiers, and introduced a state system of the sort that exists
everywhere else, but they did not quell all significant local opposition to
those decisions.

As a result of the events of 1914-22, while brining to an end Europe's
Middle Eastern Question, gave birth to a Middle Eastern Question in the
Middle East itself. The settlement of 1922 [...] resolved, as far as
Europeans were concerned, the question of what—as well as who—should
replace the Ottoman Empire; yet even today there are powerful local forces
within the Middle East that remain unreconciled to these arrangements—
and may well overthrow them.

Some of the disputes, like those elsewhere in the world, are about rulers or
frontiers, but what is typical of the Middle East is that more fundamental
claims are also advanced, drawing into question not merely the dimensions
and boundaries, but the right to exist, of countries that immediately or
eventually emerged from the British and French decisions of the early
1920s: Iraq, Israel, Jordan, and Lebanon. So at this point in the twentieth
century, the Middle East is the region of the world in which wars of
national survival are still being fought with some frequency.

The disputes go deeper still: beneath such apparently insoluble, but
specific, issues as the political future of the Kurds or the political destiny
of the Palestinian Arabs, lies the more general questions of whether the
transplanted modern system of politics invented in Europe—characterized,
among other things, by the division of earth into independent secular states
based on national citizenship—will survive in the foreign soil of the
Middle East.

In the rest of the world European assumptions are so taken for granted that
nobody thinks about them anymore; but at least one of these assumptions,
the modern belief in secular civil government, is an alien creed in a region
most of whose inhabitants, for more than a thousand years, have avowed
faith in a Holy Law that governs all of life, including government and
politics.

European statesman in the First World War era did—to some extent—recognize the problem and its significance. As soon as they began to plan their annexation of the Middle East, Allied leaders recognized that Islam's hold on the region was the main feature of the political landscape with which they would have to contend. Lord Kitchener, it will be remembered, initiated in 1914 a policy designed to bring the Moslem faith under British sway. When it looked as though that might not work—for the Sherif Hussein's call to the Faithful in 1916 fell on deaf ears—Kitchener's associates proposed instead to sponsor other loyalties (to a federation of Arabic-speaking peoples, or to the family of King Hussein, or to about-to-be-created countries such as Iraq) as a rival to pan-Islam. Indeed they framed the postwar Middle East settlement with that object (among others) in view.

However, European officials at the time had little understanding of Islam. They were too easily persuaded that Moslem opposition to the politics of modernization—of Europeanization—was vanishing. Had they been able to look ahead to the last half of the twentieth century, they would have been astonished by the fervor of the Wahhabi faith in Saudi Arabia, by the passion of religious belief in warring Afghanistan, by the continuing vitality of the Moslem Brotherhood in Egypt, Syria, and elsewhere in the Sunni world, and by the recent Khomeini upheaval in Shi'ite Iran.

Continuing local opposition, whether on religious grounds or others, to the settlement of 1922 or to the fundamental assumptions upon which it was based, explains the characteristic feature of the region's politics: that in the Middle East there is no sense of *legitimacy*—no agreement on rules of the game—and no belief universally shared in the region that within whatever boundaries, the entities that call themselves countries or the men who claim to be rulers are entitled to recognition as such. In that sense, successors to the Ottoman sultans have not yet been permanently installed, even though—between 1919 and 1922—installing them was what the Allies believed themselves to be doing.

It may be that one day the challenges to the 1922 settlement—to the existence of Jordan, Israel, Iraq, and Lebanon, for example, or to the institution of secular national government in the Middle East—will be withdrawn. But if they continue in full force, then the twentieth-century Middle East will eventually be seen to be in a situation similar to Europe's in the fifth century Adm when the collapse of the Roman Empire's authority in the West threw its subjects into a crisis of civilization that obliged them to work out a new political system of their own. The European experience suggests what dimensions of such a radical crisis of political civilization might be.

It took Europe a millennium and a half to resolve its post-Roman crisis of social and political identity: nearly a thousand years to settle on the nation-state form of political organization, and nearly five hundred years more to determine which nations were entitled to be states. Whether civilization would survive the raids and conflicts of rival warrior bands; whether church or state, pope or emperor, would rule; whether Catholic or Protestant would prevail in Christendom; whether dynastic empire, national state, or city-state would command fealty; and whether, for example, a townsman of Dijon belonged to Burgundian or the French nation, were issues painfully worked out through ages of searching and strife, during which the losers—Albigensians of Southern France for example—were often annihilated. It was only at the end of the nineteenth century, with the creation of Germany and Italy, that an accepted map of Western Europe finally emerged, some 1,500 years after the old Roman map started to become obsolete.

The continuing crisis in the Middle East in our time may prove to be nowhere near so profound or so long-lasting. But its issue is the same: how diverse peoples are to regroup to create new political identities for themselves after the collapse of an ages-old imperial order to which they had grown accustomed. The Allies proposed a post-Ottoman design for the region in the early 1920s. The continuing question is whether the peoples of the region will accept it.

The settlement of 1922, therefore, does not belong entirely or even mostly to the past; it is at the very heart of current wars, conflicts, and politics in the Middle East, for the questions that Kitchener, Lloyd George, and Churchill opened up are even now being contested be forces of arms, year after year, in the ruined streets of Beirut, along the banks of the slow-moving Tigris-Euphrates, and by the waters of the Biblical Jordan.
[...]

MANDATE

Memorandum: Future of Palestine (1915)
Herbert Samuel

The course of events opens a prospect of a change, at the end of the war, in the status of Palestine. Already there is a stirring among the twelve million Jews scattered throughout the countries of this world. A feeling is spreading with great rapidity that now, at last, some advance may be made, in some way, towards the fulfillment of the hope and desire, held with unshrinkable tenacity for eighteen hundred years, for the restoration of the Jews to the land to which they are attached by ties almost as ancient as history itself.

[...]

If the attempt were made to place the 400,000 or 500,000 Mahommedans of Arab race under a Government which rested upon the support of 90,000 or 100,000 Jewish inhabitants, there can be no assurance that such a Government, even if established by the authority of the Powers, would be able to command obedience. The dream of a Jewish State, prosperous, progressive, and the home of a brilliant civilization, might vanish in a series of squalid conflicts with the Arab population. And even if a State so constituted did succeed in avoiding or repressing internal disorder, it is doubtful whether it would be strong enough to protect itself from external aggression from the turbulent elements around it. To attempt to realise the aspiration of a Jewish State one century too soon might throw back its actual realisation for many centuries more.

I am assured that the solution of the problem of Palestine which would be much the most welcome to the leaders and supporters of the Zionist movement throughout the world would be the annexation of the country to the British Empire. I believe that the solution would be cordially welcome also to the greatest number of Jews who have not hitherto been interested in the Zionist movement. It is hoped that under British rule facilities would be given to Jewish organizations to purchase land, to found colonies, to establish educational and religious institutions, and to spend usefully the funds that would be freely contributed for promoting the economic development of the country. It is hoped also that Jewish immigration, carefully regulated, would be given preference so that in course of time the Jewish people, growing into a majority and settled in the land, may be conceded some degree of self-government [....]

It would, no doubt, be necessary to establish an extra-territorial regime for the Christian sacred sites, and to vest their possession and control in an international commission, in which France on behalf of the Catholic Church, and Russia, on behalf of the Greek Church, would have leading voices. It would be desirable also that Mahommedan sacred sites should be declared inviolable, and probably that the Governor's council should include one or more Mahommedans, whose presence would be a guarantee that Mahommedan interests would be safe-guarded.

From the standpoint of British interests there are several arguments for this policy, if wider considerations should allow it to be pursued:—

1. It would enable England to fulfill in yet another sphere her historic part of civiliser of the backward countries. Under the Turk, Palestine has been blighted. For hundreds of years she has produced neither men nor things useful to the world. Her native population is sank in squalor. Roads, harbours, irrigation, sanitation, are neglected. Almost the only signs of agricultural or industrial vitality are to be found in the Jewish and, on a smaller scale, in the German colonies. Corruption is universal in the administration and in the judiciary. The Governors, who follow one another in rapid succession, are concerned only with the amount of money they can squeeze out of the country to send to Constantinople. Under British administration all this will be quickly changed. The country will be redeemed. […] England should assume control, because by that means she can move forward the purpose for which, at bottom, her Empire in the tropics and subtropics exists.

2. The British Empire, with its present vastness and prosperity, has little addition to its greatness left to win. But Palestine, small as it is in area, bulks so large in the world's imagination, that an Empire is so great but its prestige would be raised by its possession. The inclusion of Palestine within the British Empire would add a lustre even to the British Crown. It would make a most powerful appeal to the people of the United Kingdom and the Dominions, particularly if it were avowedly a means of aiding the Jews to reoccupy the country. Widespread and deep-rooted in the Protestant world is a sympathy with the idea of restoring the Hebrew people to the land which was to be their inheritance, an intense interest in the fulfillment of the prophecies which have foretold it. The redemption also of the Christian Holy Places from the vulgarities to which they are now subject, and the opening of the Holy Land, more easily than hitherto, to the visits of Christian travellers, would add to the appeal which this policy would make to the British peoples. There is probably no outcome of the war which would give greater satisfaction to powerful sections of British opinion.

3. The importance that would be attached to this annexation by British opinions would help to facilitate a wise settlement of another of the problems which will result from the war. Although Great Britain did not enter the conflict with any purpose of territorial expansion, being in it and having made immense sacrifices, there would be profound disappointment in the country if the outcome were to be se securing of great advantages by our allies, and none by ourselves. But to strip Germany of her colonies for

the benefit of England would leave a permanent feeling of such intense bitterness among the German people as to render such a course impolitic. We have to live in the same world with 70,000,000 Germans, and we should take care to give as little justification as we can for the hatching, ten, twenty, or thirty years hence of a German war of revenge. But if Great Britain can obtain the compensations, which public opinion will demand, in Mesopotamia and Palestine and not in German East Africa and West Africa, there is more likelihood of a lasting peace.

4. The belt of desert to the east of the Suez Canal is an admirable strategic frontier for Egypt. But it would be an inadequate defence if a great European Power were established on the further side. [...] Palestine in British hands would itself no doubt be open to attack, and would bring with it extended military responsibilities. But the mountainous character of the country would make its occupation by an enemy difficult, and while this outpost was being contested time would be given to allow the garrison of Egypt to be increased and the defenses to be strengthened. A common frontier with a European neighbour in the Lebanon is a far smaller risk to the vital interests of the British Empire than a common frontier at El Ariah.

5. The course which is advocated would win for England the lasting gratitude of the Jews throughout the world. In the United States, where they number about 2,000,000, and in all the other lands where they are scattered, they would form a body of opinions whose bias, where the interest of the country of which they were citizens was not involved, would be favourable to the British Empire. [...] [H]elp given now towards the attainment of the ideal which the Jews have never ceased to cherish through so many centuries of suffering, cannot fail to secure, into a far-distant future, the devoted gratitude of a whole race, whose goodwill, in time to come, may not be without its value.
[...]
The gradual growth of a considerable Jewish community under British suzerainty, in Palestine will not solve the Jewish question in Europe. [...] But it could probably hold in time 3,000,000 to 4,000,000, and some relief would be given to the pressures in Russia and elsewhere. Far more important would be the affect upon the character of the larger part of the Jewish race who must still remain intermingled with other peoples, to be a strength or to be a weakness to the countries in which they live. Let a Jewish centre be established in Palestine; let it achieve, as I believe it would achieve, a spiritual and intellectual greatness; and insensibly, but inevitably, the character of the individual Jew, wherever he might be, would be ennobled. [...]

The Jewish brain is a physiological product not to be despised. For fifteen centuries the race produced in Palestine a constant succession of great men—statesmen and prophets, judges and soldiers. If a body be again given inn which its soul can lodge, it may again enrich the world. [...]

Principal Political Events in Palestine Since British Occupation (1946)
ANGLO-AMERICAN COMMITTEE OF INQUIRY

11th December, 1917 [...] A military administration [...] was established at the end of 1917 under a Chief Administrator subject to the orders of the Commander-in-Chief (General Allenby). This Administration, with headquarters in Jerusalem, administered southern Palestine until October, 1918, when, with the occupation of the remainder of Palestine and the armistice with the Turks, its authority was extended to the whole country. Direct rule by British officers was established. [...] The Turkish laws and systems of administration were adopted with adaptations where necessary; special regard was paid to the claims of religious institutions to administer their own affairs, the authority of the Sharia courts being confirmed and a Waqf Council being set up for the administration of endowment funds in place of the former Ministry of Awqaf in Constantinople. The objective of this military administration, pending the appointment of a permanent Government, was the preservation of the *status quo,* the avoidance of the introduction of marked changes in the laws of the country or their manner of application, and the maintenance of public services with the least disturbance of the existing order.
[...]
April 1920 (Easter Sunday). Savage attacks were made by Arab rioters in Jerusalem on Jewish lives and property. Five Jews were killed and 211 injured. Order was restored by the intervention of British troops; four Arabs were killed and 21 injured. It was reported by a military commission of inquiry that the reasons for this trouble were:—

(a) Arab disappointment at the non-fulfilment of the promises of independence which they claimed had been given to them during the war.

(b) Arab belief that the Balfour Declaration implied a denial of the right of self-determination and their fear that the establishment of a National Home would mean a great increase in Jewish immigration and would lead to their economic and political subjection to the Jews.

(c) The aggravation of these sentiments on the one hand by propaganda from outside Palestine associated with the proclamation of the Emir Feisal as King of a re-united Syria and with the growth of Pan-Arab and Pan-Moslem ideas, and on the other hand by the activities of the Zionist Commission supported by the resources and influence of Jews throughout the world.
[...]
1st May, 1921. Arabs of Jaffa murderously attacked Jewish inhabitants of the town and Arab raids were made on five Jewish rural settlements; the disorders were suppressed by the police and military forces. Forty-seven

---

46 From Anglo-American Committee of Inquiry. Report: <u>A Survey of Palestine</u>, Vol. I (1946).

Jews were killed and 146 wounded, mostly by Arabs, and 48 Arabs were killed and 73 wounded, mostly by police and military action.

A Commission of Inquiry […] found that the fundamental cause of these acts of violence was "a feeling among the Arabs of discontent with, and hostility to, the Jews, due to political and economic causes, and connected with Jewish immigration, and with their conception of Zionist policy as derived from Jewish exponents". They observed, in relation to the Zionist Commission, "a belief among the Arabs that the Commission has either desired to ignore them as a factor to be taken into serious consideration, or else has combated their interests to the advantage of the Jews". […] They maintained that the root of the trouble lay in Arab fear of the consequences of a steady increase in Jewish immigration; the Arabs regarded Jewish immigration not only as an ultimate means of Arab political and economic subjection, but also as an immediate cause of Arab unemployment. The Commission found that the Arabs were aware that Jewish predominance was envisaged not only by extremists but also by the responsible representatives of Zionism. […]

The hostility shown towards the Jews during the riots was shared by Arabs of all classes; Moslem and Christian Arabs, whose relations had hitherto been uneasy, were for once united. […]

21st February, 1922. A delegation of Arab leaders in London informed the Secretary of State for the Colonies that "the People of Palestine" could not accept the Balfour Declaration or the Mandate and demanded their national independence. They declared their refusal to co-operate in any form of government other than a government responsible to the Palestinian people and requested that "the constitution for Palestine should:

(1) Safeguard the civil, political and economic interests of the people.

(2) Provide for the creation of a national independent Government in accordance with the spirit of paragraph 4, Article 12, of the Covenant of the League of Nations.

(3) Safeguard the legal rights of foreigners.

(4) Guarantee religious equality to all peoples.

(5) Guarantee the rights of minorities.

(6) Guarantee the rights of the Assisting Power".

[…]

British White Paper on Palestine (1922)
Winston Churchill

The tension which has prevailed from time to time in Palestine is mainly due to apprehensions, which are entertained both by sections of the Arab and by sections of the Jewish population. These apprehensions, so far as the Arabs are concerned are partly based upon exaggerated interpretations of the meaning of the Declaration favouring the establishment of a Jewish National Home in Palestine, made on behalf of His Majesty's Government on 2nd November, 1917.

Unauthorized statements have been made to the effect that the purpose in view is to create a wholly Jewish Palestine. Phrases have been used such as that Palestine is to become "as Jewish as England is English." His Majesty's Government regard any such expectation as impracticable and have no such aim in view. Nor have they at any time contemplated, as appears to be feared by the Arab delegation, the disappearance or the subordination of the Arabic population, language, or culture in Palestine. They would draw attention to the fact that the terms of the Declaration referred to do not contemplate that Palestine as a whole should be converted into a Jewish National Home, but that such a Home should be founded 'in Palestine.' In this connection it has been observed with satisfaction that at a meeting of the Zionist Congress, the supreme governing body of the Zionist Organization, held at Carlsbad in September, 1921, a resolution was passed expressing as the official statement of Zionist aims "the determination of the Jewish people to live with the Arab people on terms of unity and mutual respect, and together with them to make the common home into a flourishing community, the upbuilding of which may assure to each of its peoples an undisturbed national development."

It is also necessary to point out that the Zionist Commission in Palestine, now termed the Palestine Zionist Executive, has not desired to possess, and does not possess, any share in the general administration of the country. Nor does the special position assigned to the Zionist Organization in Article IV of the Draft Mandate for Palestine imply any such functions. That special position relates to the measures to be taken in Palestine affecting the Jewish population, and contemplates that the organization may assist in the general development of the country, but does not entitle it to share in any degree in its government.

Further, it is contemplated that the status of all citizens of Palestine in the eyes of the law shall be Palestinian, and it has never been intended that they, or any section of them, should possess any other juridical status. So far as the Jewish population of Palestine are concerned it appears that some among them are apprehensive that His Majesty's Government may depart from the policy embodied in the Declaration of 1917. It is necessary, therefore, once more to affirm that these fears are unfounded, and that that Declaration, re-affirmed by the Conference of the Principle Allied Powers at San Remo and again in the Treaty of Sevres, is not susceptible of change.

During the last two or three generations the Jews have recreated in Palestine a community, now numbering 80,000, of whom about one fourth are farmers or workers upon the land. This community has its own political organs; an elected assembly for the direction of its domestic concerns; elected councils in the towns; and an organization for the control of its schools. It has its elected Chief Rabbinate and Rabbinical Council for the direction of its religious affairs. Its business is conducted in Hebrew as a vernacular language, and a Hebrew Press serves its needs. It has its distinctive intellectual life and displays considerable economic activity. This community, then, with its town and country population, its political, religious, and social organizations, its own language, its own customs, its own life, has in fact "national" characteristics. When it is asked what is meant by the development of the Jewish National Home in Palestine, it may be answered that it is not the imposition of a Jewish nationality upon the inhabitants of Palestine as a whole, but the further development of the existing Jewish community, with the assistance of Jews in other parts of the world, in order that it may become a centre in which the Jewish people as a whole may take, on grounds of religion and race, an interest and a pride. But in order that this community should have the best prospect of free development and provide a full opportunity for the Jewish people to display its capacities, it is essential that it should know that it is in Palestine as of right and not on the sufferance. That is the reason why it is necessary that the existence of a Jewish National Home in Palestine should be internationally guaranteed, and that it should be formally recognized to rest upon ancient historic connection.

This, then, is the interpretation which His Majesty's Government place upon the Declaration of 1917, and, so understood, the Secretary of State is of opinion that it does not contain or imply anything which need cause either alarm to the Arab population of Palestine or disappointment to the Jews.

For the fulfilment of this policy it is necessary that the Jewish community in Palestine should be able to increase its numbers by immigration. This immigration cannot be so great in volume as to exceed whatever may be the economic capacity of the country at the time to absorb new arrivals. It is essential to ensure that the immigrants should not be a burden upon the people of Palestine as a whole, and that they should not deprive any section of the present population of their employment. Hitherto the immigration has fulfilled these conditions. The number of immigrants since the British occupation has been about 25,000.
[…]

With reference to the Constitution which it is now intended to establish in Palestine, the draft of which has already been published, it is desirable to make certain points clear. In the first place, it is not the case, as has been represented by the Arab Delegation, that during the war His Majesty's Government gave an undertaking that an independent national government should be at once established in Palestine. This representation mainly rests upon a letter dated the 24th October, 1915, from Sir Henry McMahon, then His Majesty's High Commissioner in Egypt, to the Sharif of Mecca, now King Hussein of the Kingdom of the Hejaz. That letter is quoted as conveying the promise to the Sherif of Mecca to recognise and support the independence of the Arabs within the territories proposed by him. But this promise was given subject to a reservation made in the same letter, which excluded from its scope, among other territories, the portions of Syria lying to the west of the District of Damascus. This reservation has always been regarded by His Majesty's Government as covering the vilayet of Beirut and the independent Sanjak of Jerusalem. The whole of Palestine west of the Jordan was thus excluded from Sir Henry McMahon's pledge.

Nevertheless, it is the intention of His Majesty's government to foster the establishment of a full measure of self-government in Palestine. But they are of the opinion that, in the special circumstances of that country, this should be accomplished by gradual stages and not suddenly. [...]

The Secretary of State would point out that already the present administration has transferred to a Supreme Council elected by the Moslem community of Palestine the entire control of Moslem Religious endowments (Waqfs), and of the Moslem religious Courts. To this Council the Administration has also voluntarily restored considerable revenues derived from ancient endowments which have been sequestrated by the Turkish Government. The Education Department is also advised by a committee representative of all sections of the population, and the Department of Commerce and Industry has the benefit of the co-operation of the Chambers of Commerce which have been established in the principal centres. It is the intention of the Administration to associate in an increased degree similar representative committees with the various Departments of the Government.

The Secretary of State believes that a policy upon these lines, coupled with the maintenance of the fullest religious liberty in Palestine and with scrupulous regard for the rights of each community with reference to its Holy Places, cannot but commend itself to the various sections of the population, and that upon this basis may be built up that a spirit of cooperation upon which the future progress and prosperity of the Holy Land must largely depend.

Address to Parliament Concerning Palestine Mandate (1922)

U.K. HOUSE OF COMMONS

[Winston Churchill sought a vote of support in the House of Commons after the House of Lords rejected the Balfour Declaration. The House of Commons voted in favor of the Balfour Declaration 295 to 35].

Mr. CHURCHILL […] No doubt individual Members who have always opposed the Zionist policy—if such there be—are perfectly consistent in opposing it now, but the House, as a whole, has definitely committed itself on more than one occasion to the general proposition that we should use our best endeavours to make good our pledges and facilitate the achievement of a National Home for the Jewish people in Palestine. There never has been any serious challenge to that policy in Parliament. Pledges and promises were made during the War, and they were made, not only on the merits, though I think the merits are considerable. They were made because it was considered they would be of value to us in our struggle to win the War. It was considered that the support which the Jews could give us all over the world, and particularly in the United States, and also in Russia, would be a definite palpable advantage. […] Like other Members, I accepted and was proud to accept a share in those great transactions, which left us with terrible losses, with formidable obligations, but nevertheless with unchallengeable victory. We presented ourselves to our constituents on that basis, and on that basis we were returned. Then came the peace negotiations. They were watched throughout with the utmost vigilance by Parliament. Parliament repeatedly and deliberately approved of the arrangements which were made, and included among those arrangements was the acceptance by Great Britain of mandatory responsibility for Palestine, and with that mandatory responsibility for Palestine there was also accepted responsibility for fulfilling the promises we had made to the Zionists.

[…]

I say this: You have no right to say this kind of thing as individuals; you have no right to support public declarations made in the name of your country in the crisis and heat of the War, and then afterwards, when all is cold and prosaic, to turn round and attack the Minister or the Department which is faithfully and laboriously endeavouring to translate these perfervid enthusiasms into the sober, concrete facts of day-to-day administration. […] I appeal to the House of Commons not to alter its opinion on the general question, but to stand faithfully to the undertakings which have been given in the name of Britain, and interpret in an honourable and earnest way the promise that Britain will do her best to fulfil her undertakings to the Zionists.

[…]

At the same time that this pledge was made to the Zionists, an equally important promise was made to the Arab inhabitants in Palestine—that their civil and religious rights would be effectively safeguarded, and that they should not be turned out to make room for newcomers. If that pledge was to be acted upon, it was perfectly clear that the newcomers must bring their own means of livelihood, and that they, by their industry, by their brains, and by their money, must create new sources of wealth on which they could live without detriment to or subtraction from the well-being of the Arab population. It was inevitable that, by creating these new sources of wealth, and bringing this new money into the country, they would not only benefit themselves, but benefit and enrich the entire country among all classes and races of its population.

What sources of new wealth were, opened? In the first place, there was a greatly extended and revived agriculture. As I explained to the House when I addressed hon. Members a year and a half ago, anyone who has visited Palestine recently must have seen how parts of the desert have been converted into gardens, and how material improvement has been effected in every respect by the Arab population dwelling around. On the sides of the hills there are enormous systems of terraces, and they are now the abode of an active cultivating population; whereas before, under centuries of Turkish and Arab rule, they had relapsed into a wilderness. There is no doubt whatever that in that country there is room for still further energy and development if capital and other forces be allowed to play their part. There is no doubt that there is room for a far larger number of people, and this far larger number of people will be able to lead far more decent and prosperous lives.

Apart from this agricultural work—this reclamation work—there are services which science, assisted by outside capital, can render, and of all the enterprises of importance which would have the effect of greatly enriching the land none was greater than the scientific storage and regulation of the waters of the Jordan for the provision of cheap power and light needed for the industry of Palestine, as well as water for the irrigation of new lands now desolate. [...] It would create a new world entirely, a new means of existence. And it was only by the irrigation which created and fertilised the land, and by electric power which would supply the means of employing the Arab population, that you could take, any steps towards the honest fulfilment of the pledges to which this country and this House, to an unparalleled extent of individual commitment, is irrevocably committed.

What better steps could we take, in order to fulfil our pledge to help them to establish their national home, without breaking our pledge to the Arabs that they would not be disturbed, than to interest Zionists in the creation of this new-Palestinian world which, without injustice to a single individual, without taking away one scrap of what was there before, would endow the whole country with the assurance of a greater prosperity and the means of a higher economic and social life? [...]

Mandate for Palestine (1922)
LEAGUE OF NATIONS

Whereas the Principal Allied Powers have agreed [...] to entrust to a Mandatory selected by the said Powers the administration of the territory of Palestine, which formerly belonged to the Turkish Empire, within such boundaries as may be fixed by them; and

Whereas the Principal Allied Powers have also agreed that the Mandatory should be responsible for putting into effect the declaration originally [...] in favour of the establishment in Palestine of a national home for the Jewish people, it being clearly understood that nothing should be done which might prejudice the civil and religious rights of existing non-Jewish communities in Palestine, or the rights and political status enjoyed by Jews in any other country; and

Whereas recognition has thereby been given to the historical connection of the Jewish people with Palestine and to the grounds for reconstituting their national home in that country; and

Whereas the Principal Allied Powers have selected His Britannic Majesty as the Mandatory for Palestine; and
[...]
ART. 2. The Mandatory shall be responsible for placing the country under such political, administrative and economic conditions as will secure the establishment of the Jewish national home, [...] the development of self-governing institutions, and also for safeguarding the civil and religious rights of all the inhabitants of Palestine, irrespective of race and religion.
[...]
ART. 4. An appropriate Jewish agency shall be recognised as a public body for the purpose of advising and co-operating with the Administration of Palestine in such economic, social and other matters as may affect the establishment of the Jewish national home and the interests of the Jewish population in Palestine, and, subject always to the control of the Administration to assist and take part in the development of the country.

The Zionist organization, so long as its organization and constitution are in the opinion of the Mandatory appropriate, shall be recognised as such agency. [...]

ART. 6. The Administration of Palestine, while ensuring that the rights and position of other sections of the population are not prejudiced, shall facilitate Jewish immigration under suitable conditions and shall encourage, in co-operation with the Jewish agency referred to in Article 4, close settlement by Jews on the land, including State lands and waste lands not required for public purposes.
[...]

Memorandum to the League of Nations – Commission on the Holy Places (1922)
THE VATICAN

The Holy See raises no objection to the decision already taken by the League of Nations to entrust the Mandate for Palestine to Great Britain [....]

Nevertheless, the Holy See conceives it to be its duty to request that certain articles in the Balfour Draft should be modified, in the interest of the noble British nation, which would surely desire that the Mandate for Palestine should be administered in an atmosphere of peace and without causing any uneasiness to the religious sentiment of the people concerned.

According to these articles:

(1)   The Jews would enjoy in Palestine a privileged and preponderating position as compared with Catholics and other nationalities and creeds.

(2)   The rights of the Christian communities—and especially those of Catholics—would not be adequately safeguarded.

With regard to the first point, although in the preamble, which aims at the establishment of a national home for the Jewish people, the Balfour Draft guarantees that " nothing should be done which might prejudice the civil and religious rights of existing non-Jewish communities in Palestine"; nevertheless, it appears from the wording of certain articles that there is an intention to confer a definitely preponderating influence, from an economic, administrative, and political point of view, on the Jewish element as compared with the other nationalities and creeds.

In the Balfour Draft:

a)   A Jewish agency, which is nothing less than the very influential Zionist organization, is recognised as a public body (Article 4);

b)   This Jewish agency is given the role of co-operating with the administration of Palestine and is endowed with very wide powers, even in questions regarding "the development of the country";

c)   The immigration of Jews is encouraged (Art. 7); and care is taken to provide and to facilitate a "close settlement" for Jews, who are even to receive grants of State lands or waste lands (Art. 6); they are also to be given preference in connection with contracts for public works (Art. 11).

The effect of all these provisions of the Draft, tending to give the Jewish element a definitely preponderating influence over all the other races and creeds of Palestine, appears to be not only a serious injury to the established rights of the latter, but also to be incompatible with Article 22 of the Treaty of Versailles, which defines the nature and object of all mandates. According to this article, a Mandate is a tutelage which is assumed by some power for the benefit of "people not yet able to stand by themselves under the strenuous conditions of the modern world"; and its object is "a sacred trust of civilization", namely, the "well-being and development of such peoples".

The passages just quoted are obviously incompatible with a Mandate which would prove to be an instrument for the subjection of native Catholics and races or of religious communities, for the benefit of another nationality or creed.

As regards the second point, special attention should be directed to Article 14 of the Balfour Draft, which provides, in conformity with Article 95 of the Treaty of Sevres, for a "special Commission to study and regulate all questions and claims relating to the different religious communities."

The Holy See desires at once to state that it could never agree that this Commission should consider itself entitled to discuss the question of ownership of the Holy Places, almost all of which, for centuries—even under the Turkish domination—always remained in the undisturbed possession of Catholics.

The Holy See further ventures to remark that the Commission, as provided for in Article 14 of the Balfour Draft, would be unable to arrive at any concrete result. Since all the creeds concerned are to be represented upon the Commission, it is only too probable that violent dissensions may arise within that body, the inevitable result of which will be a combination of all the other members against those of the religion which is in possession of the particular Holy Place in question. The result will be to make any reasoned decision by Commission impossible.
[...]

The Jews in Palestine (1926)
Leonard Stein

Great Britain administers Palestine under a Mandate which she has formally undertaken to exercise on behalf of the League of Nations. [...] It is an "A" Mandate, of the type designed for the ex-Ottoman Territories in Asia, as contrasted with the former German colonies in Africa and the Pacific. In this respect Palestine is on the same footing as Syria and Iraq. Palestine, however, is *sui generis*, and the Mandate has certain distinctive features which give it a character of its own.

Of these, the first is the absence of any express provision for the eventual independence of Palestine. The Syrian Mandate requires the Mandatory "to enact measures to facilitate the progressive development of Syria and the Lebanon as independent States." A similar clause was inserted in the draft Mandate for Iraq. There is no corresponding stipulation in the Mandate for Palestine, and there is reason to believe that the omission is not accidental.

But it would be a mistake to infer that the Mandate is in this case a cloak for annexation. On the contrary, of all the mandated territories, there is none in which the Mandatory's status as trustee has been more clearly brought out. [...] [T]he situation in Palestine was much more exhaustively reviewed by the Permanent Mandates Commission. This is a body of independent experts whose duty is to watch the execution of the various Mandates and to report annually to the League Council. [...] If the Mandate for Palestine is distinguished from others of the same general type by the omission of the independence clause, that does not mean that the Mandatory ceases in any sense to be a trustee; what it means is that this is a case in which the trusteeship is deemed to be of indefinite duration.

A second distinctive feature of the Palestine Mandate is the provision made in Articles 13 and 14 for the safeguarding of the Holy Places. [...]

Under Article 13 of the Mandate, the Holy Places are withdrawn from the jurisdiction of the local authorities in Palestine and are placed under the direct control of the Mandatory Power, which is responsible solely to the League of Nations. On the other hand, the Mandatory Power has itself no authority to deal with questions in dispute. Its function is merely to prevent any disturbance of the status quo, -- a task which it has performed with punctilious exactitude. Conflicting claims -- and they are many -- are reserved for settlement under the general auspices of the League of Nations. A special Commission to be set up for this purpose is to be appointed by the Mandatory Power, but "the method of nomination, the composition and the functions of this Commission shall be submitted to the Council of the League for its approval, and the Commission shall not enter upon its functions without the approval of the Council."
[...]

A third feature of the Mandate, and much the most far-reaching in its effects, is the group of Articles dealing with the establishment in Palestine of a national home for the Jews on the basis of the Balfour Declaration.

It was on November 2, 1917, that Lord Balfour, at that time Foreign Secretary in Mr. Lloyd George's Coalition Cabinet, assured the Zionist Organization that "His Majesty's Government view with favor the establishment in Palestine of a national home for the Jewish people, and will use their best endeavors to facilitate the achievement of this object, it being clearly understood that nothing shall be done which may prejudice the civil and religious rights of the existing non-Jewish communities in Palestine or the rights and political status enjoyed by Jews in any other country."

The initiative was taken by Great Britain, but in issuing the Balfour Declaration she did not speak for herself alone. She had secured in advance the concurrence of France and Italy, and both powers proceeded to make corresponding statements on their own account. The United States had not declared war on Turkey, and it was, for that reason, hardly possible for the Declaration to be formally endorsed by the American Government. It had, however, been framed with the full knowledge and approval of President Wilson. The President had consistently supported the Zionists with the full weight of his influence and shortly after the Declaration was issued, he publicly expressed his satisfaction. In 1922 a resolution in favor of the establishment in Palestine of a Jewish national home was adopted without opposition by both Houses of Congress, and on December 3, 1925, the British and American governments ratified a Convention by which the United States agrees to the administration of Palestine by Great Britain under the terms of the Mandate [....]

Nor did the Declaration reflect a mere momentary impulse. From the earliest days of the war, the Zionists had had influential friends in the Allied Governments. Their claims were disregarded in the Anglo-French agreement of May, 1916, under which a mutilated Palestine was to play Tangier to a Moroccanized Syria. But even at that stage the Allies were aware that Zionism was a force to be reckoned with. As early as March 13, 1916, Sir Edward Grey reminded M. Sazonov that "a numerous and most influential section of Jewry in all countries would highly appreciate the proposal of an agreement concerning Palestine which would fully satisfy the Jewish aspirations." A few days later, M. Sazonov informed the British and French Ambassadors in Petrograd that "as regards Palestine, the Russian Government . . . will put forward no objection on principle to the settlement of Jewish colonists in that country." [...]

The course of Jewish immigration, excluding returning residents, can be seen from the following table:

JEWISH IMMIGRANTS INTO PALESTINE

Armistice to end of 1920 (14 months)	8,346
1921	8,517
1922	7,844
1923	7,421
1924	12,856
1925, January to October (10 months)	29,124

Total	74,108

Since the Armistice, about 5,000 Jewish refugees who left Palestine during the war have returned to their homes. If these are added to the immigrants proper, the total is brought up to about 79,000. During the same period there have been about 11,000 Jewish emigrants, of whom nearly half were pre-war residents, as distinct from recent arrivals. The result is a net Jewish immigration, including returning refugees, of (in round numbers) 68,000. In 1914, Palestine had a Jewish population of about 90,000. War, famine, emigration and forcible expulsion by the Turks left only about 55,000 survivors at the time of the Armistice. In April, 1925, it was officially estimated that there were 104,000 Jews in Palestine, and this figure must since have increased to something like 125,000, or about 15 percent of the total population. Thus the losses of the war have been more than made good, and since the beginning of 1925 Jewish immigrants have been coming in at the rate of 2,900 a month.

Of 12,856 Jewish immigrants in 1924, 10,852, or over 84 percent came from Poland and other parts of eastern and south-eastern Europe. These figures are fairly typical, though there has recently been a growing immigration of Sephardic Jews from the Balkans and from various parts of Asia. From another point of view, the character of the immigration has recently undergone a striking change. In 1922 the proportion of middle-class, as distinct from working-class, immigration was only 13 percent. This figure rose to 40.6 percent in 1924 and has shown a tendency to mount still higher in 1925. Immigrants of this type, who are not brought out to fill vacancies in the labor-market, are required by the Regulations to possess at least a moderate amount of capital. In some cases they are persons of substantial means, and they usually bring with them, not only capital, but some experience in industry or trade. Some of them settle on the land, and more would do so if land were not so scarce and land-values so inflated. On the other hand, many of the middle-class immigrants are making at least temporary homes in the towns, with the result that Palestine is going through what may almost be called an industrial revolution. In November, 1923, particulars were available of 279 Jewish industrial undertakings employing 2,331 workmen and representing a capital investment of $4,200,000. In July, 1925, the corresponding figures were 547, 4,894 and $7,585,000. Some of these enterprises are at present on an insignificant scale, but others -- such as the brick and tile factory at Jaffa and the cement works and vegetable oil factory at Haifa -- are of considerable size and are considered creditable examples of modern industrial practice. [...]

It is obvious that middle-class and working-class immigration tend to play into one another's hands, since the influx of capital for investment produces a corresponding demand for labor. Thus, in the first half of 1925, when middle-class immigration reached unparalleled proportions, more working-class immigrants entered Palestine than in the whole of the previous year. At the same time, it is felt in some quarters that the balance between town and country is being endangered by these developments, and it has also been suggested that what is really in progress is a boom which is bound to be followed by a reaction. It is true that industry has recently made more rapid strides than agriculture, though it is also true that the proportion as well as the number of Jews on the land has not only not decreased, but is appreciably larger today than it was at the end of 1922. Whether industry or agriculture is destined to predominate time alone will tell. [...]

It is, indeed, natural that agriculture should develop more slowly. The Mandate requires the Government to make unoccupied state lands available for Jewish colonization. The state lands, however, have still to be finally delimited, and all that is definitely known is that the vacant area is not as extensive as was originally assumed. [...] [A]ll but a trifling proportion of the land acquired by the Jews has had to be bought in the open market at prices which are being rapidly forced up. The Jews now hold nearly 250,000 acres of land in Palestine, of which about 50,000 acres have been acquired during the past twelve months. Again, agricultural colonization is seldom self-supporting in the early stages, and this is especially true in Palestine, where there has almost always to be heavy expenditure on preparatory work before the land becomes fit for settlement. [...]

In spite of these handicaps, the number of Jews on the land has steadily increased and now stands at about 23,000 or 21 percent of the Jewish population, as compared with 15,000 or 18 percent, at the census of October, 1922.

The Jews have not confined themselves to the promotion of industry and agriculture. They have created so extensive a network of Hebrew schools that 85 percent of the Jewish children between five and fourteen years of age are being educated, as compared with 76 percent in the case of the Christians and 14 percent in the case of the Moslems. The Jews have also opened a Technical Institute and an Institute of Agricultural Research, -- both of them the only establishments of their kind in the country, -- while the educational system is now about to be crowned by the Hebrew

University of Jerusalem, of which the first three Departments, devoted respectively to Chemistry, Medical Research and Jewish Studies, have already been opened. In coöperation with the Government and other agencies, the Jews are doing medical and sanitary work in Palestine on an extensive scale. By these and other means, they are contributing materially to the development of Palestine as a whole and to the strengthening of its social and economic fabric. They are, at the same time, enlarging and enriching their own corporate life. What is growing up in Palestine is a vigorous and many-sided Jewish society, which has its weaknesses as well as its virtues, but which has in any case its distinctive tone and color. [...]

There is in some quarters a hazy impression that if Palestine is not a Jewish State, it is at all events under Jewish administration. Nothing could be further from the truth. The following figures were given in evidence last year before the Permanent Mandates Commission of the League of Nations:

PALESTINE ADMINISTRATION

	Senior Service	*Junior Service*	*Total*
Christians	231	1,212	1,443
Moslems	76	1,943	2,019
Jews	47	764	811
Others	2	6	8
	---	------	------
Totals	356	3,925	4,281

At this time the High Commissioner was a Jew. He has since been succeeded by a Christian, Lord Plumer, and the only Jew now holding high office in the Palestine Government is the Attorney-General. [...]

Great Britain has rendered [...] two services of vital importance, and these are none the less services to the Jews because they have also been services to Palestine as a whole. She has, in the first place, kept the peace. Palestine has not been altogether free from disorder, but whatever unrest there has been is insignificant in the light of what has occurred since the war in Syria and -- in the earlier stages -- in Iraq. Since the Jaffa riots of May, 1921, Palestine has been perfectly quiet [....]

In the second place, the Government has stood firm on the vital question of immigration. If it has not conceded an unrestricted right of entry to the Jews, neither has it conceded an embargo to the Arabs. It has regulated immigration, but it has allowed it to come in in what is now a steady and growing stream. [...]

When the Balfour Declaration became known to the Arabs, they were in genuine doubt as to what might be in store for them. Their anxieties, in themselves not unnatural, were sedulously played upon by propagandists who had their own motives for making mischief in Palestine. The Damascus Nationalists took a hand in the game, and various interested parties in Europe fished diligently in troubled waters. The Civil Administration had hardly been set up before the almost inevitable explosion took place in the Jaffa district in May, 1921, when six days' rioting resulted in the loss of ninety-five Jewish and Arab lives. This is as near as post-war Palestine has ever come to serious disorder. There has since been nothing more alarming than an occasional brawl. The Arabs, however, had still to be reconciled to the new régime. They now embarked on a policy of non-coöperation on the lines familiar in India, in Cyprus and in other parts of the East. The Government was not actively opposed, but all its advances were rejected, while the Arab leaders poured forth an almost incessant stream of protests. It is not easy to say how far these leaders spoke for the Arab population at large. That they had, at one time at least, a considerable body of opinion behind them can hardly be doubted. On the other hand, the simple-minded folk who compose the bulk of the Arab population take little or no interest in public affairs. The shopkeepers were occasionally called upon to pull down their shutters when the leaders ordered a peaceful demonstration, but beyond this little was expected of the rank-and-file, and the policy of non-coöperation made no perceptible difference to their ordinary routine, any more than it prevented their betters from putting Jewish money into their pockets when there was business to be done.

The policy of the Arab leaders had, however, one important consequence. It delayed indefinitely the development of self-governing institutions. In 1922 Palestine was granted a Constitution providing for the establishment of a Legislative Council with extensive, though not unlimited, powers. Of the 23 seats on the Council, eleven were to be occupied by the High Commissioner and other British officials. The remaining twelve members were to be popularly elected on a wide franchise, with the proviso that the Jewish and Christian communities were to have two seats each. Elections were held early in 1923, but they were boycotted by the Arabs and were eventually annulled. The 1922 Constitution was not repealed, but it was left in abeyance. The Government did not, however, abandon its attempt to secure the cooperation of representative Arabs. Two successive offers were made, but both were promptly rejected. The Government had now spoken its last word. Since the end of 1923, the central administration has remained purely autocratic, though all the larger towns have their own municipal authorities, while in the rural areas there are twenty-seven elected local councils, of which twenty-three are in Arab villages.
[…]

REVOLT

The Palestine Disturbances of August, 1929 ("Shaw Commission" Report) (1930)
BRITISH COLONIAL OFFICE

There can, in our view, be no doubt that racial animosity on the part of the Arabs, consequent upon the disappointment of their political and national aspirations and fear for their economic future, was the fundamental cause of the outbreak on August last. [...]

In less than ten years three serious attacks have been made by Arabs on Jews. For eighty years before the first of these attacks there is no recorded instance of any similar incidents. It is obvious then that the relations between the two races during the past decade must have differed in some material respect from those which previously obtained. Of this we found ample evidence. The reports of the Military Court and of the local Commission which, in 1920 and in 1921 respectively, enquired into the disturbances of those years, drew attention to the change in the attitude of the Arab population towards the Jews in Palestine. This was borne out by the evidence tendered during our enquiry when representatives of all parties told us that before the War the Jews and Arabs lived side by side if not in amity at least with tolerance, a quality which today is almost unknown in Palestine.
[...]
When the terms of the Balfour Declaration became generally known the Arabs were greatly disappointed with the position in which they found themselves. In particular this was true of the Arab leaders, many of them members of a class that, under the Turkish rule, had been dominant in the country and whose sense of nationalism had been stimulated by the events of the Great War. Those leaders found not merely that they would not achieve their ambitions, but that their leadership in the country was likely to be threatened by the advent of a new and powerful element composed of a capable and progressive people.

Upon the announcement of policy in 1922 the Jews found that His Majesty's Government were not prepared to accept the exaggerated interpretations which in some quarters had been placed upon the Balfour Declaration. In consequence some sections of the Jews also in their turn were disappointed.

To the political disappointment of the Arabs there came in time to be added fear of the Jew as an economic competitor. In pre-war days the Jews in Palestine, regarded collectively, had formed an unobtrusive minority; individually many of them were dependent on charity for their living, while many of the remainder—in particular the colonists—brought direct and obvious material benefits to the inhabitants of the area in which they settled. The Jewish immigrant of the post-war period, on the other hand, is a person of greater energy and initiative than were the majority of the Jewish community of pre-war days. He represents a movement created by an important international organization supported by funds which, judged by Arab standards, seem inexhaustible. To the Arabs it must appear improbable that such competitors will in years to come be content to share the country with them. These fears have been intensified by the more extreme statements of Zionist policy and the Arabs have come to see in the Jewish immigrant not only a menace to their livelihood but a possible overlord of the future.

Fear of the Jew as an economic competitor has been intensified in two ways. The political campaign of opposition to the Jewish National Home has kept the fear present in the mind of the Arab people, and the results of Jewish enterprise and penetration have been such as to confirm their early fears and to lead them today to the opinion that ultimately they will be excluded from the soil. To some extent these two causes have reacted upon one another. If an Arab was dispossessed or was replaced in employment by a Jew, he and his friends gave public expression to his grievance; the general political opposition to the Jews was thus strengthened and, as a result, the people came to view ail economic issues in the light of political considerations and to find in them causes for complaint, sometimes even where none existed. This interplay of political and economic grievances added to the feeling of discontent. Step by step the whole Arab people become identified with their leaders in opposition to the Jewish National Home and, in consequence, united with them in a demand for self-government. They were reminded of the war-time pledges and of the constitutional position in other Arab countries; they were given to believe that, with self-government, taxation would be reduced, immigration would be checked, if not stopped, and each peasant would obtain a secure title to his land.

[…]

In other words, those consequences of Jewish enterprise which have most closely affected the Arab people have been such that the Arab leaders could use them as the means of impressing upon their followers that a continuance of Jewish immigration and land purchases could have no other result than that the Arabs would in time be deprived of their livelihood and that they, and their country, might ultimately come under the political domination of the Jews. Racial antipathy needed no other stimulus, but it was further encouraged by a spirit of mutual intolerance which has unfortunately been a marked feature of the past decade in Palestine. From the beginning the two races had no common interest. They differed in language, in religion, and in outlook. […]

If we have succeeded in conveying a correct impression of the general undercurrent of feeling in Palestine, it will be realized that an incident or a series of incidents that elsewhere would at worst lead to a local riot would be apt in that country to result in widespread disturbance. The removal of the screen from the pavement in front of the Wailing Wall on the Jewish Day of Atonement in September, 1928, was the beginning of such a series of incidents. [...]

The Wailing Wall problem, which for nearly three months had received little public notice as a political or racial question was revived in a form even more acute than ever before when, towards the end of July last, it became known that, in the light of an opinion of the Law Officers to the Crown, the Palestine Government had decided to permit the resumption of building operations that would have the effect, *inter alia*, of converting the pavement in front of the Wall into a thoroughfare. In the middle of June this decision had been communicated to the Palestine Zionist Executive, who had not contested its validity. Nevertheless, Jewish opinion throughout Palestine strongly resented it. Dissatisfaction at the earlier decisions was succeeded, as witnesses have told us, by a feeling that the Government had created a situation of humiliation for the Jewish people in Palestine. Expression to these feelings was given in the demonstration held at Tel Aviv on the 14th of August and in the Jewish procession to and demonstration at the Wailing Wall on the following day. At the Wall on the 15th of August the Zionist flag was raised, the Zionist anthem was sung, two minutes' silence was observed, and there were such cries as "The Wall is ours." The conduct of the counter demonstration by the Moslems on the following day was even more regrettable; the crowd took out petitions placed in the crevices of the Wall by Jewish worshippers and burnt these and prayer books and prayer sheets which are used in the devotional services at the Wall.

This series of incidents, culminating in the two demonstrations, roused the latent feelings of hostility and animosity between the two races, each of which regarded the demonstration of their co-religionists as the mere assertion of their lawful rights and the other demonstration as an improper trespass upon those rights. Among the Moslem Arabs throughout the country the story spread that the Jews had attacked or intended to take the Moslem Holy Places. To the general undercurrent of feeling, already intensified through excitement caused by earlier diversity of grievances. Racial antipathy, accentuated among the Arabs by a sense of religious grievance and among the Jews by a feeling of humiliation and dissatisfaction, found its outlet in a series of attacks and assaults of varying degrees of severity, which, during the week following the Moslem demonstration, were made by Arabs on Jews and by Jews on Arabs in the Old and New Cities of Jerusalem and, to a less extent, in other parts of the country. On the 23rd of August the more serious disturbances began.

The chain of circumstances connected with the Wailing Wall is unbroken from the Jewish Day of Atonement in September, 1928, up to the 23rd of

August, 1929, and must in our view, be regarded as a whole. If from this series of events some incident had to be selected as having been more than any other single incident an immediate cause of the outbreak, that incident must, in our view, be the Jewish demonstration which took place at the Wailing Wall on the 15th of August [....]

(A) General Conclusion on More Important Matters

(i) Nature of the outbreak

1. The outbreak in Jerusalem on the 23rd of August was from the beginning an attack by Arabs on Jews for which no excuse in the form of earlier murders by Jews has been established.

2. The outbreak was not premeditated. Disturbances did not occur simultaneously in all parts of Palestine but spread from the capital through a period of days to most outlying centres of population and to some rural districts.

3. [...] [T]he disturbances [...] took the form, for the most part, of a vicious attack by Arabs on Jews accompanied by wanton destruction of Jewish property. A general massacre of the Jewish community at Hebron was narrowly averted. In a few instances, Jews attacked Arabs and destroyed Arab property. These attacks, though inexcusable, were in most cases in retaliation for wrongs already committed by Arabs in the neighbourhood in which the Jewish attacks occurred.
[...]

(B) Summary of Findings as to Causes of the Outbreak of August Last

44. The fundamental cause, without which in our opinion disturbances either would not have occurred or would have been little more than a local riot, is the Arab feeling of animosity and hostility towards the Jews consequent upon the disappointment of their political and national aspirations and fear for their economic future. [...] The feeling as it exists to-day is based on the twofold fear of the Arabs that by Jewish immigration and land purchase they may be deprived of their livelihood and in time pass under the political domination of the Jews.
[...]

Letter to Dr. Chaim Weizmann (1931)

Ramsay MacDonald

[Following the Shaw Commission, the British government issued a White Paper restricting Jewish immigration and settlement development. The Zionists opposed these policies through a letter-writing campaign. This letter is in response to the Zionist opposition].

Dear Dr. Weizmann:

In order to remove certain misconceptions and misunderstandings which have arisen as to the policy of his Majesty's Government with regard to Palestine, […] I have pleasure in forwarding you the following statement of our position, which "will fall to be read as the authoritative interpretation of the White Paper on the matters with which this letter deals.
[…]
His Majesty's Government did not regard it as necessary to quote *in extenso* the declarations of policy which have been previously made, but attention is drawn to the fact that, not only does the White Paper of 1930 refer to and endorse the White Paper of 1922, which has been accepted by the Jewish Agency, but it recognizes that the undertaking of the mandate is an undertaking to the Jewish people and not only to the Jewish population of Palestine. The White Paper places in the foreground of its statement my speech in the House of Commons on the 3rd of April, 1930, in which I announced, in words that could not have been made more plain, that it was the intention of his Majesty's Government to continue to administer Palestine in accordance with the terms of the mandate as approved by the Council of the League of Nations. […]

A good deal of criticism has been directed to the White Paper upon the assertion that it contains injurious allegations against the Jewish people and Jewish labor organizations. Any such intention on the part of his Majesty's Government is expressly disavowed. It is recognized that the Jewish Agency have all along given willing cooperation in carrying out the policy of the mandate and that the constructive work done by the Jewish people in Palestine has had beneficial effects on the development and well-being of the country as a whole. His Majesty's Government also recognizes the value of the services of labor and trades union organizations in Palestine, to which they desire to give every encouragement.
[…]
We may proceed to the contention that the mandate has been interpreted in a manner highly prejudicial to Jewish interests in the vital matters of land settlement and immigration. It has been said that the policy of the White Paper would place an embargo on immigration and would suspend, if not indeed terminate, the close settlement of the Jews on the land, which is a primary purpose of the mandate. In support of this contention particular stress has been laid upon the passage referring to State lands in the White Paper, which says that "it would not be possible to make available for Jewish settlement in view of their actual occupation by Arab cultivation

and of the importance of making available suitable land on which to place the Arab cultivators who are now landless."

The language of this passage needs to be read in the light of the policy as a whole. It is desirable to make it clear that the landless Arabs, to whom it was intended to refer in the passage quoted, were such Arabs as can be shown to have been displaced from the lands which they occupied in consequence of the land passing into Jewish hands, and who have not obtained other holdings on which they establish themselves, or other equally satisfactory occupation. […] It is to landless Arabs within this category that his Majesty's Government feels itself under an obligation to facilitate their settlement upon the land. The recognition of this obligation in no way detracts from the larger purposes of development which his Majesty's Government regards as the most effectual means of furthering the establishment of a national home for the Jews…

Further, the statement of policy of his Majesty's Government did not imply a prohibition of acquisition of additional lands by Jews. It contains no such prohibition, nor is any such intended. What it does contemplate is such temporary control of land disposition and transfers as may be necessary not to impair the harmony and effectiveness of the scheme of land settlement to be undertaken. […]

Cognate to this question is the control of immigration. It must first of all be pointed out that such control is not in any sense a departure from previous policy. From 1920 onward, when the original immigration ordinance came into force, regulations for the control of immigration have been issued from time to time, directed to prevent illicit entry and to define and facilitate authorized entry. The right of regulation has at no time been challenged.

But the intention of his Majesty's Government appears to have been represented as being that "no further immigration of Jews is to be permitted as long as it might prevent any Arab from obtaining employment." His Majesty's Government never proposed to pursue such a policy. They were concerned to state that, in the regulation of Jewish immigration, the following principles should apply: viz., that "it is essential to insure that the immigrants should not be burden on the people of Palestine as a whole, and that they should not deprive any section of the present population of their employment." *(White Paper 1922.)*

In one aspect, his Majesty's Government have to be mindful of their obligations to facilitate Jewish immigration under suitable conditions, and to encourage close settlement by Jews on the land; in the other aspect, they have to be equally mindful of their duty to insure that no prejudice results to the rights and position of the non-Jewish community. It is because of this apparent conflict of obligation that his Majesty's Government have felt bound to emphasize the necessity of the proper application of the absorptive principle.

That principle is vital to any scheme of development, the primary purpose of which must be the settlement both of Jews and of displaced Arabs on the land. It is for that reason that his Majesty's Government have insisted, and are compelled to insist, that government immigration regulations must be properly applied. The considerations relevant to the limits of absorptive capacity are purely economic considerations.

His Majesty's Government did not prescribe and do not contemplate any stoppage or prohibition of Jewish immigration in any of its categories. The practice of sanctioning a labor schedule of wage-earning immigrants will continue. In each case consideration will be given to anticipated labor requirements for works which, being dependent upon Jewish or mainly Jewish capital, would not be or would not have been undertaken unless Jewish labor was available. With regard to public and municipal works failing to be financed out of public funds, the claim of Jewish labor to a due share of the employment available, taking into account Jewish contributions to public revenue, shall be taken into consideration. As regards others kinds of employment, it will be necessary in each case to take into account the factors bearing upon the demand for labor, including the factor of unemployment among both the Jews and the Arabs. Immigrants with prospects of employment other than employment of a purely ephemeral character will not be excluded on the sole ground that the employment cannot be guaranteed to be of unlimited duration.

In determining the extent to which immigration at any time may be permitted it is necessary also to have regard to the declared policy of the Jewish Agency to the effect that "in all the works or undertakings carried out or furthered by the Agency it shall be deemed to be a matter of principle that Jewish labor shall be employed." His Majesty's Government do not in any way challenge the right of the Agency to formulate or approve and endorse this policy. The principle of preferential, and indeed exclusive, employment of Jewish labor by Jewish organizations is a principle which the Jewish Agency are entitled to affirm. But it must be pointed out that if in consequence of this policy Arab labor is displaced or existing unemployment becomes aggravated, that is a factor in the situation to which the mandatory is bound to have regard.

His Majesty's Government desire to say, finally, as they have repeatedly and unequivocally affirmed, that the obligations imposed upon the mandatory by its acceptance of the mandate are solemn international obligations from which there is not now, nor has there been at any time, an intention to depart. [...]

Ramsay MacDonald

68

Memorandum Concerning Unrest in Palestine (1936)
Leland Morris

Sir: […] To understand the atmosphere which prevailed in Palestine immediately prior to April 17 when it appeared that a disturbance of the local peace was imminent, the Consulate General believes it wise to refer to its despatch No. 691 of November 25, 1935, which was submitted subsequent to the events which succeeded the discovery of an important arms importation at the port of Jaffa and which described a situation closely related to that existing at the present moment. At that time, it will be remembered, tension was high and the fear existed that an open break between Arabs and Jews would occur at any time. The situation was further involved by the activities of Sheikh Izz-Ed-Din Kassem who organized bands of political highwaymen and, in effect, challenged the police to maintain security on the roads of north Palestine. His actions were said to constitute his contribution to the organized Arab protests that the local Government was unable to discover the importers or even to put a stop to the traffic in arms. Sheikh Izz-Ed-Din's activities resulted in the death of one British constable, the wounding of another, and in the death of four members of his organization (if such it may be called) and the capture of five others. Political brigandage thereafter disappeared in Palestine until during the week of April 5, when it reappeared and helped to precipitate the present disorders.

[…]

[T]he first factor contributing to the occurrence of the disturbances was the recrudescence of political highway robbery by bands of Arabs. Although Sheikh Izz-ed-Din had been captured and executed by the police, his spirit was reinvoked to inspire the Arabs to begin again their annoying practices on the highways. There was, however, a difference in the *modus operandi* of these bands as compared with those which operated under Sheikh Izz-ed-Din. The latter worked merely to annoy the Government, whereas the former operate on what can only be described as anti-Jewish lines. On one occasion busses were stopped on the Tulkarm-Nablus Road and all the passengers were forced to alight. The only three Jews in the busses were then segregated from their fellow passengers and placed in the cab of a truck at the head of the stopped column of cars. The door of the cab was closed and the Jews were fired upon at point-blank range. Of the three, one was killed outright, one died later of wounds, and the third was severely wounded. This incident was followed the next night by a revenge killing of two Arabs by Jews in a small hut on the Petah Tikva–Ranaana Road. It is reported by the police in this respect that at 10 p.m. on April 16 a car stopped before the hut and one of its occupants knocked on the door. In response to the knock the door was opened and two persons believed by the police to be Jews entered and, finding two Arabs within, shot them both dead on sight. One was shot six times with a Browning automatic and the other five with a Parabellum. The car with its occupants then disappeared.

When these facts became known the following morning tension between Arabs and Jews reached a crucial point. The situation was rendered acute later in the morning when the Jew who had been murdered by the "terrorists" two days before was buried as a martyr in the cemetery on the outskirts of Tel Aviv. The cortege following the body worked itself into a frenzy of righteous indignation and became disorderly. The efforts of the Jewish police of Tel Aviv to restore order and control the course of the procession were unavailing. A clash ensued and the Jewish police were routed. Reserves of British police were immediately called and likewise were attacked. By this time the excitement had spread to the occupants of nearby houses who joined the fray by throwing flower pots, cement building blocks and even iron bedsteads upon the heads of the police below. At one moment it seemed as though the British police would likewise be routed and troops were ordered to stand by from the encampment at Sarafand. Fortunately, however, order was at length restored, but not until after the police had been forced to fire into the crowd and many casualties had occurred both among the police and the rioters. […]

The following day, Saturday, passed without incident, but in an atmosphere of extreme tension. The police and the military authorities prepared for serious trouble.

On Sunday their fears were justified. A large crowd of Arabs gathered in the morning before the offices of the District Commissioner in Jaffa to protest against the murder of the two Arabs killed on the 16th, and as they were milling about in the square and working themselves into a condition of frenzy two Jews appeared and were immediately set upon. The crowd of Arabs then went berserk and pursued every Jew they saw. Fortunately, not many were at hand. The crowd then turned its attention to the main Jaffa–Jerusalem highway, stopping all cars and inspecting them for Jewish passengers. Many cars were wrecked and many casualties took place [....] When order was finally restored at 3:30 in the afternoon total casualties amounted to

7 Jews killed;	2 Arabs killed;
15 Arabs wounded;	39 Jews wounded.

Monday morning dawned on a Palestine prepared for disturbances of the most serious sort. All shops were closed and traffic was at a minimum on the roads. At about 9 a.m. the police received word of fresh outbreaks in Jaffa and, as a result traffic ceased on the Jerusalem–Jaffa road and was convoyed on the Jerusalem–Nazareth road. The disturbances remained localized in the no-man's-land between Jaffa and Tel Aviv, where a platoon of the Cameron Highlanders had been stationed the day before, but a few minor incidents of stoning automobiles occurred in the Northern

District near Jenin. [...] Casualties in Jaffa on April 20 were as follows: 5 Jews killed and 26 wounded; 2 Arabs killed and 32 wounded; on that day also 2 Jews died of injuries received on the previous day.

[...]

On April 21 the situation was reported as being "easier". Nineteen persons were wounded, 14 Arabs and 5 Jews, in "isolated assaults"; a Jewish lumber yard and other buildings were fired in Jaffa; traffic was resumed under convoy on the Jerusalem–Jaffa road; a crowd of Arabs bent on invading an outlying quarter of Tel Aviv were repulsed by the police; a general strike, which in effect has been only partial, was begun by Arab shopkeepers and still continues on April 25. This strike, which is supposed to have been inspired by that of the Damascene merchants some weeks ago and which is scheduled to last "until Arab demands are met", is a most half-hearted affair unsupported by the Nashashibi element. (As far as can be determined the Arab "demands" are the traditional ones: cessation of Jewish immigration and termination of land sales to Jews.)

The most significant events of April 21 were the orations delivered by the Messrs. Rokach and Dizengoff, Vice-Mayor and Mayor of Tel Aviv respectively, before a crowd estimated at 10,000 persons who had gathered when Tel Aviv buried its dead of the day before. In the course of his oration Mr. Rokach said: "These victims have not shed their blood for nothing. This incident will open the eyes of the Jews to the necessity of joining together with renewed energy and strength ..." Mr. Dizengoff's remarks were perhaps more pointed: "Some have fallen and the living must take their places ... Many before you have made the same sacrifice. All of us are ready to make it ... You have fallen not as wrongdoers but as a sacrifice to our weakness and powerlessness ... We failed to secure enough power to keep at bay the danger which pursues us outside Palestine. Thousands have died before and thousands will yet die ... No savage force, no murders, no attacks will move us from our position which we have gained here ... You were the victims of our optimism ... This silence bears witness to the strength of our people, to the power of our answer, to your determination ..."

April 22 and 23 passed under circumstances officially described as "quiet but tense". No incident of importance occurred. [...]

Two events which occurred during these two days are, however, worthy of mention. Both are important when considering the altered Jewish attitude. During the night of April 22 a police patrol was fired upon by Jews in the Tel Aviv district; the police returned the fire and a Jew was wounded. This fact was first circulated as rumor but was later confirmed and embodied in an official communiqué to which the Jewish Agency took formal exception on the ground that the report was unfounded and the Government was therefore culpable of disseminating untruths calculated to redound to the discredit of the Jews.

The second event occurred on April 23. It was a speech made by Dr. Weizmann when opening the World Congress of Jewish Physicians, at Tel Aviv. The essence of Dr. Weizmann's remarks is contained in the following words: "This Congress is a symbol of our answer to the attacks of the last few days ... On one side the forces of destruction, the forces of the desert have arisen, and on the other stand firm the forces of civilization—but we will not be stopped." These words [...] contain Weizmann's opinion of the Arabs and his challenge to the Mandatory; both apparently honestly expressed.

[...]

In brief summary: the disturbances appear to have been begun by Jews entering a square in Jaffa which was packed by irresponsible Arabs gathered to demand the punishment of the alleged Jews who had murdered two Arabs two days previously; the district of unrest was localized in Jaffa–Tel Aviv for two days, when it spread without serious effect to the Arab nationalist centers in the north; the lukewarm attitude of the Arab leaders in general and of Nashashibi in particular appears to have prevented the spread of the disturbances and to have maintained quiet in Jerusalem [...]; the Arabs may use the present situation as a fulcrum for their demands (as was done with success in Egypt and Syria); and, finally, the situation has adduced considerable evidence to demonstrate that a significant alteration of attitude has occurred among the Jews, both individuals and officials—an attitude which implies the pushing ahead of Zionist designs in the face of all resistance, whether offered by Arab or Mandatory. In this respect the most significant fact, and one that has thus far not been mentioned in this despatch, is that the Jewish defense organization Haganah, once guarded in the utmost secrecy, is now openly boasted of as a sort of Zionist army, trained, disciplined and armed.

Respectfully yours,
Leland B. Morris

PEEL COMMISSION

The Disturbances of 1936 ("Peel Commission" Report) (1937)
BRITISH COLONIAL OFFICE

2.   The trouble began with the murder of two Jews by Arab bandits [....] The following night two Arabs were murdered [...] as an act, so the Arabs believed, of Jewish reprisal. The funeral of one of the murdered Jews [...] led to angry Jewish demonstrations. A series of assaults on Arabs in Tel Aviv began, and on the 19th April, excited by false rumours that Arabs had been killed, Arab mobs in Jaffa began attacking Jews and murdered three of them. [...]

25.   [T]he outbreak of 1936 was a repetition, to a greatly intensified degree, of the past: but there were two features of it which were quite unprecedented. The first was the attitude of the Arab officials. We have already referred to their memorandum, and we shall refer later on to the difficulty the Government experienced, as the disorders dragged on, in relying on its Arab district officers and police. The second novelty was the intrusion of the "external factor." Previous outbreaks in Palestine had excited the interest and sympathy of the neighbouring Arab peoples: but this time, not only was considerable popular feeling displayed against the British Government as well as the Jews, but a substantial number of volunteers, including the ultimate leader of the rebellion, came from Syria or Iraq, and the Arabs of Trans-Jordan were with difficulty prevented from joining in the conflict. Still more important, the Arab Governments concerned themselves for the first time in the dispute. [...] If, indeed, we were to pick out the feature of the late "disturbances" which on a general view seems to us the most striking and far-reaching, it would be the manner in which they roused the feeling of the Arab world at large against Zionism and its defenders.

26.   Only the roughest reckoning can be made of the loss occasioned by the "disturbances" to the Arab population. [...] It has been credibly estimated at 1,000 killed-mostly in fighting, since very few Arabs were murdered.

27.   On the Jewish side, the official list gives 80 Jews killed or died of wounds and 308 wounded. The figures supplied by the Jewish Agency are "82 Jews murdered, apart from nine further deaths arising out of and connected with the disturbances between April and October, 1936," and 369 Jews wounded in the same period. As to material loss, the Jewish Agency reports the destruction of 80,000 citrus trees, 62,000 other fruit trees, 64,000 forest trees, and 16,500 dunums of crops. It reckons the total cost of the injury to Jewish property at about £250,000, of which £100,000

is in respect of the destruction or damage of commercial or industrial premises in Jaffa by fire or otherwise.

[...]

43.   After examining this and other evidence and studying the course of events in Palestine since the War, we have no doubt as to what were "the underlying causes of the disturbances" of last year. They were:—

(i)   The desire of the Arabs for national independence.

(ii)   Their hatred and fear of the establishment of the Jewish National Home.

44.   We make the following comments on these two causes:—

(i)   They were the same underlying causes as those which brought about the "disturbances" of 1920, 1921, 1929, and 1933.

(ii)   They were, and always have been, inextricably linked together. The Balfour Declaration and the Mandate under which it was to be implemented involved the denial of national independence at the outset. The subsequent growth of the National Home created a practical obstacle, and the only serious one, to the concession later of national independence. It was believed that its further growth might mean the political as well as economic subjection of the Arabs to the Jews, so that, if ultimately the Mandate should terminate and Palestine become independent, it would not be national independence in the Arab sense but self-government by a Jewish majority.

[...]

CHAPTER XIX – CONCLUSIONS AND RECOMMENDATIONS

[...]

2.   We have found that, though the Arabs have benefited by the development of the country owing to Jewish immigration, this has had no conciliatory effect. On the contrary, improvement in the economic situation in Palestine has meant the deterioration of the political situation.

3.   The Palestine Government have attempted to discharge the contradictory obligations of the Mandatory under conditions of great difficulty by "holding the balance" between Jews and Arabs. Repeated attempts to conciliate either race have only increased the trouble. The situation in Palestine has reached a deadlock. [...]

4.   As regards immigration the Mandate has been fully implemented, but the attempts to regulate it have been unsatisfactory, unacceptable to

Arabs and Jews alike, and accompanied by disconcerting variations in the number of immigrants.

[...]

7.   As regards the development of local autonomy and self-governing institutions, this also has been hampered by the difficulty of combining what are virtually two civilizations in one system. The restrictions which the Mandatory Power found it necessary to impose in the interests of rural boards or backward municipalities have been resented by the larger towns. The attempts to create a local legislature have been unsuccessful and should not be revived.

[...]

CHAPTER XXIII – CONCLUSION

1.   "Half a loaf is better than no bread" is a peculiarly English proverb; and, considering the attitude which both the Arab and the Jewish representatives adopted in giving evidence before us, we think it improbable that either party will be satisfied at first sight with the proposals we have submitted for the adjustment of their rival claims. For Partition means that neither will get all it wants. It means that the Arabs must acquiesce in the exclusion from their sovereignty of a piece of territory, long occupied and once ruled by them. It means that the Jews must be content with less than the Land of Israel they once ruled and have hoped to rule again. But it seems to us possible that on reflection both parties will come to realize that the drawbacks of Partition are outweighed by its advantages. For, if it offers neither party all it wants, it offers each what it wants most, namely freedom and security.

2.   The advantages to the Arabs of Partition on the lines we have proposed may be summarized as follows:—

(i)   They obtain their national independence and can cooperate on an equal footing with the Arabs of the neighbouring countries in the cause of Arab unity and progress.

(ii)   They are finally delivered from the fear of being "swamped" by the Jews and from the possibility of ultimate subjection to Jewish rule.

(iii)   In particular, the final limitation of the Jewish National Home within a fixed frontier and the enactment of a new Mandate for the protection of the Holy Places, solemnly guaranteed by the League of Nations, removes all anxiety lest the Holy Places should ever come under Jewish control.

(iv)   As a set-off to the loss of territory the Arabs regard as theirs, the Arab State will receive a subvention from the Jewish state. It will also, in view of the backwardness of Trans-Jordan, obtain a grant of £2,000,000 from the British Treasury; and, if an arrangement can be made for the exchange of land and population, a further grant will be made for the conversion, as far as may prove possible, of uncultivable land in the Arab State into productive land from which the cultivators and the State alike will profit.

3.   The advantages of Partition to the Jews may be summarized as follows:—

(i)   Partition secures the establishment of the Jewish National Home and relieves it from the possibility of its being subjected in the future to Arab rule.

(ii)   Partition enables the Jews in the fullest sense to call their National Home their own: for it converts it into a Jewish State. Its citizens will be able to admit as many Jews into it as they themselves believe can be absorbed. They will attain the primary objective of Zionism—a Jewish nation, planted in Palestine, giving its nationals the same status in the world as other nations give theirs. They will cease at last to live a "minority life."

4.   To both Arabs and Jews Partition offers a prospect—and we see no such prospect in any other policy—of obtaining the inestimable boon of peace. It is surely worth some sacrifice on both sides if the quarrel which the Mandate started could be ended with its termination. It is not a natural or old-standing feud. An able Arab exponent of the Arab case told us that the Arabs throughout their history have not only been free from anti-Jewish sentiment but have also shown that the spirit of compromise is deeply rooted in their life. And he went on the express his sympathy with the fate of the Jews in Europe. "There is no decent-minded person," he said, "who would not want to do everything humanly possible to relieve the distress of those persons," provided that it was "not at the cost of inflicting a corresponding distress on another people." Considering what the possibility of finding a refuge in Palestine means to many thousands of suffering Jews, we cannot believe that the "distress" occasioned by Partition, great as it would be, is more than Arab generosity can bear. [...]

Arab Submission to the Permanent Mandates Commission (1937)
THE ARAB HIGHER COMMITTEE

1 – The Disappointment of the Arabs:

The Arab Higher Committee deeply regrets that it must make an immediate declaration of the extreme disappointment of the Arab people of Palestine as a result of the Royal Commission's investigations here [....] Particularly it would express in this connection its repugnance to the whole of the partition scheme, which it sincerely regards as a measure very far from being calculated or likely to establish security, restore public confidence to bring peace to this country.

2 – The Erroneous Premise of the Royal Commission that the Arab and Jewish Cases are by their Moral and Historical Nature of an Equal Weight and Urgency:

We regard as a profound error the point of view adopted by His Majesty's Government that in their mutual relations the Arabs and the Jews of Palestine stand as opposed litigants with equal rights. Though we have always repudiated any such suggestion, the Royal Commission have gone still further, and in seeking their "solution", have treated the Jewish case as the basic issue, to be considered and solved without reference to the Arab issues at stake. Accordingly, its actual and stated policy has been that His Majesty's Government must fulfill its promises to the Jews and only in the second place consider its promises to the Arabs; this, despite the solemn assertion of the Permanent Mandates' Commission and the British Government that their "dual obligations" are of equal weight. The latter assertion is itself an understatement of the Arab rights which is not justified by either morality or history. For the Arabs of Palestine are the owners of the country and lived in it prior to the British Occupation for hundreds of years and in it they still constitute the overwhelming majority. The Jews on the other hand are a minority of intruders, who before the war had no great standing in this country, and whose political connections therewith had been severed for almost 2,000 years. It is impossible to find either in logic or morality any justification for the attempt to renew this broken connection by the establishment of a so-called Jewish National Home. [...]

3 – The Situation in the Great War and the Obligations of the British Government:

The Royal Commission has at last admitted that it was the seriousness of the situation of the British Government, during the Great War, which led it to issue the Balfour Declaration to the Jews after it had already made certain promises to the Arabs. It may be that the British Government thus assumed obligations mutually exclusive of fulfillment, but this does not affect the all-important fact that the Arabs have the natural right to enjoy the freedom of self-rule in their own country; more particularly since the promises obtained from the British (for which they paid in full measure) and the obligations which they in return assumed, were but the means to the expressed end of achieving that right. [...]

4 – The Unceasing Protest of the Arabs against the Balfour Declaration:

The Arabs have never ceased since its promulgation in 1917 vigorously to repudiate the Balfour Declaration, proclaiming through every congress, party programme and delegation their steadfast rejection thereof. They have always emphasized its invalidity, its inner contradictions, the injustice of its conception and its inherent partiality. [...]

5 – The Admission by the Royal Commission of the Impossibility of Reconciling these two Obligations and the Culpability of the British Government and the Permanent Mandates Commission in Ignoring the Fact:

[...] [T]he Royal Commission [...] and the British Government [...] have admitted the impossibility of reconciling the British Government's obligations to the Arabs with those to the Jews, because they mutually conflict. The Arabs have insisted upon this irreconcilability from the inception of the Mandate and throughout the period in which a policy based upon this veritable impossibility has been implemented. We now, therefore, assert that the British Government has consciously persisted in a policy of palpable errors and recognized contradictions by mere weight of armed force, despite the unceasing gestures of protest and repudiation on the part of the Arabs, and even despite demonstrations which have cost them life and blood. This has gone on till the number of Jews in Palestine reached 400,000. This increase of Jewish population has greatly increased the complications of the Palestine problem. [...]

6 – The Recognition by the Royal Commission of the Arab Aspirations for Independence and the Repudiation of the National Home Policy since the Occupation:

The Arab Higher Committee considers it its further duty to point out that the Royal Commission has admitted in its Report that the desire of the Arabs for independence and their determined opposition to the establishment of the Jewish National Home existed from the very beginning of the British Occupation of Palestine. They further recognize that the intensity of this attitude has in no way diminished in the interim, but on the contrary, that the causes of the 1936 disturbances were but an intensification of those which had led to every demonstration made by the Arabs since 1920. The British Government, we regret to say, has persistently ignored this fact, meeting out rightful protests with armed force instead of the spirit of honest and impartial enquiry into the reasons thereof. […]

7 – The Possibility of Solving the Palestine Problem on the Basis of Justice and National Right:

[…] It must be candidly recognized that Palestine is still an Arab majority country, because the majority of its population is Arab, the majority of its property owners are Arabs and because of its unbroken historical connection with the Arabs for over 1400 years. The Jews on the other hand are even now a minority in the country. Many of them have retained their alien nationality and as such are incapable of loyalty to Palestine, being prevented from ever becoming settled here, to the degree that Arabs are, by their economic and social ties with a number of foreign countries. Palestine is not the only country where different national groups are found living side by side. In other countries, where this phenomenon is encountered, the government follows the natural principle of majority-rule with minority-protection. Therefore by analogy with existing examples, it was to be expected that the Royal Commission would suggest a solution of the Palestine problem on the basis of this natural principle which is operative in the rest of the world.

8 – The Royal Commission's Evasion of the Obvious and Natural Solution of the Palestine Problem:

[…] The suggestions put forward by the Royal Commission are the result of its considering the Jewish claims without reference to the Arab cause, and further, of sympathies aroused in it by the emotional and irrelevant references of Jewish witnesses to the sufferings of Jews in other parts of the world. The Royal Commission's resultant desire to alleviate their plight cannot but call forth our opposition when it is proposed to secure such alleviation at the cost our own racial future.

9 – The Impossibility of Solving the Problem of International Jewry through Palestine:

[…] [T]he problems of world-Jewry cannot be solved by the annexation of all or part of Palestine. For if Palestine absorbed the maximum possible numbers of Jewish immigrants, it could hold not more than a fraction of World-Jewry.

The Arab Higher Committee begs, therefore, to suggest that if the British people wish to aid the Jews from humanitarian motives, and help them forward to peace, confidence and freedom from persecution, the means to that end should not be a project by which the Arabs of Palestine will be uprooted from their country and deprived of their best land to accommodate the Jews. Rather, we would suggest, that Britain should exert its great influence for the protection of Jews and Jewish interests in countries where they now reside, or provide areas for their settlement within its own domain.

10 – The Royal Commission's Suggestion Concerning a Jewish State:

The Royal Commission recommended the establishment of an autonomous Jewish State. They propose that its limits should include the most important and fertile plain lands, almost in their entirety, the coastal region and the large agricultural area bounded by the northern frontier. In the section so delimited there are some 300,00 Jews and 325,000 Arabs. In the northern sector of this area there are districts which are entirely Arab. [...] In the plain and coastal areas to the south there are a large number of Arab villages, and the Arabs own some four times the amount of landed and immovable property which the Jews possess. [...] It has further been assessed that 7/8 of the total area of orange groves owned by the Arabs are on lands designated for the Jewish State. Furthermore in this area are hundreds of Arab mosques, churches, religious shrines, cemeteries, the object of the people's veneration, and large areas of religious "Waqf". The establishment, therefore, of a Jewish State in this area means subjecting an Arab community, the predominant element in respect of numbers and private and religious property, to the control of the Jewish State. It appears to us in the highest degree anomalous that the Royal Commission, while finding it impossible that a Jewish minority should be placed under the rule of an Arab majority, should yet find no difficulty in the reverse process or even in placing an Arab majority under a Jewish minority.
[...]
It is true that the Royal Commission states that the mosques, churches, religious sites, and "waqfs", falling within the prospective Jewish State, should receive mandatory protection. The holiness of these places, however, depends on and demands the continuance of the religious ceremonies which have in the past hallowed them. It is not without serious misgiving that we recall the fate which has befallen such religious sites and premises in villages and towns where the Jews have already acquired control of the land. Mosques and cemeteries have completely disappeared.
[...]
The proposed Jewish State would erect a barrier between Arab Palestine and Arab Syria, two areas which are linked by bonds of blood and culture which make them inherently one. This we cannot but regard as a blow aimed at Arab unity. Moreover, in the light of events past and present, we feel certain that a Jewish State in Palestine, overfilled with Jewish immigrants, must have the result of stimulating Jewish aspirations for further expansion. This idea has already been expressed by Zionist leaders. This must expose the Arab territories to East, North and South to perpetual encroachments, political and economic. The consequent friction could not but grow into an interminable struggle between Arab and Jew which must adversely affect the whole of the Near East.

[...]

13 – Imperial Intentions in Creating a Permanent Mandatory Zone:

When the impartial observer considers the formation of the proposed mandatory zone and the peculiar arrangements relating to the ports of Jaffa and Akaba it becomes clear that imperial and military considerations, rather than religious, are here at play. We cannot feel that it is by chance that the aerodromes of Lydda and Ramleh and the important railway junction at Lydda, where lines of Egypt, Haifa, Jerusalem, and Jaffa meet, fall into the mandatory zone. The strategic value of Akaba with the potential command of the Suez Canal and the Red Sea is self-evident. Although the precise relationship between Akaba and the Holy Places Enclaves is not clearly defined, it would appear that this arrangement will involve mandatory surveillance over the whole Southern part of the suggested Arab State. Wherein then lies the gift of independence? The Arabs are fully prepared to discuss reasonably with Great Britain the question of safeguarding her imperial interests and communications as in Iraq and Egypt. [...] Nor is it to be supposed that the Arabs, who resisted for the last 18 years a temporary mandate, will ever consent to submit to a permanent mandate in its place.

14 – The Arab State:

The Royal Commission has made the further proposal that the part of Palestine, that remains after the Jewish State and the Permanent Mandatory zone have been delimited, be attached to Transjordan and a single Arab State so created. The Arabs welcome any legitimate proposal or event that tends to the fulfillment of their aspiration for independence and union with other Arab countries; and they appreciate the tribute paid them by the Royal Commission as to their fitness to rule and as to the strength of the nationalist spirit among them. But they cannot and will not agree to surrendering their most productive land to allow the establishment of a Jewish State and a mandatory zone which are both in conflict with their aspirations and which threaten the existence of half the Arabs in Palestine. The comparison which the Royal Commission makes with a "surgical operation" suggests to us the thought that an amputated limb dies even though the trunk with the vital organs may live. The Arabs regard what is to be left to them of Palestine as such a limb. It is a mountainous and barren region, for the most part arid and unproductive, restricted by artificial frontiers on three sides. In agriculture it is proposed that the most productive land is to go to the Jews, while in industry and commerce the centres of life and opportunity (such as Haifa Port, the railway and the greater part of the newly constructed roads) are also to be withdrawn from the Arabs.

Deprived of its historic right of protecting the Holy Places, the Arab State would lose with it also the means of livelihood derived from the presence of pilgrims and tourists. The Arab State will further be deprived of the main agricultural industry, namely the citrus fruit belt, while it will also lose in Galilee the principal centre of olive-growing, and in the plains the important watermelon crop.

[…]

The Royal Commission, it is true, has displayed a superficial concern for the prospects and welfare of this State, which it realizes must be bankrupt from its inception. They, therefore, propose that in addition to a grant of two million pounds to Transjordan in lieu of the present annual grant, the British Treasury should make an additional grant for the purpose of developing irrigation and land settlement in the event of the so-called transfer of population being carried out. The poverty to which the Arab State would be reduced by the loss of the territory allotted to the Jewish State and the Mandatory Zone, is further indicated by the proposal that the Arab State should receive an annual subvention from the Jewish State. Apart from the fact that Jewish finance to Palestine does not inspire us with confidence as to the possibility of realizing this grant, such a system would lay the Arab State open to the continual threat of bankruptcy, and constitute in fact Jewish control over the allegedly independent Arab State. For unless it identified itself with the policy of the Jewish State in all things, every pretext would be used for with-holding this subvention. Apart from the fact that to accept any such grant would be a degradation which no Arab Government could with honor accept, we take the whole of this scheme of grants and subventions as proving beyond question that the British Government recognizes that the proposed Arab State would not possess the minimum resources necessary to support the population it is proposed to force into its narrow limits.

15 – The Arab Repudiation of the Partition Scheme:

[…] [I]f Palestine has been for the last 18 years the scene of disturbances arising out of the fears of the Arab people at the Jewish invasion and the British imperial policy which has sponsored it, it is only natural to expect that the struggle will be intensified if the Jews receive immediately many times the extent of the territory which they have been able to acquire in 15 years during which the mandate has been fully implemented.

The Arab Higher Committee is reluctant to believe that the Members of the Royal Commission and the Secretary of State for the Colonies do not recognize and appreciate the dangers which the Partition Scheme involves; or that they do not appreciate the effect it would have, not only on the Arabs, Moslem and Christian, of Palestine but on those of other countries. We therefore assert without hesitation or doubt that the peace for which the Royal Commission declares it is working and which it calls an "indispensable boon" cannot be established in this country by a continuance of these abortive experiments. We cannot but wonder what are the real motives for the insistence on further "unique political experiments"

to fulfill a fantastic political project which was born of Jewish sufferings in countries for which the Arab world has not the least responsibility.
[…]
17 – The Natural Solution of the Palestine Problem:
[…]
The Arab Higher Committee, therefore, urges that the only solution compatible with justice and a true desire for peace in the land must be based on the following principles:

    1.   The recognition of the right of the Arabs to complete independence in their own land.

    2.   The cessation of the experiment of the Jewish National Home.

    3.   The cessation of the British mandate and its replacement by a treaty similar to treaties existing between Britain and Iraq, Britain and Egypt, and between Britain and Syria, creating in Palestine a Sovereign State.

    4.   The immediate cessation of all Jewish immigration and of land-sales to Jews pending the negotiation and conclusion of the Treaty.

The Arabs are prepared to negotiate, in a reasonable spirit, the conditions under which reasonable British interests shall be safeguarded; to approve the necessary guarantees for the preservation and right of access to all Holy Places and for the protection of all legitimate rights of the Jewish population or other minorities in Palestine.
[…]

Summary of Meeting with Dr. Weizmann (1939)

Herschel V. Johnson

Sir: […] I have the honor to enclose the text of a communiqué issued last night summarizing the Jewish case as presented by Dr. Weizmann. […]

The Jewish representatives, Dr. Weizmann said, entered the present Conference with the desire to be helpful and with a full recognition of the difficulties facing the British Government. There were, however, vital interests which they had to safeguard, and rights which they could not surrender, least of all at this, the blackest hour in Jewish history.

At the root of the Jewish problem, Dr. Weizmann stated, lay the homelessness of the Jewish people who everywhere were a minority. They had preserved their identity because of their attachment to Palestine and of their hope of a return to Zion. The claim to Palestine had never been abandoned; the Jewish community there had never ceased to exist; in every age groups of Jews had worked their way back to Palestine; and for the past sixty years active resettlement had gone on. The Balfour Declaration, he said, recognized those historic facts; and in the Preamble of the Mandate international recognition was "given to the historical connection of the Jewish people with Palestine and to the grounds for reconstituting their national home in that country."

Dr. Weizmann then reviewed developments connected with the Peel and the Woodhead Reports, pointing out that the central point of the former was the proposal to partition Palestine and to set up a Jewish State and an Arab State. The Jews, he said, did not regard the proposal to divide Palestine as fulfilling the original promise of the Balfour Declaration, but they had agreed to explore the possibility of cooperating on the basis of the report because two guiding principles underlay it, namely, the Jews should have sole control of immigration in their allotted territory and they should be guaranteed there against becoming a minority. Those principles, he submitted, retained their binding force.

Moreover, the Royal Commission, he maintained, was satisfied that when the British Government issued the Balfour Declaration, it realized that a Jewish State might eventually be established in Palestine. That important statement, he asserted, ruled out any artificial restriction on Jewish immigration and any relegation to minority status. He could not conceive that after twenty years, the British Government should seek an interpretation of the Mandate which might curtail those fundamental Jewish rights. Such a departure from a moral position, he said, would shake the British Empire to its foundation, for the bonds which rivet it together are purely moral bonds, composed of mutual faith and belief in the security of promises. […]

Referring to suggestions that at the time of the Balfour Declaration, large scale immigration to Palestine was not envisaged, Dr. Weizmann asserted that this was erroneous; that Jewish distress had always been one of the foundations of the Zionist movement; but that apart from this, the Movement was built upon the homelessness of the Jews, which had itself produced the Jewish problem; and that it was essential that there should be one place where Jews should not be a fraction, an adjunct to something else, but themselves, masters of their own destinies.

Dr. Weizmann dismissed as offering little immediate relief to refugees projects for founding Jewish territorial bases elsewhere than in Palestine. The success of Jewish colonization in Palestine, he held, was due to the national and religious fervor behind the effort there and sixty years of pioneer preparation. Palestine, he asserted, was capable of absorbing hundreds of thousands of refugees, and if it could not take all, that was hardly a reason for refusing to allow it to take as many as it could.

Alluding to the alleged conflicting promises made to Jews and Arabs, Dr. Weizmann stated that the British Government had repeatedly acknowledged that no such conflict existed with regard to Western Palestine; that Sir Henry McMahon had stated this, and that Colonel T. E. Lawrence had placed on record that Mr. Churchill's settlement of 1921–22 fulfilled all Britain's promises to the Arabs "in letter and in spirit." Where there might have been a conflict of promises—in Transjordan—it had been solved 100% in favor of the Arabs.

Turning to the Arab claim that Palestine was an Arab country and should have an Arab National Government, Dr. Weizmann contended that this claim was not capable of realization. The Jews, he said, already formed one third of the population, and were responsible for two-thirds or more of the country's economic and cultural activity. The Arabs professed to fear Jewish domination. The Jews, he said, did not wish to dominate the Arabs, but would not allow themselves to be dominated.

A meeting ground beneficial to both, Dr. Weizmann believed, could, as stated, be found only on the basis of the Mandate; large-scale Jewish immigration as determined by the absorptive capacity of the country; an active policy of development; and effective safeguards against minority status.

The respective points of view of the Jews and the Arabs have now been fully set forth by the two delegations and I understand that tomorrow the actual work of negotiation will begin and that the British representatives will start discussions of the opposing claims with each delegation in an effort to ascertain where compromise is possible.
[…]

Pan Arabism and the Palestine Problem (1938)
Robert Gale Woolbert

[…] It is the British mandatory government which has become the principal object of Arab hostility. This bitter anti-British feeling is the first and most powerful impression that strikes the outsider visiting Palestine today. This means, not that animosity towards the Jews has lessened, but that the Arabs have concluded that only by the use of force can they prevent Britain from making the whole of Palestine into a Jewish State. Britain's denial of any such intention only proves to them the essential perfidy of British policy.

The Arabs fear that Palestine will be swamped by Jews. In recent years the Jewish proportion of the population has been rapidly increasing until today it constitutes thirty percent of the total. […]

In essence, then, the struggle is not (to quote the Royal Commission's Report) "an inter-racial conflict arising from an old instinctive antipathy of Arabs towards Jews." As the Report adds: "Quite obviously . . . the problem of Palestine is political. It is . . . the problem of insurgent nationalism." The Arabs are not interested in the argument that the National Home has greatly benefited them economically, even if they admit it to be true. They did not ask to be enriched; and they would much prefer, they say, that the Jews go away and leave them poor but masters in what they consider to be their own house. To prevent the Mandatory Power from letting the political control of Palestine pass to the Jews, they are prepared, if necessary, to fight.

This in a nutshell is the background for the revolt, or guerrilla war, which the Arabs began waging against the British authorities in the spring of 1936. When the Royal Commission went to Palestine in October of that year to investigate and take testimony, the Arabs boycotted it because the British Government refused to suspend Jewish immigration at once. […]

When the proposal for partition was made public a new wave of Arab protest quite naturally arose. Anti-British feeling, smouldering for several months, again flamed out. Some of the more belligerent and nationalistic Arabs were not to be restrained, and sporadic acts of terrorism were committed in spite of pleas by Arab leaders for moderation and patience. The renewed violence has been directed principally against officials in the British administration. But this time, however, the British have met arson, bombings and assassination with such stern measures as the curfew, wholesale arrests, the destruction of the houses of suspected incendiaries,

86   Used with permission of Foreign Affairs, from FOREIGN AFFAIRS, Vol. 16, No. 2 (Jan. 1, 1938); permission conveyed through Copyright Clearance Center, Inc.

the imposition of large fines and the quartering of military garrisons on towns where outbreaks occur. They have also dissolved Arab political organizations and sent prominent Arab leaders into exile.

The net result, at the time these lines are written, has been to widen the gulf between the Arabs and the British. The recent decision of the authorities to restrict Jewish immigration to the country's "political" capacity to absorb it, which if made a year ago might have led to a compromise or at least a detente, has come too late. [...]

This dilemma clearly illustrates the impossible situation into which the British got themselves by making contradictory promises to the Jews and to the Arabs during the World War. As has been aptly remarked, Palestine is the "too-much promised land." The British, in order to escape from the resulting impasse, propose that each side surrender part of what it was promised. The Jews, after much private soul-searching and public debate, have decided to accept the principle of partition on the theory that half a loaf is better than no bread at all, and in the hope that the diminutive Jewish state can in the future, near or distant, be extended to the whole of Palestine.

Precisely because they fully realize the nature of this powerful if seldom expressed hope of the Jews, the Arabs are determined to prevent partition. Let the Jews come and settle in Palestine, they say, until they constitute 35 percent -- or even 40 percent -- of the total population. But let them live there as a minority in an Arab state, not as citizens of an independent Jewish homeland.
[...]
[T]he Holy Land occupies such a central place in the religious affections and political interests of so many people throughout the world that events there are followed with a concern out of all proportion to their intrinsic importance. [...] Any happening in Palestine today may arouse the passions of Jews on six continents; and given the power wielded by individual Jews in the press, legislative assemblies and public life of many Great Powers, a shot fired in Tel Aviv may well be heard round the world.

It is a great handicap for the Arabs that they have few powerful compatriots dwelling in Christian countries who can be called upon to defend the Arab cause before the occidental world. They do, however, possess other weapons, and these they are learning to wield under the guidance of the Grand Mufti of Jerusalem, His Eminence Haj Mohammed Amin el Huseini. These weapons are Pan Arabism and Pan Islamism; for it must not be forgotten that Jerusalem, with its Haram-ash-Sherif, is one of the three sacred cities of the Moslems. [...] The dominant political tactic of the Arabs in Palestine, led by the Grand Mufti, has been to arouse the sympathy and, if possible, obtain the active assistance of the Arabs and Moslems everywhere. In short, His Eminence has tried to lift the Palestine question from its local setting and make it a Pan Arab and Pan Islamic problem.

How has the Mufti sought to accomplish this and how successful has he been? He is a man of great personal charm and astuteness, as anyone who has talked with him can testify. He is still relatively young. After having been an officer in the old Turkish army, he changed his allegiance and served with the Emir Feisal in Damascus. [...][I]n 1921 was named Mufti of Jerusalem to succeed his half brother. In the following year he was elected President of the Supreme Moslem Council for Palestine. In this position he enjoyed the control of (1) the *Waqf* funds, the income of which in 1936 was £67,000, and (2) the *Sharia*, or religious, courts. He also had supervision of orphans' funds valued at £50,000 annually. His prestige was further heightened when in 1931 he presided over a Moslem Congress in Jerusalem, at which were present 145 delegates from every corner of the Islamic world. With all this authority in his hands he had become the most powerful Arab in Palestine.

At the same time that he was consolidating his ecclesiastical position, he was also building up a political organization, called the Palestine Arab Party but generally referred to as the "Mufti's Party." [...] It is the largest but not the only Arab party in Palestine. [...]

All the Arab parties are at one, however, in their determination to oppose the creation of a Jewish national state. To cement their joint forces in a single body, in April 1936 they set up the Supreme Arab Committee (later renamed the Arab Higher Committee), of which the Mufti was elected President. Haj Amin's power thus became even greater, to the dismay of his opponents in the Opposition Party, some of whom refer to him as "the spider" or as "Rasputin." Nonetheless, they maintained a common front during the disturbances of 1936 and towards the Royal Commission. When the latter's Report was published in July 1937, the Opposition Party withdrew from the Arab Higher Committee because its leaders felt that the Report should at least be considered. During the disturbances of recent months a number of the victims of Arab terrorism have been members of the Opposition Party or Arabs who had sold land to the Jews. Many Arabs held the Mufti responsible for these acts despite the fact that he had issued public pleas for law and order. Nevertheless, the [opposing] faction is no less adamant against partition than the Mufti himself [....]

Over one-tenth of the Arab population consists of Christians of one sect or another; yet they have taken the same stand toward partition as their Moslem compatriots. [...]

This solid support from all the Arab elements put the Mufti in a very favorable situation to make trouble for the British. His accumulation of offices gave him unrivalled power in the country -- his position was described by the Royal Commission as that of an *imperium in imperio* -- while his function as the religious custodian of Jerusalem gave him great prestige among Moslems everywhere. [...] [H]e has not hesitated to make use of his high religious position in arousing Moslem sentiment against Britain.

Certain circumstances have played in the Mufti's favor. Arab anxiety over the rapid expansion of Jewish immigration was mounting to its peak at the very time British prestige in the Mediterranean was being shattered by Mussolini's behavior in the Ethiopian affair. The Arabs quite naturally concluded that Britain was not so formidable as had been supposed -- a belief later strengthened by the dilatory manner in which she went about suppressing the 1936 revolt. In another if less direct way the Ethiopian War helped raise the pitch of Arab nationalist agitation in Palestine. It will be recalled that fear of Italian aggression had finally terminated the long negotiations for Egyptian independence by the signature of the Anglo-Egyptian Alliance on August 21, 1936. A few days later, on September 9, the French signed a treaty with Syria, promising the latter virtual independence within a few years. They entered into a similar arrangement with the Lebanon Republic on November 13. Since 'Iraq had already been independent for some years, Palestine and Trans Jordan were the chief Arab states still remaining under foreign tutelage. This, of course, only further embittered the Palestine Arabs.
[...]
Perhaps the reader has become somewhat confused by the seemingly indiscriminate use of the expressions "Pan Arab" and "Pan Islamic." The two manifestly cannot be the same thing: there are 250,000,000 Moslems in the world, and of these only a fifth speak Arabic. [...] [I]t is quite incorrect to confuse the two but that this is precisely what the Arab Nationalists are constantly doing, intentionally or otherwise. The tendency was well exemplified in the speeches and resolutions of the Pan Arab Congress held at Bludan, a mountain resort in Syria, September 8-10, 1937. Among the some four hundred and fifty delegates to this picturesque gathering were Orthodox Archbishops who presumably were much more interested in Pan Arabia than in Pan Islam. [...]

The Congress had been called for the specific purpose of demonstrating Arab solidarity against the partition of Palestine. [....] Among those who attended there were no responsible statesmen in office. Pan Arabism is still too young and experimental a movement, Great Britain's power is still too dominant in the Near and Middle East, for a member of the 'Iraqi or Egyptian cabinets, for example, to participate in such an openly anti-British manifestation. Furthermore, some of the more distant Arabic-speaking countries did not, as far as I have been able to ascertain, send delegates. Since no non-Arabic-speaking country was represented it was in no sense a Pan Islamic gathering. [...]

The sole *raison d'être* of the Congress was to protest partition. That fact is reflected in the resolutions adopted, which may be summarized as follows:

1.   Palestine is Arab and its preservation as such is the duty of every Arab.

2.   All offers of peace from the British are to be rejected if they contain a vindication of Jewish political and racial demands. The Jews are to be permitted to live in Palestine only as a minority, with the same rights which minorities possess elsewhere.

3.   The Palestine Report is rejected, in particular the proposal for partition.

4.   The Palestine question can be solved only if the following steps are taken first: (a) the withdrawal of the Balfour Declaration; (b) the abolition of the Mandate; (c) the signing of a treaty creating an Arab state after the example of 'Iraq; (d) the immediate prohibition of the sale of land to Jews and of further Jewish immigration; (e) the suspension of arbitrary measures and all restraints on liberty; and (f) "The delegates pledge before God, before history, before the Arab nation and before the Islamic peoples to carry on their struggle and their efforts on behalf of the Arab cause in Palestine until it is saved and its sovereignty rests in itself."

5.   There were also resolutions calling for more intensive propaganda and for a boycott on Jews as a patriotic duty. The Executive Committee was empowered to impose a boycott on British goods and to ask other Moslem countries to do the same unless Britain altered her policy towards the Arabs.
[...]
However, in spite of these appeals to the Moslem world -- indeed, to all colonial peoples -- the only places from which substantial support can be expected in the near future are, with the possible exception of Italy, the Arab countries of the Near East and North Africa. [...]

The 'Iraqi Government has on several occasions actively intervened in the Palestine question. Typical of its attitude was its note to the Mandates Commission shortly after the Palestine Report was published, in which it vigorously protested against partition as unjust, dangerous and ineffective. The 'Iraqi Minister of Justice went on record as saying that a Jewish state would be a menace to nearby countries. There were several mass demonstrations, one of them attended by more than 50,000 people, at which the Government's stand against partition was clamorously upheld.

Syria is one of the centers of the Pan Arab agitation. One European observer not long ago reported that talks with Syrian politicians, intellectuals and businessmen revealed that "the pan Arab ideal must be regarded as the strongest and most dynamic force in the life of modern Syria." The Lebanon, being preponderantly Christian, manifests less Pan Arab sentiment than its neighbors; and it is definitely suspicious of Pan Islam. [...] The President of the Republic, Emile Eddé, is reported to have described Pan Arabism in his country as "a utopian dream of a few fanatics only." This statement is typical of the "Phœnician" policy advocated by certain Lebanese politicians, who look upon the creation of a Jewish state contiguous to the Lebanon as a reinforcement against the "Moslem peril." Still, some of the leading intellectuals of Pan Arabia are Lebanese Christians.

The Emir Abdullah of Trans Jordan, who owes his position to Britain, has been very loath to join in condemning the British policy in Palestine. He is a natural rival of the Mufti, for in the projected Arab state to be created out of Palestine and Trans Jordan there would not be room for them both. [...]

Sa'udi Arabia is said to have contributed -- unofficially -- both men and arms to the 1936 revolt in Palestine. A convention of ulemas that met at Ar-Riyadh last summer informed King Ibn Sa'ud that the creation of a Jewish state in a Moslem land could not be permitted and that he should help prevent it. Ibn Sa'ud has great respect for the religious doctors; but thus far he has been circumspect enough not to antagonize the British too openly. [...]

When on September 18 the Egyptian Foreign Minister, Wassif Boutros Ghali Pasha, delivered a speech in the League Assembly in opposition to partition, many observers were surprised. The Wafd Government was supposed not to have any interest in Palestine, or at least not to have any desire to annoy the British unnecessarily. Yet the Minister said: "The Palestinian question is engaging the closest attention of the Egyptian Government and people, because of the neighbourly relations between Egypt and Palestine, and of the religious and historical relationship which unites Egypt and the Holy Places, the bonds of fraternity based upon a common language, religion and civilisation that connect us with the people of Palestine, and also because of the close relations of alliance and friendship existing between Egypt and the United Kingdom, the mandatory power." Having made this bow to impartiality, he went on to assert that "Right and justice require that Palestine should remain in the hands of the Palestinians. This is the natural law in its simplest and clearest form." [...]

Recent reports of unrest in French North Africa have contained statements that the authorities have uncovered a Pan Arab plot to throw off European control and set up native governments. That the Tunisian, Algerian and Moroccan nationalists are striving for independence is certainly news to no one. On the other hand, the statement that leaders of those movements have proclaimed Pan Arab objectives comes somewhat as a surprise. [...]

My impression -- based on recent talks with such leaders as the Sheik Thaalbi, venerable leader of the old Destur Party in Tunisia, and Si Allal el Fassi, head of the National Reform Party in Morocco, now exiled to French Equatorial Africa -- is that among the intellectuals there is considerable sympathy for the cause of Pan Arabism and a general desire to aid the campaign of the Mufti. Some of the intellectuals have studied in Cairo and elsewhere in the Near East. Many of them possess, or have invented, long genealogies to prove their descent from the Prophet. To be an Arab, or at least to be taken for one, is a mark of great social distinction in North Africa where authentic Arabs are so few and far between. Any movement labelled "Pan Arab" therefore carries a certain appeal.

[...]

True, there have been manifestations of Pan Arab and Pan Moslem solidarity in French North Africa (the latter is probably the stronger). In Tunisia money was collected to aid the Arab cause in Palestine, while numerous letters, telegrams and delegations protested against partition. The Congress of Algerian ulemas at Oran asked the French Government's intervention to prevent the dismemberment of Palestine. In French Morocco the Higher Arab Committee's appeal for moral support was answered with prayers and addresses in the mosques, while in a letter to the Mufti the National Reform Party in Spanish Morocco announced itself ready for any sacrifice on behalf of the Arab cause.

These demonstrations do not signify that the Moors -- some of whom are in any case occupied at present in reconverting Spain to Christianity -- are about to betake themselves *en masse* to Palestine in order to save it from the Infidel. They do, however, signify that the Pan Arab and Pan Islamic banners have been raised in North Africa. [...]

British White Paper of 1939 (1939)
Malcolm MacDonald

[…] [T]he establishment of self-supporting independent Arab and Jewish States within Palestine has been found to be impracticable. It has therefore been necessary for His Majesty's Government to devise an alternative policy which will, consistent with their obligations to Arabs and Jews, meet the needs of the situation in Palestine. […]

Section I. "The Constitution"

[…] His Majesty's Government believe that the framers of the Mandate in which the Balfour Declaration was embodied could not have intended that Palestine should be converted into a Jewish State against the will of the Arab population of the country. […]

His Majesty's Government therefore now declare unequivocally that it is not part of their policy that Palestine should become a Jewish State. They would indeed regard it as contrary to their obligations to the Arabs under the Mandate, as well as to the assurances which have been given to the Arab people in the past, that the Arab population of Palestine should be made the subjects of a Jewish State against their will.
[…]
In the light of these considerations His Majesty's Government make the following declaration of their intentions regarding the future government of Palestine:

The objective of His Majesty's Government is the establishment within 10 years of an independent Palestine State in such treaty relations with the United Kingdom as will provide satisfactorily for the commercial and strategic requirements of both countries in the future. The proposal for the establishment of the independent State would involve consultation with the Council of the League of Nations with a view to the termination of the Mandate.

The independent State should be one in which Arabs and Jews share government in such a way as to ensure that the essential interests of each community are safeguarded.
[…]
Section II. Immigration

[…] [T]he extent to which Jewish immigration into Palestine is to be permitted is nowhere defined in the Mandate. But in the Command Paper of 1922 it was laid down that for the fulfilment of the policy of establishing a Jewish National Home:

"it is necessary that the Jewish community in Palestine should be able to increase its numbers by immigration. This immigration cannot be so great in volume as to exceed whatever may be the economic capacity of the country at the time to absorb new arrivals. It is essential to ensure that the immigrants should not be a burden upon the people of Palestine as a whole, and that they should not deprive any section of the present population of their employment."

In practice, from that date onwards until recent times, the economic absorptive capacity of the country has been treated as the sole limiting factor, and in the letter which Mr. Ramsay MacDonald, as Prime Minister, sent to Dr. Weizmann in February 1931 it was laid down as a matter of policy that economic absorptive capacity was the sole criterion. [...] If immigration has an adverse effect on the economic position in the country, it should clearly be restricted; and equally, if it has a seriously damaging effect on the political position in the country, that is a factor that should not be ignored. Although it is not difficult to contend that the large number of Jewish immigrants who have been admitted so far have been absorbed economically, the fear of the Arabs that this influx will continue indefinitely until the Jewish population is in a position to dominate them has produced consequences which are extremely grave for Jews and Arabs alike and for the peace and prosperity of Palestine. The lamentable disturbances of the past three years are only the latest and most sustained manifestation of this intense Arab apprehension. [...] If in these circumstances immigration is continued up to the economic absorptive capacity of the country, regardless of all other considerations, a fatal enmity between the two peoples will be perpetuated, and the situation in Palestine may become a permanent source of friction amongst all peoples in the Near and Middle East. His Majesty's Government cannot take the view that either their obligations under the Mandate, or considerations of common sense and justice, require that they should ignore these circumstances in framing immigration policy.
[...]
In all these circumstances, they believe that they will be acting consistently with their Mandatory obligations to both Arabs and Jews, and in the manner best calculated to serve the interests of the whole people of Palestine, by adopting the following proposals regarding immigration:

1.   Jewish immigration during the next five years will be at a rate which, if economic absorptive capacity permits, will bring the Jewish population up to approximately one third of the total population of the country. Taking into account the expected natural increase of the Arab and Jewish populations, and the number of illegal Jewish immigrants now in the country, this would allow of the admission, as from the beginning of April this year, of some 75,000 immigrants over the next five years. These

immigrants would, subject to the criterion of economic absorptive capacity, be admitted as follows:

  a. For each of the next five years a quota of 10,000 Jewish immigrants will be allowed on the understanding that a shortage one year may be added to the quotas for subsequent years, within the five year period, if economic absorptive capacity permits.

  b. In addition, as a contribution towards the solution of the Jewish refugee problem, 25,000 refugees will be admitted as soon as the High Commissioner is satisfied that adequate provision for their maintenance is ensured, special consideration being given to refugee children and dependents.

  c. The existing machinery for ascertaining economic absorptive capacity will be retained, and the High Commissioner will have the ultimate responsibility for deciding the limits of economic capacity. Before each periodic decision is taken, Jewish and Arab representatives will be consulted.

  2. After the period of five years, no further Jewish immigration will be permitted unless the Arabs of Palestine are prepared to acquiesce in it.
[…]

Section III. Land

[…] The Reports of several expert Commissions have indicated that, owing to the natural growth of the Arab population and the steady sale in recent years of Arab land to Jews, there is now in certain areas no room for further transfers of Arab land, whilst in some other areas such transfers of land must be restricted if Arab cultivators are to maintain their existing standard of life and a considerable landless Arab population is not soon to be created. In these circumstances, the High Commissioner will be given general powers to prohibit and regulate transfers of land. […]

The policy of the Government will be directed towards the development of the land and the improvement, where possible, of methods of cultivation. In the light of such development it will be open to the High Commissioner, should he be satisfied that the "rights and position" of the Arab population will be duly preserved, to review and modify any orders passed relating to the prohibition or restriction of the transfer of land.
[…]

Parliamentary Debate on British White Paper of 1939 (1939)

Mr. Williams [...] We have watched the rise and fall of this Palestine problem. In 1917 Jewish hopes were raised in all parts of the world. It was thought that at long last here was the Jewish Magna Charta. By 1921 Transjordan was lopped off; in 1922 free immigration became immigration on the basis of economic absorptive capacity and very properly; in 1930 land sales were restricted; in 1937 partition was accepted by the Government; in 1938 partition was rejected by the Government; and in 1939 we see the funeral of the Mandate. That is not a very proud record either for this, or for any other Government that has gone before. [...]

Mr. Crossley [...] Let me give a few facts about the Arabs. Let me first take Scandinavia as an analogy. It is very often said of the Arabs that they have this vast Kingdom, these huge fertile areas. Why cannot they give this little corner away to the Jews. Suppose that after a war the whole of Scandinavia were liberated from a tolerant but rather corrupt rule, let us say, Russia. Suppose we liberated the Norwegians and said that they should live in Norway, that the Swedish Scandinavians should live in Sweden, that the Finnish Scandinavians should live in Finland, but as for the Denmark Scandinavians, surely they could afford their little corner. Therefore we will put Jews there in large numbers. That is an exact analogy. [...]

It is true that these Arabs in Palestine have been there for 1,400 years as a settled population of peasant farmers. If ever a people were entitled to look forward to the helpful tutelage of the British Empire it is these people. This brings me to the point about the increase in the Arab population. Has this House ever realised that we brought the war to Palestine and that 300,000 Arabs in Palestine died of starvation during the war in that country—died as the result of the war which we brought to that country. That makes it more and more an obligation on us to see to their future well-being. [...]

I do not believe that a more disinterested, hard-working or honest body of men exists than the British civil servant in Palestine. It is perfectly true that they are all pro-Arab at heart. So is every soldier. They do not go there pro-Arab, but they see the things for themselves and they see that no race of men under the Colonial standard of government in the British Empire has been so harshly or so unfairly treated or has had so raw a deal as the Arabs in Palestine.
[...]
I want to say a few words about immigration. At the end of paragraph 12 there is reference to fear on the part of the Arabs of a Zionist immigration into Palestine, and hon. Members opposite will not find many of the workers in Palestine who do not share that fear. The White Paper says: "If in these circumstances immigration is continued up to the economic absorptive capacity of the country, regardless of all other considerations, a

fatal enmity between the two peoples will be perpetuated, and the situation in Palestine may become a permanent source of friction amongst all peoples in the Near and Middle East." It is a pity that they have been waiting 20 years and constantly increasing the rancour in that country before they discovered this. Later on, in paragraph 13, it is said: "It has been the hope of British Governments ever since the Balfour Declaration ... that in time the Arab population, recognizing the advantages to be derived from Jewish settlement and further development in Palestine, would become reconciled to the further growth of the Jewish National Home." What were the advantages to the Arabs? [...] [T]he average holdings for an Arab family was in dunums, or 28 acres, but all the land that is available to-day for an Arab peasant is on average from 50 to 58 dunums or 12 1/2 to 14 acres. In 1931 about a quarter of the agricultural population in Palestine, that is the Arabs, could not subsist on their holdings, now it is a half. The price of citrus has gone to nothing, trees have had to be cut down, planting is stopped, and indeed many of the old citron growers are completely ruined by the entirely non-commercial over-development of the industry. We may as well face the fact that to many of the Arabs, immigration has meant penury, a dispossession of their land, and they are not by the terms of the Jewish Agency leases even allowed to be engaged as were the Hivites of old as hewers of wood and drawers of water. There is no economic case for any further immigration whatever. Then the Government in paragraph 14 say they: "are conscious of the present unhappy plight of large numbers of Jews who seek a refuge from certain European countries, and they believe that Palestine can and should make a further contribution to the solution of this pressing world problem." There again they are putting forward an extraneous argument to which the Arabs have always naturally objected. They say why cannot Palestine be treated solely and simply as a problem to be judged by the criterion of its own wishes? In 1931 Sir John Hope Simpson reported that immigration should be drastically limited. In 1933 10,000 people were allowed in, in 1934 30,000, in 1935 42,000 and in 1936 62,000, and that was solely for political reasons. Nobody more bitterly hates the policy of the leaders of Germany than I do, but that was done for political reasons in Europe, and does it not justify the fears of the Arabs as to the possibility of an actual Zionist majority? It was also the same with land sales. It may interest hon. Members to know how these sales came about. It may be true that only one-ninth of Palestine belongs to the Jews but that one-ninth is by far the most fertile area of the country, as it happens to be the valleys of Sharon and Esdraelon. How was this land bought? Eighty per cent. of it was sold over the heads of the Arab tenants, who were forcibly dispossessed, and if anyone does not believe there is unemployment in Palestine let him go to the tin shanties about Haifa, where he will see 25,000 unemployed Arabs who have been dispossessed of their land. There is a proverb which says: The Fellah dies in his furrow. And too often the fellah dies in a tin shanty at the end of an alien town listening to the sound of a strange tongue and with hatred seated in his heart. That is not what British rule should bring;

but it is what British rule has brought to this country. I come now to the constitutional point and I would like to draw hon. Members attention to paragraph 9 on page 6 of the White Paper. It says: "The establishment of an independent State and the complete relinquishment of Mandatory control in Palestine would require such relations between the Arabs and the Jews as would make good government possible." No one in this House will quarrel with that statement if it means that if the Arabs commit murder, if their armed bands roam the country and if life and property are not safe, it is therefore right to withhold the reward of self-government. But does that phrase mean—and it is what the friends of the Arabs in this House want to know—that mere Jewish non-cooperation will deny the Arabs what have been admitted to be their legitimate aspirations? I cannot believe that most hon. Members opposite do not consider it a just aspiration for any subject race to go towards self-government. If so, by what point of logic, by what dictate of reason, by what principle of justice, can the non-cooperation of a minority refuse or cause to be refused the legitimate desires of a majority? [...]

In conclusion, I offer to the Government two truisms and one prophecy. The first of my truisms is, "Hesitate and you are lost," and the second— which is indeed more than a truism—is, "You do not ever right one wrong—the wrong that has been inflicted on the Jews in other countries— by inflicting another, the wrong inflicted on the Arabs." For that reason, I think it is best, on the whole, if the Government take the White Paper as a basis and act strongly and firmly on it. I will make this prophecy. Sooner or later, the Arabs will get their way in Palestine, if for no other reason than that they have right on their side. I know the Arabs; I have heard them abused, but they are courtly, fine, considerate gentlemen, and they are doing their best for their people. I am certain that if it is sooner, it will not be found that they either misuse their trust or prove to be other than good friends to this country. After all, they desire only to achieve what every Colonial population which has reached a certain standard of government in every part of the Empire also desires to achieve, and what no party in the House ought to deny to them—legitimate self-government in their own land.
[...]

The Great Revolt and Roots of the Middle East Conflict (2023)
Oren Kessler

During the 1930s, Arabs living under the British Mandate of Palestine challenged the increasing Jewish immigration to the territory by launching in the spring of 1936 the Arab Revolt, which "began fairly spontaneously." The Arabs, influenced by Izz ad-Din al-Qassam, a Syrian "jihadi preacher" who arrived in Palestine in the twenties to incite jihad against Jewish and British targets, attacked Jews in a "concerted nationalist uprising." Al-Qassam, who was killed as a wanted man, "becomes the first martyr icon in the Palestinian Arab pantheon." Prophetically, David Ben Gurion, "the undisputed leader of the Jews of Palestine," said at that time that "finally, the Arabs have found someone willing to die for an ideal," and predicted that there would be "dozens, hundreds, or thousands just like him."

Three "legacies" emerged from the revolt: (1) a Jewish state, in the full sense of the word, first appears on the "international agenda"; (2) the Yishuv, "the pre-state community" of Jews of British Mandate Palestine, produces a Jewish army through "British training and facilitation of arms"; and (3) Britain denies the doomed Jews of Europe entry to Palestine during World War II.

After Britain's first high commissioner for Palestine, Herbert Samuel, appointed Hajj Amin al-Husseini to the position of Grand Mufti of Jerusalem and head of the Supreme Muslim Council, Hajj Amin continued al-Qassam's violence against the Jews. The Mufti took control of the revolt by calling for a widespread Arab general strike. He threatened to continue the strike unless three demands were met: (1) ceasing all Jewish immigration to the country, (2) banning all land sales (many land-owning Arabs at that time were selling lands to Jews at inflated prices), and (3) creating a legislative assembly to reflect the then-Arab majority demographic of Mandatory Palestine. Hajj Amin's aim was to prevent Jews from becoming a majority in the Mandate through the Jewish population's rapid growth in Palestine since the early 1930s. As antisemitism escalated in European countries, Jewish immigration to Mandatory Palestine during the first half of the 1930s doubled. As a result, Jews accounted for thirty percent of the population when the revolt began.

The Arab strike lasted six months, pausing only after the British government dispatched the Peel Commission to investigate grievances. The Commission's report produced the first of the three legacies — "the first two-state solution" to appear on the international agenda. Recommending partition, the Peel Commission became the "ideological template" of "partition plans" through the present day. While Ben-Gurion

From Middle East Forum Webinar: Oren Kessler on "Palestine 1936: The Great Revolt and Roots of the Middle East Conflict", MIDDLE EAST FORUM (June 2, 2023), url: https://www.meforum.org/64487/oren-kessler-on-palestine-1936-the-great-revolt.

was privately "euphoric" about the recommendation, the Mufti rejected it outright as a "humiliation."

The Mufti, "pulling the strings of this revolt," raised the incitement level, which culminated in the assassination in 1937 of Lewis Andrews, a British proponent of the partition plan and acting governor of the Galilee. Andrews was also the highest-ranking British official to be assassinated in Mandatory Palestine. Fearing arrest by the British, Hajj Amin fled the country, and as the Arab revolt escalated in 1938, World War II was on the verge of erupting.

The British, short of manpower, trained and armed 20,000 Jews in the framework of the Notrim, "the Jewish Supernumerary Police," to counter the Arabs, thereby creating the "second major legacy" of the revolt. The establishment of this force enabled the Haganah, "the mainstream Jewish armed force," to evolve from a "glorified group of night watchmen" into the "seed of the Jewish army" facilitated by the British Empire. The Jewish army's emergence coincided with great "economic, industrial, agricultural [and] demographic gains" for the Jews. Settlements sprang up, and the Jews "formed the kernel of their state-to-be in 1939."

During that time, Britain received a temporary reprieve from the "Munich crisis" after Neville Chamberlain's government appeased Hitler by acceding to his demand that Germany take control of Czechoslovakia's Sudetenland. The respite enabled Britain to send two divisions of soldiers to quell the Arab uprising in Palestine in a "brutal" counterinsurgency. Hampered by Arab infighting that erupted in Hajj Amin's absence, the revolt ended.

Despite its muscular approach to ending the revolt, Britain pursued a policy of appeasement elsewhere in the world. Thus, concerned that Muslims in India would not side with Britain, the government convened the St. James Conference in London in 1939, which opted to placate Arab and Muslim opinion. The conference produced the White Paper, which limited the number of Jews permitted to enter Palestine, declaring "that over the next five years, only 75,000 Jews in total could come to this land. And then no more Jews could immigrate without Arab consent." The Mufti, exiled in Beirut, rejected the White Paper "for not going far enough."

To the Jews, the White Paper was a betrayal of Britain's 1917 Balfour Declaration supporting a Jewish homeland in Palestine, a rejection of the Peel Partition plan, and a death trap for their co-religionists in Europe. Yet, "despite the tremendous toll in blood that the [Arab] revolt inflicted on the Jews.... As the revolt is brought to an end and the World War begins, the Jews have that kernel and springboard of a state. And on the Arab side, it's really the mirror image."

Instead of crushing Zionism, the Arabs, with their "leadership in exile," thousands killed, thousands fleeing, and a "huge amount of bad blood within the Arab community," were themselves crushed. Kessler argues that by 1948, the "showdown" between the Jews and Arabs was won by one side and lost by the other "really nearly ten years in advance."

HOLOCAUST

Message Concerning Anti-Jewish Activity (1935)
William Dodd

Sir: [...] [T]here have been signs of an intensification of pressure upon the Jews in Germany. Fresh outbursts against the Jews in public speeches, additional discriminatory ordinances, and finally undercover work by the police all seem to furnish evidence that the State [...] is engaged in a new anti-Jewish drive.

Julius Streicher, Gauleiter of Franconia and famous as a Jewbaiter, is making a speaking tour of several German cities, a fact of significance in itself, even though many of his public utterances have to be discounted because of their very violence. Last week before a large meeting at Cologne he was acclaimed by the local Gauleiter, Grohé, as "the man who had waged war without compromise against Jewry." "Those who believe that the measures against the Jews will be relaxed, are grievously mistaken," Grohé declared. "The Jewish question will be solved once and for all along the lines recommended by the Stürmer!" (Streicher's notorious anti-Jewish paper which advocates measures little short of annihilation.)

Streicher then delivered a speech which even he evidently considered too violent for the papers to carry, particularly the foreign press, inasmuch as he left the press the alternative either of printing the full text of his address which, according to the Easier Nachrichten lasted three hours, or of publishing nothing at all. The Westdeutscher Beobachter, a reliable party organ of the west of Germany, which incidentally has just issued a special anti-Jewish number, was apparently permitted to disregard this injunction, however, and reprinted certain of Streicher's statements in brief, as follows: "To those who argue that Christ was a Jew, I would say, 'Were I to call Christ a Jew, I should be calling him a criminal.'" Entering the field of international politics, Streicher acknowledged Germany's debt to Mussolini for Fascism but warned him "that he who consorts with Jews goes with them to ruination." "We know who has prevented France from accepting Germany's outstretched hand of peace, who in Soviet Russia holds the power and plots world revolution—the Jews!" Streicher exclaimed.

[...] It may have been of some importance, moreover, that the Fxihrer himself saw fit to put the seal of his approval on Streicher's work [....] Speaking before the Kulturverein in Nurnberg on March 29, Minister of the Interior Frick said: "I should like to pay a special tribute to the very great service performed by our party comrade, Julius Streicher, who for a decade has tirelessly combatted the baleful influence of racial mixture and

Jewry, and I believe that after two years of power we stand very close to his goal."

Against the background of remarks such as these the several new measures which have recently been taken against the Jews stand out in particular prominence. Within the last fortnight orders have been issued forbidding Jewish lawyers to handle cases for the Aryan poor and excluding Jewish apprentices from the State schools for the book and publishing trades. Furthermore, the Reichsschrif tums-kammer has addressed a circular letter to, it is understood, several thousand Jewish authors, many of whom have been doing freelance work for the papers, denying them the right to publish any more of their writings on the ground that their status of non-Aryan deprived them of a sense of connection and obligation to the community. [...]

The Times also reports that a new policy has been prescribed with respect to Jewish organizations engaged in the training of young farmers. These organizations have had as one of their objects the placing of the Jewish youth upon the land in order to meet National Socialist complaints against Jewish absorption of the intellectual professions; now, however, they have been instructed to train the Jewish youth for the sole purpose of emigrating to Palestine. The same paper reports that, with a view to discouraging the repatriation in Germany of Jews who have been working abroad, many of those returning recently have been arrested at the border and informed that they would have to undergo a period of "education," preferably in a concentration camp, before they could resume their place as inhabitants in Germany.

[...]

An interesting characteristic of the new anti-Jewish campaign is that, apart from the outbursts of Gauleiters Grohé and Streicher as quoted above, it is for the most part being carried on unobtrusively. There appears as yet to be no general attempt to incite the population to excesses against the Jews and in contrast to the first anti-Semitic drive, violence on any perceptible scale is apparently being avoided. Even the fanatical Julius Streicher lately published a warning against "certain irresponsible elements who have spread rumors that the Jews were planning an attack upon the Fuhrer's life and that consequently they must be exterminated." Streicher claimed that he demanded the utmost discipline in his district and that he had recently dismissed a local leader for "undue rashness." In conversation with a journalist known to the Embassy, Dr. Goebbels made the significant statement that the "Jewish question will soon be liquidated," but denied permission that publicity be given to his remark. The new campaign seems rather to be directed at a further restriction of the Jews' legal rights. It is impossible to say at present how far the measures may be carried but it might be mentioned that announcement has been made of an early codification of the German citizenship laws and that in this connection many Jews here fear for the worst.

The Extermination Camps of Auschwitz and Birkenau ("Vrba-Wetzler" Report) (1944)

Rudolf Vrba and Alfred Wetzler

[This report was co-authored by two persons who escaped from Auschwitz-Birkenau].

AUSCHWITZ is a concentration camp for political prisoners under so-called "protective custody". [...]

AUSCHWITZ camp headquarters controls at the same time the work-camp of BIRKENAU as well as the farm labor camp of HARMENSE. All the prisoners arrive first at AUSCHWITZ where they are provided with a prisoner's immatriculation number and then are either kept there, sent to BIRKENAU or, in very small numbers, to HARMENSE. The prisoners receive consecutive numbers upon arrival. Every number is only used once so that the last number always corresponds to the number of prisoners actually in the camp. [...]

Together with the remaining Russian prisoners the Slovak Jews worked at the construction of buildings, whereas the French Jews had to do spade work. After three days I was ordered, together with 200 other Slovak Jews, to work in the German armament factories at AUSCHWITZ, but we continued to be housed in BIRKENAU. We left early in the morning returning at night and worked in the carpentry shop as well as road construction. Our food consisted of one liter of turnip soup at midday and 300 grams of bad bread in the evening. Working conditions were inconceivably hard, so that the majority of us weakened by starvation and the inedible food, could not stand it. The mortality was so high that every day our group of 200 had 30 to 35 dead. Many were simply beaten to death by the overseers—the "Capos"—during work, without the slightest provocation. The gaps in our ranks caused by these deaths were replaced daily by prisoners from BIRKENAU. Our return at night was extremely painful and dangerous, as we had to drag along over a distance of 5 kilometers our tools, firewood, heavy caldrons, and the bodies of those who had died or had been killed during the working day. With these heavy loads we were forced to maintain a brisk pace, and anyone incurring the displeasure of one of the "Capos" was cruelly knocked down, if not beaten to death. Until the arrival of the second group of Slovak men some 14 days later, our original number had dwindled to 150. At night we were counted, the bodies of the dead were piled up on flat, narrow-gauge cars or in a truck and brought to the Birch Forest (BRZEZINSKI) where they were burned in a trench several meters deep and about 15 meters long. [...]

There was no question of any medical attention or care. We had some 150 dead daily and their bodies were sent for cremation to AUSCHWITZ.

At the same time the so-called "selections" were introduced. Twice weekly, Mondays and Thursdays, the camp doctor indicated the number of prisoners who were to be gassed and then burned. These "selections" were loaded into trucks and brought to the Birch Forest. Those still alive upon arrival were gassed in a big barrack erected near the trench used for burning the bodies. The weekly "draft" in dead from "Block 7" was about 2,000, of whom 1,200 died of "natural death" and about 800 through "selection." For those who had not been "selected" a death certificate was issued and sent to the central, those who had not been "selected" a death certificate was issued and sent to the central the indication "S.B." ("Sonderbehandelt" - special treatment). Until January 15, 1943, up to which time I was administrator of "Block 7" and therefore in a position to directly observe happenings, some 50,000 prisoners died of "natural death" or by "selection."

[...]

The first male Jewish transport reaching AUSCHWITZ for BIRKENAU, was composed, as mentioned, of 1,320 naturalized French Jews bearing approximately the following numbers:

[...]

38,000 – 38,400 400 French naturalized Jews who arrived with their families

> This whole convoy consisted of about 1,600 individuals of whom approximately 200 girls and 400 men were admitted to the camp, while the remaining 1,000 persons (women, old people, children as well as men) were sent without further procedure from the railroad siding directly to the Birch Forest, and there gassed and burned. From this moment on all Jewish convoys were dealt with in the same manner. Approximately 10% of the men and 5% of the women were allotted to the camps and the remaining members were immediately gassed. This process of extermination had already been applied earlier to the Polish Jews. During long months, without interruption, trucks brought thousands of Jews from the various "ghettos" direct to the pit in the "Birkenwald."

38,400 – 39,200 800 naturalized French Jews, the remainder of the convoy was—as previously described, gassed.

39,200 – 40,000 800 Poles (Aryans), political prisoners. 150 Slovak Jews with their families.

40,000 – 40,150 Slovak Jews with their families.

> Outside of a group of 50 girls sent to the women's camp, all other members were gassed in the Birch forest. Among the 150 men who came to the camp, there was a certain "Zucker", and Sonneschein, Viliam, both from eastern Slovakia.

40,150 – 43,800 Approximately 4,000 French naturalized Jews, almost all were intellectuals; 1,000 women were directed to the women's camp, while the balance of about 3,000 persons were gassed in the usual manner.

43,800 – 44,200 400 Slovak Jews from LUBLIN[...]

44,200 – 45,000 200 Slovak Jews. The convoy consisted of 1,000 persons. A number of women were sent to the women's camp, the rest gassed in the Birch Wood. [...]

45,000 – 47,000 2,000 Frenchmen (Aryans), communists and other political prisoners, among whom were the brother of Thorez and the young brother of Leon Blum. The latter was atrociously tortured, then gassed and burned.

47,000 – 47,500 500 Jews from Holland, in the majority German emigrants. The rest of the convoy, about 2,500 persons, gassed.

47,500 – 47,800 About 300 so-called Russians under protective custody.

48,300 – 48,620 320 Jews from Slovakia. About 70 girls were transferred to the women's camp, the remainder, some 650 people, gassed in the Birch Wood. This convoy included about 80 people who had been handed over by the Hungarian police to the camp of SERED. [...]

48,000 – 64,800 15,000 naturalized French, Belgian and Dutch Jews. This figure certainly represents less than 10 percent of the total convoy. This was between July 1 and September 15, 1942. Large family convoys arrived from various European countries and were at once directed to the Birch Wood. The special squad ("Sonderkommando") employed for gassing and burning worked in day and night shifts. Hundreds of thousands of Jews were gassed during this period.

64,800 – 65,000 200 Slovak Jews. Out of this transport about 100 women were admitted to the camp, the rest of them gassed and burned. [...]

65,000 – 68,000 Naturalized French, Belgian, and Dutch Jews. Not more than 1,000 women were "selected" and sent to the camp. The others, at the lowest estimate 30,000, were gassed.

71,000 – 80,000 Naturalized French, Belgian, and Dutch Jews. The prisoners brought to the camp hardly represent 10 percent of the total transport. A conservative estimate would be that approximately 65 to 70,000 persons were gassed.
[...]
No. 80,000 marks the beginning of the systematic extermination of the Polish ghettos.

80,000 – 85,000 Approximately 5,000 Jews from various ghettos in
MLJAWA-MAKOW-ZICHENOW-LOMZA-GRODNO-BIALYSTOK.

> For fully 30 days truck-convoys arrived with-out interruption.
> Only 5,000 persons were sent to the concentration camp; all the
> others were gassed at once. The "special squad" worked in two
> shifts, 24 hours daily and was scarcely able to cope with the
> gassing and burning. Without exaggerating it may be said that out
> of these convoys some 80,000 to 90,000 received "special
> treatment." These transports also brought in a considerable amount
> of money, valuables, and precious stones.

85,000 – 92,600 6,000 Jews from GRODNO, BIALOSTOK and
CRACOW as well as 1,000 Aryan Poles. The majority of the Jewish
convoys were directly gassed and daily about 4,000 Jews were driven into
the gas chambers.

> During mid-January, 1943 three convoys of 2,000 persons, each
> from THERESIENSTADT arrived. They bore the designations
> "CU," "CR" and "R" (The meaning of these signs is unknown to
> us). These markings were also stamped on their luggage. Out of
> these 6,000 persons only 600 men and 300 women were admitted
> to the camp. The remainder were gassed.

99,000 – 100,000 End of January, 1943 large convoys of French and Dutch
Jews arrived; only a small portion of them reached the camp.

100,000 – 102,000 In February, 1943, 2,000 Aryan Poles, mostly
intellectuals.

102,000-103,000 700 Czech Aryans. Later those still alive were sent to
BUCHENWALD.

103,000 – 108,000 3,000 French and Dutch Jews and 2,000 Poles
(Aryans).

> During the month of February , 1943, two contingents arrived
> daily. They included Polish, French, and Dutch Jews, who in the
> main, were sent to the gas chambers. The number gassed during
> this month can well be estimated at 90,000.

At the end of February, 1943 a new modern crematorium and gassing plant
was inaugurated at BIRKENAU. The gassing and burning of the bodies in
the Birch Forest was discontinued, the whole job being taken over by the
four specially built crematoria. The large ditch was filled in, the ground
leveled, and the ashes used as before for fertilizer at the farm labor camp of

HERMENSE, so that today it is almost impossible to find trace of the dreadful mass murder which took place here.

At present there are four crematoria in operation at BIRKENAU, two large ones, I and II, and two smaller ones, III and IV. Those of type I and II consist of 3 parts, i.e.,: (A) the furnace room; (B) the large halls; and (C) the gas chamber. A huge chimney rises from the furnace room around which are grouped nine furnaces, each having four openings. Each opening can take three normal corpses at once and after an hour and a half the bodies are completely burned. This corresponds to a daily capacity of about 2,000 bodies. Next to this is a large "reception hall" which is arranged so as to give the impression of the antechamber of a bathing establishment. It holds 2,000 people and apparently there is a similar waiting room of the floor below. [...] Thus the total capacity of the four cremating and gassing plants at BIRKENAU amount's to about 6,000 daily.

On principle only Jews are gassed; Aryans very seldom, as they are usually given "special treatment" by shooting. Before the crematoria were put into service, the shooting took place in the Birch Wood and the bodies were burned in the long trench; later, however, executions took place in the large hall of one of the crematoria which has been provided with a special installation for this purpose.

Prominent guests from BERLIN were present at the inauguration of the first crematorium in March, 1943. The "program" consisted of the gassing and burning of 8,000 Cracow Jews. The guests, both officers and civilians, were extremely satisfied with the results and the special peep-hole fitted into the door of the gas chamber was in constant use. They were Lavish in their praise of this newly erected installation.

109,000 – 119,000 At the beginning of March, 1943, 45,000 Jews arrived form Salonika. 10,000 of them came to the camp, including a small percentage of women; some 30,000 however went straight to the cremating facility. Of the 10,000 nearly all died a short time later from a contagious illness resembling malaria. They also died of Typhus due to the general conditions prevailing in the camp.

> Malaria among the Jews and typhus took such toll among the prisoners in general that the "selections" were temporarily suspended. The contaminated Greek Jews were ordered to present themselves and in spite of our repeated warnings many of them did. They were all killed by intracardial phenol injections administered by a lance-corporal of the medical corps.
>
> Out of the 10,000 Greek Jews, some 1,000 men remained alive and were later sent, together with 500 other Jews, to do fortification

work in Warsaw. A few weeks later several hundred came back in a pitiful state and were immediately gassed. The remainder presumably died in Warsaw. 400 Greek Jews suffering from malaria were sent for "further treatment" to LUBLIN after the phenol injections had been stopped, and it appears that they actually arrived. Their fate is not known to us, but it can be taken for granted that out of the original number of 10,000 Jews not one eventually remained in the camp.

[…]

During a night shift I was able to witness for the first time how incoming convoys were handled. The transport I saw contained Polish Jews. They had received no water for days and when the doors of the freight cars were open we were ordered to chase them out with loud shouts. They were utterly exhausted and about a hundred of them had died during the journey. The living were lined up in rows of five. Our job was to remove the dead, dying, and the luggage from the cars. The dead, and this included anyone unable to stand on his feet, were piled in a heap. Luggage and parcels were collected and stacked up. Then the railroad cars had to be thoroughly cleaned so that no trace of their frightful load was left behind. A commission from the political department proceeded with the "selection" of approximately 10 percent of the men and 5 percent of the women and had them transferred to the camps. The remainder were loaded on trucks, sent to BIRKENAU, and gassed while the dead and dying were taken directly to the furnace. It often happened that small children were thrown alive into the trucks along with the dead. Parcels and luggage were taken to the warehouses and sorted out in the previously described manner.

[…]

Careful estimate of the number of Jews gassed in BIRKENAU between April 1942 and April 1944 (according to countries of origin).

Poland	(transported by truck)	approximately	300,000
	(" " train	"	600,000
Holland	....	"	100,000
Greece	....	"	45,000
France	....	"	150,000
Belgium	....	"	50,000
Germany	....	"	60,00
Yugoslavia, Italy and Norway	....	"	50,000
Lithuania	....	"	50,000
Bohemia, Moravia and Austria	....	"	30,000
Slovakia	....	"	30,000
Various camps for foreign Jews in Poland		"	300,000
		approximately	1,765,000

Refugee Crises and the Sad Legacy of the 1938 Evian Conference
(2015)
Marvin Kalb

In 1938, the refugees were mostly German Jews, squeezed out of their country—where many had lived for hundreds of years—by a cruel Nazi policy of *judenrein*, cleansing the region of Jews. Of Germany's 600,000 Jews, about 150,000 had already fled from home and country, victims of a widening Hitlerian pogrom. When Germany annexed Austria in March of that year, another 185,000 Jews left there, many seeking entry into neighboring countries or visas to the United States.

They were to be disappointed. Doors were shutting, not opening. And, after Germany absorbed the Sudetenland and then all of Czechoslovakia, another 300,000 frightened Jews joined the ranks of suddenly rootless refugees, none knowing yet that soon Adolf Hitler would launch his "Final Solution to the Jewish Question," as it was to be called, and that six million Jews would be killed during World War II, which was just around the corner. So, what to do? Where to go?

Seeking Safe Haven

Across the Atlantic was the United States, viewed in Europe (especially by the refugees) as a haven for the homeless and oppressed, as a place perfect for those seeking religious freedom. Surely, it was felt, if such a powerful president as Franklin D. Roosevelt knew about the spreading refugee crisis in Europe, he would act. He would raise quotas. He would open the door to America and encourage other nations to open theirs.

Unfortunately for the refugees, this proved to be an illusion. Roosevelt, of course, knew about the refugee crisis in Europe, but he also knew about Congress' reluctance to raise existing quotas on Jewish immigration. In those days, anti-Semitism and isolationism were entrenched in American culture and politics, and Roosevelt was clearly not ready to fight Congress on quotas or to stand as the champion of oppressed European Jews.

However, he did not wish to appear indifferent to the problem—he was under pressure to do something. But what? He decided to do what Washington politicians have often done in a pinch—he set up a committee, in this case an international conference, to study the problem and, perhaps, come up with a solution. He wanted to appear to be the leader of a global effort to help European Jews—for the United States to strike the right pose, to suggest an open door policy, while realizing at the same time that he would not fight to raise quotas for European Jews. The American door would remain closed. Let others open their doors, he hoped.

The dead duck

The conference formally opened in mid-July, 1938, in the French resort of Evian-les-Bains. Representatives from 32 nations, plus 39 private organizations, gathered for 8 days of speeches, meetings, and grand displays of good will. More than 200 journalists covered the event. It was a big deal.

The U.S. representative was not a well-known diplomat—he was a businessman, Myron C. Taylor, whose major credential was that he was one of the president's close friends. His speech, like many of the others, flowered with humanitarian appeals but contained no new ideas. He was very cautious, as if he were walking on eggs.

Taylor went only so far as to assure his colleagues that the annual immigration quotas of 30,000 for Germany and Austria could include Jewish refugees. Great Britain agreed to accept a few thousand German Jews. Australia said it would accept 15,000 over three years. Reflecting the opinion of many delegations, the Australian representative, T. W. White, explained: "As we have no real racial problem, we are not desirous of importing one."

But the food was superb, and the vistas breathtaking, and everyone tried to exude good will. In fact, if success could be measured by good will alone, the Evian Conference would have been judged a roaring success. But day after day reporters sensed a failure all but inevitable. By the end it was clear to everyone, not just to the reporters, that little had been accomplished. Hopes had been raised, and then dashed. The Evian Conference went down in history as a complete flop. Only one nation, the Dominican Republic, agreed to accept 100,000 refugees.

Hitler, not known for his humor, was supposed to have joked: "We…are ready to put all these criminals at the disposal of these countries," adding: "for all I care, even on luxury ships." In Hitler's lexicon, apparently all Jews were "criminals."
[…]

Testimony Before the United Nations Special Committee on Palestine (UNSCOP) (1947)
Chaim Weizmann

The nations of the world realized, particularly the British, American, French and Italians, that a great deal of the trouble, worry and persecution which has beset the Jews throughout their history is due to the abnormal position of the Jews in the world. What is the abnormal position of the Jews in the world? What is it characterized by? It is characterized by one thing: I think this word from what I can see from reports, has been used here quite often. I used this word for the first time in speaking before the Royal Commission. It is the "Homelessness" of the Jewish people. To that I must add a comment. I do not mean the "homelessness" of individual Jews. There are groups of Jews in the world who have very comfortable homes—the American Jews, the Jews in a great many of the Western and North-western countries, the Jews in Sweden, Denmark, France, and also there was in Germany—but as a collectivity, as an ethnic group, they are homeless. They are and they are not. They are a people and they lack the props of a people. They are a disembodied ghost. There they are with a great many typical characteristics, many strong characteristics which have not disappeared throughout centuries, thousands of years of martyrdom and wandering, and at the same time they lack the props which characterize every nation. We ask today: "What are Poles? What are French? What are Swiss?" When that is asked everyone points to a country, to certain institutions, to parliamentary institutions, and the man in the street will know exactly what it is. He has a passport. If you ask what a Jew is, well, he is a man who has to offer a long explanation for his existence. And, any person who has to offer an explanation as to what he is always suspect, and from suspicion there is only one step to hatred or contempt. […]

I gave some of the reasons for the Balfour Declaration in 1917. They were, as I said, ideal, and they were what is called "utilitarian." They also came as a result of a conception that the position of the Jew would be altered and his suffering allayed if he had a place to go to. And, if these reasons were valid in 1918, they *a fortiori* are one thousand times more valid today. I am afraid that the reasons which prompted us to make a prognosis of the Jewish problem in the years 1904, 1905, and 1906, for which we were looked upon as dreamers and stargazers who were trying to get something impossible—all these prognoses as to what was going to happen to the Jews, unfortunately more than came true. There are six million Jews dead in Europe, and hundreds of thousands of Jews are languishing today either in D.P. camps or in countries where they are not wanted. It is proof that the situation demands speedy remedy. […]

Look at the difference which has been created between the Mandate and the White Paper. The Mandate encourages settlement of the land; the White Paper not only discourages it, it stops it. The Mandate encourages intensive colonization; the White Paper discourages it. The White Paper nullifies the Mandate. That is why we have to oppose the White Paper with all the strength at our disposal.

[…]

The Mandate was born out of hope. The White Paper was born out of fear. The fear which was brought into the world by Hitler, by Nazism, by all this darkness which has covered the bright horizon of Jews before the war. This fear has found expression in a great many forms, particularly in the form of the White Paper. This fear was a result of the appeasement policy: appeasement of Germany; appeasement of the Arabs. […] The Jews in Palestine have paid for this appeasement in the form of the White Paper. […]

At the last Congress which took place in Basle, I said in my opening address, and I think it stands repeating before you today: "Whenever a new country was about to come under Gestapo rule we asked that the gates of the National Home be opened for saving as many as possible of our people from the gas-chambers. Our entreaties fell on deaf ears; it seemed that the White Paper was more sacred for some people than life itself. Sometimes we were told that our exclusion from Palestine was necessary in order to do justice to a nation endowed with seven independent territories, covering a million square miles; at other times we were informed that the admission of our refugees might endanger military security during the war. It was easier to doom the Jews of Europe to a certain death than to evolve a technique for overcoming such difficulties. […]"

I have warned the various Commissions before whom I have had the honour to speak. […] I told them in 1936: there are in this part of the world—meaning Central Europe, Germany, and other countries—people who are pent up without being able to move; the world for them is divided into two parts, the countries where they cannot live and the countries they cannot enter and they are doomed. This sombre prophecy of 1936 came true in 1942. Therefore, in the face of this terrible fact, to advise us to turn again to live among the hatreds of the present and the tombstones of the past is asking too much from flesh and blood. Only recently there has been a conspiracy discovered in France which aimed at the overthrow of the French Republic, probably by the French Nazis. One of the projects which was discovered was a detailed programme of how to exterminate the French Jews on the pattern of Hitler and his Nazis.

It is, therefore, for us no more a question of refugees alone. It is very important to save refugees. It is very important, as I pointed out, to save every Jewish soul we can, particularly now, when every Jew alive is a precious possession to us. But there are higher things at stake, and that is the survival of the Jews as a people, and this can be achieved only through independence in a Jewish State in this country in part of this country.

[…]

The Condition and Needs of Displaced Persons in Western Europe
(1945)
Earl G. Harrison

[…] I have the honor to present to you a partial report upon my recent mission to Europe to inquire into (1) the conditions under which displaced persons and particularly those who may be stateless or non-repatriable are at present living, especially in Germany and Austria, (2) the needs of such persons, (3) how those needs are being met at present by the military authorities, the governments of residence and international and private relief bodies, and (4) the views of the possibly non-repatriable persons as to their future destinations.
[…]

II. Needs of the Jews
[…]
The first and plainest need of these people is a recognition of their actual status and by this I mean their status as Jews. Most of them have spent years in the worst of the concentration camps. In many cases, although the full extent is not yet known, they are the sole survivors of their families and many have been through the agony of witnessing the destruction of their loved ones. Understandably, therefore, their present condition, physical and mental, is far worse than that of other groups.

While SHAEF (now Combined Displaced Persons Executive) policy directives have recognized formerly persecuted persons, including enemy and ex-enemy nationals, as one of the special categories of displaced persons, the general practice thus far has been to follow only nationality lines. While admittedly it is not normally desirable to set aside particular racial or religious groups from their nationality categories, the plain truth is that this was done for so long by the Nazis that a group has been created which has special needs. Jews as Jews (not as members of their nationality groups) have been more severely victimized than the non-Jewish members of the same or other nationalities.

When they are now considered only as members of nationality groups, the result is that special attention cannot be given to their admittedly greater needs because, it is contended, doing so would constitute preferential treatment and lead to trouble with the non-Jewish portion of the particular nationality group.
[…]

WISHES AS TO FUTURE DESTINATIONS

(1) For reasons that are obvious and need not be labored, most Jews want to leave Germany and Austria as soon as possible. That is their first and great expressed wish and while this report necessarily deals with other needs present in the situation, many of the people themselves fear other suggestions or plans for their benefit because of the possibility that attention might thereby be diverted from the all-important matter of

114

evacuation from Germany. Their desire to leave Germany is an urgent one. [...] They want to be evacuated to Palestine now, just as other national groups are being repatriated to their homes. They do not look kindly on the idea of waiting around in idleness and in discomfort in a German camp for many months until a leisurely solution is found for them.

(2) Some wish to return to their countries of nationality but as to this there is considerable nationality variation. [...]

(3) With respect to possible places of resettlement for those who may be stateless or who do not wish to return to their homes, Palestine is definitely and pre-eminently the first choice. Many now have relatives there, while others, having experienced intolerance and persecution in their homelands for years, feel that only in Palestine will they be welcomed and find peace and quiet and be given an opportunity to live and work. In the case of the Polish and the Baltic Jews, the desire to go to Palestine is based in a great majority of the cases on a love for the country and devotion to the Zionist ideal. It is also true however, that there are many who wish to go to Palestine because they realize that their opportunity to be admitted into the United States or into other countries in the Western hemisphere is limited, if not impossible. [...]

(4) Palestine, while clearly the choice of most, is not the only named place of possible emigration. Some, but the number is not large, wish to emigrate to the United States where they have relatives, others to England, the British Dominions, or to South America.

Thus the second great need is the prompt development of a plan to get out of Germany and Austria as many as possible of those who wish it. [...]

IV. Conclusions and Recommendations
[...]
(2) Evacuation from Germany should be the emphasized theme, policy and practice.

(a)   Recognizing that repatriation is most desirable from the standpoint of all concerned, the Jews who wish to return to their own countries should be aided to do so without further delay. [...] It cannot be overemphasized that many of these people are now desperate, that they have become accustomed under German rule to employ every possible means to reach their end, and that the fear of death does not restrain them.

(b)   With respect to those who do not, for good reason, wish to return to their homes, prompt planning should likewise be undertaken. In this connection, the issue of Palestine must be faced. Now that such large numbers are no longer involved and if there is any genuine sympathy for what these survivors have endured, some reasonable extension or modification of the British White Paper of 1939 ought to be possible without too serious repercussions. For some of the European Jews, there is no acceptable or even decent solution for their future other than Palestine. This is said on a purely humanitarian basis with no reference to ideological or political considerations so far as Palestine is concerned.

It is my understanding, based upon reliable information, that certificates for immigration to Palestine will be practically exhausted by the end of the current month (August 1945). What is the future to be? To anyone who has visited the concentration camps and who has talked with the despairing survivors, it is nothing short of calamitous to contemplate that the gates of Palestine should be soon closed.

The Jewish Agency of Palestine has submitted to the British Government a petition that one hundred thousand additional immigration certificates be made available. A memorandum accompanying the petition makes a persuasive showing with respect to the immediate absorptive capacity of Palestine and the current, actual man-power shortages there.

While there may be room for difference of opinion as to the precise number of such certificates which might under the circumstances be considered reasonable, there is no question but that the request thus made would, if granted, contribute much to the sound solution for the future of Jews still in Germany and Austria and even other displaced Jews, who do not wish either to remain there or to return to their countries of nationality.

[…]

(3)   […] Here I feel strongly that greater and more extensive efforts should be made to get them out of camps for they are sick of living in camps. In the first place, there is real need for such specialized places as (a) tuberculosis sanitaria and (b) rest homes for those who are mentally ill or who need a period of readjustment before living again in the world at large-anywhere. Some will require at least short periods of training or retraining before they can be really useful citizens.

[…]

As matters now stand, we appear to be treating the Jews as the Nazis treated them except that we do not exterminate them. They are in concentration camps in large numbers under our military guard instead of S.S. troops. […]

The Obstacles Preventing Self-Governing Institutions in Palestine
(1948)
BRITISH COLONIAL OFFICE

1939 also saw the beginning of organised attempts by large numbers of Jews to enter Palestine in excess of the permitted quota. These attempts have continued ever since, and, by exacerbating Arab resentment, have greatly increased the difficulty of maintaining law and order in Palestine. During the war the majority of these illegal immigrants were deported to Mauritius, as enemy agents might otherwise have employed this means of entering Palestine, then a vital strategic area. In 1945 these Jews were brought back from Mauritius and allowed to enter Palestine, an equivalent number being deducted from the legal quota, which on the expiry of the five-year period laid down in the White Paper of 1939, had been fixed at 1,500 a month, as war conditions had prevented the Jews from bringing in all the 75,000 immigrants permitted by the White Paper. Although this limit was reached at the end of 1945, His Majesty's Government decided to continue the quota of 1,5000 a month pending the report of the Anglo-American Commission of Enquiry, which was then starting its work. Jewish immigration has, in fact, continued at this rate ever since. In the summer of 1946 the influx of Jewish illegal immigrants exceeded the capacity of the camps in Palestine where, since the war, they had been detained pending their release under the legal quota, and the majority of those reaching Palestine waters subsequently have been sent to Cyprus for the same purpose.

The control of illegal immigration not only burdened still further the British forces in Palestine and the Royal Navy, but was also the principal cause of the steady increase in Jewish terrorist activities. These had ceased at the beginning of the war, in whose persecution both Jews and Arabs had loyally co-operated, but broke out again in 1942. From that year until the end of the war Jewish extremists carried out a number of political murders, robberies and acts of sabotage, while Haganah (an illegal military force controlled by the Jewish Agency), organised the theft of arms and ammunition from the British forces in the Middle East. Once Germany had been defeated, these activities, previously sporadic and supported by only a minority of the Jewish community, increased in scale and intensity as the efforts of terrorist gangs were supplemented by those of Haganah and assisted by members of the Jewish Agency. Communications were attacked throughout the country; Government buildings, military trains and places of entertainment frequented by Britons were blown up; and numbers of Britons, Arabs and moderate Jews were kidnapped or murdered. This wholesale terrorism has continued ever since.
[…]

From <u>Palestine: Termination of the Mandate, 15th May 1948</u>, United Kingdom Colonial Office (1948). London: His Majesty's Stationery Office.

117

Declaration Adopted at the Biltmore Hotel ("Biltmore Program") (1942)
EXTRAORDINARY ZIONIST CONFERENCE

[The Extraordinary Zionist Congress met in lieu of the Zionist Congress, which could not meet because of WWII. The Declaration was adopted by the Jewish Agency and the Inner Zionist Council].

1.   American Zionists assembled in this Extraordinary Conference reaffirm their unequivocal devotion to the cause of democratic freedom and international justice to which the people of the United States, allied with the other United Nations, have dedicated themselves, and give expression to their faith in the ultimate victory of humanity and justice over lawlessness and brute force.

2.   This Conference offers a message of hope and encouragement to their fellow Jews in the Ghettos and concentration camps of Hitler-dominated Europe and prays that their hour of liberation may not be far distant.

3.   The Conference sends its warmest greetings to the Jewish Agency Executive in Jerusalem, to the Va`ad Leumi, and to the whole Yishuv in Palestine, and expresses its profound admiration for their steadfastness and achievements in the face of peril and great difficulties …

4.   In our generation, and in particular in the course of the past twenty years, the Jewish people have awakened and transformed their ancient homeland; from 50,000 at the end of the last war their numbers have increased to more than 500,000. They have made the waste places to bear fruit and the desert to blossom. Their pioneering achievements in agriculture and in industry, embodying new patterns of cooperative endeavor, have written a notable page in the history of colonization.

5.   In the new values thus created, their Arab neighbors in Palestine have shared. The Jewish people in its own work of national redemption welcomes the economic, agricultural and national development of the Arab peoples and states. The Conference reaffirms the stand previously adopted at Congresses of the World Zionist Organization, expressing the readiness and the desire of the Jewish people for full cooperation with their Arab neighbors.

6.   The Conference calls for the fulfillment of the original purpose of the Balfour Declaration and the Mandate which recognizing the historical connection of the Jewish people with Palestine was to afford them the opportunity, as stated by President Wilson, to found there a Jewish Commonwealth. The Conference affirms its unalterable rejection of the White Paper of May 1939 and denies its moral or legal validity. The White Paper seeks to limit, and in fact to nullify Jewish rights to immigration and settlement in Palestine, and, as stated by Mr. Winston Churchill in the

118

House of Commons in May 1939, constitutes 'a breach and repudiation of the Balfour Declaration'. The policy of the White Paper is cruel and indefensible in its denial of sanctuary to Jews fleeing from Nazi persecution; and at a time when Palestine has become a focal point in the war front of the United Nations, and Palestine Jewry must provide all available manpower for farm and factory and camp, it is in direct conflict with the interests of the allied war effort.

7. In the struggle against the forces of aggression and tyranny, of which Jews were the earliest victims, and which now menace the Jewish National Home, recognition must be given to the right of the Jews of Palestine to play their full part in the war effort and in the defence of their country, through a Jewish military force fighting under its own flag and under the high command of the United Nations.

8. The Conference declares that the new world order that will follow victory cannot be established on foundations of peace, justice and equality, unless the problem of Jewish homelessness is finally solved. The Conference urges that the gates of Palestine be opened; that the Jewish Agency be vested with control of immigration into Palestine and with the necessary authority for upbuilding the country, including the development of its unoccupied and uncultivated lands; and that Palestine be established as a Jewish Commonwealth integrated in the structure of the new democratic world.

Then and only then will the age old wrong to the Jewish people be righted.

Summons to a Holy War ("Fatwa") Against Britain (1941)
Haj Amin al-Husseini

The English have tried to seize this Arab-Moslem land, but she has risen, full of dignity and pride to defend her safety, to fight for her honor and to safeguard her integrity. 'Iraq fights the tyranny which has always had as its aim the destruction of Islam in every land. It is the duty of all Moslems to aid 'Iraq in her struggle and to seek every means to fight the enemy, the traditional traitor in every age and every situation.

Whoever knows the history of the East has everywhere seen the hand of the English working to destroy the Ottoman Empire and to divide the Arab countries. British politics toward the Arab people is masked under a veil of Hypocrisy. The minute she sees her chance, England squeezes the prostrate country in her imperialist grasp, adding futile justification. She creates discord and division within a country and while feeding it in secret openly she assumes the role of advisor and trusted friend. The time when England could deceive the peoples of the East is passed. The Arab Nation and the Moslem people have awakened to fight British domination. The English have overthrown the Ottoman Empire, have destroyed Moslem rule in India, inciting one community against another; they stifled the Egyptian awakening, the dream of Mohammed Ali, colonizing Egypt for half a century. They took advantage of the Ottoman Empire to stretch out their hands and use every sort of trick to take possession of many Arab countries as happened to Aden, the 9 Districts, the Hadramut, Oman, Masqat and the Emirates of the Persian Gulf and Transjordania. The vivid proof of the imperialistic designs of the British is to be found in Moslem Palestine which, although promised by England to Sheriff Hussein has had to submit to the outrageous infiltration of Jews, shameful politics designed to divide Arab-Moslem countries of Asia from those of Africa. In Palestine the English have committed unheard of barbarisms; among others, they have profaned the el-Aqsa Mosque and have declared the most unyielding war against Islam, both in deed and in word. The Prime Minister at that time told Parliament that the world would never see peace as long as the Koran existed. What hatred against Islam is stronger than that which publicly declares the Sacred Koran an enemy of human kind? Should such sacrilege go unpunished? After the dissolution of the Moslem Empire in India and of the Ottoman Caliphate, England, adhering to the policy of Gladstone, pursued her work of destruction to Islam depriving many Islamic States both in the East and in the West of their freedom and independence. The number of Moslems who today live under the rule of England and invoke liberation from their terrible yoke exceeds 220,000,000.

Therefore I invite you, O Brothers, to join in the War for God to preserve Islam, your independence and your lands from English aggression. I invite you all to bring your weight to bear in helping 'Iraq that she may throw off the shame that torments her.

[…]

120

Memorandum Concerning the Arab League (1945)
Loy W. Henderson

September 1, 1939–December 7, 1941

The outbreak of the war in Europe brought the nationalistic aspirations of the Arabs into greater prominence, since Arab friendship was cultivated by both the Allied and the Axis powers, as a part of the struggle for the Middle East. This was particularly true of the Axis, which embarked on an elaborate propaganda campaign through the use of Arabic-language broadcasts and in other ways. The British, for their part, were also conscious of the need for Arab support, and at a moment when the British strategic position in the Middle East was particularly acute, Foreign Secretary Eden gave recognition to the newly-developing movement for Arab Union in the following statement made at the Mansion House on May 29, 1941:

> "The Arab world has made great strides since the settlement reached at the end of the last war, and many Arab thinkers desire for the Arab peoples a greater degree of unity than they now enjoy. In reaching out towards this unity they hope for our support. No such appeal from our friends should go unanswered. It seems to me both natural and right that the cultural and economic ties between the Arab countries, yes, and the political ties too, should be strengthened. His Majesty's Government for their part will give their full support to any scheme that commands general approval."

[...]
December 1941 to date

The Arab union movement was naturally given impetus by Mr. Eden's Mansion House declaration, one of the more important results being the publication early in 1943 by Nuri Pasha, then Prime Minister of Iraq of his "Blue Book" entitled *Arab Independence and Unity*. This work proposed an Arab League to be composed initially of (1) a unified Syrian state comprising Syria, Lebanon, Palestine and Trans-Jordan; and (2) Iraq, with provision for other Arab states to adhere to this League.

Early in 1943 Mr. Eden made another statement, declaring on February 24 in the House of Commons:

> "As they have already made plain His Majesty's Government would view with sympathy any move among the Arabs to promote their economic, cultural or political unity. But clearly the initiative would have to come from the Arabs themselves and so far as I am aware no such scheme which would command general approval has yet been worked out."

This declaration had the direct result of leading Nuri Pasha to write Nahas Pasha, at that time Prime Minister of Egypt, urging the latter to take the initiative in calling an Arab Congress. Shortly thereafter Nahas announced that he was starting a series of individual conferences with representatives of the Arab states for an exchange of views regarding Arab union and with a view to the eventual convening of a full-dress Arab Congress. These talks took place through the remainder of 1943 and the early part of 1944 and were attended in turn by representatives of Iraq, Trans-Jordan, Saudi Arabia, Syria, Lebanon and the Yemen. The inclusion of representatives of the Arabs of Palestine was several times considered, but no agreement could be reached on the composition of a Palestine delegation.
[...]
In September and October 1944, a preliminary Arab Conference met at Alexandria and soon developed into a full-dress meeting of the Arab States. A representative of the Arabs of Palestine was present, as were delegates from Egypt, Syria, Lebanon, Iraq, Trans-Jordan, Saudi Arabia and the Yemen, the last two as observers only.

The Conference adopted a protocol providing for the formation of a League of Arab States, in accordance with plans to be drawn up by an interim sub-committee. There were also to be subcommittees on economic, cultural, social and other matters, while in addition the Conference passed resolutions according recognition to the independence of Lebanon and affirming Arab rights in Palestine.

Subsequently, a draft constitution for the Arab League was drawn up and was embodied in a pact signed by delegates of the seven member states on March 22, 1945.The pact was accompanied by annexes providing respectively for the participation in the work of the League of a representative of the Palestine Arabs and for cooperation with certain Arab territories not members of the League (Presumably such non-independent areas as French North Africa and the Persian Gulf sheikhdoms).

In brief, the Pact of the League prohibits any resort to force among member states, provides for consultation and mutual assistance in the event of aggression against a member state, sets up a Council and a Secretary General with headquarters in Cairo, and provides for cooperation between member states in many non-political fields.

At San Francisco the members of the Arab League gave indications of a desire to work together as a definite bloc and to have their group accepted as a regional organization under Chapter VIII of the Charter.
[...]

Synopsis of Anglo-American Inquiry Committee Report (1946)
Dean Acheson
[The Anglo-American Committee of Inquiry was created to explore solutions for Jewish refugees created by the Holocaust].

Report AngloAm Committee Inquiry re Palestine will be published May 1 according to present plans. Summary of main conclusions for your strictly confidential info follows:

1.   No hope in countries other than Palestine of substantial assistance in finding homes Jews wishing or forced leave Europe. But this is world responsibility and Palestine alone cannot meet Jewish emigration needs. AmBrit Govts in association other countries should endeavor find new homes all displaced and nonrepatriable persons both Jews, non-Jews. Since most will continue live Europe, AmBrit Govts should endeavor secure basic human rights freedoms as set forth UN Charter.

2.   100,000 certificates for Jewish victims Nazi Fascist persecution should be authorized immediately for admission Palestine. Certificates awarded as far possible 1946 and actual immigration accelerated as rapidly conditions permit.

3.   Exclusive claims of Jews and Arabs to Palestine should be disposed of once for all on three principles: Jew shall not dominate Arab in Palestine and vice versa; Palestine shall be neither Jewish nor Arab state; form of govt ultimately established shall fully protect interests of Christian, Jewish, Moslem faiths under international guarantees. Ultimately Palestine to become state guarding interests of Moslems, Jews and Christians alike according fullest measure self govt consistent three principles above. Palestine as Holy Land completely different from others hence narrow nationalism inappropriate. In view ancient [and] recent history Pal neither purely Arab nor Jewish land. Jewish National Home has right to continued existence protection development. Minority guarantees would not afford adequate protection for subordinated group. Struggle for numerical majority must be made purposeless by constitution.

4.   Hostile feeling between Jews Arabs and determination of both achieve domination makes almost certain attempt establish Palestinian state or states now or some time to come would result in civil strife possibly threatening world peace. Palestine Govt should continue under mandate then UN trusteeship until hostility disappears.

5.   Mandatory or trustee should declare Arab economic, educational, political advancement in Palestine equal importance with Jewish and prepare measures bridge present gap by raising Arab standards. Perhaps advisable encourage formation Arab community on lines Jewish community.

6. Pending trusteeship agreement Mandatory should facilitate Jewish immigration while ensuring rights and position of other sections population not prejudiced. In future Pal Govt should have right decide number immigrants admitted in any period having regard to well-being of all Pal people. View disapproved that any Jew anywhere can enter Pal as of right. Any immigrant Jew entering Pal contrary its laws is illegal immigrant.

7. Land transfers regulations should be amended on basis freedom sale, lease, use of land irrespective race, community, creed. Stipulations that only members one race, community, creed may be employed in connection conveyances, leases, agreements should be made nugatory and prohibited. Govt should closely supervise holy places and localities to protect from desecration offensive uses.

8. Not competent assess value plans presented for agricultural industrial development. Such projects if successful of great benefit but require peace and cooperation adjacent Arab states. Full consultation, cooperation required from start with Jewish Agency and Arab states affected.

9. Reformation of educational system both Jews Arabs and introduction compulsory education.

10. Should be made clear beyond doubt to both Jews Arabs that attempts by violence, threats, organization or use illegal armies to prevent execution of report if adopted will be resolutely suppressed. Jewish Agency should resume cooperation with Mandatory to suppress terrorism, illegal immigration, maintain law order.

Telegram to President Truman (1946)
James F. Byrnes

59. Delsec 482. For the President from the Secretary. Bevin has given me a copy of a memorandum prepared by his Govt for his use in discussing with me the Anglo-American Committee's report on Palestine and the Jewish question of which the following is a summary:

1. A brief examination shows that the commitments involved in giving effect to the report would involve the expenditure of large sums of money and the employment of military forces to an extent beyond the capacity of His Majesty's Govt to meet alone. Before any decision is taken as to whether the report should be put into force or not the British Govt must know what assistance they can count on, obtaining from the US Govt.

2. The military burden is the more important one. Before any decision could be taken to admit 100,000 additional immigrants as recommended in the report, the illegal Jewish armies must be suppressed and there must be a general disarmament throughout Palestine. Otherwise these armies would be swollen by recruits drawn from the new immigrants. The implementation of the report would cause serious repercussions throughout the Arab world involving additional military commitments which the British Govt could not undertake alone in present circumstances.

3. The British now have an equivalent of two and one-half divisions in Palestine. The British Govt considers that adoption of the Committee's report would make necessary reinforcements of the order of two infantry divisions and one armoured brigade. There is no possibility of providing these reinforcements from British sources if they are to meet their inescapable commitments in other parts of the world. It would be necessary for American forces of the required strength to be immediately available before the policy recommended could be endorsed by the British Govt, and it would be essential to obtain a guarantee that American assistance would be sustained at full strength so long as the commitment in Palestine lasted. A token contingent would not be sufficient.

4. A conservative estimate is that the recommendations of the report would involve an expenditure of from 60,000,000 to 70,000,000 pounds in Palestine during the next couple of years if the new immigrants are to be housed and fitted into the economy of the country. Over a period of 10 years the expenditure involved would be from 115,000,000 to 125,000,000 pounds. The foregoing figures exclude the cost of development schemes such as the Jordan Valley project which is estimated to cost 76,000,000 pounds.

5. Zionists have suggested that expenditures of this nature be met from reparations allocation for the victims of Nazism but the total available from this source for both Jews and non-Jews is only about 7,500,000

pounds. Even allowing for a maximum effort by world Jewry, there will obviously be a much larger residue than the British Govt will be able to bear alone and it would be glad to know to what extent it can count on American financial assistance should it be decided to put these measures into operation.

6.   The British are convinced that they would not be in a position to put the report into operation without substantial financial and military contributions from the US Govt.

7.   Both the British and US Govts are committed to consultation with the Arabs and Jews before a new policy is adopted which fact would preclude the British Govt from giving immediate effect to the report.

8.   Consideration should be given to the form of such consultations and whether the US would be associated with the British Govt in conducting them.

9.   If the US Govt is unable to agree to assist in implementing the report the British Govt will have to consider what its future policy in Palestine is to be. Meanwhile some other state may refer the matter to the Security Council at any moment as a situation likely to endanger the maintenance of international peace and security.

10. The British Govt considers that the Committee on Refugees and Displaced Persons of the Economic and Social Council should deal with the question of the disposal of the Jews for whom immigration to Palestine has not been suggested.

[BYRNES]

Memorandum Concerning Anglo-American Committee Report (1946)
John H. Hilldring

As anticipated, the British are stalling on the Anglo-American Committee's recommendation for authorization of 100,000 immigration visas to Palestine. Mr. Attlee has announced that action upon this recommendation will be withheld pending (*a*) disarmament of the Jewish underground Army in Palestine and (*b*) guarantee of military and financial assistance by the U.S. This position is inconsistent with the Committee's recommendation, which attached no such conditions, and, in fact, is reported to be the position which was considered by the Committee but was specifically rejected by it.

Our military and political interests in Germany and Austria require that we press for immediate implementation of the Committee's recommendation. I believe that unless we exercise unremitting pressure to this end, these interests will not receive adequate representation by our Government and there will be no effective counteraction to British tactics of stalling and confusing the entire issue.

[…] In order to further our interests in Germany and Austria, i.e., to resettle the Jewish displaced persons as expeditiously as possible, I think that all the Jewish pressure should be directed against the British rather than against both U.S. and British Governments jointly. This result, I believe, can be achieved only if this Government pursues an aggressive public policy of needling the British to implement the Committee's recommendation for entry of 100,000 immediately and without reference to future action on any other aspects of the Report. […]

I suggest, therefore, that you discuss with the President the following recommendations for immediate action:

    a. A public statement by the President stressing the urgent necessity of immediate implementation of the Committee's recommendation for issuance of 100,000 immigration visas.

    b. A public offer by the U.S. Government to assume primary responsibility for movement of all of the 100,000 from Europe to Palestine. This offer should be accompanied by a statement of the President's intention to designate an outstanding U.S. citizen (preferably by name) as his Personal Representative to coordinate the movement of these persons. […] It is believed that the net cost of such an operation to the U.S. Government would be not more, and perhaps even less, than the expense of maintaining Jewish displaced persons in camps in Germany and Austria for another year.
[…]

Memorandum Concerning Jewish Displaced Persons (1946)
Gordon P. Merriam

Assistant Secretary Hilldring, in his memorandum of May 3, states that our military and political interests in Germany and Austria require that we press for immediate implementation of the Committee's recommendation, and that in order to further our interests in these countries the resettlement of Jewish displaced persons should proceed as expeditiously as possible. He advocates that this Government pursue an aggressive public policy of needling the British into issuing 100,000 immigration certificates for Palestine immediately and without reference to future action on any other aspects of the report.

This recommendation apparently fails to take into account any aspect of the complicated Palestine problem other than the European. Before any action along such lines is contemplated, the following points should be given the most serious consideration:

1.   The whole question of procedure has already been put up to the President with the Department's observation that, since the Committee's ten recommendations form a carefully integrated whole, the various parts cannot be singled out for separate treatment. At the same time we urged that the report as a whole be adopted as this Government's policy at the earliest possible moment.

2.   Until the United States Government is prepared to accept the report, which it has not yet done, its status is simply that of a recommendation. It would seem unwise for this Government to take active steps to give effect to it, either in its entirety or in part, before it is adopted as the official policy of this Government.

3.   Our policy toward, interests in, and relations with the various Arab countries in the Near East, chiefly Egypt, Syria, Lebanon, Iraq and Saudi Arabia, are of an importance which is certainly commensurate with our interest in the future of the occupied zones of Europe. The Arab reaction to the Committee's recommendations has been swift and alarming. The Arabs have singled out the recommendation for putting 100,000 Jews into Palestine for criticism of the strongest kind, and they give every indication of the intention to resist. We have many political, economic and educational interests in these countries. Our educational interests, for example, have taken more than a century to build up, and they constituted a sheet anchor in the Middle East when we were militarily weak. These American schools and colleges require Arab good will for their continuance and effectiveness. Our Near Eastern trade and petroleum interests cannot be neglected, nor the desirability of our maintaining friendly relations with the countries located in the vital Near and Middle Eastern area.

4.   According to sources in close contact with the displaced Jews of Europe, the removal of 100,000 persons from the American zones in Germany and Austria would be a temporary solution at best, as they expect the influx of DP's from the Soviet Russian zones to continue unabated and soon fill the vacuum.

5.   The fact that the Committee was bi-national and its report a joint Anglo-American undertaking would seem to preclude unilateral action of any sort on our part, certainly at this stage. If, without full consultation with the British, the President were to issue a statement similar to that recommended in the memorandum under reference, British resentment would follow as a virtual certainty, to the inevitable detriment of our long-range interests in Palestine and elsewhere. It may be recalled that the British Prime Minister reacted strongly to the President's espousal of the 100,000 recommendation in view of the fact that no accompanying commitment was made to share responsibility for the results of carrying it out.

6.   Last but not least, this Government has committed itself on various occasions to take no action involving a change in the basic situation in Palestine without full consultation with both Arabs and Jews. We have also made it known that the hearings before the Committee did not constitute this consultation. If all or part of the report were to be put into operation by us without such consultation, it would be regarded as a breach of faith which could not fail to have repercussions of a very serious nature.

Gandhi on Jews and Palestine (1946)
Mahatma Gandhi

From Harijan

Hitherto I have refrained practically from saying anything in public regarding the Jew-Arab controversy. I have done so for good reasons. That does not mean any want of interest in the question, but it does mean that I do not consider myself sufficiently equipped with knowledge for the purpose. For the same reason I have tried to evade many world events. Without airing my views on them, I have enough irons in the fire. But four lines of a newspaper column have done the trick and evoked a letter from a friend who has sent me a cutting which I would have missed but for the friend drawing my attention to it. It is true that I did say some such thing in the course of a long conversation with Mr. Louis Fischer on the subject. I do believe that the Jews have been cruelly wronged by the world. "Ghetto" is, so far as I am aware, the name given to Jewish locations in many parts of Europe. But for their heartless persecution, probably no question of return to Palestine would ever have arisen. The world should have been their home, if only for the sake of their distinguished contribution to it.

But, in my opinion, they have erred grievously in seeking to impose themselves on Palestine with the aid of America and Britain and now with the aid of naked terrorism. Their citizenship of the world should have and would have made them honoured guests of any country. Their thrift, their varied talent, their great industry should have made them welcome anywhere. It is a blot on the Christian world that they have been singled out, owing to a wrong reading of the New Testament, for prejudice against them. "If an individual Jew does a wrong, the whole Jewish world is to blame for it." If an individual Jew like Einstein makes a great discovery or another composes unsurpassable music, the merit goes to the authors and not to the community to which they belong.

No wonder that my sympathy goes out to the Jews in their unenviably sad plight. But one would have thought adversity would teach them lessons of peace. Why should they depend upon American money or British arms for forcing themselves on an unwelcome land? Why should they resort to terrorism to make good their forcible landing in Palestine? If they were to adopt the matchless weapon of non-violence whose use their best Prophets have taught and which Jesus the Jew who gladly wore the crown of thorns bequeathed to a groaning world, their case would be the world's and I have no doubt that among the many things that the Jews have given to the world, this would be the best and the brightest. It is twice blessed. It will make them happy and rich in the true sense of the word and it will be a soothing balm to the aching world.

Panchagani, July 14, 1946

Letter from Albert Einstein (1946)
Albert Einstein

Dear Sir:

I have served as witness before the Anglo-American Inquriy [sic] Commission on Palestine for the sole purpose to act in favor of our just cause. But it is, of course, impossible to prevent distortion by the press. I am in favor of Palestine being developed as a Jewish Homeland but not as a separate State. It seems to me a matter for simple common sense that we cannot ask to be given the political rule over Palestine where two thirds of the population are not Jewish. What we can and should ask is a secured bi-national status in Palestine with free immigration. If we ask more we are damaging our own cause and it is difficult for me to grasp that our Zionists are taking such an intransigent position which can only impair our cause.

Very truly yours,
Albert Einstein

Diplomatic Letter Correspondence Regarding Jewish State in the Middle East (1946-1947)
Harry Truman and King Abdul Aziz Ibn Saud

Washington, July 13, 1946.

Your Majesty: It was a great pleasure to me to receive Your Majesty's letter of May 24, 1946 containing your preliminary views regarding the report of the Anglo-American Committee of Inquiry on Palestine, which was brought to me by my good friend and former Minister to Your Majesty's Government, Colonel William A. Eddy, the day he arrived in Washington, and I wish to assure Your Majesty that it will be a very real help to me to have the benefit of Your Majesty's considered views on this most difficult question.

I am deeply gratified by the close and friendly relations which have always existed between our two Governments and between Americans and Saudi Arabs generally. Although the questions under discussion between us are not without difficulty, I sincerely trust that these relationships will remain cordial and strong in the future.

I was very pleased that Your Majesty recognized the humanitarian principles which have motivated this Government in its approach to the Palestine problem. American interest in this question is of long standing and has been accentuated by the dire and urgent needs of victims of Nazi persecution. I am very conscious of the deep significance which all Arabs attach to Palestine and I particularly welcomed the visit to Riyadh of a sub-committee of the Anglo-American Committee of Inquiry. The report of that Committee reflects the complexity of the situation in Palestine. Its unanimous recommendations made after careful and dispassionate study I feel sure you will agree call for careful consideration by all.

I am sincere in my belief that the admission to Palestine of 100,000 Jewish refugees this year would neither prejudice the rights and privileges of the Arabs now in Palestine, nor constitute a change in the basic situation. I am convinced that Palestine can absorb 100,000 additional residents through its existing economy without interfering with the present inhabitants.

I have appointed a Committee of three members of my Cabinet to ensure careful consideration of the report on our part and to advise me. To that end they will engage in discussions with the British Government. I am hopeful that the situation will be further clarified by consultations with the Arabs and the Jews and that we can remain in close touch with the interested parties on these questions.

With my sincere wishes for the continued health and happiness of Your Majesty and for the prosperity of your people, I have the honor to remain your very good friend.

* * *

October 15, 1946

Your Excellency: In my desire to safeguard and strengthen in every way possible the friendship which binds our two countries together and which existed between the late President Roosevelt and which was renewed with Your Excellency, I reiterate my feelings on every occasion when this friendship between the United States on the one hand, and my country and the other Arab countries on the other hand, is endangered, so that all obstacles in the way of that friendship may be removed.

On previous occasions I wrote to the late President Roosevelt and to Your Excellency, and explained the situation in Palestine: How the natural rights of the Arabs therein go back thousands of years and how the Jews are only aggressors, seeking to perpetrate a monstrous injustice, at the beginning, speaking in the name of humanitarianism, but later openly proclaiming their aggressiveness by force and violence as is not unknown to Your Excellency and the American people. Moreover, the designs of the Jews are not limited to Palestine only, but include the neighboring Arab countries within their scope, not even excluding our holy cities.

I was therefore astonished at the latest announcement issued in your name in support of the Jews in Palestine and its demand that floodgates of immigration be opened in such a way as to alter the basic situation in Palestine in contradiction to previous promises. My astonishment was even greater because the statement ascribed to Your Excellency contradicts the Declaration which the American Legation in Jeddah requested our Foreign Office to publish in the Government's official paper *Omm Al-Qura* in the name of the White House, on August 16, 1946, in which it was stated that the Government of the United States had not made any proposals for the solution of the Palestine problem, and in which you expressed your hope that it would be solved through the conversations between the British Government and the Foreign Ministers of the Arab States, on the one hand, and between the British Government and the third party on the other, and in which you expressed the readiness of the United States to assist the displaced persons among whom are Jews. Hence, my great astonishment when I read your Excellency's statement and my incredulity that it could have come from you, because it contradicts previous promises made by the Government of the United States and statements made from the White House.

I am confident that the American people who spent their blood and their money freely to resist aggression, could not possibly support Zionist aggression against a friendly Arab country which has committed no crime except to believe firmly in those principles of justice and equality, for which the United Nations, including the United States, fought, and for which both your predecessor and you exerted great efforts.

My desire to preserve the friendship of the Arabs and the East towards the United States of America has obliged me to expound to Your Excellency the injustice which would be visited upon the Arabs by any assistance to Zionist aggression.

I am certain that Your Excellency and the American people cannot support right, justice, and equity and fight for them in the rest of the world while denying them to the Arabs in their country, Palestine, which they have inherited from their ancestors from Ancient Times.

Abdul Aziz

* * *

Washington, October 25, 1946.

Your Majesty: I have just received the letter with regard to Palestine which Your Majesty was good enough to transmit to me through the Saudi Arabian Legation under date of October 15, 1946, and have given careful consideration to the views expressed therein.

I am particularly appreciative of the frank manner in which you expressed yourself in your letter. Your frankness is entirely in keeping with the friendly relations which have long existed between our two countries, and with the personal friendship between Your Majesty and my distinguished predecessor; a friendship which I hope to retain and strengthen. It is precisely the cordial relations between our countries and Your Majesty's own friendly attitude which encourages me to invite your attention to some of the considerations which have prompted my Government to follow the course it has been pursuing with respect to the matter of Palestine and of the displaced Jews in Europe.

I feel certain that Your Majesty will readily agree that the tragic situation of the surviving victims of Nazi persecution in Europe presents a problem of such magnitude and poignancy that it cannot be ignored by people of good will or humanitarian instincts. This problem is worldwide. It seems to me that all of us have a common responsibility for working out a solution which would permit those unfortunates who must leave Europe to find new homes where they may dwell in peace and security.

Among the survivors in the displaced persons centers in Europe are numbers of Jews, whose plight is particularly tragic in as much as they represent the pitiful remnants of millions who were deliberately selected by the Nazi leaders for annihilation. Many of these persons look to Palestine as a haven where they hope among people of their own faith to find refuge, to begin to lead peaceful and useful lives, and to assist in the further development of the Jewish National Home.

The Government and people of the United States have given support to the concept of a Jewish National Home in Palestine ever since the termination of the first World War, which resulted in the freeing of a large area of the

Near East, including Palestine, and the establishment of a number of independent states which are now members of the United Nations. The United States, which contributed its blood and resources to the winning of that war, could not divest itself of a certain responsibility for the manner in which the freed territories were disposed of, or for the fate of the peoples liberated at that time. It took the position, to which it still adheres, that these peoples should be prepared for self-government and also that a national home for the Jewish people should be established in Palestine. I am happy to note that most of the liberated peoples are now citizens of independent countries. The Jewish National Home, however, has not as yet been fully developed.

It is only natural, therefore, that my Government should favor at this time the entry into Palestine of considerable numbers of displaced Jews in Europe, not only that they may find shelter there, but also that they may contribute their talents and energies to the upbuilding of the Jewish National Home.

It was entirely in keeping with the traditional policies of this Government that over a year ago I began to correspond with the Prime Minister of Great Britain in an effort to expedite the solving of the urgent problem of the Jewish survivors in the displaced persons camps by the transfer of a substantial number of them to Palestine. It was my belief, to which I still adhere, and which is widely shared by the people of this country, that nothing would contribute more effectively to the alleviation of the plight of these Jewish survivors than the authorization of the immediate entry of at least 100,000 of them to Palestine. No decision with respect to this proposal has been reached, but my Government is still hopeful that it may be possible to proceed along the lines which I outlined to the Prime Minister.

At the same time there should, of course, be a concerted effort to open the gates of other lands, including the United States, to those unfortunate persons, who are now entering upon their second winter of homelessness subsequent to the termination of hostilities. I, for my part, have made it known that I am prepared to ask the Congress of the United States, whose cooperation must be enlisted under our Constitution, for special legislation admitting to this country additional numbers of these persons, over and above the immigration quotas fixed by our laws. My Government, moreover, has been actively exploring, in conjunction with other governments, the possibilities of settlement in different countries outside Europe for those displaced persons who are obliged to emigrate from that continent. In this connection it has been most heartening to us to note the statements of various Arab leaders as to the willingness of their countries to share in this humanitarian project by taking a certain number of these persons into their own lands.

I sincerely believe that it will prove possible to arrive at a satisfactory settlement of the refugee problem along the lines which I have mentioned above.

With regard to the possibility envisaged by Your Majesty that force and violence may be used by Jews in aggressive schemes against the neighboring Arab countries, I can assure you that this Government stands opposed to aggression of any kind or to the employment of terrorism for political purposes. I may add, moreover, that I am convinced that responsible Jewish leaders do not contemplate a policy of aggression against the Arab countries adjacent to Palestine.

I cannot agree with Your Majesty that my statement of Oct 4 is in any way inconsistent with the position taken in the statement issued on my behalf on Aug 16. In the latter statement the hope was expressed that as a result of the proposed conversations between the British Government and the Jewish and Arab representatives a fair solution of the problem of Palestine could be found and immediate steps could be taken to alleviate the situation of the displaced Jews in Europe. Unfortunately, these hopes have not been realized. The conversations between the British Government and the Arab representatives have, I understand, been adjourned until December without a solution having been found for the problem of Palestine or without any steps having been taken to alleviate the situation of the displaced Jews in Europe.

In this situation it seemed incumbent upon me to state as frankly as possible the urgency of the matter and my views both as to the direction in which a solution based on reason and good will might be reached and the immediate steps which should be taken. This I did in my statement of October 4.

I am at a loss to understand why Your Majesty seems to feel that this statement was in contradiction to previous promises or statements made by this Government. It may be well to recall here that in the past this Government, in outlining its attitude on Palestine, has given assurances that it would not take any action which might prove hostile to the Arab people, and also that in its view there should be no decision with respect to the basic situation in Palestine without prior consultation with both Arabs and Jews.

I do not consider that my urging of the admittance of a considerable number of displaced Jews into Palestine or my statements with regard to the solution of the problem of Palestine in any sense represent an action hostile to the Arab people. My feelings with regard to the Arabs when I made these statements were, and are at the present time, of the most friendly character. I deplore any kind of conflict between Arabs and Jews, and am convinced that if both peoples approach the problems before them

136

in a spirit of conciliation and moderation these problems can be solved to the lasting benefit of all concerned.

I furthermore do not feel that my statements in any way represent a failure on the part of this Government to live up to its assurance that in its view there should be no decision with respect to the basic situation in Palestine without consultation with both Arabs and Jews. During the current year there have been a number of consultations with both Arabs and Jews.

Mindful of the great interest which your country, as well as my own, has in the settlement of the various matters which I have set forth above, I take this opportunity to express my earnest hope that Your Majesty, who occupies a position of such eminence in the Arab world, will use the great influence which you possess to assist in the finding in the immediate future of a just and lasting solution. I am anxious to do all that I can to aid in the matter and I can assure Your Majesty that the Government and people of the United States are continuing to be solicitous of the interests and welfare of the Arabs upon whose historic friendship they place great value.

I also take this occasion to convey to Your Majesty my warm personal greetings and my best wishes for the continued health and welfare of Your Majesty and your people.
[…]

Harry S. Truman

* * *

November 2, 1946

Your Excellency: I have received with deep appreciation, your message of October 25, 1946 which you sent to me through the American Legation.

I value Your Excellency's friendship and that of the American people to me personally, to my country and to the rest of the Arab countries. In appreciation of the humanitarian spirit which you have shown, I have not objected to any humanitarian assistance which Your Excellency or the United States may give to the displaced Jews, provided that such assistance is not designed to condemn a people living peacefully in their land. But the Zionist Jews have used this humanitarian appeal as an excuse for attaining their own ends of aggression against Palestine:—these aims being to conquer Palestine and by achieving a majority to make it Jewish, to establish a Jewish state in it, to expel its original inhabitants, to use Palestine as a base for aggression against the neighboring Arab states, and to fulfill (other aspects of) their aggressive programs.

The humanitarian and democratic principles on which the foundations of life in the United States have been built are incompatible with enforcement on a peaceful people, living securely in their country, of foreign elements to conquer and expel the native people from their country. In the attainment of their objectives these foreign elements have confused world public opinion by appealing to the principles of humanity and mercy while at the same time resorting to force.

When the first World War was declared not more than 50,000 Jews lived in Palestine. The Arabs took up the fight on the side of Great Britain, its ally the United States and the other Allies. With the Allies, they fought in support of Arab rights and in support of the principles enunciated by President Wilson—particularly the right of self-determination. Nevertheless Great Britain adopted the Balfour Declaration and in its might embarked upon a policy of admitting Jews into Palestine, in spite of the desires of its preponderantly Arab population and in contradiction to all democratic and human principles. The Arabs protested and rebelled, but they were ever faced with a greater force than they could muster until they were obliged to acquiesce against their wishes.

When this last World War commenced the forces of the enemy were combined and directed against Great Britain. Great Britain stood alone and demonstrated a power and steadfastness which have won for her the admiration of the whole world. Her faith and courage did truly save the world from a grave danger. In those dark days the enemies of Great Britain promised the Arabs to do away with Zionism. Sensing the gravity of England's position at that time, I stood firm by her. I advised all the Arabs to remain quiet and assured them that Britain and her Allies would never betray those principles of humanity and democracy which they entered the war to uphold. The Arabs heeded my counsel and gave whatever assistance to Great Britain and her Allies they could, until victory was attained.

And now in the name of humanity it is proposed to force on the Arab majority of Palestine a people alien to them, to make these new people the majority, thereby rendering the existing majority a minority. Your Excellency will agree with me in the belief that no people on earth would willingly admit into their country a foreign group desiring to become a majority and to establish its rule over that country. And the United States itself will not permit the admission into the United States of that number of Jews which it has proposed for entry into Palestine, as such a measure would be contrary to its laws established for its protection and the safeguarding of its interests.

In your message, Your Excellency mentioned that the United States stands opposed to all forms of aggression or intimidation for the attainment of political objectives, if such measures have been applied by the Jews. You also expressed your conviction that responsible Jewish leaders do not contemplate the pursuit of an antagonistic policy toward the neighboring Arab states. In this connection I would call Your Excellency's attention to the fact that it was the British Government which made the Balfour Declaration, and transported the Jewish immigrants into Palestine under the protection of its bayonets. It was the British Government which gave

138

and still gives shelter to their leaders and accords them its benevolent kindness and care. In spite of all this the British forces in Palestine are being seared by Zionist fire day and night, and the Jewish leaders have been unable to prevent these terroristic attacks. If, therefore, the British Government (the benefactor of the Jews) with all the means at its disposal is unable to prevent the terrorism of the Jews, how can the Arabs feel safe with or trust the Jews either now or in the future!

I believe that after reviewing all the facts Your Excellency will agree with me that the Arabs of Palestine, who form today the majority in their country, can never feel secure after the admission of the Jews into their midst nor can they feel assured about the future of the neighboring states.

Your Excellency also mentioned that you were unable to understand my feeling that your last declaration was inconsistent with previous promises and declarations made by the Government of the United States. Your Excellency also mentioned the assurances which I had received that the United States would not undertake any action modifying the basic situation in Palestine without consulting the two parties. I am confident that Your Excellency does neither intend to break a promise which you have made, nor desire to embark on an act of aggression against the Arabs. For these reasons I take the liberty to express to Your Excellency quite frankly that by an act which renders the Arab majority of Palestine a minority, the basic situation would be changed. This is the fundamental basis of the whole problem. For the principles of democracy dictate that when a majority exists in a country, the government of that country shall be by the majority, and not the minority. And should the Arabs forego the right conferred upon them by their numerical superiority, they would inevitably have to forego their privilege of their own form of government. What change can be considered more fundamental! And would the American people acquiesce in the admission into the United States of foreign elements in sufficient numbers to bring about a new majority? Would such an act be considered consonant with the principles of humanity and democracy?

I am confident that Your Excellency does not intend to antagonize the Arabs, but desires their good and welfare. I also believe that the American people will not agree to acts which are contrary to democratic and human principles. Relying on your desire for frankness and candidness in our relations I am prepared to do my best to remove all sources of misunderstanding by explaining the facts not only for the sake of truth and justice but also to strengthen the bonds of friendship between Your Excellency, the American people and myself.

I trust that Your Excellency will rest assured that my desire to defend the Arabs and their interests is no less than my desire to defend the reputation of the United States, throughout the Moslem and Arab worlds, and the entire world as well. Therefore you will find me extremely eager to persist in my efforts to convince Your Excellency and the American people of the democratic and human principles involved, which the United Nations, Your Excellency and the American people all seek to implement. For this reason I trust that Your Excellency will review the present situation in an effort to find a just solution of the problem—a solution which will ensure life for those displaced persons without threatening a peaceful people living securely in their country.

[...]

Abdul-Aziz

* * *

Washington, January 24, 1947.

Your Majesty: I deeply regret my delay in replying to the further letter regarding Palestine which Your Majesty sent me on November 2, 1946 through the Saudi Arabian Legation in Washington. The delay arose from my desire that careful study be given to the points which Your Majesty raised in the letter.

The frank and friendly manner of your response to my message of October 25, 1946 is deeply appreciated. I am convinced that this response was prompted not only by your interest in the welfare of the Arab population of Palestine but also by your sincere desire that the bonds of friendship between the United States and Saudi Arabia be strengthened and that the United States follow a policy with regard to Palestine which would enhance its reputation throughout the Arab and Moslem world.

For my part I wish again to emphasize my earnest desire that the friendship between the United States and Saudi Arabia which this country values so highly will continue to grow stronger. It also is my sincere hope that friendship and cooperation between the United States and the Arab world, and indeed the whole Moslem world, will continue to increase as the realization becomes more widespread among the American people and among Arabs and Moslems that all of them are striving for the common objective of a peaceful and prosperous world based upon principles of justice and fairness.

Palestine is undoubtedly one of the most difficult problems faced by the world at the present time. The United States is anxious that this problem shall be solved in a manner that will be recognized by the world as just and fair. As I indicated to you in my message of October 25, the United States and other Powers, which as victors in the first World War bore a certain responsibility for the future of Palestine, took the position following the conclusion of that war that Palestine should be the site of a Jewish national home. There was a strong feeling in this country that the Jewish people who had made so many notable contributions to the world were entitled to a national home of their own, and it seemed appropriate that this national home should be established in a land which for thousands of years had been regarded by Jews as their spiritual home.

140

In supporting the establishment of the Jewish National Home in Palestine the United States had no thought of embarking upon a policy which would be prejudicial to the interests of the indigenous population of Palestine, and it has no such thought at the present time. The Government and the people of this country desire that the fundamental rights of both the Arab and Jewish population of Palestine shall be fully safeguarded and that in Palestine Arabs and Jews alike shall prosper and shall lead lives free of any kind of political or economic oppression. We would be firmly opposed to any solution of the Palestine problem which would permit a majority of the population to discriminate against a minority on religious, racial or other grounds. It is our belief that this problem should be solved in such a manner that the various religious and ethnic groups will have similar opportunities and freedoms regardless of which group might be in the numerical majority at any given time. I am convinced, furthermore, that the responsible Jewish groups and leaders interested in developing the Jewish National Home in Palestine have no intention of expelling now or at a later date the indigenous inhabitants of that country or of using Palestine as a base for aggression against neighboring Arab States. No people has suffered more than the Jews during recent years from aggression and intolerance. No people stands more in need of world sympathy and support at the present time. It is therefore inconceivable that responsible Jewish groups or leaders could be contemplating acts of intolerance and aggression against Arabs in Palestine or elsewhere which would be sure to arouse public opinion and to provoke indignation throughout the world. I also am convinced that the terrorist acts of certain irresponsible Jewish groups in Palestine are by no means indicative of the temper of Jews in general throughout the world or symbolic of Jewish aspirations respecting Palestine. These acts in fact are deplored by the great body of Jews who fully realize that resort to terrorism merely renders the problem of Palestine more difficult of solution.

I take this occasion again to point out that I do not consider the various statements which were made by me, including those urging that at least 100,000 Jewish refugees from Europe be admitted into Palestine, are in any way inconsistent with previous assurances or statements made by the Government of the United States. This Government has repeatedly stated that in its view there should be no change in the basic situation in Palestine without consultation with both Arabs and Jews. During the last year a number of consultations with Arabs and Jews have actually taken place. Unfortunately these consultations did not lead to any agreed solution of the Palestine problem. They have served, however, to emphasize the urgency of this problem and the necessity that a solution of it be found without protracted delay. I am confident that Your Majesty will agree with me that until decisions have been reached with regard to the future of Palestine the uncertainties which at present are at least to an extent responsible for unsettled conditions in that country will continue to exert a disturbing influence in Palestine and adjacent areas.

[…]

Harry S. Truman

* * *

Riyadh, October 26, 1947

At this critical moment, during which relations between the United States and the Arabs are clouded with doubt and suspicion, it is my duty as a close friend whose country is united to the people of the United States by several strong mutual political and economic ties to implore you before this last opportunity is missed to revise as quickly as is possible this dangerous situation which has resulted from the support your Government has lent to Zionism against the interests of the Arab peoples which may lead to the partition of Palestine into two states.

(1)   The decision of the Government of the United States to support claims of the Zionist in Palestine is an unfriendly act directed against the Arabs and, at the same time, is inconsistent with the assurances given us by the late President Roosevelt. This decision is also inconsistent with interests of the United States in these Arab countries. It is most difficult to believe that the Government of the United States can persist in its unfriendly decision.

(2)   Without doubt, the results of this decision will lead to a deathblow to American interests in the Arab countries and will disillusion the Arab's confidence in the friendship, justice and fairness of the United States.

(3)   The Arabs have definitely decided to oppose establishment of a Jewish state in any part of the Arab world. The dispute between the Arab and Jew will be violent and long-lasting and without doubt will lead to more shedding of blood. Even if it is supposed that the Jews will succeed in gaining support for the establishment of a small state by their oppressive and tyrannous means and their money, such a state must perish in a short time. The Arab will isolate such a state from the world and will lay siege to it until it dies by famine. Trade and possible prosperity of the state will be prevented; its end will be the same as that of those crusader states which were forced to relinquish coveted objects in Palestine.

(4)   Such a policy of the United States is in disagreement with its long-held reputation as a defender of friendly nations against fearfulness and aggression. This former policy of honor was seen in the support given Syria and Lebanon by the United States in expelling the tyrannous French; this same policy was followed in supporting Turkey and Greece against the aggression of their neighbors to the north.

The Arabs of Palestine had anticipated that this same policy of support in obtaining their right to decide their own destiny would be continued by the United States.

(5)   The policy followed by the United States at the present is in disagreement with its announced policy of considering matters of immigration as an internal affair of foreign states. As the Government of the United States does not permit foreign powers to dictate policy of immigration into any of the United States, why then should the Arab permit foreign states to dictate conditions of immigration into their states? Should this policy be implemented, there will be no limit to Jewish aggression, which will be continued until they become a majority in both Palestine and Trans Jordan.

(6)   As this decision is still in the hands of the United States, we hope deeply that the United States will reconsider its stand before the opportunity slips away and it becomes impossible to maintain peace and security in the Near East. The establishment of a Jewish state will be a menace to peace in the Near East. It will be cause for bloodshed and will create difficulties which will be prejudicial to the interests of the United States in the Arab countries.

* * *

November 21, 1947, 5 p.m.

Your Majesty[:] I have received your communication of Oct 26, 1947 and desire to assure Your Majesty that I have given it most careful consideration. I regret to learn of your belief that the relations between the Arabs and the United States are clouded, in view of the close ties between them which have become closer with time in view of our mutual political and economic interests.

As Your Majesty knows, the Palestine problem is now before the General Assembly of the United Nations, and it is the view of the United States Government, as stated by its representative to the appropriate organ of the United Nations on Oct 11, 1947 that the United Nations "must do everything within its power to evolve a practical solution consistent with the principles laid down in the United Nations Charter."

At the present time the members of the United Nations, all of whom are represented in the General Assembly including Saudi Arabia, which has as its representative your honored and distinguished son, are making their respective contributions to a solution of this difficult and complex question. As in any representative body of this kind, friendly and honest differences of opinions, whether held by large or small nations, should contribute to the ultimate achievement of a just and workable solution.

The approach of the Government of Saudi Arabia and of the Government of the United States to this particular matter is obviously different for several reasons; nevertheless I am firmly convinced that both Governments earnestly desire solution of international difficulties based upon reason, peace, and justice. The United States considers that the United Nations has an indispensable part to play in the solution of difficult problems such as

143

the Palestine problem, and for its part, is fully disposed to accept the decisions of the United Nations in this as in other matters which come within its jurisdiction.

One of the important factors influencing the decision of the United States Government to support the majority plan of the United Nations Special Committee on Palestine was the fact that it represented the majority views of a committee specially appointed by the United Nations to consider the question. The United States decision was not based on any desire to be unfriendly to the Arabs, and should not be construed as an unfriendly act, any more than the decision taken in this respect by other members of the United Nations. In the General Assembly the vote of the United States counts for no more than the vote of any other country, large or small.

In line with its support of the United Nations our delegation has made it clear that the United States wishes to abide by the decision of the United Nations and is confident that in conformity with the United Nations Charter all members of the United Nations will take a similar attitude.
[…]

The Problem Referred to the United Nations (1948)
BRITISH COLONIAL OFFICE

After the failure of [discussions with the Arabs and the Jews] His Majesty's Government decided that the only course now open to them was to submit the problem to the judgment of the United Nations, asking that body to recommend a solution. The reasons for this decision were explained by His Majesty's Principal Secretary of State for Foreign Affairs in a speech to the House of Commons on 18th February, 1947, in which he said:—

> "His Majesty's Government have been faced with an irreconcilable conflict of principles. There are in Palestine about 1,200,000 Arabs and 600,000 Jews. For the Jews the essential point of principle is the creation of a sovereign Jewish State. For the Arabs, the essential point of principle is to resist to the last the establishment of Jewish sovereignty in any part of Palestine. The discussions of the last month have quite clearly shown that there is no prospect of resolving this conflict by any settlement negotiated between the parties. But if the conflict has to be resolved by an arbitrary decision, that is not a decision which His Majesty's Government are empowered, as Mandatory, to take. His Majesty's Government have of themselves no power, under the terms of the Mandate, to award the country either to the Arabs or to the Jews, or even to partition it between them."

The question was accordingly placed on the agenda of the General Assembly of the United Nations, who, after a special session, appointed on 15th May, 1947, a Special Committee to investigate the problem and recommend a solution. In the course of this session the United Kingdom Delegate had explained that His Majesty's Government could not commit themselves to enforcing alone any settlement not acceptable to both Arabs and Jews.

[…] The Committee's report was considered by the General Assembly of the United Nations in September 1947, when the United Kingdom Delegate explained that His Majesty's Government were not themselves prepared to undertake the task of imposing a policy in Palestine by force of arms, and that, in the absence of a settlement, they must plan for an early withdrawal of British forces and of the British administration from Palestine. He also urged that any recommendations made by the General Assembly should be accompanied by a clear definition of the means by which they were to be carried out. These warnings were repeated throughout the Assembly's session, which closed on 29th November, 1947, with the adoption, by 33 votes to 13 with 10 abstentions, of a modified

From <u>Palestine: Termination of the Mandate, 15th May 1948</u>, United   145
Kingdom Colonial Office (1948). London: His Majesty's Stationery Office.

scheme of partition to be implemented by a Commission of five members unsupported by any police or military forces. This plan was accepted in principle by the majority of the Jews, but the Arabs announced their intention of resisting it by every means within their power and were promised full support in their resistance by Egypt, Iraq, the Lebanon, Saudi Arabia, Syria, Transjordan and the Yemen. While this plan was still being discussed, and before the vote was taken, His Majesty's Government repeatedly emphasized that, in the absence of agreement by both Arabs and Jews, they would not themselves enforce it and announced their intention to withdraw all British forces from Palestine by 1st August, 1948.

His Majesty's Government had now striven for twenty-seven years without success to reconcile Jews and Arabs and to prepare the people of Palestine for self-government. The policy adopted by the United Nations had aroused the determined resistance of the Arabs, while the States supporting this policy were themselves not prepared to enforce it. 84,000 troops, who received no co-operation from the Jewish community, had proved insufficient to maintain law and order in the face of a campaign of terrorism waged by highly organised Jewish forces equipped with all the weapons of the modern infantryman. Since the war 338 British subjects had been killed in Palestine, while the military forces there had cost the British taxpayer £100 million. The renewal of Arab violence on the announcement of the United Nations decision to partition Palestine and the declared intentions of Jewish extremists showed that the loss of further British lives was inevitable. It was equally clear that, in view of His Majesty's Government's decision not to enforce the partition of Palestine against the declared wishes of the majority of its inhabitants, the continued presence there of British troops and officials could no longer be justified.

In these circumstance His Majesty's Government decided to bring to an end their Mandate and to prepare for the earliest possible withdrawal from Palestine of all British forces. They accordingly announced, on 11th December, 1947, that the Mandate would end on 15th May, 1948, from which date the sole task of the British forces in Palestine would be to complete their withdrawal by 1st August, 1948. His Majesty's Government's decision to end the Mandate was welcomed by Arabs and Jews alike, as well as by the United Nations.

THE ELEMENTS OF THE CONFLICT

D. THE CONFLICTING CLAIMS

The Jewish case
[...]
127. The Jewish case seeks the establishment of a Jewish State in Palestine, and Jewish immigration into Palestine both before and after the creation of the Jewish State, subject only to the limitations imposed by the economic absorptive capacity of that State. [...]

The Arab Case

156. [...] The Arab case seeks the immediate creation of an independent Palestine west of the Jordan as an Arab State. [...]

157. They postulate the "natural" right of the Arab majority to remain in undisputed possession of the country, since they are and have been for many centuries in possession of the land. [...]

CHAPTER V RECOMMENDATIONS (I)
[...]
RECOMMENDATION I. TERMINATION OF THE MANDATE

It is recommended that

The Mandate for Palestine shall be terminated at the earliest practicable date.
[...]
RECOMMENDATION II. INDEPENDENCE

It is recommended that

Independence shall be granted in Palestine at the earliest practicable date.

Comment

(a) Although sharply divided by political issues, the peoples of Palestine are sufficiently advanced to govern themselves independently.

(b) The Arab and Jewish peoples, after more than a quarter of a century of tutelage under the Mandate, both seek a means of effective expression for their national aspirations.
[...]

147

RECOMMENDATION III. TRANSITIONAL PERIOD

It is recommended that

There shall be a transitional period preceding the grant of independence in Palestine which shall be as short as possible, consistent with the achievement of the preparations and conditions essential to independence.
[...]
RECOMMENDATION IV. UNITED NATIONS RESPONSIBILITY DURING THE TRANSITIONAL PERIOD

It is recommended that

During the transitional period the authority entrusted with the task of administering Palestine and preparing it for independence shall be responsible to the United Nations.
[...]
RECOMMENDATION V. HOLY PLACES AND RELIGIOUS INTERESTS

It is recommended that

In whatever solution may be adopted for Palestine,

A. The sacred character of the Holy Places shall be preserved and access to the Holy Places for purposes of worship and pilgrimage shall be ensured in accordance with existing rights, in recognition of the proper interest of millions of Christians, Jews and Moslems abroad as well as the residents of Palestine in the care of sites and buildings associated with the origin and history of their faiths.

B. Existing rights in Palestine of the several religious communities shall be neither impaired nor denied, in view of the fact that their maintenance is essential for religious peace in Palestine under conditions of independence.
[...]
RECOMMENDATION VI. JEWISH DISPLACED PERSONS

It is recommended that

The General Assembly undertake immediately the initiation and execution of an international arrangement whereby the problem of the distressed European Jews, of whom approximately 250,000 are in assembly centers, will be dealt with as a matter of extreme urgency for the alleviation of their plight and of the Palestine problem.

(a) The distressed Jews of Europe, together with the displaced persons generally, are a legacy of the Second World War. They are a recognized international responsibility. Owing however to the insistent demands that the distressed Jews be admitted freely and immediately into Palestine, and to the intense urge which exists among these people themselves to the same end, they constitute a vital and difficult factor in the solution.

(b) It cannot be doubted that any action which would ease the plight of the distressed Jews in Europe would thereby lessen the pressure of the Palestinian immigration problem, and would consequently create a better climate in which to carry out a final solution of the question of Palestine. This would be an important factor in allaying the fears of Arabs in the Near East that Palestine and ultimately the existing Arab countries are to be marked as the place of settlement for the Jews of the world.

[...]

RECOMMENDATIONS (II)

[...]

PART I. PLAN OF PARTITION WITH ECONOMIC UNION JUSTIFICATION

1. The basic premise underlying the partition proposal is that the claims to Palestine of the Arabs and Jews, both possessing validity, are irreconcilable and that among all of the solutions advanced, partition will provide the most realistic and practicable settlement, and is the most likely to afford a workable basis for meeting in part the claims and national aspirations of both parties.

2. It is a fact that both of these peoples have their historic roots in Palestine, and that both make vital contributions to the economic and cultural life of the country. The partition solution takes these considerations fully into account.

3. The basic conflict in Palestine is a clash of two intense nationalisms. Regardless of the historical origins of the conflict, the rights and wrongs of the promises and counter-promises, and the international intervention incident to the Mandate, there are now in Palestine some 650,000 Jews and some 1,200,000 Arabs who are dissimilar in their ways of living and for the time being, separated by political interests which render difficult full and effective political co-operation among them, whether voluntary or induced by constitutional arrangements.

4. Only by means of partition can these conflicting national aspirations find substantial expression and qualify both peoples to their places as

independent nations in the international community and in the United Nations.

[...]

7. Partition is the only means available by which political and economic responsibility can be placed squarely on both Arabs and Jews, with the prospective result that, confronted with responsibility for bearing fully the consequences of their own actions, a new and important element of political amelioration would be introduced. In the proposed federal-State solution. this factor would be lacking.

8. Jewish immigration is the central issue in Palestine today and is the one factor, above all others, that rules out the necessary co-operation between the Arab and Jewish communities in a single State. The creation of a Jewish State under a partition scheme is the only hope of removing this issue from the arena of conflict.

9. It is recognized that partition has been strongly opposed by Arabs, but it is felt that that opposition would be lessened by a solution which definitively fixes the extent of territory to be allotted to the Jews with its implicit limitation on immigration. The fact that the solution carries the sanction of the United Nations involves a finality which should allay Arab fears of further expansion of the Jewish State.

10. In view of the limited area and resources of Palestine, it is essential that, to the extent feasible, and consistent with the creation of two independent States, the economic unity of the country should be preserved. The partition proposal, therefore, is a qualified partition, subject to such measures and limitations as are considered essential to the future economic and social well-being of both States. Since the economic self-interest of each State would be vitally involved, it is believed that the minimum measure of economic unity is possible, where that of political unity is not.

11. Such economic unity requires the creation of an economic association by means of a treaty between the two States. The essential objectives of this association would be a common customs system, a common currency and the maintenance of a country-wide system of transport and communications.

[...]

PART Ill. City of Jerusalem

[...]

Recommendations

1. The City of Jerusalem shall be placed under an International Trusteeship System by means of a Trusteeship Agreement which shall designate the United Nations as the Administering Authority, in accordance with Article 81 of the Charter of the United Nations.

[...]

The Consequences of the Partition of Palestine (1947)
CENTRAL INTELLIGENCE AGENCY

Armed hostilities between Jews and Arabs will break out if the UN
General Assembly accepts the plan to partition Palestine into Jewish and
Arab States as recommended by the UN Special Committee on Palestine
(UNSCOP).

Inflamed by nationalism and religious fervor, Arabs in Syria, Lebanon,
Iraq, Transjordan, Egypt, and Saudi Arabia as well as Palestine are
determined to fight against any force, or combination of forces, which
attempts to set up a Jewish state in Palestine. […]

In composition, the Arab forces will vary from relatively well controlled
quasi-military bands to the loose tribal organization of the nomads. The
largest number actively engaged against the Jews at any one time will
probably be between 100,000 and 200,000. The Arabs are good guerilla
fighters, and they will be well supplied with small arms and will also
undoubtedly obtain some planes and tanks.

[…] Whatever the UN recommends, [the Zionists] will attempt to establish
a Jewish state after the British withdrawal [....] The Jews are expected to be
able to mobilize some 200,000 fighters in Palestine, supplemented to a
limited extent by volunteers and recruits from abroad. The Jewish armed
groups in Palestine are well equipped and well trained in Commando
tactics. Initially they will achieve marked success over the Arabs because
of superior organization and equipment. As the war of attrition develops,
however, the Jewish economy (severely strained by mobilization) will
break down; furthermore, the Jews will be unable continuously to protect
their fields in the face of constant harassing "hit and run" Arab attacks.
Without substantial outside aid in terms of manpower and material, they
will be able to hold out no longer than two years.
[…]
2. Political Consequences

a) INTERNAL PRESSURE ON ARAB GOVERNMENTS

1) *Nationalist Pressure*

Arab nationalism is the strongest political force in the Arab world. It grew
up in secret societies under Ottoman rule, came out into the open in the
Arab Revolt or World War I and has been the major factor in the
independence movement in the Arab world ever since. The independence
of all the Arab states in the Near East throws into high relief the continuing
mandatory status of Palestine. Because of the strong ties between the
various Arab states, political developments in any one country are of vital
concern to Arabs everywhere. Palestinian independence is, consequently

the major aim not only of the Palestinians Arabs but also of Syrians, Lebanese, Iraqis, Transjordanians, Egyptians, and Saudi Arabians. [...]

The ultimate aim of Arab nationalism is to preserve and enrich the Arab heritage while the political aims are the independence of all Arab lands and the establishment of some degree of unity among them. The nationalists regard Palestine as the chief stumbling block to the achievement of their political aims. [...] Arab national fervor is so explosive and pervasive a force that Arab government officials who recognize the political implications involved in flouting a UN decision will nonetheless have to oppose any decision for partition or run the risk of losing office.

2) *Religious Pressure*

The Arab governments are probably as greatly influenced by religious pressures as they are by nationalist pressures. [...] It is very possible that certain religious organizations will take the initiative in organizing Arab resistance in Palestine.

The Ikhwan al Muslimin (Moslem Brotherhood), with headquarters in Egypt, is an organization of young Moslems founded for the purpose of orienting Arab society in accordance with Islamic ideologies. Branches of the Ikhwan have been formed in Syria and Lebanon, and one of the most active branches is in Palestine. The Ikhwan regards Westernization as a dangerous threat to Islam and would oppose any political encroachment of Zionism on Palestine with religious fanaticism. Should a "Jihad" or Holy War, be declared, the Ikhwan would be the spearhead of any crusade. The Grand Mufti, as head of the Moslem Supreme Council, can count on the unanimous support of all members of the Ikhwan, who are assured of entrance into Paradise if they die on the field of battle.
[...]

b) PROBABLE ATTITUDES OF ARAB GOVERNMENTS

1) *Towards A Jewish State*

The Arabs violently oppose the establishment of a Jewish state in Palestine because they believe that Palestine is an integral part of the Arab world. In addition, they fear that the Jews will consolidate their position through unlimited immigration and that they will attempt to expand until they become a threat to the newly won independence of each of the other Arab countries. They believe that not only politically but also culturally the Jewish state threatens the continued development of the Islamic-Arabic civilization. For these reasons, the Arab governments will not consider any compromise, and they categorically reject any scheme which would set up a Jewish state in Palestine. [...]

c) PROBABLE ACTIONS OF ARAB GOVERNMENTS

1) *Against Palestine*

In the event of the partition of Palestine, it is unlikely that the Arab governments will openly proclaim war against the Jews. Pressure from the Arab people for an open declaration of war will be strong, but the governments doubtless realize that such a step in defiance of a decision passed by the UN would seriously jeopardize the Arab position in the UN. However, it is probable that the large numbers of Arabs from the surrounding countries will join the Arabs residing within Palestine for the war against Zionism. These Arabs will be loosely organized under national leaders and tribal sheikhs. Volunteers will leave the armies and ammunition and military equipment will find their way from the Arab armies to the resistance movement. […]

d) AIMS OF THE JEWISH STATE

1) *Consolidation*

In spite of increasing tension and hostilities between various factions in the Jewish community, it can be expected that all Jewish groups in Palestine will join forces against the Arabs in defense of the newly formed Jewish state. The chief aims of the Jewish government will be organization of defense and increased immigration.

2) *Territorial Ambitions*

In the long run no Zionists in Palestine will be satisfied with the territorial arrangements of the partition settlement. Even the more conservative Zionists will hope to obtain the whole Nejeb, Western Galilee, the city of Jerusalem, and eventually all of Palestine. The extremists demand not only all of Palestine but Transjordan as well. They have stated that they will refuse to recognize the validity of any Jewish government which will settle for anything less, and will probably undertake aggressive action to achieve their ends.

3) *Soliciting Foreign Aid*

The Zionists will continue to wage a strong propaganda campaign in the US and in Europe. The "injustice" of the proposed Jewish boundaries will be exaggerated, and the demand for more territory will be made as Jewish immigration floods the Jewish sector. In the chaos which will follow the implementation of partition, atrocities will undoubtedly be committed by Arab fanatics; such actions will be given wide publicity and even be exaggerated by Jewish propaganda. The Arabs will be accused of aggression, whatever the actual circumstances may be. […]

153

PLAN OF PARTITION WITH ECONOMIC UNION

PART I — FUTURE CONSTITUTION AND GOVERNMENT OF PALESTINE

A. TERMINATION OF MANDATE, PARTITION AND INDEPENDENCE

1. The Mandate for Palestine shall terminate as soon as possible but in any case not later than 1 August 1948.

2. The armed forces of the mandatory Power shall be progressively withdrawn from Palestine, the withdrawal to be completed as soon as possible but in any case not later than 1 August 1948.
[…]
3. Independent Arab and Jewish States and the Special International Regime for the City of Jerusalem, set forth in part III of this plan, shall come into existence in Palestine two months after the evacuation of the armed forces of the mandatory Power has been completed but in any case not later than 1 October 1948. […]

C. DECLARATION

A declaration shall be made to the United Nations by the provisional government of each proposed State before independence. It shall contain *inter alia* the following clauses:

GENERAL PROVISION

The stipulations contained in the declaration are recognized as fundamental laws of the State and no law, regulation or official action shall conflict or interfere with these stipulations, nor shall any law, regulation or official action prevail over them.

Chapter 1 – *Holy Places, religious buildings and sites*

1. Existing rights in respect of Holy Places and religious buildings or sites shall not be denied or impaired.

2. In so far as Holy Places are concerned, the liberty of access, visit and transit shall be guaranteed, in conformity with existing rights, to all residents and citizens of the other State and of the City of Jerusalem, as well as to aliens, without distinction as to nationality, subject to requirements of national security, public order and decorum.

Similarly, freedom of worship shall be guaranteed in conformity with existing rights, subject to the maintenance of public order and decorum.
[...]

Chapter 2 – *Religious and minority rights*

1. Freedom of conscience and the free exercise of all forms of worship, subject only to the maintenance of public order and morals, shall be ensured to all.

2. No discrimination of any kind shall be made between the inhabitants on the ground of race, religion, language or sex.

3. All persons within the jurisdiction of the State shall be entitled to equal protection of the laws.

4. The family law and personal status of the various minorities and their religious interests, including endowments, shall be respected.

5. Except as may be required for the maintenance of public order and good government, no measure shall be taken to obstruct or interfere with the enterprise of religious or charitable bodies of all faiths or to discriminate against any representative or member of these bodies on the ground of his religion or nationality

6. The State shall ensure adequate primary and secondary education for the Arab and Jewish minority, respectively, in its own language and its cultural traditions.

The right of each community to maintain its own schools for the education of its own members in its own language, while conforming to such educational requirements of a general nature as the State may impose, shall not be denied or impaired. Foreign educational establishments shall continue their activity on the basis of their existing rights.

7. No restriction shall be imposed on the free use by any citizen of the State of any language in private intercourse, in commerce, in religion, in the Press or in publications of any kind, or at public meetings.

8. No expropriation of land owned by an Arab in the Jewish State (by a Jew in the Arab State) shall be allowed except for public purposes. In all cases of expropriation full compensation as fixed by the Supreme Court shall be paid previous to dispossession.

1. *Citizenship.* Palestinian citizens residing in Palestine outside the City of Jerusalem, as well as Arabs and Jews who, not holding Palestinian citizenship reside in Palestine outside the City of Jerusalem shall, upon the recognition of independence, become citizens of the State in which they are resident and enjoy full civil and political rights. Persons over the age of eighteen years may opt, within one year from the date of recognition of independence of the State in which they reside, for citizenship of the other State, providing that no Arab residing in the arca of the proposed Arab State shall have the right to opt for citizenship in the proposed Jewish State and no Jew residing in the proposed Jewish State shall have the right to opt for citizenship in the proposed Arab State. The exercise of this right of option will be taken to include the wives and children under eighteen years of age of persons so opting.
[...]
PART II — BOUNDARIES*
[...]
PART III — CITY OF JERUSALEM

A. SPECIAL REGIME

The City of Jerusalem shall be established as a *corpus separatum* under a special international regime and shall be administered by the United Nations. The Trusteeship Council shall be designated to discharge the responsibilities of the Administering Authority on behalf of the United Nations.
[...]

1.   The Arab Higher Committee maintains that the partitions recommendation does not represent the sentiments of the United Nations. We cannot forget that the resolution of partition in the Ad Hoc Committee secured 25 votes only. When the matter was referred to the General Assembly on the 26th of November, there were 17 nations opposing partition. Had voting taken place on that date the partition proposal would not have obtained the required two-third majority. The Arab Higher Committee cannot forget the maneuvers made by the President of the Assembly and some delegates supporting partition in order to postpone taking votes on that day when they realized that their proposal might be defeated.

2.   The pressure put by the United States Delegation and Government on certain nations […] is nothing short of political blackmail. The following represent only a few instances:

(a)   The delegate of Siam was accepted in the Ad Hoc Committee as a vice chairman until he showed his intention to vote against partition. Then he was threatened that his credentials would be refused. As a consequence he was forced not to attend.

(b)   The delegate of Haiti on Wednesday made a very strong speech against partition, on instructions from his Government. On Saturday he circulated a note to Delegations explaining that he is voting for partition in accordance with fresh instructions from his Government. […] Being a sincere and noble man, he could not hide the fact that his Government surrendered to pressure and was forced into changing its instructions to him.

(c)   General Carlos P. Romulo, Head of Philippines delegation, on Wednesday made a very strong and courageous speech denouncing partition [....]

But on Saturday and in the absence of General Romulo there were two Philippines Delegates, each claiming different instructions – one to vote against partition as instructed by the head of his delegation, the other supporting partition according to fresh instructions from his Government. It is an established fact that strong pressure was put on the Philippines Government by the United States Government and, according to reliable information, the United States Government threatened the Philippine Government that it will not grant it the loan it is asking for if its delegation fails to support partition. […]

(d)   The Liberian delegate on the Ad Hoc Committee, Mrs. Ellen Scarborough, on the 25th of November abstained from voting

157

although it was known that the Liberian Delegates intended to vote against partition in the Assembly. Thereupon the Jewish Agency and its pressure squads threatened her with actual physical violence which caused her to ask for police protection. On Saturday, the 29th of November, due to heavy pressure on the said Government, the Liberian Delegation voted for partition.

3. This undue pressure was not limited to the aforementioned delegations, but to every other delegation and its Government abroad. [...]

4. Such flagrant interference and pressure were not exercised by the United States Government only, but also by United States Senators. [...]

5. The President of the General Assembly, Mr. Oswaldo Aranha, who being president should have been very impartial, was contrary to the traditions of presidency, influencing the Latin-American countries to vote against the Arabs. A report of a speech by him appeared in the P.M. of New York in its issue of October 9th as follows:

"Oswaldo Aranha of Brazil, President of the General Assembly warned Latin-American Delegates that failure on their part to support the United States-Soviet agreement on partition of Palestine would be a further heavy blow to the weakened United Nations. Aranha stressed the point at a recent Latin-American caucus after several delegates had declared themselves impressed with Arab claims that United Nations lacked authority under the Charter to partition any State." Without making any comment on these judicial claims, Aranha is reported to have said: "I want to impress upon all of you that they are, at best, merely juridical."

[...]

6. It is an elementary rule of law and justice that any decision [...] made or done under pressure, undue influence or duress, is null and void. The aforementioned facts prove how the partition recommendations were extorted from member states of the United Nations. The Arabs therefore consider them null and void and of no legal or moral force.

7. The Arab Higher Committee Delegation maintains that the recommendation of partition is also contrary to the letter and spirit of the United Nations Charter. The Arab Delegations have fully dealt with this point in their addresses in the Ad Hoc Committee and in the Assembly. Their arguments were unanswerable, but power politics ignored all the logic, reason and justice of their arguments and Delegations were being led by undue pressure and influence to make recommendations repugnant to the Charter.

8. The United Nations has no jurisdiction to order or recommend the Partition of Palestine. There is nothing in the Charter to warrant such

authority, consequently the recommendation of partition is *ultra vires* and therefore null and void.

9.   The Arab Delegations submitted proposals in the Ad Hoc Committee in Order to refer the whole legal issue raised for a ruling by the International Court of Justice. The said proposals were never put to vote by the president in the Assembly. The United Nations is an International body entrusted with the task of enforcing peace and justice in international affairs. How would there be any confidence in such a body if it bluntly and unreasonably refuses to refer such a dispute to the International Court of Justice?

[...]

13. In conclusion, the Arab Higher Committee Delegation wishes to stress the following:

(a)   The Arabs of Palestine will never recognize the validity of the extorted partition recommendations or the authority of the United Nations to make them.

(b)   The Arabs of Palestine consider that any attempt by the Jews or any power or group of power to establish a Jewish state in Arab territory is an act of aggression which will be resisted in self-defense by force.

(c)   It is very unwise and fruitless to ask any commission to proceed to Palestine because not a single Arab will cooperate with the said Commission.

(d)   The United Nations or its Commission should not be misled to believe that its efforts in the partition plan will meet with any success. It will be far better for the eclipsed prestige of this organization not to start on this adventure.

(e)   The United Nations prestige will be better served by abandoning, not enforcing such an injustice.

(f)   The determination of every Arab in Palestine is to oppose in every way the partition of that country.

(g)   The Arabs of Palestine made a solemn declaration before the United Nations, before God and history, that they will never submit or yield to any power going to Palestine to enforce partition. The only way to establish partition is first to wipe them out—man, woman and child.

[...]

Testimony Before UNSCOP Partition Proceedings (1947)
Chaim Weizmann

[W]e are—I think I am speaking the mind of a great many Jews, after a great deal of hardship, after a great deal of testing, after a great deal of evaluating the possibility of what we can do—for a form of partition which would satisfy the just demands of both the Jews and the Arabs. We realize that we cannot have the whole of Palestine. God made a promise; Palestine to the Jews. It is up to the Almighty to keep His promise in His own time. Our business is to do what we can in a very imperfect human way. I do not like to play on the sentiment of the distinguished Indian representative who sits here. I should say partition is *a la mode*. It is not only in small Palestine; it is in big India. But at least there you have something to partition. Here we have to do it with a microscope. There you can do it with a big knife.

What are the advantages of partition? It has, in my opinion, two great advantages. It is final and it helps to dispel some of the fears of our Arab friends. I am not saying that you would dispel easily all fears. Fear is not a matter of logic. It is a matter of emotion, and emotional reaction cannot be dispelled by logical performance. But at any rate we can do all we can in order to help in future to mitigate their fear. If it is final the Arabs will know and the Jews will know that they cannot encroach upon each other's domain. To us it means something else. It means equality of status with our Arab neighbours: the most important requisite for good relations between us and them. As long as they consider us inferior in political status they will not be anxious to make peace with us. Therefore, it is a desirable solution, although it represents, as I have already pointed out, a new and great sacrifice on the part of the Jewish people. It cannot be whittled down, it cannot be bargained down, and the part of Palestine which would remain after partition must be something in which Jews could live and into which we could bring a million and a half people in a comparatively short time. It must not be a place for graves only, or graveyards, or, as you sometimes see on very full trams, "standing room only." […]

One would be tempted now to go into details on the side of the partitioned area, if one speaks of partition. […] The area must be sufficiently adequate to absorb something in the nature of a million and a half people in addition to the present population. That is the size of the problem which is urgent at present. It must be an area which can be worked. And, I believe, speaking in general terms, if you will take a somewhat improved Peel Line (I understand that all of you have had before you the Peel Report and the "Line" which the Peel Commission offered as a basis for a Jewish State.) I say, advisedly, a somewhat improved Peel Line. This Peel Line was not fixed by the Peel Commission. It was simply an indication as to how their minds ran. They were prepared to discuss improvements, alterations, and modifications. If to this Peel area is added the area of what is usually called the Negev which I think you have visited and which in its greater part is a desert, a desert which I daresay will never be worked except by us because for us it is again a struggle of life and death to open up this area—then I think you will have created a part of Palestine which may in the future, with God's help, become a land flowing with milk and honey and give nourishment and sustenance to a sorely tried people—the Jewish people. Further, I would like to add, in my opinion, that it will also help the future development of the Arab population. I may be asked—I cannot foresee all the questions—I may be asked: "will it be troublesome? Will it produce friction and trouble?" It would be foolish on my part if I were to say, "Oh, no, it will go off quite smoothly." Nothing goes smoothly. And nothing worth doing is done without trouble. But I do believe that a great many thoughtful Arabs if they feel that this project is set into motion with all the authority, dignity and force (I do not mean military pr physical force: I mean moral force) which the United Nations command, I think the Arabs will eventually acquiesce. Probably the Mufti will not acquiesce, and some other extremists on our side may not acquiesce, but I do not think that will present an unsurmountable difficulty. Therefore, the prerequisite is to sweep away the White Paper and give us a chance to bring in a considerable population. I named a figure of a million and a half. Give us a chance of developing the derelict part of Palestine which is today the Negev. And do it, I pray with the utmost possible respect, quickly. […]

CIVIL WAR

Possible Developments in Palestine (1948)
CENTRAL INTELLIGENCE AGENCY

1. Aims in Palestine After the Partition Recommendation.

[...]

c. PLANNED ARAB COURSE OF ACTION.

[...] [T]he Arabs agreed that a Zionist state could not be tolerated in the Arab world. To prevent the formation of this state, the following general course of action was envisaged:

(1) To make military preparations, both in Palestine and the Arab states, to prevent by military action the formation and functioning of a Jewish state.

(2) To refuse to cooperate with the UN Commission in any way.

(3) To establish an independent unitary state embracing all of Palestine.

(4) To prevent further Jewish immigration until an immigration policy could be formulated by the unitary state.
[...]

d. JEWISH COURSE OF ACTION.

The Jewish plan of action after the UNGA recommendation was perfectly clearcut. While the Jewish Agency, the official representative of the Jewish community, had hoped to obtain a larger portion of Palestine, it decided to cooperate with the UN Commission in the establishment of the proposed Jewish state. In the meantime, it planned to build up its internal security forces, train an administrative corps, and propagandize the rest of the world for financial and military assistance against any Arab attempts to prevent the implementation of the UNGA recommendation. The aims, however, of the Revisionists, including Irgun Zvai Leumi and the Stern Gang, were more extreme: to fight both the British and the Arabs and to set up a Jewish state in all of Palestine and Transjordan.

2. Development of the Situation Since the Partition Recommendation.

a. UN ACTIVITY.

[...] [T]he UN Commission has made little progress, for its success was predicated on the assumption that it would receive the cooperation of the Jews, the Arabs, and the UK. Of these, only the Jews have fully cooperated. The Arabs have flatly refused to have anything to do with the

Commission, and the UK's cooperation was considerably restricted by its interpretation of its responsibilities as mandatory power. UK refusal to allow the Commission to enter Palestine before 1 May (two weeks before the termination of the mandate) will make it impossible for the Commission to establish the provisional Arab and Jewish governments by the required date of 1 April. The UK refusal to relinquish any administrative authority in Palestine until after the termination of the mandate has prevented the progressive transfer of authority to the UN Commission. The Commission has also been compelled to recognize the deplorable security situation in Palestine and realizes that it cannot attempt to carry out the recommendations of the UNGA without an adequate international police force.

b. UK ACTIVITY.

UK activity since the partition vote has been twofold. In Palestine the mandatory administration, its police, and the UK forces have been attempting to maintain internal security. They have been hampered by two main factors: (1) evacuation plans have considerably obstructed UK security measures; and (2) the UK desire not to antagonize the Arab states has prevented the implementation of full-scale security measures to repress Arab-Jewish hostilities. In spite of these reservations, UK forces have been impartial in attempting to curb Arab-Jewish hostilities. The major aims seem to have been to prevent general anarchy and full-scale war—at least until the forces themselves have withdrawn.

In the UN, the UK delegates have taken pains to acquaint the UN Commission with the difficulties of the Palestine situation. [...] They have refused, however, to assume joint responsibility with the Commission for the establishment of the new states in Palestine or to permit any development which might be interpreted as UK support of one side against the other. [...]

c. ARAB ACTIVITY.

Arab reaction to the UNGA partition plan was prompt and violent. Strikes and demonstrations led to scattered riots within Palestine, and Arab League action was instituted by the Arab states. The sporadic violence in Palestine had developed by the middle of January into more highly organized hostilities. By the beginning of February disciplined Arab bands were operating in different parts of the country, and the Arab Higher Committee claimed to be directing their activities. The nature of Arab activities indicated that until the British withdrawal Arab objectives were limited to: (1) avoiding, if possible, hostilities with the British forces; (2) purchasing and capturing essential supplies such as food, weapons, ammunition, and clothing; (3) disrupting Jewish commerce, transportation, and communications without launching full-scale attacks; (4) recruiting volunteer forces, within and without Palestine, and training them in guerrilla tactics; (5) setting up a unified military command; (6) establishing contact with Arab League channels of assistance. The entire emphasis has been on preparation for the British withdrawal, and the Arab leaders have apparently attempted to hold back their surging followers.

During a series of meetings at Sofar, Aley, and Cairo, Arab League representatives, despite differences of opinion, eventually evolved a program of action. The program, which in several particulars merely approved activities already under way, was immediately implemented and provided that: (1) the partisan movement in Palestine be supported with funds, arms, and men; (2) troops of the Arab states be stationed on the frontier of Palestine as a border watch; and (3) these armies not be sent into Palestine until after the British withdrawal. Funds were immediately raised in all the Arab states. Volunteers from Iraq, Syria, Lebanon, and Transjordan foregathered at Qatana in Syria for training; and by the middle of February over 8,000 were known to have slipped, uniformed and armed, into Palestine. Syrian, Egyptian, and Transjordan troops had been moved to the Palestine border; and Iraqi contingents were reported to be moving into Transjordan. Determined efforts were made to obtain arms and ammunition. Syria signed a contract with Skoda, and a first delivery is known to have been made.

While the Arab chain of command has not been announced, the forces will be commanded by former Syrian and Iraqi army officers and experienced guerrilla leaders.

d. JEWISH ACTIVITY.

Having won the initial victory in the acceptance by the UNGA of the partition plan, the Jews concentrated (with some exceptions) on preparing for the new state. In the face of violent Arab opposition, the Jewish Agency immediately undertook: (1) to strengthen the internal defense forces of the prospective Jewish state; (2) to organize and train an administrative corps; and (3) to cooperate with the UN in implementing the UNGA decisions. Recruiting and training for Hagana were increased; and, in spite of the fact that the mandatory refused to recognize its legality, it attempted to protect the Jewish community from Arab attacks and also acted as a local police force. In time, Hagana adopted a policy of "active" defense and carried out terrorist raids against the Arabs similar in tactics to those of the Irgun Zvai Leumi and the Stern Gang against the UK forces. These two extremist groups continued their war against the British; and although they agreed to fight the Arabs together with Hagana, they refused to accept the partition recommendation and continued to claim all of Palestine (and even Transjordan) for the Jewish state.
[…]

Telegram to UN Secretary General (1948)
King Abdullah Ibn Hussein

The calamities occurring in Palestine are beyond belief and after May the 15th will reach the pinnacle of horror. I deplore and reprobate the useless killing and attacks the one upon the other and vehemently protest against such unparalleled massacres as Deiryasseen, wherein the wombs of pregnant women were ripped open as the Jewish Agency confirmed to me by telegram but laid to the book of their dissident elements. I am nevertheless persuaded that the Jewish people as a whole desire to live in amity with the Arabs. Everything cries for intervention to halt this butchery. We now declare our readiness to give the Jews in Palestine full Arab nationality in a unitary State sharing all that we share while yet enjoying a special administration in particular areas. Thus will end the slaughter and the people will live in peace and security forever.

Letter Correspondence to the UNSCOP Principal Secretary (1948)
John Fletcher-Cooke

April 20, 1948

My dear Bunche,

May I refer you to paragraph 2 of the Incident Report for the 9th April, in which reference was made to the attack by Jews on the Arab village at Deir Yassin.

2. The following supplementary information is now available as regards this incident:—

(1) The operation is believed to have been a joint National Military Organisation—Stern Group enterprise undertaken with the knowledge of the Haganah.

(2) The deaths of some 250 Arabs, men, women and children, which occurred during this attack, took place in circumstances of great savagery.

(3) Woman and children were stripped, lined up, photographed, and then slaughtered by automatic firing and survivors have told of even more incredible bestialities.

(4) Those who were taken prisoner were treated with degrading brutality.

(5) Although the Haganah is unable to deny that it gave covering fire to the terrorists responsible for this outrage, the action as a whole has been condemned by the Jewish press and denounced by the Chief Rabbinate.

(6) Owing to other pre-occupations, the Security Forces were not in a position to act before the 14th April, for which day an air strike at Deir Yassin was arranged.

(7) On the 13th April, it became apparent that the Haganah had taken over the village from the terrorists, and the operation was, therefore, suspended.

(8) The Government of Palestine reported on the 14th April that it had not yet been possible to enter Deir Yassin and that a Jewish Police Officer sent to investigate was not allowed by the Haganah to proceed beyond Givat Shaul.

(9) A representative of the International Red Cross who visited Deir Yassin on the 11th April is said to have stated that in one cave he saw

heaped bodies of some 150 Arab men, women and children, whilst in a stronghold a further 50 bodies were found.
[…]

* * *

April 21, 1948
My dear Bunche

In your letter of the 21st April, you enclosed a copy of a cable from the President of the Jewish Community Council, Jerusalem, relating to the Arab attack on a convoy of vehicles conveying doctors and nurses and other medical personnel to Hadassah Hospital and academic staff to the University on Mount Scopus.

2. References to this attack will be found in paragraph 6 of the Incident Report for April 12th and 13th and in paragraph 3 of the Incident Report for April 14th.

3. Subsequent information received from Jerusalem indicates that as a result of this incident, Hadassah Hospital will now be evacuated and further military assistance has been sought for this.

4. In view of the statement in the third sentence of the telegram, namely, that "attack took place within 100 yards of British Army Post continuing for six hours under the very eyes of British Military personnel who failed the effective steps intervene and actually prevented Haganah Forces from coming rescue", I would invite the Commission's attention to the statement in paragraph 6 of the Incident Report for April 12th and 13th that "Security Forces went to the scene…Security forces intervened and during shooting one British Other Rank was killed and two British Other Ranks were wounded, a Deputy Superintendent of Police was seriously wounded, seven Jews were rescued from abandoned convoy vehicles". I would also point out that the corrected figures in paragraph 3 of the Incident Report for 14th April show that two British soldiers were killed, two wounded and one Jewish police officer were wounded.
[…]

* * *

April 22, 1948
My dear Bunche,

The Commission will no doubt wish to have the latest information available here about the position in Haifa.

2. Reports, which are subject to confirmation, have been received from Jerusalem to the effect that the situation in Haifa is as follows:—

(1) There has been heavy continuous fighting in Haifa Town since midday on the 21st April, after British Forces had withdrawn to positions covering the Port.

(2) Jewish attacks by night on Arab outposts at Burj Hill and Prophets' Steps and on the Telephone Exchange were successful.

(3) Khoury House, the headquarters of the Palestine Railways, was set on fire and was gutted with all records.

(4) Jewish Forces have captured Salameh Building and positions in the Station Street – Burj Hill area and are now closing in on Khamra Square.

(5) The fire in the Port caused by mortaring has been extinguished.

(6) Heavy firing continues with mortaring of the Suq (market) area, which is reported deserted.

(7) Arabs are evacuating in large numbers by sea to Acre.

(8) Total casualties are believed to be heavy, including one British Constable wounded.

(9) British Police at the Haifa lock-up are being evacuated and the prisoners released.

(10) Military authorities are helping in the evacuation with landing-craft. The above Report is dated 9.40 a.m. Palestine Time, 22nd April.
[...]

* * *

April 23, 1948
My dear Bunche,

In continuation of the letter to the 22nd April, the following additional information was included in the *Second Report on the situation in Haifa* just received from Jerusalem.

(1) After the release of prisoners from Haifa lock-up, the Arab Legion took altar the building same time later.

(2) By 1015 hours, Arab casualties had been admitted to the Amin Hospital.

(3) Hospital staff and casualties were then evacuated to the Government Hospital, Haifa.

(4) Towards midday, the fighting slackened considerably. The Jews had complete control of the Khamra Square and Stanton Street area and were firing from their positions into the Suq (market) eras. The have also appeared in strength in the eastern quarter or the town from Wadi Rushmiyah Bridge to Tel Aviv.

(5) Arab women, children and others were still being evacuated from the Suq area through the port of Haifa and other safe areas.

(6) Arabs were by this time suing for a truce and the Jews had replied that they were prepared to consider it if the Arabs stopped shooting.

(7) At 5.0 p.m., general Arab resistance had ceased in the eastern area with the exception of a few isolated spots and the Jews were in possession of the Suq as far as the Eastern Gate.

(8) In the Wadi Misnar area the battle was still going on. Arab casualties in this area are believed to be considerable.

(9) At 6.0 p.m., Arab leaders met to consider final terms laid down at a joint meeting of Arabs and Jews.
[...]

* * *

April 26, 1948
My dear Bunche,

In continuation of my letter of the 23rd April, the following additional Information was included in the *Third Report on the Situation in Haifa* just received from Jerusalem:—

(1) On the morning of the 25th April, the situation in Haifa Town was described as very much quieter and it was reported that normal life was being resumed.

(2) General Headquarters reported that some military stores trains were still being operated by the military.

(3) The Haifa workshops were still operating.

(4) It was also reported that attempts to secure a truce had failed and that the Arabs had decided to evacuate the Town.

2. The following information contained in the *Fourth Report on the Situation in Haifa* has just been received:—

(1) On the afternoon of the 25th April, the situation in Haifa Town was reported to be quiet.

(2) During the night of April 23rd/24th there was practically no shooting in the Town though a small skirmish occurred in a village outside Haifa where British troops intervened and restored order.

(3) The Arabs, especially in the poorer quarters, were continuing to evacuate but the general exodus had almost ceased.

(4) It was estimated that some five thousand persons in all had evacuated the Town.

British Police Report: Arab Flight from Haifa (1948)
DISTRICT POLICE HEADQUARTERS

Subject:—   General Situation Haifa District.

Haifa remains quiet. Yesterday produced a noticeable change in the general atmosphere and businesses and shops in the lower town were open for the first time in many days. Traffic started to move normally around the town and people returning to the places of business filled the streets. In fact, Haifa presented a more normal appearance than it had done for a long while. Some Arabs were seen moving among the Jews in the lower town and German Colony area and these were allowed free and unmolested passage. An appeal has been made to the Arabs by the Jews to reopen their shops and businesses in order to relieve the difficulties of feeding the Arab population. Evacuation was still going on yesterday and several trips were made by 'Z' craft to Acre. Roads too, were crowded with people leaving Haifa with all their belongings. At a meeting yesterday afternoon Arab leaders reiterated their determination to evacuate the entire Arab population and they have been given the loan of ten 3-ton military trucks as from this morning to assist the evacuation.

Yesterday morning a Jew attempted to pass the drop barrier of Police H.Q. facing Palmers Gate wheeling a barrow. He was shot and killed by a Police sentry.

At 0640 hrs. yesterday Tireh village was again attacked with mortar fire. Casualties and damage not known.

A report has been received from Military to the effect that at 23.50 hrs. yesterday Jews attacked Acre from the direction of Ein Hamifratz and Tall al Pukhkhar. An advance Party succeeded in demolishing three houses in the Manshiya Quarter and then heavy mortar fire was directed at the town. Several mortar bombs landed in Acre Prison and all the inmates have escaped. The British Warden staff are safe. Military proceeded to the scene and opened fire with artillery on Ein Hemifratz. The Jews thereupon withdrew and a convoy of 11 vehicles was seen proceeding in the direction of Haifa. Casualties to both sides are not known.

(A.J. Bidmead.)
for SUPERINTENDENT OF POLICE

British Position Hit in Palestine (1948)
Robert Kennedy

I was in Palestine over Easter week and even then people knew there was absolutely no chance to preserve peace. They just wanted the British out, so that a decision could be reached either way. An early departure of the British has been far more important strategically to the Jews than to the Arabs.

The City of Jerusalem has more Jews than Arabs but the immediate surrounding territory is predominately Arab. Through part of that hilly territory winds the narrow road that leads from Tel Aviv to Jerusalem.

It is by this road that the Jewish population within Jerusalem must be supplied, but it is fantastically easy for the Arabs to ambush a convoy as it crawls along the difficult pass. On my trip from Tel Aviv to Jerusalem I saw grim realities of the fact and while in Jerusalem the failure and destruction of another Jewish convoy made meat non-existent and lengthened food queues for other items.

The Arabs living in the old city of Jerusalem have kept the age-old habit of procuring their water from the individual cisterns that exist in almost every home. The Jews being more "educated" (an Arab told me that this was their trouble and now the Jews were going to really pay for it) had a central water system installed with pipes bringing fresh hot and cold water. Unfortunately for them, the reservoir is situated in the mountains and it and the whole pipeline are controlled by the Arabs. The British would not let them cut the water off until after May 15th but an Arab told me they would not even do it then. First they would poison it.

Orthodox Community

Within the Old City of Jerusalem there exists a small community of orthodox Jews. They wanted no part of this fight but just wanted to be left alone with their wailing wall. Unfortunately for them, the Arabs are unkindly disposed toward any kind of Jew and their annihilation would now undoubtedly have been a fact had it not been that at the beginning of hostilities the Haganah moved several hundred well-equipped men into their quarter.

This inability to make any long-range military maneuvers because of the presence of the British has been a great and almost disastrous handicap to the Jews. If the brief but victorious military engagement on the Tel Aviv-Jerusalem road had not taken place, the Jewish cause would have suffered such a setback as to be virtually lost. If the Haganah had waited for May 15th and the withdrawal of British troops, there would be few alive in Jerusalem today. Strong units of that body had moved into the hills on either side of that strategic road and repelled Arab counterattacks long enough for several hundred truckloads to make the 40-mile trip into the city, and then, only after threats from the British commander to use force against them, had withdrawn from their positions. [...]

Power Supply

The same basic difficulty that exists in relation to the water exists with regard to electric and power supply. Fortunately, an immediate danger is not yet present, but the Arabs have had months of preparations for a maneuver they know their opponents must eventually make.

The Jewish ghetto in the old city of Jerusalem would not have been in such an untenable position if it could have been periodically relieved, or if with a Jewish victory in that area it could have been connected with the main Jewish section in the new city.

The Jews have small settlements or community farms such as Givat Brenner in completely hostile territory. They take pride that, despite the great difficulties, they have not evacuated any of them. From the very tip of Galilee right down to the arid Negev these communities exist [....] All have their supply problems. But no great military operation can be undertaken into Arab territory to relieve the increasing Arab pressure.

Need True Facts
[...]
The British government [...] has given ample credence to the suspicion that they are firmly against the establishment of a Jewish state in Palestine.

When I was in Cairo shortly after the blowing up of the Jewish Agency [March 11, 1948] I talked to a man who held a high position in the Arab League. He had just returned from Palestine where he had, among other things, interviewed and arranged transportation to Trans-Jordan for the Arab responsible for that Jewish disaster. This Arab told him that after the explosion, upon reaching the British post which separated the Jewish section from a small neutral zone set up in the middle of Jerusalem, he was questioned by the British officers in charge. He quite freely admitted what he had done and was given immediate passage with the remark, "Nice going."

British Markings

Just before I arrived in Palestine there was the notorious story of the foundry outside of Tel Aviv. It was situated in a highly contested area and the British accused the Jews of using it as a sniper post for the Jaffa-Jerusalem road. One day the British moved in, stripping the Jews of all arms and ordered them to clear out within 10 minutes. The British had scarcely departed when a group of armed Arabs moved in, killing or wounding all the occupants. The British government was most abject in its apologies.

I came in contact personally, however, with evidence that demonstrated clearly the British bitterness toward the Jews. I have ridden in Jewish armored car convoys which the British have stopped to inspect for arms. As always, there were members of the Haganah aboard and they quickly broke down their small arms, passing the pieces among the occupants to conceal them so as to prevent confiscation. Satisfied that none existed, the convoy supposedly unarmed was allowed to pass into Arab territory. If the arms had been found and confiscated and the Arabs had attacked, there would have been but a remote chance of survival for any of the occupants. There have been many not as fortunate as we.

British Informants

When I was in Tel Aviv the Jews informed the British government that 600 Iraqi troops were going to cross into Palestine from Trans-Jordan by the Allenby Bridge on a certain date and requested the British to take appropriate action to prevent this passage. The troops crossed unmolested. It is impossible for the British to patrol the whole Palestinian border to prevent illegal crossings but such flagrant violations should certainly have led to some sort of action.

Five weeks ago I saw several thousand non-Palestinian Arab troops in Palestine, including many of the famed British-trained and equipped Arab legionnaires of King Abdullah. There were also soldiers from Syria, Lebanon, Iraq, Trans-Jordan, and they were all proudly pointed out to me by a spokesman of the Arab higher committee. He warned me against walking too extensively through Arab districts as most of the inhabitants there were now foreign troops. Every Arab to whom I talked spoke of thousands of soldiers massed in the "terrible triangle of Nablus-Tulkarem-Jenin" and of hundreds that were pouring in daily.

Oversubscribed

When I was in Lebanon and asked a dean at the American University at Beirut if many students were leaving for the fight in Palestine he shrugged and said, "Not now – the quota has been oversubscribed." When journeying by car from Jerusalem to Amman I passed many truckloads of armed Arabs and even then Jericho was alive with Arab troops. There is no question that it was taken over by the Arabs for an armed camp long before May 15.
[…]

Memorandum of Conversation Concerning Palestine (1948)
George Marshall

The President said that he had called the meeting because he was seriously concerned as to what might happen in Palestine after May 15.

Mr. Lovett gave a lengthy exposition of recent events bearing on the Palestine problem. He recalled that on the preceding Saturday, May 8, the Political Representative of the Jewish Agency, Mr. Moshe Shertok, had called upon the Secretary and himself, accompanied by Dr. Epstein. Mr. Shertok had related that the British Minister for Colonial Affairs, Sir Arthur Creech Jones, had told him that Abdullah, the King of Transjordan, might enter the Arab portions of Palestine but that there need be no fear that Abdullah's forces, centered upon the British subsidized and officered Arab Legion, would seek to penetrate Jewish areas of Palestine. Furthermore, Mr. Shertok told the Secretary that a message, a week delayed in transmission, had been received from the Jewish Agency in Palestine, recounting overtures by a Colonel Goldy, an officer of the Arab Legion, suggesting that a deal could be worked out between Abdullah and the Jewish Agency whereby the King would take over the Arab portion of Palestine and leave the Jews in possession of their state in the remainder of that country.

Mr. Lovett said that this intelligence had obviously caused an abrupt shift in the position of the Jewish Agency. Only a week before, the Jewish Agency had officially communicated to the Security Council its charges that Arab armies were invading Palestine. Likewise, only a week before, Mr. Shertok and other representatives of the Jewish Agency had seemed seriously interested in proposed articles of truce. Now, however, their attitude had shifted and they seemed confident, on the basis of recent military successes and the prospect of a "behind the barn" deal with Abdullah, that they could establish their sovereign state without any necessity for a truce with the Arabs of Palestine.

I intervened at this juncture to recall what I had told Mr. Shertok on May 8. I had stressed that it was extremely dangerous to base long-range policy on temporary military success. There was no doubt but that the Jewish army had gained such temporary success but there was no assurance whatever that in the long-range the tide might not turn against them. I told Mr. Shertok that they were taking a gamble. If the tide did turn adversely and they came running to us for help they should be placed clearly on notice now that there was no warrant to expect help from the United States, which had warned them of the grave risk which they were running.

Later during the conversation a telephone call was received from General Carter stating that a UP press despatch from Tel Aviv reported that following two interviews with me by Mr. Shertok the latter had flown to Tel Aviv bearing a personal message from me to Mr. Ben Gurion, who was styled in the press despatch as the forth-coming President of the Jewish State. The despatch likewise was reported as saying that Shertok had informed me of the intention of the Jewish Agency to establish a sovereign state on May 16.

I directed, with the President's concurrence, that no comment be made on this press story. In actual fact, no message had been sent to Mr. Ben Gurion, and I did not even know that such a person existed. Furthermore, Shertok had not told me of any intention to establish a Jewish State on May 16.

Resuming his summary of the situation, Mr. Lovett read a telegram just received from New York City, indicating that, while the United Kingdom Government was prepared to support our draft resolution, it desired that the United States give further consideration to the possibility of a commission being appointed by the General Assembly to deal with the administration of Palestine, this commission to be made up of Belgium, France and the United States.

It was generally agreed that the British had played a lamentable, if not altogether duplicitous, role in the Palestine situation and that their last-minute approaches and indications of a change in heart could have no effect upon our policy.

The President then invited Mr. Clark Clifford to make a statement. Mr. Clifford said that he had three main suggestions to offer, based upon consultation with colleagues of the White House staff.

Mr. Clifford said that he objected to the first article of our draft resolution which would place the General Assembly on record as reaffirming support of the efforts of the Security Council to secure a truce in Palestine. He said this reference was unrealistic since there had been no truce and probably would not be one. He said that on March 24, Mr. Rusk at a White House conference had estimated that a truce could be negotiated within two weeks but this goal was still not in sight. Instead, the actual partition of Palestine had taken place "without the use of outside force".

Mr. Clifford's second point was strongly to urge the President to give prompt recognition to the Jewish State after the termination of the mandate on May 15. He said such a move should be taken quickly before the Soviet Union recognized the Jewish State. It would have distinct value in restoring the President's position for support of the partition of Palestine.

Mr. Clifford's third point was that the President, at his press conference on the following day, May 13, should make a statement of his intention to recognize the Jewish State, once the provision for democratic government outlined in the resolution of November 29, had been complied with, which he assumed would be the case. The proposed statement would conclude: "I have asked the Secretary of State to have the Representatives of the United States in the United Nations, take up this subject in the United Nations with a view toward obtaining early recognition of a Jewish State by the other members of the United Nations".

The rebuttal was made by Mr. Lovett. With regard to Mr. Clifford's reference to the article on truce, Mr. Lovett pointed out that the Security Council was still seized of this matter under its resolutions of April 1, April 17 and April 23. The United States in fact was a member of the Security Council's Truce Commission on Palestine. Surely the United States could not by its unilateral act get the Security Council to drop this matter and it would be most unbecoming, in light of our activities to secure a truce.

On the question of premature recognition, Mr. Lovett said that it would be highly injurious to the United Nations to announce the recognition of the Jewish State even before it had come into existence and while the General Assembly, which had been called into special session at the request of the United States, was still considering the question of the future government of Palestine. Furthermore, said Mr. Lovett, such a move would be injurious to the prestige of the President. It was a very transparent attempt to win the Jewish vote but, in Mr. Lovett's opinion, it would lose more votes than it would gain. Finally, to recognize the Jewish State prematurely would be buying a pig in a poke. How did we know what kind of Jewish State would be set up? [...]

Mr. Lovett also failed to see any particular urgency in the United States rushing to recognize the Jewish State prior to possible Soviet recognition.

I remarked to the President that, speaking objectively, I could not help but think that the suggestions made by Mr. Clifford were wrong. I thought that to adopt these suggestions would have precisely the opposite effect from that intended by Mr. Clifford. The transparent dodge to win a few votes would not in fact achieve this purpose. [...] The counsel offered by Mr. Clifford was based on domestic political considerations, while the problem which confronted us was international. I said bluntly that if the President were to follow Mr. Clifford's advice and if in the elections I were to vote, I would vote against the President.

Mr. Lovett and I told the President that naturally after May 16 we would take another look at the situation in Palestine in light of the facts as they existed. Clearly the question of recognition would have to be gone into very carefully. [...]

The President [...] terminated the interview by saying that he was fully aware of the difficulties and dangers in the situation, to say nothing of the political risks involved which he, himself, would run.

Speech to Council of Jewish Federations (1948)

Golda Meir

*[Golda Meir led a U.S. fundraising tour to benefit the Jewish war effort.
The Jewish Agency needed $7 million to continue the war — she raised
$30 million. This speech is from her fundraising tour].*

I have had the privilege of representing Palestine Jewry in this country and
in other countries when the problems that we faced were those of building
more kibbutzim, of bringing in more Jews in spite of political obstacles
and Arab riots.

We always had faith that in the end we would win, that everything we were
doing in the country led to the independence of the Jewish people and to a
Jewish state.

Long before we had dared pronounce that word, we knew what was in
store for us.

Today we have reached a point when the nations of the world have given
us their decision — the establishment of a Jewish state in a part of
Palestine. Now in Palestine we are fighting to make this resolution of the
United Nations a reality, not because we wanted to fight. If we had the
choice, we would have chosen peace to build in peace.

Friends, we have no alternative in Palestine. The Mufti and his men have
declared war upon us. We have to fight for our lives, for our safety, and for
what we have accomplished in Palestine, and perhaps above all, we must
fight for Jewish honour and Jewish independence. Without exaggeration, I
can tell you that the Jewish community in Palestine is doing this well.
Many of you have visited Palestine; all of you have read about our young
people and have a notion as to what our youth is like. I have known this
generation for the last twenty-seven years. I thought I knew them. I realize
now that even I did not.

These young boys and girls, many in their teens, are bearing the burden of
what is happening in the country with a spirit that no words can describe.
You see these youngsters in open cars—not armoured cars—in convoys
going from Tel Aviv to Jerusalem, knowing that every time they start out
from Tel Aviv or from Jerusalem there are probably Arabs behind the
orange groves or the hills, waiting to ambush the convoy.

These boys and girls have accepted the task of bringing Jews over these
roads in safety as naturally as though they were going out to their daily
work or to their classes in the university.

We must ask the Jews the world over to see us as the front line.

All we ask of Jews the world over, and mainly of the Jews in the United States, is to give us the possibility of going on with the struggle.

When trouble started, we asked young people from the age of seventeen to twenty-five who were not members of Haganah, to volunteer. Up to the day that I left home on Thursday morning, when the registration of this age group was still going on, over 20,000 young men and women had signed up. As of now we have about 9,000 people mobilized in the various parts of the country. We must triple this number within the next few days.

We have to maintain these men. No government sends its soldiers to the front and expects them to take along from their homes the most elementary requirements—blankets, bedding, clothing.

A people that is fighting for its very life knows how to supply the men they send to the front lines. We too must do the same.

Thirty-five of our boys, unable to go by car on the road to besieged Kfar Etzion to bring help, set out by foot through the hills; they knew the road, the Arab villages on that road, and the danger they would have to face. Some of the finest youngsters we have in the country were in that group, and they were all killed, every one of them. We have a description from an Arab of how they fought to the end for over seven hours against hundreds of Arabs. According to this Arab, the last boy killed, with no more ammunition left, died with a stone in his hand.

I want to say to you, friends, that the Jewish community in Palestine is going to fight to the very end. If we have arms to fight with, we will fight with those, and if not, we will fight with stones in our hands.

I want you to believe me when I say that I came on this special mission to the United States today not to save 700,000 Jews. During the last few years the Jewish people lost 6,000,000 Jews, and it would be audacity on our part to worry the Jewish people throughout the world because a few hundred thousand more Jews were in danger. That is not the issue.

The issue is that if these 700,000 Jews in Palestine can remain alive, then the Jewish people as such is alive and Jewish independence is assured. If these 700,000 people are killed off, then for many centuries, we are through with this dream of a Jewish people and a Jewish homeland.

My friends, we are at war. There is no Jew in Palestine who does not believe that finally we will be victorious. That is the spirit of the country. We have known Arab riots since 1921 and '29 and '36. We know what happened to the Jews of Europe during this last war. And every Jew in the country also knows that within a few months a Jewish state in Palestine will be established.

We knew that the price we would have to pay would be the best of our people. There are over 300 killed by now. There will be more. There is no doubt that there will be more. But there is also no doubt that the spirit of our young people is such that no matter how many Arabs invade the country, their spirit will not falter. However, this valiant spirit alone cannot face rifles and machine guns. Rifles and machine guns without spirit are not worth very much, but spirit without arms can in time be broken with the body.

Much must be prepared now so that we can hold out. There are unlimited opportunities, but are we going to get the necessary means? Considering myself not as a guest, but as one of you, I say that the question before each one is simply whether the Yishuv, and the youngsters that are in the front line, will have to fail because money that should have reached Palestine today will reach it in a month or two months from now?

Is it possible that time should decide the issue not because Palestinian Jews are cowards, not because they are incapable, but merely because they lack the material means to carry on?

I have come to the United States, and I hope you will understand me if I say that it is not an easy matter for any of us to leave home at present—to my sorrow I am not in the front line. I am not with my daughter in the Negev or with other sons and daughters in the trenches. But I have a job to do.

I have come here to try to impress Jews in the United States with the fact that within a very short period, a couple of weeks, we must have in cash between twenty-five and thirty million dollars. In the next two or three weeks we can establish ourselves. Of that we are convinced, and you must have faith; we are sure that we can carry on.

I said before that the Yishuv will give, is giving of its means. But please remember that even while shooting is going on, we must carry on so that our economy remains intact. Our factories must go on. Our settlements must not be broken up.

We know that this battle is being waged for those not yet in the country.

There are 30,000 Jews detained right next door to Palestine in Cyprus. I believe that within a very short period, within the next two or three months at most, these 30,000 will be with us, among them thousands of infants and young children. We must now think of preparing means of absorbing them. We know that within the very near future, hundreds of thousands more will be coming in. We must see that our economy is intact.

I want you to understand that there is no despair in the Yishuv. This is true not only of the young people. I have travelled the road from Tel Aviv to Jerusalem and other roads quite a bit. I have seen these dangerous buses filled not only with young Haganah men and girls, but with old people travelling the roads as a matter of course.

When you go to Tel Aviv now, you will find the city full of life; only the shooting that you hear on the outskirts of Tel Aviv and Jaffa reminds one that the situation in the country is not normal. But it would be a crime on my part not to describe the situation to you exactly as it is.

Merely with our ten fingers and merely with spirit and sacrifice, we cannot carry on this battle, and the only hinterland that we have is you. The Mufti has the Arab states—not all so enthusiastic about helping him but states with government budgets. The Egyptian government can vote a budget to aid our antagonists. The Syrian government can do the same.

We have no government. But we have millions of Jews in the Diaspora, and exactly as we have faith in our youngsters in Palestine I have faith in Jews in the United States; I believe that they will realize the peril of our situation and will do what they have to do.

I know that we are not asking for something easy. I myself have sometimes been active in various campaigns and fund collections, and I know that collecting at once a sum such as I ask is not simple.

But I have seen our people at home. I have seen them come from the offices to the clinics when we called the community to give their blood for a blood bank to treat the wounded. I have seen them lined up for hours, waiting so that some of their blood can be added to this bank.

It is blood plus money that is being given in Palestine.

I know that many of you would be as anxious as our people to be on the very front line. I do not doubt that there are many young people among the Jewish community in the United States who would do exactly what our young people are doing in Palestine.

We are not a better breed; we are not the best Jews of the Jewish people. It so happened that we are there and you are here. I am certain that if you were in Palestine and we were in the United States, you would be doing what we are doing there, and you would ask us here to do what you will have to do.

I want to close with paraphrasing one of the greatest speeches that was made during the Second World War— the words of Churchill.

I am not exaggerating when I say that the Yishuv in Palestine will fight in the Negev and will fight in Galilee and will fight on the outskirts of Jerusalem until the very end. You cannot decide whether we should fight or not. We will. The Jewish community in Palestine will raise no white flag for the Mufti. That decision is taken. Nobody can change it. You can only decide one thing: whether we shall be victorious in this fight or whether the Mufti will be victorious. That decision American Jews can make. It has to be made quickly within hours, within days.

And I beg of you—don't be too late. Don't be bitterly sorry three months from now for what you failed to do today. The time is now.

I have spoken to you without a grain of exaggeration. I have not tried to paint the picture in false colours. It consists of spirit and certainty of our victory on the one hand, and dire necessity for carrying on the battle on the other.

I want to thank you again for having given me the opportunity at a conference that I am certain has a full agenda to say these words to you. I leave the platform without any doubt in my mind or my heart that the decision that will be taken by American Jewry will be the same as that which was taken by the Jewish community in Palestine, so that within a few months from now we will all be able to participate not only in the joy of resolving to establish a Jewish state, but in the joy of laying the cornerstone of the Jewish state.

CREATION

Israeli Declaration of Independence (1948)
PROVISIONAL COUNCIL OF ISRAEL

ERETZ-ISRAEL was the birthplace of the Jewish people. Here their spiritual, religious and political identity was shaped. Here they first attained to statehood, created cultural values of national and universal significance and gave to the world the eternal Book of Books.

After being forcibly exiled from their land, the people remained faithful to it throughout their Dispersion and never ceased to pray and hope for their return to it and for the restoration in it of their political freedom.

Impelled by this historic and traditional attachment, Jews strove in every successive generation to re-establish themselves in their ancient homeland. In recent decades they returned in their masses. Pioneers, ma'pilim and defenders, they made deserts bloom, revived the Hebrew language, built villages and towns, and created a thriving community controlling its own economy and culture, loving peace but knowing how to defend itself, bringing the blessings of progress to all the country's inhabitants, and aspiring towards independent nationhood.

In the year 5657 (1897), at the summons of the spiritual father of the Jewish State, Theodore Herzl, the First Zionist Congress convened and proclaimed the right of the Jewish people to national rebirth in its own country.

This right was recognized in the Balfour Declaration of the 2nd November, 1917, and re-affirmed in the Mandate of the League of Nations which, in particular, gave international sanction to the historic connection between the Jewish people and Eretz-Israel and to the right of the Jewish people to rebuild its National Home.

The catastrophe which recently befell the Jewish people—the massacre of millions of Jews in Europe—was another clear demonstration of the urgency of solving the problem of its homelessness by re-establishing in Eretz-Israel the Jewish State, which would open the gates of the homeland wide to every Jew and confer upon the Jewish people the status of a fully privileged member of the comity of nations.

Survivors of the Nazi holocaust in Europe, as well as Jews from other parts of the world, continued to migrate to Eretz-Israel, undaunted by difficulties, restrictions and dangers, and never ceased to assert their right to a life of dignity, freedom and honest toil in their national homeland.

In the Second World War, the Jewish community of this country contributed its full share to the struggle of the freedom- and peace-loving nations against the forces of Nazi wickedness and, by the blood of its soldiers and its war effort, gained the right to be reckoned among the peoples who founded the United Nations.

On the 29th November, 1947, the United Nations General Assembly passed a resolution calling for the establishment of a Jewish State in Eretz-Israel; the General Assembly required the inhabitants of Eretz-Israel to take such steps as were necessary on their part for the implementation of that resolution. This recognition by the United Nations of the right of the Jewish people to establish their State is irrevocable.

This right is the natural right of the Jewish people to be masters of their own fate, like all other nations, in their own sovereign State.

ACCORDINGLY WE, MEMBERS OF THE PEOPLE'S COUNCIL, REPRESENTATIVES OF THE JEWISH COMMUNITY OF ERETZ-ISRAEL AND OF THE ZIONIST MOVEMENT, ARE HERE ASSEMBLED ON THE DAY OF THE TERMINATION OF THE BRITISH MANDATE OVER ERETZ-ISRAEL AND, BY VIRTUE OF OUR NATURAL AND HISTORIC RIGHT AND ON THE STRENGTH OF THE RESOLUTION OF THE UNITED NATIONS GENERAL ASSEMBLY, HEREBY DECLARE THE ESTABLISHMENT OF A JEWISH STATE IN ERETZ-ISRAEL, TO BE KNOWN AS THE STATE OF ISRAEL.

WE DECLARE that, with effect from the moment of the termination of the Mandate being tonight, the eve of Sabbath, the 6th Iyar, 5708 (15th May, 1948), until the establishment of the elected, regular authorities of the State in accordance with the Constitution which shall be adopted by the Elected Constituent Assembly not later than the 1st October 1948, the People's Council shall act as a Provisional Council of State, and its executive organ, the People's Administration, shall be the Provisional Government of the Jewish State, to be called "Israel".

THE STATE OF ISRAEL will be open for Jewish immigration and for the Ingathering of the Exiles; it will foster the development of the country for the benefit of all its inhabitants; it will be based on freedom, justice and peace as envisaged by the prophets of Israel; it will ensure complete equality of social and political rights to all its inhabitants irrespective of religion, race or sex; it will guarantee freedom of religion, conscience, language, education and culture; it will safeguard the Holy Places of all religions; and it will be faithful to the principles of the Charter of the United Nations.

THE STATE OF ISRAEL is prepared to cooperate with the agencies and representatives of the United Nations in implementing the resolution of the General Assembly of the 29th November, 1947, and will take steps to bring about the economic union of the whole of Eretz-Israel.

WE APPEAL to the United Nations to assist the Jewish people in the building-up of its State and to receive the State of Israel into the comity of nations.

WE APPEAL—in the very midst of the onslaught launched against us now for months—to the Arab inhabitants of the State of Israel to preserve peace and participate in the upbuilding of the State on the basis of full and equal citizenship and due representation in all its provisional and permanent institutions.

WE EXTEND our hand to all neighboring states and their peoples in an offer of peace and good neighborliness, and appeal to them to establish bonds of cooperation and mutual help with the sovereign Jewish people settled in its own land. The State of Israel is prepared to do its share in a common effort for the advancement of the entire Middle East.

WE APPEAL to the Jewish people throughout the Diaspora to rally round the Jews of Eretz-Israel in the tasks of immigration and upbuilding and to stand by them in the great struggle for the realization of the age-old dream—the redemption of Israel.

PLACING OUR TRUST IN THE ALMIGHTY, WE AFFIX OUR SIGNATURES TO THIS PROCLAMATION AT THIS SESSION OF THE PROVISIONAL COUNCIL OF STATE, ON THE SOIL OF THE HOMELAND, IN THE CITY OF TEL-AVIV, ON THIS SABBATH EVE, THE 5TH DAY OF IYAR, 5708 (14TH MAY, 1948).

Statement Following the Establishment of the State of Israel (1948)
THE ARAB LEAGUE

Now that the British mandate over Palestine has come to an end, without there being a legitimate constitutional authority in the country, which would safeguard the maintenance of security and respect for law and which would protect the lives and properties of the inhabitants, the Governments of the Arab States declare the following:

First: That the rule of Palestine should revert to its inhabitants, in accordance with the provisions of the Covenant of the League of Nations and (the Charter) of the United Nations and that (the Palestinians) should alone have the right to determine their future.

Second: Security and order in Palestine have become disrupted. The Zionist aggression resulted in the exodus of more than a quarter of a million of its Arab inhabitants from their homes and in taking refuge in the neighbouring Arab countries. The events which have taken place in Palestine have unmasked the aggressive intentions and the imperialist designs of the Zionists, including the atrocities committed by them against the peace-loving Arab inhabitants, especially in Dayr Yasin, Tiberias and others. Nor have they respected the inviolability of consuls, as they have attacked the consulates of the Arab States in Jerusalem. After the termination of the British mandate over Palestine the British authorities are no longer responsible for security in the country, except to the degree affecting their withdrawing forces, and (only) in the areas in which these forces happen to be at the time of withdrawal as announced by (these authorities). This state of affairs would render Palestine without any governmental machinery capable of restoring order and the rule of law to the country, and of protecting the lives and properties of the inhabitants.

Third: This state of affairs is threatening to spread to the neighbouring Arab countries, where feeling is running high because of the events in Palestine. The Governments of the Member States of the Arab League and the United Nations are exceedingly worried and deeply concerned about this state of affairs.

Fourth: These Governments had hoped that the United Nations would have succeeded in finding a peaceful and just solution of the problem of Palestine, in accordance with democratic principles and the provisions of the Covenant of the League of Nations and (the Charter) of the United Nations, so that peace, security and prosperity would prevail in this part of the world.

Fifth: The Governments of the Arab States, as members of the Arab League, a regional organization within the meaning of the provisions of Chapter VIII of the Charter of the United Nations, are responsible for maintaining peace and security in their area. These Governments view the
186

events taking place in Palestine as a threat to peace and security in the area as a whole and (also) in each of them taken separately.

Sixth: Therefore, as security in Palestine is a sacred trust in the hands of the Arab States, and in order to put an end to this state of affairs and to prevent it from becoming aggravated or from turning into (a state of) chaos, the extent of which no one can foretell; in order to stop the spreading of disturbances and disorder in Palestine to the neighbouring Arab countries; in order to fill the gap brought about in the governmental machinery in Palestine as a result of the termination of the mandate and the non-establishment of a lawful successor authority, the Governments of the Arab States have found themselves compelled to intervene in Palestine solely in order to help its inhabitants restore peace and security and the rule of justice and law to their country, and in order to prevent bloodshed.

Seventh: The Governments of the Arab States recognize that the independence of Palestine, which has so far been suppressed by the British Mandate, has become an accomplished fact for the lawful inhabitants of Palestine. They alone, by virtue of their absolute sovereignty, have the right to provide their country with laws and governmental institutions. They alone should exercise the attributes of their independence, through their own means and without any kind of foreign interference, immediately after peace, security, and the rule of law have been restored to the country. At that time the intervention of the Arab states will cease, and the independent State of Palestine will cooperate with the (other member) States of the Arab League in order to bring peace, security and prosperity to this part of the world. The Governments of the Arab States emphasize, on this occasion, what they have already declared before the London Conference and the United Nations, that the only solution of the Palestine problem is the establishment of a unitary Palestinian State, in accordance with democratic principles, whereby its inhabitants will enjoy complete equality before the law, (and whereby) minorities will be assured of all the guarantees recognized in democratic constitutional countries and (whereby) the holy places will be preserved and the rights of access thereto guaranteed.

Eighth: The Arab States most emphatically declare that (their) intervention in Palestine was due only to these considerations and objectives, and that they aim at nothing more than to put an end to the prevailing conditions in (Palestine). For this reason, they have great confidence that their action will have the support of the United Nations; (that it will be) considered as an action aiming at the realization of its aims and at promoting its principles, as provided for in its Charter.

America, Russia, and the Window of Opportunity (1987)
Paul Johnson

[...] [O]n 14 February 1947, Bevin announced that he was handing over the whole Palestine problem to the United Nations.

That did not necessarily mean a rapid British withdrawal, however. So the terror campaign continued. A further episode, for which Begin was again responsible, proved decisive. He was opposed to Sternist-type assassinations but he insisted on Irgun's moral right to punish members of the British armed forces in the same way as Britain punished Irgun members. The British hanged and flogged. Irgun would do the same. In April 1947 three Irgun men were put on trial for an attack on the Acre prison-fortress, which freed 251 prisoners. Begin threatened retaliation if the three were convicted and hanged. They were, on 29 July. A few hours later two British sergeants, Clifford Martin and Marvyn Paice, who had been captured for this purpose, were hanged on Begin's instructions by Irgun's operations chief, Gidi Paglin. He also mined their bodies. This gruesome murder of Martin and Paice, who had committed no crime, horrified many Jews. The Jewish Agency called it 'the dastardly murder of two innocent men by a set of criminals.' (It was even worse than it seemed at the time, for it emerged thirty-five years later that Martin had a Jewish mother.) It captured unrestrained fury in Britain. A synagogue was burned down in Derby. There were anti-Jewish riots in London, Liverpool, Glasgow, and Manchester – the first in England since the thirteenth century. These in turn produced critical changes in British policy. The British had assumed that any partition would have to be supervised and enforced by them; otherwise the armies of the Arab states would simply move in and exterminate the Jews. Now they decided to get out as quickly as possible and leave Arabs and Jews to it. Thus, Begin's policy succeeded, but it involved appalling risks.

The extent of the risks depended to some extent on the two superpowers, America and Russia. In both cases the Zionists benefited from what might be called luck or divine providence, according to taste. The first was the death of Roosevelt on 12 April 1948. In his last weeks he had turned anti-Zionist, following a meeting with King Ibn Saud after the Yalta Conference. The pro-Zionist presential assistant, David Niles, later asserted: 'There are serious doubts in my mind that Israel would have come into being if Roosevelt had lived.' F.D.R.'s successor, Harry S. Truman, had a much more straightforward commitment to Zionism, part emotional, part calculating. He felt sorry for Jewish refugees. He saw Jews in Palestine as underdogs. He was also much less sure of the Jewish vote than Roosevelt. For the coming 1948 election, he needed the endorsement of Jewish organizations in such swing states as New York, Pennsylvania and Illinois. Once the British renounced their mandate, Truman pushed for the creation of a Jewish State. In May 1947 the Palestine problem came before the UN. A special committee was asked to submit a plan. It produced two. A minority recommended a federated binational state. The majority produced a new partition plan: there would be Jewish and Arab states, plus an international zone in Jerusalem. On 29 November 1947, thanks to Truman's vigorous backing, it was endorsed by the General Assembly, 33 votes to 13, with 10 abstentions.

The Soviet Union and the Arab states, followed by the international left in general, later came to believe that the creation of Israel was the work of a capitalist-imperialist conspiracy. But the facts show the reverse. Neither the American State Department nor the British Foreign Office wanted a Jewish state. They foresaw disaster for the West in the area if one were created. The British War Office was equally strong in opposition. So was the US Defense Department. Its Secretary, James Forrestal, bitterly denounced the Jewish lobby: 'No group in this country should be permitted to influence our policy to the point where it could endanger national security.' The British and American oil companies were even more vehement in opposing the new state. Speaking for the oil interests, Max Thornburg, of Cal-Tex, said that Truman had 'extinguished the moral prestige of America' and destroyed 'Arab faith in her ideals.' It is impossible to point to any powerful economic interest, in either Britain or the United States, which pushed for the creation of Israel. In both countries, the overwhelming majority of her friends were on the left.

Indeed, if there was a conspiracy to create Israel, then the Soviet Union was a prominent member of it. During the war, for tactical reasons, Stalin suspended some aspects of his anti-Semitic policies. He even created a Jewish Anti-Fascist Committee. From 1944, for a brief period, he adopted a pro-Zionist posture in foreign policy (though not in Russia itself). His reason seems to have been that the creation of Israel, which he was advised would be a socialist state, would accelerate the decline of British influence in the Middle East. When Palestine first came before the UN in May 1947, Andrei Gromyko, the Soviet Deputy Foreign Minister, caused surprise by announcing that his government supported the creation of a Jewish state, and by voting accordingly. On 13 October Semyon Tsarapkin, head of the Soviet delegation to the UN, offered members of the Jewish Agency the toast, 'To the future Jewish State', before voting for the partition plan. At the decisive General Assembly vote on 29 November the entire Soviet and American delegations worked closely together on the timetable of British withdrawal. Nor was this all. When Israel declared independence on 14 May 1948 and President Truman immediately accorded it *de facto* recognition, Stalin went one better and, less than three days later, gave it recognition *de jure*. Perhaps most significant of all was the decision of the Czech government, on Stalin's instructions, to sell the new state arms. An entire airfield was assigned to the task of air-lifting weapons to Tel Aviv.

Timing was absolutely critical to Israel's birth and survival. Stalin had the Russian-Jewish actor Solomon Mikhoels murdered in January 1948, and this seems to have marked the beginning of an intensely anti-Semitic phase in his policy. The switch to anti-Zionism abroad took longer to develop but it came decisively in the autumn of 1948. By this time, however, Israel was securely in existence. American policy was also changing, as the growing pressures of the Cold War dissolved her mood of post-war idealism and forced Truman to listen more attentively to Pentagon and State Department advice. If British evacuation had been postponed another year, the United States would have been far less anxious to see Israel created and Russia would almost certainly have been hostile. Hence the effect of the terror campaign on British policy was perhaps decisive to the entire enterprise. Israeli slipped into existence through a fortuitous window in history, which briefly opened for a few months in 1947-48. That too was luck; or providence.

[...]

INVASION

Israel's Border and Security Problems (1955)
Major-General Moshe Dayan

More than fifteen years ago a British Royal Commission had recorded the official Arab view presented by the Mufti of Jerusalem that the Jewish population of Palestine was "too large" and should be reduced by military action. In November 1947 the United Nations' recommendation for the establishment of a sovereign Jewish State in Palestine was the signal for a purposeful attempt to put this doctrine into effect. [...] On November 30, 1947, this assault began with the slaughter of 36 Jews in the first week of hostilities commenced by Palestinian Arab guerrillas. A "Liberation Army" organized by Arab Governments moved into Palestine to continue the carnage. Finally, on May 15, 1948, when the British Mandate expired, the armies of all the Arab states invaded Israel with the avowed aim of destroying her independence. Iraqi and Jordanian battalions took over the Arab half of Palestine, then pressed on toward the coastal plain while Israel stood with her back against the sea. Syrian tanks crashed into farming villages in the Upper Jordan valley. Lebanese regulars and irregulars from Syria converged upon Galilee. Egyptian forces began what was intended as a triumphal march on Tel Aviv, coming within nine miles of the city's suburbs. Aircraft bombed Israel's undefended cities. A ring of fire encircled Jerusalem and exposed its population to the horrors of bombardment, famine and siege.

There has never been any serious dispute about the origins of this assault or its aggressive character. In the spring of 1948 a United Nations Commission reported: "Powerful Arab forces are defying the resolution of the General Assembly and attempting to overthrow by force the recommendations contained therein." The authoritative international view was further expressed in the United Nations by Ambassador Warren Austin, speaking for the United States, in the Security Council, on May 22, 1948:

> ... Probably the most important and the best evidence we have on that subject is contained in the admissions of the countries whose five armies have invaded Palestine that they are carrying on a war.

> Their statements are the best evidence we have of the international character of this aggression. . . . They tell us quite frankly that their business in Palestine is political and that they are there to establish a unitary State. Of course, the statement that they are there to make peace is rather remarkable in view of the fact that they are waging war.

The American representative then invited his colleagues to determine that this "aggression of international character" constituted a breach of the peace within the meaning of Article 39 of the U.N. Charter. The fighting between May 15 and June 13, when a 30-day truce was concluded, had involved the Arab Governments in the open rejection of the Security Council's three cease-fire orders.

When the 30-day truce expired, the United Nations ordered its renewal. The Arab states refused to accede, arguing with frankness that if there were no fighting it would be impossible to prevent the State of Israel from continuing to exist. In a resolution adopted on July 15, 1948, the Security Council renewed its verdict of Arab responsibility by resolving that the Arab refusal to prolong the truce constituted a breach of international peace and security. This was the first time that such a determination under Chapter VII of the Charter had been made by the United Nations on any issue.

The repulse by ill-equipped defenders of this assault was Israel's first achievement, and it won her high renown. But both the army and the civilian population sustained cruel loss of life. Some of the patient rewards of five decades of pioneering had been ravaged. The state of Israel had come into existence in the shadow of imminent destruction, and the memories of escape from fearful dangers have attended the people of Israel from the very dawn of their independence. These memories abide with us still, and go far to explain the depth of our preoccupation with security. Nor have the Israel people ever forgotten that in their supreme ordeal they received no direct assistance from outside, although waves of sympathy flowed in from free peoples everywhere and provided a valued consolation.

The acceptance of a permanent truce in July 1948 did not signify the end of the war. Contrary to the terms of the truce and to the rulings of the United Nations Truce Supervision Board, the Egyptian Army blocked the supply road to the Jewish villages in the south and renewed the attack on Israel positions in the Negev. A convoy was sent to supply the Negev villages. It was heavily attacked by the Egyptian forces from positions secured after the truce. Seven days' more fighting ensued, which gave to the Israel forces control of Beersheba, center of the Negev, as well as of the northern Negev with the exception of the Gaza strip and the Faluja pocket. In a statement made on October 25, 1948, by the United Nations Chief of the Truce Supervision Board to the Egyptian Commander-in-chief in Gaza, he attributed the renewal of the fighting in the Negev primarily to the failure of the Egyptians to comply with Ruling No. 13 of the Truce Supervision Board regarding the passage of convoys to the Jewish villages in the south. In March 1949 the Israel forces occupied the Wadi Araba up to the Gulf of Elath and thus gained control of the Negev--a desert area which had been part of Israel since her establishment but had been unoccupied by any forces up to that time. Neither the Egyptians nor the Jordanians had ever possessed international sanction to occupy this part of Israel in the first place, and if their patrols had ever crossed or scantily supervised it prior to its occupation by Israel--a claim that was never substantiated--their expulsion was a blow against aggressive conquest.

The purpose of the Arab invasion had been the destruction of the state of Israel and the ejection of the Jewish population from the soil of Palestine. In a statement made by Azzam Pasha, then Secretary General of the Arab League, on May 15, 1948, the eve of the invasion of the Arab armies, the Arab war aim was formulated in unambiguous terms: "This," he said, "will be a war of extermination and a momentous massacre which will be spoken of like the Mongolian massacre and the crusades." Indeed, the Arab attack, especially in its first guerrilla stage, did not lack cases of disregard of the rules of war.

There are at present more than 180,000 Arabs living in the state of Israel, but not a single Jew survives in any part of Palestine that came to be occupied by the invading Arab armies. The Jewish quarter in the Old City of Jerusalem, with its ancient synagogues and monuments, was completely destroyed; even the Jewish Cemetery of the Mount of Olives was desecrated and laid waste.

[…]

Violence on the Jordan-Israel Border: A Jordanian View (1954)
Lieutenant-General J. B. Glubb

When the United Nations prepared its plan for the partition of Palestine in the autumn of 1947, it drew the demarcation line in such a manner that the Arabs to be included in the proposed Jewish state looked like being very nearly as numerous as the Jews. This indeed was the principal problem which seemed likely to face the Jewish state when it came into existence on May 15, 1948. How were the Jews to run a "Jewish state" in which nearly half the inhabitants would be Arabs?

When the British Mandate came to an end on May 15, guerrilla fighting between Jews and Arabs had already been going on for some months, as the British forces gradually dwindled. On that date the fighting became general.

Both before and after the end of the Mandate, the Israelis seized every possible opportunity to get rid of the Arabs still living in the area allotted to the Jewish state. In some cases, massacre was resorted to, as in the Arab village of Deir Yassin, where the women of the village were massacred and their bodies thrown down the wells--one morning when most of the men of the village were away at work. One such incident went a long way, and the inhabitants of neighboring villages panicked and fled.

In the course of the fighting, the Jews captured a number of Arab towns and villages, some of which were in the area allotted to the Arabs under the United Nations partition plan. In many such instances, the civil inhabitants were driven out immediately by Israeli troops or were given half an hour to leave. In some cases, all the means of transport were seized by the Israeli army, so that the inhabitants were obliged to abandon all their possessions in their homes.

In general, the Israelis were most ruthless in driving out the Arab civil population from places in the coastal plain or near Tel Aviv, then the Israeli capital. In northern Galilee, which they captured from the Syrian Army, they were far less ruthless, and most of the Arab inhabitants remained. Presumably the hilly district, far removed from vital strategic centers, was not considered to threaten the safety of the State of Israel.

It was in this manner that the Arab refugee problem came into existence. More than half the total number of refugees sought asylum in Jordan, which according to United Nations statistics now contains 450,000 refugees. The total number of inhabitants of Jordan is about 1,400,000. Thus it will be seen that the refugees constitute about one-third of the inhabitants of the country.

194   Used with permission of Foreign Affairs, from FOREIGN AFFAIRS, Vol. 32, No. 4 (July 1, 1954); permission conveyed through Copyright Clearance Center, Inc.

The general fighting in Palestine came to an end in July 1948. When all parties accepted the United Nations Armistice, the Egyptian Army was still in occupation of the Negeb (the Beersheba area) and of the Wadi Araba, the depression which runs from the Dead Sea down to the Red Sea. This area had been allotted to Israel in the United Nations partition plan, but the Israelis had failed to occupy it. On the other hand, west of Jerusalem and in northern Galilee they had occupied areas allotted by the United Nations to the Arabs.

In October 1948, the Israeli Army broke the United Nations Armistice and attacked the Egyptians. It is true that the Israelis claimed that it was the Egyptians who broke it. For 15 days before the battle began, however, the Israelis had refused to allow United Nations observers to visit the area in which their troops were concentrating. The Egyptians were taken completely by surprise, and suffered a serious reverse. The Israelis thereupon occupied the Beersheba area.

Few outsiders realize now that the whole of the southern part of Israel as it stands today was won, not in the general fighting from May to July 1948, but by a deliberate violation of the United Nations Armistice in October 1948. The Israeli Army had been able to increase its strength in the interval by consignments of arms received from behind the Iron Curtain.

Israel was to be guilty of one more breach of the United Nations Armistice. Jordan had been in military occupation of the Wadi Araba since the end of the British Mandate in May 1948, and in August 1948, as already mentioned, the United Nations had arranged an armistice. In the autumn, Jordan and Israel concluded a separate agreement of their own covering the Jerusalem area, and representatives of the two countries met in Rhodes on April 3, 1949, to conclude a new armistice. While these direct Israel-Jordan negotiations were going on in Rhodes, suspicious Israeli troop movements were observed southeast of Beersheba. The Jordan Government cabled its delegation in Rhodes instructing it to ask for an Israeli explanation. The Israeli delegation vehemently denied any military movements. Three days later, however, while negotiations were still proceeding in Rhodes, the Israeli Army launched its offensive against the Jordan forces in the Wadi Araba, in defiance of the previous armistice agreements to which the Israel Government had subscribed, in contradiction of its own assurances given only three days before, and while its own delegation was negotiating with a Jordan Government delegation in Rhodes.

[…]

195

Report to the Provisional Government Concerning Military and Political Position of Israel (1948)
David Ben-Gurion

We have three objectives: Security, a Jewish State, and a pact between the Jews and the Arabs. Our goal must be not only the achievement of the first two, but eventually of the third as well. A pact between Jews and Arabs would, I believe, guarantee the fulfilment of Zionist aspirations and cause a revolutionary change in the Arab world. In any case, it would be extremely important for us.

I start with two basic assumptions: (1) The November 29 resolution is dead, or so it appears to me. Perhaps we may find ourselves in a situation where there is no alternative but to accept the November 29 resolution as the basis for a settlement, but I fail to see any enthusiastic supporters of the resolution, and if there are none, then it is indeed dead. (2) The dispute will be settled by force. The political question now is really a *military* one. This is so even in the unlikely event that fighting is not renewed. In any circumstances, military considerations will be dominant.

The war is not yet over; there is only a truce. If war begins again, it will be a life-death struggle *for us,* but not for them. We will obviously not exterminate the Egyptian people or the Syrian people. We could, I believe, destroy the Trans-Jordan Army and that part of the Egyptian Army sent here. But it is not our intention to slaughter the Egyptian people. However, if we are defeated, they will annihilate us. The Arabs have already arrested some hundred Jewish merchants in Baghdad on the charge that they were trading with Russia, though there is no law against trading with Russia. If they were to invade Tel Aviv, I am not at all sure that they would show mercy to its inhabitants. If war does begin again, we will be fighting for our lives. We cannot allow the Arabs to return to those places that they left.

The truce will be of value to us if it lasts for two months. We cannot accomplish a great deal in a month. We would also lose something by a two-month truce, but at its conclusion we would have a better organizational structure, as well as a trained and disciplined army.

I shall begin my discussion of other political questions with the Negev. The Negev differs from every other section of the country for a very simple reason: it is a 12-million-dunam (3-million-acre) area which is both empty and desolate. In ordinary circumstances, this would certainly be no great advantage. A settled area would ordinarily have been better, but not from our point of view. From a Zionist viewpoint, an empty and desolate area is better, because we can turn it into a flourishing center of Jewish settlement. We are dealing here not only with the Negev, but with the Dead Sea. You do not have to be an expert to realize the value of the Dead Sea.

The Dead Sea is a vast treasure house, particularly the southern part. The exact location of the Dead Sea is not important. The important thing is what we can extract from it and take somewhere else. South of the Dead Sea lies a flat area, the Arava, and then, finally, the Red Sea.

It is only natural that the Arabs should want Eilat, but we also want it. The Negev is an enormous Zionist asset, and there is no substitute for it anywhere else in the Land of Israel. First of all, it is half of the Land of Israel. There is no such thing as the northern and the southern Negev. The Negev is barren and empty now, and that is why it is important. We can create there a densely populated Jewish area, perhaps with room for millions of people. Moshe Smilansky thinks that it would be possible for 2 million Jews to make a living from farming in the Negev. If he is correct, then an additional 3 million could make a living from industry. The Jews who might be settled there are, unfortunately, not yet with us. Even so, the Negev still offers very great opportunities.

The central military issue is the struggle for Jerusalem. In my opinion, the outcome will determine the fate of the Land of Israel as a whole. This is true not only because of Jerusalem's historic importance, but also because of its strategic importance. It is not only the road to Jerusalem that is at stake. The war has shown us that Jerusalem cannot survive unless it is linked geographically with the Jewish State.

A third key area, as we all understand, is western Galilee.

We must begin working in Jaffa. Arab workers must be employed there, and at the same wages as Jewish workers. An Arab should also have the right to be elected President of the State. If a Jew or a Negro does not have the right to be President of the United States then I, for one, doubt the existence of civil rights there. But war is war. We did not start the war. The Arabs attacked us in Jaffa, Haifa, etc.; and I do not want those who fled to return. Everything that happens after the war will depend on the results of the war itself. While I oppose the return of the Arabs, I am for a pact with the Arab states after the war.

Our most serious potential problem is posed by Britain. I believe that we can stand up to the Arab world and the regular armies of the Arab states. But I doubt whether we could hold our own against the British Army. Therefore, I have always been against entering into a conflict with the British Army. Even as things stand, the British government is trying to strangle us. There were British commanders in Gezer and in Jerusalem, and the Arabs are using British weapons. The British are conducting a political campaign against us, because they feel that they have the Arabs in their pockets.

We will not solve our problems with the British unless we can win their political friendship. The British are a fine people, but they have suddenly turned against us because of the country's foreign policy. Eventually they will be forced to abandon their centers of power in the Middle East, and when that happens, we will be able to establish closer relationships with our Arab neighbors. If the Arabs are willing to negotiate, we should not stipulate territorial preconditions that would make it impossible for them to do so. The very meeting with the Arabs would be of value, even if it -did not achieve any positive results. It is important that the Syrians, Egyptians and Lebanese know what we want. It is vital that we meet, and therefore no preconditions should be set. I don't know if such a meeting will take place, but we must try to bring it about. However, it will become possible only when the Arabs and Bernadotte understand that two things are not negotiable: we will not consider either abolishing the State or restricting its independence. If they are ready to sit down with us, it is important that we should meet. Therefore, no hard-and-fast rules should be set as prerequisites to a meeting.

Jewish Terrorists Assassinate U.N. Peacekeeper Count Folke Bernadotte (1995)
Donald Neff

It was 47 years ago, Sept. 17, 1948, when Jewish terrorists assassinated Count Folke Bernadotte of Sweden as he sought to bring peace to the Middle East. His three-car convoy had been stopped at a small improvised roadblock in Jewish-controlled West Jerusalem when two gunmen began shooting out the tires of the cars and a third gunman thrust a Schmeisser automatic pistol through the open back window of Bernadotte's Chrysler. The 54-year-old diplomat, sitting on the right in the back, was hit by six bullets and died instantly. A French officer sitting next to Bernadotte was killed accidentally.

The assassins were members of Lehi (Lohamei Herut Israel—Fighters for the Freedom of Israel), better known as the Stern Gang. Its three leaders had decided a week earlier to have Bernadotte killed because they believed he was partial to the Arabs. One of those leaders was Yitzhak Shamir, who in 1983 would become prime minister of Israel.

Bernadotte had been chosen the United Nations mediator for Palestine four months earlier in what was the U.N.'s first serious attempt at peacemaking in the post-World War II world. As a hero of the war, when his mediation efforts on behalf of the International Red Cross saved 20,000 persons, including thousands of Jews, from Nazi concentration camps, Bernadotte seemed a natural choice for the post. [...]

It had been only on Nov. 29, 1947 that the U.N. General Assembly had voted to partition Palestine into Arab and Jewish states. Yet, as had been widely predicted, that action had led to war. Fighting intensified after elements of five Arab armies moved into Palestine the day after Israel proclaimed its establishment on May 14, 1948. Bernadotte's first action had been to arrange a truce, which lasted from June 11 to July 9.

During the lull, Bernadotte had put forward his first proposal for solving the conflict. Instead, it was to seal his fate. Bernadotte's transgression, in the view of Jewish zealots, was to include in his June 28 proposal the suggestion that Jerusalem be placed under Jordanian rule, since all the area around the city was designated for the Arab state.

The U.N. partition plan had declared Jerusalem an international city that was to be ruled by neither Arab nor Jew. But the Jewish terrorists, including Shamir and Menachem Begin, the leader of the largest terrorist group, Irgun Zvai Leumi—National Military Organization, also known by the Hebrew acronym "Etzel"—had rejected partition and claimed all of Palestine and Jordan for the Jewish state. These Jewish extremists were horrified at Bernadotte's suggestion.

From Washington Report on Middle East Affairs (Sept. 1995).   199
Reprinted with permission.

[...]

The assassination brought an official condemnation from the Israeli government and promises of quick arrests. However, no one was ever brought to trial nor was there any nationwide outcry against the assassination. None of Lehi's leaders or the actual gunmen were ever caught, although they were clearly known to Israel's leaders.

Israel's obvious reluctance to prosecute the assassins brought the first U.N. Security Council criticism of the new country. On Oct. 19, 1948, the council unanimously passed a resolution expressing its "concern" that Israel had "to date submitted no report to the Security Council or the Acting Mediator regarding the progress of the investigation into the assassination." An official inquiry by Sweden produced a report in 1950 that charged Israel's investigation had been so negligent that "doubt must exist as to whether the Israeli authorities really tried to bring the inquiry to a positive result."

Israel later admitted the laxity of its investigation and in 1950 paid the United Nations $54,628 in indemnity for Bernadotte's murder.

The assassination and Israel's failure to punish the culprits struck a hard blow against the fledgling United Nations. The first secretary-general, Trygve Lie, said: "If the Great Powers accepted that this situation in the Middle East could best be settled by leaving the forces concerned to fight it out amongst themselves, it was quite clear that they would be tacitly admitting that the Security Council and the United Nations was a useless instrument in attempting to preserve peace." To Secretary of State George Marshall, Lie had written on May 15, 1948 that Egypt had warned him it was about to send troops beyond its borders and against the Jewish state in Palestine, saying: "My primary concern is for the future usefulness of the United Nations and its Security Council...I must do everything to prevent this, otherwise the Security Council will have...created a precedent for any nation to take aggressive action in direct contravention to the Charter of the United Nations."

But, as author Kati Marton has observed: "If the United Nations spoke with 'considerable authority' early that summer, by fall its voice was barely above a whisper in Palestine. Unwilling or unable to enforce its own decisions, the U.N. [...] became for many Israelis in Ben-Gurion's memorable putdown, 'UNO, schmuno.'" She also observed: "So muted was the world body's reaction, so lacking in any real sanctions against the Jewish state for its failure to pursue the murderers of the United Nations' mediator, that for Israel, 'world opinion' became an empty phrase."
[...]

The Security Council,

Reaffirming its previous resolutions concerning the establishment and implementation of the truce in Palestine, and recalling particularly its resolution 54 (1948) of 15 July 1948 which determined that the situation in Palestine constitutes a threat to the peace within the meaning of Article 39 of the Charter of the United Nations,

Taking note that the General Assembly is continuing its consideration of the future government of Palestine in response to the request of the Security Council in its resolution 44 (1948) of 1 April 1948,

Without prejudice to the actions of the Acting Mediator regarding the implementation of Security Council resolution 61 (1948) of 4 November 1948,

1. *Decides* that, in order to eliminate the threat to the peace in Palestine and to facilitate the transition from the present truce to permanent peace in Palestine, an armistice shall be established in all sectors of Palestine;

2. *Calls upon* the parties directly involved in the conflict in Palestine, as a further provisional measure under Article 40 of the Charter, to seek agreement forthwith, by negotiations conducted either directly or through the Acting Mediator, with a view to the immediate establishment of the armistice, including:

(a) The delineation of permanent armistice demarcation lines beyond which the armed forces of the respective parties shall not move;

(b) Such withdrawal and reduction of their armed forces as will ensure the maintenance of the armistice during the transition to permanent peace in Palestine.

Resolution 194 – The Right of Return (1948)

UNITED NATIONS GENERAL ASSEMBLY

The General Assembly,

Having considered further the situation in Palestine,
[...]
11. *Resolves* that the refugees wishing to return to their homes and live at peace with their neighbours should be permitted to do so at the earliest practicable date, and that compensation should be paid for the property of those choosing not to return and for loss of or damage to property which, under principles of international law or in equity, should be made good by the Governments or authorities responsible;
[...]

General Armistice Agreements (1949)

[Israel executed armistice agreements with Egypt, Syria, Lebanon, and Jordan. These armistices were simultaneously negotiated through similar mediation frameworks and contain very similar language. The language produced here is common to all the agreements.].

Article I

[...]

1. The injunction of the Security Council against resort to military force in the settlement of the Palestine question shall henceforth be scrupulously respected by both Parties.

2. No aggressive action by the armed forces—land, sea, or air—of either Party shall be undertaken, planned, or threatened against the people or the armed forces of the other; it being understood that the use of the term "planned" in this context has no bearing on normal staff planning as generally practiced in military organizations.

3. The right of each Party to its security and freedom from fear of attack by the armed forces of the other shall be fully respected.

4. The establishment of an armistice between the armed forces of the two Parties is accepted as an indispensable step toward the liquidation of armed conflict and the restoration of peace in Palestine.

Article II

1. In pursuance of the foregoing principles and of the resolutions of the Security Council [...] a general armistice between the armed forces of the two Parties—land, sea and air—is hereby established.

2. No element of the land, sea or air military or para-military forces of either Party, including non-regular forces, shall commit any warlike or hostile act against the military or para-military forces of the other Party, or against civilians in territory under the control of that Party; or shall advance beyond or pass over for any purpose whatsoever the Armistice Demarcation Line set forth in [...] this Agreement [...]; and elsewhere shall not violate the international frontier; or enter into or pass through the air space of the other Party or through the waters within three miles of the coastline of the other Party.

[...]

Article IV

With specific reference to the implementation of the resolutions of the Security Council [...], the following principles and purposes are affirmed:

1. The principle that no military or political advantage should be gained under the truce ordered by the Security Council is recognized.

2. It is also recognized that the basic purposes and spirit of the Armistice would not be served by the restoration of previously held military positions, changes from those now held other than as specifically provided for in this Agreement, or by the advance of the military forces of either side beyond positions held at the time this Armistice Agreement is signed.

3. It is further recognized that rights, claims or interests of a nonmilitary character in the area of Palestine covered by this Agreement may be asserted by either Party, and that these, by mutual agreement being excluded from the Armistice negotiations, shall be, at the discretion of the Parties, the subject of later settlement. It is emphasized that it is not the purpose of this Agreement to establish, to recognize, to strengthen, or to weaken or nullify, in any way, any territorial, custodial or other rights, claims or interests which may be asserted by either Party in the area of Palestine or any part or locality thereof covered by this Agreement, whether such asserted rights, claims or interests derive from Security Council resolutions [...] or from any other source. The provisions of this Agreement are dictated exclusively by military considerations and are valid only for the period of the Armistice.

Article V

1. The line described in [...] this Agreement shall be designated as the Armistice Demarcation Line and is delineated in pursuance of the purpose and intent of the resolutions of the Security Council [....]

2. The Armistice Demarcation Line is not to be construed in any sense as a political or territorial boundary, and is delineated without prejudice to rights, claims and positions of either Party to the Armistice as regards ultimate settlement of the Palestine question.

3. The basic purpose of the Armistice Demarcation Line is to delineate the line beyond which the armed forces of the respective Parties shall not move except as provided in [...] this Agreement.

4. Rules and regulations of the armed forces of the Parties, which prohibit civilians from crossing the fighting lines or entering the area between the lines, shall remain in effect after the signing of this Agreement with application to the Armistice Demarcation Line. [...]

Article XI

No provision of this Agreement shall in any way prejudice the rights, claims and positions of either Party hereto in the ultimate peaceful settlement of the Palestine question.
[...]

The Current Situation in Israel (1949)
CENTRAL INTELLIGENCE AGENCY

[…] Within little more than a year, the Israelis have set up a democratic government of their own, created an outstanding military force, driven back the Arab armies, and embarked on an ambitious economic development program. […]

Despite these successes, Israel is beset by serious problems. The attempt to create a viable economy is frankly based on the assumption that foreign aid will continue to be forthcoming for years to come. The financial costs of the war and of the current armed truce are heavy. The high rate of immigration that the government is committed to maintaining has already created economic and social strains [....] A diminution of foreign aid or failure of Israel's plans for developing both foreign markets and agricultural self-sufficiency would create major economic difficulties. Fundamental among these problems is the fact that Israel remains ostracized by the Arab states along its still undetermined borders. […]

4. Foreign Affairs

a. RELATIONS WITH THE ARAB STATES

Israel is at war with the Arab states. Although no serious hostilities have occurred since January 1949, the relationship in every other particular between the two antagonists is one of deep distrust and for the most part implacable enmity, and the threat of renewed hostilities in one sector or another is ever present. Neither diplomatic nor economic representatives are exchanged, the only official contact between Jews and Arabs being on a military level in armistice or peace negotiations. Israel's land frontiers are sealed, and trade with the Arab world is non-existent. Egypt refuses to permit ships destined for Israel to traverse the Suez Canal, and Iraq refuses to allow Iraq Petroleum Company oil to flow through the pipeline to Haifa. Although the Arabs remaining in Israel have been permitted to participate (at least nominally) in political activity, the great majority are discriminated against economically. Many have been treated as enemy aliens, and some have been, and continue to be, driven from their homes and land to swell the refugee rolls in the neighboring Arab states. Although the treatment of the indigenous Jewish communities in the Arab countries has been remarkably mild considering the passions that have been aroused, the tendency to tar all Jews with the Zionist brush has increased their fear that they will reap the whirlwind their Western-supported co-religionists have sown in Palestine.
[…]

[L]ittle basis for agreement between the Jews and Arabs exists. The main questions at issue are the Arab refugees, and Israel's frontiers. On the first question, the Arabs insist that Israel carry out the provisions of the 11 December 1948 General Assembly resolution which stated that those refugees wishing to return to their homes be permitted to do so and those who did not wish to return be compensated for their lost property. Israel, on the other hand, disclaims any responsibility for the refugees, asserting that they all fled of their own volition. Furthermore, Israel has frankly stated that the refugees have no homes to return to, inasmuch as their homes have either been destroyed or occupied by recent Jewish immigrants. Irrespective of the various arguments regarding ultimate responsibility for the refugee problem, there is little doubt that Israel has now taken deliberate steps permanently to reduce the Arab section of its population to a minimum and that, consequently, the great majority of the 800,000 Arab refugees will have to be resettled outside Israel. This fact alone will embitter relations between Israel and the Arab states for many years to come.

On the question of Israel's frontiers, the Arabs and Jews are as divided as on the refugee question. During the course of the fighting Israel occupied considerable territory allocated to the Arabs under the General Assembly partition plan, i.e. Western Galilee, a broad strip between Jerusalem and Tel Aviv, Jaffa, and areas on the Dead Sea and the Egyptian frontiers. Under the terms of the armistice agreement with Jordan, Israel took over additional territory in central Palestine. On top of all these gains, Israel has now publicly stated that it would like to obtain the Gaza strip from Egypt, additional areas in central Palestine and Jerusalem from Jordan, and possibly at some future date a strip of territory in southern Lebanon. It is, furthermore, demanding the Syrian-held salient of Mishmar hay Yarden, the only territory originally allotted to the Jews by the partition plan which is now occupied by an Arab state. […]

Although the Arab states would probably now be willing to settle for the original partition boundaries, they also have additional territorial claims. While Egypt might be willing to give up the Gaza strip, provided Israel at the same time took over responsibility for the 200,000 refugees therein, the Egyptians will probably also demand considerable territory in the Negeb in compensation. King Abdullah of Jordan continues to demand a corridor to the Mediterranean and a port thereon, as well as the former Arab towns of Jaffa, Lydda, and Ramle and Arab suburbs around Jerusalem. Syria demands that Israel give up Western Galilee and has even advanced the proposition that Eastern Galilee should also be given up in order to connect Western Galilee with Syria. […] These Israeli and Arab claims are so conflicting that it is difficult to see how they can be reconciled.
[…]

206

The Arab Refugee Problem (1949)
CENTRAL INTELLIGENCE AGENCY

The war in Palestine has produced an Arab refugee problem comparable to the Jewish DP problem which the establishment of the Jewish state was partly intended to alleviate. Although Arab-Jewish hostilities have for the most part ceased, the problem posed by the Arab refugees from Israel now in neighboring Arab lands is threatening not only the truce and the possibility of a compromise solution in Palestine but also the stability of the entire Arab world. Unless these refugees can be swiftly and adequately care for, they will swell the ranks of the Arab extremists and possibly prevent the establishment of an effective Arab-Jewish agreement for many years to come.

UN Mediator Bernadotte has estimated that the refugees number between 300,000 and 400,000. Approximately 100,000 are believed to be in Transjordan; 65,000 in Syria; 55,000 in Lebanon; 25,000 in Egypt; and the remaining 100,000 in the Arab-occupied areas of Palestine. The provisional Government of Israel has stated that it will not permit any of the refugees to return their homes until a definitive settlement of the Palestine issue has been reached and then only under such restriction that few Arabs will qualify for repatriation.

The neighboring Arab states have neither the economic resources nor the political stability to absorb the Arab refugees peacefully. The poverty of arable land in the Arab states is chronic, and no state can afford to launch large resettlement projects land reclamation. An exchange of populations might solve the problem, but such a solution would raise other serious difficulties. The eviction of the Jews from the major Arab cities, in which they form sizeable minorities, would entail further economic dislocation. If Israel were to receive the 200,000 Jews in Arab lands as well as the 200,000 DP's from Europe, its area would have to be expanded far beyond the UN partition boundaries. Such a development would still further exacerbate Arab feelings and would, therefore, contribute little to no ultimate solution of the Palestine issue.

Temporary relief for the Arab refugees can be facilitated through substantial assistance from the Internation Red Cross, the International Refugee Organization, and the Arab League. However, a permanent solution of the problem, involving the whole question of the future of Palestine, would probably require positive action by the UN.

Palestinians in Jordan, 1948-1967
Jalal Al Husseini

After the 1948 Palestine War, the geographic and demographic structures of Jordan were entwined with those of Palestine. In April 1950 the Hashemite Kingdom of Jordan formally annexed the former Palestinian districts of Jenin, Nablus, Tulkarm, Ramallah, East Jerusalem, and Hebron (thereafter grouped under the label of "West Bank") that had fallen under its control during the conflict. Unlike the other Arab countries that hosted Palestinian refugees, Jordan granted citizenship to both indigenous West Bankers and Palestinian refugees. The 1954 Nationality Law stipulated that citizenship would be granted to "any person who, not being Jewish, possessed Palestinian nationality before 15 May 1948 and resides ordinarily in the Hashemite Kingdom of Jordan on the publication date of this law."

In May 1946, the Emirate of Transjordan (i.e. the East Bank of the Jordan River) had gained independence from Great Britain and was named the Hashemite Kingdom of Jordan. As a result of the "unification of the two Banks," Jordan's land mass grew by 5,640 km^2 (a mere 1/16th of the Transjordan territory). The demographic and political impacts of the unification were more significant, however: In 1949, the West Bank had a population of 740,000, including 280,000 refugees, and the East Bank had a population of 470,000, including 70,000 refugees. Taken together, the population of Jordan exceeded 1.2 million inhabitants, two-thirds of whom were of Palestinian origin (Jordanian-Palestinians).

The annexation of the West Bank by Jordan was supported by some Palestinians, who were coopted into abandoning the nationalist stream of Palestinian politics led by the Mufti of Palestine Haj Amin al-Husseini. The union materialized through the "gentlemen's agreement" concluded between King Abdullah I and pro-Hashemite Palestinian notables in a series of conferences. During the Jericho Conference held on 1 December 1948, which was attended by mayors of several West Bank towns, the conference participants asked Jordan to annex the regions of Palestine it actually administered.

The assimilation of the Palestinians within Jordan was facilitated by their integration in the country's political system. […] In January 1952, a new constitution enacted by the Parliament promoted the equality of all Jordanians before the law, regardless of their race, language or religion. The "Jordanization" process was reinforced through a "de-Palestinization" policy: the term "Palestine" was banned from all official documents in May 1950, and Jordan's official school curriculum promoted the idea of the unified Kingdom as a "little Arab homeland."

A Qualified Assimilation

Yet, from the outset the Palestinian refugees were politically singled out as persons claiming a "right of return" to their original homes. [...] Until the mid-1960s, references to Palestine were coupled with the principle of the right of return, which rapidly became a rallying cry within the entire Arab world that all Arab states, including Jordan, were compelled to endorse publicly.

This also entailed espousing the Palestinian refugees' view of UNRWA, the UN agency established in 1949 "to carry out direct relief and works programmes" for registered Palestinian refugees, most of whom were farmers and unskilled workers, while promoting their socioeconomic reintegration in the local economies. Conceived by the United Nations as a humanitarian agency, UNRWA soon came to symbolize the international community's commitment to solve the refugee issue along the guidelines of Resolution 194.

Because of the politicization of UNRWA's mandate, a sizeable segment of Jordan's population was thus granted two potentially conflictual sources of identification: Jordan, as a (temporary) state; and Palestine, the homeland to which they aspired to return. The resulting ambiguity has been most palpable among camp refugees (18 percent of the refugee population in Jordan): categorized as the neediest refugees, they are often regarded as the guardians of the memory of the "lost Palestine" and of Palestinian identity in exile, and the ultimate custodians of the "right of return." As a result, although they hold full Jordanian citizenship, their socioeconomic status as structurally underprivileged people has brought Jordanian observers to deny them the Jordanian-Palestinian label in favor of the "Palestinian" or "Palestinian refugee" labels.

A Durable Coexistence

The hybrid political status of the "Jordanian-Palestinians" neither prevented their integration nor genuinely destabilized the Kingdom. Nationalist Palestinians resented Jordan's annexation of the West Bank and the ensuing naturalization of the Palestinian refugees and of West Bank residents. This resentment was reflected in the assassination of King Abdullah I in Jerusalem in 1951. [...]

Despite these tensions, the key objectives of Jordan's assimilatory policies were fulfilled. One of them aimed at the Palestinians' full involvement in the country's development, and more particularly that of the East Bank that benefitted from the bulk of public investments in the 1950s and 1960s. Demographic data illustrate the steady migration of the West Bankers toward the East Bank, mainly Amman [....]

Plunder in the Holy Land (1950)
Henry Cattan

"We lost everything," say Palestine refugees – "and time will not bring acceptance of Israel's gun-point thievery." Here a Palestinian legal authority tells why.

[...]

The Israeli success over the unorganized Arab inhabitants of Palestine [...] enabled the Israelis to seize 70% of the area of Palestine—that is, almost double the area allotted to them by the United Nations. [...] They now occupy whole Arab cities, tens of thousands of Arab homes and thousands of Arab villages with their lands and groves.

The majority of the Israeli population today lives in Arab houses. Over 90% of the Israeli cultivation live on Arab-owned land. Arab citrus and olive groves which were taken over by the Israeli government account for the largest percentage of the government's income from foreign exports.
[...]

The first fact that must be considered is the ownership of such areas occupied by Israel beyond the limits and boundaries assigned to them. The following table gives this information:

Area	Arabs	Jews	State or Other
Western Galilee	87%	3%	10%
Jerusalem Area	99%	1%	
Ramleh and Lydda Areas	77%	14%	9%
Hebron Area	96%	1%	3%

The figures just quoted are [...] based on official figures and records of ownership of land.
[...]

The value of Arab properties now seized by the Israelis is tremendous. Although no proper estimate has ever been made of such properties yet the figure runs between 15 and 16 billion dollars.

In 1950 the UN Conciliation Commission for Palestine set up a Committee of Experts to evaluate Arab properties in Israel. This Committee, disregarding market prices and established values, proceeded to evaluate Arab agricultural lands and urban properties on the basis of their notional tax value as it stood in the tax books as of the year 1947. Instead of attempting to ascertain what the value was, it attempted to lay down what the value should be naturally, in favor of Israel.

By this arbitrary method, the Committee arrived at the ridiculous figure of 100 million sterling, a sum which represents about 2½% of the real market value of Arab properties in Israel. The figure suggested by this Committee is equivalent to confiscation rather than compensation.

210

When one recalls that the Jews had before the of the Mandate, spent several times that amount in order to acquire less than 7% of the land of Palestine, one clearly realizes that the figure suggested is quite unreasonable as being the value of the remainder of the area, with the addition of a few Arab cities like Jerusalem. Jaffa, Haifa, Lydda, Ramleh, and Safad, and a few thousand villages and thousands of orange, olive and fruit groves. It goes without saying that this incongruous evaluation was rejected by the Arabs.

At present, many persons, unaware or unconscious of the magnitude of Arab assets in Palestine, talk of compensation. Even if the principle of compensation were to be acceptable to Arab refugees—a fact which the Arabs do not concede because the Arabs prefer to recover their homes and lands rather than be compensated—therefore the compensation if it is to be adequate and commensurate with the value of such properties is clearly beyond the financial means of Israel.

In any event, the question of compensation in respect of Arab properties cannot be considered in relation to Arab properties in Jerusalem (which is subject to internationalization) or to areas of Palestine occupied by Israel beyond the boundaries of the UN resolution on partition. Any discussion as to compensation in such areas is an indirect attempt to attribute to Israel title to territories held by it in contravention of and in contemptuous defiance to resolutions of this international assembly. The questions of compensation should, therefore, be so circumscribed.

Moreover, compensation can only be discussed when the Arab refugees are allowed to exercise the right, recognized in principle by the UN but denied in practice by Israel, of returning to their homes. Only in the case of such refugees as decline to exercise the right to return would the question of compensation arise.

[…]

Arab properties are at present vested in the Israeli Custodian of Absentee Properties. Absentee means Palestine Arabs and includes subjects or residents of Lebanon, Egypt, Syria, Saudi Arabia, Jordan, Iraq, or Yemen. The Custodian leases and administers Arab properties, he may even, in certain cases, sell or transfer the right of ownership thereto. The produce of vested properties is itself vested in the Custodian. Such produce is charged with taxes, rates, administration expenses and repairs.

Such is the picture in relation to real property. The question of movables is somewhat different. It is well known that by reason of the sudden aggravation of events in 1948, most of the refugees left their homes, shops and businesses without being able to take any of their effects or belongings with them. Some 200,000 Arab homes were looted by Israel and Israelis. Some of those homes were rich, full of silver, carpets and furs; many were modest, many more were poor.

The fact however, remains that an organized and general pillage of Arab homes occurred which left no traces of the effects and belongings of over 900,000 Arabs. The same story may be told of the contents of thousands of Arab stores, shops and offices. Some goods were seized by the Israeli authorities but the larger part was allowed to be pillaged.

[...]

The General Assembly of the United Nations, on December 11, 1948, passed a resolution recommending the following measures:

(1) That refugees be permitted to return to their homeland;

(2) That compensation be paid in respect of the properties of those that do not wish to return;

(3) That compensation be paid in respect of damages and losses relating to property which is recoverable in accordance with principles of international law, equity and justice from the governments or authorities concerned.

What has happened since the date of that resolution? **Nothing!** Not one refugee was permitted to return and not one piastre was paid as compensation. Israel is not disposed to permit Arab refugees to return to their homes or to pay them compensation.

[...]

Israel has, however, been doing a lot. It has destroyed some two hundred villages (including their churches and mosques) and wiped them completely from the surface of the earth [....] It has uprooted thousands of acres of Arab orange groves.

It is actively and gradually confiscating Arab properties. This is how it is done. In March 1953, Israel passed the Land Acquisition Law. Under this law, power is given to expropriate Arab properties and register them in the name of the Israeli authorities. A nominal amount as compensation is evaluated in favor of the owner and then such amount is vested in the Custodian. This method of acquisition of the properties of Arab refugees is made to look, in appearance, like a legal expropriation, but in fact and in substance, it is a blatant confiscation. Arab properties are thus gradually passing into Israeli ownership without the UN lifting a finger or raising its voice.

The Arabs do not recognize Israel. Nor do they recognize anything done by it. Whether it take the form of expropriation or confiscation Israel is literally settled in another man's home. It has bolted the door and fixed guns at all windows fearing the return of the owner and his family. This large scale robbery of the homeland of a million Arab refugees will never be accepted. Such an injustice cannot go unrequited.

[...]

212

Violence on the Jordan-Israel Border: A Jordanian View (1954)
Lieutenant-General J. B. Glubb

The Israeli conquest of the Negeb (the Jews spell the word Negev) produced a new wave of refugees who sought asylum in Jordan. This was not the case, however, in the neighborhood of Beersheba; although that district was principally inhabited by Arab tribes, these were farmers despite the fact that they lived in tents. Homogeneous tribal communities like these did not panic and take to flight as did the individual citizens of the towns and villages further north. Israel took over control of the Beersheba area, but the tribes remained on their lands.

In the subsequent two years the great majority of these tribes were evicted by the Israeli authorities. Since such an eviction was contrary to the terms of the armistice signed at Rhodes it was not carried out by direct military action. The tribes were living and cultivating their own lands, but the Mandatory Government had not yet carried out complete land settlement of the area. Consequently individuals did not hold title deeds for their land, although the boundaries of tribal areas had been demarcated. This situation gave the Israeli authorities an opportunity. They began on various pretexts to move these tribes from place to place. They refused to admit the right of the tribes to ownership of tribal lands, and ordered them to live in other and less fertile areas. In some cases, tribes were allowed to plough and sow their land, and when the crop was above ground, the tribe was moved to another area and the crop was harvested by the Jews.

By such means life was made economically impossible for the Beersheba Arab tribes. At this stage, hints were dropped that perhaps the tribesmen would be happier in Jordan. If the suggestion was not welcomed they were moved once more, perhaps to a rocky hillside where life was virtually impossible. Eventually when a tribe "opted" to migrate into Jordan, the Israeli Government was careful to secure a signature from the chief to the effect that they had migrated voluntarily. In this manner the Israeli Government succeeded in getting rid of most of the tribes of the Beersheba plains and in taking over their lands. There is no doubt that this action was contrary to the spirit of the armistice. It was carried out by making life administratively and economically impossible for the Arabs in question. [...]

Let us now return to the refugees from the cities and villages of the coastal plain and the foothills of Judaea and Samaria. When the fighting ended with the signature of the Israel-Jordan armistice agreement in April 1948, most of these refugees were huddled in camps or scattered in caves in the rocky hills of Judaea and Samaria. Many of them could actually see their homes and their farms, their cottages and their possessions in their houses. In a great many cases, families had become divided. Old people unable to

Used with permission of Foreign Affairs, from FOREIGN AFFAIRS, Vol. 32, No. 4 (July 1, 1954); permission conveyed through Copyright Clearance Center, Inc.

escape had stayed behind. A wife had fled with her children when her husband had been away at work, and so on.

A naïve idea also prevailed amongst Arab villagers when the armistice was signed that the troubles were over and they could now go home and resume their normal lives. [...] [N]o sooner was the Rhodes armistice signed in April 1949 than a number of the refugees walked across the armistice line into Israel and made for their homes. All or nearly all were unarmed, and their intentions were perfectly innocently to collect their possessions, to search for their relatives or just plainly to "go home." The presence of these Arabs in Israel had, however, caused the Jews one of their principal anxieties at the beginning. They had got rid of them by ruthless methods, and they were certainly not going to allow them back.

[...] A great number of them were shot dead, without question or answer, by the first Israeli patrol they met. Others were maltreated or tortured.

[...] Israeli violence did not put an end to "infiltration." Instead, the innocent attempts of the refugees to find their relatives or to collect their property [...] assumed the proportions of a problem.

When it became clear that the Israelis would shoot on sight any Arab who crossed the armistice line, the number of persons crossing with no evil intent decreased. But the few who for one reason or another still went did so fully armed, and if they saw Israelis coming they shot first. What might have been a passport offense, a nuisance, was unnecessarily magnified by the brutal methods employed.

Not all so-called infiltrators were of this type, however. By occupying the Beersheba area down to the Gulf of Aqaba, Israel had severed the land passage joining Asia to Africa. The so-called Gaza strip, formerly a part of Palestine, was cut off from Arab Palestine and Jordan. There was no way of getting from Jordan, Syria or Lebanon to Gaza and to Egypt except by air, for such as could afford it. Those who could not pay for an air passage walked across the Israel-held Beersheba area in the hours of darkness. They did so for many reasons, but they did not do so to injure the Jews-- merely because they had business on the other side. Some were engaged in perfectly legitimate trade, and drove pack animals loaded with rice, sugar or consumer goods. Some were smugglers. Some were traffickers in forbidden drugs. Some came from Gaza to Jordan to look for work. None of these persons who crossed the Beersheba area wished to attack the Jews, but Israeli patrols frequently intercepted and killed them. And as the numbers of killed increased, so did the numbers of embittered persons mount up. Men whose fathers, brothers, sons or even wives and daughters had been killed on the Gaza caravans longed for revenge. Some of them went back to kill a Jew to pay off the debt. [...]

The armistice line itself produced other varieties of "infiltration." In many cases, the line divided a man's home from his orchard. If he went out to pick an apple in his own garden, he was shot dead as an infiltrator. […] The resulting incidents were described by the Israelis as armed incursions of bandits.

There were other sorts of "infiltration." A certain Arab family had remained in Israel, and they had a son 15 years old. The boy refused to finish his education in Israel. He "infiltrated" into Jordan and went to college. At vacation times, he "infiltrated" back to Israel to see his parents. Or take another example. The women of the Moslem Arab tribes of South Palestine were used to being veiled and to wearing long sweeping skirts. They could not at once accustom themselves to wearing the European clothes and short skirts which were the only ones to be bought in Israel. Their husbands "infiltrated" to Jordan to buy them their traditional Arab clothes. Such examples could be multiplied almost indefinitely. Most of these cases were the inevitable result of the sudden violent bisection of a country which had been one for eight centuries. Inevitably all sorts of complicated problems and conflicting interests required settlement. […]

When the Israeli Government discovered that shooting the infiltrators did not put an end to infiltration, they took refuge in military reprisals. These at first were on a small scale. A party of eight or ten Israeli soldiers would cross into Jordan and approach a small village; the first one or two persons encountered would be killed, and the patrol would return across the armistice line. Sometimes the patrols came across at night and threw hand grenades into the windows of houses, sometimes killing women and children in their beds. In these reprisals the Israelis almost invariably killed the innocent.

The Israeli Government, seeing that its reprisals by military patrols were not effective, did not apparently conclude that its policy was wrong. It decided to use more force. Platoon attacks by the Israeli Army became the order of the day. Against these military attacks on their villages, the Jordan authorities organized the National Guard to defend the villages. The Israeli platoon attacks were repulsed. The Israelis then stepped up their reprisals by using companies of infantry supported by mortars. The Jordan Government then began to put barbed-wire entanglements around frontier villages. The Israeli Army replied by using battalions, bombarding the villages with mortars and using detachments of engineers to blow a path through the barbed wire. Other engineers carried prepared charges, which they laid in the captured village and blew down the houses into heaps of rubble.
[…]
Jordan has constantly pressed for frequent meetings of police officers all up and down the border line. It is confident that by steady police coöperation of this kind, together with full exchange of information

between the two police forces, infiltration can be reduced to a minimum. On one or two occasions when Israeli and Jordanian police officers on either side of the border have "got together," incidents in their area have virtually ceased, a fact which seems amply to confirm the Jordan thesis. But Jordan has been preaching for five years to deaf ears.

In the absence of coöperation from Israel, Jordan has made the most strenuous efforts to prevent civilians from crossing the line. A great many arrests have been made in the past five years, and many hundreds of persons are in prison on charges of infiltration. […]

In this connection, it is worthy of note that in international practice every nation is responsible for the prevention of illegal entry into its frontiers. If a Canadian citizen should enter the United States illegally, the Government of the United States does not make a diplomatic protest to Canada. It merely tightens up its own frontier precautions. Israel, however, claims on the contrary that Jordan is solely responsible for preventing Jordanians from entering Israel illegally. Jordan constantly expresses her readiness to coöperate with Israel in doing so. But Israel, while refusing such coöperation in practical terms, claims that Jordan is solely to blame. […]

It is not my intention, however, to deny that infiltration has taken place in the past and that thefts of farm animals, water piping and a few other items have occurred. The articles stolen are usually such as are left out in the fields at night. But reference to United Nations statistics reveals that a high proportion of articles stolen are returned by the Jordan police. As against these thefts, Israeli Army patrols have an awkward habit of driving off Jordanian flocks of sheep. On the whole, the value of property lost by the two sides is often roughly the same. There is, however, a difference. Thefts from Israel by Jordanians are carried out by thieves, who are nearly all destitute refugees evicted from Israel. The looting of Jordan flocks is carried out by patrols of the Israeli Army.

The activities of the Israeli Army are not, however, limited to the occasional looting of sheep. Infinitely more serious, and in fact the root of the whole problem, are the military attacks on Jordanian villages carried out by units of the Israeli Army. The now notorious attack on Qibya village in October 1953 was only a peculiarly bloody example of the kind of "reprisal" attack carried out again and again by the Israeli Army for the past five years. In these attacks, men, women and children are slaughtered indiscriminately. Sometimes also the village is deliberately destroyed with explosives.

[…] As an Arab delegate recently said in New York, "Israel cannot shoot her way to peace."
[…]

216

Israel's Border and Security Problems (1955)
Major-General Moshe Dayan

The effects of geographical vulnerability are aggravated by the fierce antagonism directed against Israel across her embattled frontiers. There is no other state in the world community whose very right to existence is so persistently challenged by all its contiguous neighbors. This is not the classic pattern of international conflict in which neighboring peoples recognize each other's statehood but are divided by specific disputes which they have failed to reconcile. The hostility of the Arab Governments towards Israel is more fundamental. [...]

In 1949 a series of armistice agreements were concluded under United Nations auspices between Israel and each of the Arab states which had participated in the war, with the exception of Iraq. [...]

No sooner had the Arab states recovered from the shock of Israel's successful resistance than they began to question the character of the Armistice Agreements as a phase in the progress towards a final settlement. So far from regarding them as an arrangement "to facilitate the transition to permanent peace," the Arab signatories, in a joint statement issued on April 1, 1950, pledged themselves not to conduct peace negotiations with Israel and declared that any Arab state doing so would be treated as a traitor and an outcast. Subsequent policy has been in full accord with that declaration. [...]

This concept of Israel as a temporary bridgehead to be eliminated by war or blockade still dominates Arab official utterances. "In demanding the restoration of the refugees to Palestine," wrote Muhammad Salah-ad-Din, a former Foreign Minister of Egypt, "... the Arabs intend to annihilate the State of Israel." No less outspoken was King Saud in a statement made in Riadh soon after his accession to the throne: "The only way which the Arab states must go is to draw Israel up by her roots. Why should we not sacrifice 10,000,000 out of 50,000,000 Arabs so that we may live in greatness and honor?" Against this mood of war and revenge, reason has little chance of prevailing. "The Jews are our enemies," Baghdad Radio told its listeners on June 28, 1949, "and it does not matter how peace-loving they may be. We shall never cease to prepare for the day of reckoning, for the second round, when the Jews will be driven off our soil." [...]

Nor has Arab hostility been confined to warlike propaganda. From the very inception of the state of Israel, an economic boycott has been enforced against it by the Arab states, of which the most significant aspect is the closing of the Suez Canal to all Israel shipping and the interference with the passage of ships of other nations carrying cargoes to Israel. This action of the Egyptian Government is a violation of the Constantinople

Convention of 1888 under which the power contiguous to the Suez Canal is bound to keep the Canal "always ... free and open in time of war as in time of peace to every vessel of commerce or of war without distinction of flag." The Security Council of the United Nations on September 1, 1951, ruled that under the Armistice Agreement neither party could assert that it was actively a belligerent or entitled to exercise the right of visit, search and seizure. The Council found that Egyptian interference with the passage through the Suez Canal of goods destined for Israel was "inconsistent with the purpose of the Armistice Agreement" and "an abuse of the exercise of the right of visit, search and seizure." It called upon Egypt to terminate all such restrictions. No heed has been paid to this decision and the Egyptian blockade has recently taken the form of the flagrant seizure of an unarmed Israel ship in the international waterway.

A widely ramified boycott machinery has been set up with headquarters in Cairo to prevent trade between the Arab states and Israel, indeed between Israel and other countries. International firms trading with Israel are blacklisted, airlines and shipping companies are denied servicing in Arab airports and harbors if they maintain contact with Israel. [...] Danger to international air traffic has been caused by the refusal of Arab airports to provide flight information to aircraft proceeding to or from Israel. The boycott of the Arab states against Israel extends even to the denial of information on the movement of infectious diseases or locusts. [...]

Moreover, Israel faces these manifold dangers with no sure prospect of assistance from any quarter. Israel is not integrated into any system of defense pacts or security guarantees. The Arab League Collective Security Pact, the British treaties with Iraq, Jordan and Egypt, the defense association growing up around Turkey and Pakistan, and American arms and agreements in the Middle East are all oriented exclusively towards the Arab states and are based on Israel's exclusion. [...]

This policy of one-sided reinforcement of Israel's neighbors appears to the Israel people as a deviation from the best standards of international morality or prudence. It also implies a retreat by the Western Powers from the undertakings contained in the Tripartite Declaration of May 1950, under which they pledged themselves to maintain the military balance between the Arab states and Israel and to enable "Israel and the Arab states" (not the Arab states alone) to contribute to the defense of the area against aggression.

These policies increase the existing advantage which the Arabs possess as a result of their geographic and demographic preponderance. They have vast expanses of territory and vital strategic strongpoints. They have huge resources of oil. They have enormous reserves of manpower. Their financial and economic resources are vastly superior to those of Israel. These advantages may or may not be reflected in their current military posture. But this is of small moment. In discussing a regional security problem the criterion is one of basic potential, not of current military strength; and in such terms the Arab states possess an advantage even without the treaties and arms agreements showered on them and withheld from Israel by the United States and Britain. [...]

It is against this background that the specific problem of border insecurity, of marauding and infiltration, should be viewed. An intermittent guerrilla war on Israel's borders, especially those with Jordan and the Egyptian-occupied Gaza-strip, is the spearhead of comprehensive hostility. [...]

The process of "infiltration" began in the period immediately following the conclusion of the Armistice Agreements. It was at first a sporadic trickle of illegal crossings actuated in part by motives of family reunion. Efforts made by Israel to regulate this movement by agreement with the Arab states failed owing to the Arab refusal to legalize any transit of persons between their respective territories and Israel. As a result, these illegal crossings became a regular practice, which after a time degenerated into wholesale infiltration accompanied by theft and smuggling. The Government of Israel first took no steps to suppress this movement, regarding it as a temporary phase. It also put into operation an official scheme of its own for the reunion of Arab families separated by the war, and as a result several thousand Arabs have rejoined their kinsfolk in Israel. Contrary to expectations, however, the movement showed no sign of abating. Thefts, robbery, hold-ups and eventually murder and sabotage became of frequent occurrence. As the border region became more tense with constant violence, the Israeli villagers in the area were authorized to organize their own defense against invaders.

It has been asserted quite wrongly that this infiltration is conducted primarily by refugees. The nightly incursions into Israel territory, which in most cases show careful planning, are not the work of destitute refugees but of highly trained gunmen acting on paramilitary lines. They openly sell their booty in the markets of the Arab border towns, not infrequently sharing their gains with the appointed organs of security. In a number of cases, where the Israel authorities supplied to the Arab Governments data on the identity and the crimes of the infiltrators, these were not brought to trial, and only rarely have the stolen goods been returned.

There can be little doubt that much of this guerrilla war is of a military character. The targets chosen, the form of attack, the types of arms used and the methods employed indicate that many of these raids are planned on military lines. The setting of mines, the ambushing of watchmen and firing at guards are clearly not the work of hapless refugees. In more than one case the raids have been well synchronized and carefully planned military operations executed with a high degree of precision. This campaign affords first class opportunities for instructing men in guerrilla tactics, gathering military information and making the raiders familiar with the territory in which the "second round" may one day be fought.

The dimensions which the guerrilla war against Israel has assumed in recent years may be gathered from the following data. From 1949 to the middle of 1954 there have been an average of 1,000 cases of infiltration per month along the several frontiers, the majority of them on the Israel-Jordan border. The number of clashes with armed marauders on the latter border alone amounted during the last four years to 1,069, the incidents of theft, burglary and armed robbery to 3,573. Livestock, seed, fertilizers, agricultural implements and irrigation pipes have been among the principal booty of these marauding expeditions. Miles of telephone wires have been stolen and telephone poles destroyed, while the cutting of electric wires has seriously interfered with agricultural and industrial activities. All this material damage, however, is overshadowed by the fearful toll of human life. On the Jordan border alone 513 Israelis were killed and wounded during the past four years. […]

Many of the attacks have occurred not along the "frontier" but deep inside Israel territory. The innumerable wadis and tracks covered by sand make it easy for raiders to enter and escape undetected. Not infrequently Israel watchmen and border police wounded by shots have been dragged across the frontier and cruelly done to death, their mutilated bodies then being presented as evidence of Israel aggression against Jordan. The Jordan Government has distributed arms and ammunition to village youths in the border areas, labelling them "National Guards," without effective control or training. Its agreement has not yet been received for any radical measures to stop guerrilla activities along the border, such as the regular policing of the area, the division of no man's land or the marking of the armistice line. According to a report of the Chief of Staff of the Truce Supervision Organization to the Secretary-General of the U.N., dated October 30, 1952, no effective system of frontier demarcation could be set up "since the Jordan authorities have been unwilling to agree to any 'permanent' scheme for the marking of the demarcation line." According to the same report, "an Israel survey team engaged in the marking of the border was fired on from Jordan-controlled territory," and the "officer in charge of the surveying team was seriously wounded." This has happened in many instances. The case of the Lebanese frontier, which is clearly marked by cairns placed every few hundred yards and where the local gendarmerie maintains order, indicates that where there is a will, an end can be put to violence across the border. […] In July 1954 the United States, Britain and France proposed the demarcation of the frontier and the erection of barriers as a measure to prevent infiltration and reprisals. This suggestion was accepted by Israel and again rejected by Jordan. […]

A serious situation, second in gravity only to that on the Jordan frontier, has developed in recent months on the Egyptian border. Though the constant raids into Israel territory across the Egyptian armistice line do not, like those from Jordan, operate in populous areas, they have created in the wide expanses of the Negev a state of insecurity necessitating exceptional measures of vigilance to safeguard the lives and property of the rural population. Many of these raids reveal paramilitary training and careful reconnaissance of the ground and of the local farmers' habits. Flocks numbering many hundred heads of sheep have been driven off, plantations uprooted and vital communications mined. A special problem is presented by the Bedouin in the area. The Egyptian authorities frequently employ their own Bedouin for attacks on the Israeli Bedouin, particularly at times of political tension.

[…]

Another measure intended to stop infiltration was the Agreement reached on March 5, 1951, between Israel and Jordan for the holding of regular meetings of local commanders for settling border problems, exchanging information on marauders, arranging for the return of stolen property and providing for the return of persons who had inadvertently strayed across the unmarked line. After a year's trial it became clear, however, that the Jordanian authorities had no intention of coöperating effectively in the prevention of marauding. Stolen property was for the most part sold openly in Jordan market places and was returned only in very exceptional cases. On January 8, 1953, Israel informed the Jordanians that it saw no purpose in continuing this Agreement. In June 1953 Israel took the initiative in proposing a new Local Commanders' Agreement, following a suggestion made by Secretary of State Dulles. The Jordanians were reluctant, but in the end grudgingly signed it. The new Agreement, too, remained a dead letter. Very little was done by the Jordan police to return stolen property and apprehend marauders even when their names were officially communicated to them by the Israel authorities. Israel also proposed the setting up of telephone lines in exposed districts, such as the area of Al-Kubeibe-Latrun, to facilitate a speedy exchange of information. This proposal, too, was first held up and then rejected. The Israel authorities also suggested that in certain areas the armistice line be redrawn, so as to enable villagers to work on their fields without crossing the border. In this matter, too, the Jordanians have maintained their negative attitude.

[…] Israel has no aggressive designs against her neighbors. If she had, she could have had many opportunities in recent years, when Arab states were weakened by internal disturbances and coups d'état. There has been a scrupulous abstention by Israel from exploiting these instabilities. Nor would an aggressive Israel support American and British proposals for reinforcing the armistice demarcation line as a tangible barrier to movement from either side. Israel urgently needs peace for economic development and for accomplishing the great task of absorbing the 700,000 Jewish refugees who have come from all parts of the world--including 350,000 immigrants driven by intolerance from Arab lands. […]

In these circumstances the basic question is clearly not one of procedure but of policy. Does there exist any international influence which can overcome the comprehensive negation which the Arab Governments have chosen to adopt? Refusal to discuss peace; refusal to develop the Armistice Agreement into more lasting accords; refusal to review the Armistice Agreement under Article XII; refusal to confer with Israel under Article VIII of the Armistice; refusal by Jordan to attend the Security Council's meetings under Article 35 of the Charter; refusal to mark the frontier; refusal to erect barriers to infiltration; refusal to restrain the eruption of marauding bands across the frontier; refusal to desist from inflammatory propaganda and incitement; refusal by Egypt to abandon an illicit blockade--all this together adds up to a political attitude which will surely have to be modified if the tension in the Middle East is to be relieved. Until then the Israel Defense Forces will face a heavy task, and face it virtually alone as the solitary effective means for safeguarding Israel's physical integrity.

Zionist Logic (1964)
Malcolm X

The Zionist armies that now occupy Palestine claim their ancient Jewish prophets predicted that in the "last days of this world" their own God would raise them up a "messiah" who would lead them to their promised land, and they would set up their own "divine" government in this newly-gained land, this "divine" government would enable them to "rule all other nations with a rod of iron."

If the Israeli Zionists believe their present occupation of Arab Palestine is the fulfillment of predictions made by their Jewish prophets, then they also religiously believe that Israel must fulfill its "divine" mission to rule all other nations with a rod of irons, which only means a different form of iron-like rule, more firmly entrenched even, than that of the former European Colonial Powers.

These Israeli Zionists religiously believe their Jewish God has chosen them to replace the outdated European colonialism with a new form of colonialism, so well disguised that it will enable them to deceive the African masses into submitting willingly to their "divine" authority and guidance, without the African masses being aware that they are still colonized.

Camouflage

The Israeli Zionists are convinced they have successfully camouflaged their new kind of colonialism. Their colonialism appears to be more "benevolent," more "philanthropic," a system with which they rule simply by getting their potential victims to accept their friendly offers of economic "aid," and other tempting gifts, that they dangle in front of the newly-independent African nations, whose economies are experiencing great difficulties. During the 19th century, when the masses here in Africa were largely illiterate it was easy for European imperialists to rule them with "force and fear," but in this present era of enlightenment the African masses are awakening, and it is impossible to hold them in check now with the antiquated methods of the 19th century.

The imperialists, therefore, have been compelled to devise new methods. Since they can no longer force or frighten the masses into submission, they must devise modern methods that will enable them to maneuver the African masses into willing submission.

The modern 20th century weapon of neo-imperialism is "dollarism." The Zionists have mastered the science of dollarism: the ability to come posing as a friend and benefactor, bearing gifts and all other forms of economic

Used with permission of Socialist Viewpoint Publishing, from SOCIALIST VIEWPOINT, Vol. 4, No. 5 (May/June 2005) (originally published in *The Egyptian Gazette*, September 17, 1964)

aid and offers of technical assistance. Thus, the power and influence of Zionist Israel in many of the newly "independent" African nations has fast-become even more unshakeable than that of the 18th century European colonialists...and this new kind of Zionist colonialism differs only in form and method, but never in motive or objective.

At the close of the 19th century when European imperialists wisely foresaw that the awakening masses of Africa would not submit to their old method of ruling through force and fears, these ever-scheming imperialists had to create a "new weapon," and to find a "new base" for that weapon.

Dollarism

The number one weapon of 20th century imperialism is Zionist dollarism, and one of the main bases for this weapon is Zionist Israel. The ever-scheming European imperialists wisely placed Israel where she could geographically divide the Arab world, infiltrate and sow the seed of dissension among African leaders and also divide the Africans against the Asians.

Zionist Israel's occupation of Arab Palestine has forced the Arab world to waste billions of precious dollars on armaments, making it impossible for these newly independent Arab nations to concentrate on strengthening the economies of their countries and elevate the living standard of their people.

And the continued low standard of living in the Arab world has been skillfully used by the Zionist propagandists to make it appear to the Africans that the Arab leaders are not intellectually or technically qualified to lift the living standard of their people...thus, indirectly inducing Africans to turn away from the Arabs and towards the Israelis for teachers and technical assistance.

"They cripple the bird's wing, and then condemn it for not flying as fast as they."

The imperialists always make themselves look good, but it is only because they are competing against economically crippled newly independent countries whose economies are actually crippled by the Zionist-capitalist conspiracy. They can't stand against fair competition, thus they dread Gamal Abdul Nasser's call for African-Arab Unity under Socialism.

Messiah?

If the "religious" claim of the Zionists is true that they were to be led to the promised land by their messiah, and Israel's present occupation of Arab Palestine is the fulfillment of that prophesy: where is their messiah whom their prophets said would get the credit for leading them there? It was

224

[United Nations mediator] Ralph Bunche who "negotiated" the Zionists into possession of Occupied Palestine! Is Ralph Bunche the messiah of Zionism? If Ralph Bunche is not their messiah, and their messiah has not yet come, then what are they doing in Palestine ahead of their messiah?

Did the Zionists have the legal or moral right to invade Arab Palestine, uproot its Arab citizens from their homes and seize all Arab property for themselves just based on the "religious" claim that their forefathers lived there thousands of years ago? Only a thousand years ago the Moors lived in Spain. Would this give the Moors of today the legal and moral right to invade the Iberian Peninsula, drive out its Spanish citizens, and then set up a new Moroccan nation...where Spain used to be, as the European Zionists have done to our Arab brothers and sisters in Palestine?

In short the Zionist argument to justify Israel's present occupation of Arab Palestine has no intelligent or legal basis in history...not even in their own religion. Where is their Messiah?

The Law of Return (1950)
GOVT. OF ISRAEL

Right of Aliyah
1. Every Jew has the right to come to this country as an oleh.

Oleh's visa
2. (a) Aliyah shall be by oleh's visa.
(b) An oleh's visa shall be granted to every Jew who has expressed his
desire to settle in Israel, unless the Minister of Immigration is satisfied
that the applicant

> (1) is engaged in an activity directed against the Jewish people;
> or
> (2) is likely to endanger public health or the security of the
> State.

Oleh's certificate
3. (a) A Jew who has come to Israel and subsequent to his arrival has
expressed his desire to settle in Israel may, while still in Israel, receive
an oleh's certificate.
(b) The restrictions specified in section 2(b) shall apply also to the
grant of an oleh's certificate, but a person shall not be regarded as
endangering public health on account of an illness contracted after his
arrival in Israel.

Residents and persons born in this country
4. Every Jew who has immigrated into this country before the coming
into force of this Law, and every Jew who was born in this country,
whether before or after the coming into force of this Law, shall be
deemed to be a person who has come to this country as an oleh under
this Law.

Implementation and regulations
5. The Minister of Immigration is charged with the implementation of
this Law and may make regulations as to any matter relating to such
implementation and also as to the grant of oleh's visas and oleh's
certificates to minors up to the age of 18 years.

Address to the Egyptian National Assembly (1967)
Gamal Abdel Nasser

Israel used to boast a great deal, and the Western Powers, headed by the United States and Britain, used to ignore and even despise us and consider us of no value. But now that the time has come—and I have already said in the past that we will decide the time and place and not allow them to decide— we must be ready for triumph and not for a recurrence of the 1948 comedies. We shall triumph, God willing.

Preparations have already been made. We are now ready to confront Israel. They have claimed many things about the 1956 Suez war, but no one believed them after the secrets of the 1956 collusion were uncovered— that mean collusion in which Israel took part. Now we are ready for the confrontation. We are now ready to deal with the entire Palestine question.

The issue now at hand is not the Gulf of Aqaba, the Straits of Tiran, or the withdrawal of the UNEF, but the rights of the Palestine people. It is the aggression which took place in Palestine in 1948 with the collaboration of Britain and the United States. It is the expulsion of the Arabs from Palestine, the usurpation of their rights, and the plunder of their property. It is the disavowal of all the UN resolutions in favor of the Palestinian people.

The issue today is far more serious than they say. They want to confine the issue to the Straits of Tiran, the UNEF and the right of passage. We demand the full rights of the Palestinian people. We say this out of our belief that Arab rights cannot be squandered because the Arabs throughout the Arab world are demanding these Arab rights.

[…] The United States and Britain are partial to Israel and give no consideration to the Arabs, to the entire Arab nation. Why? Because we have made them believe that we cannot distinguish between friend and foe. We must make them know that we know who our foes are and who our friends are and treat them accordingly.

If the United States and Britain are partial to Israel, we must say that our enemy is not only Israel but also the United States and Britain and treat them as such. If the Western Powers disavow our rights and ridicule and despise us, we Arabs must teach them to respect us and take us seriously. Otherwise all our talk about Palestine, the Palestine people and Palestinian rights will be null and void and of no consequence. We must treat enemies as enemies and friends as friends.
[…]

Soviet Policy and the 1967 Arab-Israeli War (1970)
CENTRAL INTELLIGENCE AGENCY

Prelude to War—May 1967

RUMOR FEEDS TENSION

[...] On 12 May Israeli Prime Minister Ekshol, in a sharply worded statement, warned Syria that it faced severe counteraction if it did not halt terrorist incursions into Israel. Shortly thereafter, word spread through the area that Israel was concentrating forces on the Syrian border and was poised to launch an attack on Syria. The report was untrue. In fact Israel did not reinforce its frontiers and mobilize its reserves until *after* the UAR began its military build-up.

The origin of the report is not clear; it apparently did not originate with either the Syrians or Egyptians, both of whom were given the information by the Soviets. It is possible that the Israelis themselves floated the rumor hoping to induce the Soviets to persuade the Syrians to stop their provocative actions. In any event, the Soviets did not appear particularly concerned about establishing the validity of the report. [...]

On 13 May a message was sent through Egyptian channels to Cairo from Moscow. It stated that Soviet Deputy Foreign Minister Semenov had told the Egyptians that Israel was preparing a ground and air attack on Syria— to be carried out between 17 and 21 May. It stated that the Soviets had advised the UAR to be prepared, to stay calm, and not to be drawn into fighting with Israel, and that they had advised the Syrians to remain calm and not give Israel the opportunity for military operations. The message also said that the USSR favored informing the Security Council before Israel took military action against Syria. [...] The Arabs were to take the information but not the advice.
[...]
Soviet motivation for spreading a flimsy and unsubstantiated report as explosive as this one is not clear. Even if they knew the facts of the story to be untrue, the Soviets might in fact have feared that, as a result of Eshkol's speech, an Israeli reprisal attack of some sort against Syria was likely to occur shortly. If so, they may have hoped to push the UAR toward a firm and open commitment to come to Syria's aid, reasoning that such a commitment might deter Israel from further raids. It is also possible that the Soviets hoped to frighten the Syrians into modifying their policies by convincing them that they faced an Israeli attack otherwise.* In either case, they were proved wrong. If they did believe the report, they had made an intelligence blunder; if, as seems more likely, they did not believe the story or had fabricated it and were using it to prod either Nasir or the Syrians, they misjudged the effect it would have. The story did not restrain the

---

228 * This supports the view that Israel itself might have started the rumor.

Syrians, and it provoked a far more aggressive reaction from Nasir than Moscow expected or desired.

BUILD-UP OF UAR FORCES

Nasir apparently believed the reports given him by the Soviet Union,* and the mobilization of UAR forces deployed against Israel followed. Nasir may have had reasons of his own for proceeding as he did, but the report spread by the Russians gave him a justification. According to the Egyptian press, an emergency had been declared in the UAR in order "to put teeth into the mutual defense pact with Syria." In public statements Nasir repeatedly stressed that UAR military preparations were in response to the threat of an Israeli attack on Syria. This apparently was designed to direct Israeli attention to the Egyptian border, and at the same time help bolster Nasir's image as the leader of the Arab world.

On 17 May Nasir requested the withdrawal of UNEF from Sinai and the Gaza Strip; he subsequently demanded that these forces be withdrawn from the UAR entirely. On 18 May UAR forces began to occupy UN observation posts in Sinai. UN forces were not equipped to respond and the following day Secretary General U Thant agreed to complete withdrawal.** By 22 May, Egyptian soldiers had completely replaced the UN forces.

Nasir's demand that the UN forces be withdrawn and U Thant's compliance served several purposes. With the UNEF buffer removed, Egyptian forces could respond more quickly in case of an Israeli attack on Syria. Nasir's demand also undercut Jordanian charges that the UAR had been hiding behind a UN shield. And, getting UN forces out of the UAR, particularly out of the symbolic and strategic post at Sharm ash-Shaykh, bolstered Nasir's prestige and Arab pride.

[...]

NASIR CLOSES THE GULF OF AQABA

By 22 May 1967, the day the small UNEF force was withdrawn from Sharm ash-Shaykh, Nasir announced that the UAR had closed the Gulf of Aqaba to Israeli shipping and to ships of all other countries bringing

---

* Nasir's willingness to believe the reports at this time may have been   229
influenced by the Israeli air attacks on Syria in April as well as by Eshkol's
sharp warning in May.

** The UN forces had been stationed in the UAR after the 1956 war;
units in Sharm ash-Shaykh, a point southwest of the Strait of Tiran at the
mouth of the Gulf of Aqaba, had been a token of assurance of safe passage for
Israeli ships through the strait. The control of the Strait of Tiran had been a
source of friction between the Arabs and Israelis since 1949; in that year,
following the armistice, Egypt installed guns near Sharm ash-Shayk,
overlooking the strait. In the 1956 campaign, Israel captured the post
commanding the strait. In the face of U.S. and Soviet pressure it subsequently
withdrew its forces.

strategic cargoes to Israel. The next day, Ekshol repeated the Israel position that Egyptian interference with Israeli shipping in the Gulf would be considered an act of aggression. On 26 May Israel warned that it would not wait indefinitely for an end to the Egyptian blockade and the withdrawal of Arab troop concentration on its borders. By then, the Israeli armed forces were near peak mobilization.

Nasir's actions during the month of May probably were influenced by bad information concerning Arab military strength and the extent of Soviet backing. But the false report of Israel's plans to attack Syria, by triggering Nasir's decision to mobilize, played a major role in Nasir's actions. If he believed that Israel planed an attack on Syria and that the UAR would have to respond, his mobilization and his demand for a withdrawal of UNEF forces might have been intended as deterrents.

However, Nasir's decision to blockade the Gulf of Aqaba raised the pitch of the crisis to new and dangerous levels. His speeches indicated that he believed Israel would respond to the blockade and that the UAR was equipped to handle an Israeli attack. On 26 May he stated

> … Recently we have felt strong enough that if we were to enter a battle with Israel, with God's help, we could triumph. On this basis we decided to take actual steps…. Taking over Sharm ash-Shaykh … meant that we were ready to enter a general war with Israel.

Though he indicated that the UAR would not initiate an attack, he declared that if Israel attacked either Syria or the UAR.

> …. The battle will be a general one and our basic objective will be to destroy Israel.

While Nasir was publicly stating that Israel would have to respond and that the UAR could then handle Israel militarily, it seems likely that Nasir in fact believed that Israel would not attack and that he would make major political gains for only a modest risk.

[…]

On The Brink

NATURE OF SOVIET SUPPORT FOR THE ARABS

Reports on specific Soviet commitments to the Arabs are confusing; it appears that Soviet assurances were always kept vague and thus were open to misinterpretation by the Arabs. The only fairly clear commitment the Soviets made was to support the Arabs if the United States intervened on behalf of Israel—and even here the extent and type of assistance were not clear. […]

Whatever his interpretation of the actual Soviet commitment, Nasir apparently felt that it was sufficient. He seems to have believed that Soviet support would only be needed to prevent a recurrence of 1956—when Western forces assisted Israel. He apparently felt that the United States could restrain Israel and also seemed confident that the Arabs could cope with Israel militarily if necessary. Nasir's confidence in Egypt's military capability seems to have been at least partially shared by the Soviets.... [T]he Soviets overestimated the Arab ability to employ its military strength, and ... the Soviets had made a bad estimate of Arab capabilities.... However, the most important Soviet error at this point would appear to have been their failure to foresee an Israeli attack.

SOVIETS URGE RESTRAINT—TOO LITTLE TOO LATE

During the period between the announcement of the blockade of the Gulf of Aqaba and the outbreak of war, Soviet policy apparently was based on the assumption that Israel would not attack if the situation remained static. On the one hand, the Soviets gave encouragement to the Arabs and left open the possibility that they would support the Arabs in the event of war; on the other hand, they sought gently to restrain the Arabs from further proactive actions. There is no indication that they ever attempted to persuade Nasir to lift the blockade. Anxious to avoid war — and at the same time retain the atmosphere of tension from which they felt they could benefit, the Soviets urged the Arabs only that degree of restraint they felt necessary to keep the situation from boiling over into war.
[...]
Soviet attempts to restrain the Arabs were limited, however, and suggest that they were concerned not so much about a possible Israeli retaliation for closure of the Gulf of Aqaba, as they were about further Arab actions which in turn might lead to war. Their late May attempts to convince the Arabs that Israel was not going to attack apparently referred back to the original untrue report of a planned Israeli attack on Syria, rather than to the possibility of a retaliatory attack for closure of the gulf.

POSITIONS HARDEN

In the last days of May, Nasir began to settle his differences with the more conservative Arab nations, a situation most feared by Israel and, by the beginning of June, the Egyptian and Israeli positions were completely intransigent. On 1 June Israeli Labor Minister Yigal Alon insisted that some protection of Israel's borders from terrorist attacks, the withdrawal of Egyptian troop concentrations along the border, and the lifting of the blockade were necessary conditions to avoid an "inevitable" military clash. On 2 June UAR Foreign Minister Riyad announced that the Suez Canal would be closed to anyone who tried to break the blockade.

Most available information indicates that the Israeli attack at dawn on 5 June came as complete surprise to the Soviets…. The timing of the attack certainly surprised the Arabs. After the war Nasir blamed this unpreparedness on the fact that the United States had indicated it would try to restrain Israel. And Nasir, as well as the Soviets, apparently was convinced Israel would not attack without U.S. approval.

The Outbreak of War

ISRAEL ATTACKS; THE USSR REACTS

Israel's attack on the UAR came in the morning on 5 June 1967. Surprise enabled the Israeli air force to virtually eliminate the Egyptian air force on the ground, and Israeli forces advanced with little trouble into Sinai and the Gaza Strip. By 6 June Israeli forces were well on their way to the Suez; on 7 June they captured Sharm ash-Shaykh; and on 8 June Israel claimed complete control of Sinai. The war with Jordan began later in the day on 5 June. After Jordanian forces seized UN headquarters in Jerusalem, Israel launched air and ground attacks along the armistice line and Israeli forces swept toward the Jordan River. Israel had virtually destroyed the Syrian air force on 5 June, but did not begin her ground attack against Syria until 9 June; by the time of cease-fire with the Syrians, Israeli forces has penetrated about 10 miles into Syria and occupied the Golan Heights.
[…]

The Khartoum Resolutions (1967)

LEAGUE OF ARAB STATES

1. The conference has affirmed the unity of Arab ranks, the unity of joint action and the need for coordination and for the elimination of all differences. The Kings, Presidents and representatives of the other Arab Heads of State at the conference have affirmed their countries' stand by and implementation of the Arab Solidarity Charter [....]

2. The conference has agreed on the need to consolidate all efforts to eliminate the effects of the aggression on the basis that the occupied lands are Arab lands and that the burden of regaining these lands falls on all the Arab States.

3. The Arab Heads of State have agreed to unite their political efforts at the international and diplomatic level to eliminate the effects of the aggression and to ensure the withdrawal of the aggressive Israeli forces from the Arab lands which have been occupied since the aggression of June 5. This will be done within the framework of the main principles by which the Arab States abide, namely, no peace with Israel, no recognition of Israel, no negotiations with it, and insistence on the rights of the Palestinian people in their own country.

4. The conference of Arab Ministers of Finance, Economy and Oil recommended that suspension of oil pumping be used as a weapon in the battle. However, after thoroughly studying the matter, the summit conference has come to the conclusion that the oil pumping can itself be used as a positive weapon, since oil is an Arab resource which can be used to strengthen the economy of the Arab States directly affected by the aggression, so that these States will be able to stand firm in the battle. The conference has, therefore, decided to resume the pumping of oil, since oil is a positive Arab resource that can be used in the service of Arab goals. It can contribute to the efforts to enable those Arab States which were exposed to the aggression and thereby lost economic resources to stand firm and eliminate the effects of the aggression. The oil-producing States have, in fact, participated in the efforts to enable the States affected by the aggression to stand firm in the face of any economic pressure.

5. The participants in the conference have approved the plan proposed by Kuwait to set up an Arab Economic and Social Development Fund on the basis of the recommendation of the Baghdad conference of Arab Ministers of Finance, Economy and Oil.

6. The participants have agreed on the need to adopt the necessary measures to strengthen military preparation to face all eventualities.

7. The conference has decided to expedite the elimination of foreign bases in the Arab States.

Resolution 242 – The Situation in the Middle East (1967)
UNITED NATIONS SECURITY COUNCIL

The Security Council,

Expressing its continuing concern with the grave situation in the Middle East,

Emphasizing the inadmissibility of the acquisition of territory by war and the need to work for a just and lasting peace in which every State in the area can live in security,

Emphasizing further that all Member States in their acceptance of the Charter of the United Nations have undertaken a commitment to act in accordance with Article 2 of the Charter,

   1. *Affirms* that the fulfilment of Charter principles requires the establishment of a just and lasting peace in the Middle East which should include the application of both of the following principles:

      i.   Withdrawal of Israel armed forces from territories occupied in the recent conflict;

      ii.   Termination of all claims or states of belligerency and respect for and acknowledgement of the sovereignty, territorial integrity and political independence of every State in the area and their right to live in peace within secure and recognized boundaries free from threats or acts of force;

   2. *Affirms further* the necessity

     (a)   For guaranteeing freedom of navigation through international waterways in the area;

     (b)   For achieving a just settlement of the refugee problem;

     (c)   For guaranteeing the territorial inviolability and political independence of every State in the area, through measures including the establishment of de-militarized zones;

   3. *Requests* the Secretary-General to designate a Special Representative to proceed to the Middle East to establish and maintain contacts with the States concerned in order to promote agreement and assist efforts to achieve a peaceful and accepted settlement in accordance with the provisions and principles in this resolution;
[...]

1967 | The Six-Day War was a Watershed in Middle Eastern History (2017)
Asher Susser

The 1967 War was a watershed in Middle Eastern history. Israelis call it the Six-Day War, which is symbolic of the euphoric sense of victory that Israeli Jews felt in the aftermath of the war. The Arabs don't call it the Six-Day War; for them it's the 'June War', or the '67 War'. It was the most humiliating of defeats for the Arabs in modern times, maybe of all time.

First of all, the war wasn't just a defeat in the battlefield. The war was also a horrendous defeat for the idea of Arab nationalism or pan-Arabism or Nasserism – whatever you want to call it. It showed that it was an empty vessel. A whole generation of Arabs had hung on every word of Abdel Nasser. The Palestinians were great believers in Nasser as the man who would deliver Palestine. Almost overnight, it all came to naught.

Nasser had, in theory, the formula for Arab modernisation and success: Arab unity, Arab socialism, and alliance with the Soviet Union in the Cold War. This was to be the panacea for Arab ills and for the modernisation of the Arab world. I think many Israelis don't realise the extent to which the war of 1967 was an utter shock and humiliation for the Arabs and for the Egyptians in particular.

From Arab Nationalism to State Interest and Islamism

There was a void in the aftermath of 1967 which was filled by two simultaneous but contradictory developments. One was the reassertion of raison d'etat – state interest. Once pan-Arabism was seen as 'pie in the sky' it became every more legitimate to pursue state interest unabashedly: Egypt first, Jordan first, Palestine first. So Egypt made war with Israel again, and then peace with Israel, each time serving purely Egyptian territorial state interests. For the Arab states involved in the 1967 war with Israel, the defeat was the beginning of thinking seriously about withdrawing from the conflict with Israel. After the Yom Kippur War of 1973 we saw the gradual withdrawal of the Arab states from the conflict with Israel. Essentially, the Arab world post-67 has left the Palestinians to fend for themselves. The Palestinians spoke with ever greater emphasis after 1967 of what in Arabic is called 'the independence of decision'. They said: 'the Arabs have disappointed us, we Palestinians must fend for ourselves, we must be our own independent decision makers.' By taking this position the Palestinians took ever more responsibility for their own fate. But that also paved the way for the Arab states to actually let them go, in the spirit of 'You want to be more independent, be our guests'. The Arab states walked away from the conflict, leaving the Palestinians to fend for their own raison d'etat.

The second trend that filled the void after 1967 was Islamic politics. The Islamists could now say with a lot of credibility: 'We told you so. All this secular Arab nationalism is not going to get us anywhere. Islam is the solution, not secular nationalism.' Arab nationalism was never favoured by the Islamists for the very good reason that Arab nationalism was actually an aircraft carrier for secularisation. Arab nationalism, at least in theory, is a secular ideology, uniting people based on the language they speak, not their religion. Arabism is about Muslims and Christians being Arabs. Islamism has the opposite effect, reasserting the sectarian differences which Arabism actually papered over. Now you're talking about Sunni and Shi'a, Muslims and non-Muslims. This reassertion of Islamism has eroded and in some cases even partly dissolved the Arab state: Iraq and Syria are two examples.

1967 and the Creation of the 'Israel-Palestine Conflict'

What impact did the Six-Day War have on the Arab-Israeli conflict?

First, Israel appeared in the Arab mind – in the aftermath of 1967 even more than before – as a monument to Arab inadequacy, Arab failure. Second, we saw the return of the Palestinians to the front of the stage. It is no longer the 'Arab-Israeli conflict'; it's the 'Palestinian-Israeli conflict'. After 1967 the Palestinians were very much in control of their destiny, a dramatic turn of events. Third, the Arab states fought their last war with Israel in 1973. There has been no inter-state war between Arab states and Israel for 44 years. Once Egypt made its peace with Israel, there was no longer an Arab war option. Arab states could not make war with Israel without Egypt.

So the Palestinians, left on their own, faced the brunt of Israeli power in the war of 1982 in Lebanon. You know, there is a direct but unintended connection between that war and the Oslo peace process. The people who went to war in 1982 against the Palestine Liberation Organisation (PLO) in Lebanon, didn't intend to go to Oslo, and the people who went to Oslo from Israel condemned the war in Lebanon. But it was the crushing the PLO in Lebanon that created the reality in which, 10 years later, the PLO had no choice but to enter into a negotiation with Israel on the basis of UN Security Council Resolution 242.

The Palestinians never accepted 242 when it was passed in November 1967. No surprise there: the words 'Palestine' or 'Palestinians' do not appear in 242. In November 1967 the Palestinians were not the autonomous player that they became in later years. The resolution created the principle of 'land for peace'; Israel was supposed to give back the land it took in 1967 to the states it took it from. That is, to give the West Bank back to Jordan, not to create a Palestinian state. Israel's withdrawal from the territories it occupied in 1967 is not unconditional – it's land for peace.

Israel is not required to withdraw from the West Bank unilaterally, unconditionally. It is only supposed to withdraw if the Arab side makes peace with Israel. In effect, 242 is very mindful of Israel's security needs and is recognition by the international community that 1967 was a war of self-defence.

The International Community Draws a Line

In 242 we see what Zionism is in the eyes of the international community. In 1967, Israel was seen as a representation of Zionism as a great project of historical self-defence of the Jewish people against their horrific past. Israel's legitimacy was based on this vision of Zionism as self-defence, in which the Zionists and Israel agreed to the partition of Palestine into two states. 242 followed the logic of the partition resolution of 1947; it speaks of all states in the region having the right to secure and recognised boundaries. So 242 was the beginning of the Arab states' – if we're talking about Egypt and Jordan—willingness to come to terms with Israel in a way that did not exist before 1967.

The PLO never accepted 242 until 1988, and even then in a very convoluted way. Why? Because the Arab-Israeli conflict is divided into two major packages of issues that have to be negotiated, the 1967 questions and the 1948 questions. 242 only dealt with the 1967 file. Other issues – the origins of which are in 1948, and which are not so important to the Arab states, but are critically important to the Palestinians, most obviously the refugee question and the right of return—were not dealt with.

In the negotiations between the Israelis and the Palestinians for the two-state solution, as far as the Palestinians are concerned, there must be some element of intrusion into Israel: the refugee question. And Israel requires some element of intrusion into the state of Palestine: security. These mutual intrusions, so to speak, make a deal so difficult to attain.

The Rise of Settlerist Neo-Zionism

Another legacy of 1967 is the beginning of the Israeli settlement project, and the creation of a new kind of Zionism, what I would call settlerist neo-zionism. This is a Zionism no longer about self-defence and partition, but about the messianic, religious redemption of the land and a rejection of the idea of partition. And this is where Israel clashes with the international community.

Look at UN Security Council Resolution 2334, and look at the speech by then US Secretary of State John Kerry, both in December 2016. You can see a very clear distinction between a critique of the Israel occupation and the settlements, but not of Israel proper. There is an actual endorsement of

Israel proper, in both the resolution and the Kerry speech. Kerry speaks about refugee return, as did the Clinton parameters of 2000, only in the framework of a two-state solution, preserving the nature of Israel as the state of the Jewish people. That means refugees will return to Palestine not to Israel.

The critique in 2334 of the settlements as a 'flagrant violation of international law' calls upon all states to distinguish in all their relevant dealings between the territory of the state of Israel and the territories occupied since 1967. In other words, Israel pre-1967, in 78 per cent of Palestine, is entirely accepted as fully legitimate by the international community.

This was not the situation pre-1967. In the mid-1950s, Israel was called upon by the great powers to give up parts of the Negev in exchange for peace with Nasser, which never came to any fruition. But now there is an international consensus which has emerged on the contours of two states, and in this there is no erosion of Israel as the nation state of the Jewish people. Therefore the international community is in agreement with the Palestinians on the 1967 questions but not on the 1948 questions. The Palestinians therefore have the full support of the international community when it comes to settlements and dividing Jerusalem, but not on refugee return.

The Threat of Arab Weakness

Today's Middle East is not what Israel's founding fathers expected. David Ben-Gurion and his generation were a pessimistic lot. They thought that Israel would find it extremely difficult, if not impossible, to manage the potential power of the Arab states. They feared those states would modernise, and with their huge populations and relative wealth they would create massive armies with the support of the Soviet Union. Israel, with its very small population, would find it very difficult to maintain a conventional balance of power. Israel went nuclear because of this belief in the long-term power of the Arab world.

Well, the Arab states did not get stronger and stronger. They got weaker and weaker. The war of 1967 was an indication of precisely that. And since 1967 they have got even weaker. Israel is now confronted not by the power of the Arab states that the founding fathers feared, but with Arab weakness.

The defeat in 1967 was itself a symptom of the decline of the Arabs due to their failure to modernise successfully. There are a series of reports written by Arab scholars for the UN – the Arab Human Development Reports. These reports are eloquent about the reason for the crisis of the Arabs: the three great deficits of political freedom, first world education systems and gender equality. These deficits have resulted in weak Arab economies;

especially weak in the sphere of innovation, which requires freedom of thought, creative thinking and good universities. So Arab economics lag far behind the Western world in a globalised era.

And all this is worsened by the lack of gender equality. If women are not well educated and not incorporated into the workforce for reasons of tradition, you have two consequences: economies where almost half the population doesn't work; and women who are not involved in the workforce and have low education tend to have large families.

Add all this together and you have poorly preforming economies with rapidly growing populations, which is a recipe for disaster. This is not a prediction; we are going through it now. That is what the Arab Spring was about, the clash between the forces of modernity and tradition, and the failure to modernise successfully.

There is now an Arab human disaster: state failure, sectarian conflict, millions of refugees, economic crisis, collapsing health systems. And this is a disaster that the Arab states are not going to overcome any time soon. Even Egypt, which has overcome its internal instability, is still a country suffering from profound economic difficulties. However stable Egyptian President Abdel Fattah al-Sisi has made Egypt, overcoming Egypt's economic difficulties is not on the cards any time soon.

What is Israel to do with Arab disarray and disorder? The threat from this Arab world of disarray is from non-state actors who are benefiting from the weakness of the states: Hezbollah and Hamas and ISIS and their ilk. And there is the threat from Iran too.

Main Issues in a Middle East Settlement (1967)
CENTRAL INTELLIGENCE AGENCY

1.   The outlook for settlement between Arabs and Israelis is dim indeed. Their respective positions on almost all questions are poles apart and emotions are running high. Arab policy towards Israel remains adamantly hostile. For many years, no Arab leader--except Bourguiba, who scarcely counts in this context--has considered it politically possible to contemplate the recognition of Israel. The Arab leaders are fully aware of magnitude of their defeat, but they do not draw the conclusion that they must acknowledge it. Hence, anything in the nature of peace negotiations is highly unlikely. The Arabs may feel compelled to sign some form of armistice agreements, but they may for a long time resist even this step if-- as is likely--the price is significant concessions to Israel. But the shock of their swift and overwhelming defeat has, for the most part, probably prevented them from making decisions on all but immediate matters, and they are reduced to hoping that international pressures will somehow force the Israelis to withdraw from occupied territory.

2.   As for the Israelis, promptly after their dramatic victory, they began talking about direct negotiations leading to Arab recognition of Israel and an overall settlement. Israel's great objectives are to break the pattern of the last two decades, to gain Arab recognition of its right to exist, and assurances against further terrorism and other harassment. There are clearly divided counsels within Israel on the strategy and tactics of achieving these goals. The hardliners, represented by Dayan, have the advantage of being identified by many Israelis as the architects of Israel's victory, and their promises have strong domestic appeal because they emphasize what Israel wants and feels it has won, with little regard to what might have to be conceded in the face of international pressures or opinion. Even if Dayan is forced out of the cabinet, Israel will probably remain largely impervious to external pressures to withdraw from occupied areas for months to come, unless there is unexpectedly quick progress toward a settlement tolerable to Israel. [...]

3.   In the longer run, however, Israel faces a painful dilemma. The Israelis may hope that the Arabs (and the Soviets) will draw the "correct" conclusion from the recent war, and that a new order will emerge in the area which will involve acceptance of the Israeli state and assurances for its security. But so far there are few indications that any such new order is emerging, and unless it does, Israeli must sooner or later face the problem of how to assure its security. Eventually, Israel is probably prepared to trade much of its captured territory in return for security arrangements. Experience does not incline the Israelis to put faith in guarantees by the great powers and certainly not in the effectiveness of UN arrangements. And while the Arabs may reluctantly enter into some more formal armistice arrangements, the chances remain slight that any significant Arab

leader will undertake to associate himself with the kind of binding agreement that Israel wants and feels it must have.
[...]

6. No matter what the Israelis offer by way of a new order in Palestine or movement on the refugee question, the Arabs will press for a return to something as close to the status quo ante as they can get. In the process, there will be intense maneuvering, not only between Arabs and Israelis, but also among the Arab states. Husayn and Nasir have neither the same interests at stake nor the same attitudes, and the Syrians are something else again. In addition, there will be considerable controversy and haggling between the regional adversaries and the great powers. The overall outcome is obscure, but it is possible to isolate and analyze contrasting positions on certain of the main specific issues, and to suggest where chances of accommodation now appear best, and where they do not. [...]

II.   Jerusalem

A. Israel's Position	B. Jordan's Position	C. Chance of Compromise
Israel is moving rapidly to absorb Arab Jerusalem into its own city administration. It is asserting sovereignty over the entire city. It is prepared to concede some form of international supervision of the Christian and Muslim holy places.	Jordan wants the Old City returned to its control. Failing this, it could acquiesce in an internationalization of the Old City, but to surrender Jerusalem to Israeli control permanently would be politically difficult, and perhaps disastrous for Husayn.	There is some slight room for compromise here. Israel is certain to reject the return of the Old City to Jordanian control, because this could deny its citizens access to the Jewish holy places. There is at most a less than even chance that Israel could be forced to relinquish the Old City to some form of international control, but it would require formidable international pressures and be a long slow battle.

III.   West Bank of Jordan

A. Israel's Position

Though Israel will insist on some relatively minor border gains, it will almost certainly decide that it cannot absorb the entire West Bank with its 850,000 Arab inhabitants. Hence, Israel probably will push for some special arrangement for this area, possibly in the form of an autonomous state linked to Israel. Israel would probably demand demilitarization of any areas of the West Bank left under Jordanian control.

B. Jordan's Position

Jordan will undoubtedly demand return of the entire West Bank, which it probably believes necessary if Jordan is ever to become economically self-sufficient. Husayn fears that the loss of West Jordan would mean loss of his throne, too.

C. Chance of Compromise

Jordan probably would be willing to accept some border rectification, e.g. surrendering a part of the Latrun Salient. Husayn probably also would agree to arms limitation for areas of the West Bank under his control, especially if Egypt and Syria were doing the same on their borders. Such concessions would probably satisfy Israel's minimum demands in this area. Jordan would be likely to agree to an autonomous status for the West Bank only if Cairo were to agree to a comparable status for Gaza.

IV.   The Gaza Strip

A. Israel's Position

Israel will resist return to Egyptian control of the Gaza Strip with its 400,000 Arabs. Israel would like to retain Gaza, if the bulk of its Arab population went elsewhere. It might offer generous terms to the local Arabs in return for their acquiescence in re-settlement. Failing that, Israel might turn to some type of autonomous status, like that discussed for the West Bank, for this area, which has never been formally incorporated into Egypt.

B. Egypt's Position

Aside from a general demand to return to pre-hostilities armistice lines, Egypt has given no indication of what it might consider a suitable disposition of the Gaza Strip. Cairo would like to regain control of it, and in any case, to have a large voice in the Gaza through puppets in the various· Palestine refugee organizations.

C. Chance of Compromise

It is conceivable, though hardly likely, that Egypt would agree to a UN administration of Gaza. Ultimate Egyptian policy on this issue is hard to estimate; it may depend largely on the type of government Cairo has in the next few months.

Israel, under strong outside pressure, might agree to accept international administration of the area, though not on behalf of Cairo.

242

V. Access to Eilat Through the Strait of Tiran

A. Israel's Position

Israel will insist on freedom of passage through the Strait of Tiran guaranteed either by its own physical control of at least one shore of the Strait or by an international guarantee of compelling force, i.e. one which included the US and the USSR and which specifically excluded Egyptian military domination of the Strait.

B. Egypt's Position

The Egyptians will advance the claim to control of the Strait, but without great determination. The Egyptians are aware that the USSR will not support restrictions on passage. Even during the fighting, Egypt appeared willing to concede free passage in exchange for Israeli withdrawal.

C. Chance of Compromise

The chances here look reasonably good. Israel will insist on holding the Strait by force at least until the UAR agrees to free passage. The USSR is likely to urge the UAR to give in on this point. Cairo will thus probably accede to some formula which permits Israeli access, but legally recognizes the Strait as Egyptian territorial water.

VI. The Suez Canal

A. Israel's Position
1. Reopening the Canal

Israel is aware that continued closure of the canal hurts Egypt's economy and is willing to put economic pressure on Egypt by keeping forces along the canal, while asserting that it would do nothing to impede navigation.

B. Egypt's Position

Egypt refuses to undertake work to clear the canal as long as Israeli troops are along its eastern edge.

C. Chance of Compromise

Egypt probably won't open the canal at all until Israeli troops are withdrawn at least some distance from it.

2. Israeli Transit

Israel will try to link freedom of navigation through the canal with freedom of navigation through the Strait of Tiran. Canal transit rights, however, are mainly a matter of face for the Israelis, and they will probably use the issue of canal transit as a bargaining counter. Most Israeli trade goes from its Mediterranean ports to Europe. Trade

Egypt will be adamant against granting Israel the right of transit.

The two parties probably won't come to grips with this issue. Nasir would find it almost impossible to agree to Israeli passage. The Israelis probably recognize this situation and in the final analysis may not push this issue strongly. Compromise is possible only in the unlikely eventuality of an agreement covering between Israel and the Far East can be handled at least as cheaply and just as readily through the Port of Eilat.

several international waterways.

VII.   Sinai

A. Israel's Position	B. Egypt's Position	C. Chance of Compromise
The Israelis will hold Sinai as a bargaining position but they do not want it and in the end will consent to return almost all of it to Egyptian rule. The Israelis will probably ask for it to be demilitarized, possibly under international inspection. The Israelis may exploit oil produced from Egyptian fields as an inducement to bring the UAR to settlement.	Egypt will demand unconditional return of the Sinai.	Nasir probably would agree to informal demilitarization, but would be likely to refuse any formal commitment on this score. Israel would be content with a demilitarized zone along its border, say 20 to 50 miles wide.

[...]

IX.   The Refugees

(Although not a product of the late war, the status and future of some 1,300,000 Arab refugees from the 1948-49 fighting are certain to be considered in the efforts to settle Arab-Israeli problems.)

A. Israel's Position	B. Arab Position	C. Chance of Compromise
Israel opposes return of refugees in more than small numbers, lest the ethnic balance of the state be adversely affected. Israel has floated the idea of an autonomous Arab state (the West Bank, and perhaps Gaza) which would provide place for many refugees to resettle and call home. Israel would be ready to cooperate in a scheme whereby each refugee would be given a one-	The Arabs insist that the refugees be permitted to exercise the right to choose between returning to their homes or getting compensation for land and property if they do not. Arab leaders will be reluctant to accede to a scheme which in practice permitted, say, only 10-15 percent of the refugees actually to return. A Palestine state, if established at Arab, rather than Israeli,	Israeli occupation of the West Bank and Gaza may permit some progress in getting a number of refugees out of the camps. Moreover, the experience of living under Israeli control may convince others that repatriation is not an attractive option. However, the obstacles in the way of an overall resolution of the refugee problem are enormous and are probably insuperable.

time choice between repatriation and resettlement outside of Israel with compensation, as long as the process assured that the vast majority accepted the latter.

initiative would have some support.

TERRITORIES

Arab Territories Under Israeli Occupation (1967)
CENTRAL INTELLIGENCE AGENCY

Approximately 1,150,000 Arab civilians were estimated to be in Israeli-occupied areas of Jordan, Syria, and Egypt on 1 September 1967. Prior to the war, the population of these areas was about 1.6 million.

As a result of the mass exodus of Arabs to Jordan's East Bank fewer than 750,000 remain of the approximately 930,000 persons who resided on the West Bank prior to 5 June. [...]

Of the more than 400,000 in the Gaza Strip and the 50,000 in Sinai when the war started, only 35,000 were able to cross the Suez Canal ahead of the Israelis. Gaza residents continue to go to east Jordan through Israel and the West Bank, however, with more than 4,000 crossing before 1 September. [...]

After investigating Syrian charges that the Israelis had made "systematic efforts to expel the entire original population" from the occupied portion of Syria, the UN special representative concluded that whatever the policy of the Israeli Government may have been as regards the population, it seemed clear that "certain actions authorized or allowed by local military commanders were an important cause of flight."

In regard to similar charges concerning the civilian population on the West Bank, the special representative stated that although there was no indication that persons had been physically forced to cross to the East Bank, there had been reports of acts of intimidation by the Israeli armed forces and of Israeli attempts--using loudspeakers--to suggest to the population that "they might be better off on the East Bank." The representative concluded, however, that the main factor in the exodus from the West Bank had clearly been the inevitable impact of hostilities and military occupation as such, particularly when no measures of reassurance were taken.

Administration of Occupied Areas
[...]
Contrary to a UN General Assembly resolution, the Old City of Jerusalem has, for all intents and purposes, been incorporated into the state of Israel. The members of the former municipal council of the Old City, which has been dissolved by the Israelis, have refused even to discuss meeting in a combined council under Israeli rule inasmuch as this might be construed as recognition of Israeli sovereignty over the Old City.

In the remainder of the West Bank, however, the Israelis have to a large extent used the administrative structure established by the Jordanians. Local municipal councils have continued to administer essential services, such as health, utilities, and public welfare. In cases where the local council has been unable to cope with a problem, the Israeli military governor has provided whatever assistance is necessary. In this connection, some hospital patients have been evacuated from the West Bank to Israel, fuel has been sent from Israel to the West Bank, and local road construction and works projects for the unemployed that had been started before the war are now continuing with Israeli assistance. [...]

Arab Resistance and Israeli Reaction

The Israeli occupation is viewed by Arab residents of the occupied areas with varying degrees of dislike. In all the occupied areas, however, Arab resistance has in general been non-violent in nature and has mostly taken the form of civil disobedience.

West Bank Arabs engaging in civil disobedience are by and large members of an urban minority who before the war comprised only 25 to 30 percent of the West Bankers, and are even less numerous now as more townsmen than villagers have fled. [...]

The most serious resistance has been the failure of most West Bank teachers to report for the opening of the fall school term. [...] The teachers charge that Israeli educational authorities have deleted religious passages and phrases from textbooks; the Israelis counter that they have banned or altered only textbooks containing anti-Jewish material. The teachers' action, however, probably stems primarily from a desire to demonstrate a more general dissatisfaction with the Israeli presence in the area.

Israeli authorities from the first have demonstrated their readiness to act against uncooperative elements, including those who periodically refuse to cooperate with the occupying authorities. In recent weeks, they have adopted an increasingly harder line toward those advocating resistance. On 31 July, four prominent West Bank political figures--including Anwar al-Khatib, former governor of the Jerusalem district--were identified as signers of a petition calling for non-cooperation with Israeli authorities. Arrested for "obstructing law and order," they have been exiled to towns in Israel for three months.

In early September, the Israeli commander of West Bank forces issued an order prohibiting oral or written attempts to influence public opinion that might harm or disturb safety and order. Violators are subject to a large fine and ten years imprisonment. Persons communicating with the enemy in any way are liable to five years imprisonment. On 23 September, the president and acting chief justice of the High Muslim Court in Jerusalem was deported to the East Bank on charges of inciting noncooperation with Israeli authorities. By moving against the spiritual leader of the West Bank Arabs, the Israelis have indicated that they are willing to adopt extreme measures in dealing with dissidence.

Residents of the occupied territories have become increasingly tense as time passes without any movement toward ending the Israeli occupation or settling the political future of the West Bank.... a higher volume of violent incidents as local Arabs become increasingly annoyed by the petty irritations of life under occupation by members of an essentially alien culture.

Israeli authorities state that a rash of incidents in early September was the work of Palestinian terrorists based in Syria rather than an indication of indigenous sentiment. Nonetheless, some measure of aid and assistance must have been given to the terrorists by the indigenous population. Israeli reaction to these acts of violence has been swift and harsh, including the demolition of houses belonging to people suspected of aiding the saboteurs. Israeli officials have stated that the captured terrorists will be tried by military courts which will have authority to mete out the death penalty.

Israeli Views on the Future of the Occupied Territories

Israeli authorities have not made an official policy statement with respect to the eventual status of the occupied territories, presumably because they do not want to jeopardize any eventual negotiations with the Arabs. Individual Israeli views, including those of cabinet members, vary widely-- except with regard to the status of the Old City of Jerusalem, which almost all Israelis insist must remain under Israeli control.
[...]
The establishment in late September of Israeli settlements on the West Bank and on the Syrian heights is probably intended primarily as a warning to the Arabs that in the absence of any progress towards negotiations, Israel may move towards permanent possession of the area.

Outlook

Meanwhile, as the frustration of the Arabs in the occupied territories increases, acts of violence seem likely to increase against both the Israelis and the Arabs cooperating with them. Israeli security forces, however, are capable of suppressing any dissident elements and maintaining order.

Gaza Strip: A Primer (1979)
CENTRAL INTELLIGENCE AGENCY

[...] On 15 May 1948 the British mandate was terminated and the Arab-Israeli war began. Egyptian forces entered Gaza city, which became the headquarters of the Egyptian expeditionary force in Palestine. The area of Egyptian control was reduced by the fighting to a narrow strip of coastal territory 25 miles long that became known as the Gaza Strip. Its borders were demarcated in the Egyptian-Israeli armistice of 24 February 1950 [....]

During the 1948 fighting, the Strip became a haven for Palestinian refugees. Egypt did not annex the territory after the armistice, but administered it through governors whose rule is remembered as harsh.

Between 1949 and 1956 there was a gradual escalation of violence between inhabitants of Gaza and the neighboring Israelis. Israel temporarily occupied the area during the 1956 war, but relinquished control to Egypt in March 1957 under US and UN pressure.

Anti-Israeli activity accelerated in the Strip in the mid-1960s with the formation of the Palestine Liberation Organization. [...]

Israel regards the Gaza Strip as an anomaly. In its view it has neither the emotional and historical associations of the West Bank nor is it part of Egypt. But because of its proximity to Israel's populous coastal plain, Israeli leaders strongly believe they must retain some measure of control over the area to prevent it from again becoming a staging base for Palestinian terrorist attacks.

Egypt presently considers Gaza its responsibility until Gaza achieves self-determination as part of an independent Palestinian state or as a self-governing entity. Cairo does not include annexation of the Strip among the options available to Egypt, in part because of the large refugee population in Gaza.
[...]
Geography
[...]
Water supply is precarious; it is dependent on wells tapping underground aquifers fed by rainfall seepage. Average annual rainfall is about 14 inches.

Gaza has no known commercially exploitable natural resources and no natural harbor.

Human Resources

The Gaza Strip, with about 2,000 persons per square mile according to a 1967 census, is among the more densely populated areas of the world. [...]

It is a young population, with nearly half the people under 15 years of age. […]

The influx of refugees raised the population from 72,000 in 1946 to 280,000 in 1949; the natural increase of the 1948 refugee population is largely responsible for the area's current population of more than 400,000, of whom the refugees comprise over 80 percent. About 60 percent of the refugees continue to live in the eight camps administered by the United Nations Relief and Works Agency (UNRWA). The camp refugees, especially, remain a distinct social and political element that has not been absorbed into the surrounding communities, regarding themselves as temporarily separated from their homeland.
[…]

The Economic Setting

Gaza is basically a commercial center, with some agricultural activity and a few small industrial plants. Surrounded by the wastes of the Sinai and the Negev, Gaza has a poor location as a transportation crossroads. At present, the economy is almost totally dependent on labor, trade, transportation, and power ties to the Israeli economy.

[…] Per capita annual income is estimated at $500 to $700. (Jordan's is near $500 and Egypt's around $300.) Growth of real gross national product since 1968 has averaged an impressive 13 percent annually.

The rise of the standard of living in Gaza is less a product of economic development than a derivative of full employment and worker remittances from abroad. Full employment became possible after 1968 when Israel allowed Gaza's surplus labor to work in Israel, mostly as unskilled day laborers in the construction and agricultural sectors. About half of the employed labor force works in Israel—mostly as unskilled day laborers in the construction and agricultural sector.

Worker earnings from Israel—roughly $100 to 150 million annually—account for perhaps 40 percent of GNP. In 1978, per capita GNP surpassed $700, well above the average for less developed countries.

Such unemployment as does exist in Gaza is centered, ironically, among the better educated, because the demand in Israel is for cheap, unskilled labor.
[…]

Agriculture is Gaza's most important economic sector, accounting for 26 percent of employment, 28 percent of the gross domestic product, and about 90 percent of all export earnings. Industry is mostly restricted to traditional crafts, small workshops, and assembly operations for Israeli manufacturers.

Political Dynamics

Gaza is administered by an Israeli military governor assisted by 130 civilian technical personnel and 150 Israeli Defense Force personnel who supervise a local police force of several hundred.

Gaza has no elected officials—the last election was in 1964—and organized political activity is banned. Local government is provided by Arab mayors in four municipalities and seven villages, each assisted by a council. Mayors and councilmen are appointed by the Israeli governor.

The governor meets regularly with about 30 Gazan notables, the mayors, and the heads of the city councils. Israel allows Gazan officials some leeway in local matters and patronage power in return for a degree of cooperation. The officials are wary of appearing openly to be doing Israel's bidding because Gazans tolerate but do not accept Israeli rule.

Because political organizations are banned, most political activity takes place in ostensibly nonpolitical societies. [...]

UNRWA

The local Arab administrators of the UNRWA program, who are relatively free of both Israeli influence and that of the traditional power structure, constitute another political force in Gaza. The UNRWA group's importance would probably increase if Gaza were faced with the practical problems of self-government because UNRWA has the experience and machinery to administer the area.

Local UNRWA officials are drawn almost exclusively from among the refugees. They preside over a multimillion-dollar operation that is in constant touch with the population through the administration of schools and hospitals; control of housing, food, and vocational training; and the dispensation of considerable patronage. It is the most thoroughly organized, largest, and best funded administrative structure in the Strip.
[...]

West Bank: A Handbook (1983)
CENTRAL INTELLIGENCE AGENCY

___

<u>Geography and History</u>

The West Bank refers to that portion of Palestine that was annexed by
Jordan in 1950 and that has been occupied by Israel since the 1967 war
with the Arab states. Roughly the size of Delaware, the territory extends
130 kilometers from Janin in the north to Hebron in the south, and as
much as 55 kilometers from the Jordan River in the east to the foothills
overlooking the coastal plain of Israel.
[…]
WATER RESOURCES

The scarcity of water in most parts of the West Bank constrains both
agriculture and urban development in the region. As a result, water use has
become a contentious issue between the resident Palestinians and the
occupying Israelis.
[…]
TERRITORIAL CLAIMS

Palestinian Arab and Israeli claims and contentions over the West Bank
are based on several concerns. From the Palestinian perspective the area
is an important part of their homeland, controlled by a foreign,
colonialist power. For most Israelis, the West Bank is seen as a
strategic asset, affording Israel territorial depth against a possible Arab
attack from the east and protecting the densely populated coastal strip.
Both peoples share a religious and historical attachment to the West
Bank. […]

The war of 1948 forced far-reaching modifications in the UN partition
plan. The Arab state envisaged by that plan failed to emerge, and the
territory it was to have occupied was divided among Israel, Transjordan,
and Egypt by the armistice agreements of 1949. […] Trans-jordan
acquired 5,700 square kilometers, which it formally annexed a year
after the conclusion of the armistice, transforming itself into the state of
Jordan. […] Jerusalem was divided between Israel and Jordan.
[…]
Organizations dedicated to the liberation of Palestine—and to the
destruction of Israel—soon proliferated throughout the Palestinian
refugee communities in the Middle East. Jordan was unable to prevent
many of these groups from carrying out guerrilla or terrorist raids into
Israel from West Bank territory. […]

PALESTINIAN SOCIETY, LANDS, AND VILLAGES

Palestinian society on the West Bank is essentially agrarian.
Historically, Arab village life and agriculture were regulated by the

252

Islamic code's agrarian system. This system classified land into one of several categories: *mulk*, those limited areas of private ownership; *metruka*, communal land used for grazing, wood lots, roads, and other public concerns; *mawat*, abandoned land claimed by no one; *miri*, state land leased to private owners, particularly farmers; and *waqf*, land consecrated through religious institutions for welfare purposes.

[...]

REFUGEE CAMPS

[...]

The history of these camps dates back to the 1948 war and immediately thereafter, when hundreds of thousands of Palestinians left Israel for the Arab nations. Thinking they would soon be able to return, many resettled as close to their homes, particularly in the West Bank, which absorbed several hundred thousand displaced persons. Approximately 130,000 of them established residence in what were expected to be temporary camps. Permanent camps, however, soon were constructed by UNRWA [....]

The Economy

AGRICULTURE

Agriculture has always been the primary sector in the West Bank economy, but modern agricultural methods have been introduced on a large scale only in the past 16 years of Israeli administration. During this period, production of nearly all agricultural products has substantially increased. This has occurred despite a halving of the farm labor force, expropriation of land and deprivation of water resources by Israeli authorities, and market restrictions—both in Israel and Jordan. [...]

Politics

ISRAELI OCCUPATION AND POLICIES

The Israeli occupation of the West Bank since 1967 has triggered a number of changes in the region's society. The economic links that developed between Israel and the West Bank have significantly affected the income and employment of the territory's residents and led to the emergence of a politically more sophisticated middle class. The international controversy over the territory's future status has made it more difficult for West Bankers to ignore political issues. [...]

Development of Israeli Policy

Israeli policy toward the West Bank has undergone significant changes since 1967. When the West Bank first came under Israeli control, most Israelis probably expected that the territory—with the exception of

Jerusalem—would eventually be returned to Jordan in exchange for Amman's recognition of Israel. Military occupation authorities confined themselves largely to serving as proxy administrators of Jordanian law. The lack of significant political activity by Palestinians in the West Bank was as much due to policies and habits established under Jordanian rule as it was to Israeli restrictions. [...]

In the mid-1970s, however, the West Bank's military government assumed a more active role in the politics of the territory and attempted to direct the emerging political aspirations of West Bank residents into channels the Israelis thought would be constructive. During the voting for village and municipal leaders in 1975 and 1976, the military administration took great pains to ensure that the elections were relatively open and democratic. Israeli officials who advocated this liberalization of West Bank politics believed that the elections would produce a new echelon of moderate West Bank leaders who would cooperate with the military government and who could compete with the PLO for the allegiance of West Bank residents.

Most of the mayors who were elected in the 1976 municipal elections, however, openly sympathized with the PLO. [...]

PALESTINIAN POLITICS
[...]
Despite the political evolution there in the last few years, the West Bank largely remains a traditional, rural-based society. More than half of the territory's nonrefugee residents, for example, still live in villages of 3,000 people or less. For most West Bankers, even those living in the larger urban areas, family or clan ties are the most important factors in their lives. Even the city of Nablus—the largest and most politically active West Bank town—is essentially an overgrown agricultural market center whose inhabitants are either still farmers or not far removed from the rural lifestyle.
[...]
As in most traditional societies, the majority of the West Bank's residents are more concerned about earning a living for themselves and their families than they are about political affairs that often do not affect them directly. The group in West Bank society that is most likely to act on its political beliefs is the educated elite. White-collar workers, professionals, teachers, students, and journalists—who are the cutting edge of political activity in most traditional societies—are a growing force on the West Bank. [...]

The West Bank Elite and the PLO
[...]
Despite their increasing numbers, the West Bank's educated elites have had little direct political impact on the territory. This is due in large part to the ban on political parties in the West Bank. During the late 1970s the

mayors and municipal councils did reflect the views of most West Bank professionals, but since the Israeli crackdown on municipal leaders, the West Bank elite has lacked even that channel for expressing its political views.

[...]

Security Aspects

WEST BANK'S INTERNAL SECURITY

[...]

The military government also has had considerable success in containing civil disturbances in the territory, but the resentment that many West Bankers harbor against the Israelis makes a certain level of unrest inevitable. Much of the violence is cyclical in nature, and tensions are often highest during anniversaries commemorating important events in the history of Palestinian nationalism. The highly vocal and nationalistic school-age population poses a special problem for Israeli authorities, and the opening days of school terms are often marked by protests and demonstrations.

The military government has dealt forcefully with civil unrest, and it has not hesitated to employ its discretionary powers of arrest and detention to contain disturbances. The IDF has also followed a policy of punishing entire groups for the actions of individuals by, for example, razing homes when one family member is guilty of offenses. [...]

TERRORISM

Before the Six-Day War, Palestinian groups and, during the 1950s, even the Jordanian Army randomly shelled Israel's coastal plain from the Judean and Samarian hills, and armed bands frequently crossed into Israel to carry out terrorist attacks. After the Israeli occupation of the West Bank, the IDF succeeded in clearing out much of the PLO's infrastructure from the territory. Israeli settlements built in the Jordan River Valley were in part intended to help monitor and stop PLO infiltration from Jordan, although the actual border patrolling has been performed by IDF units. [...]

The influx of West Bank laborers to Israel during the early and mid-1970s, however, has provided the PLO with a new means of carrying out terrorist attacks inside Israel. The large number of West Bankers who work in Israel travel freely and regularly across the border. Rather than rely on more easily detectable bands of terrorists, the PLO now depends largely on individuals who deposit simple bombs in busy Israeli urban areas and disappear from the scene long before an explosion occurs. [...]

In spite of the sharp differences in Israel over settlements and over the degree to which Israel can afford to compromise in West Bank negotiations, there is virtually universal agreement that the territory is vital to Israel's security. No political faction of any significance would agree to a treaty that did not permit an Israeli military presence on the West Bank.

The Israelis stress the importance of denying the territory to potentially hostile military forces. They note that Israel's pre-1967 border with Jordan constituted one of the least defensible boundaries imaginable. It left Arab forces in control of high ground overlooking a coastal plain only 15 to 30 kilometers wide on which 75 percent of the Jewish population and half of Israel industry are located. An armor thrust from the Arab hills could theoretically have divided Israel and seriously challenged its defense. The West Bank itself offered ideal sanctuaries for a campaign of irregular warfare.
[…]
Jerusalem

The status of Jerusalem is recognized as the most difficult of any of the issues that must be resolved by the parties to the Arab-Israeli dispute. By more or less general agreement, consideration of Jerusalem will be one of the final items on any negotiating agenda. […]

Jerusalem is comprised of the Old City, a walled area that contains sites considered sacred by Judaism, Christianity, and Islam; the Arab area outside the walls north and east of the Old City; the primarily Jewish area to the west known as the New City; and the area of the West Bank that was incorporated into Jerusalem in 1967, consisting of Arab villages and new Jewish housing developments.

Jews and Muslims consider one part of the city to be especially sacred: the raised area of 14 hectares in the southwest corner of the walled city called the Temple Mount by the Jews because within this area the Temple once stood. The Western Wall, frequently referred to as the Wailing Wall, is part of the retaining wall around the raised area and is considered holy in Jewish tradition because of its proximity to the inner sanctuary of the Temple. Located on the Temple Mount—called Haram al-Sharif by the Muslims—are the al-Aqsa Mosque and the Dome of the Rock, which according to Muslim tradition is built over the spot from which Muhammad ascended to heaven.

The conflict between the forces of Israel following its creation as an independent state in May 1948 and the armed forces of the Arab states left Jerusalem a divided city, with Jordanian forces holding the Old City and the adjacent areas to the north and east and the Israeli forces in control of the New City. The 1967 war brought the entire city, as well as the West Bank, the Sinai Peninsula, and the Golan Heights in Syria, under Israeli control.

Jerusalem is the focal point and symbol of Israeli identity. For most Israelis, the reunification of the city marked the completion of the creation of the Jewish state. They are determined that Jerusalem remain a united city, under exclusive Israeli sovereignty, and the capital of Israel. The third most sacred city in the world for Muslims, after Mecca and Medina, Jerusalem is also of paramount importance to most Arabs.

Since the 1967 war, the Israeli Government has taken a series of actions that are clearly intended to make the reunification of Jerusalem irreversible. This process of Israelization, or "creating facts" as the Israelis have termed it, has involved annexation, expropriation, and the construction of housing for Israeli Jews in the expropriated areas. In June 1967 the Knesset approved a series of decrees greatly expanding the municipal boundaries northeast, east, and south of the city and annexing the entire area to Israel. In 1968 and 1970 large tracts of land in the newly expanded city were expropriated by the Israelis. Several major housing projects for Israeli Jews were subsequently established on the expropriated land. The effect of this action has been to separate Arab Jerusalem from the West Bank. Some government offices, including the Ministry of Justice, the Supreme Court, and the Israeli National Police, were transferred to East Jerusalem shortly after the 1967 war, an action intended to strengthen Israeli claims to Jerusalem as its permanent capital.
[...]
Since 1967 the Israeli position on Jerusalem has been that continued Israeli control over the expanded city is not negotiable. Although government spokesmen have stated that the future of the city will be discussed in direct negotiations, they have avoided giving details on what might be offered the Arabs, and it is clear that no government is prepared to compromise Israeli sovereignty over the united city.
[...]
For the most part, the Arab states publicly have adopted a hardline position on Jerusalem. Although Jordanian King Hussein in early 1972 indicated that he would agree to Israeli sovereignty over the Armenian Quarter as well as the Jewish Quarter and the Western Wall plaza, he subsequently toughened his position and called for the return of all East Jerusalem to Arab sovereignty. Saudi Arabia and Egypt have also called for Israeli withdrawal from East Jerusalem. Nevertheless, recognizing that even under extreme pressure Israel is unlikely to agree to the return of East Jerusalem to Arab control, we believe that at least some Arab states, particularly Egypt and Jordan, may be prepared to compromise on the ultimate status of the city.
[...]

Israeli Development of Occupied Arab Territories (1969)
CENTRAL INTELLIGENCE AGENCY

Israeli settlers entered the occupied territories shortly after the conclusion of the June 1967 war. By November 1969, they had established 22 new settlements and had moved into the Arab towns of East Jerusalem and Hebron. While most of the settlements were founded to serve as military outposts, they have for some time now been assigned such nonmilitary functions as the development of agricultural and mineral resources and the promotion of tourism. [...]

Israeli Approach to Development
[...]

2. Among the organizations cooperating in the development of the occupied territories are the Israel Defense Forces (IDF), which are responsible for territorial administration. The Settlement Department of the quasi-official Jewish Agency, which raises funds throughout the world to support immigrant absorption, settlement, and land reclamation, is responsible for planning and carrying out all rural settlement in Israel. [...]

West Bank

10. Eight Israeli settlements have been established on the West Bank, despite the presence of 600,000 to 650,000 Arab residents. Five of these settlements are in the Jordan Valley, two are south of Jerusalem, and one is in the former demilitarized zone west of Jerusalem. [...] In addition, a group of Israelis has settled in Hebron, and several hundred others have moved into East Jerusalem. The West Bank sector of the Jordan Valley contains marginal agricultural land, and estimates differ on the availability of potentially cultivable acreage. [...]

11. Security is a primary concern on the West Bank. Settlement activity in the thinly populated Jordan Valley appears to reflect ideas expressed in the "Allon Plan," which calls for a 10- to 15-mile-wide "security zone" west of the Jordan River. Control of this zone would be maintained by up to 20 settlements if the plan is fully implemented. [...]

The Gaza Strip and Al 'Arish

12. Problems faced by Israel in the Gaza Strip and the adjoining Al 'Arish area concern the administration of an economically depressed area where the population, primarily refugee, exceeds 350,000. Payments from UNRWA have been the major source of income for most people in the Gaza Strip; the local nonrelief economy rests mainly on the export of citrus fruit. An attempt is being made by Israel to improve the production, grading, and packing of export fruit in order to improve the acceptance of Gaza products in Israeli markets. Programs

have also been initiated to improve the quality of grazing animals, to increase the production of nuts and dates, and to expand the fishing industry. In July 1969 [...] $2,285,714 (IL 8,000,000) had been made for the development of textile and service industries. [...]

Sinai

13. [...] Physical conditions severely limit agricultural potential, and most of the 45,000 to 50,000 local Arabs, two-thirds of whom are in the vicinity of Al'Arish on the Mediterranean Coast, exist at a subsistence level. Israeli development here has been geared largely to security requirements. [...]

17. Two nahals and a kibbutz have been established on the Mediterranean coast of the Sinai Peninsula and two more settlements have been authorized. Five army camps are being completed in central and western Sinai. [...]

18. Israel's most profitable economic venture in the occupied Arab territories is the exploitation of the oil fields on the Gulf of Suez. During 1968 Israel lifted some 3,920,000 barrels (560,000 tons) of crude oil from 16 offshore wells [....]

Conclusions

20. Israel's activity in the occupied territories reflects her strong concern for security and her readiness for the eventuality of a long-term occupation. Expenditures to date and projected activity indicate a systematic but flexible plan of development [....] The nature of activity in western Sinai for instance, indicates a recognition that the occupation may be terminated on short notice; Israeli development activities in the Jordan Valley and the Golan Heights, and activities associated with Sharm ash Shaykh at the entrance to the Gulf of Aqaba, on the other hand, give no such indication of impermanence.

21. Israel clearly regards a strong presence in the occupied territories as essential to a firm negotiating position. At the same time, it recognizes that selective exploitation and development of the territories can generate income during the stalemate. The overall pace of development suggests that so long as there is no settlement of Arab and Israeli differences, Israel's presence in occupied territory will probably continue to grow.

22. Security aside, Israeli withdrawal from the occupied territories at this time would not result in substantial losses. After a few years of continuing investment of time, money, and effort, however, the potential costs incident to a withdrawal might be more than the Israeli Government would be willing to accept.

PALESTINE LIBERATION ORGANIZATION ("PLO")

The Guerilla Threat in The Middle East (1968)
TIME MAGAZINE

The revolution of Fatah exists! It exists here, there and everywhere. It is a storm, a storm in every house and village.

Faithful and unfailing as the muezzin's call from the minaret, that heady cry goes out nightly from a radio station in Cairo to the Arab lands. It is the "Voice of El Fatah," speaking for the Arab commando organization whose bands of raiders cross each night into hated Israel, bent on bringing death, destruction and terror. To Arabs huddled in wind-chilling refugee tents outside Amman, sipping thick coffee in the drawing rooms of Damascus, or lounging in the common rooms of the American University of Beirut, the Voice brings welcome—if often inaccurate—news. The fight against Israel continues, it asserts, despite the Arabs' humiliating defeat in last year's war. Each night new Arab heroes are born, fresh revenge is meted out to Israel, a portion of Arab pride is restored. Amid the breathless bulletins and the florid rhetoric of propaganda, there are the underground's customary coded messages: "M.H.: the bird is back in the cage"; "Attention Green Lion: the gift has been received."

On Fatah's signal, a band of Arabs sets out across the Jordan River on rafts made from tractor tires, carrying their Russian-made Kalashnikov assault rifles in waterproof inner tubes. In the darkness they land, make their way inland, plant a mine, ambush an Israeli patrol or throw a grenade, then scramble as best they can for home. The odds are heavily against their making it back, for many are caught or killed by efficient Israeli security forces. But the rewards are high, as posthumous compensations go. They are martyrs to all Arabs, their photographs and tales of their exploits are displayed in Cairo and Amman. Under the rules of jihad, or holy war, proclaimed against Israel by Moslem leaders from 34 countries last October, those Arabs who fall in battle are accorded the reverence of prophets and go straight to paradise.

The Elements of Instability

The Fatah is one of several similar clandestine organizations. While no one can be sure of the exact numbers involved, Fatah is the most prominent and the largest of them. To the Israelis, the raiders are terrorists and thugs, inept and indiscriminate in their missions. To the Arabs, they are freedom fighters in the best guerrilla tradition, skilled in the arts of the commando and the saboteur. The world knows them best as the fedayeen, meaning "men of sacrifice," a disparate group of clandestine plotters often at odds with one another, who play a large part in keeping the Middle East on the edge of war.

There is no more perilously unstable area in the world. Israel, despite its overwhelming victory in last year's war, grows increasingly frustrated as it finds peace with its encircling Arab neighbors still beyond reach. The Arab countries, their armies and air forces rebuilding with major Soviet aid and advice, refuse to accept fully their defeat or abandon completely their long-range goal of eliminating Israel. The more responsible Arab leaders, including Egypt's Gamal Abdel Nasser and Jordan's King Hussein, know that any early attack on Israel would only result in another resounding defeat. But in a measure they are prisoners of their Arab masses, long fed on the oratory of hate and revenge and embittered by the 26,000 sq. mi. of Arab territory—taken from Jordan, Syria and Egypt—now occupied by the Israelis.

Despite their common adversity, the Arabs are as quarrelsome and mistrustful of one another as ever. Iraq, for example, has sent troops to bolster shattered Jordan's defenses against Israel, and King Hussein worries about the Iraqis in his midst almost as much as he does about Israel. The U.S. is committed to peace in the area and to Israel's right to exist; but also vitally needs to establish better relations with the Arabs, most of whom regard America as simply the backer and ally of Israel. In this situation, Washington can do little beyond attempting to keep a reasonable balance of arms among the antagonists. Meanwhile, the Soviet Union, more influential in the Arab world than ever because of its arms shipments, has staked its own claim to the use of the Mediterranean for its expanding navy, sharply increasing the danger of a direct U.S.-Russian confrontation on the high seas should a new Middle East war break out.

For more than twelve months, United Nations Special Representative Gunnar Jarring has patiently sought grounds for agreement, and at least succeeded in becoming an intermediary whom both sides trust and through whom they have begun, in a fashion, to talk to each other. In the bitter history of Arab-Israeli relations, that is no mean accomplishment. Though his mandate was due to expire this month, both sides want him to stay on the job. One of the reasons is that Israel's stunning victory in the Six-Day War introduced at least a small element of reality into the Middle East impasse. Before the 1967 war, the only issue was Israel's existence, a matter clearly not negotiable at a conference table between the Israelis and the Arabs. But the matter of recovering the occupied territories is negotiable—theoretically. In the discussions with Jarring, the Israelis so far refuse to give up any of the occupied territories without guarantees of progress toward a full Middle East settlement. The Arabs in turn so far refuse to talk about a settlement until the Israelis return the Arab lands. [...]

It is in this tense milieu that the Arabs' "men of sacrifice" operate, in a defiant effort to exploit its instabilities to their own ends. The fedayeen, who owe no fealty to any government, are responsible only to themselves, and view any settlement as a betrayal and a disaster. They possess the power to sting Israel into repeated reprisals, and perhaps to whip Arab popular opinion to such a pitch that not even Nasser with all his prestige might dare a settlement with Israel. In Jordan, their primary staging area, they constitute virtually a state-within-a-state and could probably topple King Hussein and take over his splintered kingdom if they chose. [...]

The Palestinian Diaspora

The primary sources of fedayeen strength are the Palestinian refugees, now 1,500,000 strong, who for 20 years have been a scattered and forlorn people, possessing neither a country nor any say in the harsh events profoundly affecting them. Dispossessed of their homes, lands and sense of nationhood when Israel was founded in 1948, they dispersed throughout the Middle East. They endured the scorn of their host populations toward outsiders, although the most skilled and educated came to dominate many areas of Arab intellectual and commercial life. Those that did not assimilate settled in crowded camps, mostly in Jordan and the Gaza Strip, where they lived a miserable, subsistence life, fed by the United Nations Relief and Works Agency.

For 20 years they have been pawns in Arab politics, nourished on promises of a return to Palestine and a passionate hatred of Israel. Today the camps house 540,000, including 350,000 new refugees who fled the occupied territories after the June War. The camps seethe with frustration and anger, and provide a rich source of recruits for fedayeen. Says the mother of one dead commando: "I am proud that he did not die in this camp. The foreign press comes here and takes our pictures standing in food queues, and they publish them and say 'Look at this nation of beggars.' This is no life. I am proud to send my second son to replace the first, and I am already preparing my eight-year-old boy for the day when he can fight too."

With the fanaticism and desperation of men who have nothing to lose, the fedayeen have taken the destiny of the Palestinians into their own hands. Peace in the area would hurt their cause by removing the support of other Arabs. They have no brotherly concern for the ambitions of Nasser—and certainly not for, as one fedayeen communique puts it, the "slave traffickers in the U.N. lobbies" and their efforts to act as mediators in the Middle East.

In the aftermath of the Arab defeat, the fedayeen are today the only ones carrying the fight to Israel. The guerrillas provide an outlet for the fierce Arab resentment of Israel and give an awakened sense of pride to a people accustomed to decades of defeat, disillusionment and humiliation. In the process, the Arabs have come to idolize Mohammed ("Yasser") Arafat, a leader of El Fatah fedayeen who has emerged as the most visible spokesman for the commandos. An intense, secretive and determined Palestinian, he is enthusiastically portrayed by the admiring Arab press as a latter-day Saladin, with the Israelis supplanting the Crusaders as the hated—and feared—foe.

It was the Israeli victory last year that, as one fedayeen commander puts it, "handed us the Arab people on a golden platter." Students quit their classes to sign up as terrorists. Doctors abandoned their practices in Beirut and Cairo to come to Jordan to attend wounded fedayeen. Arab businessmen offered supplies and purchased weapons, and the Saudi and Kuwait governments began diverting to fedayeen coffers funds usually contributed to Jordan's budget. Individual contributions by the thousands poured in from Arabs throughout the Middle East and those abroad; the wife of Saudi Arabia's King Feisal sent $4,500. In the coffee bars of Beirut, young Arabs peddle El Fatah stamps, to be used like Christmas seals, bearing a picture of a burned child and the words "Shalom and Napalm"—a reference to the use of napalm by Israelis in last August's reprisal raid on the Jordanian town of Salt. Other stamps show a guerrilla fighter, a monument to martyrs or Jerusalem, with the slogan: "Palestinian Resistance." The money raised, of course, goes to buy bullets.

Contributing to the fedayeen mystique is their shadowy organization, which somehow manages to appear to be everywhere in the Arab countries. At the airport of Amman, dark-suited youths sidle up to customs officers as crates marked "Palestine Nation, Amman" or "Freedom Fighters against Israel, Amman" are unloaded, and whisper, "For the fedayeen." Customs formalities are cut short, and the supplies are whisked away. The goods may be headed for any one of more than 50 bases maintained by the fedayeen in the Jordanian mountains east of Wadi Araba, the desert valley that stretches from the Dead Sea to the Gulf of Aqaba.

No one knows how many Arab commandos roam about in that desolate stretch, from which raiders set out nightly, but estimates range upward from 10,000. Besides their base camps, there are other installations as well. The fedayeen maintain at least a dozen underground field hospitals and supply depots, as well as training camps for ash-bals, or tiger cubs— refugee children who are taught the art of guerrilla war beginning at age eight.

Ambassador Extraordinary

The fedayeen are most secretive of all about their high command, though the largest organization, Arafat's El Fatah, is said to be ruled by a committee of wealthy civilians in Damascus. Nor does anyone really know very much about Yasser Arafat, though everyone in the Arab world knows who he is. As El Fatah grew and felt the need for a visible spokesman, he became its ambassador extraordinary to the Arab world, its chief fund raiser and its field commander in Jordan. Arafat (his code name is Abu Ammar) sits at a wooden desk in his headquarters in Amman, dealing with a procession of couriers like a general on a field of battle, which in a sense he is. When a guerrilla comes in to report a successful raid, Arafat's eyes, bulging almost to the panes of the dark glasses he wears day and night, dance with delight. He speaks softly and turns aside all questions about himself: "Please, no personality cult. I am only a soldier. Our leader is Palestine. Our road is the road of death and sacrifice to win back our homeland. If we can not do it, our children will, and if they cannot do it, their children will."

Arafat's career in a way mirrors the history and thrust of the fedayeen. Born in Jerusalem, he spent his early childhood in a house within a stone's throw of the Wailing Wall. The area today is marked by the Israelis for bulldozing. Of that prospect, Arafat says bitterly: "We will see that our homes are rebuilt." Descended from Palestinian nobility, Arafat learned early what dispossession meant. According to one story widely told in the Middle East, his family has been disinherited of enormous wealth for 150 years through a legal tangle that deprived it of land once owned in downtown Cairo. Arafat's father spent a lifetime trying to reclaim the land in the Egyptian courts but was overruled first by King Farouk and then Nasser. There are those who suspect that that may be one factor in Arafat's occasional lack of enthusiasm for Egypt's ruler.

A teenage gunrunner in the 1948 war with Israel, Arafat afterward enrolled at Fuad I (now Cairo) University, where he majored in civil engineering— and in Palestinian nationalism as president of the Palestine Student Federation. After graduating, he worked in Kuwait, editing an ultranationalist magazine on the side. In 1955, he appeared in Cairo attending officers' school, where he specialized in explosives. He graduated as a lieutenant just in time to share in another Arab defeat, at Suez a year later.

That debacle only confirmed Arafat's conviction that the Arabs could never defeat the Israelis with conventional armies. Throughout the 1950s, he had organized "cells" among Palestinian students abroad and studied the techniques of Algerian guerrillas. At that time, Nasser had organized forerunners of today's fedayeen among Palestinians in the Gaza Strip, and used them to stir up the border, a role they took on with sufficient enthusiasm to help bring about Israel's decision to launch the 1956 war. After Suez, El Fatah was founded as a strictly Palestinian force outside Nasser's reach.

Not until 1964 was El Fatah ready for its first raid, sabotaging an Israeli water-pumping station. It was an "experimental era," recalls Arafat, when

El Fatah staged only one raid a week, testing out attack techniques, taking notes on Israeli defenses and reaction times, and filing away the information to be used in future battle plans. "We were also experimenting with public opinion all through this period," Arafat's top aide told TIME Correspondent Edward Hughes last week. According to the dictum of Mao Tse-tung, guerrilla fighters must be able to live among a friendly population like fish in water. But El Fatah at that time "had no audience. Without the people to listen to us, we had no sea to swim in—the fish had no oxygen."

The Expansion of the War

After last year's war, El Fatah found itself not only swimming in popular support but also possessed of a sudden bequest of weapons left by the retreating Arab armies. The battlefields were littered with arms, and for two weeks, El Fatah teams took camels into the Sinai desert to collect machine guns, rifles, grenades and bazookas before the Israeli salvage squads. Four heavy trucks were found in Golan, along with two tons of ammunition and weapons. A Bedouin offered to sell 150 Kalashnikov rifles for $140. El Fatah gave him twice as much. Another Bedouin found a Syrian helicopter and built a tent to hide it for the El Fatah men. But when they arrived, they had no helicopter pilot along, so the craft was destroyed. A cache of eight tons of TNT, too heavy to carry away, was buried in the Sinai: "We don't have to carry explosives into that area. It's there waiting for us," Arafat says.

By August 1967, El Fatah was ready to try to launch an underground revolt among the Arabs on the now occupied West Bank. Hundreds of guerrillas trekked across the Jordan River, only to be rounded up by Israeli forces. To head off any future attempts, the Israelis blew up the homes of any Palestinians who cooperated with Arafat's men. El Fatah's next phase was a campaign that sent smaller groups to hide in caves or live with sympathetic Arabs, and venture out at night to set mines or time bombs. Israel hit back at their riverside guerrilla camps, forcing El Fatah to move its bases farther in land. Despite these setbacks, the fedayeen have been able to step up their operations to as many as two dozen a day. Though El Fatah hotly rejects being called terroristic, it has also turned increasingly to attacking Israel's civilian population. The methods are brutal and indiscriminate, random terrorism for terrorism's sake without any military value —a bomb in a crowded cinema, a grenade thrown in a schoolyard, a mine planted for anyone who comes along. [...]

By laying down a strict policy of staying out of Arab politics on the ground that, as Arafat says, "one enemy at a time is enough," El Fatah has so far been able to operate independently in the host Arab countries— chiefly Jordan. Disputes with rival fedayeen organizations are another matter, and on one occasion two groups of raiders almost shot it out, each thinking the other was Israeli. Last month, the fedayeen set up a council to coordinate raids between El Fatah and its two chief rivals, the Palestine Liberation Force and the Popular Front for the Liberation of Palestine, or P.F.L.P. (inevitably pronounced "flop" by Westerners on the scene), a militantly leftist merger of several splinter organizations on the scene.

Training for Terror

From the refugee camps, and from universities that are often staffed with zealous Palestinian professors, come a steady stream of several hundred recruits a month—more, in fact, than El Fatah can handle. It accepts Palestinians for the most part, and only those who pass rigorous medical tests and an examination by a team of psychiatrists. A recruit must also pass a final, brutal test of fortitude. He is handed a large box containing the body of a newly killed dog, still bleeding profusely. As the blood seeps out, he is told, "Inside this box is a wounded comrade. Take it and carry it around the block and bring it back here." The recruit is not inclined to ask questions. If he vomits or faints on the spot, he is gently steered to an easier job as a courier, or told to go home and simply spy on his neighbors. If he passes, he is sent to one of dozens of different training camps in Jordan, Syria, Lebanon and Iraq.

Outside Amman, children, aged eight to twelve, from the *Baq'aa* refugee camp, are trained in commando techniques. They are given rigorous calisthenics and obstacle-course training, taught to handle rifles and machine guns, and instructed where the larynx, heart, liver and intestines are located, the better to thrust a dagger in the right place. Daughters of dead fedayeen are sent to schools run by the "Martyr Family Welfare Service," where they are taught to chant: "I have broken my chains. I am the daughter of Fatah! We are all commandos." Refugee women are trained in first aid and in handling weapons.
[...]
These days El Fatah hardly has time to fight as it copes with the avalanche of aid. Stacks of bandages, food and ammunition are piled everywhere. Sometimes, the arriving shipments include beer. It is not drunk: the fedayeen sell it and use the money to purchase arms. Some of the fedayeen weapons are purchased directly, but some are contributed by Arab governments, particularly Egypt, Iraq, and Syria, which help out in other ways as well. A Syrian raider captured by the Israelis revealed that he had been trained by Egyptian army officers.
[...]
To the fedayeen, the model and example is the Algerian revolution. For ideology, they look to its apostle, Frantz Fanon, the late Martinique-born Negro psychiatrist, who preached in *The Wretched of the Earth* that for oppressed and colonized people of the world "violence is a cleansing force. It frees the native from his inferiority complex and from his despair and inaction; it makes him fearless and restores his self-respect."

266

In the view of the Palestinians, Israel is an imperialist colonial power occupying their land. With no hope of driving the Israelis out themselves, the Palestinians aim to provoke Israel into taking so much territory that in finally chokes on a glut of Arabs within its borders. Moreover, says Arafat, "the very process of Israeli expansion will extend the war of liberation into all the countries bordering on the occupied territories, and they will take up the struggle in defense of their own existence"—perhaps with Russia this time drawn in on the Arab side.

The Catalogue of Violence

To that fantastic end, the fedayeen have staged some 1,000 incidents over the last year, and killed or wounded over 900 Israelis. When a school bus struck one of their mines last March, 28 children were wounded and two adults killed. In August, the guerillas managed to terrorize the population of Jerusalem and in the bargain set off an anti-Arab riot by a series of grenade attacks. In September, they struck for the first time at Tel Aviv, where a commando bomb in a wastebasket outside the bus station killed one Israeli and wounded another ten.

[...]

The Israeli Assessment

To the guerillas' disadvantage, the bleak, rocky West Bank, where they target most of their operations, does not provide good cover, and the Israelis are a formidably efficient enemy. They claim to have killed or captured 2,650 fedayeen and tend to dismiss them as amateurs. "We cannot dignify them with the name guerilla or commando," says an Israeli officer. "The Arabs who cross over show no daring. In that respect, they are nowhere near Viet Cong standards." The Israelis do respect Arafat, however. Their intelligence network has twice reported him on Israeli soil, and twice he escaped a dragnet. "Anyone who can do that has to be pretty shrewd," admits an Israeli intelligence officer grudgingly.

The newest Israeli countermeasure is an electronic barrier that stretches about 40 miles along the Jordan River Valley. [...] It consists of an outer line of 8-ft.-high barbed wire and an inner, 5-ft.-high line 10 yds. away. The space between is laced with mines. At irregular intervals along the fence are strung electronic sensing devices, which raise an alarm in adjacent guard posts when an infiltrator tries to cross. The guards in turn alert nearby army units, equipped to react quickly with helicopter and powerful searchlights.

There are signs that Israeli traditional response to commando activity, a retaliation raid in massive force, only serves to steel the will of the fedayeen and win them new allies among the Jordanian people. Last March, an armored column of more than 1,000 Israeli men punched across the Jordan River to destroy a guerilla base at Karamah. They succeeded, but Karamah became the fedayeen Alamo. In the furious battle, as El Fatah recounts it, one youth strapped a bundle of TNT around his waist and jumped on an Israeli tank, blowing himself up with it. From the surrounding hills, the regular Jordanian army poured a withering fire on Israeli troops, who had to fight their way home, taking high casualties. Jordan's King Hussein went on television after the battle ended and declared, in words that have since been taken up as a rousing slogan throughout the Arab countries. "I think we may reach a position where we are all fedayeen."

Thus, for all the Israelis' contempt for the raiders, there is evidence that they are worried. Recently, Israel closed the Allenby Bridge over the Jordan River to truck traffic, reversing its own policy of keeping connections between Jordan and the West Bank open. Now trucks coming from Jordan must unload on one side, and the goods are reloaded into Israeli vehicles on the other side, all under the watchful eye of police. [...] At Israeli schools, teachers are now being lectured on anti-terrorists tactics and given courses in first aid, and schoolchildren are instructed in how to identify mines. Cinema ushers and janitors are undergoing training to learn how to take precautions against bombs. [...] Yehoshafat Harkahi, a former chief of Israeli intelligence, warns that "subversion may become a feature of our lives for a length of time that no one can foresee. It might become like the toll of traffic accidents modern societies have to pay." Over the long run, there, perhaps a danger that the fedayeen campaign may strike severe blows at Israeli democracy, as ever more repressive measures are required to hold down terrorism.

The Dilemma for the U.S.

Yet there are many in the Middle East who believe that the fedayeen pose the greatest long run threat not to Israel but rather to Hussein and Nasser. In Jordan, the fedayeen in a recent showdown with the King won the right to run their own military show without interference from the Jordanian army (TIME, Nov. 22). So great is the popular groundswell for the movement that no Arab leader dares condemn it or openly talk peace on any terms that Israel might be likely to accept. Israel has not helped by its policy of holding each Arab government responsible for the acts of the fedayeen launched from its territory—though it is hard to see what else Israel could do. Caught between the Israelis and their own militant populations, Arab leaders could be pushed to extremes to which they do not want to go. Lest he appear less militant than the guerillas, Nasser has sent half of Egypt's 141st battalion to southern Jordan and last October Egyptian forces launched an artillery attack on Israel for no other apparent purpose than to silence sniping at home about his comparative lack or zeal against Israel.
[...]

The PLO: Past, Present and Future (1980)
Dr. Asad Abdul-Rahman and Rashid Hamid

The Palestine Liberation Organization is the broad organizational framework within which all Palestinian organizations—commando groups, trade unions, professional associations, as well as prominent national figures—converge to work for the achievement of Palestinian national goals. […]

1. The Historical Context

After the 1948 war, the Palestinians were in the unusual situation of possessing a high level of national consciousness without the national and political institutions to embody it. Their national identity was a dominant theme of their everyday life. In the eyes of those Palestinians, who found themselves suddenly uprooted from their normal rhythm of life, and plunged into the situation of refugees in the surrounding countries, all the daily problems of survival—finding work, food, or shelter—arose directly from the fact that they were Palestinians exiled by the Israelis from their homeland. At all levels of political and national socialization in this traumatic situation. Palestinian consciousness was retained and extended: Palestinians lived among other Palestinians or other Arabs in exile; they remembered Palestine through personal experience and through the accounts of families and relatives; and they identified themselves as Palestinians with a common historical and contemporary experience with a deep attachment to their land. Those who were politically active, were committed to parties working for the Palestinian cause in one way or another.

Palestinian aspirations for the future, both political and personal, crystalized in most cases into a single goal that received almost universal support in the community—that of the return. This was, in fact, a right that was internationally acknowledged by the United Nations resolutions passed annually with the approval of Israel's major ally, the United States, though not implemented by Israel. […]

Palestinian consciousness might be high, but partly because of the abnormal situation of dispersal in which Palestinians found themselves, their political organization was initially very limited. Their old, traditional leadership, comprising the Arab Higher Committee led by the Mufti of Jerusalem, had been discredited by the disasters of 1947-48. In the Diaspora, the Palestinians were not able to fill that political vacuum because of the organizational difficulties arising from their being dispersed, and because they were subjected to the laws and regulations of the host countries which had no interest in encouraging a separate national political organization among them.

From The First United Nations Seminar on the Question of Palestine: The 269 Inalienable Rights of the Palestinian People. Arusha, Tanzania.

Most Palestinians found themselves under the sovereignty of Jordan, which had annexed the West Bank, the largest and most important of the three areas of Palestine remaining in the hands of the Arabs after planting the "State of Israel" in Palestine in 1948. Apart from this, the Gaza Strip was administered, but not annexed, by the Egyptians. The third and smallest area of the unusurped parts of Palestine (al-Himma) was administered by Syria. These territories covered about 21 per cent of the original mandated territory. Tens of thousands of Palestinians were either dispersed in Lebanon, Syria, Kuwait, Iraq and other Arab and non-Arab countries or lived under Israeli military rule.

The different areas in which Palestinians were located had a different effect on their freedom to conduct nationalist activities. Palestinian activities in Jordan were kept within the Hashemite framework. Their serious opposition, especially through pan-Arab groups, was repressed. In contrast, there was a basic difference with the Gaza Strip (administered by Egypt). There the Palestinians fully exposed to Arab nationalist ideas and much Palestinian activism arose (e.g. the creation of al-Fateh). Elsewhere, Palestinian activism tended to be linked with one of the political trends that existed in the neighboring countries, especially movements such as Nasserism, the Ba'th, the Arab Nationalists' Movement or the Syrian National Party. Most Palestinians saw the recovery of their homeland as dependent upon the achievement of Arab power through Arab unity; they therefore identified with pan-Arab parties, which they believed to be seriously committed to the Palestinian cause.
[…]
[T]he major reasons for the upsurge of Palestinian political activity in the 1960's lay in two events that seemed to alter the political environment. The first was the break-up of the United Arab Republic, the union between Egypt and Syria that had marked the high-point of pan-Arab nationalism to which Palestinian political activists had been committed. This shook their belief in the possibility of quick Arab unity, particularly when, following close on its heels came the attainment of independence by Algeria in 1962 after a long, bitter, and costly revolution.

This seemed to indicate that Arab unity might not be a prerequisite for liberation and that a nation could struggle successfully against foreign settlers by relying mainly on its own resources. Hitherto oriented mainly towards the Arab states, certain Palestinians now began to emphasize self-reliance. Groups for the liberation of Palestine sprung up from among those Palestinians who had been politically active in someway or another in the Arab world. […]

The first significant resolutions on the subject were those of the First Arab Summit conference [....] It adopted, according to its own communique, "practical resolutions necessary to ward off the existing Zionist danger in the technical and defence fields and to organize the Palestinian people to

270

enable them to carry out their role in liberating their homeland and determining their destiny. In February of that year, late Ahmad Shuqairy, who had been appointed representative of Palestine at the Arab League [...] toured Arab countries at the request of the Summit Conference, announcing that a Palestine National Council (also known as Assembly or Congress) would be summoned in Jerusalem in May 1964. [...]

2. Establishment of the PLO

[...]

The [Palestinian National] Council, in its concluding session on June 1, 1964, adopted certain key resolutions creating an infrastructure, that affected the Palestinian community in several fields: military, financial, political and administrative. The Palestine Liberation Organisation was officially proclaimed with the goal (not spelled out in any detail) of the liberation of Palestine. [...]

3. The Commandoes Come to Power

The aftermath of the 1967 war created a new situation for the Palestinians. Israel now occupied the whole of Palestine, parts of Syria and Egypt. Arab military activity against Israel, previously opposed by almost all Arab regimes, now appeared inevitable in order to regain at least those territories. This situation opened up new possibilities for the Palestinians, and especially those organizations outside the PLO that had already been carrying out guerilla activities against Israel. These organizations, at least, had not been tarnished by the defeat of the regular armies, and their military tactics seemed to present a viable alternative to those of the Arab conventional armed forces. When Israel dug in on the West Bank and Gaza, the support among the Palestinians community at large for the guerillas increased rapidly as they begun active resistance against the Israelis.

[...]

On the initiative of Fateh, a meeting of commando organizations was held in Cairo on January 17-20, 1968, with the result that a Permanent Bureau, composed of the eight attending organizations was constituted. [...] In an attempt to keep up with the commandos, the PLO created its own guerilla unit, the Popular Liberation Forces, in March 1968. A meeting held between the PLO, Fateh, and the PFLP in Beirut in the same month had, however, resulted in an agreement that would give the commandos half of the seats in a new 100-seat National Council to be convoked soon. This move recognized the new realities of the prestige and support enjoyed by the commando organizations among Palestinians.

[...]

The new National Council demanded freedom of movement for commandos in the countries surrounding Israel, called for support for the PLA and rejected UN Security Council resolution 242, which made no reference to the Palestinians or their national rights. [...]

The dominance of the commandoes in the PLO had then become obvious. Military collaboration between themselves and the PLO leadership was established by the creation of a Military Co-ordination Council in Amman in October 1968. The next session of the Palestine National Council was held in February 1969. It resulted in the election of Yasser Arafat, the leader of Fateh as Chairman of the new Executive Committee. [...]

4. Major Institutions of the PLO

THE NATIONAL COUNCIL AND THE CENTRAL COUNCIL:

The most important of the institutions within the PLO is the National Council, the Palestinian equivalent of a parliament. Members of the Council are nominated by a committee of the preceding Council after wide-ranging consultations with the commando organisations, the Palestinian unions and professional organisations, and leading Palestinian individuals in all walks of life. [...]

Constitutionally, the Council is the supreme authority formulating policies and programmes for the PLO. [...]

THE EXECUTIVE COMMITTEE

The National Council selects the Palestinian "Cabinet", the PLO Executive Committee, from its own members. [...]

The Executive Committee performs four major functions. It represents the Palestinian people officially, it supervises the various bodies of the PLO; it issues directives, draws up programmes, and takes decisions on the organisation of the PLO, provides these do not contradict the National Charter; finally, it executes the financial policy of the PLO and prepares its budget. [...]

THE NATIONAL FUND:

[...] Revenues for the fund come from the following sources: (1) a fixed tax levied on Palestinians by the Arab governments in whose countries they reside; (2) financial contributions by the Arab governments and peoples; (3) loans and contributions Arab governments and friendly nations; (4) any additional sourced approved by the Council.
[...]
The Palestine National Fund receives all revenues and finances the PLO according to an annual budget prepared by the Executive Committee and approved by the National Council. It also develops the Fund's revenues and supervises the expenditures of the PLO and its organs.

The PLO maintains a regular military force known as the Palestine Liberation Army (PLA). It was established in accordance with the resolutions of the First National Council which provided for the constitution of special military units in co-operation and co-ordination with the United Arab Command. The PLO Executive Committee was to work towards the enrollment of Palestinians in Arab military colleges and institutions, the mobilization of all Palestinian capabilities, and the preparation of the Palestinians for a war of liberation. Moreover, the first Council called for the formation of capable commando units, though these did not come into existence until 1968.

[...]

The resistance organizations that constitute the PLO have their own guerilla units. These, however, operate autonomously and are controlled by their own organizations, not by the PLO itself. The PLO's own guerilla unit, the Popular Liberation Forces, founded in 1968, had only a short existence.

[...]

SOCIAL, EDUCATIONAL, AND INFORMATION BODIES:

[...]

Palestinian trade unions are democratic organisations in which officials are elected by their respective members. All unions are linked to the PLO in several ways. The unions are represented by delegates in the Palestine National Council and are also engaged in day-to-day co-operation with the PLO. The PLO department for popular organizations, whose staff includes representatives of the unions, deals with the regular problems encountered by Palestinian workers and professionals. The PLO offers help to these unions in fields ranging from finance to intercession with Arab governments (e.g. on behalf of the right of Palestinian workers to work in Arab countries where they are refugees without work permits).

In the field of medical services, the major institution affiliated with the PLO is the Palestine Red Cross Society (PRCS), established in 1969. [...]

The PRCS renders medical services to the Palestinian people – civilians and commando alike. It operates several hospitals in Syria, Lebanon and Egypt; and many clinics in the villages of South Lebanon. [...]

Educationally, the PLO has organized an educational programme for Palestinian students in Kuwait. This programme was necessitated by the unusually large number of Palestinians of school age resident there as a result of the large influx of Palestinians into Kuwait following the 1967 war. The programme provides educational opportunities for 38 per cent of school-age Palestinian children in the country, at considerable cost. The PLO Planning Centre also has an educational section that has evolved a philosophy of Palestinian education and designed educational materials for

Palestinian children. It organizes summer programmes and courses for Palestinian teachers, and had built several model kindergartens.

The PLO assumes responsibility for the welfare of the children of commandos killed in battle. The most significant of the organizations dedicated to this end is the Association of Workshops for the Children of Palestinian Martyrs, first established by Fateh in January 1970. It offers vocational training for orphans or children from fatherless families, but has the additional economic purpose of producing ready-made clothes, furniture and embroidery for the population of refugee camps at prices consistent with the very low income of these camps.

The PLO has a number of information offices and its own newspaper, Filastin al-Thawra (Palestine Revolution) and news agency (WAPA). It also operates a major institution for the documentation and study of the Palestinian question. This is the PLO Research Centre, established in Beirut in 1965, which possesses a huge library and extensive archives. It has published over 400 books on the Palestine problem and issues an Arabic intellectual monthly journal, Shu'un Filastiniya (Palestine Affairs).

Conclusion
[...]
PLO policy has been defined in terms of the total liberation of Palestine. In 1969, at its sixth session, the Palestine National Council declared their goal to mean the establishment of a democratic state in all of Palestine, free from all forms of racial and religious discrimination. Following the 1973 war, when moves towards peace negotiations became more serious than ever before, the PLO chose to define its attitude towards any settlement that would restore the Palestinian territories occupied in 1967 by Israel. The result was a decision by the twelfth session of the National Council (June 1-9, 1974) to adopt a ten-point transitional political programme, which stated that in the case of an Israeli withdrawal from the West Bank and the Gaza Strip, the PLO would accept the establishment of a national authority in these two parts of Palestine. This moderate attitude has crystalized in more concrete resolutions in the last two meetings of the National Council hold respectively in March 1977 and January 1979. According to the resolutions of these two Councils, the PLO seeks to establish a Palestinian independent state on any liberated part of Palestine and in accordance with the UN resolution 3236. Should Israel withdraw from the occupied Palestinian land, the highly developed infrastructure of the PLO will greatly facilitate its task of establishing the long-waited Palestinian State.

Palestine Arab Terrorist Organizations (1974)
CENTRAL INTELLIGENCE AGENCY

1. The tradition of terrorism in Arab-Israeli relations extends back into the 1920's and '30's. Before the Arab-Israeli war of 1948–49, terrorism was the principal weapon of both Arabs and Jews in harassing the British authorities in Palestine. In the early 1950's, the Arab governments organized paramilitary commando groups—fedayeen—which undertook raiding and sabotage missions into Israel. […]

The PLO

2. As official support of terrorist operations ceased, many Palestinian Arabs became increasingly frustrated at the relative lack of aggressiveness toward Israel on the part of Arab governments. There was persistent agitation among Palestinians throughout the Arab world for some kind of representative organization, and this culminated in 1964 in the formation of the Palestine Liberation Organization (PLO). The PLO received the formal sanction of the League of Arab States at an Arab summit meeting that year.

3. The organization is a kind of Palestinian government in exile but it has been careful to avoid such a designation because of King Husayn's well-founded suspicion that it posed a threat to his authority in west Jordan. The PLO's activities are mainly political and military; it has tried, for example, to form a "Palestine Liberation Army" around a core of Palestinian units which had been formed over the years in the Egyptian, Syrian, and Iraqi armies. Nasir exercises considerable influence over the PLO, though he does not completely control its leaders. […]

4. The PLO's long-range plans for opposing the Israelis initially omitted sponsorship of terrorist operations into Israel. PLO leaders and sponsors recognized that such operations would provoke Israeli retaliation, and very possibly lead to a war for which the Arab governments are still not ready. This policy was a source of frustration to many activist Palestinians, and it led to the emergence of the present generation of terrorist groups. The PLO has failed to persuade these groups to submit to over-all PLO direction, and, to meet their competition, has within the past few months felt compelled to undertake such activities on its own. […]

Fatah

5. The most prominent of the terrorist groups is Fatah (a reverse acronym of the Arabic for "Palestine Liberation Movement"). Fatah is sometimes also known by the name of its commando arm, Asifa (Storm). Fatah appears to be descended from a clandestine Palestinian organization—now inactive — which was formed in the mid-1950's. Some of its members had connections with the Muslim Brotherhood, a conservative, strongly anti-

Nasir politico-religious movement. Fatah also may have had links with the Arab Higher Committee of Hajj Amin al-Husayni, the ex-Grand Mufti of Jerusalem, with whom the Brotherhood collaborated in regard to Palestine affairs.

6. In its present incarnation, Fatah emerged publicly in January 1965, when it claimed responsibility for terrorist incidents in Israel. Its leaders had previously participated in the organization of the PLO, but had become disenchanted. They are also disgusted with the continuing inability of most Arab governments to act decisively toward Israel, and are wary of any official control which might curtail Fatah's operations.

7. Syria, the most bellicose of the Arab states, is the one government whose policy comes closest to Fatah's violently anti-Israeli line. Damascus supports Fatah by providing it with a base for its operations, training facilities, and a propaganda outlet. The infiltrations into Israel, however, have been undertaken from Jordanian and Lebanese territory, since those borders are more easily traversed. This has occurred without the approval of either the Jordanian or the Lebanese government. Most of Fatah's financial support comes from wealthy Palestinians living in Kuwait and Saudi Arabia.

8. The number of people who participate in Fatah, as well as in other terrorist organizations, is unknown and probably fluctuates. Many of the terrorists are professional thugs or smugglers, and some were active against Israel in 1955–56. The Israelis say Fatah has been responsible for 61 sabotage incidents. Israeli Foreign Minister Eban recently stated, however, that Fatah had been inactive for about six weeks.

The PLF

9. A rival Palestinian terrorist organization called the "Palestinian Liberation Front" (PLF) has been credited by the Israelis with the 12 November road mining incident which triggered the Israeli raid into Jordan the next day. Jordanian officials also suspected the PLF of having perpetrated that incident, and they had begun a search for those responsible at the time Israel attacked. Little is known about the PLF. Like Fatah, it apparently aims at provoking a general Arab-Israeli war, but it is reputed to be more skilled in its operations. PLF members are said to regard Fatah as an organization of publicity seekers.

10. Some "terrorism" in Israel is more or less spontaneous. For years, Arab smugglers and crossborder operators have occasionally clashed with Israeli security forces. Incidents of this sort have been much reduced as the Israelis' security measures have been tightened. The organized, professional terrorism of the Fatah, the PLF, and of the PLO's new arm, poses problems for Israeli authorities that have no easy solution.

Arab States' Influence on the Palestine Liberation Organization (1978)

CENTRAL INTELLIGENCE AGENCY

Key Points

- PLO leader Yasir Arafat attempts to maintain good relations with as many states as possible in order to avoid overdependence on any single state, and to obtain greater material support and political backing.

- The need for such a broad base of support partially inhibits the PLO from actions that would conflict seriously with the policies of important patron states.

- The PLO often is a prisoner of inter-Arab politics and is rarely able to influence major political developments in the Middle East directly.

- Sympathy for the Palestinians' claims against Israel is nearly universal in the Arab World, however, and no Arab leader can openly abandon the Palestinian cause without risking serious censure or worse.

- Syria wields more influence over the PLO than any other Arab state, and in many instances holds veto power over PLO policies. Without the support of other Arab states, however, Damascus would be reluctant to attempt to impose unpalatable terms on the PLO in a Middle East settlement.

- Saudi Arabia possesses considerable financial leverage over Fatah and the PLO but generally has avoided using the blatant pressure tactics employed by other Arab states.

- Iraq and Libya are able to exercise control over some Palestinian extremist groups, but have only marginal influence with Fatah and Palestinian moderates.

Background

The establishment of the Palestine Liberation Organization was proposed by Egypt and Jordan during an Arab summit conference in Cairo in 1964 as a demonstration of militancy designed to offset a Syrian call for war with Israel. From its inception the organization was dependent upon the Arab states for arms and financial aid, and was used by them to further their various political objectives.

Following the June 1967 war the Palestinians gradually asserted their independence from Arab state control. Several factors accounted for this transformation:

- Conventional Arab military forces were humiliated during the war, leaving the Palestinian guerrillas as the only force capable of continuing the struggle against Israel.

- The war generated a large new group of Palestinian refugees from the West Bank, thus offering the guerillas new recruits and focusing world attention on the Palestinian question.

- By February 1969 Yasir Arafat's Fatah had assumed control of the PLO and the organization gained wider popular appeal in the Arab world.

Support for the Palestinian cause, if only on the verbal level, is considered by many Arabs to be an important test of one's commitment to Arab nationalism. [...]

Arafat and other PLO leaders have successfully capitalized on the popular appeal of their cause. By playing one government off against another, Arafat has managed to maintain for himself, and to a lesser extent for the PLO, a degree of independence that is remarkable given his organization's dependence on external support and lack of a secure territorial base. [...]

The PLO attempts to improve its bargaining position by winning and maintaining the support of states outside the Middle East as well. PLO leaders of all stripes consider the political support of the USSR important, and consult frequently with Soviet officials. [...]

Those Arab states who help keep the Palestinian issue alive also cynically exploit it to advance their own more narrow political goals. Iraqi and Libyan support for radical groups within the PLO is designed to further their particular interests, as is Syria's controlling role over Saiqa. Support provided to Fatah by these and other states is of course meant to enhance the donor's influence as well.

The Arab states are generally able to control the overt activities of the Palestinian activist groups within their borders. Jordan is the most notable example in this regard although it required several months of sporadic but bloody fighting in 1970 and 1971 before the government brought the Palestinians to heel. Syria allows the Palestinians the use of some military training facilities and gives them other forms of material support, but has quickly curtailed such assistance when at odds with the PLO. Similar facilities provided to the Palestinians in other Arab states are equally tenuous. Lebanon remains the last relatively independent base of operations for the Palestinians. Here they have taken advantage of a weak national government to maintain a strong military presence despite attempts by various parties, including Syria, to limit their freedom of action.

The Palestinian Charter (1968)

PALESTINIAN NATIONAL COUNCIL

[The Palestinian Charter was originally created in 1964 when the PLO was created, and was updated following the 1967 war].

Article 1: Palestine is the homeland of the Palestinian Arab people and an integral part of the great Arab homeland, and the people of Palestine are part of the Arab nation.

Article 2: Palestine with its boundaries that existed at the time of the British mandate is an integral regional unit.

Article 3: The Palestinian Arab people possesses the legal right to its homeland, and when the liberation of its homeland is completed they will exercise self-determination solely according to its own will and choice.

Article 4: The Palestinian personality is an innate, persistent character that is transmitted from parents to children. The Zionist occupation, and the dispersal of the Palestinian Arab people as a result of the disasters that befell it, do not deprive them from their Palestinian personality and affiliation and do not nullify that.

Article 5: The Palestinians are the Arab citizens who were living permanently in Palestine until 1947, whether they were expelled or remained there. Whoever is born to a Palestinian father after that date, within Palestine or outside is a Palestinian.

Article 6: Jews who were living permanently in Palestine until the beginning of the Zionist invasion will be considered Palestinians.

Article 7: The Palestinian affiliation and the material, spiritual and historical ties with Palestine are permanent realities. The upbringing of the Palestinian individual in an Arab and revolutionary fashion, the undertaking of all means of forging consciousness and training the Palestinians, in order to acquaint him profoundly spiritually and materially with his land, and prepare him for the conflict and armed struggle, as well as for the sacrifice of his property and life to restore his homeland, until the liberation is achieved is a national duty.

Article 8: The phase in which the people of Palestine is living is that of national struggle for the liberation of Palestine. Therefore the contradictions among the Palestinian national forces are of minimal importance that must be suspended in the interest of the main conflict between Zionism and Colonialism on the one side and the Palestinian Arab people on the other. On this basis, the Palestinian masses, whether in the homeland or in exile, organizations and individuals, comprise one national front which acts to restore Palestine and liberate it through armed struggle.

Article 9: Armed struggle is the only way to liberate Palestine and is therefore a strategy and not a tactic. [...]

Article 10: Fedaeyeen's action forms the nucleus of the popular Palestinian war of liberation. This requires its promotion, extension and protection, and the mobilization of all the Arab and Palestinian masses and scientific capacities of the Palestinians, their organization and involvement in the armed Palestinian revolution to ensure the continuation of the revolution, its advancement and victory.

Article 11: The Palestinians will have three mottoes: National unity, mobilization, and liberation.

Article 12: The Palestinian Arab people believes in Arab unity. In order to fulfill its role in realizing this, it must preserve, in this phase of national struggle, its Palestinian personality and the conscience, thereof increase consciousness of its consistence and resist any plan that tends to disintegrate or weaken it.

Article 13: Arab unity and the liberation of Palestine are two complementary aims. Each one paves the way for the realization of the other. [...]

Article 14: The destiny of the Arab nation, indeed the very Arab existence, depends on the destiny of the Palestinian issue. The endeavor and effort of the Arab nation to liberate Palestine flows from this connection. [...]

Article 15: The liberation of Palestine from the Arab viewpoint is a national duty to repulse the Zionist, imperialist invasion from the great Arab homeland and to purge it from the Zionist presence. This full responsibility falls upon the Arab nation, peoples and governments, with the Arab Palestinian people at their lead. [...]

Article 16: The liberation of Palestine from a spiritual viewpoint will prepare an atmosphere of tranquility and peace for the Holy Land in the shade of which all the holy places, will be safeguarded, and freedom of worship and free access to all will be guaranteed without distinction or discrimination of race, color, language or, religion. [...]

Article 17: The liberation of Palestinian from a human point of view will restore to the Palestinian human being dignity, glory and freedom. [...]

Article 18: The liberation of Palestine from an international point of view, is a defensive act necessitated by the requirements of self-defense. [...]

Article 19: The partition of Palestine in 1947 and the establishment of Israel is null and void from the very beginning, whatever time has elapsed because it was done contrary to the wish of the people of Palestine and their national right to their homeland and contradicts with the principles embodied in the charter of the UN, the first of which is the right of self-determination.

Article 20: The Balfour Declaration, the mandate document and what has been based upon them are considered null and void. The claim of a historical or spiritual tie between Jews and Palestine does not tally with the historical realities nor with the constituencies of statehood in their true sense. Judaism in its character as a religion of revelation, is not a nationality with an independent existence. Likewise, the Jews are not one people with an independent personality. They are rather citizens of the states to which they belong.

Article 21: The Palestinian Arab people in expressing itself through the armed Palestinian revolution, rejects every solution that is a substitute for a complete liberation of Palestine. and rejects all alternative plans that aim at the settlement of the Palestinian issue or its internationalization.

Article 22: Zionism is a political movement organically related to the world imperialism and is hostile to all movements of liberation and progress in the world. It is a racist and fanatic movement in its formation, aggressive, expansionist, and colonialist in its aims, fascist and nazi in its means. Israel is the tool of the Zionist movement and is a human and geographic base for the world imperialism. It is a concentration and a way for imperialism to the heart of the Arab homeland, to strike at the hopes of the Arab nation for liberation, unity and progress.

Article 23: The demands of security peace and the requirement of truth and justice oblige all states that maintain friendly relations with people, and loyalty of citizens to their homeland, to consider Zionism an illegitimate movement and to prohibit its existence and activity.

Article 24: The Palestinian Arab people believes in the principle of justice, freedom, sovereignty, self-determination, human dignity and the right of peoples to exercise them.

Article 25: To realize the aims of this charter and its principles the Palestine Liberation Organization will undertake its full role in liberating Palestine.

Article 26: The Palestinian Liberation Organization which represents the forces of the Palestinian revolution, is responsible for mobilizing the Palestinian Arab people in their struggle to restore their homeland, liberate it, and exercise the right of self-determination on it. This responsibility extends to all military, political and financial matters, and all else that the Palestinian issue requires on the Arab and international arena.

Article 27: The Palestine Liberation Organization will cooperate with Arab states, each according to its capacities and will maintain neutrality in their mutual relations in light of the requirements of the battle for the liberation, and will not interfere in the internal affairs of any Arab state.

Article 28: The Palestinian Arab people affirms the originality and independence of its national revolution and rejects every manner of interference, guardianship or subordination.

Article 29: The Palestinian Arab people possesses the prior and original right for liberating and restoring its homeland and form its relations with other states according to the latter's stands on the Palestinian issue the extent of their support for the Arab Palestinian people in their revolution to realize their aims.

Article 30: The fighters and carriers of arms in the battle of liberation are the nucleus of the popular army which will be the protection arm of the Palestinian Arab people.

Article 31: This organization shall have a flag, oath, and anthem all of which will be determined in accordance with a special system.

Article 32: To this charter is attached a law known as the basic law of the Palestine Liberation Organization, in which the organization's structure is determined, its committees, institutions and the special function of every one of them, and all the requisite duties assigned to them in accordance with this charter.

Article 33: This charter cannot be amended except by a two-thirds majority of all the members of the National Assembly in a special session called for this purpose.

Address to the United Nations (1974)
Yasser Arafat

As a result of the collusion between the Mandatory Power and the Zionist movement and with the support of some countries, this General Assembly early in its history approved a recommendation to partition our Palestinian homeland. This took place in an atmosphere poisoned with questionable actions and strong pressure. The General Assembly partitioned what it had no right to divide -- an indivisible homeland. When we rejected that decision, our position corresponded to that of the natural mother who refused to permit King Solomon to cut her son in two when the unnatural mother claimed the child for herself and agreed to his dismemberment. Furthermore, even though the partition resolution granted the colonialist settlers 54 percent of the land of Palestine, their dissatisfaction with the decision prompted them to wage a war of terror against the civilian Arab population. They occupied 81 percent of the total area of Palestine, uprooting a million Arabs. Thus, they occupied 524 Arab towns and villages, of which they destroyed 385, completely obliterating them in the process. Having done so, they built their own settlements and colonies on the ruins of our farms and our groves. The roots of the Palestine question lie here. Its causes do not stem from any conflict between two religions or two nationalisms. Neither is it a border conflict between neighboring States. It is the cause of people deprived of its homeland, dispersed and uprooted, and living mostly in exile and in refugee camps.
[...]
Those who call us terrorists wish to prevent world public opinion from discovering the truth about us and from seeing the justice on our faces. They seek to hide the terrorism and tyranny of their acts, and our own posture of self-defense.

The difference between the revolutionary and the terrorist lies in the reason for which each fights. For whoever stands by a just cause and fights for the freedom and liberation of his land from the invaders, the settlers and the colonialists cannot possibly be called terrorist, otherwise the American people in their struggle for liberation from the British colonialists would have been terrorists; the European resistance against the Nazis would be terrorism, the struggle of the Asian, African and Latin American peoples would also be terrorism, and many of you who are in this Assembly hall were considered terrorists. [...] As to those who fight against the just causes, those who wage war to occupy, colonize and oppress other people, those are the terrorists. Those are the people whose actions should be condemned, who should be called war criminals: for the justice of the cause determines the right to struggle.
[...]
The Palestinian people produced thousands of physicians, lawyers, teachers and scientists who actively participated in the development of the Arab countries bordering on their usurped homeland. They utilized their income to assist the young and aged amongst their people who remained in

the refugee camps. They educated their younger sisters and brothers, supported their parents and cared for their children. All along, the Palestinian dreamt of return. Neither the Palestinian's allegiance to Palestine nor his determination to return waned; nothing could persuade him to relinquish his Palestinian identity or to forsake his homeland. The passage of time did not make him forget, as some hoped he would. When our people lost faith in the international community, which persisted in ignoring its rights, and when it became obvious that the Palestinians would not recuperate one inch of Palestine through exclusively political means, our people had no choice but to resort to armed struggle. [...]

In the past 10 years of our struggle, thousands of martyrs and twice as many wounded, maimed and imprisoned were offered in sacrifice, all in an effort to resist the imminent threat of liquidation, to regain our right to self-determination and our undisputed right to return to our homeland. With the utmost dignity and the most admirable revolutionary spirit, our Palestinian people has not lost its spirit in Israeli prisons and concentration camps or when faced with all forms of harassment and intimidation. It struggles for sheer existence and it continues to strive to preserve the Arab character of its land. Thus it resists oppression, tyranny and terrorism in their ugliest forms.

It is through our popular armed struggle that our political leadership and our national institutions finally crystallized and a national liberation movement, comprising all the Palestinian factions, organizations and capabilities, materialized in the Palestine Liberation Organization.

Through our militant Palestine national liberation movement, our people's struggle matured and grew enough to accommodate political and social struggle in addition to armed struggle. The PLO was a major factor in creating a new Palestinian individual, qualified to shape the future of our Palestine, not merely content with mobilizing the Palestinians for the challenges of the present.

The PLO can be proud of having a large number of cultural and educational activities, even while engaged in armed struggle, and at a time when it faced increasingly vicious blows of Zionist terrorism. We established institutes for scientific research, agricultural development and social welfare, as well as centers for the revival of our cultural heritage and the preservation of our folklore. Many Palestinian poets, artists and writers have enriched Arab culture in particular and world culture generally. Their profoundly humane works have won the admiration of all those familiar with them. In contrast to that, our enemy has been systematically destroying our culture and disseminating racist, imperialist ideologies; in short, everything that impedes progress, justice, democracy and peace.

The PLO has earned its legitimacy because of the sacrifice inherent in its pioneering role, and also because of its dedicated leadership of the struggle. It has also been granted this legitimacy by the Palestinian masses, which in harmony with it have chosen it to lead the struggle according to its directives. The PLO has also gained its legitimacy by representing every faction, union or group as well as every Palestinian talent, either in the National Council or in people's institutions. This legitimacy was further strengthened by the support of the entire Arab nation, and it was consecrated during the last Arab Summit Conference, which reiterated the right of the PLO, in its capacity as the sole representative of the Palestinian people, to establish an independent national State on all liberated Palestinian territory.

[...]

I am a rebel and freedom is my cause. I know well that many of you present here today once stood in exactly the same resistance position as I now occupy and from which I must fight. You once had to convert dreams into reality by your struggle. Therefore you must now share my dream. I think this is exactly why I can ask you now to help, as together we bring out our dream into a bright reality, our common dream for a peaceful future in Palestine's sacred land.

As he stood in an Israeli military court, the Jewish revolutionary, Ahud Adif, said: "I am no terrorist; I believe that a democratic State should exist on this land." Adif now languishes in a Zionist prison among his co-believers. To him and his colleagues I send my heartfelt good wishes.

And before those same courts there stands today a brave prince of the church, Bishop Capucci. Lifting his fingers to form the same victory sign used by our freedom-fighters, he said: "What I have done, I have done that all men may live on this land of peace in peace." This princely priest will doubtless share Adif's grim fate. To him we send our salutations and greetings.

Why therefore should I not dream and hope? For is not revolution the making real of dreams and hopes? So let us work together that my dream may be fulfilled, that I may return with my people out of exile, there in Palestine to live with this Jewish freedom-fighter and his partners, with this Arab priest and his brothers, in one democratic State where Christian, Jew and Muslim live in justice, equality and fraternity.

Is this not a noble dream worthy of my struggle alongside all lovers of freedom everywhere? For the most admirable dimension of this dream is that it is Palestinian, a dream from out of the land of peace, the land of martyrdom and heroism, and the land of history, too.

[...]

In my formal capacity as Chairman of the PLO and leader of the Palestinian revolution I proclaim before you that when we speak of our common hopes for the Palestine of tomorrow we include in our perspective all Jews now living in Palestine who choose to live with us there in peace and without discrimination.

In my formal capacity as Chairman of the PLO and leader of the Palestinian revolution I call upon Jews to turn away one by one from the illusory promises made to them by Zionist ideology and Israeli leadership. They are offering Jews perpetual bloodshed, endless war and continuous thralldom.

We invite them to emerge from their moral isolation into a more open realm of free choice, far from their present leadership's efforts to implant in them a Masada complex.

We offer them the most generous solution that we might live together in a framework of just peace in our democratic Palestine.

In my formal capacity as Chairman of the PLO I announce here that we do not wish one drop of either Arab or Jewish blood to be shed; neither do we delight in the continuation of killing, which would end once a just peace, based on our people's rights, hopes and aspirations had been finally established.

In my formal capacity as Chairman of the PLO and leader of the Palestinian revolution I appeal to you to accompany our people in its struggle to attain its right to self-determination. This right is consecrated in the United Nations Charter and has been repeatedly confirmed in resolutions adopted by this august body since the drafting of the Charter. I appeal to you, further, to aid our people's return to its homeland from an involuntary exile imposed upon it by force of arms, by tyranny, by oppression, so that we may regain our property, our land, and thereafter live in our national homeland, free and sovereign, enjoying all the privileges of nationhood. Only then can we pour all our resources into the mainstream of human civilization. Only then can Palestinian creativity be concentrated on the service of humanity. Only then will our Jerusalem resume its historic role as a peaceful shrine for all religions.

I appeal to you to enable our people to establish national independent sovereignty over its own land.

Today I have come bearing an olive branch and a freedom fighter's gun. Do not let the olive branch fall from my hand. I repeat: do not let the olive branch fall from my hand.

War flares up in Palestine, and yet it is in Palestine that peace will be born.

286

Resolution 3237 – PLO Observer Status (1975)
UNITED NATIONS GENERAL ASSEMBLY

The General Assembly,

Having considered the question of Palestine,

Taking into consideration the universality of the United Nations prescribed in the Charter,

Recalling its resolution 3102 (XXVIII) of 12 December 1973,

Taking into account Economic and Social Council resolutions 1835 (LVI) of 14 May 1974 and 1840 (LVI) of 15 May 1974,

Noting that the Diplomatic Conference on the Reaffirmation and Development of International Humanitarian Law Applicable in Armed Conflicts, the World Population Conference and the World Food Conference have in effect invited the Palestine Liberation Organization to participate in their respective deliberations,

Noting also that the Third United Nations Conference on the Law of the Sea has invited the Palestine Liberation Organization to participate in its deliberations as an observer,

1. *Invites* the Palestine Liberation Organization to participate in the sessions and the work of the General Assembly in the capacity of observer;

2. *Invites* the Palestine Liberation Organization to participate in the sessions and the work of all international conferences convened under the auspices of the General Assembly in the capacity of observer;

3. *Considers* that the Palestine Liberation Organization is entitled to participate as an observer in the sessions and the work of all international conferences convened under the auspices of other organs of the United Nations;

4. *Requests* the Secretary-General to take the necessary steps for the implementation of the present resolution.

Anti-Terrorism Act of 1987 (1987)

GOVT. OF U.S.A.

Sec. 1002—Findings; Determinations.

a) FINDINGS.—The Congress finds that—

   1) Middle East terrorism accounted for 60 percent of total international terrorism in 1985;

   2) the Palestine Liberation Organization (hereafter in this chapter referred to as the "PLO") was directly responsible for the murder of an American citizen on the Achille Lauro cruise liner in 1985, and a member of the PLO's Executive Committee is under indictment in the United States for the murder of that American citizen;

   3) the head of the PLO has been implicated in the murder of a United States Ambassador overseas;

   4) the PLO and its constituent groups have taken credit for, and been implicated in, the murders of dozens of American citizens abroad;

   5) the PLO covenant specifically states that "armed struggle is the only way to liberate Palestine, thus it is an overall strategy, not merely a tactical phase";

   6) the PLO rededicated itself to the "continuing struggle in all its armed forms" at the Palestine National Council meeting in April 1987; and

   7) the Attorney General has stated that "various elements of the Palestine Liberation Organization and its allies and affiliates are in the thick of international terror".

b) DETERMINATIONS.—Therefore, the Congress determines that the PLO and its affiliates are a terrorist organization and a threat to the interests of the United States, its allies, and to international law and should not benefit from operating in the United States.

Address at Outbreak of War (1973)
Hafez al-Assad

Oh citizens, oh our intrepid soldiers, non-commissioned officers and officers, oh sons of our defiant people.

With my regards to every one of you, I address in you the authentic Arab spirit, the spirit of courage and heroism, the spirit of exertion and sacrifice, the spirit of self-sacrifice and giving. In address in you the affection for the homeland for which you have had a natural disposition, and the faith in the cause that you have been determined to defend.

Since around a week ago the enemy has been mobilizing and preparing, thinking that it will inflict a treacherous strike on us, and we have been awake, staying up, observing their movements and rests, and we are prepared and ready to repel their new likely aggression. For we have not allowed them to take us by surprise, and our armed forces have hurried to give them the appropriate response, and our brothers in Egypt have not allowed them to take them by surprise, so the great army of Egypt has hurried to defend the dignity of Egypt and the dignity of the Arab Ummah.

So regards to our army and our people, and regards to the army of Egypt and the great Arab people of Egypt, and it is necessary for me in these decisive moments to direct regards from the heart to these intrepid military personnel who have come to our area from the brotherly Maghreb in order to participate in the battle of glory and dignity, and to offer the blood in generosity alongside their brothers in Syria and Egypt, so they have embodied in that the unity of the Ummah and the unity of fate and the sanctity of the aim.

We today are waging the battle of honor and glory defending our precious land, our glorious history, the heritage of the fathers and forefathers. We are waging the battle of faith in God and ourselves and with solid determination and decisive determination that victory should be our ally in that. Israel has transgressed and has been struck by deception and arrogance has filled the heads of the officials in it, so they have intensely engaged in the crime and savored the way of aggression, as their hearts are filled with black hatred for our people and humanity, and they are overcomes by a thirst for bloodshed, and their steps are guided by a disdain for the principles of humanity and its supreme example and the international resolutions and laws. The likes of these people are the likes of those who preceded them from the warmongers, who do not stop at a limit and do not desist unless they are deterred by the peoples believing in their right, and defending in the path of their freedom and existence. And as we

Translated by Aymenn Jawad Al-Tamimi. From https://www.aymennjawad.org. Reprinted with permission.

carry out our duty in defending our land and the honor of our Ummah, we are prepared to expend every sacrifice and accept every hardship in the path of the victory of the truth and victory of the principles, and in the path of the reign of just peace.

Oh citizen brothers,

The hardships are a test of the metal of the peoples and testing their authenticity, and whenever the Ummah faces an increase in hardship, the pure metal appears and the firmly-rooted authenticity is confirmed. Indeed you are the sons of an Ummah known over the course of history for stances of manliness and defiance, stances of heroism and self-sacrifice, sons of an Ummah that has carried the message of light and faith to the regions of the Earth, and the world has acknowledged it without exception for the highest qualities and most noble ethics. So oh descendants of Abu Bakr, Omar, Othman and Ali (may God be pleased with them), oh descendants of Khalid and Abu Obeida, Amr, Sa'ad and Salah al-Din: indeed the conscience of our Ummah calls on us and the souls of our martyrs encourage us to embody the meanings of Yarmouk, Qadisiya, Hateen and Ayn Jalut, and indeed the masses of our Ummah from the Ocean to the Gulf gaze with their eyes and hearts upon our great steadfastness, and all of them are full of hope and trust that we are proceeding to victory.

Oh our intrepid soldiers, non-commissioned officers and officers, we are people of right and people of a just cause, and God gives victory to the one who is on right and the one who defends and upholds his right. Indeed you today are defending the honor of the Arab Ummah and protecting its dignity and protecting its existence, and you are making sacrifices so that the coming generations may live delighted and at ease. And the will of the Lofty and Powerful is that your jihad should be in this day of the days of the distinguished month, the month of Ramadan, the month of jihad, the month of the Badr expedition, the month of the day of al-Fatah, the month of victory: a clear page in the history of our armed forces that we add to the multiple pages of heroism and self-sacrifice that they have written with the blood of the pious martyrs in the history of our area and our homeland. Our forefathers were victorious by faith in sacrifice, and competing with each other for martyrdom in defense of the religion of God and the message of truth. And indeed you today by your heroic acts and your courage, draw inspiration from this spirit and revive it and revive through it the traditions of our glorious Ummah.

Your arms before you are a trust, so use them well, and the honor of the Arab soldier is a trust on your necks, so protect the trust, and the future of our people is in your custody, so expend the impossible in defense of it. And indeed our people—the hearts of whose sons are filled with fervor—stand behind you in one rank protecting your back lines and supporting your jihad with all they have. And behind them are the masses of our Arab

Ummah that I think only take the stance that the nationalist obligation in this decisive stage dictates. And behind them afterwards in the world are multiple friends supporting our right and supporting our cause and supporting our struggle.

We are not people who desire killing and destruction, but rather we are repelling killing and destruction from ourselves. We are not aggressors and we have never been aggressors, but rather we are and remain repelling the aggression from ourselves. We do not want death for anyone, but rather we repel death from our people. We love freedom and want it for us and others besides us. And we defend today so that our people may enjoy their freedom. We are advocates of peace, and we work for the sake of peace for our people and all the peoples of the world. And today we defend so that we may live in peace. So proceed on the blessing of God and if God supports you no one can overcome you. And peace be upon you.

Memorandum Regarding Arab-Israeli Fighting (1973)
Henry Kissinger

Fighting broke out on the Egyptian and Syrian fronts at about 2:00 Middle East time (8:00 a.m. Washington). Tension had been building for several days as a result of the high state of Egyptian alert and Syrian troop redeployments. Yesterday the Soviets began to fly transport planes into Damascus and Cairo to take dependents out of the area, apparently in anticipation of imminent conflict. Early this morning the Israelis, reversing their earlier assessment, told us that they had firm intelligence that a coordinated Egyptian-Syrian attack would take place before nightfall.

The Course of the Fighting

The Israelis told us that they would not open hostilities, and we have no reason to believe that they did. Their reconnaissance planes were active just prior to the outbreak of the fighting, however, and our intelligence sources are not exactly sure how the battle began. In the first day of combat, most of the fighting has been along the cease-fire lines. The Israelis appear to have attained control of the air, but have not bombed Arab airfields or made deep raids beyond the cease-fire lines. The Egyptians have managed to cross the Suez Canal in a few areas, and are trying to maintain their toeholds in the Sinai. Israeli counterattacks against these positions can be expected during the night. The Israelis will be very reluctant to accept a cease-fire with a return to the status quo ante.

On the Syrian front there has been intense fighting, but Syrian forces have not penetrated Israeli anti-tank defenses. Jordan has remained outside the battle. Casualties are not yet known, but the Egyptians have admitted losing ten aircraft. Soviet military moves in the area have not been provocative thus far.

Diplomatic Steps

As soon as we learned of the likelihood of hostilities, I contacted Ambassador Dobrynin and told him the Israelis had told us they would not open hostilities. I also talked to the Israelis, who reassured me there would be no preemptive strike. Subsequently, I saw the Egyptian and Syrian Foreign Ministers. We sent messages to Kings Hussein and Faisal as well. Once hostilities had begun, we explored the possibility of gaining Soviet support for a Security Council meeting that would call for a cease-fire with a return to the status quo ante. We have had no reply and have not formally asked for a Security Council meeting.

The WSAG met this morning to consider what step we should take to protect US interests. It will meet again this afternoon. US forces in the Mediterranean have been alerted, but have not been moved as yet.

Critical Issues

Thus far American citizens in the Middle East seem to be safe and there have been no threats of an Arab oil boycott. If fighting resumes tomorrow and the Arabs suffer serious setbacks, both these US interests could be endangered.

On the diplomatic front we face a possible issue of how to handle a call for a cease-fire in place. The Israelis would be very reluctant to accept a cease-fire that left any of the occupied territories in Arab hands, but we could encounter strong international pressures to urge the Israelis not to reopen hostilities tomorrow.

Nickel Grass (1998)
Walter J. Boyne

One of the most critical but least celebrated airlifts in history unfolded over a desperate 32 days in the fall of 1973. An armada of Military Airlift Command aircraft carried thousands of tons of materiel over vast distances into the midst of the most ferocious fighting the Middle East had ever witnessed—the 1973 Arab–Israeli War. MAC airlifters—T-tailed C-141s and C-5As—went in harm's way, vulnerable to attack from fighters, as they carved a demanding track across the Mediterranean, and to missiles and sabotage, as they were off-loading in Israel.

Though not as famous as the 1948–49 Berlin Airlift or as massive as the 1990–91 Desert Storm airlift, this 1973 operation was a watershed event. Code-named "Nickel Grass," it restored a balance of power and helped Israel survive a coordinated, life-threatening Soviet–backed assault from Egypt and Syria. It proved the Air Force concept of global mobility based on jet-powered transport aircraft. The airlift also transformed the image of the C-5 from that of expensive lemon to symbol of US might.

A quarter of a century ago, in summer and fall 1973, the Mideast seethed with tensions. Six years earlier, in June 1967, Israeli forces conquered vast swaths of land controlled by Egypt, Syria, and Jordan. Cairo and Damascus failed over the years to persuade or force Israel to relinquish its grip on the land and, by 1973, the stalemate had become intolerable. Egypt's Anwar Sadat and Syria's Hafez al-Assad meticulously planned their 1973 offensive, one they hoped would reverse Israeli gains of the earlier war and put an end to Arab humiliation. The war was set to begin on the holiest of Jewish religious days, Yom Kippur.

Trapped by Complacency

The Arab states had trained well and Moscow had supplied equipment on a colossal scale, including 600 advanced surface-to-air missiles, 300 MiG-21 fighters, 1,200 tanks, and hundreds of thousands of tons of consumable war materiel. On paper, the Arabs held a huge advantage in troops, tanks, artillery, and aircraft. This was offset, in Israeli minds, by the Jewish state's superior technology, advanced mobilization capability, and interior lines of communication. Despite unmistakable signs of increasing Arab military capability, Israeli leaders remained unworried, even complacent, confident in Israel's ability to repel any attack.

The Israeli government became unequivocally convinced of impending war just hours before the Arab nations attacked at 2:05 p.m. local time, Oct. 6. Prime Minister Golda Meir, despite her immense popularity, refused to use those precious hours to carry out a pre-emptive attack; she was concerned that the US might withhold critical aid shipments if Washington perceived Israel to be the aggressor.

On the southern front, the onslaught began with a 2,000-cannon barrage across the Suez Canal, the 1967 cease-fire line. Egyptian assault forces swept across the waterway and plunged deep into Israeli–held territory. At the same time, crack Syrian units launched a potent offensive in the Golan Heights. The Arab forces fought with efficiency and cohesion, rolling over or past shocked Israeli defenders. […]

Day 4 of the war found Israel's once-confident military suffering from the effects of the bloodiest mauling of its short, remarkably successful existence. Egypt had taken the famous Bar Lev line, a series of about 30 sand, steel, and concrete bunkers strung across the Sinai to slow an attack until Israeli armor could be brought into play. Egyptian commandos ranged behind Israeli lines, causing havoc. In the north, things looked equally bad. The Syrian attack had not been halted until Oct. 10.

Grievously heavy on both sides were the losses in armored vehicles and combat aircraft. Israeli air-power was hard hit by a combination of mobile SA-6 and the man-portable SA-7 air-defense missiles expertly wielded by the Arabs. The attacking forces were also plentifully supplied with radar-controlled ZSU-23-4 anti-aircraft guns. Israeli estimates of consumption of ammunition and fuel were seen to be totally inadequate. However, it was the high casualty rate that stunned Israel [....]

The shock was accompanied by sheer disbelief at America's failure to comprehend that the situation was critical. Voracious consumption of ammunition and huge losses in tanks and aircraft brought Israel to the brink of defeat, forcing the Israelis to think the formerly unthinkable as they pondered their options.
[…]
Shifting Scenarios

[…] Nixon, in response to a personal plea from Meir, had made the crucial decision Oct. 9 to re-supply Israel. However, four days would pass before the executive office could make a final decision on how the re-supply would be executed.

Initially, planners proposed that Israel be given the responsibility for carrying out the entire airlift. (Israel did use eight of its El Al commercial airliners to carry 5,500 tons of materiel from the US to Israel.) Israel attempted to elicit interest from US commercial carriers, but they refused to enlist in the effort, concerned as they were about the adverse effects Arab reaction would have upon their businesses. MAC's inquiries with commercial carriers received the same negative response. Then, it was suggested that MAC assist the Israeli flag carrier by flying the material to

Lajes, the base on the Portuguese Azores islands in the Atlantic, where it could be picked up by Israeli transports.

The US dithered in this fashion for four days. Then, on Oct. 12, Nixon personally decided that MAC would handle the entire airlift. Tel Aviv's Lod/Ben-Gurion air complex would be the off-load point.

"Send everything that can fly," he ordered.

[...]

Fighters All the Way

The threat of Arab interception was real, and the US Navy's Sixth Fleet acted as protector until the transports came within about 200 miles of Israel. There Israeli air force fighters took over. [...]

The first C-5 (Tail No. 00461) to land at Lod touched down at 22:01 Zulu. It carried 97 tons of 105 mm howitzer shells, and it arrived at a time when Israeli forces were down to their last supplies of ammunition. Another 829 tons would be delivered in the next 24 hours. Even as Israeli workers unloaded those first cargo airplanes, huge formations of Israeli and Egyptian armor, maneuvering just 100 miles to the southwest, were locked in a desperate tank battle that would prove to be the largest clash of armor since the World War II Battle of Kursk.

[...]

The first C-141 (Tail No. 60177) to arrive at Lod landed at 23:16 Zulu. The aircraft carried more ammunition but, more importantly, it delivered Strobaugh and his ALCE crew. The group ultimately numbered 55, all of whom worked 12 hours a day, seven days a week. They were given three 40K loaders as well as locally improvised unloading gear.

[...]

The original 4,000-ton airlift requirement grew daily. After the first day, USAF set the daily flow requirement at four C-5s and 12 C-141s. After Oct. 21, it raised the aircraft flow level to six C-5s and 17 C-141s and maintained it there until Oct. 30, when the demand began to drop.

The continuous flow of aircraft on the long flights was tough on the aircrews, but MAC was judicious in its positioning of relief crews for the C-141 and using augmented crews on the C-5. A special pool of navigators was created for the vital but tedious task of navigating the Mediterranean.

To the Offensive

Because it eliminated the need to husband ammunition and other consumable items, the continuous flood of US war materiel enabled Israeli forces to go on the offensive in the latter stages of the war. In the north, Israel's ground forces recovered all territory that had been lost and began to march on Damascus. In the Sinai, tank forces led by Maj. Gen. Ariel

Sharon smashed back across the Suez, encircled the Egyptian Third Army on the western side of the canal, and threatened Ismailia, Suez City, and even Cairo itself.

Egypt and Syria, which had previously rejected the idea of a negotiated settlement, now felt compelled on Oct. 22 to agree to the arrangement hammered out by Washington and Moscow with the goal of preventing the total destruction of the trapped Egyptian army. Israel was reluctant to comply immediately, wishing to gain as much as possible before a cease-fire.

The Soviet Union, faced with Israel's continuing offensive, raised the stakes. Moscow declared to the United States that, if the US could not bring Israel to heel, it would take unilateral action to dictate a settlement. On Oct. 24, the United States, in order to intensify the image of risk in Soviet minds and keep Soviet forces out of the crisis, responded by taking its armed forces to a worldwide DEFCON III alert, implying readiness for nuclear operations, if necessary.

Fortunately, after several abortive efforts, an effective cease-fire finally took hold Oct. 28.

Israel suffered 10,800 killed and wounded—a traumatic loss for a nation of some 3 million persons—plus 100 aircraft and 800 tanks. The Arab nations suffered 17,000 killed or wounded and 8,000 prisoners, and lost 500 aircraft and 1,800 tanks.

The airlift officially ended Nov. 14. By then, the Air Force had delivered 22,395 tons of cargo—145 missions by C-5 Galaxy and 422 missions by C-141 Starlifter. The C-5s delivered about 48 percent of the tonnage but consumed 24 percent less fuel than the C-141s. Included in the gross cargo tonnage was a total of 2,264.5 tons of "outsize" materiel, equipment that could be delivered only by a C-5. Among these items were M-60 tanks, 155 mm howitzers, ground radar systems, mobile tractor units, CH-53 helicopters, and A-4E components.

The airlift had been a key to the victory. It had not only brought about the timely resupply of the flagging Israeli force but also provided a series of deadly new weapons put to good use in the latter part of the war. These included Maverick and TOW anti-tank weapons and extensive new electronic countermeasures equipment that warded off successful attacks on Israeli fighters. [...]

"For generations to come," said Golda Meir not long after the war's end, "all will be told of the miracle of the immense planes from the United States bringing in the material that meant life for our people."

Resolution 338 — Ceasefire in the Middle East (1973)
UNITED NATIONS SECURITY COUNCIL

The Security Council

1. Calls upon all parties to the present fighting to cease all firing and terminate all military activity immediately, no later than 12 hours after the moment of the adoption of this decision, in the positions they now occupy;

2. Calls upon the parties concerned to start immediately after the cease-fire the implementation of Security Council resolution 242 (1967) in all of its parts;

3. Decides that, immediately and concurrently with the cease-fire, negotiations shall start between the parties concerned under appropriate auspices aimed at establishing a just and durable peace in the Middle East.

Half a century has passed since the 1973 October War, yet which side emerged victorious from this pivotal conflict remains an open question that is still debated endlessly both globally and in the Middle East. Military strategists often couch the answer in terms of territories gained or lost, or as a function of military and human cost. Political scientists and practitioners of diplomacy focus more on whether the optimum goals of conclusive victory of one side over the other were achieved, or whether all outstanding problems between the parties were settled.

Both criteria are inappropriate. Victory or defeat is not determined by hard tangible assets, nor can success or failure be assessed in absolute terms given the fog of war and the complexities of negotiations on reaching a settlement to the conflict. Assessing the outcome of war hinges on the question of whether the respective parties ended up in better or worse circumstances in its aftermath, and whose predetermined objectives were achieved. It is important in this respect to underscore that the use of force is a tool to achieve a core political objective.

Addressing the "who won" question requires revisiting the politico-military environment before October 1973, Egypt's objectives for going into the war, as well as the negotiating process after the guns went silent. […]

The Prelude to War

Late Egyptian President Anwar Sadat firmly believed that his country needed to vigorously embrace modernity and socioeconomic development. He also understood that the interminable Arab-Israeli conflict was imposing a heavy toll on Egypt.
[…]
Sadat assumed office following Nasser's sudden death in September 1970. Disappointed and uncomfortable with his relations with the Soviet Union and concerned about domestic political opposition, Sadat publicly floated several peace initiatives to Israel including opening the Suez Canal to international shipping if Israeli forces were to withdraw fifty kilometers eastward from the canal zone. He also sent his national security adviser Hafez Ismail to meet Kissinger twice in 1973 in the hopes that the latter would serve as an interlocutor in negotiations between Egypt and Israel. Sadat's overtures, however, were received with disinterest by both the Israelis and the Americans, neither of whom took Sadat seriously at the time. Both the Israelis and the Americans miscalculated that Sadat did not possess any agency, and they shared a sense of hubris flowing from Israel's perceived military dominance that obviated any need to negotiate.

With his efforts falling on deaf ears, and his personal domestic credibility increasingly eroding, Sadat had the foresight to conclude that Egypt needed to militarily demonstrate a seriousness of purpose in order to change the political paradigm. That would surely spur negotiations. At the same time, he also wisely understood that given Israeli's military superiority, it would be unrealistic to attempt a complete liberation of the occupied Sinai by military means. His objective was to initiate a limited targeted military operation with calculated objectives against a stronger adversary for the purpose of creating a more conducive negotiating paradigm. […]

The United States, the Soviet Union, and Israel had no appetite to negotiate peace in the Middle East before the 1973 War. Washington and Moscow were focused on superpower détente, while Israel basked in a sense of invincibility, its forces secure behind the supposedly impenetrable Barlev defense fortifications on the eastern bank of the Suez Canal. None of the other parties wanted war, or even seriously considered that Egypt possessed a war option.

Sadat, on the other hand, wanted to negotiate peace, and initiating military operations with the specific objective of initiating negotiations was a means to an end. Syria decided to join a military coalition with Egypt, although it remains unclear whether it felt it could liberate the Golan Heights militarily or, like Sadat, was intent on engaging militarily to create a window for negotiations. It is my firm conviction that Egypt emerged as the biggest winner from the 1973 War because Sadat's immediate goal was achieved, irrespective of the final disposition of forces at the time of the ceasefire or the conclusion of diplomatic negotiations.

The Aftermath of War

[…] I vividly remember how the 1967 defeat was a severe blow to Egypt that shattered its self-confidence. On the other hand, the 1973 war was a profoundly traumatic event for Israel, and shocked the United States and the Soviet Union into realizing that Egypt's military initiative was a game changer in the Middle East. […]

Perhaps more importantly, the war restored a sense of confidence and pride among the Egyptian people. This is difficult to quantify, but it was an invaluable pivot point and an indispensable precondition for dealing with the intricacies and complexities of balancing relations with the Soviet Union, the United States, and the Arab World, as well as negotiating with Israel.

The 1973 War was invaluable in creating a geopolitical paradigm which fostered negotiations between the Arabs, particularly with respect to Egypt and Israel. Without the war, negotiations would have been questionable considering the highly stagnant pre-1973 geopolitical environment. Given

Sadat's specific war aims, the immediate consequences of the 1973 War were very much aligned with Egypt's objectives, more so than with any of the other parties to the conflict.

[…]

The Israelis ultimately gained from the war as well, albeit after having to swallow some bitter medicine and undergo serious and painful reflection. Having been forced to abandon their sense of invincibility, Israel's reassessment of its place, which was prompted by the war, opened the door for negotiations that would conclude with several peace agreements with Arab states. It is important to note here that these agreements did not come about because of any premeditated willingness by Israel but as a direct consequence of the 1973 conflict.

[…]

The strategic landscape of the Middle East was thus profoundly changed as a result of the war. The ultimate agent of that change was Sadat's determination to develop a limited war option to force an Israeli—and American—reassessment, prompting both to consider negotiations seriously. The United States and the Soviet Union did not want Egypt and Syria to initiate the 1973 War, nor for that matter were they always supportive of different Arab negotiating positions or tactics. Sadat's strategy thus underscores the importance of regional parties reserving the ability to take independent national decisions, irrespective of relations with friend or foe.

[…]

Pivoting From War to Peace

The Geneva Peace Conference on the Middle East took place in Switzerland from December 21-23, 1973, under the aegis of the United Nations and the sponsorship of the United States and Soviet Union. Egypt welcomed the co-sponsorship but insisted that it be under UN auspices because this reaffirmed the legal basis for conflict resolution. Interestingly, Jordan participated even though it had not joined the war effort, while Syria absented itself. This raised questions regarding Syria's motivation, but more importantly, it was a grave mistake for the Syrians because it was the first indication that the Arab front was not politically united.

The United States brokered two Egyptian-Israeli disengagement agreements in 1974 and 1975, as well as a disengagement agreement between Syria and Israel in 1974, all signed in the context of the reconvened Geneva Conference. Because the United States and Soviet Union were focused on having their respective allies militarily disengage, Jordan did not get a disengagement agreement as it was not a party to the war. […]

Sadat and the Egyptian foreign policy establishment wanted a comprehensive Arab-Israeli peace, including a Palestinian state where Palestinians could express their national identity. Both were adamant that all occupied Egyptian territory without exception would be returned to Egypt. I remember years later former Israeli President Ezer Weizman recounting to a group, which included myself, that the Israelis found Sadat's and Egypt's negotiating styles perplexing. They were surprised that the initial and concluding positions on fundamentals like territory were identical and unwavering, while the Israelis would always exaggerate requests or inflate problems to create room for negotiations and justifications for compromises made. The difference is simple and profound: put simply, Egypt had sovereign international borders and respected international law while Israel's borders were not legally defined and over the years had shown very little respect for international law.

I believe that the October War created a negotiating paradigm, induced a sense of national confidence on the Arab side that enhanced its negotiating position, generated a higher level of respect toward Arab demands, and forced a sliver of Israeli realism. It also established a higher sense of international priority to the Arab-Israeli conflict, including the Palestinian cause, which became prominent on the international agenda, leading to then-PLO Chairman Yasser Arafat addressing the UN General Assembly in New York on November 13, 1974.

A Still Elusive Comprehensive Peace
[...]
From the outset, the Arabs have complained bitterly about Kissinger's pro-Israeli bias. Equally important, if not more so, it was evident that he never attempted or wanted to achieve Arab-Israeli peace. His declared objective was to establish "order" to allow him to manage relations with the Soviet Union. This is explicitly confirmed in numerous books by and about Kissinger, including most recently by Martin Indyk's in his comprehensive book on Kissinger's Middle East diplomacy *Master of the Game*. Consequently, it is unquestionable that Kissinger did not invest in peacemaking and intentionally limited the prospects for peace that could have been realized as the result of the paradigm shift brought about by the October War. This served Israel's interests but was mostly a Kissingerian U.S. objective. Over-dependence on the United States, and increasingly on Kissinger himself given his leading role as a result of the turmoil of the closing Nixon years, was a major mistake made by the Arabs despite the validity of their objectives.

Another egregious mistake years later was to move the peace process out of the aegis of the United Nations to that of the superpowers, and subsequently to the sole supervision of the United States. This undermined the centrality of the sole internationally recognized framework of Arab-Israeli peacemaking embodied in the principle of "land for peace"—a phrase used as a euphemism for Security Council Resolution 242. Ultimately, with the breakdown of the Soviet Union and changing circumstances including American administrations less committed to a two-state solution, a distorted Israeli concept of "Peace for Security" and now "Arab-Israeli peace before Israeli-Palestinian Peace" is unabashedly promoted by the Israeli government.

[...]

Opposition to Sadat's Post-War Diplomacy

There have been vehement voices of opposition in Egypt and the Arab World to Sadat's strategy of agreeing to peace with Israel; some have even unjustifiably questioned his sincerity in pursuing comprehensive peace. Sadat was a courageous and astute politician and strategist who focused on the bigger picture—the war would not have happened without him—whereas the Israeli approach was dominated by a security-focused obsession with micro-level details.

Sadat and his Foreign Minister Ismail Fahmy held each other in high respect and were quite close. Both wanted a change in direction for Egypt's foreign policy as well as a comprehensive Arab-Israeli peace. How best to deal with Israel and Egypt's relations with global powers was nonetheless a contentious subject between Sadat and Fahmy. Sadat was a courageous leader focused on the big picture. Fahmy was a strategically seasoned diplomat and highly acclaimed negotiator. Ultimately, however, the latter resigned in objection to Sadat's 1977 Jerusalem visit because of his strong conviction that this would feed into Israeli negotiating tactics of divide and conquer and only lead to a bilateral peace agreement between the two countries. Bilateral peace would leave Israel free to completely ignore all other issues thereafter, making comprehensive peace unachievable. Israel stayed true to its practices and did little to accommodate Sadat's magnanimous gestures.

[...]

ROI for Middle Eastern Peace

[...]

Numerous efforts and permutations developed thereafter, including—but not exclusively—the Palestinian-Israeli Oslo process. Negotiations with limited participants are normally easier to manage and even more efficient tactically, especially with Israel's penchant for detail. It is also clear, however, that the more we compartmentalized tracks and isolated them, the more difficult it was to resolve the core Palestinian-Israeli issues at the heart of the conflict, particularly when there exists a strategic imbalance of power.

Looking back at the outcome of the October 1973 War, one cannot deny that it was historic in its numerous consequences. It was all the more so because the geopolitical environment of the time was not conducive to bold decision-making. Most of all, the war opened the door for negotiations between regional parties big and small.

[...]

Israel's 1973 October War: A 50-Year Perspective (2023)
Itamar Rabinovich

During the past five decades, the Middle East has been shaped by several significant events and developments: the Iranian Revolution (1979), the fall of the Soviet Union (1991), the two Gulf wars (1991 and 2003), the Egyptian-Israeli peace treaty (1979), and the Oslo Process (1993-1995), to name a few. Among these events, the October War of 1973 (the "Yom Kippur War" as it is known in Israel, and the "October War" in Egypt and Syria) stands out as particularly influential.

A limited Egyptian-Syrian partnership

Egypt and Syria launched the October War on October 6, 1973. The Egyptian-Syrian partnership was limited. Syria's President Hafez al-Assad did not fully share Egyptian President Anwar Sadat's war aims. Sadat had in mind a limited war, a crossing of the Suez Canal, and the establishment of an Egyptian presence on the canal's eastern bank in order to force Israel and the United States to enter into a diplomatic process designed to redress the consequences of the 1967 Six-Day War. The initial attack was unexpectedly successful. Sadat devised an effective strategy of using advanced Soviet surface-to-air missiles to neutralize Israel's air force and armored units. He was also successful in surprising Israel and was unexpectedly aided by the mindset that affected the judgment of Israel's intelligence community and political leadership.

That mindset meant that in the view of the leadership of Israel's military intelligence, and part of the political leadership, capabilities were confused with intentions. In their view, Egypt would be unable to defeat Israel militarily and therefore was unlikely to start a war in which it was bound to suffer a defeat. It took Israel just over two weeks to recover and turn the tide of war. By the time a cease-fire was imposed by American and Soviet pressure, Israel had crossed the Suez Canal, threatened to decimate the Egyptian Third Army (a major part of the Egyptian military's war contingency), and in the northern front reached the environs of Damascus. The war ended with a series of agreements culminating in the Egyptian-Israeli and Syrian-Israeli disengagement agreements of 1974.

Israel's national trauma

The October War inflicted a national trauma on Israel. The intelligence failure, the surprise, the weak performance of the Israel Defense Forces during the war's first few days, the large number of casualties, the dependence on resupply from the United States, and the huge economic cost mobilized the Israeli public against the Golda Meir government. There was a recognition that the massive victory of 1967 created in Israel a hubris that contributed to the setback of 1973. It also realized that the war could have been prevented had Israel accepted Sadat's peace feelers between 1971 and 1973. [...]

As in other crises, the accounting happened later, when in 1977 the Israeli public voted the Labor Party out of office and elected Menachem Begin and his right-wing Likud Party. It was the first change of power in Israel after nearly 30 years of statehood, preceded by another three decades of Labor Party hegemony in the pre-state Zionist movement.

The beginning of an Arab-Israeli peace process

The post-October War diplomacy, led by the U.S. Secretary of State Henry Kissinger, also marked the beginning of an Arab-Israeli peace process. All previous efforts to settle the conflict, beginning in 1948, were short-lived and unsuccessful. But the mood created in both Egypt and Israel and Kissinger's unusual skills shaped the transition from war to peacemaking. In Egypt and other parts of the Arab world, the feeling was that if Israel could not be defeated even after an initial setback, there was no prospect of an Arab military victory over Israel.

In Egypt though, the war was and is described as a victory, and the crossing of the Suez Canal is glorified as "The Crossing," implying that a wide gap was victoriously crossed. This sense of achievement played an important role in enabling Sadat to carry his country into peacemaking with Israel. Sadat had wanted to disengage from the conflict with Israel since his assumption of power. His original concept of peace with Israel was more limited than the eventual outcome of the Camp David Accords, but he ended up signing a full-fledged peace agreement with Israel. The end of the Egyptian-Israeli military conflict was a huge asset in Israel's national security equation.

In Israel, the course and cause of the war had a sobering effect on the public and the political system, thus enabling three prime ministers — Meir, Rabin, and later Begin — to make the concessions necessary for the interim agreements of 1974 and 1975, and eventually to the Camp David Accords of 1978. The war and its aftermath did not bring an end to the Arab-Israeli conflict, but it marked the beginning of a peace process that continued to unfold in the coming decades. It also marked the decision of several Arab states to distinguish — without necessarily admitting it — between their own state interests and their commitment to the Palestinian cause. In the short term, the October War contributed to the empowerment of the Palestinian Liberation Organization (PLO) and the Palestinian National Movement.

The war's impact on the Middle East

In the regional politics of the Middle East, Sadat's decision to move from a limited ending of the war into a peace process pitted Syria, his wartime partner, against Egypt. Under Assad's leadership, a powerful and coherent Syrian state was built for the first time since independence. Assad sought hegemony in the Levant over Lebanon, Jordan, and the Palestinians, and cultivated an Arab coalition against Sadat and his policies. [...]

The October War and Washington's support of Israel also led Saudi Arabia to deploy for the first time the "oil weapon" and announce an oil embargo on the United States, leading oil prices to quadruple. It was a turning point in the relationship between the oil-producing countries in the Middle East, the Western consumers, and the international oil companies, and it channeled huge revenues into the coffers of the Gulf countries. [...]

The war and postwar diplomacy contributed to the completion of Egypt's move from the Soviet to the American orbit. Kissinger had argued in the Washington policy debate of the late 1960s that the United States should pressure Israel to give up on territories captured from Egypt and Syria only when these two countries had shifted from a pro-Russian to a pro-American orientation. He was unsuccessful with Syria, but fully successful with Egypt, thus completing one of the most dramatic diplomatic coups of the Cold War in the Middle East. The United States established itself as the only power, as distinct from the Soviet and European unions, capable of dealing with both Israel and its Arab adversaries and promoting the next phases of the Arab- Israeli peace process.
[...]

Trends in Inter-Arab Cooperation Over the Next Decade and the Implications for Israel (1976)

CENTRAL INTELLIGENCE AGENCY

The second Sinai agreement has clearly weakened this Arab unity and sapped Arab political as well as military strength against Israel, at least for the near term. Some Israelis now take satisfaction in claiming that for the first time in their history they are the reason not for unity among the Arabs but for serious division. It is precisely this division in Arab ranks--a division that leaves Egypt temporarily neutralized and the other belligerents thereby weakened--that Prime Minister Rabin outlined in late 1974 as the first and most important step in Israel's strategy for the following seven years. Rabin's object: to gain time by numbing the Arabs while Israel's strength is augmented and the West's dependence on Arab oil diminishes.

[…]

The Case for Arab Unity versus Division

[…]

Before the 1973 war, the Arabs rarely exhibited, even in a loose sense, an effective, positive unity. Their solidarity was always a negative one--a united rejection of Israel, a united refusal to consider peace with Israel, a united refusal even to negotiate with Israel. An emotional and ideological outlook unified the Arabs in blind opposition to any compromises and made a peace settlement impossible.

At the same time, clear division among the Arabs is no more likely to facilitate a settlement than is unbending unity. The Arabs are so militarily and economically inter-dependent that, without a common purpose, they lose both military and political strength and, if the past is any precedent, tend to retreat in their weakness into increased radicalism. Moves toward a settlement by one Arab state that fail to offer hope to the others tend to increase the militancy of the dissatisfied and to swing Arab opinion in favor of the aggrieved. The net effect is to place increased pressure on the state that has left the fold, diminishing its willingness to maintain the separate policy that originally brought division.

Progress toward a peace settlement thus can be facilitated from the Arab side only if the Arabs exhibit a loose solidarity of purpose somewhere between the rigid unity that characterized their policy toward Israel in the past, and the complete fragmentation that Israel seems to desire. The Arabs achieved progress in negotiations following the 1973 war because they showed a reasonable degree of positive, purposeful unity but were able to temper this with tactical flexibility. Negotiations were facilitated precisely because the Arabs had a common strategic goal in mind but were not inhibited by a fully united and therefore binding view of the tactics to be pursued in achieving the goal.

[…]

Egypt's engagement in separate negotiations is indicative of a trend toward pragmatic concentration on separate national, as opposed to pan-Arab, goals that is true to one degree or another of all Arab states. At the same time, Syria's move toward closer coordination with the Palestinians and Jordan in reaction to its frustration in negotiations is indicative of a lingering tendency to seek comfort in inhibiting political rigidity. The tug of war between these conflicting tendencies is likely to be the salient political feature in the Arab world as further attempts are made to negotiate an Arab-Israeli settlement, and the outcome will in large measure determine whether a settlement is possible.

[...]

The Domestic Situation as a Factor

[...]

This trend toward greater concentration on domestic priorities has been at the expense of previous Arab striving toward pan-Arab unity and at the expense, in some measure, of a unified Arab strategy against Israel. [...] In a subtle way, domestic priorities in the states on the periphery of the Arab-Israeli conflict have served to divert attention from what was formerly the single policy issue that animated all Arabs. The confrontation states maneuverability has thereby been increased, lessening pressure on them to act only within the constraints of a rigid pan-Arab policy that allowed little room for compromise or difference of tactics.

To say that the Arabs are now more interested in furthering domestic rather than pan-Arab goals is not to say, however, that they have rid themselves of an emotional commitment to the struggle with Israel and particularly to the Palestinian cause or that they are so completely dedicated to their separate national goals that they are willing or able to pursue totally in-dependent paths in pursuit of separate peace settlements with Israel.

Indeed, precisely the same concentration on domestic priorities that has given the Arab states some room for individuality also prevents them from being totally independent of each other. President Sadat's almost single minded purpose is to develop Egypt economically, but to do this he must achieve a durable and honorable peace and at the same time attract the financial assistance of the wealthy oil states in the Arab world. The two goals are compatible only if his idea of peace also satisfies the demands of the other Arabs and specifically of the oil states--Saudi Arabia chief among them. Egypt cannot, in short, afford economically to settle for an Egyptian-Israeli peace. A settlement that did not satisfy all of the confrontation states, as well as the Palestinians and Saudi Arabia, would very probably result in a cut-off of vital economic assistance and thus undermine the very economic progress that is Egypt's prime reason for seeking peace.

[...] In the case of peripheral states like Saudi Arabia, domestic concerns of an entirely different nature dictate a continued solidarity with the mainstream of the Arab cause. For the very reason that Saudi Arabia is a conservative monarchy with vast oil wealth for the taking in any power grab, its identification with the Arab cause is a matter of self-preservation. While a strong element of genuine dedication to the struggle against Israel governs Saudi solidarity with the Arabs, this is also in no small measure governed by a desire to deny an issue to potential domestic malcontents and outside agitators who might readily stir up opposition if the Saudis withheld their economic weapons from the Arab struggle.

[…]

The Psychology of Arabism

[…]

No Arab country wants to appear to be turning its back on the Palestinians, and the Arab country that most loudly champions the Palestinian cause on the grounds that Palestinian interests are being ignored can succeed in winning a large measure of Arab sympathy to its side. Syria is attempting this in the present situation. One of its chief objects in maintaining its steady criticism of Egypt for signing the second Sinai agreement is to win support and to prevent the Arabs from supporting Egypt's position. The Syrians have not fully succeeded; most Arabs are not convinced, despite their growing doubts about Egypt's intentions, that Cairo has permanently abandoned the Arab or the Palestinian cause, as Syria charges. But Damascus has successfully played on these doubts and on the emotionalism of the issue to prevent any Arab from openly backing Egypt or from speaking out against the Syrian position.

By allying itself with the Palestinians, Syria has guaranteed the purity of its Arab credentials, and no other Arab is willing to appear any less true to the cause. Should the day ever come that Syria is so dissatisfied with the pace and course of negotiations that it rejects the concept of negotiations altogether, it would undoubtedly be able to take large numbers of the other Arabs with it in a unified policy opposing accommodation with Israel, and the position of those still desiring talks would be untenable.

[…]

Israel's Policies--The Key to Arab Pragmatism

No single factor will be as important in determining the degree of Arab solidarity and the flexibility or inflexibility of Arab policies in the future as Israel's own actions. No amount of domestic strength, of independence from Arab doles, of unemotional pragmatism in policy-making, or of Saudi recommendations for moderation will keep the Arabs from uniting in a rigid policy toward negotiations if Israel does not give the Arabs a return for their readiness to negotiate.

Pragmatism and the give-and-take of negotiations are still unfamiliar concepts to the Arabs, and there remains a strong emotional resistance to making concessions to Israel. This has lately been evidenced by the Syrians' and the Palestinians' horrified reaction to Egypt's concessions in the Sinai agreement and by Egypt's own insistence that it in fact made no concessions. That the Arabs have engaged in negotiations at all is entirely a function of two factors: the increased self-confidence that pride in their military accomplishments in 1973 has given them, and the fact that it has been demonstrated by the US and Israel through three rounds of disengagement negotiation that flexibility can bring tangible benefits in the form of territory returned. If those tangible benefits no longer appear to be forthcoming, not only will Arab self-confidence be sapped, thus heightening their inhibitions about negotiations, but they will be convinced that in fact flexibility on their part does not pay off.

The Arabs still feel more comfortable with a policy that is rigid and rhetorically militant, and they will retreat to the comfortable if the unfamiliar does not produce results. Only Israel can maintain Arab flexibility by demonstrating that this is a productive policy; only Israel, by making territorial concessions itself, can prevent the Arabs from returning to the unified, uncompromising Arab policy that would make a peace settlement impossible.

Conclusion
[...]
The Arabs are in fact heavily inter-dependent, militarily, economically, and politically.

By an accident of fate their resources are scattered in such a way as to make it virtually impossible for any one state to act with complete independence against the wishes of the others. Egypt and Syria need each other militarily and politically to pose a credible military threat to Israel. Both need the financial largesse of Saudi Arabia for their own economic well-being, and the Saudi oil weapon is critical to the success of their politico-military strategy against Israel. Saudi Arabia, in its turn, needs good relations with the confrontation states and the Palestinians if it is to maintain its influence in Arab councils and its credibility as a good Arab. Jordan needs the friendship of either Egypt or Syria as protection against the slings and arrows of other Arabs who oppose its Palestinian policy, and, in the normal course of Arab relations, either Syria or Egypt is usually seeking Jordan's friendship to protect its flanks against criticism from the other. The Palestinians are totally at the mercy of the other Arabs--whether of Lebanon for the haven it provides, of Syria and Egypt for political suste-nance, or of Saudi Arabia and other oil states for financial support.

The very fact of this interdependence, and its practical grounding, make it an enduring phenomenon. It is likely that there will never be [a] major Arab-Israeli war in which the resources of most Arab states are not called into service in some measure. It is equally likely that there will never be an Arab-Israeli peace that does not give reasonable satisfaction to all the Arab principals and have at least the implicit blessing of the main peripheral states. The Arabs are now--and are likely to be for the foreseeable future--

militarily, economically, and emotionally incapable of making peace or war with Israel individually.

[...]

The tendency toward a degree of self-interested independence and separateness can be nurtured only if the one issue that unites the Arabs is removed as a focus for their common attention. That issue is Israel's occupation of Arab territories, and by continuing its hold on those territories Israel itself gives the Arabs a cause for unity and solidarity that they would not otherwise have. A decade hence the Arabs will be better educated, more sophisticated, probably economically more powerful, and undoubtedly militarily stronger than they are now. If peace has not been achieved, they are likely also to be more emotionally determined to achieve it their way, and they will not hesitate to concentrate their resources on their common antagonist.

CAMP DAVID

Speech to Knesset (1977)
Anwar Sadat

1 have borne — and I still bear — the exigencies of a historic responsibility. For this purpose I declared some years back, on February 4, 1971 to be exact, that I was ready to sign a peace agreement with Israel. It was the first declaration — ever to be made by an Arab responsible official since the onset of the Arab-Israeli conflict.

Moved by all these motivations which were dictated by the responsibility of leadership, I called on October 16, 1973, before the Egyptian People's Assembly, for the convening of an international conference to decide upon a just and durable peace. This came at a time when 1 was not in the position of one begging for peace or seeking a cease-fire.

Moved by all these motivations, which were dictated by the duty of history and leadership, we signed the first, then the second disengagement agreements in Sinai. Next, we tried both the closed and open doors, seeking a path which could lead to a durable and just peace. We bared our heart to the nations of the entire world to enable them to understand our motivations and objectives, and to convince them once and for all that we are advocates of justice and peace-makers.

Moved by all these reasons, I have decided to come to you with an open mind and heart, and with a conscious free will, to establish a durable peace based on justice. [...]

Let us be frank with one another as we answer the big question; How can we achieve a durable and just peace?

I came to you carrying my clear and frank answer to this question so that the Israeli people may hear it, to have the entire world and those whose sincere voices reach my ears listen to it, hoping that in the end the outcome, expected by millions from this history-making meeting, would materialize.

Before I make public my answer, allow me to assure you that my clear and frank answer rests on several facts, that everyone cannot help but recognize.

First fact: Nobody can have happiness at the expense of the wretchedness of others.

Second fact: I have never spoken, and I will never speak in two different ways. I have not and will never, adopt a two-faced policy. I have never conferred with anybody except through one language, one policy and one face.

Third fact: Direct confrontation and the straight line are the shortest and most successful road to clear-cut objectives.

Fourth fact: The call for a durable and just peace based on respect of the U.N. resolutions, has been adopted today by the entire world and has become a cogent expression of the international community's will, either in the official capitals where policy and decisions are made, or on the level of world public opinion which influences the processes of policy and decision-making.

Fifth fact: Which may be the most salient and clear-cut of all facts, is that the Arab Nation is not seeking a durable and just peace from a position of weakness or instability. On the contrary, it possesses all the potentialities of power and stability. Hence its word emanates from a genuine will to achieve peace, a word that proceeds from a civilized awareness that in order to avert a definite catastrophe for us and for you and for the entire world, we have no other alternative but to establish a durable and just peace; a peace that cannot be shaken by storms, or tampered through doubts or shaken by ill and distorted intentions.

Proceeding from these facts, I would like, while wishing to bring you to see the image as I conceive it, to sincerely warn you against thoughts that might occur to you. The commitment to be frank compels to say the following:

First: I did not come to you to conclude a separate agreement between Egypt and Israel, for this has no place in Egyptian policy. The problem does not concern Egypt and Israel alone. Hence, any separate peace between Egypt and Israel or between any of the front-line States and Israel is bound to fall short of establishing a durable and just peace in the entire area. Furthermore, it would not be possible to achieve the just and durable peace so pressingly advocated by the entire world in the absence of a just solution to the Palestinian problem even though peace may have achieved between all the front-line States and Israel.

Second: I did not come to you seeking a partial peace in the sense that we put an end to the state of belligerency at this stage, shelving the whole problem to be tackled at a later stage.

This will not be the radical solution leading us to durable peace. In addition to this, I did not come to you to agree upon a third disengagement in Sinai, or the Golan and the West Bank, for this would only mean that we are postponing the lighting of the fuse to a future date.

It would also mean that we lack the courage to face up to peace and we are too weak to shoulder the burden and responsibilities of a durable and just peace. I came here to you to build together a durable and just peace and to prevent any Arab or Israeli bloodshed. For this reason I declared that I was ready to go to the end of the world. Let me now answer the big question: How can we achieve a just and durable peace?

In my opinion, and I am declaring it to the entire world from this rostrum, the answer is neither impossible nor difficult, in spite of long years of blood feuds, malevolence, hatred and bringing up generations on complete estrangement and chronic antagonism.

The answer is not difficult, nor is it impossible, if we only were to tread the straight line with sincerity and faith. You want to co-exist with us in this part of the world, and I tell you quite sincerely: We welcome you among us in all peace and security.

This, in itself, constitutes a sharp turning point, a landmark in a historic and decisive change.

In the past we rejected you and we had our reasons and claims.

Yes,

We refused to meet you — in any place.

Yes,

We used to describe you as so-called Israel.

Yes,

We attended the same international conferences or organizations. Our representatives never — and still do not — exchange greetings. This took place and is still taking place. One of our conditions in any talks was a mediator who met each party.

Yes,

On these lines, the first and second disengagement talks took place. Our representatives at the first Geneva Conference met without ever exchanging a single word.

Yes, this has taken place.

But, I tell you today, and declare to the whole world, that we accept to

314

live with you in durable and just peace. We do not want to encircle each other with rockets ready to destroy or with missiles of feuds and hatred.

I have declared more than once that Israel has become an established fact recognized by the entire world. The two super-powers have committed themselves to security and the safe-guarding of its existence. And since we really and sincerely want peace, we welcome you to live among us in real peace and security.
[...]
To tell you the truth, peace cannot be real unless it rests on justice and not on the occupation of the land of others. It is not right that you should demand for yourselves what you deny to others. In all frankness, and in the spirit that impelled me to come to you today, I say to you: You should give up once and for all the dreams of conquest, and the belief that force is the best way to deal with the Arabs. You should assimilate the lessons of confrontation between us. Expansion will gain you nothing.

So that we may speak dearly, our land is not subject to bargaining nor is it a topic of debate.

Our national and regional soil is to us like the sacred valley in which God spoke to Moses. None of us can, nor would, give up one inch of that soil, nor would we accept the principle of discussing, or bargaining about it.

Let me tell you truthfully: Today we have a good chance for peace, an opportunity that cannot be repeated, if we are really serious in the quest for peace. If we throw or fritter away, this chance, the curse of mankind and the curse of history, will befall the one who plots against it.

What is peace for Israel?

That it should live in security and safety in the area with its Arab neighbors.

To such logic I say, Yes.

That, Israel should live within its borders secure from any aggression.

To such logic I say, Yes.

That Israel should obtain all the guarantees that ensure for it these two facts.

To such demand I say, Yes.

I declare that we accept all international guarantees you may imagine, and from whoever you may choose.

I declare that we accept all guarantees you may want from the two superpowers, or from the five Big Powers, or from some of them.

I repeat quite clearly, we accept any guarantees you may want, because, in return, we will have the same guarantees.

To sum up: When we ask, What is peace for Israel?

The answer will be, that Israel should live within its borders in peace and security with its Arab neighbors, within the framework of all the guarantees it may want, and which are given to the other party.

But how can this be achieved?

How can we reach this result, so as to achieve a just and lasting peace? There are certain facts that have to be faced with courage and clear vision.

There are Arab territories which Israel occupied, and still occupies, by armed force. We insist on complete withdrawal from these territories, including Arab Jerusalem — Jerusalem which I came to as the city of peace, the city which will always be the living embodiment of the co-existence among the believers of the three religions.

It is inadmissible that anyone should conceive special status of Jerusalem within the framework of annexation or expansion. Jerusalem must be a free city, open to all the faithful.

More important than this, this city should not be separated from those who chose it for centuries as their place for living and working.

Instead of awakening the hatreds of the Crusades, we should revive the Spirit of Omar Ibn El Khattab and Salah Eldine — the spirit of tolerance and respect for rights.

Moslem and Christian places of worship are not only for the performance of religious rites, but a living testimony to our uninterrupted existence in this place, politically, spiritually and intellectually.

Here let no one make a mistake about the importance and reverence that we, Christians and Moslems, attach to Jerusalem.

Let me tell you, without any hesitation, that I did not come to you under this dome to request you to withdraw forces from the occupied territories.

316

Complete withdrawal from the Arab territories occupied in 1967 is a logical and undisputed matter. No one should plead for that.

Any talk about a just and lasting peace, any step to guarantee our living together in this part of the world in peace and security, while you occupy Arab land by armed force would be meaningless. There can be no peace built on the occupation of the land of others.

Yes.

This is elementary, indisputable, if the intentions are good and the endeavour is earnest for a just and lasting peace for our generation and the generations to come.

As for the Palestine cause, no one can deny that this is the crux of the whole problem. No one in the whole world today can accept slogans raised here in Israel, ignoring the existence of the Palestinian people, and even questioning where is that people?

The cause of the Palestinian people, and the legitimate rights of the Palestinian people, are no longer ignored or denied by anybody. No thinking mind can conceive that this should be ignored or denied.

It is a reality which the international community, west and east, has supported and recognized in international documents and official communiques. It will not do anybody any good to turn deaf ears to its resounding: voice or to close his eyes to its historic truth. Even the United States of America, your prime ally, which bears the maximum commitment to protect the existence and security of Israel, and which provides Israel all moral, material and military aid, even the United States has elected to face the facts and the reality, and to admit that the Palestinian people have legitimate rights, that the Palestine question is the heart and crux of the conflict, and that as long as this issue remains unsolved the conflict can only continue to aggravate and to reach new dimensions.

In all faith I tell you that peace cannot be achieved without the Palestinians. It would be a grave error with unpredictable consequences to ignore or brush aside this cause.

I shall not review past events since the Balfour Declaration sixty years ago, for you are well aware of the facts.

If you have found legal and moral justification for the establishment of a national home on land that did not all belong to you, you should all the more understand the insistence of the Palestinian people to re-establish their State on their land.

When some extremists call on the Palestinians to give up this noble aim, they are in fact asking them to give up their identity and abandon every hope in the future. I hail the Israeli voices that have called for recognition of the rights of the Palestinian people so as to achieve and guarantee peace. Therefore, I say to you, ladies and gentlemen, there is no use in refusing to recognize the Palestinian people and their right to establish a State and to return.

We, Arabs, have gone before through this experience with you and with the reality of the Israeli presence. The conflict led us from one war to another, from victims to more victims, until today, we and you, are on the brink of a terrible abyss; a frightful disaster, unless, we seize the chance together, today, for a just and lasting peace.

You should face the reality courageously, as I have faced it. No problem can be solved by evading it or keeping aloof from it. No peace can be established by trying to impose fantasy concepts to which the whole world has turned its back, and announced its unanimous call for the respect of rights and facts.

There is no need to enter a vicious circle on Palestinian rights. There is no gain in creating obstacles. That would only delay peace, or kill peace. As I have told you, no one can be happy at the expense of the misery of others. Direct confrontation of a problem and the straight line are the shortest and most practical way to reach the clear target. And direct confrontation with the Palestinian problem, the only language to deal with it for a just and lasting peace, is the establishment of their State.

With all the international guarantees you request, there should be no fear of a new-born State that would need aid from all the countries of the world for its establishment.

When the bells of peace ring, there will be no hand to beat the drums of war, and if there is any, it shall be soundless. Conceive — with me — a peace agreement in Geneva, which we herald to a world thirsty for peace. A peace agreement based on the following:

First: Termination of the Israeli occupation of the Arab territories occupied in 1967.

Second: Achievement of the basic rights of the Palestinian people and their right to self-determination, including the right to establish their own State.

Third: The right of each State in the area to live in peace within secure borders guaranteed by agreed upon procedures that would ensure the proper security of international borders, in addition to appropriate international guarantees.

Fourth: All the States of the area should be committed to conduct their relations with one another, according to the aims and principles of the United Nations Charter, particularly, not to resort to the use of force, and to resolve any differences among them through peaceful means.

Fifth: Termination of the present state of belligerency in the area.

Ladies and gentlemen,

Peace is not a signature endorsing written lines. It is a new writing of history. Peace is not a contest in trumpeting for it, only to defend any passions or to conceal any ambitions. Peace, in its essence, is a giant struggle against passions and ambitions.
[...]
I have chosen to depart from all precedents and traditions practised by belligerent countries, although the Arab territories are still occupied. My announcement about my readiness to come to Israel was a major surprise that stirred many feelings, astounded many minds, and though some doubted the intention, despite all this, I made my decision with all the spiritual clarity and purity of faith, in true expression of the will of my people. I chose this difficult course, which in the view of many is the most difficult.

I chose to come to you with an open heart and an open mind. I chose to give this great impetus to all the world efforts for peace. I chose to present to you, in your own house, the pure facts, free from bias or prejudice;

Not to manoeuvre;

Not to win a round;

But to win together, the major and most serious battle in modern history.

The battle for a just and lasting peace.
[...]
Peace be upon you.

West Bank: Opinion on Sadat's Plan (1977)
CENTRAL INTELLIGENCE AGENCY

Egyptian President Sadat has been unable to get West Bank and Gaza Palestinian leaders to endorse his peace initiatives publicly, despite significant support for his efforts among Palestinians living in the occupied territories. The local leaders want to avoid further divisions in the Palestinian movement, and they are skeptical about Israel's willingness to withdraw to its 1967 borders.

Egyptian officials have asked representatives from Gaza and the West Bank to visit Cairo to discuss Sadat's initiative, but no major figure has accepted. We have no evidence that Egypt has formally invited any West Bank representatives to the proposed Cairo conference.

A few conservative West Bank leaders, notably Bethlehem Mayor Ilyas Frayj who met with Sadat in Jerusalem, have commented favorably on Sadat's policy....

Before Sadat's arrival in Jerusalem, many West Bank notables received threats, presumably from Fatah sympathizers, warning them not to meet with the Egyptian President. Some low-level representatives from Gaza and the Sinai will visit Cairo soon, however, according to press reports from Egypt and Israel.

There is substantial popular sentiment in favor of Sadat's initiatives. Palestinians in the occupied territories were initially skeptical about Sadat's trip to Israel but approved of his firm statement of the Arab cause to the Knesset. Many are now supporting Sadat and criticizing Syria.

Sadat's initiatives have given rise to unrealistic popular expectations among the Palestinians of an easy peace settlement that will end the Israeli occupation. Even among the usually more radical student population large numbers are enthusiastically backing Sadat. This feeling could rapidly evaporate if the Cairo conference does not produce forward movement on the West Bank question.
[...]

Framework for Peace in the Middle East (Camp David Accords) (1978)
THE ARAB REPUBLIC OF EGYPT AND THE STATE OF ISRAEL

Muhammad Anwar Al-Sadat, President of the Arab Republic of Egypt, and Menachem Begin, Prime Minister of Israel, met with Jimmy Carter, President of the United States of America, at Camp David from September 5 to September 17, 1978, and have agreed on the following framework for peace in the Middle East. They invite other parties to the Arab-Israeli conflict to adhere to it.

PREAMBLE

The search for peace in the Middle East must be guided by the following:

—The agreed basis for a peaceful settlement of the conflict between Israel and its neighbors is United Nations Security Council Resolution 242, in all its parts.

—After four wars during thirty years, despite intensive human efforts, the Middle East, which is the cradle of civilization and the birthplace of three great religions, does not yet enjoy the blessings of peace. The people of the Middle East yearn for peace so that the vast human and natural resources of the region can be turned to the pursuits of peace and so that this area can become a model for coexistence and cooperation among nations.

—The historic initiative of President Sadat in visiting Jerusalem and the reception accorded to him by the Parliament, government and people of Israel, and the reciprocal visit of Prime Minister Begin to Ismailia, the peace proposals made by both leaders, as well as the warm reception of these missions by the peoples of both countries, have created an unprecedented opportunity for peace which must not be lost if this generation and future generations are to be spared the tragedies of war.

—The provisions of the Charter of the United Nations and the other accepted norms of international law and legitimacy now provide accepted standards for the conduct of relations among all states.

—To achieve a relationship of peace, in the spirit of Article 2 of the United Nations Charter, future negotiations between Israel and any neighbor prepared to negotiate peace and security with it are necessary for the purpose of carrying out all the provisions and principles of resolutions 242 and 338.

—Peace requires respect for the sovereignty, territorial integrity and political independence of every state in the area and their right to live in peace within secure and recognized boundaries free from threats or acts of force. Progress toward that goal can accelerate movement toward a new era of reconciliation in the Middle East marked by cooperation in promoting economic development, in maintaining stability, and in assuring security.

—Security is enhanced by a relationship of peace and by cooperation between nations which enjoy normal relations. In addition, under the terms of peace treaties, the parties can, on the basis of reciprocity, agree to special security arrangements such as demilitarized zones, limited armaments areas, early warning stations, the presence of international forces, liaison, agreed measures for monitoring, and other arrangements that they agree are useful.

FRAMEWORK

Taking these factors into account, the parties are determined to reach a just, comprehensive, and durable settlement of the Middle East conflict through the conclusion of peace treaties based on Security Council resolutions 242 and 338 in all their parts. Their purpose is to achieve peace and good-neighborly relations. They recognize that, for peace to endure, it must involve all those who have been most deeply affected by the conflict. They therefore agree that this framework as appropriate is intended by them to constitute a basis for peace not only between Egypt and Israel, but also between Israel and each of its other neighbors which is prepared to negotiate peace with Israel on this basis. With that objective in mind, they have agreed to proceed as follows:

A. WEST BANK AND GAZA

1. Egypt, Israel, Jordan and the representatives of the Palestinian people should participate in negotiations on the resolution of the Palestinian problem in all its aspects. To achieve that objective, negotiations relating to the West Bank and Gaza should proceed in three stages:

(a) Egypt and Israel agree that, in order to ensure a peaceful and orderly transfer of authority, and taking into account the security concerns of all the parties, there should be transitional arrangements for the West Bank and Gaza for a period not exceeding five years. In order to provide full autonomy to the inhabitants, under these arrangements the Israeli military government and its civilian administration will be withdrawn as soon as a self-governing authority has been freely elected by the inhabitants of these areas to replace the existing military government. To negotiate the details of a transitional arrangement, the Government of Jordan will be invited to join the negotiations on the basis of this framework. These new arrangements should give due consideration both to the principle of self-government by the inhabitants of these territories and to the legitimate security concerns of the parties involved.

(b) Egypt, Israel, and Jordan will agree on the modalities for establishing the elected self-governing authority in the West Bank and Gaza. The delegations of Egypt and Jordan may include Palestinians from the West Bank and Gaza or other Palestinians as mutually agreed. The parties will negotiate an agreement which will define the powers and responsibilities of the self-governing authority to be exercised in the West Bank and Gaza. A withdrawal of Israeli armed forces will take place and there will be a redeployment of the remaining Israeli forces into specified security locations. The agreement will also include arrangements for assuring internal and external security and public order. A strong local police force will be established which may include Jordanian citizens. In addition, Israeli and Jordanian forces will participate in joint patrols and in the manning of control posts to assure the security of the borders.

(c) When the self-governing authority (administrative council) in the West Bank and Gaza is established and inaugurated, the transitional period of five years will begin. As soon as possible, but not later than the third year after the beginning of the transitional period, negotiations will take place to determine the final status of the West Bank and Gaza and its relationship with its neighbors, and to conclude a peace treaty between Israel and Jordan by the end of the transitional period. These negotiations will be conducted among Egypt, Israel, Jordan, and the elected representatives of the inhabitants of the West Bank and Gaza. Two separate but related committees will be convened: one committee, consisting of representatives of the four parties which will negotiate and agree on the final status of the West Bank and Gaza, and its relationship with its neighbors, and the second committee, consisting of representatives of Israel and representatives of Jordan to be joined by the elected representatives of the inhabitants of the West Bank and Gaza, to negotiate the peace treaty between Israel and Jordan, taking into account the agreement reached on the final status of the West Bank and Gaza. The negotiations shall be based on all the provisions and principles of UN Security Council resolution 242. The negotiations will resolve, among other matters, the location of the boundaries and the nature of the security arrangements. The solution from the negotiations must also recognize the legitimate rights of the Palestinian people and their just requirements. In this way, the Palestinians will participate in the determination of their own future through:

1. The negotiations among Egypt, Israel, Jordan and the representatives of the inhabitants of the West Bank and Gaza to agree on the final status of the West Bank and Gaza and other outstanding issues by the end of the transitional period.

2. Submitting their agreement to a vote by the elected representatives of the inhabitants of the West Bank and Gaza.

3. Providing for the elected representatives of the inhabitants of the West Bank and Gaza to decide how they shall govern themselves consistent with the provisions of their agreement.

4. Participating as stated above in the work of the committee negotiating the peace treaty between Israel and Jordan.

2. All necessary measures will be taken and provisions made to assure the security of Israel and its neighbors during the transitional period and beyond. To assist in providing such security, a strong local police force will be constituted by the self-governing authority. It will be composed of inhabitants of the West Bank and Gaza. The police will maintain continuing liaison on internal security matters with the designated Israeli, Jordanian, and Egyptian officers.

3. During the transitional period, representatives of Egypt, Israel, Jordan, and the self-governing authority will constitute a continuing committee to decide by agreement on the modalities of admission of persons displaced from the West Bank and Gaza in 1967, together with necessary measures to prevent disruption and disorder. Other matters of common concern may also be dealt with by this committee.

4. Egypt and Israel will work with each other and with other interested parties to establish agreed procedures for a prompt, just and permanent implementation of the resolution of the refugee problem.

B. EGYPT—ISRAEL

1. Egypt and Israel undertake not to resort to the threat or the use of force to settle disputes. Any disputes shall be settled by peaceful means in accordance with the provisions of Article 33 of the Charter of the United Nations.

2. In order to achieve peace between them, the parties agree to negotiate in good faith with a goal of concluding within three months from the signing of this Framework a peace treaty between them, while inviting the other parties to the conflict to proceed simultaneously to negotiate and conclude similar peace treaties with a view to achieving a comprehensive peace in the area. [...]

C. ASSOCIATED PRINCIPLES

1. Egypt and Israel state that the principles and provisions described below should apply to peace treaties between Israel and each of its neighbors— Egypt, Jordan, Syria and Lebanon.

2. Signatories shall establish among themselves relationships normal to states at peace with one another. To this end, they should undertake to abide by all the provisions of the Charter of the United Nations. Steps to be taken in this respect include:

(a) full recognition;

(b) abolishing economic boycotts;

(c) guaranteeing that under their jurisdiction the citizens of the other parties shall enjoy the protection of the due process of law.

3. Signatories should explore possibilities for economic development in the context of final peace treaties, with the objective of contributing to the atmosphere of peace, cooperation and friendship which is their common goal.

4. Claims Commissions may be established for the mutual settlement of all financial claims.

5. The United States shall be invited to participate in the talks on matters related to the modalities of the implementation of the agreements [....]

6. The United Nations Security Council shall be requested to endorse the peace treaties and ensure that their provisions shall not be violated. The permanent members of the Security Council shall be requested to underwrite the peace treaties and ensure respect for their provisions. They shall also be requested to conform their policies and actions with the undertakings contained in this Framework.

After Camp David (1978)
CENTRAL INTELLIGENCE AGENCY

Reaction in the Middle East this week to the announcements following the Camp David summit ranged from optimism in Israel and Egypt to outrage among the Palestinians. Most leaders in the area, however, have been notably cautious in their initial responses.

Most Israelis are pleased with the outcome. Several leading figures in Prime Minister Begin's ruling Likud bloc have expressed cautious optimism, and some of Begin's most outspoken critics in the "Peace Now" movement and opposition parties are supporting him. The agreement has been sharply criticized only by a vocal minority on the right who have expressed strong opposition to the removal of any of Israel's Sinai settlements. According to a survey by an Israeli polling organization, however, about 60 percent of the Israeli public approves abandoning Israel's Sinai settlements as part of a peace agreement with Egypt.

An informal count this week of about 70 Knesset deputies showed that two-thirds support the Camp David accords. Barring a major Israeli-Egyptian dispute over interpretation, as many as 100 of the 120 Knesset members will approve the agreements.

In Egypt, too, the early reaction to the agreements has been favorable. [...] The ... segment of the population, which forms an important part of President Sadat's power base, believes the policy of reliance on the US has been vindicated and is so far not particularly worried about what other Arabs think. Some ... Egyptians, however, are concerned that real problems lie ahead in Egypt's relations with other Arab states.

The Saudis, while describing the Camp David framework for a settlement as an "unacceptable formula for a definitive peace," have taken a less negative attitude toward Sadat's effort to regain the Sinai. Riyadh announced before Secretary Vance's arrival on 21 September that as long as Arab higher interests are not contradicted, Saudi Arabia does not believe it has the right to interfere with an Arab country's efforts to regain its lost territory through military or peaceful means. The Saudis, as they have in the past, stressed their interest in Israeli withdrawal from Jerusalem, and the need for new efforts toward Arab unity.

Jordan's King Hussein has been holding his cards closely. In a statement just before Secretary Vance's visit he announced that Jordan would not be bound by the Camp David agreements but he did not flatly rule out a Jordanian role in a West Bank - Gaza arrangement. He called for a comprehensive settlement involving total Israeli withdrawal from the West Bank, Gaza, and East Jerusalem, and recognition of the right of the Palestinian people to determine their own destiny.

326

Hardline Arabs

The hardline Arabs have made no secret of their distaste for the Camp David results. At a meeting in Damascus, leaders of Syria, Algeria, Libya, South Yemen, and the Palestine Liberation Organization—members of the "Steadfastness Front" formed last December to oppose the Egyptian peace initiative—condemned Sadat for betraying the Arab cause by making a separate peace with Israel.

In his public remarks to the Front, Syrian President Assad charged Sadat with abandoning the Arab cause by agreeing to a separate peace with Israel. Assad has always feared that a bilateral Egyptian-Israeli deal would permit Israel to remain intransigent on the Palestinian question and the Golan Heights. Many Syrians are particularly unhappy that the Camp David accords do not mention the Golan issue.

The Syrians were clearly encouraged by the Jordanian and Saudi statements. Assad apparently hopes to develop an Arab consensus of hardliners and moderates to isolate Sadat. At the same time, Assad wants to maintain his image of being favorable to a comprehensive peace agreement; his willingness to meet with Secretary Vance is intended in part to serve this end.

Some of the strongest criticism has come from the leaders of the PLO. The group's Executive Committee termed the Camp David agreements a "complete capitulation" by Sadat and called on Palestinians everywhere to strike and demonstrate against "the conspiracy," and urged Egyptians to rise in defense of their national dignity. The committee threatened "fair punishment" to those who declare their support for the accords.

Treaty of Peace (1979)
THE ARAB REPUBLIC OF EGYPT AND THE STATE OF ISRAEL

Convinced of the urgent necessity of the establishment of a just, comprehensive and lasting peace in the Middle East in accordance with Security Council Resolutions 242 and 338;

Reaffirming their adherence to the "Framework for Peace in the Middle East Agreed at Camp David," dated September 17, 1978;

Noting that the aforementioned Framework as appropriate is intended to constitute a basis for peace not only between Egypt and Israel but also between Israel and each of its other Arab neighbors which is prepared to negotiate peace with it on this basis;

Desiring to bring to an end the state of war between them and to establish a peace in which every state in the area can live in security;

Convinced that the conclusion of a Treaty of Peace between Egypt and Israel is an important step in the search for comprehensive peace in the area and for the attainment of the settlement of the Arab-Israeli conflict in all its aspects;

Inviting the other Arab parties to this dispute to join the peace process with Israel guided by and based on the principles of the aforementioned Framework;

Desiring as well to develop friendly relations and cooperation between themselves in accordance with the United Nations Charter and the principles of international law governing international relations in times of peace;

Agree to the following provisions in the free exercise of their sovereignty, in order to implement the "Framework for the Conclusion of a Peace Treaty Between Egypt and Israel".

Article I. 1. The state of war between the Parties will be terminated and peace will be established between them upon the exchange of instruments of ratification of this Treaty.

2. Israel will withdraw all its armed forces and civilians from the Sinai behind the international boundary between Egypt and mandated Palestine, as provided in the annexed protocol (Annex I), and Egypt will resume the exercise of its full sovereignty over the Sinai.

3. Upon completion of the interim withdrawal provided for in Annex I, the Parties will establish normal and friendly relations, in accordance with article III (3).

Article II. The permanent boundary between Egypt and Israel is the recognized international boundary between Egypt and the former mandated territory of Palestine, as shown on the map at Annex II, without prejudice to the issue of the status of the Gaza Strip. The Parties recognize this boundary as inviolable. Each will respect the territorial integrity of the other, including their territorial waters and airspace.

Article III. 1. The Parties will apply between them the provisions of the Charter of the United Nations and the principles of international law governing relations among states in times of peace. In particular:

    a.   They recognize and will respect each other's sovereignty, territorial integrity and political independence;

    b.   They recognize and will respect each other's right to live in peace within their secure and recognized boundaries;

    c.   They will refrain from the threat or use of force, directly or indirectly, against each other and will settle all disputes between them by peaceful means.

2. Each Party undertakes to ensure that acts or threats of belligerency, hostility, or violence do not originate from and are not committed from within its territory, or by any forces subject to its control or by any other forces stationed on its territory, against the population, citizens or property of the other Party. Each Party also undertakes to refrain from organizing, instigating, inciting, assisting or participating in acts or threats of belligerency, hostility, subversion or violence against the other Party, anywhere, and undertakes to ensure that perpetrators of such acts are brought to justice.

3. The Parties agree that the normal relationship established between them will include full recognition, diplomatic, economic and cultural relations, termination of economic boycotts and discriminatory barriers to the free movement of people and goods, and will guarantee the mutual enjoyment by citizens of the due process of law. The process by which they undertake to achieve such a relationship parallel to the implementation of other provisions of this Treaty is set out in the annexed protocol (Annex III).

Article IV. 1. In order to provide maximum security for both Parties on the basis of reciprocity, agreed security arrangements will be established including limited force zones in Egyptian and Israeli territory, and United

Nations forces and observers, described in detail as to nature and timing in Annex I, and other security arrangements the Parties may agree upon.

2. The Parties agree to the stationing of United Nations personnel in areas described in Annex I. The Parties agree not to request withdrawal of the United Nations personnel and that these personnel will not be removed unless such removal is approved by the Security Council of the United Nations, with the affirmative vote of the five Permanent Members, unless the Parties otherwise agree.

3. A Joint Commission will be established to facilitate the implementation of the Treaty [....]

4. The security arrangements provided for in paragraphs I and 2 of this article may at the request of either Party be reviewed and amended by mutual agreement of the Parties.

Article V. 1. Ships of Israel, and cargoes destined for or coming from Israel, shall enjoy the right of free passage through the Suez Canal and its approaches through the Gulf of Suez and the Mediterranean Sea on the basis of the Constantinople Convention of 1888, applying to all nations. Israeli nationals, vessels and cargoes, as well as persons, vessels and cargoes destined for or coming from Israel, shall be accorded non-discriminatory treatment in all matters connected with usage of the canal.

2. The Parties consider the Strait of Tiran and the Gulf of Aqaba to be international waterways open to all nations for unimpeded and non-suspendable freedom of navigation and overflight. The Parties will respect each other's right to navigation and overflight for access to either country through the Strait of Tiran and the Gulf of Aqaba.

Article VI. 1. This Treaty does not affect and shall not be interpreted as affecting in any way the rights and obligations of the Parties under the Charter of the United Nations.

2. The Parties undertake to fulfill in good faith their obligations under this Treaty, without regard to action or inaction of any other party and independently of any instrument external to this Treaty.

3. They further undertake to take all the necessary measures for the application in their relations of the provisions of the multilateral conventions to which they are parties, including the submission of appropriate notification to the Secretary-General of the United Nations and other depositaries of such conventions.

4. The Parties undertake not to enter into any obligation in conflict with this Treaty.

5. Subject to Article 103 of the United Nations Charter, in the event of a conflict between the obligations of the Parties under the present Treaty and any of their other obligations, the obligations under this Treaty will be binding and implemented.

Article VII. 1. Disputes arising out of the application or interpretation of this Treaty shall be resolved by negotiations.

2. Any such disputes which cannot be settled by negotiations shall be resolved by conciliation or submitted to arbitration.

Article VIII. The Parties agree to establish a claims commission for the mutual settlement of all financial claims.

Article IX. [...]

2. This Treaty supersedes the Agreement between Egypt and Israel of September, 1975.
[...]

The Arab-Israeli Military Balance: Impact of the Egyptian-Israeli Peace Treaty (1979)
CENTRAL INTELLIGENCE AGENCY

The Egyptian-Israeli peace treaty, establishing the basis for Egypt's eventual withdrawal from the Arab military ranks arrayed against Israel, has significantly reduced the military threat to Israel. Although Egyptian participation in future Arab-Israeli hostilities cannot be ruled out by the existence of the treaty, any effective participation by Egypt will be made more difficult and risky by the ongoing deterioration of its military capabilities and by military factors set in motion by the treaty. Since Israel can defeat all Arab forces, [...] the absence of the largest Arab military power and one battlefront will give Israel an overwhelming military superiority over the remaining Arab states.

Israel's widening margin of military superiority may encourage it to more aggressively pursue its policy goals, by striking hard at any perceived Arab provocations and manifesting less concern about the reactions of the Arab states, including Egypt. Israel views the Arabs as unwilling to risk an escalation of any fighting to a wider conflict [....]

The Arabs on the Golan Heights-Jordan Valley front could become stronger, but, without Egypt, there is little they can do over the next five years to substantially improve their military position relative to Israel.

- The Arab states will not be able to absorb enough weapons to compensate for the loss of Egypt's inventories; even Iraq's contribution of all of its forces would be insufficient.
- The Arabs cannot compensate for their significantly diminished numbers through qualitative increases in the operational effectiveness of their armed forces.
- The impact of new, advanced weapons received by the Arabs is likely to be offset by low Arab operational capabilities and effective Israeli countermeasures and weapon systems.

Arab improvements also will be constrained by several less important factors:

- Syria cannot pose a significant offensive threat to Israel as long as a substantial part of its Army remains deployed in Lebanon.
- Iraq has military requirements at home—heightened by events in Iran—to which it must devote significant numbers of units.
- Israel now would be able to assign more forces to interdiction of Iraqi forces en route to the Golan Heights-Jordan Valley front.

- Despite shared opposition to the peace treaty, mutual suspicions and traditional rivalries will continue to beset Arab attempts at unity.

These problems pose major impediments to the development before 1984 of Arab forces capable of effectively challenging Israel on the Golan Heights-Jordan Valley front. [...]

Israel will find it difficult over the next five years to maintain the quality of its forces while absorbing large amounts of new equipment. Direct competition by the military with the civilian economy for Israel's limited supply of skilled manpower already has forced the lowering of some military standards. [...]

US-Israeli Differences Over the Camp David Peace Process (1982)
CENTRAL INTELLIGENCE AGENCY

1.   In anticipation of a new US peace initiative the Israeli cabinet warned last Sunday that it will reject any effort to amend the Camp David Agreements (CDA). The stage is set for a bruising US-Israeli confrontation in which a key issue will be defining the meaning of the Camp David Agreements.

-- From the day the agreements were signed in September 1978 Israel has taken a narrow, legalistic, approach to their interpretation.
-- US officials have privately argued that the CDA are open to wider interpretation (a view shared by Egypt) but have never presented this view publicly.

2.   The most critical issue concerns the ultimate political status of the West Bank and Gaza. Prime Minister Begin asserts that the CDA rule out the emergence of a Palestinian state. In Begin's view, the agreements "guarantee that under no condition" can a Palestinian state be created.

-- In practice Begin effectively rules out any exercise of Palestinian self-determination except one that continues Israel's preeminent position in the West Bank. Moreover, he has made clear that Israel will press its own claim to sovereignty to the occupied territories in the future.
-- In fact the CDA does not prejudge the final status of the occupied territories. Their status is to be settled in talks held after a transitional Self-Governing Authority is created. As the Jerusalem Post noted on Monday, "nothing is ruled out in advance under Camp David, all options are to remain open."

3.   The key immediate difference is over what role should be given the Self-Governing Authority (SGA) which is to run the West Bank and Gaza during the interim 5-year transition period while these territories' final status is negotiated between the SGA, Israel, Egypt, Jordan, and the US. Begin's view is that the SGA should be a solely administrative authority regulating the affairs of the Arab inhabitants and leaving control of the territory and all key security issues with Israel. In sum, autonomy is for people not territory and therefore does not prejudice Israel's territorial claims to the West Bank.

-- The agreements themselves are purposefully vague, however, about the "powers and responsibilities" of the SGA and leave it to the parties (US, Egypt, Israel) to "negotiate an agreement" to "define the powers." Moreover, the CDA are vague about whether autonomy applied to people and/or land. In some clauses it refers to autonomy for "the inhabitants" but in others it deals with the West Bank and Gaza as territorial entities (for example as areas from which Israeli military role is to be withdrawn) and calls for "full" autonomy.

-- Egypt has always maintained that the CDA call for an autonomy agreement that gives the SGA legislative as well as administrative powers. Cairo argues -- probably correctly -- that a narrowly defined agreement will never attract broad Palestinian or Arab support.

4.   Israel has already defined its views on all the key issues and in each case makes a narrow interpretation:

-- Jewish settlements are to remain under Israeli control and not be subject to the SGA. The SGA could not prevent new settlements and territorial expansion of existing ones (115 settlements currently).
-- Water rights would be allocated by joint Israeli-SGA agreement. If agreement is not reached, the status quo -- which benefits Israel -- prevails.
-- Land rights would also be under joint control (Israel currently controls 1/3 of all West Bank land).
-- Security issues, internal and external, would be under sole Israel control, with only minor police rights given to SGA.
-- East Jerusalem is not considered part of West Bank and its Arab inhabitants are not eligible to vote for SGA.

In fact on all of these points the agreements are either vague or silent. Jordan's role in the peace process is dealt with, however; Amman was specifically "invited to join the negotiations" to establish the SGA on the basis of Camp David. Therefore, there is no reason to accept Israeli arguments that the US is prohibited from putting forth its own interpretations.

5.   A likely Israeli tactic will be to argue that the US and Egypt both promised to make no alteration in the Camp David approach last April during the talks before Israel returned the Sinai. In fact, President Reagan promised "to pursue" the negotiations "for full autonomy" and agreed that the CDA is "the only agreed plan" to resolve the Palestinian issue. These commitments do not prevent the US from giving its own interpretation of the CDA.

-- Israeli leaders, including Begin, have often warned that Israel will formally annex the West Bank if, in its judgement, the Camp David process is abrogated. The bottom line for US policy is to argue persuasively that Camp David is a broad framework within which the US can and must put forward its own views on key issues in order to attract other Arab states (Jordan) to the negotiating table.

Basic Law: Jerusalem, Capital of Israel (1980)
GOVT. OF ISRAEL

Jerusalem, Capital of Israel
1. Jerusalem, complete and united, is the capital of Israel.

Seat of the President, the Knesset, the Government and the Supreme Court
2. Jerusalem is the seat of the President of the State, the Knesset, the Government and the Supreme Court.

Protection of Holy Places
3. The Holy Places shall be protected from desecration and any other violation and from anything likely to violate the freedom of access of the members of the different religions to the places sacred to them or their feelings towards those places.

Development of Jerusalem
4. (a) The Government shall provide for the development and prosperity of Jerusalem and the well-being of its inhabitants by allocating special funds, including a special annual grant to the Municipality of Jerusalem (Capital City Grant) with the approval of the Finance Committee of the Knesset.

(b) Jerusalem shall be given special priority in the activities of the authorities of the State so as to further its development in economic and other matters

(c) The Government shall set up a special body or special bodies for the implementation of this section

Area of the jurisdiction of Jerusalem (Amendment no. 1)
5. The jurisdiction of Jerusalem includes, as pertaining to this basic law, among others, all of the area that is described in the appendix of the proclamation expanding the borders of municipal Jerusalem beginning the 20th of Sivan 5727 (June 28, 1967), as was given according to the Cities' Ordinance.

Prohibition of the transfer of authority (Amendment no. 1)
6. No authority that is stipulated in the law of the State of Israel or of the Jerusalem Municipality may be transfered either permanently or for an allotted period of time to a foreign body, whether political, governmental or to any other similar type of foreign body.

The Security Council,

Recalling its resolution 476 (1980),

Reaffirming again that the acquisition of territory by force is inadmissible,

Deeply concerned over the enactment of a "basic law" in the Israeli Knesset proclaiming a change in the character and status of the Holy City of Jerusalem, with its implications for peace and security,

Noting that Israel has not complied with resolution 476 (1980),

Reaffirming its determination to examine practical ways and means, in accordance with the relevant provisions of the Charter of the United Nations, to secure the full implementation of its resolution 476 (1980), in the event of non-compliance by Israel,

1. *Censures* in the strongest terms the enactment by Israel of the "basic law" on Jerusalem and the refusal to comply with relevant Security Council resolutions;

2. *Affirms* that the enactment of the "basic law" by Israel constitutes a violation of international law and does not affect the continued application of the Geneva Convention relative to the Protection of Civilian Persons in Time of War, of 12 August 1949, in the Palestinian and other Arab territories occupied since June 1967, including Jerusalem;

3. *Determines* that all legislative and administrative measures and actions taken by Israel, the occupying Power, which have altered or purport to alter the character and status of the Holy City of Jerusalem, and in particular the recent "basic law" on Jerusalem, are null and void and must be rescinded forthwith;

4. *Affirms also* that this action constitutes a serious obstruction to achieving a comprehensive, just and lasting peace in the Middle East;

5. *Decides* not to recognize the "basic law" and such other actions by Israel that, as a result of this law, seek to alter the character and status of Jerusalem and calls upon:

    a. All Member States to accept this decision;

    b. Those States that have established diplomatic missions at Jerusalem to withdraw such missions from the Holy City;

[...]

LEBANON

The 1970-71 Civil War (1987)
CENTRAL INTELLIGENCE AGENCY

For several years after the 1967 war, Palestinian guerrillas in Jordan exercised considerable political and military influence. Their popularity in the refugee camps was substantial, and even young children were recruited into paramilitary youth groups. During the period 1966-70, Palestinian groups launched guerilla attacks against Israel from Jordanian territory that were met with brutal retaliation by Israeli forces. The Palestinian movement in Jordan—led at the time by George Habbash's Popular Front for the Liberation of Palestine—reached its peak in 1970 and severely threatened the Hashemite monarchy.

In September 1970, also known as Black September, the Jordanian Army fought a 10-day civil war with Palestinian guerillas led by Habbash, who succeeded in persuading Fatah leader Yasir Arafat to involve his forces in the heavy fighting. This ended with an agreement, signed in Cairo, under which the guerrillas recognized Jordanian sovereignty and the King's authority and agreed to withdraw their forces from towns and villages. Some fighting continued, however, until 19 July 1971, when the Jordanian Army won a major victory over Habbash's men in the 'Aljun area. Most of the several thousand Palestinian commandos thereafter relocated to Lebanon.
[…]

338 From Central Intelligence Agency. Report: The Palestinian State in the East Bank (July 1, 1987).

Palestinians in Lebanon: Troubled Past and Bleak Future (1983)
CENTRAL INTELLIGENCE AGENCY

Historical Background

[...]

The PLO in Lebanon. Establishment of the PLO in 1964 and of its fighting units in the late 1960s helped bring about the first notable improvements in living conditions for the Palestinians in Lebanon. By 1969 the PLO had wrested control of the refugee camps from Lebanese authorities and was improving conditions in the camps, by installing electricity and running water, for example. UNRWA's charter limited its role in the camps to providing education, food, medical services, and some assistance in building refugee shelters. The UNRWA camps became places to recruit additional commandos for the PLO, which was commencing cross-border operations into Israel.

The PLO's growing power and its attacks on Israeli towns in the Galilee aroused concern in Lebanon and led to violent clashes in 1969 when the Lebanese Army attempted to curb PLO activities in the south. Lebanese Army and PLO representatives, meeting later that year in Cairo, forged the Cairo Accords, which were intended to formalize the presence of the PLO in Lebanon yet prevent it from interfering in internal Lebanese affairs. The PLO, however, reneged on its part of the bargain and increasingly asserted its military and economic control over much of southern Lebanon, especially the so-called Fatah Land on the western slopes of Mount Hermon.

The arrival of the PLO's political leadership and militia from Jordan in 1970-71 created further problems for the Lebanese. As the refugee camps in the south became armed PLO strongholds, they increasingly became targets of Israeli attacks. Moreover, the strengthening of the Palestinian presence in Lebanon drew the PLO rejectionists into Lebanese politics, usually on the side of leftist Muslim groups. This involvement aggravated the crisis between Lebanese Christians and Muslims that erupted into the 1975-76 civil war. When the PLO and the leftists appeared to be gaining the upper hand, Syrian President Assad, determined to keep a rough balance of power between the warring factions, intervened on the side of the Christians—an action ultimately approved by the Arab League.

The civil war and Syrian intervention set the PLO back militarily and politically. Although it retained some positions in Muslim West Beirut, the bulk of its forces were pushed into southern Lebanon where they became wedged between the Israelis to the south and the Syrians to the north. [...]

Impact of the Israeli Invasion

The Israeli invasion of Lebanon in June 1982 disrupted the entire Palestinian structure in southern Lebanon and Beirut. PLO strongholds were destroyed and tens of thousands of civilians were dispersed throughout the countryside. PLO fighters trapped in West Beirut were ultimately forced into exile in eight other Arab countries.

The main targets in the Israeli push north were the crowded Palestinian refugee camps and other Palestinian concentrations in southern Lebanon. [...] Most Palestinians in the south between the ages of 16 and 60—the most economically productive segment of the population—have fled, been killed, or taken prisoner by the Israelis.

The siege of West Beirut was particularly devastating for the Palestinians. Two months of Israeli shelling and bombing leveled large areas of the southern part of the city and its suburbs. The Fakhani district, Ar Ramlah al-Bayda, Burj al Barajinah, Al Awzai, and the refugee camps where the Palestinians lived were especially hard hit. According to press reports, most of the refugees fled the camps for the relative safety of the Ras Bayrut commercial district where they took cover in abandoned apartment buildings, office buildings, movie theaters, parking garages, and even public parks. The Israelis then pounded "suspect PLO concentrations" in the district.

Displacement of Palestinians. Estimates of the number of Palestinians killed, wounded, or made homeless by the Israeli invasion vary widely. Lebanese Government and United Nations sources suggest that 10,000 to 20,000 were killed and tens of thousands were wounded. In December the UNRWA Commissioner General claimed that the number of homeless Palestinians in the Beirut area and in the south numbered about 90,000, of which 55,000 were in the Sidon and Tyre areas. The Israeli Government, in contrast, reported only 30,000 homeless. Earlier, UNRWA had estimated that an additional 12,000 Palestinians were in the Bekaa Valley and that a few thousand had fled to neighboring Syria.
[...]
The loss or separation of a large share of adult males from Palestinian families—especially in the refugee camps—complicates the refugee resettlement issue. Those separated include the 8,500 PLO fighters, many of whom were recruited in the Lebanese UNRWA camps where they lived with or near their families before the invasion. An estimated 13,000 others are still in the north and in the Bekaa Valley and may be sent abroad as part of any Lebanese peace agreement. According to the International Committee of the Red Cross, an additional 5,300 alleged PLO members or sympathizers are being held prisoner at the Ansar prison camp near An Nabatiyah. [...]

Outlook

[...]

The Lebanese Government blames the Palestinians for the civil strife of recent years and wants them out of Lebanon. Realizing that expelling them all is impractical, the Lebanese Government, according to its spokesmen, will attempt to deport those Palestinians who lack proper papers. We believe this could be some 50,000 to 100,000, although one Lebanese official said the number may be as high as 250,000. Press accounts of government searches of the refugee camps in Beirut indicate that the process has already begun. UNRWA officials, according to a press report, claim that 15,000 to 20,000 Palestinians from the Beirut camps had voluntarily left the country by December 1982.

Integration of the Palestinians into Lebanese society is implausible because it is opposed by almost all Lebanese, particularly the Christian and Shia communities, according to reporting from the US Embassy. The Palestinians themselves would probably be apprehensive about such a move because they would feel neither accepted nor safe. To the extent the Palestinians use their own financial resources to build homes in the camps, they will not want to lose their investment unless they are offered a better prospect. Many cling to the hope of eventually returning to a Palestinian homeland.

If foreign forces withdraw, Palestinians can expect harsh treatment in any areas controlled by the present, Phalange-dominated Lebanese Government. The deeply rooted animosities between the Lebanese and Palestinians make isolated incidents against Palestinians likely, and widespread violence between the two groups cannot be ruled out. Official harassment to encourage emigration probably will include denials of work permits, arrests and detentions, and further destruction of refugee housing at the slightest pretext. Such policies may bring increasing numbers of Palestinian civilians to try to join relatives who were expelled or have settled abroad, but all such attempts will be subject to the policies of the host governments.

An Israeli-Palestinian Peace (1982)
Harold H. Saunders

Given the summer's immersion in day-to-day death and destruction in Lebanon, we need to begin putting the Israeli-Palestinian War of 1982 in larger perspective. For better or worse, it will mark a turning point in the history of Israel, in the course of Arab-Israeli relations, in U.S.-Israeli relations, in the political character and orientation of important Middle Eastern states, and in the U.S. position in that critical area.
[...]
The initially stated Israeli war aim was to clear a zone in southern Lebanon of weapons and fighters within reach of northern Israel. This war aim—"Peace for Galilee"—was understandable in view of past attacks on Israel's northern communities and the growing stockpile of Palestinian equipment in the region.

Within a few days, as Israeli forces moved rapidly north to lay siege to Beirut, Israel's stated war aims were expanded to include the eviction from Lebanon of the military presence and political headquarters of the Palestine Liberation Organization. This aim had a plausible basis as part of protecting Israel's physical security; it also conformed to the widespread desire of most Lebanese to be rid of the disruptive PLO apparatus there.
[...]
But the ultimate political objectives of Israel's leaders did not stop there. The physical removal of the PLO apparatus from Lebanon was seen as a means to a larger end—one frankly avowed in the statements of these leaders for several months. That end was the destruction of the organized Palestinian movement. With a fragmented and dispersed PLO, Israeli leaders foresaw the Palestinian population in the West Bank and Gaza—deprived of outside moral support—coming to accept permanent Israeli control there, in a situation in which much of that Palestinian population could be induced (or gradually coerced) to migrate across the Jordan River into Jordan.

In short, the most important Israeli objective was to resolve the Palestinian problem once and for all, by making the remaining Palestinians merely an ethnic minority within an enlarged Israel, and ultimately by transforming Jordan into a Republic of Palestine, with an accepted Palestinian diaspora elsewhere. As Foreign Minister Yitzhak Shamir has stated frankly in these pages, the only Palestinian "homeland" is to be Jordan, as "eastern Palestine."

Thus, the Israeli-Palestinian War was fought mainly over whether an organized Palestinian movement would survive in order to negotiate peace between Israelis and Palestinians as two people with equal rights. It was not fought only to determine how many Palestinian fighters should be where in Lebanon. The Palestinians' objective was to emerge from the fighting in some way that would prove that even Israel's military might could not destroy the Palestinian national movement or impose Israel's solution on it.

[…]

As this is written, it seems clear that Israel has achieved its war aim of evicting the PLO headquarters and military presence from Lebanon, and that the practical situation there will lend itself to lasting achievement of the war aim of militarily securing Israel's northern communities. […]

But it is critical that no one be derailed into thinking that the Arab-Israeli-Palestinian conflict has been or will be resolved in Lebanon. The war did not destroy Palestinian nationalism, and four million Palestinians remain in the Middle East and elsewhere.

What this invasion has done is to firmly establish the need for Israeli-Palestinian peace on the peacemaker's agenda along with peace between Israel and its neighboring states. The future of Lebanon is indeed of crucial importance—and, as we shall see, cannot even in itself be separated from the future of the Palestinian issue. […]

The war has posed the issue sharply: Will the Israeli-Palestinian conflict be resolved by negotiation in the near future or by force over time? Will Israel impose its sovereignty over the remaining land west of the Jordan River occupied in 1967? Will the Palestinians dedicate themselves to continued warfare? Or will both parties commit themselves to achieve peace in the land west of the Jordan, as envisioned at Camp David, through fair negotiations involving Israelis and Palestinians?

[…]

First, this war has again demonstrated that, in Arab words, "Israel is the superpower of the Middle East." With Egypt absent, there is no Arab military constraint on Israeli leaders who are willing to use their power to the fullest and who seem to believe that Israel's future can be assured by force alone. As just noted, Israel's attack on Syria's Soviet-supplied air defense missiles seemed designed to show that the Arabs could not rely on Moscow for help. Israel's open dismissal of President Reagan's repeated appeals to stop the bombardment of Beirut and to give the negotiations conducted by Ambassador Philip Habib a chance seemed designed to show the Arabs that they could not expect the United States to impose peace on Israel.

In Arab eyes, Israeli military encirclement of an Arab capital and the related Israeli objective of remaking the political life of an Arab country imposed a new character on what they see as Israeli expansionism. Thoughtful Arabs, looking to the future, put high on their agendas the need to show Israel that it cannot count on getting its way by force. In the end, most Arabs still look to the United States to reestablish some restraining influence over an Israel they regard as out of control.

Second, a central question is how the Palestinians will emerge. If an organized Palestinian movement survives in the aftermath of the war, preserving what institutions exist in the Palestinian community and able to play a political role, a peace process could begin sooner than if the movement is atomized or divided by internecine struggles. If Palestinian leadership were eventually to settle in Cairo rather than Damascus, it would receive greater support in pursuing a political course. Whether leadership committed to peace or to a continued guerrilla campaign emerges from the crisis, and whether most Arab states will agree that Palestinian military action from Lebanon and terrorism elsewhere should cease, will depend heavily on whether Palestinians and other Arabs see a real diplomatic alternative.

Ambassador Habib, to his great credit, seems to have kept the door open for Palestinian leadership to build a new future. The Palestinian movement is not dead politically. In some Arab eyes the PLO has emerged from the crisis as the only heroic party, having demonstrated that Israel with all of its power could not destroy the symbol and the organization of Palestinian nationalism. [...]

Third, with the headquarters and military arm of the PLO gone, Lebanon can return to dealing with the problems which were already beginning to divide it before the new PLO influx that began in the early 1970s. [...]

Fourth, it is necessary to assess carefully the attitudes of the Arab states. The war has not changed the readiness of Egypt, Jordan, and some other moderate Arabs to pursue peace with Israel on a reciprocal basis or to work with the United States toward that end, but it has caused all of them to question seriously whether Israel will negotiate a just peace and whether the United States will take a position independent of Israel's. It is widely believed that the United States acquiesced in Israel's invasion of Lebanon, and few Arabs believe that the United States could not have prevented Israel's heavy bombardments.
[...]
Much has been made of the reluctance of Arab states to accept the PLO apparatus now being evacuated from Beirut. And it is clear that each of these states will be careful to assure that the PLO does not come close to achieving within its borders the independent strength it achieved in Jordan in 1970 or subsequently in Lebanon.

But this does not mean that Arab support for Palestinian self-determination and a state in the West Bank and Gaza, or for the PLO as the only organization which speaks for the Palestinians, has declined. Even those Arab governments and groups that have come to accept the existence of

344

Israel, within essentially its pre-1967 boundaries, likewise accept and support, however belatedly in historic terms, the reality and force of Palestinian demands for a homeland of their own. In their view, that homeland should include the West Bank and Gaza, which would be freed if Israel withdrew from territories occupied in the 1967 War. In the wake of the 1982 war, there is already much evidence that underlying Arab support for the Palestinian cause has been increased by Israel's conduct of the war.

Moreover, there are often practical reasons for such support from Arab governments, especially those with large Palestinian populations. They see a dispersed Palestinian people as a politically disruptive force as long as their aspiration for a homeland of their own is unfulfilled. For that reason, among the others just stated, they will continue to press for an Israeli-Palestinian peace. [...]

In sum, the war has created, or intensified, attitudes that are often conflicting and that could now move in either direction. On the one hand, they could be channeled to produce a new process leading toward an Arab-Israeli-Palestinian peace. The Administration in Washington is again becoming directly engaged in the problems of the Middle East. Israel has demonstrated clearly what its objectives are, and has posed sharply for the United States the question of what the U.S.-Israeli relationship has become. The PLO has been forced to face the fact that its only hope for achieving its objectives is through political and diplomatic effort. Moderate Arab governments are deeply enough concerned about the radicalization of the Middle East that they may be prepared to support a Palestinian peace initiative.

Peace can come, however, only if statesmen work hard at it. The new balance of forces if left alone could more likely harden into the causes of a new and more terrible conflict before the 1980s end. After each major conflict-in 1949, 1956, 1967, 1973-opportunities have briefly existed for leaders of vision. The psychological humiliations in 1949 and 1967 made it harder for Arab leaders to negotiate. Limited Arab successes in 1973 opened the door to negotiation. If Israel's crushing military actions were now to be followed by a continued application of force by Israel in Lebanon, and the unchecked continuation of Israel's present policies in the West Bank and Gaza—so that there existed no apparent possibility of movement toward a negotiated resolution of the Palestinian issue—the 1982 war will have left the parties further apart than ever. We could look forward only to all the possibilities and dangers this would entail, including Arab alienation from the United States and progressive radicalization in the Arab world, and organized and unorganized violence growing both in the Middle East and elsewhere.
[...]

The Israeli invasion of Lebanon, to repeat, was designed to destroy once and for all any hope among the people of the West Bank and Gaza that the process of shaping the Palestinian people into a nation could succeed. It was designed to break any final resistance to total Israeli control and to pave the way for making life so difficult for those who valued their freedom and political self-expression that they would eventually leave for Jordan.

For their part, neither the Arab states (apart from Egypt and Jordan) nor the PLO have been prepared formally to accept Israel's existence as a state. Such acceptance of Israel is indeed central to peaceful resolution of the conflict.

[...]

Today, in Israel, there may be serious challenge to a definition of the Palestinian problem which acknowledges both Israeli and Palestinian claims in the same land. Many Israelis fear that accepting a Palestinian claim would dilute their own claim to all the land west of the Jordan River. Again and again in Israel one hears the sincerely stated view of early settlers that the Palestinians were doing little with the land when the Jewish settlers came. In their view, the Palestinians became active only when they wanted to share in gains the Israeli settlers were achieving. Arab states, they recall, either did not regard the Palestinians as a separate people or did not support them in establishing a state of their own when Jordan controlled the West Bank, and Egypt controlled Gaza, from 1949 until 1967.

Palestinian nationalism, in their view, is the product of terrorism and intimidation by the PLO under Yasser Arafat, and with the PLO's defeat in Lebanon, Palestinian nationalism will decline as an effective political force. The Israelis from the beginning of Jewish settlement in Palestine have either set aside the question of their long-term relationship with the Palestinian Arabs or have vaguely envisioned some kind of coexistence which Israel would dominate. Even those who are prepared to accept partitioning the land west of the Jordan River between Jews and Arabs for the most part see the Arab role being played by Jordan and not by Palestine Arabs acting independently. Most Israelis have never thought of a negotiated settlement with Palestinian Arabs as an equal partner.

At the same time, Israelis are not monolithic in support of their government's plan to assert Israel's claim of sovereignty over all the land west of the Jordan River. Many other Israelis see Israel facing an impossible future if they pursue that course. Incorporating 1.2 million Palestinian Arabs within Israel along with those already there, with appropriate civil and political rights, would eventually produce a large enough Arab population to destroy the Jewish state.

346

Incorporating those Palestinians without civil and political rights would require measures that would violate the principles and practice of human rights which are at the heart of Jewish tradition. And driving large numbers of Palestinians out of the West Bank and Gaza by force or pressure goes against the moral code and self-image of their country held by many if not most in Israel, as well as among its supporters abroad.

Palestinians and other Arabs, wherever they are, strongly hold the view that Israel will achieve peace only when Israel comes to terms fairly with the Palestinian people and respects their right to self-determination as the Jewish people have enjoyed their own. The rights of Palestinians as a people are belatedly recognized in some form by a majority of the world's governments. Palestinians do not want a state in Jordan, because it is not the land of their fathers. They do not understand why Zionists, who rejected a Jewish homeland in Africa, fail to comprehend why Palestinians want a homeland in the land where their homes have historically been. They do not understand how an Israeli Prime Minister who led violent resistance against British rule can credibly voice moral outrage at the people Israelis displaced when those people assert their rights through the means available to them. They do not understand how a Jewish government with centuries of persecution behind it could think that attacking several thousand Palestinian fighters could destroy the nationalist determination of almost four million people. They do not understand how Jews, of all people, can be insensitive to what it means to be a stateless person.
[…]

The Fatah Mutiny: Implications for the Peace Process (1983)
CENTRAL INTELLIGENCE AGENCY

Arafat faces a serious loss of confidence in his leadership among Palestinians at large and within the PLO. The mutiny remains confined to several hundred officers and men in the Bekaa Valley and Damascus, but many other Fateh members are sympathetic to the rebels' cause. There is a widespread feeling that Arafat has lost touch with the fighters in Lebanon and that his practice of trying to be all things to all people has resulted in drift and incoherence in PLO policy. Many Fateh members who have not overtly supported the rebellion have concluded that it was necessary to demonstrate to Arafat his increasing isolation.

[…]

Most Fateh members apparently have concluded that the political option for achieving Palestinian self-determination is effectively closed, given their perception that the US is unable to force Israel to bargain over the status of the West Bank and Gaza and that Israel in any event will not allow an independent PLO seat at the bargaining table.

[…]

Arafat's talks with Hussein broke down when the Fateh Central Committee almost unanimously rejected a tentative agreement Arafat had reached with Hussein providing for the creation of a negotiating team comprised of Jordanians and non-PLO Palestinians. The Committee members insisted that the PLO should have a direct role in any negotiations and a guarantee that talks would result in Palestinian self-determination.

[…] Support for negotiations even among the Palestinians normally considered moderate has become synonymous with a sell-out of the Palestinian cause. A reversion to hardline and confrontational tactics, even at the cost of being drawn into the Syrian orbit, appears the only alternative.

Arafat is being held accountable for the failure of his efforts over the years to mobilize international support behind a negotiated solution to the Palestinian issue based on the establishment of a Palestinian state in the West Bank and Gaza, at least as an interim settlement. The US Embassy in Damascus, based on discussions with local observers and Western journalists, believes the guerilla mystique still motivates the majority of young PLO fighters. Arafat's pursuit of the diplomatic path had caused him to wander far from the mystique, but he had nothing to show for his efforts, leaving Fatah fighters confused and unenthusiastic about his leadership. The militants in Fatah and in the other PLO guerilla groups believe their preference for reliance on armed struggle has been vindicated.

The effect of the rebellion will alter for a long-time and perhaps permanently the approach of Fatah and the PLO to the peace process. If Arafat is to survive, he will have to appease his critics by adopting more hardline policies aligned with those of Syria and abandon his efforts to arrange a common negotiating position with Jordan.

[…]

Implications for the Arab States

The weakening of the PLO's moderate wing has revived the fears of the moderate Arab states that they will eventually face a radicalized PLO backed by hardline Arab states and bent on their destruction as well as the elimination of Israel. A senior Saudi Foreign Ministry official told the US Deputy Chief of Mission earlier this month that the Saudis believe PLO proponents of military action, including terrorism, will gain the upper hand. The moderate Arabs have depended on Arafat to control the radicals and particularly to prevent terrorism against the Arab states. […]

Implications for Israel

We believe the Israelis are pleased with the unrest in Fatah because they believe it will loosen the PLO's hold on West Bankers and perhaps lead moderate leaders in the occupied territories to consider joining the Camp David autonomy talks or enter into direct negotiations with Israel. Moreover, radical pressure on Arafat to drop his diplomatic approach almost certainly will lead to diminished international pressure on Israel to accommodate Palestinian demands and will spare Tel Aviv the difficult decisions it would face if Arafat did agree to recognize Israel.

… Israel realizes that a return to terrorism will decrease the PLO's acceptability as a negotiating partner and thereby further erode international pressure on Israel to deal with the Palestinians.

Implications for the West Bank

The split within Fatah and the likelihood of increased Syrian and radical influence over the PLO will provide more evidence to West Bank moderates that the PLO cannot be counted on to end the Israeli occupation. West Bank leaders, however, are unlikely to emerge as a credible Palestinian voice in support of the peace process. They will probably conclude that enhanced radical influence in the PLO increases the threat to the personal safety of any Palestinian that strays from the PLO line. The West Bankers' assessment that Israel at best is prepared to grant only limited autonomy is likely to restrain whatever inclination some West Bank leaders might have to join negotiations.

The West Bankers' frustration with both the PLO and local moderates will probably cause increasing numbers to join the Muslim-Brotherhood. The Brotherhood over the past year has become more active in the occupied territories and attracted many new recruits.

[…]

INTIFADA

The Impact of Unrest in the Israeli-Occupied Territories (1988)
CENTRAL INTELLIGENCE AGENCY

The spontaneous, broad-based Palestinian uprising underway in the West Bank and Gaza Strip since 9 December demonstrates that young Arabs in the occupied territories have decided to take their fate into their own hands. Although the PLO and some Islamic groups belatedly have attempted to assert a leadership role, the uprising remains essentially a grassroots, popular resistance lacking strong central leadership. [...]

Palestinian unrest in the West Bank and Gaza since early December has reached an extent unprecedented in Israel's twenty-year occupation of the territories. The uncoordinated disturbances have featured widespread daily demonstrations, commercial strikes, stone throwings, firebombings, and isolated attempts to attack Israeli soldiers. The uprising erupted in early December in Gaza: when rumors spread that a traffic accident in which an Israeli driver killed four Palestinians was a deliberate act of revenge for the murder of an Israeli shopping in Gaza the previous month. Palestinian violence occurred mostly in Gaza in December; since mid-January most of the trouble has been in the West Bank. Israeli Arab citizens also staged several demonstrations in Israel proper against the Israeli occupation as well as for left political groups such as Peace Now and the Israeli Communist Party.

Israel, slow to realize the magnitude of the problem, has attempted to stifle the unrest through harsh repressive measures. Since 9 December Israeli troops have killed at least 65 Palestinians, claiming that Israeli lives were endangered by mobs with stones, molotov cocktails, knives, and sticks. No Israeli soldiers or civilians have been killed in the disturbances.

In our view, the continuing outburst reflects years of pent-up frustration by large numbers of Palestinians in the territories, who since 1967 have been denied political self-expression and, especially in Gaza, lived in conditions of poverty and squallor. According to numerous reports, the protests-- which spread from refugee camp to camp, from village to village--have been largely spontaneous, lacking any central or even regional leadership.

Since early January, Palestinian activists have sought to coordinate the disturbances, [...] but these efforts have not achieved broad coordination of what remain mostly localized outbursts of unrest. [...] Even within the towns, villages, and refugee camps there appears to be little coordination of activities among the many neighborhood committees. [...]

350

PLO Preempted

The PLO was caught by surprise by the unrest, according to US Embassy reporting and responded belatedly by trying to funnel assistance to Palestinians in the territories and claim credit for the disturbances. [...]

We believe that the primary goal of the PLO at this stage is to encourage West Bankers and Gazans to prolong the violence so that the Palestinian issue remains a priority item on the international agenda. At the same time, we believe the PLO leaders are alarmed by the prospect that their irrelevance to the unrest will undermine the PLO's claim to leadership of the Palestinians.
[...]

Israeli Military and Political Reactions

Israel continues its two-track response of using firm measures to contain the unrest while considering proposals for Arab-Israeli negotiations. [...]

Israeli leaders from the start defined the unrest in the territories as a problem of law and order and reacted by steadily increasing the number of troops there and allowing liberal use of force. By the end of December, the number of troops had nearly tripled from the usual two thousand in the Gaza Strip. Forces were at least doubled in the West Bank, and in both places units among the elite Golani and Givati brigades were added to the normal border police and reservists.

Israel has employed a series of increasingly forceful steps to contain the unrest, which so far have not been effective except in Gaza, where most Palestinians are residents of easily isolated refugee camps. Tear gas, large-scale arrests, curfews, selected deportation of agitators, shootings, and beatings have been used by the Israelis, but to no avail. In our opinion, shooting deaths and indiscriminate beatings of Palestinians by the Israelis have aggravated Palestinian unrest.
[...]

IDF Preparing for the Long-Haul
[...]

Despite their reservations, Israeli commanders are determined to do whatever is necessary to restore order. Israeli Chief-of-Staff, Lieutenant General Dan Shomron, has publicly conceded that the military never prepared itself for such widespread violence in the occupied territories and has admitted deep frustration with the military's inability to cope with the unrest. Since the initial wave of disturbances, however, the Israeli military has sought to minimize the use of lethal force by encouraging the graduated use of forceful riot control measures, ranging from warnings through the use of tear gas, rubber bullets and water cannons, and eventually--when warranted--live ammunition. The last action, according to the US Embassy, also is graded to include firing warning shots in the air, firing at the legs of rioters, and finally lethal fire when troops believe they are in physical danger.

The military has adopted other measures aimed both at limiting the number of shooting fatalities and at intimidating the population. Although highly controversial, the mass beatings policy was implemented by Defense Minister Rabin in early January to punish rioters directly and harshly in hopes of deterring other potential rioters. Besides beatings, other forms of collective punishment such as arrests, detentions, curfews, and midnight raids on homes of suspected agitators also have become standard tactics.

The military has admitted that excesses associated with the beatings have occurred but insists these are "deviations" and that transgressors will be disciplined. The military's concern about excesses has led it to dispatch army psychologists to the field to assess soldier behavior. Growing involvement by extremist Israeli settlers in clashes has added an explosive new clement, and several Israeli papers report a growing trend of frustrated Israeli troops developing anti-Arab feelings and spoiling for a fight. [...]

The View from Arab Capitals

We believe Arab leaders see the unrest as the most serious challenge so far to Israel's occupation of the West Bank and Gaza Strip and the beginning of a new era in populist Palestinian resistance. For most Arab states, the extensive international criticism of Israel's handling of the unrest, perceived strains in US-Israeli relations, and renewed US activism in the Arab-Israeli peace-seeking process have been welcome developments.

Still, the Arabs are aware that events in the territories are beyond their control and even that of the PLO, and they appear uncertain about how to exploit the unrest. [...]

    -- Jordan and Egypt almost certainly are concerned that rising expectations and militancy among Palestinians living in the territories make it more difficult for PLO and other Palestinian leaders to make concessions required for movement.
    -- Amman and Cairo probably also fear that Palestinian extremists are uninterested in incremental diplomatic advances and will thwart progress by stepping up the violence.

Arab regimes are more worried about growing agitation among their own large Palestinian populations, according to US Embassy reporting. [...]

Intifadeh: The Palestinian Uprising (1988)
Don Peretz

When demonstrations against the Israeli occupation erupted in Gaza last December 8-9, few Israeli politicians or military commanders expected them to last very long. They were perceived as merely another in the sporadic series of "riots" that had periodically—and only briefly each time—annoyed Israeli authorities since 1967 in the Gaza Strip, the West Bank ("Judea and Samaria") and the Golan Heights.

Soon it became clear that these disturbances were quite unlike those of the previous twenty years. Within days the Gaza unrest spilled over into the West Bank, and the authorities lengthened their estimate of the time required to suppress it: a few weeks, perhaps even a month or two. By late February, as the rioting continued, Defense Minister Yitzhak Rabin and his army commanders grew more impressed with the fundamental grievances behind the uprising, which in their judgment could be addressed only through a political solution, not by military force. Some field officers and members of the General Staff even adopted an Arabic term, *intifadeh* (uprising), used by the Palestinians themselves, to describe what was happening.

[…]

The *intifadeh* differs from previous disturbances in its intensity, its pervasiveness and its leadership. In mid-November 1987, a U.N. official in Gaza predicted—almost to the day—when the uprising would occur, for he perceived it as inevitable after twenty years of occupation, frustration and Palestinian disillusionment with larger political forces that seemed incapable of ending or even ameliorating their plight. Among the objects of their anger were not only the Israelis, the Americans and the United Nations, but all Arab regimes and at times the bureaucracy of the Palestine Liberation Organization (PLO).

Even the most benign policies could not deflect the mounting anger and frustration bred in the generation raised under occupation. Well over half the Palestinian population of the occupied territories has lived all their lives under Israeli domination, and most have lived in this situation for nearly all their lives. True, Palestinians have always lived under oppressive rule, initially Ottoman, then British and, since 1948, Israeli, Egyptian or Jordanian. But regardless of Egyptian or Jordanian harshness, rule by Israel seemed another matter altogether. Palestinians considered it far more degrading to live under a non-Arab regime, no matter what benefits, if any, that regime might offer.

By the end of 1987 frustration among Palestinian youth could not be controlled, even by the cooler heads among the older generation, the traditional "notables" or the occupation forces with their threats of

Used with permission of Foreign Affairs, from FOREIGN AFFAIRS, Vol. 66, No. 5 (June 1, 1988); permission conveyed through Copyright Clearance Center, Inc.

increasing use of force. Despite promises to "improve the quality of life" from the Reagan Administration, Israeli Foreign Minister Shimon Peres and King Hussein of Jordan, the number of university students who had to accept menial labor in Israel was increasing. Young Palestinians, among the best educated groups in the Middle East, had only limited opportunities to apply their higher skills, especially since the return of thousands of workers from the Gulf states following cutbacks in oil production during the early 1980s.

The population of the occupied territories has been increasing at a rapid rate, faster than anticipated by Palestinian or Israeli demographers, resulting in teeming villages, towns and refugee camps. Stifling pressures of life in this cramped environment have been exacerbated by policies that restrict the expansion of Arab urban areas and have placed some 50 percent of land and most water sources under Israeli control, frequently at the disposal of the new Jewish settlers.

Discontent with deteriorating economic and social conditions has been politicized in what the Israeli press has characterized as "schools of hatred": the Israeli prisons and detention centers where tens of thousands have been held, for periods ranging from a day to a decade or more. According to Israeli estimates, some 300,000 arrests have occurred in the occupied territories since 1967. […]

The *Jerusalem Post* has described Ansar 2, one of the new detention centers for rock-throwers in Gaza, as "perhaps the single most efficient operational institution for the indoctrination of Gaza youth." The treatment received by inmates in Ansar 2 and in other detention centers is more likely to breed new terrorists than to teach political moderation. Twenty years of direct, daily contact with occupation authorities has, perhaps more than any other factor, created deeply ambivalent feelings of resentment and irrepressible frustration.

Added to the overflow of bitterness caused by the experiences of daily life in the territories was the Palestinians' feeling of abandonment by the outside world, particularly by their Arab brethren, who did little to end the recent "war of the camps" in Lebanon where Palestinians, many of them relatives of those in the occupied territories, were besieged for months by the Shi'ite Amal militia. The Arab League summit in Amman during November 1987 produced little apparent support for the Palestinians. Although the meeting was convened to deal with the Gulf war, Palestinians in the territories perceived the secondary attention it devoted to their problem as a slight, an attempt to avoid confronting the Palestinian issue head on.

By December these economic, social and political frustrations needed only a chance spark to create the long-anticipated explosion. It was provided by a relatively minor incident in which an Israeli military vehicle ran down and killed four Gaza laborers. Wild rumors spread that the Palestinians were killed intentionally, in retaliation for the stabbing death of an Israeli in Gaza the day before. The incident precipitated spontaneous anti-Israeli demonstrations by school-age youths in a Gaza refugee camp. When the army arrived to put down the riots, soldiers were stoned, in what soon became a routine. Throwing stones, iron bars, insults and an occasional Molotov cocktail at the security forces has since become the hallmark of the *intifadeh*. Flying the banned Palestinian flag is another challenge to authority; when the flag is unavailable or confiscated, any public display of the national colors—red, white, green and black—is recognized as tantamount to a demonstration of resistance against Israeli rule.

What began as sporadic protest by random groups of restless youth not only spread, but developed into an organized resistance movement with an underground leadership, a definite political objective, and a well-planned and integrated strategy. From rock throwing, insults and the illegal display of national colors and patriotic slogans, tactics were devised to extend participation to the entire Palestinian community. […]

As the *intifadeh* rose from random violence, the ad hoc leaders confirmed their resolve to refrain from using "hot" weapons including guns and explosives, although Israeli intelligence and rumor among Palestinians indicated that caches of small arms were hidden throughout the territories. It was evident that they would be no match against the overwhelming weaponry of the Israel Defense Forces (IDF). Furthermore, passive resistance or small-scale violence gave the Palestinians a decided public relations advantage in the Western media, where sympathy was swayed by images of heavily armed troops with tanks, armored vehicles, helicopters and tear gas confronting unarmed civilians using only the weapons they could tear up from the streets. This disparity in the weapons available to each side assured a certain measure of restraint: the Palestinians refrained from killing Israeli soldiers, and the Israelis limited their use of force, at least for the first months. True, scores of Arab homes were destroyed in retaliation for anti-Israeli actions or suspected actions; there were beatings; tear gas was used on a wide scale; Palestinians were shot. But no villages were destroyed, and there were no mass expulsions or executions.
[…]
Israeli attempts to stem the uprising through thousands of arrests and imprisonments brought no quick respite. The larger the number of arrests, the wider the *intifadeh*. […]

In the first round of struggle between occupied Palestinians and the Israeli army the former seemed to have maintained the advantage. It was not a military victory but a political-social one. The *intifadeh* took Israel by surprise, creating political turmoil within the country; it raised Palestinian national consciousness, created a new sense of solidarity and once again focused world attention on the Palestine problem. But there was a heavy price, not only in casualties, but in the precarious economies of the West Bank and Gaza.

[...]

Many Israeli myths previously used to obscure rational analysis of relations with the Arabs are being deflated. This has led to a reevaluation among Israelis of the PLO reality. Arguments about refusing to negotiate with the PLO because it is "terrorist" are more frequently disputed in the press now than before. Several retired generals and mainstream politicians, while not commending the PLO, now hold that it is not merely a terrorist organization but a political one as well, and one with which Israelis may soon have to enter dialogue. Likud's boycott of the PLO is probably motivated less by repugnance for terrorism than by fear that recognition will imply an acknowledgment of Palestinian political rights.

The *intifadeh* has dispelled most notions that a liberal or enlightened occupation can be sustained. Hardly any Israeli newspaper or politician boasts any longer of benefits Israel has brought to the occupied territories, as they did just a few months ago. [...] Most Israeli factions have recognized that continued occupation will require harsh, even brutal measures, and that if there ever was an enlightened occupation, its time has passed. Reporting to the Knesset Foreign Affairs and Security Committee recently, Defense Minister Rabin termed the uprising a continuation of the 1982 war against the PLO in Lebanon, a war that many saw as a strategic mistake. But Prime Minister Shamir, who was one of the architects of that campaign, still regards it as an accomplishment; he characterizes the *intifadeh* as part of the continuing Arab war "against the existence of the State of Israel," definitely not civil disobedience against the occupation. Consequently, he asserts, the uprising must be fought as would any other war for Israel's survival.

[...]

Neither supporters nor opponents of annexation can deny that the uprising has redivided Eretz Israel ("the Land of Israel") along the pre-June 1967 frontiers. For all practical purposes the Green Line (demarcating the 1949 armistice frontiers with Jordan and Egypt), which former Prime Minister Menachem Begin declared in 1977 "no longer exists," has been reconstituted. At the time, Begin declared the line had "vanished forever," so that Israelis could "coexist with the Arabs in Eretz Israel." Now the army frequently reimposes the old barriers, preventing Jews, except settlers with homes there, from crossing to the territories, and noncitizen Palestinians from entering pre-1967 Israel. Even Jerusalem, enthusiastically described by its mayor, Teddy Kollek, as a united city of Jews and Arabs, is no longer united in daily life. For the past several months the former Jordanian sectors have withdrawn into isolation as their Palestinian residents have closed down shops, schools and most public activity. Today few Jews venture into the inhospitable Arab quarters.

356

The reemerging Green Line has severed many of the economic links with the territories developed during the past twenty years. The economic warfare used by both sides is less disadvantageous to Israelis than to the Palestinians. The most visible manifestation is that many of the 110,000 to 120,000 Arab workers from Gaza and the West Bank no longer report for work in Israel. This hurts most in construction, agriculture and services—industries in which up to 40 percent of the labor force is Arab. In response to the Palestinian boycott and army barriers, the Ministry of Labor now authorizes several Israeli employers to import foreign workers. In some industries experiments have begun with mechanization and automation to replace low-paid Arab workers.

[...]

The *intifadeh* has drawn international attention to the Palestine problem, from which it had recently been diverted by the Gulf war and tensions in Afghanistan and Central America. Events in the occupied territories have raised the Palestine issue to high priority within the European Community and reactivated the Reagan Administration's Middle East peace initiatives. During March the European Parliament adopted resolutions critical of Israeli policies in the territories, leading to protests from Jerusalem against European "encouragement" of the PLO. The 12-nation parliament also voted overwhelmingly against ratifying a series of trade agreements with Israel.

[...]

The net result of these events is re-Palestinianization of a conflict which began in the 1920s and 1930s as a struggle between Palestinian Jews and Palestinian Arabs. After establishment of Israel in 1948 the conflict was internationalized, between Israel and the neighboring Arab states. Since December the action has again centered in Palestine itself, between the two peoples most directly involved in struggle for control of the country.

[...]

Unfortunately the *intifadeh* also indicates that Palestinian-Israeli relations are at an impasse. The minimum that the inhabitants of the territories are now willing to accept is full self-determination and total withdrawal by Israel, demands that no mainstream Israeli party or political leader will concede. [...] Nor has the Israeli public overcome its fear of an independent Palestinian state. While demonstrating Palestinian determination and courage, the *intifadeh* has also deepened Israeli apprehensions about whether an independent Palestine would remain a peaceful neighbor.

[...]

Address to the Nation of Jordan (1988)
King Hussein bil Talal

I send you greetings and am pleased to address you in your cities and villages, in your camps and dwellings, in your institutions of learning, and in your places of work. I would like to address your hearts and minds in all parts of our beloved Jordanian land. This is all the more important at this juncture, when we have initiated—after seeking God's help and after thorough and extensive study—a series of measures to enhance Palestinian national orientation and highlight Palestinian identity; our goal is the benefit of the Palestinian cause and the Arab Palestinian people.

Our decision, as you know, comes after 38 years of the unity of the two banks, and fourteen years after the Rabat Summit resolution designating the Palestine Liberation Organization (PLO) as the sole legitimate representative of the Palestinian people. It also comes six years after the Fez Summit resolution that agreed unanimously on the establishment of an independent Palestinian state in the occupied West Bank and the Gaza Strip as one of the bases and results of the peaceful settlement.
[…]
I reviewed the facts preceding the Rabat resolution, as you recall, before the Arab leaders in the Algiers Extraordinary Summit last June. It may be important to recall that one of the main facts I emphasized was the text of the unity resolution of the two banks of April 1950. This resolution affirms the preservation of all Arab rights in Palestine and the defense of such rights by all legitimate means without prejudicing the final settlement of the just cause of the Palestinian people—within the scope of the people's aspirations and of Arab cooperation and international justice.

Among these facts, there was our 1972 proposal regarding our concept of alternatives, on which the relationship between Jordan on the one hand and the West Bank and Gaza on the other, may be based after their liberation. Among these alternatives was the establishment of a relationship of brotherhood and cooperation between the Hashemite Kingdom of Jordan and the independent Palestinian state in case the Palestinian people opt for that. Simply, this means that we declared our clear-cut position regarding our adherence to the Palestinian people's right to self- determination on their national soil, including their right to establish their own independent state, more than two years before the Rabat Summit resolution. This will be our position until the Palestinian people achieve their complete national goals, God willing.

The relationship of the West Bank with the Hashemite Kingdom of Jordan in light of the PLO's call for the establishment of an independent Palestinian state, can be confined to two considerations: First, the principle consideration pertaining to the issue of Arab unity as a pan-Arab aim, which Arab peoples aspire to and want to achieve. Second, the political consideration pertaining to the extent of the Palestinian struggles from the continuation of the legal relationship to the Kingdom's two banks. Our answer to the question, "why now?", also derives from these two factors, and the background of the clear and constant Jordanian position on the Palestinian cause, as already outlined.

Regarding the principled consideration, Arab unity between any two or more countries is an option of any Arab people. This is what we believe. Accordingly, we responded to the wish of the Palestinian people's representatives for unity with Jordan in 1950. From this premise, we respect the wish of the PLO, the sole and legitimate representative of the Palestinian people, to secede from us as an independent Palestinian state. We say that while we fully understand the situation, nevertheless, Jordan will remain the proud bearer of the message of the Great Arab Revolt, adhering to its principles, believing in one Arab destiny, and committed to joint Arab action.

Regarding the political consideration, since the June 1967 aggression we have believed that our actions and efforts should be directed at liberating the land and the sanctities from Israeli occupation. Therefore, we have concentrated all our efforts over the past twenty-one years of occupation on that goal. We did not imagine that maintaining the legal and administrative relationship between the two banks could constitute an obstacle to liberating the occupied Palestinian land. Hence, in the past and before we took measures, we did not find anything requiring such measures, especially since our support for the Palestinian people's right to self-determination was clear.

Lately, it has transpired that there is a general Palestinian and Arab orientation which believes in the need to highlight the Palestinian identity in full in all efforts and activities that are related to the Palestine question and its developments. It has also become clear that there is a general conviction that maintaining the legal and administrative links with the West Bank, and the ensuing Jordanian interaction with our Palestinian brothers under occupation through Jordanian institutions in the occupied territories, contradicts this orientation. It is also viewed that these links hamper the Palestinian struggle to gain international support for the Palestinian cause of a people struggling against foreign occupation.

In view of this line of thought, which is certainly inspired by genuine Palestinian will, and Arab determination to support the Palestinian cause, it becomes our duty to be part of this direction, and to respond to its requirements. After all, we are a part of our nation, supportive of its causes, foremost among which is the Palestinian cause. Since there is a general conviction that the struggle to liberate the occupied Palestinian land could be enhanced by dismantling the legal and administrative links between the two banks, we have to fulfill our duty, and do what is required of us.

At the Rabat Summit of 1974 we responded to the Arab leaders' appeal to us to continue our interaction with the Occupied West Bank through Jordanian institutions, to support the steadfastness of our brothers there. Today we respond to the wish of the Palestine Liberation Organization, the sole legitimate representative of the Palestinian People, and to the Arab orientation to affirm the Palestinian identity in all its aspects. We pray to God that this step be a substantive addition to the intensifying Palestinian struggle for freedom and independence.

Brother Citizens,

These are the reasons, the considerations, and the convictions that led us to respond favorably to the wish of the PLO, and to the general Arab direction consistent with it. We cannot continue in this state of suspension, which can neither serve Jordan nor the Palestinian cause. We had to leave the labyrinth of fears and doubts, towards clearer horizons where mutual trust, understanding, and cooperation can prevail, to the benefit of the Palestinian cause and Arab unity. This unity will remain a goal which all the Arab peoples cherish and seek to realize.

At the same time, it has to be understood in all clarity, and without any ambiguity or equivocation, that our measures regarding the West Bank concern only the occupied Palestinian land and its people. They naturally do not relate in any way to the Jordanian citizens of Palestinian origin in the Hashemite Kingdom of Jordan. They all have the full rights of citizenship and all its obligations, the same as any other citizen irrespective of his origin. They are an integral part of the Jordanian state to which they belong, on whose soil they live, and in whose life and various activities they participate. Jordan is not Palestine and the independent Palestinian state will be established on the occupied Palestinian territory after its liberation, God willing. There the Palestinian identity will be embodied, and there the Palestinian struggle shall come to fruition, as confirmed by the glorious uprising of the Palestinian people under occupation.

If national unity in any country is dear and precious, it is for us in Jordan more than that. It is the basis of our stability and the cause of our development and prosperity, as well as the foundation of our national security and the source of our faith in the future. It is also a living embodiment of the principles of the Great Arab Revolt which we inherited and whose banner we are proudly carrying. It is also a living example of constructive plurality and a sound nucleus of wider Arab unity.

Based on that, safeguarding national unity is a sacred duty that will not be compromised. Any attempt to undermine it, under any pretext, would only help the enemy carry out his policy of expansion at the expense of Palestine and Jordan alike. Consequently, true nationalism lies in bolstering and fortifying national unity. Moreover, the responsibility to safeguard it falls on every one of you, leaving no place in our midst for sedition or treachery. With God's help, we shall be as always, a united cohesive family, whose members are joined by bonds of brotherhood, affection, awareness, and common national objectives.

It is most important to remember, as we emphasize the importance of safeguarding national unity, that stable and productive societies, are those where orderliness and discipline prevail. Discipline is the solid fabric that binds all members of a community in a solid, harmonious structure, blocking all avenues before the enemies, and opening horizons of hope for future generations.

The constructive plurality which Jordan has lived since its foundation, and through which it has witnessed progress and prosperity in all aspects of life, emanates not only from our faith in the sanctity of national unity, but also in the importance of Jordan's pan-Arab role. Jordan presents itself as the living example of the merger of various Arab groups on its soil, within the framework of good citizenship, and one Jordanian people. This paradigm that we live on our soil gives us faith in the inevitability of attaining Arab unity, God willing.

In surveying contemporary tendencies, it becomes clear that the affirmation of national identity does not contradict the attainment of unitary institutional formats that can enjoin Arabs as a whole. There are living examples within our Arab homeland that attest to this, as there are living examples in foreign regions. Foremost among them is the European Community, which now seeks to realize European political unity, having successfully completed the process of economic complementarity among its members. It is well known that the bonds linking the Arabs are far greater than those linking European nations.

[...]

To display any doubts that may arise out of our measures, we assure you that these measures do not mean the abandonment of our national duty, either towards the Arab-Israeli conflict, or towards the Palestinian cause. Nor do they mean a relinquishing our faith in Arab unity. As I have stated, these steps were taken only in response to the wish of the Palestine Liberation Organization, the sole legitimate representative of the Palestinian people, and the prevailing Arab conviction that such measures will contribute to the struggle of the Palestinian people and their glorious uprising. Jordan will continue its support for the steadfastness of the Palestinian people, and their courageous uprising in the occupied Palestinian land, within its capabilities. I have to mention, that when we decided to cancel the Jordanian development plan in the occupied territories, we contacted, at the same time, various friendly governments and international institutions, which had expressed their wish to contribute to the plan, urging them to continue financing development projects in the occupied Palestinian lands, through the relevant Palestinian quarters.

Jordan, dear brothers, has not nor will it give up its support and assistance to the Palestinian people, until they achieve their national goals, God willing. No one outside Palestine has had, nor can have, an attachment to Palestine, or its cause, firmer than that of Jordan or of my family. Moreover, Jordan is a confrontation state, whose borders with Israel are longer than those of any other Arab state, longer even than the combined borders of the West Bank and Gaza with Israel.

In addition, Jordan will not give up its commitment to take part in the peace process. We have contributed to the peace process until it reached the stage of a consensus to convene an international peace conference on the Middle East. The purpose of the conference would be to achieve a just and comprehensive peace settlement to the Arab Israeli conflict, and the settlement of the Palestinian problem in all its aspects. We have defined our position in this regard, as everybody knows, through the six principles which we have already made public.

Jordan, dear brothers, is a principal party to the Arab-Israeli conflict, and to the peace process. It shoulders its national responsibilities on that basis.

I thank you and I repeat my heartfelt wishes to you, beseeching Almighty God to help us, guide us, enable us to please Him, and to grant our Palestinian brothers victory and success. He is the best of helpers.

May God's peace and blessings be upon you.

Palestinian Declaration of Independence (1988)
PALESTINIAN NATIONAL COUNCIL

On the same terrain as God's apostolic missions to mankind and in the land of Palestine was the Palestinian Arab people brought forth. There it grew and developed, and there it created its unique human and national mode of existence in an organic, indissoluble and unbroken relationship among people, land and history.

With epic tenaciousness in terms of place and time, the people of Palestine fashioned its national identity. Its steadfast endurance in its own defense rose to preternatural levels, for despite the ambitions, covetousness and armed invasions which deprived that people of an opportunity to achieve political independence, and which were prompted by the allure of this ancient land and its crucial position on the intersecting boundaries of powerful nations and civilizations, it was the constancy with which the people adhered to the land that gave that land its identity and which imbued its people with the national spirit.

Nourished by many strains of civilizations and a multitude of cultures and finding inspiration in the texts of its spiritual and historical heritage, the Palestinian Arab people has, throughout history, continued to develop its identity in an integral unity of land and people and in the footsteps of the prophets throughout this Holy Land, the invocation of praise for the Creator high atop every minaret while hymns of mercy and peace have rung out with the bells of every church and temple.

From generation unto generation, the Palestinian Arab people has not ceased its valiant defense of its homeland, and the successive rebellions of our people have been a heroic embodiment of its desire for national independence.

At a time when the modern world was fashioning its new system of values, the prevailing balance of power in the local and international arenas excluded the Palestinians from the common destiny, and it was shown once more that it was not justice alone that turned the wheels of history.

The deep injury already done the Palestinian people and therefore aggravated when a painful differentiation was made: a people deprived of independence, and one whose homeland was subjected to a new kind of foreign occupation, was exposed to an attempt to give general currency to the falsehood that Palestine was "a land without a people". Despite this falsification of history, the international community, in article 22 of the Covenant of the League of Nations of 1919 and in the Lausanne Treaty of 1923, recognized that the Palestinian Arab people was no different from the other Arab peoples detached from the Ottoman State and was a free and independent people.

Despite the historical injustice done to the Palestinian Arab people in its displacement and in being deprived of the right to self-determination following the adoption of General Assembly resolution 181 (II) of 1947, which partitioned Palestine into an Arab and a Jewish State, that resolution nevertheless continues to attach conditions to international legitimacy that guarantee the Palestinian Arab people the right to sovereignty and national independence.

The occupation of Palestinian territory and parts of other Arab territory by Israeli forces, the uprooting of the majority of Palestinians and their displacement from their homes by means of organized intimidation, and the subjection of the remainder to occupation, oppression and the destruction of the distinctive features of their national life, are a flagrant violation of the principle of legitimacy and of the Charter of the United Nations and its resolutions recognizing the national rights of the Palestinian people, including the right to return and the right to self-determination, independence and sovereignty over the territory of its homeland.

In the heart of its homeland and on its periphery, in its places of exile near and far, the Palestinian Arab people has not lost its unwavering faith in its right to return nor its firm belief in its right to independence. Occupation, carnage and displacement have been unable to dispossess the Palestinians of their consciousness and their identity – their epic struggle has endured, and the formation of their national character has continued with the growing escalation of the struggle. The national will has established its political framework; and that is the Palestine Liberation Organization, the sole, legitimate representative of the Palestinian people, as recognized by the international community and represented in the United Nations and its institutions and in other international and regional organizations. Founding itself on a belief in inalienable rights, on the Arab national consensus and on international legitimacy, the Palestine Liberation Organization has assumed leadership in the battles of a great people fused in an exemplary national unity and in a legendary and steadfast resistance to carnage and encirclement within its homeland and outside. To the Arab national consciousness and to that of the entire world, the epic of the Palestinian resistance has manifested itself as one of the most conspicuous national liberation movements of the age.

The great popular uprising now mounting in the occupied territories, together with the legendary steadfastness of the camps within and outside the homeland, have raised mankind's grasp of the true nature of the Palestinian issue and of Palestinian national rights to a level higher than that of full and mature comprehension, have brought down the final curtain on an entire epoch of falsification and conscientious indifference and have beleaguered the official Israeli mentality, prone as it is to appeal to arguments based on mythology and to resort to intimidation in its denial of Palestinian existence.

With the uprising, with the escalation of the revolutionary struggle and with the accumulation of revolutionary experience wherever the struggle is in progress, the Palestinian conjuncture reaches a sharp historical turning point. The Palestinian Arab people asserts once more its inalienable rights and its demand to exercise those rights in its Palestinian homeland.

By virtue of the natural, historical and legal right of the Palestinian Arab people to its homeland, Palestine, and of the sacrifices of its succeeding generations in defense of the freedom and independence of that homeland,

Pursuant to the resolutions of the Arab Summit Conferences and on the basis of the international legitimacy embodied in the resolutions of the United Nations since 1947, and

Through the exercise by the Palestinian Arab people of its right to self-determination, political independence and sovereignty over its territory:

The Palestine National Council hereby declares, in the Name of God and on behalf of the Palestinian Arab people, the establishment of the State of Palestine in the land of Palestine with its capital at Jerusalem.

The State of Palestine shall be for Palestinians, wherever they may be therein to develop their national and cultural identity and therein to enjoy full equality of rights. Their religious and political beliefs and human dignity shall therein be safeguarded under a democratic parliamentary system based on freedom of opinion and the freedom to form parties, on the heed of the majority for minority rights and the respect of minorities for majority decisions, on social justice and equality, and on non-discrimination in civil rights on grounds of race, religion or color or as between men and women, under a Constitution ensuring the rule of law and an independent judiciary and on the basis of true fidelity to the age-old spiritual and cultural heritage of Palestine with respect to mutual tolerance, coexistence and magnanimity among religions.

The State of Palestine shall be an Arab State and shall be an integral part of the Arab nation, of its heritage and civilization and of its present endeavor for the achievement of the goals of liberation, development, democracy and unity. In affirming its commitment to the Pact of the League of Arab States and its concern for the strengthening of joint Arab action, the State of Palestine calls upon the members of the Arab nation for their assistance in achieving its *de facto* emergence by mobilizing their capacities and intensifying the efforts made to bring the Israeli occupation to an end.

The State of Palestine declares its commitment to the purposes and principles of the United Nations, to the Universal Declaration of Human Rights and to the policy and principles of non-alignment.

The State of Palestine, in declaring that it is a peace-loving State committed to the principles of peaceful coexistence, shall strive, together with all other States and peoples, for the achievement of a lasting peace based on justice and respect for rights, under which the human potential for constructive activity may flourish, mutual competition may center on life-sustaining innovation and there is no fear for the future, since the future bears only assurance for those who have acted justly or made amends to justice.

In the context of its struggle to bring peace to a land of peace and love, the State of Palestine calls upon the United Nations, which bears a special responsibility towards the Palestinian Arab people and its homeland, and upon the peace-loving States and peoples of the world and those that cherish freedom to assist it in achieving its goals, in bringing the plight of its people to an end, in ensuring the safety and security of that people and in endeavoring to end the Israeli occupation of Palestinian territory.

The State of Palestine further declares, in that connection, that it believes in the solution of international and regional problems by peaceful means in accordance with the Charter of the United Nations and the resolutions adopted by it, and that, without prejudice to its natural right to defend itself, it rejects the threat or use of force, violence and intimidation against its territorial integrity and political independence or those of any other State.

On this momentous day, the fifteenth day of November 1988, as we stand on the threshold of a new era, we bow our heads in deference and humility to the departed souls of our martyrs and the martyrs of the Arab nation who, by virtue of the pure blood shed by them, have lit the glimmer of this auspicious dawn and who have died so that the homeland might live. We lift up our hearts so that they may be filled with light from the radiance of the hallowed uprising, of the epic resistance of those in the camps, in the dispersion and in exile, and of those who have borne the manner of freedom: our children, our elders and our youth; our prisoners, detainees and wounded based on the hallowed soil and in every camp, village and city; the valiant Palestinian women, the guardians of our life and our survival and keepers of our eternal flame. To the spirits of our righteous martyrs, to the masses of our Palestinian Arab people and our Arab nation and to all free and honorable men, we give our solemn pledge to continue the struggle for an end to the occupation and the establishment of sovereignty and independence. We call upon our great people to rally to the Palestinian flag, to take pride in it and to defend it so that it shall remain forever a symbol of our freedom and dignity in a homeland that shall be forever free and the abode of a people of free men.

In the name of God, the Merciful, the Compassionate
"Say: 'O God, Master of the Kingdom, Thou givest the Kingdom to whom Thou wilt, and seizest the Kingdom from whom Thou wilt, Thou exaltest whom Thou wilt, and Thou abasest whom Thou wilt; in Thy hand is the good; Thou art powerful over everything ..."
Almighty God has spoken the truth

Israel and the Palestinians: Prospects for the Uprising and the Peace Process (1989)

CENTRAL INTELLIGENCE AGENCY

Palestinian Perspectives on Key Issues

Palestinians believe the uprising has forced Israel, the Arab governments, and the United States to confront the Palestinian national movement for the first time. West Bank and Gaza residents believe it has transformed the Palestinians into the agents of their own destiny. Palestinians demand that the uprising lead to tangible results that will end the Israeli occupation and eventually establish a Palestinian state. This demand produces both anxiety that the uprising may fail to achieve its objectives and determination not to lose opportunities for progress. Although economic hardships have increased, these problems are unlikely to cause a reduction of the disorders or make West Bank and Gaza Palestinians more likely to accept the Israeli initiative for local elections.

The uprising and the changing international environment have heightened PLO confidence in its ability to negotiate with Israel and to achieve a Palestinian state. Growing Soviet activism in the region and improving US-Soviet relations also have encouraged the PLO. Most Palestinians have replaced the PLO's old idea of a secular, democratic state of Palestine (incorporating Israel and the occupied territories) with the concept of a two-state solution.

PLO-West Bank Relations

The symbiotic relationship between the PLO and the Palestinian leaders in the occupied territories will continue. The PLO realizes that the uprising has shifted attention and power in the Palestinian movement from the more prominent diaspora personalities—the "outsiders"—to underground, new leaders—the "insiders"—in the West Bank and Gaza. Nevertheless, both insiders and outsiders have their own legitimacy: the insiders through their role in the uprising and the outsiders through their recognition among Palestinians as authentic representatives. [...]

Insiders will not blindly take orders from the PLO, but they will listen to it. Although insider leaders have given a mandate to the PLO, the insiders can exercise restrictive and "corrective" influence. Discussions between the groups, therefore, will remain a two-way street. PLO leaders, for their part, are confident that the insiders will remain loyal to the PLO, but they are listening closely to insider demands. [...]

Insiders and outsiders agree that a political settlement has to be reached, that concessions will have to be made, and that direct negotiations with the Israeli Government will be required. Both believe that interim

368

arrangements are acceptable only if they are part of a plan to reach a comprehensive solution. Both Palestinian camps also agree that the sorts of interim measures the Israelis are talking about are an unacceptable Israeli ploy to ward off the pressure generated by the uprising.
[…]

Policy Changes and Steps Toward Moderation
[…]

PLO Chairman Yassir Arafat is in a strong position. His priorities are to keep the Palestinian movement relatively unified and to remain its leader. He is a pragmatist and proven survivor who has reacted to the uprising by lining up with the more pragmatic Palestinians living under Israeli occupation and not with the hardline ideologues in the diaspora.

By directly addressing an American audience through its actions in recent months, the PLO hopes that it has prepared the way for an active US role in the settlement process. This orientation reflects the PLO's hope that the United States will try to change Israel's position or, by virtue of its dialogue with the PLO, that it will help to break open the political debate in Israel on dealing with the Palestinians.

The dialogue with the United States helps Arafat and is a key element in his efforts to gain international recognition. He uses it to consolidate his dominant position in the PLO and to cope with PLO hardliners, especially fundamentalists. The fundamentalists will become a serious problem if local leaders of the uprising and the PLO fail to make progress toward a settlement. […]

PLO Positions
[…]

- PLO leaders believe that an international conference eventually will be necessary to forge a coalition in its favor that is strong enough to compensate for its lack of leverage on Israel. The conference will require careful preparation. It could be merely a ratifying mechanism for agreements reached in other forums.

- The PLO is eager for direct talks with Israeli officials, but it realizes that Israel will need time to accustom itself to talking with the PLO.

- Because the uprising provides the PLO's only leverage on Israel, the PLO will make no commitment to stop it before negotiations begin. We believe that the PLO could not halt the uprising altogether. The PLO, however, could increase or decrease the scale of the disorders, depending on how well preliminary negotiations were going.

[…]

<u>Violence and Terrorism</u>

Actions by Syria and Palestinian splinter groups in particular, and by Libya and Iran to a lesser degree, will play a central role in the future of the US-PLO dialogue. All have a major interest in the collapse of the dialogue and will try to undermine it, especially if they see movement toward a solution that ignores their interests. Many extremist non-PLO Palestinian organizations [...] will try to stage terrorist actions both outside and inside Israel and the occupied territories. The effect of these incidents on the dialogue will depend on Arafat's willingness to condemn them. Nevertheless, a successful terrorist strike against an Israeli target would generate strong reaction against the PLO regardless of which groups were involved.

Hardliners within the PLO [...] will continue to test the limits of Arafat's prohibitions on terrorism. Their actions will include continued infiltration of guerrillas into Israel from southern Lebanon, which has become a focal point for Shia fundamentalism and radical Palestinian activity directed against the Israelis and their Lebanese allies. [...]

Continued violence will be accompanied by disputes between the United States and Israel over the definition of terrorism and whether PLO elements played a role in a particular incident. For many Israelis, Arafat is ultimately responsible for all acts of violence by Palestinians, which the Israelis lump together as terrorism. For the United States, however, the identity of the perpetrators will often be difficult to determine and responsibility hard to pin down.
[...]
<u>The Changing Situation</u>

Dramatic changes in the political environment surrounding the peace process have occurred over the past 18 months.

The Uprising. The Palestinian uprising in the West Bank and Gaza shows no signs of ending. It is sustainable at present levels by the Palestinians and tolerable to the Israelis. Nonetheless, it is forcing both sides to reassess how they deal with each other.

Jordan's Disengagement. King Husayn has made clear, as recently as his visit to the United States in April 1989, that Jordan will not play a central role in the peace process at this time. The King has given a qualified endorsement of the idea of elections in the West Bank and Gaza, but only in the context of a process leading to negotiations on the final status of the occupied territories.

Palestinian Movement Toward Moderation. Despite differences in emphasis between the inhabitants of the West Bank and Gaza and the Palestinian diaspora, the leadership of the Palestinian movement has

370

reached a consensus in favor of recognition of Israel, acceptance of UN Resolution 242, and renunciation of terrorism. It wants direct negotiations with the Israeli Government and is prepared to accept interim steps, including autonomy, as long as they are tightly linked to reaching a final settlement. Moderate Palestinians, however, worry that the mood among activists in the occupied territories will turn more violent if the PLO's efforts toward accommodating Israel and the United States produce no movement toward a comprehensive settlement.

Shifting Israeli Views. The uprising has intensified the political debate in Israel over territorial compromise, dealing with the Palestinians, and coping with the violence in the occupied territories. The US dialogue with the PLO has increased pressure on the Israeli Government to counter the perception that the PLO—but not Israel—is ready to talk.

[...]

OSLO

Israel-PLO Mutual Recognition Letters (1993)
Yasser Arafat and Yitzhak Rabin

Yitzhak Rabin, Prime Minister of Israel
Mr. Prime Minister,

The signing of the Declaration of Principles marks a new era in the history of the Middle East. In firm conviction thereof, I would like to confirm the following PLO commitments:

The PLO recognizes the right of the State of Israel to exist in peace and security.

The PLO accepts United Nations Security Council Resolutions 242 and 338.

The PLO commits itself to the Middle East peace process, and to a peaceful resolution of the conflict between the two sides and declares that all outstanding issues relating to permanent status will be resolved through negotiations.

The PLO considers that the signing of the Declaration of Principles constitutes a historic event, inaugurating a new epoch of peaceful coexistence, free from violence and all other acts which endanger peace and stability. Accordingly, the PLO renounces the use of terrorism and other acts of violence and will assume responsibility over all PLO elements and personnel in order to assure their compliance, prevent violations and discipline violators.

In view of the promise of a new era and the signing of the Declaration of Principles and based on Palestinian acceptance of Security Council Resolutions 242 and 338, the PLO affirms that those articles of the Palestinian Covenant which deny Israel's right to exist, and the provisions of the Covenant which are inconsistent with the commitments of this letter are now inoperative and no longer valid. Consequently, the PLO undertakes to submit to the Palestinian National Council for formal approval the necessary changes in regard to the Palestinian Covenant.

Sincerely,

Yasser Arafat
Chairman, The Palestine Liberation Organization

* * *

Yasser Arafat, Chairman, The Palestinian Liberation Organization

Mr. Chairman,

In response to your letter of September 9, 1993, I wish to confirm to you that, in light of the PLO commitments included in your letter, the Government of Israel has decided to recognize the PLO as the representative of the Palestinian people and commence negotiations with the PLO within the Middle East peace process.

Yitzhak Rabin
Prime Minister of Israel

Declaration of Principles on Interim Self-Government Arrangements
(1993)
STATE OF ISRAEL AND PALESTINE LIBERATION ORGANIZATION

The Government of the State of Israel and the PLO team (in the Jordanian-Palestinian delegation to the Middle East Peace Conference) (the "Palestinian Delegation"), representing the Palestinian people, agree that it is time to put an end to decades of confrontation and conflict, recognize their mutual legitimate and political rights, and strive to live in peaceful coexistence and mutual dignity and security and achieve a just, lasting and comprehensive peace settlement and historic reconciliation through the agreed political process. Accordingly, the two sides agree to the following principles:

Article I: AIM OF THE NEGOTIATIONS

The aim of the Israeli-Palestinian negotiations within the current Middle East peace process is, among other things, to establish a Palestinian Interim Self-Government Authority, the elected Council (the "Council"), for the Palestinian people in the West Bank and the Gaza Strip, for a transitional period not exceeding five years, leading to a permanent settlement based on Security Council resolutions 242 (1967) and 338 (1973). It is understood that the interim arrangements are an integral part of the whole peace process and that the negotiations on the permanent status will lead to the implementation of Security Council resolutions 242 (1967) and 338 (1973).

Article II: FRAMEWORK FOR THE INTERIM PERIOD

The agreed framework for the interim period is set forth in this Declaration of Principles.

Article III: ELECTIONS

1. In order that the Palestinian people in the West Bank and Gaza Strip may govern themselves according to democratic principles, direct, free and general political elections will be held for the Council under agreed supervision and international observation, while the Palestinian police will ensure public order.

2. An agreement will be concluded on the exact mode and conditions of the elections in accordance with the protocol attached as Annex I, with the goal of holding the elections not later than nine months after the entry into force of this Declaration of Principles.

3. These elections will constitute a significant interim preparatory step toward the realization of the legitimate rights of the Palestinian people and their just requirements.

Article IV: JURISDICTION

Jurisdiction of the Council will cover West Bank and Gaza Strip territory, except for issues that will be negotiated in the permanent status negotiations. The two sides view the West Bank and the Gaza Strip as a single territorial unit, whose integrity will be preserved during the interim period.

Article V: TRANSITIONAL PERIOD AND PERMANENT STATUS NEGOTIATIONS

1.   The five-year transitional period will begin upon the withdrawal from the Gaza Strip and Jericho area.
2.   Permanent status negotiations will commence as soon as possible, but not later than the beginning of the third year of the interim period, between the Government of Israel and the Palestinian people's representatives.
3.   It is understood that these negotiations shall cover remaining issues, including: Jerusalem, refugees, settlements, security arrangements, borders, relations and cooperation with other neighbors, and other issues of common interest.
4.   The two parties agree that the outcome of the permanent status negotiations should not be prejudiced or preempted by agreements reached for the interim period.

Article VI: PREPARATORY TRANSFER OF POWERS AND RESPONSIBILITIES

1.   Upon the entry into force of this Declaration of Principles and the withdrawal from the Gaza Strip and the Jericho area, a transfer of authority from the Israeli military government and its Civil Administration to the authorized Palestinians for this task, as detailed herein, will commence. This transfer of authority will be of a preparatory nature until the inauguration of the Council.
2.   Immediately after the entry into force of this Declaration of Principles and the withdrawal from the Gaza Strip and Jericho area, with the view to promoting economic development in the West Bank and Gaza Strip, authority will be transferred to the Palestinians in the following spheres: education and culture, health, social welfare, direct taxation and tourism. The Palestinian side will commence in building the Palestinian police force, as agreed upon. Pending the inauguration of the Council, the two parties may negotiate the transfer of additional powers and responsibilities, as agreed upon.

Article VII: INTERIM AGREEMENT

1. The Israeli and Palestinian delegations will negotiate an agreement on the interim period (the "Interim Agreement").
2. The Interim Agreement shall specify, among other things, the structure of the Council, the number of its members, and the transfer of powers and responsibilities from the Israeli military government and its Civil Administration to the Council. The Interim Agreement shall also specify the Council's executive authority, legislative authority in accordance with Article IX below, and the independent Palestinian judicial organs.
3. The Interim Agreement shall include arrangements, to be implemented upon the inauguration of the Council, for the assumption by the Council of all of the powers and responsibilities transferred previously in accordance with Article VI above.
4. In order to enable the Council to promote economic growth, upon its inauguration, the Council will establish, among other things, a Palestinian Electricity Authority, a Gaza Sea Port Authority, a Palestinian Development Bank, a Palestinian Export Promotion Board, a Palestinian Environmental Authority, a Palestinian Land Authority and a Palestinian Water Administration Authority and any other Authorities agreed upon, in accordance with the Interim Agreement, that will specify their powers and responsibilities.
5. After the inauguration of the Council, the Civil Administration will be dissolved, and the Israeli military government will be withdrawn.

Article VIII: PUBLIC ORDER AND SECURITY

In order to guarantee public order and internal security for the Palestinians of the West Bank and the Gaza Strip, the Council will establish a strong police force, while Israel will continue to carry the responsibility for defending against external threats, as well as the responsibility for overall security of Israelis for the purpose of safeguarding their internal security and public order.

Article IX: LAWS AND MILITARY ORDERS

1. The Council will be empowered to legislate, in accordance with the Interim Agreement, within all authorities transferred to it.
2. Both parties will review jointly laws and military orders presently in force in remaining spheres.

Article X: JOINT ISRAELI-PALESTINIAN LIAISON COMMITTEE

In order to provide for a smooth implementation of this Declaration of Principles and any subsequent agreements pertaining to the interim period, upon the entry into force of this Declaration of Principles, a Joint Israeli-

Palestinian Liaison Committee will be established in order to deal with issues requiring coordination, other issues of common interest and disputes.

Article XI: ISRAELI-PALESTINIAN COOPERATION IN ECONOMIC FIELDS

Recognizing the mutual benefit of cooperation in promoting the development of the West Bank, the Gaza Strip and Israel, upon the entry into force of this Declaration of Principles, an Israeli-Palestinian Economic Cooperation Committee will be established in order to develop and implement in a cooperative manner the programmes identified in the protocols attached as Annex III and Annex IV.

Article XII: LIAISON AND COOPERATION WITH JORDAN AND EGYPT

The two parties will invite the Governments of Jordan and Egypt to participate in establishing further liaison and cooperation arrangements between the Government of Israel and the Palestinian representatives, on the one hand, and the Governments of Jordan and Egypt, on the other hand, to promote cooperation between them. These arrangements will include the constitution of a Continuing Committee that will decide by agreement on the modalities of admission of persons displaced from the West Bank and Gaza Strip in 1967, together with necessary measures to prevent disruption and disorder. Other matters of common concern will be dealt with by this Committee.

Article XIII: REDEPLOYMENT OF ISRAELI FORCES

1. After the entry into force of this Declaration of Principles, and not later than the eve of elections for the Council, a redeployment of Israeli military forces in the West Bank and the Gaza Strip will take place, in addition to withdrawal of Israeli forces carried out in accordance with Article XIV.
2. In redeploying its military forces, Israel will be guided by the principle that its military forces should be redeployed outside populated areas.
3. Further redeployments to specified locations will be gradually implemented commensurate with the assumption of responsibility for public order and internal security by the Palestinian police force pursuant to Article VIII above.

Article XIV: ISRAELI WITHDRAWAL FROM THE GAZA STRIP AND JERICHO AREA

Israel will withdraw from the Gaza Strip and Jericho area, as detailed in the protocol attached as Annex II.

Article XV: RESOLUTION OF DISPUTES

1. Disputes arising out of the application or interpretation of this Declaration of Principles, or any subsequent agreements pertaining to the interim period, shall be resolved by negotiations through the Joint Liaison Committee to be established pursuant to Article X above.

2. Disputes which cannot be settled by negotiations may be resolved by a mechanism of conciliation to be agreed upon by the parties.

3. The parties may agree to submit to arbitration disputes relating to the interim period, which cannot be settled through conciliation. To this end, upon the agreement of both parties, the parties will establish an Arbitration Committee.

Article XVI: ISRAELI-PALESTINIAN COOPERATION CONCERNING REGIONAL PROGRAMMES

Both parties view the multilateral working groups as an appropriate instrument for promoting a "Marshall Plan", the regional programmes and other programmes, including special programmes for the West Bank and Gaza Strip, as indicated in the protocol attached as Annex IV.

Article XVII: MISCELLANEOUS PROVISIONS

1. This Declaration of Principles will enter into force one month after its signing.

2. All protocols annexed to this Declaration of Principles and Agreed Minutes pertaining thereto shall be regarded as an integral part hereof.

Treaty of Peace (1994)

PREAMBLE

The Government of the State of Israel and the Government of the Hashemite Kingdom of Jordan,

Bearing in mind the Washington Declaration, signed by them on 25th July,1994, and which they are both committed to honor;

Aiming at the achievement of a just, lasting and comprehensive peace in the Middle East based on Security Council resolutions 242 and 338 in all their aspects;

Bearing in mind the importance of maintaining and strengthening peace based on freedom, equality, justice and respect for fundamental human rights, thereby overcoming psychological barriers and promoting human dignity;

Reaffirming their faith in the purposes and principles of the Charter of the United Nations and recognizing their right and obligation to live in peace with each other as well as with all states, within secure and recognized boundaries;

Desiring to develop friendly relations and co-operation between them in accordance with the principles of international law governing international relations in time of peace;

Desiring as well to ensure lasting security for both their States and in particular to avoid threats and the use of force between them;

Bearing in mind that in their Washington Declaration of 25th July, 1994, they declared the termination of the state of belligerency between them;

Deciding to establish peace between them in accordance with this Treaty of Peace;

Have agreed as follows:

Article 1. Establishment of Peace

Peace is hereby established between the State of Israel and the Hashemite Kingdom of Jordan (the "Parties") effective from the exchange of the instruments of ratification of this Treaty.

Article 2. General Principles

The Parties will apply between them the provisions of the Charter of the United Nations and the principles of international law governing relations among states in time of peace. In particular:

1. They recognize and will respect each other's sovereignty, territorial integrity and political independence;

2. They recognize and will respect each other's right to live in peace within secure and recognized boundaries;

3. They will develop good neighborly relations of co-operation between them to ensure lasting security, will refrain from the threat or use of force against each other and will settle all disputes between them by peaceful means;

4. They respect and recognize the sovereignty, territorial integrity and political independence of every state in the region;

5. They respect and recognize the pivotal role of human development and dignity in regional and bilateral relationships;

6. They further believe that within their control, involuntary movements of persons in such a way as to adversely prejudice the security of either Party should not be permitted.

Article 3. International Boundary

1. The international boundary between Israel and Jordan is delimited with reference to the boundary definition under the Mandate [....]

2. The boundary [...] is the permanent, secure and recognized international boundary between Israel and Jordan, without prejudice to the status of any territories that came under Israeli military government control in 1967.
[...]

Article 4. Security

1. a. Both Parties, acknowledging that mutual understanding and co-operation in security-related matters will form a significant part of their relations and will further enhance the security of the region, take upon themselves to base their security relations on mutual trust, advancement of joint interests and co-operation, and to aim towards a regional framework of partnership in peace.
[...]

380

2.   The obligations referred to in this Article are without prejudice to the inherent right of self-defense in accordance with the United Nations Charter.

3.   The Parties undertake, in accordance with the provisions of this Article, the following:

a.   To refrain from the threat or use of force or weapons, conventional, non-conventional or of any other kind, against each other, or of other actions or activities that adversely affect the security of the other Party;

b.   To refrain from organizing, instigating, inciting, assisting or participating in acts or threats of belligerency, hostility, subversion or violence against the other Party;

c.   To take necessary and effective measures to ensure that acts or threats of belligerency, hostility, subversion or violence against the other Party do not originate from, and are not committed within, through or over their territory (hereinafter the term "territory" includes the airspace and territorial waters).

4.   Consistent with the era of peace and with the efforts to build regional security and to avoid and prevent aggression and violence, the Parties further agree to refrain from the following:

a.   Joining or in any way assisting, promoting or co-operating with any coalition, organization or alliance with a military or security character with a third party, the objectives or activities of which include launching aggression or other acts of military hostility against the other Party, in contravention of the provisions of the present Treaty;

b.   Allowing the entry, stationing and operating on their territory, or through it, of military forces, personnel or materiel of a third party, in circumstances which may adversely prejudice the security of the other Party.

5.   Both Parties will take necessary and effective measures, and will co-operate in combating terrorism of all kinds. The Parties undertake:

a.   To take necessary and effective measures to prevent acts of terrorism, subversion or violence from being carried out from their territory or through it and to take necessary and effective measures to combat such activities and all their perpetrators;

b. Without prejudice to the basic rights of freedom of expression and association, to take necessary and effective measures to prevent the entry, presence and operation in their territory of any group or organization, and their infrastructure, which threatens the security of the other Party by the use of, or incitement to the use of, violent means;

c. To co-operate in preventing and combating cross-boundary infiltrations.

[...]

Article 5. Diplomatic and Other Bilateral Relations

1. The Parties agree to establish full diplomatic and consular relations and to exchange resident ambassadors within one month of the exchange of the instruments of ratification of this Treaty.

2. The Parties agree that the normal relationship between them will further include economic and cultural relations.

Article 6. Water

With the view to achieving a comprehensive and lasting settlement of all the water problems between them:

1. The Parties agree mutually to recognize the rightful allocations of both of them in Jordan River and Yarmouk River waters and Araba/Arava ground water in accordance with the agreed acceptable principles, quantities and quality as set out in Annex II, which shall be fully respected and complied with.

2. The Parties, recognizing the necessity to find a practical, just and agreed solution to their water problems and with the view that the subject of water can form the basis for the advancement of co-operation between them, jointly undertake to ensure that the management and development of their water resources do not, in any way, harm the water resources of the other Party.

3. The Parties recognize that their water resources are not sufficient to meet their needs. More water should be supplied for their use through various methods, including projects of regional and international co-operation.

4. In light of paragraph 3 of this Article, with the understanding that co-operation in water-related subjects would be to the benefit of both Parties, and will help alleviate their water shortages, and that water issues along their entire boundary must be dealt with in their totality, including the possibility of trans-boundary water transfers, the Parties agree to search

for ways to alleviate water shortages and to co-operate in the following fields:

    a.   Development of existing and new water resources, increasing the water availability, including co-operation on a regional basis as appropriate, and minimizing wastage of water resources through the chain of their uses;

    b.   Prevention of contamination of water resources;

    c.   Mutual assistance in the alleviation of water shortages;

    d.   Transfer of information and joint research and development in water-related subjects, and review of the potentials for enhancement of water resources development and use.

[...]

Article 7. Economic Relations

1.   Viewing economic development and prosperity as pillars of peace, security and harmonious relations between states, peoples and individual human beings, the Parties, taking note of understandings reached between them, affirm their mutual desire to promote economic co-operation between them, as well as within the framework of wider regional economic co-operation.

2.   In order to accomplish this goal, the Parties agree to the following:

    a.   To remove all discriminatory barriers to normal economic relations, to terminate economic boycotts directed at the other Party, and to co-operate in terminating boycotts against either Party by third parties;

    b.   Recognizing that the principle of free and unimpeded. flow of goods and services should guide their relations, the Parties will enter into negotiations with a view to concluding agreements on economic co-operation, including trade and the establishment of a free trade area or areas, investment, banking, industrial co-operation and labor, for the purpose of promoting beneficial economic relations, based on principles to be agreed upon, as well as on human development considerations on a regional basis. These negotiations will be concluded no later than 6 months from the exchange of the instruments of ratification of this Treaty;

    c.   To co-operate bilaterally, as well as in multilateral forums, towards the promotion of their respective economies and of their neighborly economic relations with other regional parties.

Article 8. Refugees and Displaced Persons

1. Recognizing the massive human problems caused to both Parties by the conflict in the Middle East, as well as the contribution made by them towards the alleviation of human suffering, the Parties will seek to further alleviate those problems arising on a bilateral level.

2. Recognizing that the above human problems caused by the conflict in the Middle East cannot be fully resolved on the bilateral level, the Parties will seek to resolve them in appropriate forums, in accordance with international law, including the following:

    a. In the case of displaced persons, in a quadripartite committee together with Egypt and the Palestinians;

    b. In the case of refugees,

        i. In the framework of the Multilateral Working Group on Refugees.

        ii. In negotiations, in a framework to be agreed, bilateral or otherwise, in conjunction with and at the same time as the permanent status negotiations pertaining to the Territories referred to in Article 3 of this Treaty;

    c. Through the implementation of agreed United Nations programmes and other agreed international economic programmes concerning refugees and displaced persons, including assistance to their settlement.

Article 9. Places of Historical and Religious Significance and Interfaith Relations

1. Each Party will provide freedom of access to places of religious and historical significance.

2. In this regard, in accordance with the Washington Declaration, Israel respects the present special role of the Hashemite Kingdom of Jordan in Muslim Holy shrines in Jerusalem. When negotiations on the permanent status will take place, Israel will give high priority to the Jordanian historic role in these shrines.

3. The Parties will act together to promote interfaith relations among the three monotheistic religions, with the aim of working towards religious understanding, moral commitment, freedom of religious worship, and tolerance and peace.

Article 10. Cultural and Scientific Exchanges

The Parties, wishing to remove biases developed through periods of conflict, recognize the desirability of cultural and scientific exchanges in all fields, and agree to establish normal cultural relations between them. Thus, they shall, as soon as possible and not later than 9 months from the exchange of the instruments of ratification of this Treaty, conclude the negotiations on cultural and scientific agreements.

Article 11. Mutual Understanding and Good Neighborly Relations

1. The Parties will seek to foster mutual understanding and tolerance based on shared historic values, and accordingly undertake:

   a. To abstain from hostile or discriminatory propaganda against each other, and to take all possible legal and administrative measures to prevent the dissemination of such propaganda by any organization or individual present in the territory of either Party;

   b. As soon as possible, and not later than 3 months from the exchange of the instruments of ratification of this Treaty, to repeal all adverse or discriminatory references and expressions of hostility in their respective legislation;

   c. To refrain in all government publications from any such references or expressions;

   d. To ensure mutual enjoyment by each other's citizens of due process of law within their respective legal systems and before their courts.

2. Paragraph 1 (a) of this Article is without prejudice to the right to freedom of expression as contained in the International Covenant on Civil and Political Rights.
[...]

Article 25. Rights and Obligations

1. This Treaty does not affect and shall not be interpreted as affecting, in any way, the rights and obligations of the Parties under the Charter of the United Nations.

2. The Parties undertake to fulfil in good faith their obligations under this Treaty, without regard to action or inaction of any other party and independently of any instrument inconsistent with this Treaty. For the purposes of this paragraph, each Party represents to the other that in its opinion and interpretation there is no inconsistency between their existing treaty obligations and this Treaty.

3.   They further undertake to take all the necessary measures for the application in their relations of the provisions of the multilateral conventions to which they are parties, including the submission of appropriate notification to the Secretary General of the United Nations and other depositories of such conventions.

4.   Both Parties will also take all the necessary steps to abolish all pejorative references to the other Party, in multilateral conventions to which they are parties, to the extent that such references exist.

5.   The Parties undertake not to enter into any obligation in conflict with this Treaty.

6.   Subject to Article 103 of the United Nations Charter, in the event of a conflict between the obligations of the Parties under the present Treaty and any of their other obligations, the obligations under this Treaty will be binding and implemented.
[…]

Address to Knesset on Ratification of Oslo Peace Accords (1995)
Yitzhak Rabin

Today, the Government presents to the Knesset the "Israeli-Palestinian Interim Agreement on the West Bank and the Gaza Strip." The Government will seek the Knesset's approval and will view the Knesset's decision as a vote of confidence in the Government.
[...]
The agreement before you is the continuation of the implementation of the agreements which were signed between the Government of Israel and the Palestinians. The first agreement which was brought to you was the Declaration of Principles, which was signed in Washington on 13 September 1993.

The second agreement which was presented to you is called the Cairo Agreement, which was signed in Cairo on 4 May 1994. Both of these agreements were ratified by the Knesset.

Mr. Chairman,

Both of the previous agreements and the third which was submitted today, separately and together, give expression to the policy of the current Government and to its path of promoting peace in the Middle East. As is known, when we formed the Government over three years ago, we said that we would aspire to reach a permanent solution to the Palestinian-Arab-Israeli conflict. And today, this Government brings, in addition to the signing of the peace treaty with the Hashemite Kingdom of Jordan -- which would not have been achieved without the agreement with the Palestinians -- a significant breakthrough in resolving the Palestinian-Israeli conflict and an attempt to put an end to decades of terrorism and blood.

Members of Knesset,

We are striving for a permanent solution to the unending bloody conflict between us and the Palestinians and the Arab states.

In the framework of the permanent solution, we aspire to reach, first and foremost, the State of Israel as a Jewish state, at least 80% of whose citizens will be, and are, Jews.

At the same time, we also promise that the non-Jewish citizens of Israel -- Muslim, Christian, Druze and others -- will enjoy full personal, religious, and civil rights, like those of any Israeli citizen. Judaism and racism are diametrically opposed.

We view the permanent solution in the framework of the State of Israel which will include most of the area of the Land of Israel as it was under the rule of the British Mandate, and alongside it a Palestinian entity which will be a home to most of the Palestinian residents living in the Gaza Strip and the West Bank.

We would like this to be an entity which is less than a state and which will independently run the lives of the Palestinians under its authority. The borders of the State of Israel, during the permanent solution, will be beyond the lines which existed before the Six-Day War. We will not return to the 4 June 1967 lines.

And these are the main changes, not all of them, which we envision and want in the permanent solution:

A. First and foremost, united Jerusalem, which will include both Ma'ale Adumim and Givat Ze'ev -- as the capital of Israel, under Israeli sovereignty, while preserving the rights of the members of the other faiths, Christianity and Islam, to freedom of access and freedom of worship in their holy places, according to the customs of their faiths.

B. The security border of the State of Israel will be located in the Jordan Valley, in the broadest meaning of that term.

C. Changes which will include the addition of Gush Etzion, Efrat, Beitar, and other communities, most of which are in the area east of what was the "Green Line," prior to the Six Day War.

D. The establishment of blocs of settlements in Judea and Samaria, like the one in Gush Katif.
[...]
The way in which Israel will implement the agreement so as to achieve its political goals regarding the permanent solution and the security of the settlements and Israelis in the territories will ensure the continuation of daily life and security, both for the Israeli side and for the Palestinian side.

The first stage of the redeployment of IDF forces will be done in order to enable the Palestinians to hold elections for the Palestinian Council and its chairman without the IDF being permanently present inside Palestinian communities.

The first stage of this redeployment of IDF forces will be carried out in three areas in order to enable the Palestinians to hold elections for the Palestinian Council, and for its Chairman, without the IDF being permanently present in Palestinian communities:

Area A -- or the "brown" area; the redeployment of IDF forces will be carried out in three areas -- will include the municipal areas of the six cities -- Jenin, Nablus, Tulkarm, Kalkiliya, Ramallah, and Bethlehem.

Responsibility for civilian security in this area will be transferred to the Palestinian Authority.

Area B -- or the "yellow" area -- includes almost all of the 450 towns and villages in which the Palestinians of the West Bank live. In this area, there will be a separation of responsibilities. The Palestinians will be responsible for managing their own lives, and Israel will have overall responsibility for the security of Israelis and the war against the terrorist threat. That is, IDF forces and the security services will be able to enter any place in Area B at any time.

The third area, Area C, or the "white" area -- is everywhere that is not included in the areas that have been mentioned until now. In this area are the Jewish settlements, all IDF installations, and the border areas with Jordan. This area will remain under IDF control.

Areas A and B constitute less than 30% of the area of the West Bank. Area C, which is under our control, constitutes more than 70% of the area of the West Bank.

However, I must bring it to the attention of the Members of the Knesset that we have committed ourselves to an additional redeployment, in three stages, beyond the redeployment that I have already mentioned. The redeployment will be carried out according to a timetable, with each stage being carried out after the previous stage. The first will be approximately six months, beginning from the establishment of the Palestinian Council after the elections.

I must emphasize that we have not committed ourselves, and I repeat, we have not committed ourselves to the scope of the redeployment at each stage. Most importantly, it was defined in the agreement that the restrictions on the completion of the redeployment are issues that will be discussed during the negotiations on the permanent settlement, as is stated in the Agreement itself, and I quote: "During the further redeployment phases to be completed within 18 months from the date of the inauguration of the Council, powers and responsibilities relating to territory will be transferred to Palestinian jurisdiction that will cover West Bank and Gaza Strip territory, except for issues that will be negotiated in the permanent status negotiations."

Several words about what the current agreement says about the permanent agreement, and I quote from the agreement itself; the words speak for themselves:

1. "Permanent status negotiations will commence as soon as possible, but not later than May 4, 1996, and will end no later than May 4,1999, between the Parties. It is understood that these negotiations shall cover remaining

issues, including: Jerusalem, refugees, settlements, security arrangements, borders, relations and cooperation with other negotiations, and other issues of common interest."

That is, among the criteria to be taken into account in every discussion on continuing the redeployment, with the consent of the Palestinians, according to this agreement, the criteria of the final agreement constitute considerations concerning the redeployment, continuing the redeployment.

2. "Nothing in this Agreement shall prejudice or preempt the outcome of the negotiations on the permanent status to be conducted pursuant to the DOP. Neither Party shall be deemed, by virtue of having entered into this Agreement, to have renounced or waived any of its existing rights, claims, or positions."

"Neither side shall initiate or take any step that will change the status of the West Bank and the Gaza Strip pending the outcome of the permanent solution negotiations."

I want to remind you: we committed ourselves, that is, we came to an agreement and committed ourselves before the Knesset, not to uproot a single settlement in the framework of the interim agreement and not to hinder building for natural growth.

Members of Knesset,

We are aware of the fact that the Palestinian Authority has not -- up until now -- honored its commitment to change the Palestinian Covenant and that all of the promises on this matter have not been kept. I would like to bring it to the attention of the members of the house that I view these changes as a supreme test of the Palestinian Authority's willingness and ability, and the changes required will be an important and serious touchstone vis-a-vis the continued implementation of the agreement as a whole.
[...]
Here before you are additional details from the agreement which was achieved through great effort:

* The passage of police forces from Area A, which is entirely under the control of the Palestinians, to Area B, in which there are authorities shared by Israel and the Palestinians, requires the permission of the joint coordination apparatus, the DCO. This means that there will be no passage of Palestinian police without Israeli approval.

* The passage of Palestinian Police forces in uniform and/or armed from the 25 Palestinian villages in which police stations will be located to the

rest of Area B will require coordination and approval from the Joint District Coordination Office.

* There will be a deployment of Israeli-Palestinian liaison offices in the area. These liaison offices will employ joint mobile units for needs which will arise on the ground.

I should further emphasize that activity for providing security measures for the Israeli communities -- fences, peripheral roads, lighting, gates -- will continue on a wide scale. Bypass roads will be built, whose purpose will be to enable Israeli residents to move about without having to pass through Palestinian population centers in places which will be transferred to the responsibility of the Palestinian Authority. In any case, the IDF will not carry out a redeployment from the first seven cities before the bypass roads are completed. In all, investment in the bypass roads will be about NIS 500 million.

The responsibility for external security along the borders with Egypt and Jordan, as well as control over the airspace above all of the territories and Gaza Strip maritime zone, remains in our hands.

Members of Knesset,

The road to reconciliation leads through the prisons. In our prisons, there are currently more than five thousand Palestinian prisoners who, in accordance with the Government's decision, will be released. Detainees and prisoners who are included on condition that they fall into the following categories: female detainees, and prisoners who have served more than two-thirds of their sentence, detainees and/or prisoners accused of or imprisoned due to security crimes that did not result in death or serious injury. What follows from this is that murderers of Jews or those who have wounded them seriously will not be released. Detainees and prisoners accused or convicted of non-security criminal offenses, and also citizens of Arab states held in Israel until implementation of expulsion orders against them.

We will also examine the release of prisoners and detainees over 50 years of age, and 18 years of age or less, who have remained in prison 10 or more years, and prisoners and detainees who are infirm and unhealthy.

But, consistent with the categories which I described before, no detainee or prisoner will be released unless he signs a commitment to obey the law, to not commit acts of terrorism and involvement in them. We have had experience, following the Cairo Agreement, and hundreds remained in jail because they refused to sign.
[...]

Ten days after the signing of the agreement in Washington, the redeployment will begin -- in the first stage, the withdrawal of Civil Administration representative offices will begin in 14 Palestinian communities. The overall timetable will be completed within two weeks after the signing of the Agreement.

The agreement includes dozens and hundreds more details, among them, elections, including the manner of voting by the Palestinians in united Jerusalem who did not want Israeli citizenship as proposed to them by Israeli governments, water, electricity, expansion of the Jericho area by 10% without affecting the lives of the residents of the Jordan Valley, safe passage and more. In the time available today, we cannot relate to every detail separately and you will see that all of these matters are addressed in the Agreement before you.
[...]
Today we may be opening a new stage in the annals of the Jewish people and the State of Israel. We know the chances. We know the risks. We will do our best to expand the chances and reduce the risks.

From the depths of our heart, we call upon all citizens of the State of Israel, certainly those who live in Judea, Samaria, and the Gaza Strip, as well as the Palestinian residents to give the establishment of peace a chance, to give the end of acts of hostility a chance, to give another life a chance, a new life. We appeal to Jews and Palestinians alike to act with restraint, to preserve human dignity, to behave in a fitting manner,-- and to live in peace and security.
[...]

Learning from Rabin (2020)
Richard Haass

[…] [T]he assassination of Israeli Prime Minister Yitzhak Rabin 25 years ago by a right-wing Jewish extremist almost certainly was a turning point in the Middle East. The reason is clear: Rabin may well have been the only Israeli leader of his generation both willing and able to make peace with the Palestinians living under Israeli occupation. […]

By contrast, Rabin's rival and successor, Shimon Peres, had the desire to make peace, but his very enthusiasm undermined his ability to rally skeptical Israelis behind him. Rabin's reluctance proved invaluable. And several subsequent Israeli prime ministers, including the incumbent, Binyamin Netanyahu, possessed the hardline credentials to make a deal with the Palestinians, in the sense that the anti-communist Richard Nixon could broker the US breakthrough with China a half-century ago. But, unlike Nixon, they lacked the desire to do so on terms that had any chance of being accepted.

This is not to say that Rabin would have succeeded had he lived. It takes two to make peace. […] Peace requires leaders who are both willing and able to compromise and sustain their commitments. And here it is not obvious that Rabin had a viable partner in Yasir Arafat, although it is instructive that Rabin ultimately judged that it was worth pursuing, because only Arafat possessed the authority to make a deal.

What also made Rabin remarkable was his openness to change. As Israel's defense minister from 1984 to 1990, he imposed harsh measures on Palestinians living in Israeli-occupied territories and cracked down on violent protest. I was working on the Middle East at the White House at the time. When I challenged Rabin on the wisdom of saying Israel would break the bones of the protesters, he responded, "What would you have us do? Kill them?"

For Rabin, it was a legal and political necessity to maintain order, but it was also a moral imperative to minimize the loss of life. […]

Over time, however, Rabin concluded that force alone would not succeed. He came to see political and economic incentives as essential as well. And in his second term as prime minister, he accepted the Palestine Liberation Organization as a negotiating partner despite its history of terrorism, and approved the 1993 and 1995 Oslo Accords that established a path designed to bring about ever greater political autonomy for Palestinians.

As we know, the Oslo Accords were never implemented in full. Rabin was assassinated, subsequent attempts at negotiating peace failed, Arafat died, and no Palestinian state materialized.
[…]

From PROJECT SYNDICATE. Reprinted with permission.

Camp David Created Oslo, Which Killed the Palestinian Struggle
(2018)
Ahmed Abu Artema

During the secret Oslo negotiations between Israel and the Palestinian Liberation Organization (PLO), lawyer Joel Singer was sent by the Israeli government to ask the Palestinian negotiators 100 questions.

One of the questions he asked was whether the Palestinians would agree to Israeli settlers remaining in their lands. The answer was "Yes".

"I wasn't surprised to get 100 answers to my 100 questions. But I was shocked not to get a single Palestinian question in return," Singer is reported to have said.

After he finished his interrogation of the Palestinian officials, Singer reportedly told then Israeli Foreign Minister Shimon Peres: "Mr. Foreign Minister, if we don't make an immediate deal with these people, we are complete idiots."

This short anecdote illustrates well what the Oslo Accords signed on the White House lawn on September 13, 1993, were really about.

This was a deal made by unequal adversaries, with one exploiting the weakness of the other in order to impose its demands.

The Oslo Accords effectively put an end to the PLO's struggle for the liberation of Palestine and facilitated the occupation by making it less costly for the Israeli state. The establishing of the Palestinian Authority relieved Israel of the burden of providing for the needs of the Palestinian people. It also set up a Palestinian-run security body which took up policing the Palestinians, making it easier for Israel to control them and suppress the popular struggle.

The status of Jerusalem and the right of return of Palestinian refugees were left out of the negotiations, allowing Israel to strengthen its grip on illegally occupied Palestinian land.

But the ground for the disaster that the Oslo Accords proved to be was prepared 15 years earlier when Egyptian President Anwar al-Sadat signed the Camp David agreement with the Israeli occupation President Menachem Begin on September 17, 1978.

That day marks the beginning of the long process of normalisation of relations between Israel and the Arab states. It was the day, Arab leaders put behind revolutionary ideas and the taboo of negotiations with the Israelis and opted for pragmatism and self-interest.

This left the PLO no choice but to pursue the same path. In this sense, Oslo was born in Camp David and it was Arab states like Egypt that helped it mature. They also kept it alive after it was signed. In May 1994, Israeli Prime Minister Yitzhak Rabin and PLO Chairman Yasser Arafat met in Cairo to negotiate an agreement on Gaza and Jericho, part of the Oslo process.

When Arafat tried to resist at the signing ceremony, al-Sadat's successor, Egyptian President Hosni Mubarak, reportedly leaned over and shouted in his face "Sign, you dog!"

It is this type of attitude that a number of Arab states have maintained towards the Palestinians and their leaders over the past few decades.

Looking back on the negotiations in Oslo and Camp David, one can see that all of Israel's demands were met and it remains the clear winner of both "peace" initiatives.
[…]
However, the worst impact of Camp David and the Oslo Accords has been the division and despair that they have sown among the Palestinians. Today, the Palestinian people seem to have lost their national compass – the relationship with the occupiers is no longer one of a political struggle for freedom and self-determination.

There is also a growing gap between the people and their political leadership. The Palestinian political elite can no longer speak in the name of struggle, nor in the name of Palestinian statehood. It is now driven solely by self-interest and self-enrichment and it struggles to preserve the status quo in order to ensure its political survival.
[…]

CAMP DAVID II

Camp David and After: An Interview with Ehud Barak (2002)
Benny Morris

The call from Bill Clinton came hours after the publication in *The New York Times* of Deborah Sontag's "revisionist" article [...] on the Israeli–Palestinian peace process. Ehud Barak, Israel's former prime minister, on vacation, was swimming in a cove in Sardinia. Clinton said (according to Barak):

> What the hell is this? Why is she turning the mistakes we [i.e., the US and Israel] made into the essence? The true story of Camp David was that for the first time in the history of the conflict the American president put on the table a proposal, based on UN Security Council resolutions 242 and 338, very close to the Palestinian demands, and Arafat refused even to accept it as a basis for negotiations, walked out of the room, and deliberately turned to terrorism. That's the real story—all the rest is gossip.

Clinton was speaking of the two-week-long July 2000 Camp David conference that he had organized and mediated and its failure, and the eruption at the end of September of the Palestinian intifada, or campaign of anti-Israeli violence, which has continued ever since and which currently plagues the Middle East, with no end in sight. Midway in the conference, apparently on July 18, Clinton had "slowly"—to avoid misunderstanding—read out to Arafat a document, endorsed in advance by Barak, outlining the main points of a future settlement. The proposals included the establishment of a demilitarized Palestinian state on some 92 percent of the West Bank and 100 percent of the Gaza Strip, with some territorial compensation for the Palestinians from pre-1967 Israeli territory; the dismantling of most of the settlements and the concentration of the bulk of the settlers inside the 8 percent of the West Bank to be annexed by Israel; the establishment of the Palestinian capital in East Jerusalem, in which some Arab neighborhoods would become sovereign Palestinian territory and others would enjoy "functional autonomy"; Palestinian sovereignty over half the Old City of Jerusalem (the Muslim and Christian quarters) and "custodianship," though not sovereignty, over the Temple Mount; a return of refugees to the prospective Palestinian state though with no "right of return" to Israel proper; and the organization by the international community of a massive aid program to facilitate the refugees' rehabilitation.

Arafat said "No." Clinton, enraged, banged on the table and said: "You are leading your people and the region to a catastrophe." A formal Palestinian rejection of the proposals reached the Americans the next day. The summit sputtered on for a few days more but to all intents and purposes it was over.

Barak today portrays Arafat's behavior at Camp David as a "performance" geared to exacting from the Israelis as many concessions as possible without ever seriously intending to reach a peace settlement or sign an "end to the conflict." "He did not negotiate in good faith, indeed, he did not negotiate at all. He just kept saying 'no' to every offer, never making any counterproposals of his own," he says. Barak continuously shifts between charging Arafat with "lacking the character or will" to make a historic compromise [...] and accusing him of secretly planning Israel's demise while he strings along a succession of Israeli and Western leaders and, on the way, hoodwinks "naive journalists"—in Barak's phrase—like Sontag and officials such as former US National Security Council expert Robert Malley [....] According to Barak:

> What they [Arafat and his colleagues] want is a Palestinian state in all of Palestine. What we see as self-evident, [the need for] two states for two peoples, they reject. Israel is too strong at the moment to defeat, so they formally recognize it. But their game plan is to establish a Palestinian state while always leaving an opening for further "legitimate" demands down the road. For now, they are willing to agree to a temporary truce à la Hudnat Hudaybiyah [a temporary truce that the Prophet Muhammad concluded with the leaders of Mecca during 628–629, which he subsequently unilaterally violated]. They will exploit the tolerance and democracy of Israel first to turn it into "a state for all its citizens," as demanded by the extreme nationalist wing of Israel's Arabs and extremist left-wing Jewish Israelis. Then they will push for a binational state and then, demography and attrition will lead to a state with a Muslim majority and a Jewish minority. This would not necessarily involve kicking out all the Jews. But it would mean the destruction of Israel as a Jewish state. This, I believe, is their vision. They may not talk about it often, openly, but this is their vision. Arafat sees himself as a reborn Saladin— the Kurdish Muslim general who defeated the Crusaders in the twelfth century—and Israel as just another, ephemeral Crusader state.

Barak believes that Arafat sees the Palestinian refugees of 1948 and their descendants, numbering close to four million, as the main demographic-political tool for subverting the Jewish state.

Arafat, says Barak, believes that Israel "has no right to exist, and he seeks its demise." Barak buttresses this by arguing that Arafat "does not recognize the existence of a Jewish people or nation, only a Jewish religion, because it is mentioned in the Koran and because he remembers seeing, as a kid, Jews praying at the Wailing Wall." This, Barak believes, underlay Arafat's insistence at Camp David (and since) that the Palestinians have sole sovereignty over the Temple Mount compound (Haram al-Sharif—the noble sanctuary) in the southeastern corner of Jerusalem's Old City. Arafat denies that any Jewish temple has ever stood there—and this is a microcosm of his denial of the Jews' historical connection and claim to the Land of Israel/Palestine. Hence, in December 2000, Arafat refused to accept even the vague formulation proposed by Clinton positing Israeli sovereignty over the earth beneath the Temple Mount's surface area.

[…]

Repeatedly during our prolonged interview, conducted in his office in a Tel Aviv skyscraper, Barak shook his head—in bewilderment and sadness—at what he regards as Palestinian, and especially Arafat's, mendacity:

> They are products of a culture in which to tell a lie…creates no dissonance. They don't suffer from the problem of telling lies that exists in Judeo-Christian culture. Truth is seen as an irrelevant category. There is only that which serves your purpose and that which doesn't. They see themselves as emissaries of a national movement for whom everything is permissible. There is no such thing as "the truth."

Speaking of Arab society, Barak recalls: "The deputy director of the US Federal Bureau of Investigation once told me that there are societies in which lie detector tests don't work, societies in which lies do not create cognitive dissonance [on which the tests are based]." Barak gives an example: back in October 2000, shortly after the start of the current Intifada, he met with then Secretary of State Madeleine Albright and Arafat in the residence of the US ambassador in Paris. Albright was trying to broker a cease-fire. Arafat had agreed to call a number of his police commanders in the West Bank and Gaza, including Tawfik Tirawi, to implement a truce. Barak said:

> I interjected: "But these are not the people organizing the violence. If you are serious [in seeking a cease-fire], then call Marwan Bargouti and Hussein al-Sheikh" [the West Bank heads of the Fatah, Arafat's own political party, who were orchestrating the violence. Bargouti has since been arrested by Israeli troops and is currently awaiting trial for launching dozens of terrorist attacks].

> Arafat looked at me, with an expression of blank innocence, as if I had mentioned the names of two polar bears, and said: "Who?

Who?" So I repeated the names, this time with a pronounced, clear Arabic inflection—"Mar-wan Bar-gou-ti" and "Hsein a Sheikh"—and Arafat again said, "Who? Who?" At this, some of his aides couldn't stop themselves and burst out laughing. And Arafat, forced to drop the pretense, agreed to call them later. [Of course, nothing happened and the shooting continued.]

But Barak is far from dismissive of Arafat, who appears to many Israelis to be a sick, slightly doddering buffoon and, at the same time, sly and murderous. Barak sees him as "a great actor, very sharp, very elusive, slippery." He cautions that Arafat "uses his broken English" to excellent effect.

Barak was elected prime minister, following three years of Benjamin Netanyahu's premiership, in May 1999 and took office in July. He immediately embarked on his multipronged peace effort—vis-à-vis Syria, Lebanon, and the Palestinians—feeling that Israel and the Middle East were headed for "an iceberg and a certain crash and that it was the leaders' moral and political responsibility to try to avoid a catastrophe." He understood that the year and a half left of Clinton's presidency afforded a small window of opportunity inside a larger, but also limited, regional window of opportunity. That window was opened by the collapse of the Soviet Empire, which had since the 1950s supported the Arabs against Israel, and the defeat of Iraq in Kuwait in 1991, and would close when and if Iran and/or Iraq obtained nuclear weapons and when and if Islamic fundamentalist movements took over states bordering Israel.

Barak said he wanted to complete what Rabin had begun with the Oslo agreement, which inaugurated mutual Israeli–Palestinian recognition and partial Israeli withdrawals from the West Bank and Gaza Strip back in 1993. A formal peace agreement, he felt, would not necessarily "end the conflict, that will take education over generations, but there is a tremendous value to an [official] framework of peace that places pacific handcuffs on these societies." Formal peace treaties, backed by the international community, will have "a dynamic of their own, reducing the possibility of an existential conflict. But without such movement toward formal peace, we are headed for the iceberg." He seems to mean something far worse than the current low-level Israeli–Palestinian conflagration.

Barak says that, before July 2000, IDF intelligence gave the Camp David talks less than a 50 percent chance of success. The intelligence chiefs were doubtful that Arafat "would take the decisions necessary to reach a peace agreement." His own feeling at the time was that he "hoped Arafat would rise to the occasion and display something of greatness, like Sadat and Hussein, at the moment of truth. They did not wait for a consensus [among their people], they decided to lead. I told Clinton on the first day [of the summit] that I didn't know whether Arafat had come to make a deal or just to extract as many political concessions as possible before he, Clinton, left office."

Barak dismisses the charges leveled by the Camp David "revisionists" as Palestinian propaganda. The visit to the Temple Mount by then Likud leader Ariel Sharon in September 2000 was not what caused the intifada, he says.

> Sharon's visit, which was coordinated with [Palestinian Authority West Bank security chief] Jibril Rajoub, was directed against me, not the Palestinians, to show that the Likud cared more about Jerusalem than I did. We know, from hard intelligence, that Arafat [after Camp David] intended to unleash a violent confrontation, terrorism. [Sharon's visit and the riots that followed] fell into his hands like an excellent excuse, a pretext.

As agreed, Sharon had made no statement and had refrained from entering the Islamic shrines in the compound in the course of the visit. But rioting broke out nonetheless. The intifada, says Barak, "was preplanned, pre-prepared. I don't mean that Arafat knew that on a certain day in September [it would be unleashed]. [...] It wasn't accurate, like computer engineering. But it was definitely on the level of planning, of a grand plan."

Nor does Barak believe that the IDF's precipitate withdrawal from the Security Zone in Southern Lebanon, in May 2000, set off the intifada. "When I took office [in July 1999] I promised to pull out within a year. And that is what I did." Without doubt, the Palestinians drew inspiration and heart from the Hezbollah's successful guerrilla campaign during 1985–2000, which in the end drove out the IDF, as well as from the spectacle of the sometime slapdash, chaotic pullout at the end of May; they said as much during the first months of the intifada. "But had we not withdrawn when we did, the situation would have been much worse," Barak argues:

> We would have faced a simultaneous struggle on two fronts, in Palestine and in southern Lebanon, and the Hezbollah would have enjoyed international legitimacy in their struggle against a foreign occupier.

The lack of international legitimacy, Barak stresses, following the Israeli pullback to the international frontier, is what has curtailed the Hezbollah's attacks against Israel during the past weeks. [...]

As to the charge raised by the Palestinians, and, in their wake, by Deborah Sontag, and Malley and Agha, that the Palestinians had been dragooned into coming to Camp David "unprepared" and prematurely, Barak is dismissive to the point of contempt. He observes that the Palestinians had had eight years, since 1993, to prepare their positions and fall-back positions, demands and red lines, and a full year since he had been elected to office and made clear his intention to go for a final settlement. By 2002, he said, they were eager to establish a state,

> which is what I and Clinton proposed and offered. And before the summit, there were months of discussions and contacts, in Stockholm, Israel, the Gaza Strip. Would they really have been more "prepared" had the summit been deferred to August, as Arafat later said he had wanted?

One senses that Barak feels on less firm ground when he responds to the "revisionist" charge that it was the continued Israeli settlement in the Occupied Territories, during the year before Camp David and under his premiership, that had so stirred Palestinian passions as to make the intifada inevitable:

> Look, during my premiership we established no new settlements and, in fact, dismantled many illegal, unauthorized ones. Immediately after I took office I promised Arafat: No new settlements—but I also told him that we would continue to honor the previous government's commitments, and contracts in the pipeline, concerning the expansion of existing settlements. The courts would force us to honor existing contracts, I said. But I also offered a substantive argument. I want to reach peace during the next sixteen months. What was now being built would either remain within territory that you, the Palestinians, agree should remain ours—and therefore it shouldn't matter to you—or would be in territory that would soon come under Palestinian sovereignty, and therefore would add to the housing available for returning refugees. So you can't lose.

But Barak concedes that while this sounded logical, there was a psychological dimension here that could not be neutralized by argument: the Palestinians simply saw, on a daily basis, that more and more of "their" land was being plundered and becoming "Israeli." And he agrees that he allowed the expansion of existing settlements in part to mollify the Israeli right, which he needed quiescent as he pushed forward toward peace and, ultimately, a withdrawal from the territories.

Regarding the core of the Israeli-American proposals, the "revisionists" have charged that Israel offered the Palestinians not a continuous state but a collection of "bantustans" or "cantons." "This is one of the most embarrassing lies to have emerged from Camp David," says Barak.

> I ask myself why is he [Arafat] lying. To put it simply, any proposal that offers 92 percent of the West Bank cannot, almost by definition, break up the territory into noncontiguous cantons. The

West Bank and the Gaza Strip are separate, but that cannot be helped [in a peace agreement, they would be joined by a bridge].

But in the West Bank, Barak says, the Palestinians were promised a continuous piece of sovereign territory except for a razor-thin Israeli wedge running from Jerusalem through from Maale Adumim to the Jordan River. Here, Palestinian territorial continuity would have been assured by a tunnel or bridge:

> The Palestinians said that I [and Clinton] presented our proposals as a diktat, take it or leave it. This is a lie. Everything proposed was open to continued negotiations. They could have raised counter-proposals. But they never did.

Barak explains Arafat's "lie" about "bantustans" as stemming from his fear that "when reasonable Palestinian citizens would come to know the real content of Clinton's proposal and map, showing what 92 percent of the West Bank means, they would have said: 'Mr. Chairman, why didn't you take it?'"

In one other important way the "revisionist" articles are misleading: they focused on Camp David (July 2000) while almost completely ignoring the follow-up (and more generous) Clinton proposals (endorsed by Israel) of December 2000 and the Palestinian– Israeli talks at Taba in January 2001. The "revisionists," Barak implies, completely ignored the shift—under the prodding of the intifada—in the Israeli (and American) positions between July and the end of 2000. By December and January, Israel had agreed to Washington's proposal that it withdraw from about 95 percent of the West Bank with substantial territorial compensation for the Palestinians from Israel proper, and that the Arab neighborhoods of Jerusalem would become sovereign Palestinian territory. The Israelis also agreed to an international force at least temporarily controlling the Jordan River line between the West Bank and the Kingdom of Jordan instead of the IDF. (But on the refugee issue, which Barak sees as "existential," Israel had continued to stand firm: "We cannot allow even one refugee back on the basis of the 'right of return,'" says Barak. "And we cannot accept historical responsibility for the creation of the problem.")

Had the Palestinians, even at that late date, agreed, there would have been a peace settlement. But Arafat dragged his feet for a fortnight and then responded to the Clinton proposals with a "Yes, but…" that, with its hundreds of objections, reservations, and qualifications, was tantamount to a resounding "No." Palestinian officials maintain to this day that Arafat said "Yes" to the Clinton proposals of December 23. But Dennis Ross, Clinton's special envoy to the Middle East, in a recent interview […], who was present at the Arafat–Clinton White House meeting on January 2, says that Arafat rejected "every single one of the ideas" presented by Clinton, even Israeli sovereignty over the Wailing Wall in Jerusalem's Old City. And the "Palestinians would have [had] in the West Bank an area that was contiguous. Those who say there were cantons, [that is] completely untrue." At Taba, the Palestinians seemed to soften a little—for the first time they even produced a map seemingly conceding 2 percent of the West Bank. But on the refugees they, too, stuck to their guns, insisting on Israeli acceptance of "the right of return" and on Jerusalem, that they have sole sovereignty over the Temple Mount.

Several "revisionists" also took Barak to task for his "Syria first" strategy: soon after assuming office, he tried to make peace with Syria and only later, after Damascus turned him down, did he turn to the Palestinians. This had severely taxed the Palestinians' goodwill and patience; they felt they were being sidelined. Barak concedes the point, but explains:

> I always supported Syria first. Because they have a [large] conventional army and nonconventional weaponry, chemical and biological, and missiles to deliver them. This represents, under certain conditions, an existential threat. And after Syria comes Lebanon [meaning that peace with Syria would immediately engender a peace treaty with Lebanon]. Moreover, the Syrian problem, with all its difficulties, is simpler to solve than the Palestinian problem. And reaching peace with Syria would greatly limit the Palestinians' ability to widen the conflict. On the other hand, solving the Palestinian problem will not diminish Syria's ability to existentially threaten Israel.

Barak says that this was also Rabin's thinking. But he points out that when he took office, he immediately informed Arafat that he intended to pursue an agreement with Syria and that this would in no way be at the Palestinians' expense. "I arrived on the scene immediately after [Netanyahu's emissary Ronald] Lauder's intensive [secret] talks, which looked very interesting. It was a Syrian initiative that looked very close to a breakthrough. It would have been very irresponsible not to investigate this because of some traditional, ritual order."

The Netanyahu-Lauder initiative, which posited an Israeli withdrawal from the Golan Heights to a line a few kilometers east of the Jordan River and the Sea of Galilee, came to naught because two of Netanyahu's senior ministers, Sharon and Defense Minister Yitzhak Mordechai, objected to the proposed concessions. Barak offered then President Hafiz Assad more, in effect a return to the de facto border of "4 June 1967" along the Jordan River and almost to the shoreline at the northeastern end of the Sea of Galilee. Assad, by then feeble and close to death, rejected the terms, conveying his rejection to President Clinton at the famous meeting in Geneva on March 26, 2000. Barak explains,

Assad wanted Israel to capitulate in advance to all his demands. Only then would he agree to enter into substantive negotiations. I couldn't agree to this. We must continue to live [in the Middle East] afterward [and, had we made the required concessions, would have been seen as weak, inviting depredation].

But Barak believes that Assad's effort, involving a major policy switch, to reach a peace settlement with Israel was genuine and sincere.

Barak appears uncomfortable with the "revisionist" charge that his body language toward Arafat had been unfriendly and that he had, almost consistently during Camp David, avoided meeting the Palestinian leader, and that these had contributed to the summit's failure. Barak:

> I am the Israeli leader who met most with Arafat. He visited Rabin's home only after [the assassinated leader] was buried on Mount Herzl [in Jerusalem]. He [Arafat] visited me in my home in Kochav Yair where my wife made food for him. [Arafat's aide] Abu Mazen and [my wife] Nava swapped memories about Safad, her mother was from Safad, and both their parents were traders. I also met Arafat in friends' homes, in Gaza, in Ramallah.

Barak says that they met "almost every day" in Camp David at mealtimes and had one "two-hour meeting" in Arafat's cottage. He admits that the time had been wasted on small talk—but, in the end, he argues, this is all part of the "gossip," not the real reason for the failure. […] "The right time for a meeting between us was when things were ready for a decision by the leaders…." Barak implies that the negotiations had never matured or even come close to the point where the final decision-making meeting by the leaders was apt and necessary.

Barak believes that since the start of the intifada Israel has had no choice—"and it doesn't matter who is prime minister" (perhaps a jab at his former rival and colleague in the Labor Party, the dovish-sounding Shimon Peres, currently Israel's foreign minister)—but to combat terrorism with military force. The policy of "targeted killings" of terrorist organizers, bomb-makers, and potential attackers began during his premiership and he still believes it is necessary and effective, "though great care must be taken to limit collateral damage.[" ....]

Barak supported Sharon's massive incursion in April—"Operation Defensive Wall"—into the Palestinian cities […] but suggests that he would have done it differently:

> More forcefully and with greater speed, and simultaneously against all the cities, not, as was done, in staggered fashion. And I would argue with the confinement of Arafat to his Ramallah offices. The

present situation, with Arafat eyeball to eyeball with [Israeli] tank gun muzzles but with an insurance policy [i.e., Israel's promise to President Bush not to harm him], is every guerrilla leader's wet dream. But, in general, no responsible government, following the wave of suicide bombings culminating in the Passover massacre [in which twenty-eight Israelis were murdered and about 100 injured in a Netanya hotel while sitting at the seder] could have acted otherwise.

But he believes that the counter-terrorist military effort must be accompanied by a constant reiteration of readiness to renew peace negotiations on the basis of the Camp David formula. He seems to be hinting here that Sharon, while also interested in political dialogue, rejects the Camp David proposals as a basis. Indeed, Sharon said in April that his government will not dismantle any settlements, and will not discuss such a dismantling of settlements, before the scheduled November 2003 general elections. Barak fears that in the absence of political dialogue based on the Camp David–Clinton proposals, the vacuum created will be filled by proposals, from Europe or Saudi Arabia, that are less agreeable to Israel.

Barak seems to hold out no chance of success for Israeli–Palestinian negotiations, should they somehow resume, so long as Arafat and like-minded leaders are at the helm on the Arab side. He seems to think in terms of generations and hesitantly predicts that only "eighty years" after 1948 will the Palestinians be historically ready for a compromise. By then, most of the generation that experienced the catastrophe of 1948 at first hand will have died; there will be "very few 'salmons' around who still want to return to their birthplaces to die." (Barak speaks of a "salmon syndrome" among the Palestinians—and says that Israel, to a degree, was willing to accommodate it, through the family reunion scheme, allowing elderly refugees to return to be with their families before they die.) […] He seems to be saying that revolutionary movements' zealotry and dogmatism die down after the passage of three generations and, in the case of the Palestinians, the disappearance of the generation of the *nakba*, or catastrophe, of 1948 will facilitate compromise.

I asked, "If this is true, then your peace effort vis-à-vis the Palestinians was historically premature and foredoomed?"

Barak: "No, as a responsible leader I had to give it a try."

In the absence of real negotiations, Barak believes that Israel should begin to unilaterally prepare for a pullout from "some 75 percent" of the West Bank and, he implies, all or almost all of the Gaza Strip, back to defensible borders, while allowing a Palestinian state to emerge there. Meanwhile Israel should begin constructing a solid, impermeable fence around the evacuated parts of the West Bank and new housing and settlements inside

Israel proper and in the areas of the West Bank that Israel intends to permanently annex (such as the Etzion Block area, south of Bethlehem) to absorb the settlers who will be moving out of the territories. He says that when the Palestinians will be ready for peace, the fate of the remaining 25 percent of the West Bank can be negotiated.

Barak is extremely troubled by the problem posed by Israel's Arab minority, representing some 20 percent of Israel's total population of some 6.5 million. Their leadership over the past few years has come to identify with Arafat and the PA, and an increasing number of Israeli Arabs, who now commonly refer to themselves as "Palestinian Arabs," oppose Israel's existence and support the Palestinian armed struggle. A growing though still very small number have engaged in terrorism, including one of the past months' suicide bombers. Barak agrees that, in the absence of a peace settlement with the Palestinians, Israel's Arabs constitute an irredentist "time bomb," though he declines to use the phrase. At the start of the intifada Israel's Arabs rioted around the country, blocking major highways with stones and Molotov cocktails. In response, thirteen were killed by Israeli policemen, deepening the chasm between the country's Jewish majority and Arab minority.

The relations between the two have not recovered and the rhetoric of the Israeli Arab leadership has grown steadily more militant. One Israeli Arab Knesset member, Azmi Bishara, is currently on trial for sedition. If the conflict with the Palestinians continues, says Barak, "Israel's Arabs will serve as [the Palestinians'] spearpoint" in the struggle:

> This may necessitate changes in the rules of the democratic game …in order to assure Israel's Jewish character.

He raises the possibility that in a future deal, some areas with large Arab concentrations, such as the "Little Triangle" and Umm al-Fahm, bordering on the West Bank, could be transferred to the emergent Palestinian Arab state, along with their inhabitants:

> But this could only be done by agreement—and I don't recommend that government spokesmen speak of it [openly]. But such an exchange makes demographic sense and is not inconceivable.

[…]

At one point in the interview, Barak pointed to the settlement campaign in heavily populated Palestinian areas, inaugurated by Menachem Begin's Likud-led government in 1977, as the point at which Israel took a major historical wrong turn. But at other times Barak pointed to 1967 as the crucial mistake, when Israel occupied the West Bank and Gaza (and Sinai and the Golan Heights) and, instead of agreeing to immediate withdrawal from all the territories, save East Jerusalem, in exchange for peace, began to settle them. Barak recalled seeing David Ben-Gurion, Israel's founder and first prime minister (1948–1953 and 1955– 1963), on television in June 1967 arguing for the immediate withdrawal from all the territories occupied in the Six- Day War in exchange for peace, save for East Jerusalem.

> Many of us—me included—thought that he was suffering from [mental] weakness or perhaps a subconscious jealousy of his successor [Levi Eshkol, who had presided over the unprecedented victory and conquests]. Today one understands that he simply saw more clearly and farther than the leadership at that time.

How does Barak see the Middle East in a hundred years' time? Would it contain a Jewish state? Unlike Arafat, Barak believes it will, "and it will be strong and prosperous. I really think this. Our connection to the Land of Israelis is not like the Crusaders'. […] Israel fits into the zeitgeist of our era. It is true that there are demographic threats to its existence. That is why a separation from the Palestinians is a compelling imperative. Without such a separation [into two states] there is no future for the Zionist dream."

Interview with Yasser Arafat (2002)
PUBLIC BROADCASTING SERVICE (PBS)

The film starts with the funeral of Yitzhak Rabin. I wanted to ask you, how did you feel that day, looking at this funeral of Rabin, your comment.

My partner. It was very, very difficult and painful for me personally, and for all the Palestinians, and many of his friends all over the world. ...

Then we had the big moment, when we had the impressions that the peace process was going very well. We had the withdrawal from the Palestinian towns, Ramallah, Jenin, Nablus. And [in the film] we show you in Bethlehem on the roof of the church. And you made a very beautiful speech. Do you remember how you felt at that moment?

Look, I am sorry to say that they are escalating their military activities again and stole our cities and towns and villages and camps against all our people. You can see by yourself the humiliation which our people are facing on all the checkpoints. And not only that, they had destroyed many of our establishments....

I am speaking about now. But this gave us how the whole attitude ... had changed while we're — I will give you one example. When my partner Rabin was obliged to close Gaza Strip, when we started Gaza, Jericho first, I was astonished when he sent me money. I told him, "Why you are sending this money for?" He said, "For job creations. Otherwise, these laborers will be against you and against me."

And this is a very important point to which I want to stress upon, that the most important thing for the Palestinians and for the Israelis and for the whole Middle East area is to return back to protect the peace of the brave which I had signed with my partner, Rabin, and to live together as we had decided, in our state and in their state. And Jerusalem to be the capital of two states, as Rome is the capital of two states. The capital of His Holiness, the Pope, and the capital of the Italian government; Brussels, the capital of the European Union, and the capital of Belgium.

Mr. President, let's go back to the election of Netanyahu. Before, everybody told you, "Help Peres, because Netanyahu will be a catastrophe." And after the election, the same people came back to you and told you Netanyahu was pragmatic, you can make business with him, you can make an agreement with him. You were worried about the election of Netanyahu. You believed this guy can make an agreement with you?

The Likud Party, not to forget that they were — the majority of them, not all of them, but a big section of them — were against the Oslo agreement.

How did you feel when you shake the hand of Netanyahu for the first time in Erez [in September 1996]?

Not to forget, not only shaking hand. We had many agreements with him; Hebron agreement, as an example. We had completed it with him. The Wye River agreement.

... The Hebron Agreement was very important because it was signed by the Israeli right, for you?

It was very important, no doubt. And also, we went to Wye River and we signed another agreement under the supervision of President Clinton. And not Netanyahu alone; Netanyahu and Sharon. They were together.

Sharon refused to shake your hand?

Never mind. But in the end, both of us accepted the agreement.

You said to several people in Wye River at the beginning, "This man, Netanyahu, will not implement the agreement." You believed it?

The most important thing [was] that a part of Wye River agreement had been implemented, not all of it. This is one of the most important facts.

When you heard that the Israelis were packing their luggage and going — remember, they made this exercise in Wye River. You believed they would stay or they would go?
[...]
No. It was clear and obvious that they want to squeeze me and to squeeze the Palestinian delegation. But the time had passed and they returned back to the negotiations under the supervision of President Clinton and the full participation of the American administration in every details.

Though it was in the last night and moment where you got up from the table, and President Clinton also, and left Netanyahu alone because Netanyahu told you, "Give me Jabali [the Palestinian police chief] or make Jabali disappear, Ghazi Jabali." Do you remember that?

Yes, I remember. But it had been solved, the most important thing and we have this agreement of Wye River. And we cannot forget the effort which had been done by His Excellency President Clinton.
[...]
When Barak was elected, you were very hopeful. ...

Not to forget that we were trying to do all our best with him. I will give you many examples. We went many times [to] the White House, have discussions in the White House. And after that in Camp David, and after that, in Paris. You remember? And after that, in Sharm el-Sheik, and after that, […] in Taba.

Can we go over these examples? It's the first meeting in Erez. You came out in a very bad mood because Barak told you he does not want to make the third redeployment. Remember that?

He delayed it, no doubt. And we then implemented the second agreement of Wye River.

At first, you didn't want to go straight to the final-status talks. Why?
[…]
No, no, no. I was insisting to follow-up all the details in the interim period and the final status.

After Sharm el-Sheik, everything started again to go. But then the Israelis stopped negotiating because they started negotiations with Syrians. You were worried that this might delay the Palestinian track?

No…. The agreement with the Jordanians, as an example, didn't stop us. Any agreement with any Arab countries will not stop us. But he used it to lose time. But, definitely, we are not against it…. We had agreed upon from the beginning in Madrid Conference [is] the implementation of [U.N. resolutions] 242 and 338 and 425 for Lebanon. And we were not alone there. Many Arab countries had attended the conference. Many international high leaders had attended this conference. And everywhere there was a very important attitude to push the peace in the Middle East.

You started two tracks [of] negotiations with the Israelis: [Israeli negotiator] Oded Eran with [Palestinian negotiator] Yasser Abed Rabbo and also Shlomo Ben-Ami with Abu Ala; and also the Stockholm track. One was important. One was less important. What did you achieve in Stockholm?

Many of our understanding had been discussed in Stockholm. But, sorry to say that this had been stopped…. I will tell you one example on Barak. You remember after our very important discussion which we had made it under the supervision of [France's] President Chirac in his office?

In October?

In his office. And with the participation of the Americans, headed by [U.S. Secretary of State Madeleine] Albright, and with the participation of Mr. Kofi Annan [of the U.N.], and the Israeli and Palestinian delegations. And we have very important discussions. And we arrive to very important platform, which we continued. After that, the details of it, until half past four in the early morning.

And we had agreed upon that we will go to Sharm el-Sheik to sign it with the presence of President [Hosni] Mubarak [of Egypt]. The Palestinian delegation arrived there. The American delegation arrived there. But we stayed there more than six hours. At last, they received a note that he [Barak] will not come.
[...]
Let's go back if I may before Camp David. Albright came to Ramallah. You had two or three meetings with her. The Israelis wanted a summit. What did you tell her? You told Albright you are not ready. You think they are not ready for a summit.

... Simply, I told her, before this, we are in need of the accurate preparation so that not to make any confrontation. And this had been used not only between us and them; this had been used in all negotiations all over the world. The preparation is very important for any negotiations.

You remember, the Americans and the Vietnamese continued about five years in Paris until they arrived to the final agreement. And she had accepted, with me, for the preparation. But we had been surprised when they started directly.

Before that, the Israelis didn't give what they promised — the three villages, Abu Dis?

Oh, not only Abu Dis, this had been even accepted by the Knesset. And in spite of that, Barak didn't implement it. This had been discussed in the Knesset. And the Knesset accepted it. And in spite of that, he didn't—

The Americans told us that you saw Clinton the beginning of June, before Albright was here. And you told him that, because you didn't get the villages, because Barak didn't implement, you didn't believe anymore in Barak. You lost confidence.

Actually, the most important thing, for your information, many activities had been agreed upon with Barak, as I had mentioned to you the agreements which had been done in the presence of President Chirac, and in the presence of Albright, and in the presence of Kofi Annan. He escaped and didn't accept to attach us in Sharm el-Sheik, while he had agreed upon with the Egyptians to sign it there in the presence of President Mubarak.

And not only that, when he gave permission for Sharon to visit the Haram as-Sharif [the Muslim name for the Temple Mount], I went to his house.... I told him not to forget that your hero, Moshe Dayan, when he occupied

411

East Jerusalem, some fanatic figures raised the Israeli flag. He came by himself and took it over and gave a very important order to prevent these visits. I mentioned it to him [Barak]. "Why you aren't doing it now?" Why he didn't visit Sharm el-Sheik when he was the second man after Netanyahu? Why he didn't visit it when he was a hero of the Israeli army after the '73 war. … Why he didn't do it during Begin? Why he didn't do it when Shamir was there? Why he is doing it now and you accepting? And you had to put in your consideration that this visit will make a big story, not only with us, [but] with all the Muslims all over the world.

He didn't listen to me. And the visit had been done. And the army, the next day, also followed up. And some of them had been, our players had been killed, 19 had been killed. And more than 70 had been wounded.

If I may go back to Camp David? You couldn't accept the proposals in Camp David. Why?

Because there are some points which, if you are in my place, you will not accept it. I will give you the control … of the airspace. … And also, I accepted for them … early-warning station. … Early warning station, three, with the participation of the Americans and the participation of the Palestinians.

But they are insisting to have, also, big — not only military, big military bases with all armaments in Jordan Valley under their control. What's the meaning of that? And also, the borders between us and the Egyptians. Who can accept that? I told him, OK. Why not to be like Sinai, international forces headed by the Americans? Or like Syria, Golan Heights, or like south Lebanon, also international forces? Why only the Palestinians will accept your conditions? And not only that, some very critical points for our sacred Christian and Muslim holy places. As an example, the control of the Armenian quarter with all its churches. Who can accept this? I told him, "You have to remember" — in front of Clinton — "I cannot betray my brothers to the Armenians." And also, they have to control the area in which Santa Maria church is there. … And they didn't reply.

Also, they have the sovereignty beyond the Harem as-Sharif. And we have the control over the Harem as-Sharif. Who can accept this? For this, if you remember, when I returned, I asked for immediate meeting for the Committee of Jerusalem of the Islamic Conference. And for the first time, I asked His Majesty, the King of Morocco, King Mohammed VI, that special representatives for all the mosques and for all the churches in Jerusalem will participate with us. And he accepted.

And after that, they had participated also in the Islamic Conference, took place in Qatar. And the meeting of the Foreign Affairs, Islamic Foreign— And recently, in the meeting also of Jerusalem which took place recently,

412

one week ago in Morocco, and I offered to them what had been offered to me. And this had been refused.

They say the Jewish temple is under the Harem.

I am giving you one example. During all this period of occupation this part, they had excavated everywhere. And no one single stone from the temple had been found.... But I had accepted, officially, the Jewish Quarter and the passage to the Jewish Quarter, and the passage to the Wailing Wall. And this is the holy places which had been given to them by the British Committee ...

The parameters of Clinton in December, 94, 96 percent of the West Bank. In Jerusalem–

Ninety?

Between 94 and 96.

No, no, no. They were speaking about, in the beginning, in Camp David, they were speaking about 88. Then we stressed pushing, pushing. They said, "OK, 92." I told them, "I accept." But to mix what? In value and in the area, not only to give me desert in the same value. No. The value and the size.

Then we get in December the parameters of Clinton. ... You had the phone call from Clinton. And you go to the United States, to Washington, to talk with Clinton about his parameters. ... What did you tell Clinton? Did you accept his parameters?

I had received a letter from him and I replied him in details about what can be done from our side which would be accepted by the Arab nation and by the Christians and by the Muslims. Because these sacred holy places are not only for the Palestinians; it is for all Muslims and for all Christians. And I asked some explanation of what had been written in his letter about it.

You wrote about the refugees.

Yes.

What was your position on the refugees?

I told him, this had been accepted from the beginning by the Americans, by the whole world. It was the resolution of the United Nations, General Assembly 194. And I told him, in spite of that, "Let us start as we had agreed upon with the displaced refugees of '67." Specially, there is a committee of the four: Jordanian, Egyptians, Israelis, Palestinians. And we were working with it.

But it had been stopped. I told him, "Let us return back to what had been agreed upon, to push for the displaced. And the refugees, let us start directly with our refugees in Lebanon because they are suffering. They haven't the ability to work according to the laws." In 60 or 71 or 68 posts, they haven't the ability to work.

And also to solve the Lebanese problem, President Clinton asked me how many [refugees] they are. I told him, when I was there, they were 480,000. But I had heard now they are about 301,000. But it had been informed to me later upon, they are about 220,000. And, in general, this had been discussed, but not settled completely.

They could have come back to Israel?

Yes, according to [U.N. Resolution] 194.

But the Israelis said this makes for them a big demographic problem.

He had mentioned this. I gave him what had been written. It is still in my pocket, what has been written in Ha'aretz, that more than 62 percent of those who came from the Soviet Union areas, which are now different countries, 62 percent are not Jews. The majority of them, more than 90 percent of them, are Christians and around 10 percent of them are Muslims. ... Then how [does] the Christian or the Muslim who is coming from Soviet Union have the right to go to our homes? And the Palestinian Christians and the Palestinian Muslims haven't the right to their homes?

At one of your talks with President Clinton, you told him, "If I have the state, with Jerusalem as a capital, with the Haram, the demographic problem of Israel will be solved." Remember that?

Yes. Do you know how many Palestinians are there in East Jerusalem? More than 270,000. They will return back as Palestinians. But the most important difference is not about when I discuss about the displaced and of Lebanon; it was not the main issue. The main issue was the holy sacred places and the area.

This must be solved first?

Yes.

Then you can find solution for the others?

We have to find the solutions for them together. This is what had been discussed in details with President Clinton, with Barak, who was very … excited. And he stayed three days in his villa not accepting to meet anybody or to leave it. And, in spite of that, we continue with the rest of his delegation.

Then after Camp David, there were secret negotiations between Gilead Sher and Saeb Erekat.

Until now, I didn't stop any contacts with the Israelis. Security meeting yesterday, … with the American participation, with the speaker of the Knesset and the speaker of our … council, … and Abu Ala, recently it was in Paris. The first meeting was with Prime Minister Jospin, and the second meeting was President Chirac. And also Sharon, and also permanent contacts with his son, Omri. And also, the talks is still going. Recently, yesterday, in New York, between Abu Ala and Mr. Shimon Peres.

Two more questions for the history, which is very important because you are part of this history. Why couldn't you stop the intifada the way you succeeded, you with the Israelis, in stopping the problem of '96 after the tunnel? After the tunnel, you succeeded.

I told you I succeeded. And I succeeded many times. But they started the field of the thorns, military plan. And the … "hell plan." And now, the rolling plan, escalating, escalating, escalating. What the meaning of their tanks some meters far of here? Thirty meters or 25 meters? Approximately.

How do you deal with these tanks here?

It is not the first time.... You remember the big battle which they had mentioned that the tanks had advanced 10 meters in the … area, while the length of the tank is 13.6 meters with its gun? The most important thing [is] not myself. The most important thing [is] how to let our people feel that they are living not under occupation, not under humiliation, not under poverty. Do you know that they had reserved all of our precious taxes, which is more now than $1 billion? It is our taxes. And they had kicked out 132 laborers working in Israel, now for 16 months.

And not only that, they had destroyed many of our factories. Not only that, they had uprooted approximate 50 percent of our olive trees.... What is the meaning of that? How many thousands of families have lost their income? And also, they are bulldozing the farms everywhere and destroying the houses everywhere, and the infrastructures, including some hospitals, and some schools, and including some holy places.

What are you negotiating with Abu Mazen with Sharon? What are the negotiations advancing?

415

This is a new start. We hope that … it is not only for his visit to Washington. We hope that it will continue. We didn't stop any contacts. You remember we sent a delegation when Yossi Bellin [a leader of the Israeli left] accept to participate with us in the negotiations under the supervision of President Mbeki. President Mbeki is also representing, as he is the president of South Africa and also the [non-aligned movement].

You believe you could have made an agreement in Taba? Or it was too late because of the elections?

It was — No. But we had arrived. If there was a time — We had agreed upon that, after the election, we will continue. And we were hoping that within maximum six weeks, we will finish it.

The new American administration is not helpful?

Not to forget, he is a new president and he is in need of time, as any new president. And the same time, what had happened in last September was a disaster for the whole world. And, for your information, as you remember, I was the first to send my condolences for him and we declared our donation. Again, it's this dramatic, what had been done from these fanatic groups.

On one hand, you have Abu Mazen, Abu Ala talking to Sharon. On the other hand Sharon [says] he regrets not having killed you. [Ed. Note: In an interview with an Israeli newspaper published in February 2002, Sharon reportedly said that he regretted not having killed Arafat in Lebanon in 1982. When Israel invaded Lebanon that year, Sharon was Israel's defense minister.]

As I have mentioned to you, I am not looking for myself. I am looking to find something concrete for our people to live freely in their independent state as all other people all over the world. You know that we are now essentially the only people who are under occupation? Who can accept this? And where? In the Terra Santa? Can this be accepted for the whole world?

The peace, in the land of peace, in the Terra Santa, is not only for the Palestinians. It's for the Palestinians, for the Israelis, for the whole Middle East area, for the whole world.

Address to the Palestinian Central Council Concerning PLO-Israel Negotiations (2000)
Mahmoud Abbas

We went to Camp David carrying our well-known positions, positions that were adopted by several of our legislative bodies. The positions we adopted are, in our point of view, the minimum that we can accept. They are positions that are based on United Nations Resolutions 242, 338 and 194. They are based on agreements signed between the Israelis and us, they are based on Israeli documents concerning the 1948 nakba (catastrophe) and the forced expulsion of Palestinians from their homes, and they are based on UN Security Council resolutions dealing with Jerusalem and Jewish settlements.

We stressed to the Americans that for a summit at such a level to succeed it must be prepared for and prepared for well. We cautioned that because of the lack of preparation the prospect of its failure is high. The Americans agreed that a summit that this level needed preparation and they agreed with us that time must be given for preparations. We agreed with Secretary Albright that would have two weeks to prepare. We were later surprised by a telephone call from President Clinton inviting us to a summit that was to be held within a week.

We were faced with two choices, to go knowing very well that the summit will fail and that the Americans may blame us for its failure, or to refuse to attend and be accused of sabotaging the peace process. So we took the first choice.

We went to Camp David not to say NO to the Americans and the world Zionists. We went to say YES to a lasting and just peace. To say YES to international legitimacy and when we failed to reach that, we said NO. Again, we did not go to Camp David to not reach an agreement or to reject points for the sake of rejection so that it would be said that we stood strong. We went to reach an agreement; we dealt with every issue with a strong desire to reach an agreement that would end this conflict that has lasted the entire century.

To assist us in this effort we brought to Camp David eight young, bright legal advisors and maps experts who, on request were ready to present documentation and advise which they had been preparing for such occasions. We feel very proud of these fine, energetic lawyers in who we have great trust and are very happy to have on our side.

Through the Americans the Israelis presented their vision on Jerusalem. They envisioned a Jerusalem where some villages around the city would come under Palestinian sovereignty. Neighborhoods outsides the walled the Old City would remain under Israeli sovereignty with the Palestinians having some type of self-rule. The quarters inside the Old City would be divided. The Jewish and Armenian Quarters will be sliced away from the Muslim and Christian Quarters, which will be ruled under a special system. In their attempt to sell this to the Palestinians, they threw in sovereign headquarters for the Palestinian President inside the Old City.

Israel refused to accept moral and legal responsibility for the plight of the refugees. Israel only showed willingness to allow several hundreds to return every year on humanitarian causes. As for compensation, Israel said any fund that will be established would also compensate Jews who left Arab countries.

On borders, Israel demanded control over the Palestinian borders with Jordan and Egypt. Israel also asked to control 15-20 percent of the Jordan River and a sector of the Jordan Valley. Israel also wants to annex 10.5 percent of the West Bank to absorb the settlements. But all West Bank settlements do not sit on more than 1.8 percent.

Israel says it needs 3-5 army bases for monitoring and intervention purposes. Israel also demands that the air space be completely under its control. It asked for a presence at all international entry points to monitor persons, products and weapons. As for the state of Palestine, it must be a demilitarized state.

If we were to summarize the positions of both, the Palestinians and Israel it would be as follows:

Security: The Israelis want control over a part of the Jordan Valley for a maximum 12-year period. That would keep the current military bases and settlements there untouched. The Israelis asked for six bases in the West Bank and three military monitoring areas. Israel demanded it have a presence at the international crossings (to monitor those entering and leaving the area). Israel also demanded the entire air space and electro-magnetic space to be under its control. The Palestinians said they would accept an international force or a multi-national force on the borders. What we won't accept is an Israeli presence, in any form on Palestinian territory.

Borders: Israel wants to carve out 15-20 percent of the Jordan River and Dead Sea border and to annex 10.5 percent of West Bank Land. The Palestinians rejected any carving of borders. Light border amendments and an exchange of lands equal in quantity and quality that does not exceed 2 percent is acceptable.

Refugees: The Israelis agree to contribute to an international fund to be established for the compensation of Palestinian refugees. However, Israel wants the fund to compensate Jews who came to the country from Arab states. Israel agrees to the return of hundreds of refugees under a family reunification plan or on humanitarian cases. The Palestinians want Israel to take moral and legal responsibility for the refugee crisis. UN Resolution 194 must be accepted so that all refuges are guaranteed the right of return, and by return we mean to Israel. Refugees who chose to return and those who do not must be compensated. The Absentee Treasurer created in Israel in 1949 to administer refugee money is responsible for the compensation. Host countries should also be compensated. An international fund could be established but that fund would only be responsible for part of the compensation. We refuse to mix the issue of Palestinian refugees with Jews immigrants.

Jerusalem: Jerusalem, occupied in 1967, is the city within the walls that includes the Haram al-Sharif, the Holy Sepulcher, and the Muslim, Christian, and Armenian quarters. It is also the city outside the walls, with neighborhoods like Sheikh Jarrah. Musrara, Damascus Gate, Saleh Eldin Street and others.

The Israeli position divides Jerusalem into several sections and gave each section a different legal status.

1-THE WALLED CITY: The Haram al-Sharif: Israel to have sovereignty and the Palestinians will be given guardianship The Muslim, Christian, and Armenian Quarters: to remain under Israeli sovereignty A Palestinian presidential complex inside the Muslim Quarter that will be given sovereign power.

2- OUTSIDE THE WALLED CITY: sovereignty remains with Israel with municipal functions over these neighborhoods to be carried out by the municipality of Abu Dis. With the exception of two villages, villages surrounding Jerusalem, most of which are area B, will come under Palestinian sovereignty. Israel will have a road that runs through the villages linking them to areas under their sovereignty. The Palestinians will only have one road linking them to the Haram.

THE PALESTINIAN POSITION: All of east Jerusalem should be returned to Palestinian sovereignty. The Jewish Quarter and Western Wall should be placed under Israeli authority not Israeli sovereignty. An open city and cooperation on municipal services.

This is our summary of the results of the Camp David negotiations. But the Israelis had a different understanding that was revealed in subsequent local meetings. Israel wants 10.5 percent of the West Bank and rejects the idea of a land exchange. Israel wants 5 monitoring posts with three roads leading to them. Three Israeli administered early warning systems with a Palestinian liaison officer present at the stations. Israeli control over 8

percent of the Jordan Valley for a 12-15 year period. No right of return to Israel. Israel may accept the return of 10,000 Palestinians over a 15-year period under a family reunification plan. Air space to come under Palestinian sovereignty but will be controlled by Israel through guiding systems. An end to the conflict. A demilitarized Palestinian state
Jerusalem: The same position as in Camp David.

This is the Israeli position as told to us ten days ago. It shows that there are fundamental differences in the positions and that the gaps between the two sides remain very wide.

A declaration of an independent state is a right our people can execute at any time. In 1988, when we declared our state in exile, more than 100 countries recognized that declaration. But recognition of a state on the ground is different that that of a state in exile. And though many nations have said they are in favor of an independent state many hinted of the necessity to declare once prepared on the ground and or after an agreement between the sides is reached. And so we must now stop and think.

Committing to a date has its positive side, it shows that dates and promise are respected and kept, but such a commitment must be based on good preparations not emotional reactions.

We need to carefully study the Israeli response to the declaration. If Israel were to respond negatively, we need to study what measures she will take and how will we respond to these measures.

The Israel-PLO Accord Is Dead (1995)
Amos Perlmutter

THE FAILURE OF OSLO

The Declaration of Principles signed by Israel and the Palestine Liberation Organization (PLO) at the White House on September 13, 1993, is for all intents and purposes dead. The repeated atrocities by Palestinian suicide bombers, including the grisly death of 20 Israeli soldiers in Beit Lid and the murder of 22 civilians in downtown Tel Aviv, serve only as dramatic illustrations of just how ineffectual the so-called Oslo accord has become. As it stands now, the whole Oslo process is unraveling, jolted by a wave of fundamentalist terrorism that deepens the prevailing pessimism among even dovish Israelis.

The original treaty—not to mention the high hopes behind it—has been so altered by both the PLO and Israel as to have become barely recognizable. Israeli plans for limited but continued West Bank settlement caused an international outcry after the expansion of Efrat, a settlement near Bethlehem. Israel has so far refused to withdraw the Israeli Defense Forces from the West Bank's major cities before the Palestinian elections for their autonomy authority, which should have been held months ago. Fifty-nine Israelis have been killed in the past nine months by suicide bombers from Islamic Jihad and Hamas, the Islamic resistance movement. For their part, many Palestinians bitterly complain that Israel has not given up anything and call the IDF's withdrawal from the turbulent Gaza Strip a blessing for Israel. They excoriate Israel's Labor-led government for refusing even to clear the handful of militant settlers out of downtown Hebron after one American-born fanatic massacred 29 worshipers in Hebron's Ibrahimi mosque. The Declaration of Principles has increasingly become a document that reflects neither reality nor probability.

This is not what the handful of Israeli and Palestinian negotiators had in mind when they secretly hammered out the accord in Norway. The pact called for an IDF withdrawal from Gaza and the West Bank town of Jericho, which would then fall under the civilian control of a Palestinian autonomy government headed by PLO Chairman Yasir Arafat. All Israeli settlements would remain intact, and the new Palestinian police would work together with the IDF to guarantee internal security and fight Hamas. In nine months, the IDF would redeploy throughout the remainder of the West Bank to prepare for Palestinian elections and the extension of autonomy to the entire West Bank. The most contentious issues— settlements, refugees, borders, Palestinian statehood, security, and Jerusalem—would be deferred until another set of talks, scheduled to begin in the third year of autonomy. The Declaration of Principles itself was accompanied by mutual recognition between Israel and the PLO, once the bitterest of enemies, and by a commitment from Arafat to end terrorism and remove calls for Israel's destruction from the PLO charter. Taken together, the Oslo accords represented a bold bid for a lasting reconciliation between Palestinians and Israelis, and promised to usher in a new era of regional peace.

The debate over Oslo's provisions, however, has divided the Palestinian nationalist movement. Those Palestinians who support Oslo do not trust Israel. On the other hand, the rejectionist front believes that this is no time for diplomacy, and that the military struggle with Israel must be continued until all of Palestine—including pre-1967 Israel—is liberated. Arafat, once the symbol of Palestinian nationalism, has become tarnished goods.

The Oslo accord is also being met with increased doubt and hostility in Israel. Immediately after the dramatic White House handshake, Israel was ready to return most of the territories it took during the Six Day War of 1967 in exchange for real peace. But the Israeli public is now deeply suspicious of the aims of the Palestinian nationalist movement. The only person who still seriously believes in Oslo is its adoptive father, Israeli Foreign Minister Shimon Peres. Polls demonstrate the growing strength of the rightist Likud, which promises a harsh anti-terror campaign and rejects territorial compromise. […]

EYELESS IN GAZA

Oslo's flaws have many roots, including weak and inconsistent PLO leadership, conflicting strategies, and faulty negotiating techniques. First, the continued weakening of the peace process is partly owed to the absence of authoritative and authentic Palestinian leadership. Arafat has isolated himself in his office in Gaza City and has scarcely set foot in Jericho since his arrival in the self-rule zones. He long ago lost the support of Palestinian intellectuals in the territories. Today, however, just about everyone is opposed to him in one way or another. In his recent book, even Abu Mazen, the chief PLO negotiator in Oslo, bitterly criticizes Arafat. Worse, a generation of radical Palestinian nationalists and Muslim fundamentalists has emerged in the occupied territories to violently oppose Oslo, demanding the destruction of Israel proper and an end to land-for-peace diplomacy.

Second, Israel and the PLO approached the negotiations from completely different angles. Coming to terms with the Palestinians was the basis for Rabin's winning 1992 election platform, but Labor designed its solutions and drew up its maps in a political and intellectual vacuum. The problem was that the Israeli negotiators designed the parameters of the process around Israeli needs and demands. On timing, Israel wanted the process to evolve in stages; on space, the final decisions on boundaries, settlements, and Jerusalem would be made later; and on the prickly issue of Palestinian

422

sovereignty—well, that would be dealt with last, because the whole issue was a serious electoral danger to Rabin.

The Palestinian agenda, on the other hand, was almost exactly the opposite. On timing, Arafat pushed a sooner-rather-than-later agenda. Arafat has repeatedly proclaimed that every inch of territory evacuated by the Zionist enemy will become Palestinian. On space, the Palestinians would not surrender an inch of territory, which meant no border rectifications, no settlers, and, above all, no united Israeli-dominated Jerusalem. As for statehood, the end of the process would see total Palestinian sovereignty over all of the West Bank and Gaza, including East Jerusalem. The differences between the two sides have actually widened since Oslo, given Arafat's ever more provocative and reckless pronouncements since 1993.

The critical Israeli errors stem from ignoring basic rules of negotiating. Frustrated by the grindingly slow talks with the Palestinian negotiating team in Washington, Peres leaped at the Norway back channel to the PLO. In 1993, however, the leadership of the intifada was more vibrant than the all-but-moribund PLO, which had lost most of its funding from the Persian Gulf states and much of its international credibility by backing Iraq's 1990 invasion of Kuwait. Nevertheless, after the West Bankers' negotiating team in Washington presented what seemed to Rabin unacceptable demands regarding settlements and Jerusalem, Rabin chose to accept Arafat's offer to postpone all of the thorniest issues until later. Arafat's less threatening offer enticed Rabin to catapult the fading apparatchiks and anachronistic terrorists of the PLO in Tunis back into the foreground.

The entire exercise led to some fundamental errors. Rabin accepted the Oslo concept after Peres and other senior Foreign Ministry diplomats persuaded themselves, and then a reluctant Rabin, that Arafat could deliver. The Rabin government acted despite extensive Israeli intelligence showing that Arafat was patently weak, did not represent the new Palestinian generation in the territories, and was in fact commonly despised by the intifada's veterans.

Moreover, the divisive permanent status issues—Jerusalem, borders, and settlements—have repeatedly come to the forefront. The interim phase also represents an ongoing invitation for Oslo's foes—extremist Israeli settlers and Palestinian radicals—to try to derail the process, as bloodily as necessary. The trust between the two old adversaries that the interim stage was supposed to build is nowhere in sight. If anything, what confidence existed has been eroded by the interim phase.

The process could collapse completely over the issue of Jerusalem, which is just what Oslo was designed to avert. Israelis will not accept a divided Jerusalem as their capital, nor will the Palestinians accept anything less than the establishment of East Jerusalem as their capital and Palestinian—

not Jordanian—control over the city's Islamic shrines. Both sides continue to thrust Jerusalem onto the agenda, which could make the holy city the straw that breaks the camel's back. Faisal al-Husseini, one of the West Bank leaders of Arafat's al-Fatah movement, is clandestinely establishing a Palestinian foreign office and other departments in Jerusalem. The city's mayor, however, is Ehud Olmert, an opportunistic young Likud leader determined to turn East Jerusalem into an Arab ghetto amid Jewish Jerusalemites. For his part, Arafat time and again speaks of Jerusalem as the capital of Palestine, while Rabin repeatedly assures Israelis that Jerusalem will remain Israel's eternal, indivisible capital.

HAMAS RULES

In essence, Rabin ended up negotiating with the weakest of all parties among politically active Palestinians: Arafat's Tunis-based PLO. This approach may have appealed to a former general like Rabin, but it was exactly wrong politically. The Palestinians in the West Bank and Gaza, as public opinion polls have demonstrated, reject the Oslo process; about 70 percent of the Palestinians either do not trust or totally reject the Oslo process. [...]

In contrast to the weak and discredited PLO, Islamic radicalism and the intifada have created a powerful Palestinian-Arab movement that currently represents Palestinian nationalism [....] Now that hopes for an independent Palestinian state have been rekindled, the hard-liners are unwilling to accept even an Israeli return to its 1967 borders. Both the intifada radicals and Hamas, as well as their ruthless terrorist wings, continue to speak of Jerusalem as their capital and pamphleteer on the ouster of Jews from historic Palestine. At the point in history where the Palestinians finally might have fulfilled their dream of statehood, an aggressive movement, fueled by small but fanatical militant cells and violently opposed to Oslo, has emerged to challenge the fading Arafat and his PLO.

[...] In effect, Rabin anointed Arafat as the Palestinian people's leader at exactly the point when he was failing to be that leader. Arafat and Fatah now have no alternative to Oslo, which has come to define the PLO's center. In February, the PLO Executive Committee resolved to continue implementing Oslo, despite strong outside opposition.

The reinvigorated and radicalized post-Oslo Palestinian nationalist movement, as heir to the intifada, brawls and sprawls and thrashes about with great fury, but lacks significant leaders. The leadership of the movement is talented and well-educated (both in Western secular venues and through traditional Islamic schooling) but lacks standout personalities or anyone as charismatic as the once-legendary Arafat. They represent all the secular classes—lawyers, academics, doctors, journalists, engineers, and members of the media—and are also prominent among the traditional

424

classes of religious preachers and teachers. Ideologically, the new leaders call incessantly for total Arab domination of Palestine and for the continuation of the armed struggle against Israel. They advocate ousting settlers by the use of terror, seek to make Jerusalem the Palestinian capital, and reject any form of democratic government. Their maximalist aspirations carry with them a patriotic, religiously flavored euphoria that can translate into a willingness to die for the cause.

Moreover, Hamas controls the education system in Gaza from kindergarten through high school, as well as the religious schools, mosques, and the Islamic universities in Gaza and Jerusalem. Thee Islamists' social services amount to Gaza's welfare state, providing for the people even as Arafat pampers his security services and bureaucrats. In the West Bank, Hamas could probably gain 30 to 40 percent of the vote for the self-government administration. This is a prospect that chills Arafat enough that he, like the Israeli government, would like to postpone the elections as long as possible.

Like it or not, however, Hamas and the intifada generation represent maximalist but popular aspirations of the Palestinian people. [...]

APRES NOUS, LA DELUGE
[...]
The 1996 [Israeli] elections could also produce a refutation of Rabin's Oslo policy and the emergence of Netanyahu of the Likud as prime minister. The Likud accepts the concept of autonomy, as adopted by former Israeli Prime Minister Menachem Begin in the 1979 Camp David peace treaty with Egypt. Netanyahu says he favors continuing negotiations with the Palestinians, but about autonomy, not Palestinian statehood. Obviously that will not be accepted by Arafat, which would make it the final blow to the Oslo process. The consequences for Israel would be dire. The intifada could restart with even greater vigor than before, accompanied by more terrorism and continuous attacks on the settlements. The likely Likud defense minister, Ariel Sharon, would handle the revolt in the most brutal way, which would return the Jewish state to its pre-Labor status as an international pariah state [....]

A Likud victory would also strengthen the Palestinian radicals. Arafat, an accommodator who leads by consensus, will move in their direction and become the international spokesman of Palestinian rage, something he did very well before Oslo. His propaganda machinery should not be underestimated. He could well return to the old Tunis posture of confrontation.
[...]

Oslo is Dead, Long Live the Peace Process (2023)
Marwan Bishara

The Israeli-Palestinian peace agreement, reached in Oslo and signed in Washington, DC in 1993, aimed to achieve peace within five years. However, after failing and resurging several times, the process ultimately led to a more violent occupation and culminated in a more entrenched system of apartheid. [...]

Five primary factors were behind the failure of the Oslo process.

First and foremost, Oslo failed because it yielded a "hegemonic peace" that privileged the Israeli occupiers, discriminated against the occupied Palestinians, and paved the way for more instability and violence. It allowed Israeli leaders to dictate the peace timetables, deadlines and overall implementation of its interim agreements to the detriment of Palestinian security and independence. From the outset, the Palestine Liberation Organization (PLO) was forced to recognise Israel as a fully-fledged state occupying 78 percent of historic Palestine. Israel, however, refused to recognise the Palestinian state on the remaining 22 percent of the land and merely acknowledged the PLO as the sole representative of the Palestinian people. While Israel said it accepted Washington's "vision" of a two-state solution, on the eve of the 2003 United States war on Iraq, it did so with numerous debilitating reservations and only to help keep up the appearance of pax Americana.

Second, the process failed because the US was not a fair or credible sponsor for it. Washington has been for decades Israel's foremost patron, and remains so today. At times it did play the role of "good cop" against Israel's "bad cop" in negotiations, but its goal has always been to ensure a compromise was reached between the US and Israel, not necessarily between Israelis and Palestinians. The latter had to accept any outcome graciously or get reprimanded.

Third, it failed because Israel's illegal settlements continued to expand unabated after 1993. On occasion, the US registered its displeasure, but Israel merely rolled its eyes and continued building. By 2003, the number of settlers had doubled, and by 2023 it had more than quadrupled. [...] This has "necessitated" greater Israeli military presence in the occupied territories, and led to greater incitement, friction and violence.

Fourth, under the guise of Oslo, Israel connected its many illegal settlements through bypass roads, development projects and security networks, rendering its occupation irreversible and a two-state solution practically unworkable. In the process, it created two legal systems in the occupied territories: a superior one for the Jewish settlers and an inferior one for the indigenous Palestinians. Within 10 years of the signing of the first Oslo Accord, Israel had already divided the Palestinian territories into 202 separate cantons, diminishing the Palestinians' access to employment, health and education.

Fifth, Israel refused to engage in any meaningful discussion about the five important "permanent status" issues: settlements that have kept on expanding; refugees who remained stranded away from their homes; borders that were de facto erased; security that Israel refused to relinquish; and the future of Jerusalem, which Israel annexed.

Long story short, after seven long years of inconsequential interim agreements, unhindered settlement expansion and violent repression followed by the failure of a hastily convened summit at Camp David, the Oslo process came to a dead end and led to a second Palestinian Intifada in 2000.

But there seems to be no letting go of the Oslo addiction. Despite all its follies, fantasies and failures, Israeli, Palestinian, American, Arab and all the other leaders with a stake in the game are holding on to Oslo's phantom. Why?

Well, the Israelis have every reason to not let go of a process that has served only to strengthen the Jewish state and legitimise its illegal colonial activities while weakening and dividing the Palestinians. For example, from 1995 to 1999, Israel's gross domestic product (GDP) rose by almost 50 percent, while its population rose by only 10 percent. [...]

Palestinian President Mahmoud Abbas and his cohorts in the Palestinian Authority are also reluctant to give Oslo up because the disastrous peace process is their very raison d'être. Unelected, unpopular, and illegitimate, they've used the Oslo process to gain international support and hold onto power.

As for the US, continuing to sponsor the peace process is a way of ensuring lasting influence over the region and maintaining the charade of pax Americana.

For Arab autocrats, the charade of the peace process absolves them from doing anything for Palestine, which remains the most important regional cause on the Arab street. It also provides them with a pretext to normalise relations with Israel in return for greater American support.
[...]

The Middle East: No More Treaties (1996)
Richard Haass

BETWEEN PEACE AND WAR

It has been a remarkable five years in the Middle East. Beginning in October 1991, when Arabs and Israelis first met face to face in Madrid, it went on to include two Israeli-PLO accords, an Israeli-Jordanian peace treaty, two grand regional economic conferences, the repeal by the U.N. General Assembly of the 1975 resolution equating Zionism with racism, serious peace negotiations between Israel and Syria, and decisions by several Arab states and many other governments around the world to establish diplomatic relations with Israel. [...]

That era, if five years can be said to qualify as an era, is over. [...]

FROM MADRID TO OSLO

What made the era of treaties and other agreements possible, above all, was the end of the Cold War and the trauma of the Persian Gulf War. Arab governments lost their Soviet benefactor, and Iraq, the center of secular Arab radicalism, was thrashed on the battlefield. Meanwhile, most Arab governments came to accept Israel as a permanent, if not welcome, reality. Palestinians faced two additional problems: the PLO lost its Arab financial backers in the Persian Gulf region when it made the mistake of backing Saddam Hussein in his bid to conquer Kuwait, and the Palestinian uprising, or intifada, was losing steam.
[...]
[T]he 1993 Oslo agreement, which gave Palestinians effective control of Gaza and Jericho, and its 1995 successor, which extended Palestinian authority to the major cities of the West Bank. Neither Yitzhak Shamir nor Yitzhak Rabin had been able to strike a deal with Palestinian "insiders," who proved both unwilling and unable to negotiate in the absence of explicit participation by the PLO. What made Oslo possible was Israeli willingness to accept the PLO as a negotiating partner, along with the PLO's willingness to accept a step-by-step process with no guarantee of where it would end -- and a shared perception that both sides would have to take matters into their own hands, given that the United States no longer appeared to be an active and forceful mediator.

The first Oslo agreement, signed on the South Lawn of the White House in September 1993, also yielded a formal peace treaty between Israel and Jordan as an unexpected dividend. What prompted the October 1994 treaty was a change in Jordan's political calculus: it would lose all influence over the future of Jerusalem and the Palestinians unless it entered into a peace treaty with Israel. In addition, Yasir Arafat's and the PLO's open willingness to come to terms with Israel made such a step for Jordan's monarch less risky.

[…] Israel and the PLO began "final status" talks just before Israel's recent election. […] The issues of final status are the most difficult: Jerusalem, Palestinian control of territory and statehood, the right of millions of Palestinian refugees to return home, and water. These issues would be difficult and perhaps impossible to negotiate even if all sides had the will to do so. […]

Today, there is neither the will nor the ability to conclude an Israeli-Palestinian final status agreement -- that is, peace. The PLO leadership fears it will lose support and, in the end, legitimacy, if it is seen to compromise important political goals. There is the additional fear that Hamas and other Islamic radical groups would gain at the expense of the PLO if anything were done to weaken the Palestinian claim to Jerusalem. It is often safer to espouse dreams that are whole than to accept inevitably incomplete realities. For its part, the new Likud government of Benjamin Netanyahu campaigned on a platform, subsequently enshrined in government guidelines, that opposes a Palestinian state, the right of return for Palestinian refugees, and any dilution of exclusive Israeli sovereignty over a united Jerusalem. For Israelis, too, it is politically less risky to live with an imperfect status quo than to contemplate controversial alternatives. […]
Agreements that have already been reached further reduce the prospects for treaties. There is less urgency now than before. The status quo is better than it was five years ago and is in many ways tolerable -- possibly more tolerable than the risks of compromise. Similarly, the passage of time has hurt the prospects for peace. The psychological impact of the demise of the Soviet Union and the outcome of the Persian Gulf War has waned. So, too, has the stature of the United States. […]

There is an obvious danger in all this. The current situation in the Middle East -- armed deterrence between Israel and Syria, together with a patchwork quilt of Palestinian population centers, Jewish settlements, and Israeli-controlled land -- is neither stable nor sustainable. […] [A]utonomy must continue to grow in both breadth and depth, or the current modus vivendi will collapse.

The collapse would be costly. Palestinians would suffer a loss of autonomy, increased economic hardship, and a future of open-ended occupation. But it would be no better for Israelis, who, in addition to facing the expense of occupation and increased terror, would forfeit a chance to gain economic access to the region. Fewer resources would be available to focus on the emerging and ultimately more worrisome threats to Israel's security posed by Iran and Iraq. A radicalization of Palestinian and Israeli politics alike would result; any chance for peace would be postponed if not destroyed. [...] But it would be wrong to equate poor or even negligible prospects for agreements with an end either to the peace process or to peace itself. At a minimum, history shows that, thanks to deterrence, it is possible to maintain "no war, no peace" for extended periods. There is a level or plateau between a solution and peace on the one hand and collapse and conflict on the other. Establishing such a plateau and making it stable ought to be the purpose of the next era of diplomacy.

DIPLOMACY FOR A NEW ERA

It may help to think of Middle East peace over the past five years as a stock whose price has soared: a correction is inevitable. The goal of American diplomacy ought to be to minimize the size of the correction and avoid giving back all the hard-earned gains. Succeeding in this effort will demand accepting the notion that diplomacy can still achieve progress in the absence of treaties and other formal agreements. Formal pacts are just one tool of diplomacy, not a synonym for it. Three alternatives stand out: unilateralism, confidence-building measures, and signaling. All three can and should be used, to avert the worst and even to bring about some gain.

Israel and the Palestinians should focus on a mixture of unilateralism and confidence-building measures to implement and supplement existing agreements. Palestinians currently control day-to-day life in Gaza and all the principal West Bank cities except Hebron. Israel and the Palestinians have joint responsibility for roughly 450 villages and towns that comprise one-fourth of the occupied territories. Israel still has sole control of the remaining two-thirds, an area that includes the bulk of its settlements, military installations, and so-called state lands. In October 1995, the second Oslo agreement called for further Israeli withdrawals from this last territorial zone at regular intervals. Accomplishing just that would be an important confidence-building measure. [...]

For its part, the Palestinian leadership must do everything possible to deal with the security threat to Israel. No one can expect 100 percent success -- Netanyahu is wrong when he says that "peace means the absence of violence" -- but Israel has every right to expect 100 percent effort. Palestinian leaders should resist calls for a new intifada. Here Israel can help its own case. Israel is more likely to get what it wants in the way of the antiterrorist cooperation in a context of increasing rather than contracting autonomy. Such a context would make sustaining popular support for tough measures while diminishing the appeal of radicals easier for the Palestinian authority.
[...]

430

ARAB PEACE INITIATIVE

Statement Presenting the Arab Peace Initiative (2002)
Abdullah bin Abdulaziz al-Saud

In spite of all that has happened—and what still may happen—the primary
issue in the heart and mind of every person in our Arab and Islamic nation
is the restoration of legitimate rights in Palestine, Syria and Lebanon.

These rights, which are bound to the cherished occupied lands, cannot be
erased from memory, nor will the passage of time diminish their
importance. No right is lost that has an advocate behind it. Those who
follow the intifada of our brothers in Palestine, which has the support of all
Arabs and Muslims, realize that steadfastness will not wither, that bravery
will not retreat, and that justice will prevail.

Every person in Palestine—young and old—understands that the way to
the liberation of his land and soil is either through steadfastness and
struggle, or a just and comprehensive peace. It is therefore incumbent on
the Israeli government to realize and understand this and deal with it by
embarking on a new path, and that is the path of peace.

My dear brethren: the noble people of the Arab and Islamic nation: when
the Arabs opted for peace as a strategic choice, they did not do so out of
crippling desperation or debilitating weakness, and Israel is mistaken if it
believes that it can impose an unjust peace by force.

We embarked upon the peace process with open eyes and clear minds, and
we have not accepted then, nor will we accept now, that this process is
transformed into a non-binding obligation imposed by one party on the
other. Peace is a free and voluntary choice made by two equal parties, and
it cannot survive if it is based on oppression and humiliation.

The peace process is based on a clear principle: land for peace. This
principle is accepted by the international community as a whole, and is
embodied in U.N. Security Council resolutions 242 and 338, and was
adopted by the Madrid conference in 1991. It was confirmed by the
resolutions of the European Community and other regional organizations,
and re-emphasized once more this month, by U.N. Security Council
resolution 1397.

My esteemed brethren: it is clear in our minds, and in the minds of our
brethren in Palestine, Syria and Lebanon, that the only acceptable objective
of the peace process is the full Israeli withdrawal from all the occupied
Arab territories, the establishment of an independent Palestinian state with

al-Quds al-Shareef (East Jerusalem) as its capital, and the return of refugees.

Without moving towards this objective, the peace process is an exercise in futility and a play on words and a squandering of time which perpetuates the cycle of violence. The return to the negotiating table is a meaningless endeavor if the negotiations do not produce tangible and positive results, as has been the case for the past 10 years.

Allow me at this point to directly address the Israeli people, to say to them that the use of violence, for more than 50 years, has only resulted in more violence and destruction, and that the Israeli people are as far as they have ever been from security and peace, notwithstanding military superiority and despite efforts to subdue and oppress.

Peace emanates from the heart and mind, and not from the barrel of a cannon, or the exploding warhead of a missile. The time has come for Israel to put its trust in peace after it has gambled on war for decades without success. Israel, and the world, must understand that peace and the retention of the occupied Arab territories are incompatible and impossible to reconcile or achieve.

I would further say to the Israeli people that if their government abandons the policy of force and oppression and embraces true peace, we will not hesitate to accept the right of the Israeli people to live in security with the people of the region.

We believe in fighting in self-defense and to deter aggression. But we also believe in peace when it is based on justice and equity, and when it brings an end to conflict. Only within the context of true peace can normal relations flourish between the people of the region and allow the region to pursue development rather than war and destruction.

Dear brethren, in light of the above, and in this place with you and amongst you, and with your backing and that of the Almighty, I propose that the Arab summit put forward a clear and unanimous initiative addressed to the United Nations Security Council based on two basic issues: normal relations and security for Israel in exchange for full withdrawal from all occupied Arab territories, recognition of an independent Palestinian state with al-Quds al-Shareef (East Jerusalem) as its capital, and the return of refugees. At the same time, I appeal to all friendly countries throughout the world to support this noble humanitarian proposal which seeks to remove the danger of destructive wars and the establishment of peace for all the inhabitants of the region, without exception.
[...]

432

The Arab Peace Initiative: Why Now? (2008)
Gabrielle Rifkind

Setting the Scene

When the API was originally conceived, the thinking within the Arab world was that there were insufficient incentives for Israel to make the concessions that Palestinians could accept and survive. The realities were that the Palestinians had nothing in the way of incentives to offer the Israelis. At the time, the US had neither the political will nor the ability to bridge the gap. It was in this context that 22 Arab countries concluded that a durable peace would have to be comprehensive — involving all Arab states which held the key to Israel's security rather than only the Palestinians.

There was a growing realisation in some circles that the Israeli-Palestinian conflict could not be sustainably resolved without reference to its regional context. The approach needed to be as inclusive as possible. It was recognised that many key actors across the region had a stake in the conflict and this would entail including them in a robust framework for regional stability. This offered the opportunity to re-conceptualise the conflict not as an obstacle to peace and development in the Middle East but as a catalyst for transforming relations within the region.

The launch of the API six years ago and its re-affirmation in 2007 and 2008 has ignited little public interest in Israel. The API has not had much impact in the wider international arena either, despite holding out the promise of full peace and normal relations with Israel in exchange for Israel's withdrawal from the territories it captured in 1967. On the face of it, the API reflects a dramatic shift in the Arab position from the famous 'three noes' of Khartoum in September 1967 to a complete acceptance of Israel into the Middle East.

The API arguably provides Israel with what it has been seeking since its inception. It has been said that such a proposal, had it been put forward several years ago, would have had Israelis dancing in the streets. Why, then, has it had them barely stirring in their seats? It has also been said that public opinion in Israel towards the API ranges between those who have never heard of it and those who do not believe a word of it. [...]

Tragic Timing for the Launch of the API in 2002

The peace process is characterised by missed opportunities, broken promises and optimistic moments shattered by violence and a hardening of attitudes. An opportunity now presents itself in the reinvigoration of the API. When the Initiative was first presented in 2002, the Arab world took a step in which it formally acknowledged the right of the Israeli people to

From OXFORD RESEARCH GROUP. Reprinted with permission from author.

433

live in peace and security alongside other people in the region. It was a proactive effort on behalf of 22 Arab nations to solve the conflict by not only addressing Arab needs but the needs of the Israelis as well.

The timing of the presentation of what was originally dubbed the Saudi Peace Initiative was a tragedy. On 27 March 2002, on the eve of the opening session of the Beirut Arab Summit during which the API would be launched, a suicide bomber blew himself up in the dining room of a seaside hotel in Israel killing around 30 people. It was the worst timing possible for those who were trying to end Israel's occupation through peaceful means. The elation felt by those who had worked so hard to create the API, a major historic achievement, was short-lived as the plans to start promoting the Initiative to the Israelis and the western publics were aborted almost immediately. Operation 'Defensive Shield', the largest military operation in the West Bank since 1967, was launched by the Israelis on 29th March, only one day after the Initiative was unveiled by the Arab League. The level of the conflict was so intense that it was impossible even to hear the offer placed on the table.
[…]

What Does the API Offer?

The API is "a proactive effort on behalf of 22 Arab nations to solve the conflict by not only addressing Arab needs but the needs of the Israelis." It claims to emanate "from the conviction of the Arab countries that a military solution to the conflict will not achieve peace or provide security for the parties" and requests Israel to "reconsider its policies and declare that a just peace is its strategic option as well." It calls upon Israel to affirm:

- Full Israeli withdrawal from all the territories occupied since 1967, including the Syrian Golan Heights, to the 4 June 1967 lines as well as the remaining occupied Lebanese territories in the south of Lebanon.
- Achievement of a just solution to the Palestinian refugee problem to be agreed upon in accordance with UN General Assembly Resolution 194.
- The acceptance of the establishment of a sovereign independent Palestinian state on the Palestinian territories occupied since 4 June 1967 in the West Bank and Gaza Strip, with East Jerusalem as its capital.

From Arab countries, it asks affirmation of the following:

- Consider the Arab-Israeli conflict ended, and enter into a peace agreement with Israel and provide security for all the states of the region.

- Establish normal relations with Israel in the context of this comprehensive peace.

The API is a collective offer to end the conflict with security guarantees for all states in the region, including Israel. This is significant because, for the first time, Israel is assured that its security will be guaranteed not only by its immediate neighbours but by all Arab states. Also, for the first time, the Arab world has committed itself to an agreed-upon solution to the refugee problem, addressing Israel's concern that Arabs would demand that four million refugees be sent to Israel and thus obliterate Israel's Jewish identity.

Some have nevertheless argued that the Arab League does not propose much more than what it would have done any way if Israel had reached a resolution of its conflicts with the Palestinians and Syria. The argument continues that the API was presented as if to say that if Israel acts positively according to the API, the Arab League would press groups such as Hamas and Hizballah towards the same principles. Indeed, senior Arab participants at the Oxford roundtable have confirmed that the Arab League worked to elicit public commitment from Hamas' leadership that it would not depart from the Arab consensus — with the understanding that regarding Israel this consensus is the API. Moreover, Hamas' Prime Minister Haniyeh accepted the Arab League's invitation to its 2007 Riyadh meeting, reaffirming the Arab commitment to the API. Marwan Muasher, a lead drafter of the API, possibly alluded to this when he wrote that in the context of a comprehensive agreement with all the Arab world the role of Hamas and Hezbollah will become marginal.
[…]

THE SECOND INTIFADA

Arafat and the Second Intifada (2013)
Elliott Abrams

The PLO and Palestinian Authority (PA) have long denied that Arafat was behind the violence, instead calling the second intifada a spontaneous uprising. This claim was endorsed in the so-called Mitchell report, the "Sharm el-Sheikh Fact-Finding Committee" of 2001: "We have no basis on which to conclude that there was a deliberate plan by the PA to initiate a campaign of violence at the first opportunity...."

That story began to fall apart for good in 2010, when Hamas leader and co-founder Mahmoud al-Zahar stated that "President Arafat instructed Hamas to carry out a number of military operations in the heart of the Jewish state after he felt that his negotiations with the Israeli government then had failed."

Now there is an additional source: Arafat's widow, Suha. In an interview in December on Dubai TV she said this:

> Yasser Arafat had made a decision to launch the Intifada. Immediately after the failure of the Camp David [negotiations], I met him in Paris upon his return, in July 2001 [sic]. Camp David has failed, and he said to me: "You should remain in Paris." I asked him why, and he said: "Because I am going to start an Intifada. They want me to betray the Palestinian cause. They want me to give up on our principles, and I will not do so. I do not want Zahwa's friends in the future to say that Yasser Arafat abandoned the Palestinian cause and principles. I might be martyred, but I shall bequeath our historical heritage to Zahwa [Arafat's daughter] and to the children of Palestine.

The debate over Arafat's role should be over. Many Palestinian leaders have always understood it to be a phony, in any event. I recall a conversation about five years ago with one PA official, whom I asked whether he shared the fears expressed then in the press about a new intifada. No, he replied, because such things do not start spontaneously. The last one started when the Palestinian leadership decided to start it, but the current leadership is against violence--so there will be no intifada.

Let's hope that remains true. But meanwhile, there should be no doubt about the origin of the second intifada: it happened when Yasir Arafat decided that more violence was useful to him. That case is closed.

The New Palestinian Revolt (2001)
Chris Hedges

The new intifada is reverberating throughout the Middle East, rattling the dusty and inefficient Arab regimes in Cairo and Damascus, emboldening extremist Arab states such as Iraq, and weakening the power of Yasir Arafat's Palestinian Authority. Most important, it foreshadows a day of reckoning for Israel when it will have to decide between the swift establishment of a sovereign Palestinian state including in some manner East Jerusalem, and a prolonged, debilitating conflict.
[…]
In Palestinian eyes, the peace process is not providing more autonomy from Israel and will not do so until the Jewish settlements are gone. For Palestinians, the Israeli occupation will not have ended until they control their own roads, borders, and economy. An enduring peace requires sovereignty over East Jerusalem and the al-Aqsa Mosque, sacred land that was in Muslim hands from the seventh century until 1967. An acceptable settlement must also provide either an agreement for the return of Palestinian refugees who fled Israel or compensation for the property and homes that they left behind. Unless these changes occur, the Palestinians appear set to go on fighting, especially after the failure of Oslo.
[…]
And just as the first intifada was directed not only against the Israelis but also against the Palestinian bourgeoisie—the shopkeepers and business owners in Gaza City—this new intifada has twin targets. Armed militias, increasingly beyond the control of Arafat's Fatah movement, are once again collecting "war taxes" from frightened shopkeepers. But this time, Arafat's own organization is targeted along with the Palestinian middle class. In the days following Israel's helicopter attacks, Palestinian mobs burned shops and hotels selling alcohol—owned by Arafat's corrupt and despised Palestinian Authority officials.
[…]
Those who speak for the Palestinians today are found in mosques, not the air-conditioned offices of Arafat's seaside compound. The secular heroes of the old intifada have been replaced by bearded Islamic warriors who trigger powerful suicide bombs and embrace an asceticism that stands in stark contrast to Fatah's hedonism and corruption.
[…]
HARDENED OBJECTIVES

The economic squeeze is taking its biggest toll on Arafat. The first intifada swept away the cautious and passive Palestinian leadership that had accommodated, or at least not challenged, the Israeli authorities after 1967. Arafat's Fatah took control. Now, under threat from the new wave of violence, Arafat is working hard to make sure that this revolt does not

Used with permission of Foreign Affairs, from FOREIGN AFFAIRS, Vol. 80, No. 1 (Jan. 1, 2001); permission conveyed through Copyright Clearance Center, Inc.

replace him with Hamas activists. Hamas has nonetheless become venerated as the vanguard in the struggle against the Jewish state.

Arafat's stature began to slip after he signed the 1993 Oslo accords, which were wrenchingly painful for the Palestinians. By signing, Arafat recognized the legitimacy of Israel, formally ending Palestinian claims to Israeli land that had been home to many of his people for generations. He gave up nearly 30 percent of the territory that the original 1948 U.N. partition plan had defined as Palestinian, leaving his bifurcated state with little more than 20 percent of what was once the British Mandate of Palestine.

Many Palestinians believe that by signing the Oslo accords, Arafat deprived them of a capital in Jerusalem, a return of refugees, and an end to the expansion of the Jewish settlements. Indeed, over the past decade of peace negotiations, the number of Israeli settlers has nearly doubled. The 1993 accords stipulated a partial Israeli withdrawal from the occupied territories, after which a five-year transitional period of negotiations toward a final-status agreement should begin. Palestinians were angered when Oslo-mandated deadlines for the Israeli withdrawal passed unfulfilled; the Israelis said that Arafat was not living up to the terms of the agreement. Thus, it began to appear to most Palestinians that Israel would withhold even the promised 20 percent. Indeed, Israel still occupies more than 80 percent of Gaza and the West Bank.

This despair, coupled with declining incomes, created a more radical, militant population. Compromise obviously did not work. After signing Oslo, Arafat was excoriated in the Arab press in ways that might have stunned even his right-wing critics in Israel. He had become the Arab world's Marshal Philippe Petain, the leader of France's collaborationist Vichy government during World War II. As time went by and Prime Minister Binyamin Netanyahu's Likud government let the peace process stagnate, Arafat's stock continued to plummet. As Hamas carried out suicide bombings in Israel and Hezbollah attacked Israeli forces in southern Lebanon—eventually forcing Israel to withdraw—it seemed that Arafat's secular Fatah movement was fading into the twilight. His decision to jail Hamas activists did not improve his popularity.

Palestinian men, filled with rage and economic despair, grew impatient with Fatah's conciliation, as well as its nepotism and corruption, and embraced the harsher methods and rhetoric of the Islamists. After all, they argued, such tactics worked for Hezbollah in southern Lebanon.

When Barak came to power in June 1998, a lot of time—perhaps too much—had been lost. The suicide bombings and lengthy closures had seen Israeli companies replace Palestinian workers with Filipinos, Chinese, and Romanians. The real per capita GDP for the West Bank and Gaza declined

438

36 percent between 1992 and 1996, due to falling incomes and the explosive population growth. In the 1980s, unemployment averaged just 5 percent; that figure is now well above 40 percent and is still climbing. Israel's per capita income is $17,000, whereas the Palestinians' is less than $2,000.

[...]

It was a beleaguered Arafat who arrived at Camp David in July 2000. He had cut a deal with the Israelis in Oslo that had not, in his eyes, been fulfilled. He had been stranded, he felt, by the heir of assassinated Prime Minister Yitzhak Rabin. And at Camp David, he was faced with an all-or-nothing Israeli peace proposal that would have left the Palestinians with a mutated statelet in five chunks, all subject to Israeli fiat. In pushing for a final-status agreement, Barak and President Clinton had ignored Arab, European, and Palestinian warnings that such a move could destroy the peace process.

Arafat saw himself as vulnerable on the issues of Jerusalem, the refugees' right of return, and the disposition of occupied land. So he walked away. If he wanted to remain the Palestinians' leader, it was his only choice. The mood in the territories had reached a feverish pitch, and Arafat correctly read the political landscape when others did not. He was cheered at home and throughout the Arab world for his decision.

[...]

The Palestinian position has now hardened, leaving little chance for a return to the Oslo process. Palestinian leaders talk only of U.N. Security Council Resolution 242, which calls on Israel to withdraw from the territory it occupied following the Six-Day War and for all the states in the region to recognize and respect each other's borders.

"This intifada has changed the basis of negotiations," Marwan Barghouthi, a leader of Arafat's Fatah faction in the West Bank, said recently in a speech at Bir Zeit University. "We will not return to the negotiations and become hostages to the Israelis and the Americans without having any action on the ground. The aim of this intifada is clear: the return of refugees, ending occupation, gaining independence and sovereignty, and establishing Palestinian sovereignty over Jerusalem."

THE NEW WARRIORS

[...]

These ragtag fighters, members of a Palestinian militia known as the *tanzim* ("organization" in Arabic), will largely determine whether the battles with Israel continue. The police of the Palestinian Authority, whether out of sympathy or impotence, often watch passively as *tanzim* members fire toward Israeli positions in spots such as the Nezarim junction in Gaza or at Ramallah in the West Bank, often provoking a withering and deadly Israeli response.

[...]

Palestinians have acquired large numbers of automatic weapons over the past couple of years. During the first intifada it was rare to find guns in the hands of protesters. It was even rarer to see them used against Israelis. But the streets of Gaza are now awash with a wide variety of guns, some of which look like they belong in a museum. Israel has permitted the ruling Palestinian Authority to obtain some light weapons, but many more have been smuggled in from Jordan, Egypt, and even Israel, militia leaders say.

Tanzim commanders say they will mount a protracted guerrilla war against Israel, a war of attrition modeled on Hezbollah's efforts in southern Lebanon. They point out that many of the inhabitants of the Israeli settlements around Ramallah, Gilo, and three settlements in Gaza— Nezarim, Kefar Darom, and Morag—have fled, despite the deployment of Israeli tanks and armored personnel carriers intended to protect them.

"We know that the Israelis have powerful weapons," said Abu Abed, who spent five years in Israeli jails, "but we are willing to take losses they would never accept. Hezbollah, with little more than light weapons, drove Israel out of Lebanon. We, with nothing more than rocks, forced them to return part of our land. With our guns we are ready to liberate all of Palestine and our capital, holy Jerusalem."

AN UNWINNABLE WAR?

Rather than defeating the Palestinians, Israel may be slowly defeating itself. The inclusive, liberal dreams of Israel's Zionist founders have mutated into an occupation from which the Israelis find it difficult to extract themselves. Unlike the wars of 1967 and 1973, Israel today is fighting not against armies but against a subject people. Palestinians, and increasingly Israeli Arabs as well, are the enemy.

Comparison can be found in the war over Algerian independence in the late 1950s and early 1960s. The French fought valiantly and brutally in Algeria. They won the military contest but by the end could no longer justify to themselves or the outside world that it was worth being there. They had few allies when it was over. The political, emotional, and financial costs for France were enormous.
[…]

RAPHAËL KRAFFT: The bus attack on last Wednesday was maybe the start of a new era for the Palestinian resistance to concentrate its attacks into the Occupied Territories. It has been interpreted by Israelis as an attack inside Israel, which is a negation of occupation. How will — will the resistance keep on going this way, including Hamas and Islamic Jihad?

MARWAN BARGHOUTI: Yeah, from the first day, our strategy in Fatah and the Tanzim, to concentrate our struggle in the Occupied Territories. And we call everybody to prevent any kind of attacks inside Israel. We do believe it's preferable to continue the struggle in the Occupied Territories and to targeting the Israeli occupation, including the settlers. I think this is the strategy. And I hope that Hamas and Islamic Jihad and all the groups will concentrate their struggle against the occupation here. But when the Israelis are continue in their massacres, assassinations, destroying the Palestinian headquarters and etc., I think this was the result that lead Hamas and the others to attack the Israelis inside Israel.

RAPHAËL KRAFFT: So, you believe that in the near future Hamas and Islamic Jihad are going to strike again inside Israel?

MARWAN BARGHOUTI: No, I hope they will not do that. I hope that they will concentrate the struggle and the attacks against the Israeli occupation inside the Occupied Territories. But I think it's very difficult to keep this strategy when the Israelis are continue to bombing the Palestinian cities under the Palestinian Authority control, because the Israelis should respect our areas. And if they are enter in everywhere, bomb everywhere, killing the civilians, children, women and etc., then I think this will lead for more Palestinian reactions. And when this criminal prime minister in Israel, Sharon, when he decided to assassinate or liquidate any leader, he decided how many Israelis will be killed in the same time.

RAPHAËL KRAFFT: Since the start of the Intifada, the Palestinian resistance has shown a sort of policy of restraint in its fight during the Bethlehem occupation by not using heavier weapon, like RPG-7. Do you believe that it is time for the Palestinian resistance to go forward and escalate?

MARWAN BARGHOUTI: You know that we should not go to fight the Israelis in their power points. We should prevent their power, and we should always find a way how to fight them, how to defeat them in another places. And I think this should be the main strategy for the Palestinian people. And I think that always the resistance will continue. There is an occupation. It will continue. Never they can achieve security by tanks, —

RAPHAËL KRAFFT: What is the —

MARWAN BARGHOUTI: — by force, by assassinations, by closure, by these things. So, I do believe that the resistance will continue. The Palestinians are patient enough, and they know very well that this is long fighting. It's not for one month or two months or one year or two years. It will take long time. So they should be patient and keep their power.

RAPHAËL KRAFFT: What is the state of the relationship between Fatah, DFLP and the Islamic Jihad and Hamas on the field?

MARWAN BARGHOUTI: Yeah, we are working together, and we have coordination and cooperation in the political fields in the activities of the Intifada. There is not any kind of coordination in military activities. Some cases, individual cases, local relations or coordination in some places, in all over the West Bank and Gaza. But in central level, there is not any kind of this coordination in military activities, because it's very difficult. It's impossible. It's impossible for anybody to do that.

RAPHAËL KRAFFT: This new tactic Israel is putting forward by doing lightning incursions, arresting people, killing people in arms, does it weaken how — in which way does it weaken the resistance? In which way are you — is the resistance touched by that?

MARWAN BARGHOUTI: Yeah, yeah, yeah. Of course, it has its effect on the people and on the Palestinian people, on the Palestinian Intifada and the resistance, and on the Palestinians generally. You know that during every day there, every night, the Israelis bomb by aircrafts, by Apache, by tanks, and they arrest a lot of people, killing, assassinations, demolish houses, cut or uprooting trees, and the closure and etc. And the tanks are not for more than 200 meters from Mr. Arafat's office. And they are trying to pressure. But I do believe that this will not [break] the Palestinian Intifada or Palestinian resistance. The resistance will continue. And the Israelis, by this way, criminal way, they will lead the Palestinians for strong and more reactions against the Israelis. We are trying to give chance for the international efforts to be succeeded to stop this comprehensive war. But all the international and European, regional Arab efforts to stop Sharon were failed 'til now.

RAPHAËL KRAFFT: The attack on the bus killed settlers. They're illegal here in the Occupied Territories. But still they are civilians, and international law forbids —

MARWAN BARGHOUTI: No, no.

RAPHAËL KRAFFT: — the killing of civilians.

MARWAN BARGHOUTI: No, they are not civilians. The settlers are not civilians. They are part of the Israeli occupation. They are armed people. They have — their existence here is illegal. This is the point, not why you are fighting against them. The question: Why are they here? Why they confiscate the land and build their settlements by force, by tanks, by weapons, by killing the people? So, I think it's — to targeting the settlers, it's legitimate. And I think who are responsible of these victims, between if they are women or children, are the criminal Sharon. And these people should be in Tel Aviv, in Israel. Why they are here? What they are doing here? They are occupation.

RAPHAËL KRAFFT: You know that the mediatic war is much more favorable to Israel, and the bus attack of Wednesday night has been announced by all the media as like an attack against civilian in Israel. Don't you —

MARWAN BARGHOUTI: It's not. No.

RAPHAËL KRAFFT: I know. I know it's not. I know it's not. But taking this in consideration, don't you believe that targets should be focused on Israeli soldiers?

MARWAN BARGHOUTI: No, no, no. I think everything is legitimate against the Israelis in every centimeter in the Occupied Territories in '67 borders. It has to be very clear. All the Israelis are legal targets in the Occupied Territories, all the Israelis, because they are not hosteds. They are not coming as hosteds for the Palestinians.

RAPHAËL KRAFFT: "Invited."

MARWAN BARGHOUTI: They are not invited. They are coming by tanks, as settlers, as criminals, and their existence here illegal. And we have the right to fight against the occupation, including the settlers. The settlers are armed people. All of them are armed people. And a lot of Palestinians were killed by the Israeli settlers. And you cannot distinguish between the Israeli soldiers and the settlers. They are the same. They are in the same settlement. It became like military camps and etc. And the soldiers are living there. In the day, they are working. And at night, they are working as soldiers and etc.

And I think, of course, we don't like to see any children, any women to be killed, any people. And I would like to reach for peace without any killing, without this fighting, without these victims, without the bloodshed from the two sides. And we worked well during seven years ago to enhance, to encourage the peace between the two sides. I was one of the prominent people who lead the Palestinian groups for [inaudible] Israelis, intellectuals, the professors, academics, members of Knesset and parliamentarians, politicians, everybody. We were trying.

But happened during seven years? They toyed the Palestinians. They're playing on the Palestinians. They laugh at the Palestinian people. They doubled the number of the settlement [inaudible] in Jerusalem, keeping with our —

RAPHAËL KRAFFT: I know of that. What do —

MARWAN BARGHOUTI: They did every, every this terror. And it should be very, very clear. The Israeli occupation are terror act. They are — this is the top of the terrorism in the world. There is no terrorism more than the occupation.

RAPHAËL KRAFFT: What do you think about Mr. Yasser Arafat's reaction condemning the bus attack last Wednesday?

MARWAN BARGHOUTI: I can understand. I can understand the position of Mr. Arafat. And I don't accept. I think it's legal to attack all the Israelis here in the West Bank and Gaza, including East Jerusalem. And I hope that everybody will prevent any attacks inside Israel, because the borders of the Palestinian state, it's the '67 borders. And if the Israelis killing everybody, in Ramallah, in everywhere, why should we respect them?

RAPHAËL KRAFFT: Well, do you — how would I say? What is your relationship today with Mr. Arafat? The resistance in the West Bank is quite weak at the moment.

MARWAN BARGHOUTI: Yeah, good, good, good. Good relation. And I met with him every night, every day. And I think we should support him and his decisions, to help him. The situation are very critical, and we are in very critical time in these days. They are trying to kill him. They are trying to destroy him, by political destroying and his authority and etc. So, we call all the Palestinian political factions to give support for Mr. Arafat.

RAPHAËL KRAFFT: Don't you think that this game Yasser Arafat has been playing, or been being forced to play, in between the international public opinion, in between the Israeli public opinion and the Palestinian public opinion, by weak — by condemning such attacks, has weakened the resistance?

MARWAN BARGHOUTI: I think it has its effects, of course. But we can understand how much the situation are very critical. And we know how much the situation is very difficult, but I do believe we will pass these difficulties, like we did during 15 months. And the Israelis will discover that they are, by these massacres, doing in Salfit, in Beit Hanoun, in everywhere in the West Bank and Gaza, there will be high price for their crimes.

Palestinian Intifada: How Israel Orchestrated a Bloody Takeover
(2020)
Ali Adam

The second Intifada—commonly referred to by Palestinians as al-Aqsa Intifada—began after then-Israeli opposition leader Ariel Sharon sparked the uprising when he stormed al-Aqsa Mosque compound in occupied East Jerusalem with more than 1,000 heavily armed police and soldiers on September 28, 2000.

The move sparked widespread outrage among Palestinians who had just marked the anniversary of the 1982 Sabra and Shatila massacre, for which Sharon was found responsible for failing to stop the bloodshed, following Israel's invasion of Lebanon.

But prior to Sharon's controversial move, frustration and anger had risen year after year among Palestinians on the backdrop of the refusal of successive Israeli governments to abide by the Oslo Accords and end the occupation.

Diana Buttu, a Ramallah-based analyst and former adviser to the Palestinian negotiators on Oslo, told Al Jazeera: "Everybody, including the Americans, were warning the Israelis that the Palestinians are reaching a boiling point, and you need to calm down. Instead, they turned up the fire even more.

"Sharon's visit was the spark that lit up the Intifada, but the groundwork was laid in the years before that."

Under the Oslo agreement by May 4, 1999, there was supposed to be an independent Palestine, Buttu noted, adding from the start of negotiations in 1993 until the start of the Intifada "what we saw was a fast expansion of Israel's settlements".

"In fact, we saw that the number of settlers doubled from 200,000 to 400,000 just in that short period from 1993 to the year 2000. You can see that what was happening on the ground was designed to ensure that there wasn't going to be an independent Palestinian state," she said.

'Israeli solutions'

The tensions and the frustration had also risen after the failure of the Camp David Peace talks that were held in July 2000, where then-Palestinian leader Yasser Arafat and Israeli Prime Minister Ehud Barak failed to reach a peace agreement because of disagreements over the status of Jerusalem, territorial contiguity, and the right of return for Palestinian refugees.

Hani al-Masri, director-general of Masarat, the Palestinian Center for Policy Research and Strategic Studies, added: "The main reason behind the Intifada was that Israeli leaders wanted to punish Arafat and the Palestinians to force them to accept the Israeli solutions that are similar to the status quo of occupation. They wanted to force the Palestinians' consciousness to accept what Israel wants.

"The Palestinians wanted through the Intifada to improve the post-Oslo conditions that reached a low point in the Camp David Summit where Arafat was demanded to give up on Jerusalem and the refugees issue."

Wasel Abu Yusuf, a senior Palestinian official and member of the Executive Committee of the Palestine Liberation Organization (PLO) said: "The political horizon was closed in face of the Palestinians after the Camp David summit where Israel sought to deprive the Palestinians of their capital in East Jerusalem, the right of return for the Palestinians, as well as territorial contiguity.

"Israel wanted through Sharon's visit to provoke the Palestinians into a violent reaction. The Israelis thought that dealing a severe military blow to the Palestinians would lower their political demands in the negotiations in the aftermath of Camp David summit."

How Israel exacerbated violence in the second Intifada

The first days of the uprising were characterised by large non-violent demonstrations that included civil disobedience and some stone-throwing. It started in Jerusalem and quickly spread to the occupied West Bank and East Jerusalem.

The demonstrations were met with excessive force from the Israeli authorities that included rubber-coated bullets and live ammunition. Soon thereafter followed military incursions involving helicopters and tanks into heavily populated Palestinian areas.

During the first few days of the second Intifada, it is estimated Israeli soldiers fired about 1.3 million rounds of ammunition, as revealed by Amos Malka, then-director of Israeli military intelligence. This occurred despite the fact that violence by Palestinians in the early weeks was minimal.

"The Israeli violence showed that the Israelis were not interested in a quick end to the conflict," Abu Yusuf said. "The fact that Israel shot over a million bullets, caused great losses to Palestinian lives, and stepped over the Muslim holy places all shows that Israel wanted to militarise the Intifada. The excessive use of force that the Israeli army exercised was intended to drag the Palestinians into a military confrontation."

446

Buttu said Israel's leaders wanted a distraction from the building of settlements. "It was a cover for everything they had wanted to do since."

In the first five days of the Intifada, 47 Palestinians were killed and another 1,885 were wounded. Amnesty International found the majority of Palestinian casualties were civilian bystanders, and 80 percent of those killed in the first month posed no life-threatening danger to Israeli forces. Five Israelis were killed by Palestinians during the same period.

Analysts have long argued excessive use of force was the reason why the phase of Palestinian popular resistance in the Second Intifada ended quickly and was replaced by armed rebellion.
[...]
Mass casualties

When talking about the second Intifada, Israelis would talk about the Palestinian suicide bombings, but observers say it was not until more than a month of Palestinians enduring lethal military attacks that some resorted to self-sacrificing violence.

At least 4,973 Palestinians were killed over the course of the Second Intifada. Among them were 1,262 children, 274 women and 32 medical personnel, according to the Palestinian Center for Human Rights.

More than 10,000 children were wounded during the five years of the Intifada, according to the Defence for Children International, a Swiss-based independent organisation dedicated to promoting and protecting children's rights.

In addition to the deaths and injuries, the Israeli army demolished more than 5,000 Palestinians homes and dam- aged another 6,500 beyond repair, according to the Palestinian Center for Human Rights.
[...]
During the Intifada years, the Palestinians made attempts to end the violence but the Israelis rejected the overtures.

In February 2003, Israeli sources revealed a proposal submitted by the Palestinian Authority to Israel. It pledged to completely stop all attacks against Israel in return for the gradual withdrawal of the Israeli occupation to the pre-Intifada locations.

In 2002, Palestinian leaders repeated their efforts to end the military confrontation when Arafat endorsed the Arab Peace Initiative launched by Saudi Arabia. Israel, on the other hand, ignored the proposal and continued its military operations.
[...]

Hostage to 9/11 (2006)
Dr. Mahdi Abdul Hadi

Five years ago, on September 11, I was giving a lecture at Bethlehem University when the news from New York filtered through. Once the scale of what had happened became clear I turned to address my audience angrily.

"This," I said, "is the collapse of the status quo, the collapse of trust and it spells the end of the usual norms. Things will no longer be the same and we, the Arab-Islamic world, will be on the defensive for a long time."

Five years later the world has fundamentally changed. 9/11 brought us the twin cultures of fear and war to govern not only US-Arab/Muslim relations, but also the Palestinian-Israeli conflict.
[…]
9/11 brought the issues of religious identity and national identity, i.e. faith and patriotism, to the fore. But rather than reflecting carefully about what these meant, they were distorted and twisted by all sides in this new climate of fear and vengeance to promote a perverse political aim that was best summed up by Bush's own "with us or against us" dictum.
[…]
Further, forcing people to choose between their cultural-religious identity or being "with us" leaves them no option at all. Angry young generations, who've lived under oppressive and corrupt regimes, can turn nowhere in their desire for justice, whether religiously informed or not, and instead are now willing to sacrifice their lives, something made easy after creating a new meaning for martyrdom, in this void that is created by a black and white world.
[…]
The Palestinian-Israeli conflict has become hostage to 9/11. Once the peculiarities of this conflict were subsumed by the "war against terror", room for international pressure, understanding and compromise was gone. Israel was allowed a free hand to exercise its military superiority, which, in the absence of any political plan, achieved only that: killing more Palestinians, taking more of their land, dehumanizing their daily lives and all of that for no observable reason or aim.

On the Palestinian side, meanwhile, Yasser Arafat's leadership and legitimate resistance in general were immediately branded terrorism. Thus, with no political allies, no restraint on Israel and already a part of those "against us", Palestinians have few options but to object, reject and deny.
[…]

Address Concerning Second Intifada (2002)
Ariel Sharon

For eighteen months Israel has been under bitter and bloody attack, initiated by our Palestinian neighbors. We have paid a high price in blood, solely because of our honest wish to live in peace with them, and because of our belief that they want the same.
[...]
On my first day in office, I sent a personal letter to Arafat. I offered a practical proposal to the end the violence, and reiterated our wish for peace. I promised that we did not intend to harm innocent civilians, and suggested ways to ease their suffering. I extended my hand in peace, and my hand was rejected.

Since then we have made an endless number of efforts to reach a cease-fire: we tried to ease security measures — and each time we lifted a closure, opened a road and withdrew the I.D.F., we were immediately answered with horrific terrorist attacks; we accepted the Mitchell plan, which includes painful compromises for Israel; we accepted the Tenet plan; we even waived the most elementary demand for seven days of quiet — we did not even get seven hours free of an attempt to perpetrate a murderous suicide attack; we cooperated with General Zinni [...] but Arafat rejected all his proposals and carried on with his reign of terror.
[...]
In talks with various world leaders, I presented our ideas for the political settlement possible after the cessation of terror. We presented Israel's honest wish for a peace that will bring honor, prosperity and security for both peoples.

However, Arafat chose a different path. We know which path his is. He assumed, and still assumes, that he will be able to defeat Israel and break its spirit. In our sensitivity to the sanctity of human life and in our openness for political debate, he sees basic weakness. By way of blood and horror he wants to force Israel into a unilateral withdrawal to its 1967 borders, including Jerusalem, thereby achieving his aims through violence, and he is not averse to using any means.

The government of Israel has thus decided to instruct the I.D.F. and other security forces to embark on Operation Defensive Shield, which has one goal: uprooting the terrorist infrastructure which Arafat built to continue attacking us.

I.D.F. soldiers and officers have been given clear orders: to enter cities and villages which have become havens for terrorists; to catch and arrest terrorists and, primarily, their dispatchers and those who finance and support them; to confiscate weapons intended to be used against Israeli citizens; to expose and destroy terrorist facilities and explosives, laboratories, weapons production factories and secret installations. The orders are clear: target and paralyze anyone who takes up weapons and tries to oppose our troops, resists them or endanger them — and to avoid harming the civilian population.

All the aforementioned should have been carried out by the Palestinian Authority, according to its agreements with Israel, and as they were requested to do by all the responsible leaders in the world. Only when it transpired that the Palestinian Authority was not willing to fulfill its promises, that it is infested with terror, and that it has factually turned into an authority which is actively involved in terror — only then, having no other choice, were we forced to act.
[…]
We never intended and do not intend to permanently reoccupy Palestinian cities. After the I.D.F. completes all its missions, it will withdraw, in accordance with the instructions of the government, to defined security zones. In my talks with President Bush, and recognizing his sincere wish for peace in our region, I have promised to make every effort to accelerate our military activities, and to withdraw our forces from those places in which our actions have been completed.

In these security zones, our forces will deploy to constitute a buffer between Palestinian territories and our territories, in order to prevent any penetration into Israeli communities, attacks on Israeli citizens, and threats to our security. Correspondingly, our forces will be prepared to precisely target anyone who tries to contrive this war of terrorism against us, regardless of his identity, status or position.
[…]
From here, I address the leaders of the Middle East. Terrorism threatens not only Israel. It threatens you as well. It does not lead to peace — terrorism is the enemy of peace and stability. […]

From here, I address the leaders of the Free World. You must remember that leniency toward terrorists is the same as a green light to terrorists, who have already proven that they do not distinguish between blood and blood, between a Jewish victim and any other victim. You cannot fight terrorism on the one hand, and condemn the victims of terrorism on the other. There is absolutely no equivalence between those who send teenage suicide bombers to kill and maim, and those who take self-defense actions and try to uproot the infrastructure of terrorism. Only your stand against terrorism and actual sanctions against its perpetrators in the Palestinian Authority, and primarily Arafat, will enable you to make a real contribution to the advancement of peace in the Middle East.
[…]

78)   [...] [T]erritory is considered occupied when it is actually placed under the authority of the hostile army, and the occupation extends only to the territory where such authority has been established and can be exercised.

The territories situated between the Green Line and the former eastern boundary of Palestine under the Mandate were occupied by Israel in 1967 during the armed conflict between Israel and Jordan. [...] All these territories (including East Jerusalem) remain occupied territories and Israel has continued to have the status of occupying Power.
[...]

82)   According to the description in the report and the Written Statement of the Secretary-General, the works planned or completed have resulted or will result in a complex consisting essentially of:

(1) a fence with electronic sensors;
(2) a ditch (up to 4 metres deep);
(3) a two-lane asphalt patrol road;
(4) a trace road (a strip of sand smoothed to detect footprints) running parallel to the fence;
(5) a stack of six coils of barbed wire marking the perimeter of the complex.

[...]

83)   [...] The works deviate more than 7.5 kilometres from the Green Line in certain places to encompass settlements, while encircling Palestinian population areas. A stretch of 1 to 2 kilometres west of Tulkarm appears to run on the Israeli side of the Green Line. Elsewhere, on the other hand, the planned route would deviate eastward by up to 22 kilometres. In the case of Jerusalem, the existing works and the planned route lie well beyond the Green Line and even in some cases beyond the eastern municipal boundary of Jerusalem as fixed by Israel.

84)   On the basis of that route, approximately 975 square kilometres (or 16.6 per cent of the West Bank) would, according to the report of the Secretary-General, lie between the Green Line and the wall. This area is stated to be home to 237,000 Palestinians. If the full wall were completed as planned, another 160,000 Palestinians would live in almost completely encircled communities, described as enclaves in the report. As a result of the planned route, nearly 320,000 Israeli settlers (of whom 178,000 in East Jerusalem) would be living in the area between the Green Line and the wall.

85)   Lastly, it should be noted that the construction of the wall has been accompanied by the creation of a new administrative regime.

Thus in October 2003 the Israeli Defence Forces issued Orders establishing the part of the West Bank lying between the Green Line and the wall as a "Closed Area". Residents of this area may no longer remain in it, nor may non-residents enter it, unless holding a permit or identity card issued by the Israeli authorities. [...]

115)   In this regard, Annex II to the report of the Secretary-General, entitled "Summary Legal Position of the Palestine Liberation Organization", States that "The construction of the Barrier is an attempt to annex the territory contrary to international law" and that "The de facto annexation of land interferes with the territorial sovereignty and consequently with the right of the Palestinians to self-determination." This view was echoed in certain of the written statements submitted to the Court and in the views expressed at the hearings. *Inter alia,* it was contended that:

> "The wall severs the territorial sphere over which the Palestinian people are entitled to exercise their right of self-determination and constitutes a violation of the legal principle prohibiting the acquisition of territory by the use of force."

In this connection, it was in particular emphasized that "[tlhe route of the wall is designed to change the demographic composition of the Occupied Palestinian Territory, including East Jerusalem, by reinforcing the Israeli Settlements" illegally established on the Occupied Palestinian Territory. It was further contended that the wall aimed at "reducing and parcelling out the territorial sphere over which the Palestinian people are entitled to exercise their right to self-determination".

116)   For its part, Israel has argued that the wall's sole purpose is to enable it effectively to combat terrorist attacks launched from the West Bank. Furthermore, Israel has repeatedly stated that the Barrier is a temporary measure. It did so *inter alia* through its Permanent Representative to the United Nations at the Security Council meeting of 14 October 2003, emphasizing that "[the fence] does not annex territories to the State of Israel," and that Israel is "ready and able, at tremendous cost, to adjust or dismantle a fence if so required as part of its political settlement". Israel's Permanent Representative restated this view before the General Assembly on 20 October and 8 December 2003. On this latter occasion, he added:

> "As soon as the terror ends, the fence will no longer be necessary. The fence is not a border and has no political significance. It does not change the legal status of the territory in any way.".

[...]

119)   The Court notes that the route of the wall as fixed by the Israeli Government includes within the "Closed Area" (see paragraph 85

above) some 80 per cent of the settlers living in the Occupied Palestinian Territory. Moreover, it is apparent from an examination of the map [...] that the wall's sinuous route has been traced in such a way as to include within that area the great majority of the Israeli settlements in the occupied Palestinian Territory (including East Jerusalem).

120) As regards these settlements, the Court notes that Article 49, paragraph 6, of the Fourth Geneva Convention provides: "The Occupying Power shall not deport or transfer parts of its own civilian population into the territory it occupies." That provision prohibits not only deportations or forced transfers of population such as those carried out during the Second World War, but also any measures taken by an occupying Power in order to organize or encourage transfers of parts of its own population into the occupied territory.
[...]

121) Whilst the Court notes the assurance given by Israel that the construction of the wall does not amount to annexation and that the wall is of a temporary nature, it nevertheless cannot remain indifferent to certain fears expressed to it that the route of the wall will prejudge the future frontier between Israel and Palestine, and the fear that Israel may integrate the settlements and their means of access. The Court considers that the construction of the wall and its associated régime create a "fait accompli" on the ground that could well become permanent, in which case, and notwithstanding the formal characterization of the wall by Israel, it would be tantamount to *de facto* annexation.

122) The Court recalls moreover that, according to the report of the Secretary-General, the planned route would incorporate in the area between the Green line and the wall more than 16 per cent of the territory of the West Bank. Around 80 per cent of the settlers living in the Occupied Palestinian Territory, that is 320,000 individuals, would reside in that area, as well as 237,000 Palestinians. Moreover, as a result of the construction of the wall, around 160,000 other Palestinians would reside in almost completely encircled communities.

In other terms, the route chosen for the wall gives expression *in loco* to the illegal measures taken by Israel with regard to Jerusalem and the settlements, as deplored by the Security Council. There is also a risk of further alterations to the demographic composition of the Occupied Palestinian Territory resulting from the construction of the wall inasmuch as it is contributing [...] to the departure of Palestinian populations from certain areas. That construction, along with measures taken previously, thus severely impedes the exercise by the Palestinian people of its right to self-determination, and is therefore a breach of Israel's obligation to respect that right.
[...]

133) That construction, the establishment of a closed area

between the Green Line and the wall itself and the creation of enclaves have moreover imposed substantial restrictions on the freedom of movement of the inhabitants of the Occupied Palestinian Territory (with the exception of Israeli citizens and those assimilated thereto). Such restrictions are most marked in urban areas, such as the Qalqiliya enclave or the City of Jerusalem and its suburbs. They are aggravated by the fact that the access gates are few in number in certain sectors and opening hours appear to be restricted and unpredictably applied. [...]

There have also been serious repercussions for agricultural production, as is attested by a number of sources. According to the Special Committee to Investigate Israeli Practices Affecting the Human Rights of the Palestinian People and Other Arabs of the Occupied Territories

> "an estimated 100,000 dunums [approximately 10,000 hectares] of the West Bank's most fertile agricultural land, confiscated by the Israeli Occupation Forces, have been destroyed during the first phase of the wall construction, which involves the disappearance of vast amounts of property, notably private agricultural land and olive trees, wells, citrus grows and hothouses upon which tens of thou- sands of Palestinians rely for their survival".

Further, the Special Rapporteur on the situation of human rights in the Palestinian territories occupied by Israel since 1967 states that "Much of the Palestinian land on the Israeli side of the Wall consists of fertile agricultural land and some of the most important water wells in the region" and adds that "Many fruit and olive trees had been destroyed in the course of building the barrier". The Special Rapporteur on the Right to Food of the United Nations Commission on Human Rights states that construction of the wall "cuts off Palestinians from their agricultural lands, wells and means of subsistence". In a recent survey conducted by the World Food Programme, it is stated that the situation has aggravated food insecurity in the region, which reportedly numbers 25,000 new beneficiaries of food aid.

It has further led to increasing difficulties for the population concerned regarding access to health services, educational establishments and primary sources of water. This is also attested by a number of different information sources. Thus the report of the Secretary-General states generally that "According to the Palestinian Central Bureau of Statistics, so far the Barrier has separated 30 localities from health services, 22 from schools, 8 from primary water sources and 3 from electricity networks." The Special Rapporteur of the United Nations Commission on Human Rights on the situation of human rights in the Palestinian territories occupied by Israel since 1967 states that "Palestinians between the Wall and Green Line will effectively be cut off from their land and workplaces, schools, health clinics and other social services." In relation specifically to water resources, the Special Rapporteur on the Right to Food of the United

454

Nations Commission on Human Rights observes that "By constructing the fence Israel will also effectively annex most of the western aquifer system (which provides 51 per cent of the West Bank's water resources)." [...]

At Qalqiliya, according to reports furnished to the United Nations, some 600 shops or businesses have shut down, and 6,000 to 8,000 people have already left the region. The Special Rapporteur on the Right to Food of the United Nations Commission on Human Rights has also observed that "With the fence/wall cutting communities off from their land and water without other means of subsistence, many of the Palestinians living in these areas will be forced to leave." In this respect also the construction of the wall would effectively deprive a significant number of Palestinians of the "freedom to choose [their] residence". In addition, however, in the view of the Court, since a significant number of Palestinians have already been compelled by the construction of the wall and its associated régime to depart from certain areas, a process that will continue as more of the wall is built, that construction, coupled with the establishment of the Israeli settlements mentioned in paragraph 120 above, is tending to alter the demographic composition of the Occupied Palestinian Territory.

134)   To sum up, the Court is of the opinion that the construction of the wall and its associated régime impede the liberty of movement of the inhabitants of the Occupied Palestinian Territory (with the exception of Israeli citizens and those assimilated thereto) as guaranteed under Article 12, paragraph 1, of the International Covenant on Civil and Political Rights. They also impede the exercise by the persons concerned of the right to work, to health, to education and to an adequate standard of living as proclaimed in the International Covenant on Economic, Social and Cultural Rights and in the United Nations Convention on the Rights of the Child. Lastly, the construction of the wall and its associated régime, by contributing to the demographic changes referred to in paragraphs 122 and 133 above, contravene Article 49, paragraph 6, of the Fourth Geneva Convention and the Security Council resolutions cited in paragraph 120 above.
[...]

137)   To sum up, the Court, from the material available to it, is not convinced that the specific course Israel has chosen for the wall was necessary to attain its security objectives. The wall, along the route chosen, and its associated régime gravely infringe a number of rights of Palestinians residing in the territory occupied by Israel, and the infringements resulting from that route cannot be justified by military exigencies or by the requirements of national security or public order. The construction of such a wall accordingly constitutes breaches by Israel of various of its obligations under the applicable international humanitarian law and human rights instruments.
[...]

139)   [...] Article 51 of the Charter [of the United Nations] thus

recognizes the existence of an inherent right of self-defence in the case of armed attack by one State against another State. However, Israel does not claim that the attacks against it are imputable to a foreign State.

The Court also notes that Israel exercises control in the Occupied Palestinian Territory and that, as Israel itself states, the threat which it regards as justifying the construction of the wall originates within, and not outside, that territory. The situation is thus different from that contemplated by Security Council resolutions 1368 (2001) and 1373 (2001), and therefore Israel could not in any event invoke those resolutions in support of its claim to be exercising a right of self-defence.

Consequently, the Court concludes that Article 51 of the Charter has no relevance in this case.
[...]

    142)   In conclusion, the Court considers that Israel cannot rely on a right of self-defence or on a state of necessity in order to preclude the wrongfulness of the construction of the wall resulting from the considerations mentioned in paragraphs 122 and 137 above. The Court accordingly finds that the construction of the wall, and its associated régime, are contrary to international law.
[...]

DISENGAGEMENT

Israeli Disengagement Plan (2004)
GOVT. OF ISRAEL

     I.   Background - Diplomatic and security significance

[...]

The State of Israel believes it must take action to improve the current situation. The State of Israel has reached the conclusion that there is currently no partner on the Palestinian side with whom progress can be made on a bilateral process. Given this, a four-stage disengagement plan has been drawn up, based on the following considerations:

A. The stalemate embodied in the current situation is damaging; in order to break the stalemate, the State of Israel must initiate a process that is not dependent on cooperation with the Palestinians.

B. The aim of the plan is to bring about a better security, diplomatic economic and demographic reality.

C. In any future permanent arrangement, there will be no Israeli presence in the Gaza Strip. On the other hand, it is clear that some parts of Judea and Samaria (including key concentrations of Jewish settlements, civilian communities, security zones and areas in which Israel has a vested interest) will remain part of the State of Israel.

D. The State of Israel supports the efforts of the United States, which is working along with the international community, to promote the process of reform, the establishment of institutions and improving the economic and welfare conditions of the Palestinian people, so that a new Palestinian leadership can arise, capable of proving it can fulfill its obligations under the road map.

E. The withdrawal from the Gaza Strip and from the northern part of Samaria will reduce interaction with the Palestinian population.

F. Completion of the four-stage disengagement plan will negate any claims on Israel regarding its responsibility for the Palestinian population of the Gaza Strip.

G. The process of graduated disengagement does not detract from existing agreements between Israel and the Palestinians. The relevant security arrangements will remain in force.

H. International support for the four-stage disengagement plan is widespread and important. This support is vital in ensuring that the Palestinians fulfill their obligations in terms of fighting terror and implementing reforms, in accordance with the road map. Only then will the sides be able to resume negotiations.

II.   Key points of the plan

a.   The Gaza Strip

1. The State of Israel will withdraw from the Gaza Strip, including all Israeli settlements, and will redeploy outside the area of the Strip. [...]

2. Once the move has been completed, there will be no permanent Israeli military presence in the evacuated territorial area of the Gaza Strip.

3. As a result of this, there will be no basis to the claim that the Strip is occupied land.

b.   Judeau and Samaria

1. The State of Israel will withdraw from northern Samaria (four settlements: Ganim, Kadim, Sa-Nur and Homesh) as well as all permanent military installations in the area, and will redeploy outside the evacuated area.

2. Once the move has been completed, there will be no permanent Israeli military presence in the area.

3. The move will provide Palestinian territorial contiguity in the northern parts of Samaria.

4. The State of Israel, along with the international community, will help improve the transportation infrastructure in Judea and Samaria, with the goal of providing continuous transport for Palestinians in Judea and Samaria.

5. The move will make it easier for Palestinians to live a normal life in Judea and Samaria, and will facilitate economic and commercial activity.

c.   The Process

The withdrawal process is slated to end by the end of 2005.

The settlements will be split into the following four groups:

1. Group A - Morag, Netzarim, Kfar Darom

458

2. Group B - The four settlements in northern Samaria (Ganim, Kadim, Sa-Nur and Homesh).

3. Group C - The Gush Katif bloc of settlements.

4. Group D - The settlements in the northern Gaza Strip (Alei Sinai, Dugit and Nissanit)

The necessary preparations will be undertaken in order to implement the four-stage disengagement plan (including administrative work to set relevant criteria, definitions and preparation of the necessary legislation.)

The government will discuss and decide separately on the evacuation of each of the above-mentioned groups.

> d.   The Security Fence

The State of Israel will continue to construct the security fence, in accordance with the relevant cabinet decisions. In deciding on the route of the fence, humanitarian considerations will be taken into account.

> III.   The security reality after the evacuation

> a.   The Gaza Strip

1. The State of Israel will monitor and supervise the outer envelope on land, will have exclusive control of the Gaza airspace, and will continue its military activity along the Gaza Strip's coastline.

2. The Gaza Strip will be completely demilitarized of arms banned by current agreements between the sides.

3. The State of Israel reserves the basic right to self-defense, which includes taking preventive measures as well as the use of force against threats originating in the Gaza Strip.

> b.   The West Bank

1. After the evacuation of the northern Samaria settlements, there will be no permanent military presence in that area.

2. The State of Israel reserves the basic right to self-defense, which includes taking preventive measures as well as the use of force against threats originating in the area.

3. Military activity will remain in its current framework in the rest of the West Bank. The State of Israel will, if circumstances allow, consider reducing its activity in Palestinian cities.

4. The State of Israel will work to reduce the number of checkpoints throughout the West Bank.

IV.   Military infrastructure and installations in the Gaza Strip and the northern Samaria region

All will be dismantled and evacuated, except for those that the State of Israel decides to transfer to an authorized body.

V.   The nature of the security assistance to the Palestinians

The State of Israel agrees that in coordination with it, consulting, assistance and training will be provided to Palestinian security forces for the purpose of fighting terror and maintaining the public order. The assistance will be provided by American, British, Egyptian, Jordanian or other experts, as will be agreed upon with Israel.

The State of Israel stresses that it will not agree to any foreign security presence in Gaza or the West Bank without its consent.
[…]

VII.   Real estate

In general, houses belonging to the settlers, and other sensitive structures such as synagogues will not be left behind. The State of Israel will aspire to transfer other structures, such as industrial and agricultural facilities, to an international third party that will use them for the benefit of the Palestinian population.

The Erez industrial zone will be transferred to an agreed-upon Palestinian or international body.

The State of Israel along with Egypt will examine the possibility of setting up a joint industrial zone on the border between Israel, Egypt and the Gaza Strip.

VIII.   Infrastructure and civilian arrangements

The water, electricity, sewage and communications infrastructures will be left in place.

As a rule, Israel will enable the continued supply of electricity, water, gas and fuel to the Palestinians, under the existing arrangements and full compensation.

The existing arrangements, including the arrangements with regard to water and the electromagnetic area, will remain valid.

IX.   The activity of the international civilian organizations

The State of Israel views very favorably continued activity of the international humanitarian organizations and those that deal will civil development, which aid the Palestinian population.

The State of Israel will coordinate with the international organizations the arrangements that will make this activity easier.

The State of Israel suggests that an international mechanism (such as the AHLC) be set up, in coordination with Israel and international bodies, that will work to develop the Palestinian economy.

X.   Economic arrangements

In general, the economic arrangements that are currently in effect between Israel and the Palestinians will remain valid. These arrangements include, among other things:

A. The movement of goods between the Gaza Strip, Judea and Samaria, Israel and foreign countries.

B. The monetary regime.

C. The taxation arrangements and the customs envelope.

D. Postal and communications arrangements.

E. The entry of workers into Israel in accordance with the existing criteria.

In the long run, and in accordance with the Israeli interest in encouraging Palestinian economic independence, The State of Israel aspires to reduce the number of Palestinian workers entering Israel, and eventually to completely stop their entrance. The State of Israel will support the development of employment sources in the Gaza Strip and in the Palestinian areas in the West Bank, by international bodies.

XI.   The international crossing points

a. The international crossing point between the Gaza Strip and Egypt

1. The existing arrangements will remain in force.

461

2. Israel is interested in transferring the crossing point to the "border triangle," south of its current location. This will be done in coordination with the Egyptian government. This will allow the expansion of the hours of activity at the crossing point.

> b. The international crossing points between Judea and Samaria, and Jordan.

The existing arrangements will remain in force.

XII. The Erez crossing point

The Erez crossing point will be moved into the territory of the State of Israel according to a timetable that will be determined separately.

XIII. Summary

The implementation of the four-stage disengagement plan will bring about an improvement in the situation and a break from the current stagnation. If and when the Palestinian side shows a willingness, an ability and an implementation of actions to fight terrorism, a full cessation of terror and violence and the carrying out of reforms according to the roadmap, it will be possible to return to the track of discussions and negotiations.

Israel's New Strategy (2006)
Barry Rubin

The emerging new policy is based on a broad Israeli recognition that holding on to the West Bank and the Gaza Strip is simply not in Israel's interest, despite the fact that the Palestinian leadership has been uninterested in and incapable of making peace and that both Fatah and Hamas will use that land to try to launch attacks on Israel. The territories no longer serve a strategic function for Israel, given the unlikelihood of a conventional attack by Arab state armies, and Israel could better defend its citizens by creating a strong defensive line rather than by dispersing its forces. Moreover, because a comprehensive peace deal is not likely to be reached for many years, the territories are no longer of value as bargaining chips. During the long era before the Palestinians will be organized and moderate enough to make peace, Israel has to set its own strategy based on these realities.

TERRITORY FOR PEACE?

The international situation changed drastically in the 1990s [....]

At first, it seemed that such changes—plus an accumulation of Palestinian defeats and internal troubles—would push Palestinian leaders, Syria, and most Arab states toward a peace agreement with Israel. The peace process was an experiment to see if this would in fact happen. In 2000, both Syria and the Palestinians (under the Clinton plan and the Camp David accords) rejected peace, proving those expectations wrong.

That result, most Israelis concluded, was not a product of some misunderstanding, U.S. or Israeli intransigence, a slight diplomatic misstep, or a need to make minor changes in the deal being offered. On the contrary, the Palestinian and Syrian leaderships were simply not ready for peace—because of radical forces and ideologies, hard-line personalities, extremist goals, and the fact that the conflict bolstered dictators who would otherwise have faced serious domestic problems. With their own hopes shattered, Israelis from across the political spectrum reluctantly accepted that the conflict would endure for a long time.

The Israeli response to this realization was defined by a historic Israeli debate over national strategy, the perceived lessons of the Oslo experience, and the Israelis' analysis of Palestinian political realities. A sector of the Israeli public had always wanted to keep the territories captured in the 1967 Six-Day War for religious or nationalist reasons, but this was always a minority position and not—except in the case of East Jerusalem—government policy. The real galvanizing arguments for retaining the territories were strategic and diplomatic: first, holding on to the West Bank and the Gaza Strip gave Israel strategic depth, which it could use to defend itself against a conventional military attack; and second, the territories could be used as bargaining chips when there was a Palestinian partner ready to make a lasting peace—"territory for peace," as the slogan went. [...]

This position was rational for several reasons. For much of Israel's history, the main strategic threat to the country was a conventional war on its borders with Arab states. In this context, it was vital to possess the West Bank, especially, in order to control the Jordan Valley and use the north-south ridges to its west as positions to defend against an attack by Iraqi, Jordanian, Saudi, or Syrian forces. Holding the territories also gave Israel a buffer against Palestinian terrorists striking from across the border, a threat magnified from irritating to existential by the fact that such forces had Arab and Soviet-bloc help. At the same time, it was assumed that those "behind" Israel's defensive lines—West Bank and Gaza Palestinians—would present only a limited security problem.

That strategic concept worked very well for 20 years—until the first intifada in the late 1980s—and reasonably well for another decade. As time wore on and many Israelis came to believe that there was a real possibility of a negotiated resolution, the "territory for peace" argument became even stronger. That notion was the basis of the 1993 Oslo agreement with the PLO. Prime Minister Yitzhak Rabin, Foreign Minister Shimon Peres, and other Israeli leaders thought that yielding territory would be the confidence-building measure that would persuade the Palestinians that Israel was ready for a deal.
[...]

PARADIGM SHIFT
[...]

Meanwhile, other Arab regimes—challenged by Islamists and strategically weak—started to be willing to sacrifice some of their support for the Palestinians in exchange for improved relations with the United States. Even if they would not make peace with Israel, they also did not want war, and their support for the Palestinians hit rock bottom. And all of this reinforced the trends set off by the ending of the Cold War and the consequent shift in the international balance of power. Israel's security environment started to look very different. Arab armies and arms appeared less dangerous, and occupying territory became less important than having clear defensive lines that did not enclose a hostile population.

What emerged from the shock of the failure of Oslo and the five-year-long terrorist war that followed was a new synthesis in Israeli thinking: a national consensus along centrist lines, drawing ideas from across the political spectrum. From the left came the idea that Israel should withdraw from the captured territories, dismantle many of the settlements, and accept an independent Palestinian state in exchange for real peace. This melded

464

with the right's belief that there would be no partner with whom to make real peace for a long time to come.

These two notions fused into a new paradigm, which dominates Israeli politics and thinking today, even as the Palestinians stick to a policy that combines weakness and intransigence. Although the Israelis' most optimistic hopes have been dashed, most Israelis now believe that the situation can actually be made more secure with the right approach.

The Israeli military played a considerable role in developing this new viewpoint. Its main mission, the generals concluded, had become patrolling the West Bank and the Gaza Strip, where it protected roads and settlements while combating terrorists on terms largely set by the enemy. Not only did this stretch forces too thin, but it also sacrificed the strategic advantages Israel held. Moreover, protecting Israeli territory and citizens was made harder by the lack of a discernible or defensible boundary. This problem could not be remedied as long as the army was required to defend every Jewish settlement and deal with a large, hostile civilian population.

The idea of a defense based on a clear line laid out along advantageous terrain was far more attractive to strategists. [...]

GO IT ALONE

This was the context in which Sharon decided on complete withdrawal from the Gaza Strip and the dismantling of several West Bank settlements. As the next step, during the 2006 election campaign, his successor, Olmert, announced a policy of "convergence," in which Israel would withdraw from most of its remaining positions in the West Bank, dismantle many more settlements, and consolidate those "settlement blocs" that it intended to claim in the future.
[...]
Certainly, Israel had never wanted the Gaza Strip for much except defensive purposes. In 1992, at the start of talks with the PLO, Israel's opening offer included turning over the Gaza Strip to Palestinian rule. Since 1994, most of the territory had been under PA control. A decade later, the Israelis were reluctant to withdraw not because of any intrinsic desire for that territory, but because of their concern that the area would become a base for attacking Israel. Many also worried that withdrawal from Gaza would be taken as a precedent for giving up all of the West Bank and be claimed by terrorists as a victory, thereby inspiring more terrorism and undercutting Israel's efforts to bargain about anything else. [...]

Sharon had a number of a strong motives for taking such a great political and strategic risk. He wanted his legacy to show that he was a moderate who sought peace and left his country more secure. But he recognized

Israel's need for a sustainable strategic stance as long as a comprehensive diplomatic solution remained out of reach. He came to realize that holding territory was no longer strategically advantageous (and was perhaps detrimental in a long war of attrition) and accepted the demographic reality that Israel, if it did not change its approach, would soon be ruling over an Arab population outnumbering its own Jewish population. Sharon also wanted to put the ball in the Palestinians' court by forcing them to show whether they could govern a territory that was, for most practical purposes, a state. Turning over the Gaza Strip, said Weisglass, meant there were "no more excuses. ... The whole world is asking what they intend to do with this slice of land." In the end, Israel even turned over control of the Gazan-Egyptian border to the PA. In response to the argument that holding on to land provided a bargaining chip in negotiations, Sharon simply asked, What is the value of having bargaining chips when there is no one with whom to bargain?

Meanwhile, Sharon believed that security fences would offer a viable line to which Israeli forces could withdraw and that, having won the 2000-2005 war, Israel could redeploy its troops on its own terms—the result of a victory over terrorism rather than a defeat by it. [...]

The basic elements of the new paradigm now constitute the program of Israel's new government and probably will for a long time. Israel wants peace. It is ready to be flexible, to take risks and make concessions, and to agree to a Palestinian state in most of the West Bank and all of the Gaza Strip. The goal is not occupation but security and the right to exist as a society not under foreign attack. [...]

Olmert's "convergence" policy is the expression of these beliefs. In an April 9 interview with *The Washington Post*, Olmert offered a succinct summary of that policy: Settlements outside the security fence will eventually be removed and their residents "converged into the blocs of settlements that will remain under Israeli control. ... The rest of the territories will not have any Israeli presence and will allow territorial contiguity for a future Palestinian state." Israel's goal, which it will seek on an interim basis, is to have borders fairly close to, but not precisely coinciding with, those of the pre-1967 period.

A key factor in this defensive orientation will be completion of the security fence to protect Israel from attack, but with efforts taken to minimize Palestinian suffering, including altering the fence's route in response to Palestinian suits in Israeli courts. Another vital element will be Israel's retention of the right of military action to prevent terrorist attacks, including missile firings, and to ensure that those carrying out such operations will not be able to do so in future.
[...]

Israel's "Disengagement" plan from the Gaza Strip states that once fully enacted "there will be no basis to the claim that the Strip is occupied land," even though the Plan envisages indefinite Israeli military and economic control over the Gaza Strip. over the Gaza Strip.

[…]

II. THE GAZA STRIP REMAINS OCCUPIED TERRITORY EVEN IMPLEMENTATION OF THE "DISENGAGEMENT" PLAN

    A. ISRAEL WILL RETAIN EFFECTIVE CONTROL OVER THE GAZA STRIP AND WILL THEREFORE REMAIN THE OCCUPYING POWER

Under the "Disengagement" Plan, Gazans will still be subjected to the effective control of the Israeli military. Although Israel will supposedly remove its *permanent* military presence, Israeli forces will retain the ability and right to enter the Gaza Strip at will.

Further, Israel will retain control over Gaza's airspace, sea shore, and borders. Under the Plan, Israel will unilaterally control whether or not Gaza opens a seaport or an airport. Additionally, Israel will control all border crossings, including Gaza's border with Egypt. And Israel will "continue its military activity along the Gaza Strip's coastline." Taken together, these powers mean that all goods and people entering or leaving Gaza will be subject to Israeli control.

Finally, Israel will prevent Gazans from engaging in international relations. Accordingly, if it enacts the "Disengagement" Plan as envisaged, Israel will effectively control Gaza—administratively and militarily. Therefore, Israel will remain the Occupying Power of the Gaza Strip.

    B. ISRAEL WILL REMAIN THE OCCUPYING POWER OF THE GAZA STRIP SO LONG AS ISRAEL RETAINS THE ABILITY TO EXERCISE AUTHORITY OVER THE STRIP

In *The Hostages Case,* the Nuremburg Tribunal expounded upon The Hague Regulations' basic definition of occupation in order to ascertain when occupation ends. It held that "[t]he test for application of the legal regime of occupation is not whether the occupying power fails to exercise effective control over the territory, but whether it has the ability to exercise such power." In that case, the Tribunal had to decide whether Germany's occupation of Greece and Yugoslavia had ended when Germany had ceded de facto control to non-German forces of certain territories. Even though Germany did not actually control those areas, the Tribunal held that Germany indeed remained the "occupying power"—both in Greece and

Yugoslavia generally and in the territories to which it had ceded control—since it could have reentered and controlled those territories at will.

Similarly, Israel will retain ultimate authority over Gaza and to a much greater degree than Germany in *The Hostages Case:* The Israeli military expressly reserves itself the right to enter the Gaza Strip at will. Further, Israel will not just retain the *ability* to exercise control over Gaza, but it will also retain *effective* control over Gaza's borders, air and sea space, overall security, and international relations.
[…]

III. THE STRATEGY BEHIND THE DISENGAGEMENT PLAN

A. THE DISENGAGEMENT PLAN DEMOGRAPHICALLY MOTIVATED

Israel's greatest battle is not against "terrorism," but against demography. Statistical analyses project that Palestinian Christians and Muslims will comprise the majority of persons in Israel and the Occupied Palestinian Territories by the year 2020. If Israel wants to remain a "Jewish state," then it will be very difficult to maintain its Jewish identity if an ethno/religious minority continues to rule over an ethnic majority. Israeli journalist David Landau noted in a statement made to a British journalist that the Gaza plans represents "the simplest, crudest solution [to Israel's demographic time bomb]: to dump Gaza and its 1.3 million Arabs in the hope that that would 'buy' [Israel] 50 more years."

Therefore, one of the primary motivations behind Israel's "Disengagement" Plan is to "dump" 1.3 million non-Jews while illegally confiscating as much Palestinian land in the West Bank as possible.

B. ISRAEL SEEKS TO CONSOLIDATE GAINS IN THE WEST BANK IN EXCHANGE FOR "CONCESSIONS" IN GAZA

While the world publicly debates the "Disengagement" Plan, Israel has been constructing the Wall in the Occupied West Bank. The Wall severs Palestinians from their lands, communities, and homes, while illegally appropriating more land and natural resources for Israeli colonies. In addition, Israel continues to expand illegal colonies in the Occupied West Bank. […]

The success of Israel's strategy became evident during a press conference on April 14, 2004, when U.S. President Bush, ostensibly in an effort to support the Gaza Plan, endorsed Israel's plans to keep illegal West Bank colonies (which he termed "Israeli population centers") in any permanent status agreement. […]

[T]he West Bank settlements that Israel would keep "in exchange" for its unilateral withdrawal from Gaza house tens of thousands of illegal colonists and stretch many miles into Occupied Palestinian Territory. In fact, just as Israel has evacuated 8,500 settlers from the occupied Gaza Strip and parts of the northern West Bank, it has embarked on plans to make room for 30,000 new settlers this year alone, primarily in and around occupied East Jerusalem.

Thus, Israel will demographically, and perhaps permanently, entrench its presence in the West Bank. Therefore, the Gaza withdrawal plan has less to do with what Israel is giving up in Gaza and more to do with what Israel plans on taking from the West Bank.

IV.   CONCLUSION: CONSTRUCTIVE SOLUTIONS

Israel will retain effective military, economic, and administrative control over the Gaza Strip and will therefore continue to occupy the Gaza Strip— even after implementation of its "Disengagement Plan" as proposed. Because Israel will continue to occupy Gaza, it will still be bound by the provisions of 1907's Hague Regulations, the Fourth Geneva Convention and relative international customary law.

This is not to say, however, that removing Gaza's settlers or reducing the Israeli military presence in and around the Gaza Strip could not usher in a better age for Palestinians and Israelis alike. Palestinians appreciate any movement on Israel's part towards compliance with international law. Compliance with international law brings Palestinians closer to liberation and the region closer to stability. By providing non-violent channels to achieve fair results, international law helps silence extremist positions and activity while bringing both sides closer to a negotiated peace. Additionally, respect for international law affirms the credibility of more powerful nations who routinely invoke it as the legitimate basis for their own actions.

Israel's "Disengagement" Plan however does not represent a good faith effort at advancing peace. Rather, Israel is selectively complying with some international legal standards in the Gaza Strip to preempt criticism for massive violations in the West Bank (including East Jerusalem). In so doing, Israel ensures that the conflict will continue and perhaps intensify. If Israel maintains effective control over the Gaza Strip, denying it the ability to develop internally or trade externally, Gaza could become a greater humanitarian disaster than it already is. Or if Israel eventually proclaims Gaza the "State of Palestine," the freedom guaranteed under international law might become ever more distant for Palestinians elsewhere.

[…]

Lessons from the Gaza Disengagement (2006)
Mohammed Dajani

It has now become generally accepted that the 1993 Oslo process is dead and the Oslo vision of a territorially contiguous Palestinian state is not on the Israeli agenda. In an interview with Haaretz on October 8, 2004, senior advisor to former prime minister Ariel Sharon, Dov Weissglas, stated: "The significance of the disengagement plan is the freezing of the peace process. [...] Effectively, this whole package called the Palestinian state, with all that it entails, has been removed indefinitely from our agenda." He went on to add: "When you freeze that process, you prevent the establishment of a Palestinian state, and you prevent a discussion of the refugees, the borders and Jerusalem [...] disengagement supplies the amount of formaldehyde that is necessary so there will not be a political process with the Palestinians."

Such statements fuel Palestinian resolve to liberate the homeland, egged on by the militant Islamic groups. Rocket attacks and Israeli reprisals continue. It is not only the radical movements such as Hamas, Islamic Jihad and the Popular Resistance Committees who claim that terrorism brought results, but also the hard-liners within Fatah. The contention is that armed struggle paid off, and suicide bombers, missiles, mortar, and Qassam rockets are what eventually forced the Israelis out of the Gaza Strip, ending 38 years of military occupation. The Hamas leadership, in an open challenge to the then-Fateh-led Palestinian Authority (PA), claimed it was their armed struggle that had led Israel to evacuate the settlements, and vowed not to lay down their weapons until the Israeli occupation ended. Al-Aqsa Martyrs Brigades, the military wing of Fateh, jumped on the bandwagon declaring that "the arms of resistance are legitimate, and that the Gaza withdrawal was achieved through resistance and steadfastness." Pursuing this logic, they argue that what worked for Gaza would work for the West Bank and East Jerusalem, and may eventually work for the rest of Palestine. As a result, violence continues, especially in the Gaza Strip, and it is paralyzing its economy and development, eroding international support, and demoralizing the public.

This situation has invited Israeli reprisals, and the Gaza Strip is presently besieged by Israeli troops making it the world's largest open air prison. This is very easy to implement since Israel still maintains full control over the Strip's border crossings, airspace and sea. For each rocket attack, Israeli forces retaliate by shelling Gaza as a form of collective punishment.

During the decades of occupation, the various Israeli prime ministers have contemplated dropping this "hot potato" called Gaza, and offered it on a silver platter first to Egypt and later to Jordan. Both countries declined through their diplomatic channels. Benny Morris, author of The Birth of the Palestinian Refugee Problem Revisited, and professor of history at Ben-Gurion University in Beersheba, pointed out that "the embattled settlers may have screamed that Prime Minister Ariel Sharon was expelling Jews from part of Eretz Yisrael, 'the land of Israel,' but the Gaza Strip was never part of the Jewish state."

A report prepared by Mark Heller and Shalom Harari, entitled The Effects of Disengagement on Palestinian Politics and Society, published by the Jaffee Center for Strategic Studies of Tel Aviv University, predicted that the disengagement is highly likely to lead to an eruption of terrorism in the West Bank and to exacerbate political, economic and social chaos among the Palestinians. They maintained that it may also provide Hamas with a favorable environment in which to build a larger militia. Their strategic assessment was that Gaza would serve as a training ground for terrorists and a support base for weapon smuggling and local arms production, and will offer a safe haven for wanted terrorists and their senior commanders. The report also predicted that the current Palestinian leadership would ultimately "fail the test" of running their Israel-free Gaza Strip effectively and responsibly, and would squander any international aid they may receive. Heller and Harari proved to be right in their assessment that the disengagement would exacerbate political, economic and social chaos among the Palestinians, basically because it was based on unilateralism.

A Measure of Optimism
[…]
Israeli unilateralism is viewed as a historic precedent in which the average Israeli crossed the psychological barrier that settlements won't ever be dismantled because, as the settlers argued, "this land is God's gift to the Jewish people," and is "the land of the Fathers," in what is considered Eretz Israel.
[…]
Lessons Learned

* Unilateralism works. It managed to speed the disengagement process. However, it worked because the PA cooperated to make it work. The expectation that the unilateral withdrawal would be chaotic, messy and would, at the last moment, be called off did not materialize. A decision was made and implemented. Thus, unilateralism works; coordinated unilateralism works better, but negotiated unilateralism works best.

* Unilateralism undermined the position of the moderate Palestinian forces while strengthening the radical militant and religious organizations, such as Hamas who claimed victory for the armed struggle.

* Unilateralism is a policy that only serves short term interests. Israeli Prime Minister Ehud Olmert was elected on a pledge to unilaterally set new borders for an expanded Israeli state, by annexing large portions of

Palestinian territories believing that this would create a de facto situation. However, on the long term, such policies would prove a stumbling bloc in future peace negotiations.

* Unilateralism embodies concessions without reciprocity. Israel left Gaza without getting in return, quid pro quo, any commitment to peace or security from the Palestinians.

* The Gaza unilateral disengagement policy placed the issue of settlements on the negotiating table.

* The power of the religious groups and the settlers in Israel is overrated. In the confrontation between the secular state and the religious state, the secular state won. In the confrontation between the democratic state and the settler state, the democratic state won.

* U.S. leverage on Israel continues to remain high. Sharon held to his position despite strong pressure from his Likud Party largely because President George W. Bush, who was having low approval ratings at home, needed the disengagement to succeed to help boost his image.

* Financial incentives, enticing compensation packages, coupled with acceptable alternatives worked well with Gaza's 8,500 settlers. This sets a useful precedent to follow, not only for most of the settlers in the West Bank and East Jerusalem, but also for the Palestinian refugees in Palestine and the diaspora.

* The disengagement represented a painful experience for the Israeli people, yet they realized that this was a necessary step to ensure the security and stability of their country. Sharon defended his decision to withdraw from Gaza and parts of the northern West Bank by saying that it's for the good of Israel, and that Israel would emerge from it a stronger country, since the disengagement plan would shorten Israel's lines of defense on its southern border.

* Unilateralism is a game two can play. The Palestinians may learn from the Israeli unilateralism and move toward taking their own unilateral decision to declare their Palestinian state in the West Bank and the Gaza Strip with East Jerusalem as its capital.

* Unilateralism will not achieve a comprehensive sustainable peace. It takes both sides on a winding and potentially treacherous road.
[...]

RISE OF HAMAS

The Covenant of the Islamic Resistance Movement (Hamas) (1988)
HAMAS

<u>PART I — DEFINITION OF THE MOVEMENT:</u>

<u>Article One</u> (Ideological Premises): The path of the Islamic Resistance Movement is the path of Islam, from which it draws its principles, concepts, terms and worldview with regard to life and man. […]

<u>Article Two</u> (Relationship with Muslim Brotherhood): The Islamic Resistance Movement is the branch of the Muslim Brotherhood in Palestine. […]

<u>Article Six</u> (Distinctiveness and Independence): The Islamic Resistance Movement is uniquely Palestinian. It has faith in Allah and adopts Islam as its way of life. It acts to fly the banner of Allah over all of Palestine, because people of all religions can live in the shadow of Islam in tranquility and security for their lives, property and rights. However, in the absence of Islam a conflict develops that injustice, corruption grows, more conflicts are created, and wars will break out. How great is the Muslim poet Muhammad Iqbal, who wrote:

> "When faith is lost there is no safety and no life for anyone who does not revive religion. He who is content with life without religion has made obliteration of the self his life's companion."

<u>Article Seven</u> (The Universality of the Islamic Resistance Movement): […]

The Islamic Resistance Movement is one of the links in the chain of the struggle against the Zionist invaders. […]

Moreover, if the links have been distant from each other and if obstacles, placed by those who are the lackeys of Zionism in the way of the fighters obstructed the continuation of the struggle, the Islamic Resistance Movement aspires to the realization of Allah's promise, no matter how long that should take. The Prophet, Allah bless him and grant him salvation, has said:

> "The Day of Judgement will not come about until Moslems fight Jews and kill them, when the Jew will hide behind stones and trees. The stones and trees will say O Moslems, O Abdulla, there is a Jew behind me, come and kill him. […] (related by al-Bukhari and Moslem).

Article Eight (The Slogan of Hamas): Allah is its goal, the Prophet its model, the Koran its Constitution, Jihad its path and death for the case of Allah its most sublime belief.

PART II — OBJECTIVES:

Article Nine (Causes and Goals): The Islamic Resistance Movement was born in an era in which Islam was absent from daily life. As a result, balances were upset, concepts were confused, values altered and evil people took power. Injustice and darkness prevailed, cowards behaved like tigers, homelands were taken by force and people were driven out and wandered purposelessly all over the earth. The Country of Truth disappeared and was replaced by the Country of Falsehood, nothing was left in its rightful place. [...]

As to the goals, they are: a war to the death against falsehood, conquering it and stamping it out so that truth may prevail, homelands may be returned and the call of the muezzin may be heard from the turrets of the mosques, announcing the institution of an Islamic state, so that Muslims might return and everything return to its rightful place, with the help of Allah,

> "...and if Allah had not prevented men, the one by the other, verily the earth had been corrupted: but Allah is beneficient towards his creatures." (The Cow - verse 251).

[...]

PART III — STRATEGIES AND METHODS:

Article Eleven (The Strategy of the Islamic Resistance Movement – Palestine is an Islamic Waqf): The Islamic Resistance Movement believes that the land of Palestine is a religious Islamic Waqf for all Muslims until Resurrection Day. It is forbidden to relinquish it or any part of it or give it up or any part of it. [...]

> "Verily, this is a certain truth. Wherefore praise the name of thy Lord, the great Allah." (The Inevitable - verse 95).

Article Twelve (Homeland and Nationalism as Seen by the Islamic Resistance Movement): Nationalism, from the point of view of the Islamic Resistance Movement, is part of the religious creed. Nothing in nationalism is more significant or deeper than in the case when an enemy should tread Moslem land. Resisting and quelling the enemy become the individual duty of every Moslem, male or female. [...]

Article Thirteen (Peaceful Solutions, Initiatives and International Conferences): Initiatives, and so-called peaceful solutions and international conferences to find a solution to the Palestinian problem, contradict the

Islamic Resistance Movement's ideological position. Giving up any part whatsoever of Palestine is like ignoring a part of religion. [...]

> "the Jews will never be pleased with you, nor will the Christians, until you have followed their religion. Say therefore, Allah's guidance is the only true guidance. But if you were to follow their desires after the knowledge that has come to you, then you would find no one to protect or guard you from Allah" (The Cow - verse 120).

There is no solution to the Palestinian problem except jihad. [...]

Article Fourteen (The Three Circles): The problem of the liberation of Palestine has three spheres: the Palestinian, the pan-Arab and the Islamic. Each has a role to play in the struggle against the Zionists. Neglecting one of the spheres is a terrible mistake and shameful ignorance, for Palestine is Islamic land. [...]

> "Verily ye are stronger than they, by reason of the terror cast into their breasts from Allah. This, because they are not people of prudence." (The Emigration - verse 13).

Article Fifteen (Jihad for the Liberation of Palestine is a Personal Duty): The day that enemies usurp part of Moslem land, Jihad becomes the individual duty of every Moslem. In face of the Jews' usurpation of Palestine, it is compulsory that the banner of Jihad be raised. [...]

Article Twenty (Social Solidarity): Islamic society is one of solidarity. The Messenger of Allah, be Allah's prayer and peace upon him, said:

> What a wonderful tribe were the Ash'aris! When they were overtaxed, either in their location or during their journeys, they would collect all their possessions and then would divide them equally among themselves.

This is the Islamic spirit which ought to prevail in any Muslim society. A society which confronts a vicious, Nazi-like enemy, who does not differentiate between man and women, elder and young ought to be the first to adorn itself with this Islamic spirit. Our enemy pursues the style of collective punishment of usurping people's countries and properties, of pursuing them into their exiles and places of assembly. It has resorted to breaking bones, opening fire on women and children and the old, with or without reason, and to setting up detention camps where thousands upon thousands are interned in inhuman conditions. In addition, it destroys houses, renders children orphans and issues oppressive judgements against thousands of young people who spend the best years of their youth in the darkness of prisons. The Nazism of the Jews does not skip women and children, it scares everyone. They make war against people's livelihood, plunder their moneys and threaten their honor. In their horrible actions they mistreat people like the most horrendous war criminals. Exiling people from their country is another way of killing them. As we face this misconduct, we have no escape from establishing social solidarity among the people, from confronting the enemy as one solid body, so that if one organ is hurt the rest of the body will respond with alertness and fervor. [...]

Article Twenty-Two (The Forces Which Support the Enemy): Our enemies planned their deeds well for a long time to achieve whatever they have, employing the factors influencing the course of events. Therefore, they acted to pile up huge amounts of influential material resources, which they utilized to fulfill their dream. Thus, by means of their money, have taken over the international communications media: the news agencies, newspapers, publishing houses, broadcasting stations, etc. They used their money to incite revolutions in various places all over the world for their own interests and to reap the fruits thereof. They were behind the French Revolution, the Communist Revolution and most of the revolutions we have heard about. They used their money to found secret organizations and scattered them all over the globe to destroy other societies and realize the interests of Zionism. These organizations include the Freemasons, the Rotary clubs, the Lions Club, The Sons of the Covenant and others. They are all destructive espionage organizations which, by means of money, succeeded in taking over the imperialist countries and encouraged them to take over many other countries to be able to completely exploit their resources and spread corruption.

Their involvement in local and world wars can be spoken of without fear of embarrassment. In fact, they were behind the First World War, through which achieved the abolishment of the Islamic Caliphate, made a profit and took over many of the sources of wealth. They got the Balfour Declaration and established the League of Nations to be able rule the world. They were also behind the Second World War, in which they made immense profits by buying and selling military equipment, and also prepared the ground for the founding of their state. They ordered the establishment of the United Nations and the Security Council which replaced the League of Nations, to be able to use it to rule the world. No war takes place anywhere in the world without them behind the scenes having a hand in it.

> "So often as they shall kindle a fire for war, Allah shall extinguish it; and they shall set their minds to act corruptly in the earth, but Allah does not like the corrupt." (The Table - verse 64).

[...]

PART IV — OUR POSITIONS ON:

[...]

Article Twenty-Seven (The Palestine Liberation Organization): The PLO is among the closest to the Hamas, for it constitutes a father, a brother, a relative, a friend. Can a Muslim turn away from his father, his brother, his relative or his friend? Our homeland is one, our calamity is one, our destiny is one and our enemy is common to both of us. Under the influence of the circumstances which surrounded the founding of the PLO, and the ideological confusion which prevails in the Arab world as a result of the ideological invasion which has swept the Arab world since the rout of the Crusades, and which has been reinforced by Orientalism and the Christian Mission, the PLO has adopted the idea of a Secular State, and so we think of it. Secular thought is diametrically opposed to religious thought. Thought is the basis for positions, for modes of conduct and for resolutions. Therefore, in spite of our appreciation for the PLO and its possible transformation in the future, and despite the fact that we do not denigrate its role in the Arab-Israeli conflict, we cannot substitute it for the Islamic nature of Palestine by adopting secular thought. For the Islamic nature of Palestine is part of our religion, and anyone who neglects his religion is bound to lose.

> "And who forsakes the religion of Abraham, save him who befools himself.?" (The Cow - verse 130).

The day The Palestinian Liberation Organization adopts Islam as its way of life, we will become its soldiers, and fuel for its fire that will burn the enemies.
[...]
Article Twenty-Eight (Position on Arab and Islamic Countries): The Zionist invasion is a vicious invasion. It does not refrain from resorting to all methods, using all evil and contemptible ways to achieve its end. It relies greatly in its infiltration and espionage operations on the secret organizations it gave rise to, such as the Freemasons, The Rotary and Lions clubs, and other sabotage groups. All these organizations, whether secret or open, work in the interest of Zionism and according to its instructions. They aim at undermining societies, destroying values, corrupting consciences, deteriorating character and annihilating Islam. It is behind the drug trade and alcoholism in all its kinds so as to facilitate its control and expansion.

Therefore, the Arab states bordering Israel are required to open their borders to the jihad warriors belonging to the Arab/Muslim nations, so that they may fulfill their role and join their efforts to those of the Muslim brethren in Palestine.

With regard to the other Arab/Muslim nations, they are required to facilitate the passage of the jihad warriors through their territory, which is the very least they can do. [...]

Article Thirty (Position on Nationalist and Religious Groups and Organizations, Intellectuals, and the Arab and Islamic world): Writers, intellectuals, media people, orators, educators and teachers, and all the various sectors in the Arab and Islamic world – all of them are called upon to perform their role, and to fulfill their duty, because of the ferocity of the Zionist offensive and the Zionist influence in many countries exercised through financial and media control, as well as the consequences that all this lead to in the greater part of the world.

Indeed, jihad is not limited to bearing arms and fighting the enemy face to face. A good word, a good article, an effective book, support and aid – if the intentions are pure – so that Allah's banner becomes supreme, all constitute the essence of jihad for the sake of Allah.

> "Whosoever mobilizes a fighter for the sake of Allah is himself a fighter. Whosoever supports the relatives of a fighter, he himself is a fighter." (related by al-Bukhari, Moslem, Abu-Dawood and al-Tarmadhi).

Article Thirty-One (Followers of the Other Religions: The Islamic Resistance Movement is a Humane Movement): The Islamic Resistance Movement is a humane movement which respects human rights. It is committed to the tolerance of Islam toward the followers of other religions. It is not hostile to them but only so far as they are hostile to it or whoever stands in its way to make it fail or frustrate is efforts.
[…]
Article Thirty-Two (The Attempt to Isolate the Palestinian People): World Zionism and the forces of imperialism are trying in a subtle way and with carefully studied planning, to remove the Arab states, one by one, from the sphere of the conflict with Zionism, in order to finally face the Palestinian people only.

The aforementioned forces have already removed Egypt to a large extent, through the treacherous Camp David accords. They are now trying to draw other Arab states into similar agreements, so that they may also be outside the conflict.

Therefore the Islamic Resistance Movement calls upon the Arab and Muslim peoples to act in all seriousness and with all diligence to frustrate that monstrous plan and to alert the masses to the danger in leaving the sphere of confrontation with Zionism: today it is Palestine and tomorrow part of another country or other countries. The Zionist plan has no limit; after Palestine the Zionists aspire to expand to the Nile and the Euphrates. Once they have devoured the region they arrive at, they will aspire to spread further and then on and on. Their plan appears in *The Protocols of the Elders of Zion*, and their present conduct is the best proof of what we are saying. Therefore, leaving the conflict with the Zionists is high treason, and cursed be he who does that,

"Whoever retreats before them on that day – unless he does so to return and fight again, or to join the other warriors – will have Allah's wrath visited upon him and hell will be his abode. What a wretched fate!" (The Spoils - verse 16).

Therefore, all forces and resources must be pulled together to confront this vicious Nazi Mongol invasion, lest homelands be lost, residents expelled, corruption spread all over the earth and all religious values destroyed. [...]

Part V — The Testimony of History

Article Thirty-Four (Confronting Aggressors Throughout History): [...]

The greedy have coveted Palestine more than once and they raided it with armies in order to fulfill their covetousness. Multitudes of Crusades descended on it, carrying their faith with them and waving their Cross. They were able to defeat the Muslims for a long time, and the Muslims were not able to redeem it until their sought the protection of their religious banner; then, they unified their forces, sang the praise of their God and set out for Jihad under the Command of Saladin al-Ayyubi, for the duration of nearly two decades, and then the obvious conquest took place when the Crusaders were defeated and Palestine was liberated.

> "Say unto those who believe not, Ye shall be overcome, and thrown together into hell; an unhappy couch it shall be." (The Family of Imran - verse 12).

This is the only way to liberation, there is no doubt in the testimony of history. That is one of the rules of the universe and one of the laws of existence. Only iron can blunt iron, only the true faith of Islam can vanquish their false and falsified faith. Faith can only be fought by faith. Ultimately victory is reserved to the truth, and truth is victorious.

> "Our word hath formerly been given unto our servants the apostles; that they should certainly be assisted against the infidels, and that our armies should surely be the conquerors." (Those Who Rank Themselves - verses 171-172).

[...]

Palestinian Elections: Trip Report (2006)
Jimmy Carter

For the third time, The Carter Center agreed to monitor the elections in the West Bank and Gaza, beginning in January 1996, with the choice of Yasir Arafat as president and 88 members of the Palestinian Authority. A year ago, Mahmoud Abbas was chosen to replace the deceased Arafat, and this new election would result in 132 members being chosen to comprise the parliament. Although the result of previous campaigns was predictable, the entry of Hamas candidates brought unprecedented uncertainty and drama to these hard fought contests.

As an organization that refuses to recognize the legitimacy of Israel and calls for violence as a means to achieve its political goals, Hamas has shown great success in local elections held during the past year. Fatah, the party of Arafat and Abbas, has become vulnerable because of its political ineffectiveness and alleged corruption, and many of its old line leaders have been replaced by younger candidates who are mostly loyal to Marwan Bargouti, a militant who is serving five concurrent life sentences in an Israeli prison. Another major factor is that both Israel and the United States have ignored Abbas as an acceptable negotiating partner, debasing him as an ineffective leader in the search for peace.

Late polls indicated that about 35 percent of the parliamentary seats would go to Hamas candidates. Unless there is a dramatic moderation of its policies, even this modest involvement would preclude any initiation of peace talks between Israelis and Palestinians (already absent for 3-1/2 years) and could terminate hundreds of millions of dollars in humanitarian aid from the United States, Europe, and other sources that have been channeled through the Palestinian government.
[...]
Rosalynn and I then had an extensive discussion with Ehud Olmert, acting prime minister, whom we have known for more than 20 years. [...]

Naturally, he will continue Sharon's policies, and made it plain that he would resume peace talks with Abbas, but only if radical Palestinian groups are completely disarmed (a hopeless prospect).
[...]
We drove to Ramallah to meet with the leaders of the Central Election Commission, one of the most honest and effective I have ever known, and then met with Palestinian President Mahmoud Abbas. Although he expressed confidence in the outcome of the election, he was obviously distressed at having been bypassed or ignored in the "peace process." He pointed out that the Palestinian economy was in a shambles, that his government would have difficulty meeting February payrolls and had a $900 million deficit. Israeli policy had precluded the training and equipping of his security force, with only 10 percent of its personnel being armed and equipped with communications equipment.
480

On election day, Rosalynn and I visited 25 polling sites, in East Jerusalem and its outskirts, Hebron, Ramallah, and Jericho. It seemed obvious to us and other observers that the election was orderly and peaceful and that there was a clear preference for Hamas candidates even in historically strong Fatah communities. Even so, we were all surprised at the enormity of the Hamas victory.

They won such a clear majority of parliamentary seats (76 of 132 members) that the Fatah government immediately announced their resignation.

I decided to remain for an extra day to assess the situation and to discuss the future with key leaders. I went to Ramallah and found President Abbas willing to remain as president during the three years remaining in his term but in a quandary about how to deal with the Hamas victory, the formation of a new government, the near bankruptcy of his government, and uncertainty about Israeli policies. He was justifiably proud of the honest, fair, and safe election process. Hamas leaders had expressed their desire to form a unity government with Fatah and the smaller independent parties, but his intention was not to cooperate with them. I urged him to reconsider.

He informed me that there were not enough funds available to meet his February payrolls for teachers, police, nurses, and other social workers, and any reduction in funds because of the election results would be disastrous. He felt that one of the major factors in the voting had been his apparent ineffectiveness as a result of being ignored by Israel and the Quartet leaders. He reminded me that there had been no opportunity for a Palestinian leader to participate in peace talks for almost four years. In our Ramallah office, I learned that the major Hamas leaders were all in Gaza and that there was some question about their being able to come to Ramallah or anywhere else in the West Bank to form a government and to administer Palestinian affairs in the future.

This was hard to believe, so I called the Prime Minister's office and was told that no Hamas party member would be given a pass to change location anywhere within the occupied territories. This would prevent the results of the election from being implemented, and could provoke an intense reaction and perhaps violence among all Palestinians, regardless of party. I informed the U.S. Consul General, who said he had not heard of this policy, and he promised to inform the ambassador, the State Department, and the White House.

Can Hamas Be Tamed? (2006)
Michael Herzog

Hamas' involvement in the democratic process may strike many as a profound irony. After all, the group fields a private army, embraces violence as a political tool, regularly orchestrates terrorist attacks, and is dedicated to the destruction of Israel and the establishment of an Islamist state ruling the territory of Israel and the PA. Granting Hamas legitimate political status and access to the prerogatives of state power seems to be asking for trouble.

[...]

Hamas was founded in 1987 as an offshoot of the pan-Islamic Muslim Brotherhood movement. It sought to address Palestinian nationalist aspirations and grievances from an Islamic perspective; its name, which means "strength," "bravery," and "zeal" in Arabic, is also an acronym for Harakat al-Muqawama al-Islamiya, or the Islamic Resistance Movement.

The group's ideology was set forth in its 1988 covenant, which remains operative to this day. The covenant defines Palestinian nationalism and the conflict with Israel in religious terms: the land of Palestine "from the river to the sea" is considered an Islamic waqf, an "endowment," and so no Muslim has the right to cede any part of it. The covenant explicitly calls for the obliteration of the state of Israel through the power of the sword and portrays the Jews as the source of all evil in the world. Freemasons, Rotarians, and members of organizations similar to theirs are denounced as Zionist agents, and they too are threatened with obliteration. The covenant stipulates that peace between Muslims, Christians, and Jews should only be permitted "under the wing of Islam."

Soon after its founding, Hamas became a major player in both Palestinian-Israeli relations and domestic Palestinian politics, pursuing a dual agenda through the parallel development of an operational and a social wing. The former now oversees hundreds of militants devoted to armed struggle against Israel and is in the process of building a backup militia of several thousand. It has been responsible for countless acts of terror -- from abductions and murders to suicide bombings and rocket attacks -- which have killed hundreds of Israelis, most of them civilians. The group's social arm (dawa), meanwhile, has developed a network of charities and religious, educational, and cultural institutions, positioning Hamas as an attractive provider of social services and an alternative to the hapless and corrupt PA.

Unlike, say, the Irish Republican Army (IRA), Hamas does not have an explicit separation between its military and its political wing. All its branches answer to the same organizational authority, which makes the principal decisions on terror operations as well as on political, social, and

482 Used with permission of Foreign Affairs, from FOREIGN AFFAIRS, Vol. 85, No. 2 (Mar. 1, 2006); permission conveyed through Copyright Clearance Center, Inc.

other policies. Hamas does, however, recognize both an "internal" leadership, living inside the Palestinian territories, and an "external" one, living outside, primarily in Damascus. (The latter seems attuned less to the practical realities on the ground than to the radical environment in the region.)

Arafat believed that it was possible to pursue diplomacy with and violence against Israel simultaneously, and he wanted to avoid major conflict within the Palestinian community. As a result, he tolerated Hamas' opposition to the peace process in both word and deed as long as the group did not directly challenge Oslo's foundations or his own political authority. He tried to co-opt the movement while keeping it at arm's length.

When Arafat died in November 2004, Hamas calculated that the time had come to step forward as a political party and make a bid for legitimate political power. This decision was driven by a number of factors, including the PA's disarray following years of chaotic and corrupt leadership; the weak position of Arafat's successor as president, Mahmoud Abbas; the opportunity to claim credit for Israel's disengagement from Gaza and a share of that territory's subsequent management; and Hamas' own growing reputation as an effective social-service provider and militia.

Abbas made Hamas' decision easier, first by campaigning in the January 2005 presidential election on a platform that clearly differentiated the ruling Fatah Party's appeal from Hamas' (by emphasizing nonviolence and the PA's monopoly on arms) and then by failing to translate the broad mandate he received into serious reforms or effective governance. Sensing its moment, last March, Hamas accepted a temporary cease-fire with Israel in return for Abbas' agreement to incorporate the group into both the Palestine Liberation Organization and the PA's electoral system. Because the deal did not require Hamas to disarm or abandon violence permanently and promised the movement some formal input (through the PLO) in determining Palestinian negotiating positions on final-status issues such as the repatriation of refugees, it rewarded Hamas' violent course and eroded Abbas' own political standing. But the Palestinian leader apparently felt he had little choice, thanks to his own weakness.

It took U.S. and Israeli policymakers some time to focus their attention on this emerging challenge, and when they did, it was too late to do much about it. Although Washington has consistently denounced Hamas' ideology and militancy, it decided not to let these concerns stand in the way of the 2006 Palestinian legislative elections. "This is going to be a Palestinian process, and I think we have to give the Palestinians some room for the evolution of their political process," noted Secretary of State Condoleezza Rice last September. Washington accepted Abbas' assertion that political participation will either transform Hamas or marginalize it. [...]

From the moment Hamas entered the field, polls consistently indicated that it would earn at least a third of the vote and possibly much more in the elections. Its popularity, according to the same polls, stems less from widespread support for its extremist ideology than from dissatisfaction with the PA's corruption and the stagnant Palestinian economy. Understanding this situation well, Hamas ran on a platform stressing reform and good governance rather than ideological struggle. With such a practical appeal and (following its sweeping victory in December's municipal elections) its day-to-day responsibility for the living conditions of almost a third of the population in the territories, Hamas clearly positioned itself as a plausible, and formidable, alternative to the old PA leadership.

[...]

[C]o-optation through political participation is not a given, but rather depends on the existence of certain conditions in the local political context. No Islamist movement has renounced violence or moderated its ideology of its own volition; when one has done so at all, it has been for lack of a better alternative. It appears that at least three factors need to be present for co-optation to occur: the existence of a strong, healthy, and relatively free political system into which the Islamists can be absorbed; a balance of power tilted against the Islamists that forces them to play by moderate rules; and sufficient time for co-optation to take effect.

[...]

Unfortunately, if one looks closely at the case of Hamas, hardly any of these potentially moderating factors are present. Elections in the PA may be relatively free. But Palestinian political, security, and other institutions are a chaotic mess, and the pragmatic political center, represented by Fatah, is in complete disarray. Hamas is launching its political career in the legislative and executive branches without having disarmed and is quite possibly stronger than the rest of the state apparatus. Despite Abbas' occasional promises that he will force Hamas to disarm, no domestic player will be able to check the group's extremist tendencies, nor will any rules or safeguards be in place to proscribe unacceptable behavior.

[...]

The ongoing Palestinian-Israeli conflict, meanwhile, adds fuel to the fire of domestic Palestinian turmoil and to extremism. It provides an excuse for tolerating private armies within the PA and enhances the legitimacy of Hamas' rejectionist stance. Opinion polls show that although most Palestinians disagree with Hamas' ideological extremism and support a two-state solution to the conflict, they also accept the notion of "armed struggle" as a legitimate route to get there, citing the Israeli withdrawal from Gaza as an example of what such pressure can achieve. This complicated preference structure gives Hamas a perverse incentive to disrupt progress in diplomatic negotiations, since the normalization of Palestinian-Israeli relations could well lessen Hamas' appeal. As long as its military and political power enhance each other, Hamas will be able to fend off pressures to disarm and will derail progress toward peace. [...]

BLOCKADE

The Blockade: Introduction and Overview (2009)
UNITED NATIONS FACT-FINDING MISSION ON THE GAZA CONFLICT

312. The series of economic and political measures imposed against the Gaza Strip began around February 2006 with the Hamas electoral victory in the legislative elections. [...] Hamas took over effective power in the Gaza Strip on 15 June 2007. Shortly thereafter Israel declared the Gaza Strip a "hostile territory," enacting a series of economic, social and military measures purportedly designed to isolate and strangle Hamas. These have made a deep impact on the population's living standards.

313. The blockade comprises measures such as the closure of border crossings, sometimes completely for a number of days, for people, goods and services, and for the provision of fuel and electricity. The closure has had severe effects on trade and general business activity, agriculture and industry in the Gaza Strip. Electricity and fuel that are provided from Israel are essential for a broad range of activities from business to education, health services, industry and agriculture. Further limits to the fishing area in the sea adjacent to the Gaza Strip were fixed and enforced by Israel, negatively impacting on fishing activities and the livelihood of the fishing community. Israel also established a buffer zone of variable and uncertain width along the border, together with a sizeable no-go area in the northern part of the Gaza Strip where some Israeli settlements used to be situated. [...] The creation of the buffer zone has forced the relocation of a number of factories from this area closer to Gaza City, causing serious environmental concerns and potential health hazards for the population. People's movements have also been drastically restricted, with only a few businesspeople allowed to cross on a very irregular and unpredictable basis.

314. Because of the occupation, which created so many ties of dependence, and for other geographic, political and historical reasons, the availability of goods and services as well as the carrying-on of daily life in the Gaza Strip are highly dependent on Israel and its policies regarding the area. Food and other consumable items as well as fuel, electricity, construction materials and other items are traded from or through Israel. [...] There are five crossing points between Israel and the Gaza Strip: Erez (basically dedicated to the transit of people), Nahal Oz (for fuel), Karni (for grains), Kerem Shalom (for goods) and Sufa (for goods). Israeli control of these crossings has always been restrictive for the Gaza population. Since the beginning of the blockade [...] not only has the measure of restriction increased, but control has been exercised arbitrarily,

From Human Rights in Palestine and Other Occupied Arab Territories: 485
Report of the United Nations Fact-Finding Mission on the Gaza Conflict, UN
Doc. A/HRC/12/48 (Sep. 25, 2009).

resulting in uncertainty of access even for those items purportedly allowed entry by Israel.

315. Movement of people through the Erez crossing to Israel and the Rafah crossing to Egypt has been almost completely blocked. Exceptions include unpredictable and irregular permission for emergency medical evacuations, access to diplomats and international humanitarian staff and only limited access to some businesspeople.

316. The movement of goods has been restricted to imports of basic humanitarian supplies through the Kerem Shalom crossing point as well as to a limited quantity of fuel. The quantities of goods allowed into the Gaza Strip have not only been insufficient to meet local demands, they also exclude several items essential for the manufacturing of goods and the processing of food products, as well as many other goods that are needed. This is compounded by the unpredictable way in which crossings are managed. Neither the list of items allowed into the Gaza Strip nor the criteria for their selection are made known to the public.

317. [...] [T]he blockade had resulted in a significant reduction in the number of trucks allowed through the crossings. The number of trucks is considered a fair measure of the amount of imports into or exports from the Gaza Strip. [...]

318. The 2005 Agreement of Movement and Access called for a daily flow of some 400 trucks in and out of Gaza by the end of 2006, which was already lower than before the second intifada, but not even that level was ever reached. [...]

319. In effect, economic activity in the Gaza Strip was severely affected because of the blockade. [...] The private sector, particularly the manufacturing industry, has suffered irreparable damage.

320. The blockade and freeze on the movement of goods imposed by Israel have spurred a black market economy in the Gaza Strip that provides basic consumables but is unreliable and unaffordable for the majority of the people. The tunnels built under the Gaza-Egypt border have become a lifeline for the Gaza economy and the people. Increasing amounts of fuel (benzine and diesel) come through those tunnels as well as consumables. [...]

321. The blockade has also included measures relating to access to the sea and airspace. [...] The only airfield in Gaza has been closed and a project to rebuild the small airport was suspended after the seizure of power by Hamas. Israel keeps total control over Gaza's airspace. [...]

70. [...] The naval blockade is often discussed in tandem with the Israeli restrictions on the land crossings to Gaza. However, in the Panel's view, these are in fact two distinct concepts which require different treatment and analysis. First, we note that the land crossings policy has been in place since long before the naval blockade was instituted. In particular, the tightening of border controls between Gaza and Israel came about after the take-over of Hamas in Gaza in June 2007. On the other hand, the naval blockade was imposed more than a year later, in January 2009. Second, Israel has always kept its policies on the land crossings separate from the naval blockade. The land restrictions have fluctuated in intensity over time but the naval blockade has not been altered since its imposition. Third, the naval blockade as a distinct legal measure was imposed primarily to enable a legally sound basis for Israel to exert control over ships attempting to reach Gaza with weapons and related goods. This was in reaction to certain incidents when vessels had reached Gaza via sea. We therefore treat the naval blockade as separate and distinct from the controls at the land crossings. [...]

71. [...] Israel has faced and continues to face a real threat to its security from militant groups in Gaza. Rockets, missiles and mortar bombs have been launched from Gaza towards Israel since 2001. More than 5,000 were fired between 2005 and January 2009, when the naval blockade was imposed. [...] It seems obvious enough that stopping these violent acts was a necessary step for Israel to take in order to protect its people and to defend itself. Actions taken by Israel in turn have had severe impacts on the civilian population in Gaza. [...]

72. [...] The Israeli report to the Panel makes it clear that the naval blockade as a measure of the use of force was adopted for the purpose of defending its territory and population, and the Panel accepts that was the case. It was designed as one way to prevent weapons reaching Gaza by sea and to prevent such attacks to be launched from the sea. Indeed there have been various incidents in which ships carrying weapons were intercepted by the Israeli authorities on their way to Gaza. While the attacks have not completely ceased since the time of the imposition of the naval blockade, their scale and intensity has much decreased over time. [...] Although a blockade by definition imposes a restriction on all maritime traffic, given the relatively small size of the blockade zone and the practical difficulties associated with other methods of monitoring vessels (such as by search and visit), the Panel is not persuaded that the naval blockade was a disproportionate measure for Israel to have taken in response to the threat it faced.
[...]

From <u>Report of the Secretary-General's Panel of Inquiry on the 31 May 2010 Flotilla Incident</u> (Sep. 2, 2011).   487

77. Important humanitarian considerations constrain the imposition of a naval blockade. For one, it would be illegal if its imposition was intended to starve or to collectively punish the civilian population. However, there is no material before the Panel that would permit a finding confirming the allegations that Israel had either of those intentions or that the naval blockade was imposed in retaliation for the take-over of Hamas in Gaza or otherwise. On the contrary, it is evident that Israel had a military objective. The stated primary objective of the naval blockade was for security. It was to prevent weapons, ammunition, military supplies and people from entering Gaza and to stop Hamas operatives sailing away from Gaza with vessels filled with explosives. This is regardless of what considerations might have motivated Israel in restricting the entry of goods to Gaza via the land crossings, an issue which as we have described above is not directly related to the naval blockade. It is also noteworthy that the earliest maritime interception operations to prevent weapons smuggling to Gaza predated the 2007 take-over of Hamas in Gaza. The actual naval blockade was imposed more than one year after that event. These factors alone indicate it was not imposed to punish its citizens for the election of Hamas.

78. [...] As this report has already indicated, we are satisfied that the naval blockade was based on the need to preserve Israel's security. Stopping the importation of rockets and other weapons to Gaza by sea helps alleviate Israel's situation as it finds itself the target of countless attacks, which at the time of writing have once again become more extensive and intensive. On the other hand, the specific impact of the naval blockade on the civilian population in Gaza is difficult to gauge because it is the land crossings policy that primarily determines the amount of goods permitted to reach Gaza. One important consideration is the absence of significant port facilities in Gaza. The only vessels that can be handled in Gaza appear to be small fishing vessels. This means that the prospect of delivering significant supplies to Gaza by sea is very low. Indeed, such supplies were not entering by sea prior to the blockade. [...] Smuggling weapons by sea is one thing; delivering bulky food and other goods to supply a population of approximately 1.5 million people is another. Such facts militate against a finding that the naval blockade itself has a significant humanitarian impact. [...]

Gaza-Egypt Border Restrictions Worsening Humanitarian Situation of Palestinians, says UN (2013)

UN NEWS

The Egyptian-controlled Rafah Crossing is Gaza's main gateway to the outside world, following the long-term restrictions imposed on the crossings controlled by Israel [....]

However, recent action by Egypt to counter illegal activities and insecurity in the Sinai have included imposing "severe" restrictions on the movement of people through the Rafah Crossing and closing down smuggling tunnels under the Egyptian-Gaza border.

At the same time, there has been only limited easing of the ongoing restrictions imposed at legitimate crossing points from Israel.

"Consequently, an already fragile humanitarian situation in the Gaza Strip has worsened," states the report.

When open, the operating hours at the Rafah Crossing are four hours a day, six days per week – reduced from nine hours, seven days per week. Only authorized travellers have been permitted to cross, including foreign nationals, people holding visas, and patients officially referred for medical treatment abroad.

"As a result, the vast majority of Gazans, who do not meet these criteria, are unable to cross," the report points out. "On average, fewer than 400 people per day have crossed in both directions since July 2013, about 29 per cent of the numbers who crossed in the first half of 2013."

The report also notes that most of the illegal tunnels under the Egyptian-Gaza border – the main channel for the supply of construction materials and fuel – have been shut down. As of 21 September, only an estimated 10 tunnels were believed to be operating, down from approximately 300 prior to June.

The Gaza Power Plant has been forced to reduce electricity production and may shut down completely, if adequate fuel supplies are not urgently made available.

Fuel shortages and increased power outages, according to OCHA, are "significantly" impacting the provision of essential services, shortages of construction materials are impeding maintenance and rehabilitation of essential service infrastructure, and restricted access for people through Rafah Crossing is impeding access to specialized health services abroad. [...]

EU Funded Water Pipelines Despite Hamas Boast it Could Turn Them into Rockets (2023)
Joe Barnes

The European Union helped to build more than 30 miles of water pipelines for Palestinians despite Hamas terrorists boasting of their ability to forge an arsenal of home-made rockets from pipes.

Brussels has poured almost €100 million into pipeline projects in territories controlled by the Islamist group over the last decade, a Telegraph analysis of the bloc's foreign aid found.
[…]

Aid decision followed 'tetchy' meeting
[…]

In 2021 footage emerged of Hamas terrorists excavating pipes from the desert that were eventually fashioned into home-made rockets.

Their main armament has been the Qassam rocket, assembled from industrial piping, makeshift rocket fuel of sugar and potassium nitrate fertiliser and commercially available explosives.

On Saturday, Hamas claimed it launched at least 5,000 rockets before mounting a ground assault across the border.

While the Telegraph cannot independently verify the exact weapons used in the mass bombardment, it has raised fears over whether Western-donated building supplies could have been used to manufacture some of the munitions.
[…]

Between the period of 2015 and 2022, the EU contributed to multiple schemes to help deliver fresh water to Palestinian territories.

The first of which was the "completion of an 18-kilometre (11-mile) pipeline" to provide 75,000 Palestinians with clean, drinking water in Gaza, alongside Unicef.

The pipeline transported desalinated seawater from a plant to the settlements of Khan Yunis and Rafah in southern Gaza, where it was estimated that 95 per cent of water was unfit for human consumption.

Another scheme delivered 2.6 miles of pipelines as part of a sewage treatment plant in Tubas, Tayasir and Aqqaba, south of known Hamas hotspot Jenin.

By the next year, EU humanitarian aid missions had further delivered some 16 miles of water pipelines to Palestine territory.
[…]

UN Suspends Aid Operation After Second Hamas-Linked Theft of Supplies (2009)

UN NEWS

Secretary-General Ban Ki-moon demanded that Hamas immediately return the food to the UN Relief and Works Agency for Palestine Refugees in the Near East (UNRWA), which said its suspension would remain in force until such a return and "the Agency is given credible assurances from the Hamas government in Gaza that there will be no repeat of these thefts."
[…]
He reiterated Security Council calls for the unimpeded provision and distribution of humanitarian aid, including food, fuel and medical treatment, throughout Gaza.

The seizures followed repeated UNRWA warnings that not nearly enough food and other vital supplies were getting through because of Israel's closure of most crossing points into Gaza. Just hours before the latest seizure, UNRWA Director of Operations in Gaza John Ging had warned that the Agency would suspend operations if there was a repeat.

Although the amount stolen in the first seizure was small, "it's massive in its significance because they've crossed a red line," Mr. Ging said.

During the night of 5 February 10 truckloads of flour and rice were taken from the Palestinian side of the Kerem Shalom Crossing into Gaza, UNRWA said in a statement. "They had been imported from Egypt for collection by UNRWA today," it added. "The food was taken away by trucks contracted by the Ministry of Social Affairs. Two hundred metric tons of rice and 100 metric tons of flour were taken."

On Tuesday, 3,500 blankets and over 400 food parcels were taken at gunpoint from a distribution store in Beach Camp in Gaza. Hamas said it would give out the aid itself and Mr. Ging yesterday told Hamas to "stop the nonsense that they've been coming out with trying to justify what they did and accept that it was an egregious error."
[…]

DEVOLUTION

Why I Blew the Whistle About Palestine (2011)
Ziyad Clot

In Palestine, the time has come for national reconciliation. On the eve of
the 63rd commemoration of the Nakba – the uprooting of Palestinians that
accompanied the creation of Israel in 1948 – this is a long-awaited and
hopeful moment. Earlier this year the release by al-Jazeera and the
Guardian of 1,600 documents related to the so-called peace process caused
deep consternation among Palestinians and in the Arab world. Covering
more than 10 years of talks (from 1999 to 2010) between Israel and the
PLO, the Palestine papers illustrated the tragic consequences of an
inequitable and destructive political process which had been based on the
assumption that the Palestinians could in effect negotiate their rights and
achieve self-determination while enduring the hardship of the Israeli
occupation.

My name has been circulated as one of the possible sources of these leaks.
I would like to clarify here the extent of my involvement in these
revelations and explain my motives. I have always acted in the best interest
of the Palestinian people, in its entirety, and to the full extent of my
capacity.

My own experience with the "peace process" started in Ramallah, in
January 2008, after I was recruited as an adviser for the negotiation support
unit (NSU) of the PLO, specifically in charge of the Palestinian refugee
file. That was a few weeks after a goal had been set at the Annapolis
conference: the creation of the Palestinian state by the end of 2008. Only
11 months into my job, in November of that year, I resigned. By December
2008, instead of the establishment of a state in Palestine, I witnessed on
TV the killing of more than 1,400 Palestinians in Gaza by the Israeli army.

My strong motives for leaving my position with the NSU and my
assessment of the "peace process" were clearly detailed to Palestinian
negotiators in my resignation letter dated of 9th November 2008.

The "peace negotiations" were a deceptive farce whereby biased terms
were unilaterally imposed by Israel and systematically endorsed by the US
and EU. Far from enabling a negotiated and fair end to the conflict, the
pursuit of the Oslo process deepened Israeli segregationist policies and
justified the tightening of the security control imposed on the Palestinian
population, as well as its geographical fragmentation. Far from preserving
the land on which to build a state, it has tolerated the intensification of the
colonisation of the Palestinian territory. Far from maintaining a national
cohesion, the process I participated in, albeit briefly, was instrumental in

creating and aggravating divisions among Palestinians. In its most recent developments, it became a cruel enterprise from which the Palestinians of Gaza have suffered the most. Last but not least, these negotiations excluded for the most part the great majority of the Palestinian people: the seven million Palestinian refugees. My experience over those 11 months in Ramallah confirmed that the PLO, given its structure, was not in a position to represent all Palestinian rights and interests.

Tragically, the Palestinians were left uninformed of the fate of their individual and collective rights in the negotiations, and their divided political leaderships were not held accountable for their decisions or inaction. After I resigned, I believed I had a duty to inform the public.

Shortly after the Gaza war I started to write about my experience in Ramallah. In my 2010 book, *Il n'y aura pas d'Etat Palestinien* (There will be no Palestinian State), I concluded: "The peace process is a spectacle, a farce, played to the detriment of Palestinian reconciliation, at the cost of the bloodshed in Gaza." In full conscience, and acting independently, I later agreed to share some information with al-Jazeera specifically with regard to the fate of Palestinian refugee rights in the 2008 talks. Other sources did the same, although I am unaware of their identity. Taking these tragic developments of the "peace process" to a wider Arab and western audience was justified because it was in the public interest of the Palestinian people. I had – and still have – no doubt that I had a moral, legal and political obligation to proceed accordingly.

Today, I am relieved that this first-hand information is available to Palestinians in the occupied Palestinian territory, in Israel and in exile. In a way, Palestinian rights are back in their holders' possession and the people are now in a position to make enlightened decisions about the future of their struggle. I am also glad that international stakeholders to the Israeli-Palestinian conflict can access these documents. The world can no longer overlook that while Palestinians' strong commitment to peace is genuine, the fruitless pursuit of a "peace process" framed according to the exclusive conditions of the occupying power leads to compromises which would be unacceptable in any other region of the globe.

Finally, I feel reassured that the people of Palestine overwhelmingly realise that the reconciliation between all their constituents must be the first step towards national liberation. The Palestinians from the West Bank and the Gaza Strip, the Palestinians in Israel and the Palestinians living in exile have a common future. The path to Palestinian self-determination will require the participation of all in a renewed political platform.

The Occupied Palestinian Territory: the Gaza Strip
[...]
2. OVERVIEW OF ISRAEL'S MILITARY OPERATIONS IN THE GAZA STRIP AND
CASUALTIES

29. Israel deployed its navy, air force and army in the operation it
codenamed "Operation Cast Lead". The military operations in the Gaza
Strip included two main phases, the air phase and the air-land phase, and
lasted from 27 December 2008 to 18 January 2009. The Israeli offensive
began with a week-long air attack, from 27 December until 3 January
2009. The air force continued to play an important role in assisting and
covering the ground forces from 3 January to 18 January 2009. The army
was responsible for the ground invasion, which began on 3 January 2009,
when ground troops entered Gaza from the north and the east. [...] The
navy was used in part to shell the Gaza coast during the operations. [...]

30. Statistics about Palestinians who lost their lives during the military
operations vary. Based on extensive field research, non-governmental
organizations place the overall number of persons killed between 1,387 and
1,417. [...]

31. According to the Government of Israel, during the military operations
there were four Israeli fatalities in southern Israel, of whom three were
civilians and one a soldier. [...] In addition, nine Israeli soldiers were
killed during the fighting inside the Gaza strip, four of whom as a result of
friendly fire.
[...]
4. OBLIGATION ON PALESTINIAN ARMED GROUPS IN GAZA TO TAKE
FEASIBLE PRECAUTIONS TO PROTECT THE CIVILIAN POPULATION AND
CIVILIAN OBJECTS

35. [...] The Mission was faced with a certain reluctance by the persons it
interviewed in Gaza to discuss the activities of the armed groups. On the
basis of the information gathered, the Mission found that Palestinian armed
groups were present in urban areas during the military operations and
launched rockets from urban areas. It may be that the Palestinian
combatants did not at all times adequately distinguish themselves from the
civilian population. The Mission found no evidence, however, to suggest
that Palestinian armed groups either directed civilians to areas where
attacks were being launched or that they forced civilians to remain within
the vicinity of the attacks.

494 From Human Rights in Palestine and Other Occupied Arab Territories:
Report of the United Nations Fact-Finding Mission on the Gaza Conflict, UN
Doc. A/HRC/12/48 (Sep. 25, 2009).

36. Although the incidents investigated by the Mission did not establish the use of mosques for military purposes or to shield military activities, it cannot exclude that this might have occurred in other cases. The Mission did not find any evidence to support the allegations that hospital facilities were used by the Gaza authorities or by Palestinian armed groups to shield military activities or that ambulances were used to transport combatants or for other military purposes. [...] While the conduct of hostilities in built-up areas does not, of itself, constitute a violation of international law, Palestinian armed groups, where they launched attacks close to civilian or protected buildings, unnecessarily exposed the civilian population of Gaza to danger.

5. OBLIGATION ON ISRAEL TO TAKE FEASIBLE PRECAUTIONS TO PROTECT THE CIVILIAN POPULATION AND CIVILIAN OBJECTS IN GAZA

37. [...] The Mission acknowledges the significant efforts made by Israel to issue warnings through telephone calls, leaflets and radio broadcasts, and accepts that in some cases, particularly when the warnings were sufficiently specific, they encouraged residents to leave an area and get out of harm's way. [...] The Mission also examined the practice of dropping lighter explosives on roofs (so-called roof knocking). It concludes that this technique is not effective as a warning and constitutes a form of attack against the civilians inhabiting the building. [...]

6. INDISCRIMINATE ATTACKS BY ISRAELI FORCES RESULTING IN THE LOSS OF LIFE AND INJURY TO CIVILIANS

41. The Mission examined the mortar shelling of al-Fakhura junction in Jabaliyah next to a UNRWA school, which, at the time, was sheltering more than 1,300 people. The Israeli armed forces launched at least four mortar shells. One landed in the courtyard of a family home, killing 11 people assembled there. Three other shells landed on al-Fakhura Street, killing at least a further 24 people and injuring as many as 40. The Mission examined in detail statements by Israeli Government representatives alleging that the attack was launched in response to a mortar attack from an armed Palestinian group. While the Mission does not exclude that this may have been the case, it considers the credibility of Israel's position damaged by the series of inconsistencies, contradictions and factual inaccuracies in the statements justifying the attack.
[...]

7. DELIBERATE ATTACKS AGAINST THE CIVILIAN POPULATION

43. The Mission investigated 11 incidents in which the Israeli armed forces launched direct attacks against civilians with lethal outcome. The facts in all bar one of the attacks indicate no justifiable military objective. The first two are attacks on houses in the al-Samouni neighbourhood south of Gaza City, including the shelling of a house in which Palestinian civilians had

been forced to assemble by the Israeli armed forces. The following group of seven incidents concern the shooting of civilians while they were trying to leave their homes to walk to a safer place, waving white flags and, in some of the cases, following an injunction from the Israeli forces to do so. [...]

44. These incidents indicate that the instructions given to the Israeli armed forces moving into Gaza provided for a low threshold for the use of lethal fire against the civilian population. The Mission found strong corroboration of this trend in the testimonies of Israeli soldiers collected in two publications it reviewed.
[...]

8. THE USE OF CERTAIN WEAPONS

48. Based on its investigation of incidents involving the use of certain weapons such as white phosphorous and flechette missiles, the Mission, while accepting that white phosphorous is not at this stage proscribed under international law, finds that the Israeli armed forces were systematically reckless in determining its use in built-up areas. [...]

9. ATTACKS ON THE FOUNDATIONS OF CIVILIAN LIFE IN GAZA: DESTRUCTION OF INDUSTRIAL INFRASTRUCTURE, FOOD PRODUCTION, WATER INSTALLATIONS, SEWAGE TREATMENT PLANTS AND HOUSING

50. [...] Already at the beginning of the military operations, el-Bader flour mill was the only flour mill in the Gaza Strip still operating. The flour mill was hit by a series of air strikes on 9 January 2009, after several false warnings had been issued on previous days. The Mission finds that its destruction had no military justification. [...] The Mission also finds that the destruction of the mill was carried out to deny sustenance to the civilian population [....]

51. The chicken farms of Mr. Sameh Sawafeary in the Zeytoun neighbourhood south of Gaza City reportedly supplied over 10 per cent of the Gaza egg market. Armoured bulldozers of the Israeli armed forces systematically flattened the chicken coops, killing all 31,000 chickens inside, and destroyed the plant and material necessary for the business. The Mission concludes that this was a deliberate act of wanton destruction not justified by any military necessity and draws the same legal conclusions as in the case of the destruction of the flour mill.

52. The Israeli armed forces also carried out a strike against a wall of one of the raw sewage lagoons of the Gaza wastewater treatment plant, which caused the outflow of more than 200,000 cubic metres of raw sewage onto neighbouring farmland. The circumstances of the strike suggest that it was deliberate and premeditated. The Namar wells complex in Jabaliyah consisted of two water wells, pumping machines, a generator, fuel storage,

a reservoir chlorination unit, buildings and related equipment. All were destroyed by multiple air strikes on the first day of the Israeli aerial attack. The Mission […] found no grounds to suggest that there was any military advantage to be had by hitting the wells and noted that there was no suggestion that Palestinian armed groups had used the wells for any purpose. […]

53. During its visits to the Gaza Strip, the Mission witnessed the extent of the destruction of residential housing caused by air strikes, mortar and artillery shelling, missile strikes, the operation of bulldozers and demolition charges. In some cases, residential neighbourhoods were subjected to air-launched bombing and to intensive shelling apparently in the context of the advance of Israeli ground forces. In others, the facts gathered by the Mission strongly suggest that the destruction of housing was carried out in the absence of any link to combat engagements with Palestinian armed groups or any other effective contribution to military action. Combining the results of its own fact-finding on the ground with UNOSAT satellite imagery and the published testimonies of Israeli soldiers, the Mission concludes that, in addition to the extensive destruction of housing for so-called operational necessity during their advance, the Israeli armed forces engaged in another wave of systematic destruction of civilian buildings during the last three days of their presence in Gaza, aware of their imminent withdrawal. […]

54. The attacks on industrial facilities, food production and water infrastructure investigated by the Mission are part of a broader pattern of destruction, which includes the destruction of the only cement-packaging plant in Gaza (the Atta Abu Jubbah plant), the Abu Eida factories for ready-mix concrete, further chicken farms and the al-Wadiyah Group's food and drinks factories. The facts ascertained by the Mission indicate that there was a deliberate and systematic policy on the part of the Israeli armed forces to target industrial sites and water installations.

10. THE USE OF PALESTINIAN CIVILIANS AS HUMAN SHIELDS

55. The Mission investigated four incidents in which the Israeli armed forces coerced Palestinian civilian men at gunpoint to take part in house searches during the military operations. The men were blindfolded and handcuffed as they were forced to enter houses ahead of the Israeli soldiers. […] The Mission concludes that this practice amounts to the use of Palestinian civilians as human shields and is therefore prohibited by international humanitarian law. […]

11. Deprivation of Liberty: Gazans detained during the Israeli military operations of 27 December 2008 to 18 January 2009

56. During the military operations, the Israeli armed forces rounded up large numbers of civilians and detained them in houses and open spaces in Gaza and, in the case of many Palestinian men, also took them to detention facilities in Israel. In the cases investigated by the Mission, the facts gathered indicate that none of the civilians was armed or posed any apparent threat to the Israeli soldiers. [...]

60. In addition to arbitrary deprivation of liberty and violation of due process rights, the cases of the detained Palestinian civilians highlight a common thread of the interaction between Israeli soldiers and Palestinian civilians which also emerged clearly in many cases discussed elsewhere in the report: continuous and systematic abuse, outrages on personal dignity, humiliating and degrading treatment contrary to fundamental principles of international humanitarian law and human rights law. The Mission concludes that this treatment constitutes the infliction of a collective penalty on these civilians and amounts to measures of intimidation and terror. [...]

12. Objectives and strategy of Israel's military operations in Gaza

61. [...] According to official Government information, the Israeli armed forces have an elaborate legal advice and training system in place, which seeks to ensure knowledge of the relevant legal obligations and support to commanders for compliance in the field. The Israeli armed forces possess very advanced hardware and are also a market leader in the production of some of the most advanced pieces of military technology available, including unmanned aviation vehicles (UAVs). They have a very significant capacity for precision strikes by a variety of methods, including aerial and ground launches. Taking into account the ability to plan, the means to execute plans with the most developed technology available, and statements by the Israeli military that almost no errors occurred, the Mission finds that the incidents and patterns of events considered in the report are the result of deliberate planning and policy decisions.

62. The tactics used by the Israeli armed forces in the Gaza offensive are consistent with previous practices, most recently during the Lebanon war in 2006. A concept known as the Dahiya doctrine emerged then, involving the application of disproportionate force and the causing of great damage and destruction to civilian property and infrastructure, and suffering to civilian populations. The Mission concludes from a review of the facts on the ground that it witnessed for itself that what was prescribed as the best strategy appears to have been precisely what was put into practice. [...]

13. THE IMPACT OF THE MILITARY OPERATIONS AND OF THE BLOCKADE ON THE PEOPLE OF GAZA AND THEIR HUMAN RIGHTS
[...]

66. [...] [T]he military operations destroyed a substantial part of the economic infrastructure. As many factories were targeted and destroyed or damaged, poverty, unemployment and food insecurity further increased dramatically. The agricultural sector similarly suffered from the destruction of farmland, water wells and fishing boats during the military operations. [...]

67. [...] Even before the military operations, 80 per cent of the water supplied in Gaza did not meet the World Health Organization's standards for drinking water. The discharge of untreated or partially treated wastewater into the sea is a further health hazard worsened by the military operations.
[...]
Israel

1. IMPACT ON CIVILIANS OF ROCKET AND MORTAR ATTACKS BY PALESTINIAN ARMED GROUPS ON SOUTHERN ISRAEL

103. Palestinian armed groups have launched about 8000 rockets and mortars into southern Israel since 2001. [...]

104. Between 18 June 2008 and 18 January 2009, rockets fired by Palestinian armed groups in Gaza have killed three civilians inside Israel and two civilians in Gaza [....] Reportedly, over 1000 civilians inside Israel were physically injured as a result of rocket and mortar attacks, 918 of whom were injured during the time of the Israeli military operations in Gaza.
[...]
107. The rocket and mortar fire has also had an adverse impact on the economic and social life of the affected communities. [...]

108. The Mission has determined that the rockets and, to a lesser extent, the mortars fired by the Palestinian armed groups are incapable of being directed towards specific military objectives and have been fired into areas where civilian populations are based. The Mission has further determined that these attacks constitute indiscriminate attacks upon the civilian population of southern Israel and that, where there is no intended military target and the rockets and mortars are launched into a civilian population, they constitute a deliberate attack against a civilian population. [...]

Reconsidering the Goldstone Report on Israel and War Crimes (2011)
Richard Goldstone

We know a lot more today about what happened in the Gaza war of 2008-09 than we did when I chaired the fact-finding mission appointed by the U.N. Human Rights Council that produced what has come to be known as the Goldstone Report. If I had known then what I know now, the Goldstone Report would have been a different document.

The final report by the U.N. committee of independent experts — chaired by former New York judge Mary McGowan Davis — that followed up on the recommendations of the Goldstone Report has found that "Israel has dedicated significant resources to investigate over 400 allegations of operational misconduct in Gaza" while "the de facto authorities (i.e., Hamas) have not conducted any investigations into the launching of rocket and mortar attacks against Israel."

Our report found evidence of potential war crimes and "possibly crimes against humanity" by both Israel and Hamas. That the crimes allegedly committed by Hamas were intentional goes without saying — its rockets were purposefully and indiscriminately aimed at civilian targets.

The allegations of intentionality by Israel were based on the deaths of and injuries to civilians in situations where our fact-finding mission had no evidence on which to draw any other reasonable conclusion. While the investigations published by the Israeli military and recognized in the U.N. committee's report have established the validity of some incidents that we investigated in cases involving individual soldiers, they also indicate that civilians were not intentionally targeted as a matter of policy.

For example, the most serious attack the Goldstone Report focused on was the killing of some 29 members of the al-Simouni family in their home. The shelling of the home was apparently the consequence of an Israeli commander's erroneous interpretation of a drone image, and an Israeli officer is under investigation for having ordered the attack. While the length of this investigation is frustrating, it appears that an appropriate process is underway, and I am confident that if the officer is found to have been negligent, Israel will respond accordingly. The purpose of these investigations, as I have always said, is to ensure accountability for improper actions, not to second-guess, with the benefit of hindsight, commanders making difficult battlefield decisions.

500 From Former Chair of the UN Fact-Finding Mission on the Gaza Conflict, "Reconsidering the Goldstone Report on Israel and War Crimes," Washington Post, 1 April 2011, Richard Goldstone, JOURNAL OF PALESTINE STUDIES, Vol. 40, No. 4, © 2011 Institute for Palestine Studies, reprinted by permission of Informa UK Limited, trading as Taylor & Francis Group, www.tandfonline.com on behalf of 2011 Institute for Palestine Studies.

While I welcome Israel's investigations into allegations, I share the concerns reflected in the McGowan Davis report that few of Israel's inquiries have been concluded and believe that the proceedings should have been held in a public forum. Although the Israeli evidence that has emerged since publication of our report doesn't negate the tragic loss of civilian life, I regret that our fact-finding mission did not have such evidence explaining the circumstances in which we said civilians in Gaza were targeted, because it probably would have influenced our findings about intentionality and war crimes.

Israel's lack of cooperation with our investigation meant that we were not able to corroborate how many Gazans killed were civilians and how many were combatants. The Israeli military's numbers have turned out to be similar to those recently furnished by Hamas (although Hamas may have reason to inflate the number of its combatants).

As I indicated from the very beginning, I would have welcomed Israel's cooperation. The purpose of the Goldstone Report was never to prove a foregone conclusion against Israel. I insisted on changing the original mandate adopted by the Human Rights Council, which was skewed against Israel. I have always been clear that Israel, like any other sovereign nation, has the right and obligation to defend itself and its citizens against attacks from abroad and within. Something that has not been recognized often enough is the fact that our report marked the first time illegal acts of terrorism from Hamas were being investigated and condemned by the United Nations. I had hoped that our inquiry into all aspects of the Gaza conflict would begin a new era of evenhandedness at the U.N. Human Rights Council, whose history of bias against Israel cannot be doubted.

Some have charged that the process we followed did not live up to judicial standards. To be clear: Our mission was in no way a judicial or even quasi-judicial proceeding. We did not investigate criminal conduct on the part of any individual in Israel, Gaza or the West Bank. We made our recommendations based on the record before us, which unfortunately did not include any evidence provided by the Israeli government. Indeed, our main recommendation was for each party to investigate, transparently and in good faith, the incidents referred to in our report. McGowan Davis has found that Israel has done this to a significant degree; Hamas has done nothing.

Some have suggested that it was absurd to expect Hamas, an organization that has a policy to destroy the state of Israel, to investigate what we said were serious war crimes. It was my hope, even if unrealistic, that Hamas would do so, especially if Israel conducted its own investigations. At minimum I hoped that in the face of a clear finding that its members were committing serious war crimes, Hamas would curtail its attacks. Sadly, that has not been the case. Hundreds more rockets and mortar rounds have been directed at civilian targets in southern Israel. That comparatively few Israelis have been killed by the unlawful rocket and mortar attacks from Gaza in no way minimizes the criminality. The U.N. Human Rights Council should condemn these heinous acts in the strongest terms.

In the end, asking Hamas to investigate may have been a mistaken enterprise. So, too, the Human Rights Council should condemn the inexcusable and cold-blooded recent slaughter of a young Israeli couple and three of their small children in their beds.

[…] Our report has led to numerous "lessons learned" and policy changes, including the adoption of new Israel Defense Forces procedures for protecting civilians in cases of urban warfare and limiting the use of white phosphorus in civilian areas. The Palestinian Authority established an independent inquiry into our allegations of human rights abuses — assassinations, torture and illegal detentions — perpetrated by Fatah in the West Bank, especially against members of Hamas. Most of those allegations were confirmed by this inquiry. Regrettably, there has been no effort by Hamas in Gaza to investigate the allegations of its war crimes and possible crimes against humanity.
[…]

Operation Pillar of Defense, 2012

Operation Cast Lead concluded in January 2009 when Israel declared a unilateral cease-fire and the UN Security Council adopted Resolution 1860 to enforce it. Hamas and Israel largely maintained the cease-fire until early 2011. In March 2011, Hamas began conducting periodic rocket and IED attacks against Israel, leading to short periods of intensified violence. In April and August 2011 and in March and June 2012, more than 140 rockets were fired on Israel. In response, the Israeli Air Force (IAF) responded with targeted killings of militants, attacks on rocket launching squads, and strikes on tunnels used for smuggling weapons. [...] By October 2012 [...] the infrequent bursts of fire turned into prolonged violence with barely any lulls. [...]

THE ROAD TO WAR: INTERNAL RIVALRIES AND REGIONAL TURMOIL

The main reason for the increase in violence was the emergence and strengthening of various armed groups in Gaza—other than Hamas and PIJ [....] These groups were ideologically and often organizationally affiliated with al-Qaeda and Islamist groups in Egypt's Sinai Peninsula and did not necessarily consider themselves bound by the rules of the Hamas-Israel cease-fire.

Such groups posed a dilemma for Hamas. On one hand, as an Islamist and Palestinian nationalist organization, Hamas sought to maintain its reputation as committed to Israel's destruction through "armed resistance" and defend itself from accusations that it was collaborating with Israel. On the other hand, as the governing body of Gaza, Hamas needed to maintain order and control violence in the Strip. [...] The balance proved difficult to maintain. When these militant groups stepped up their attacks, Israel responded gradually with preventive air strikes and interceptive strikes against jihadist leaders. As tensions escalated [...] Hamas began to enable and fund attacks by these smaller factions and even joined in and claimed public responsibility for attacking Israel.
[...]
Tit-for-Tat Dynamic Turns into Full-Scale Military Confrontation
[...]
Israel launched Operation Pillar of Defense [...] [on] November 14, with the assassination of Ahmed Jabari (head of the Izzedine al-Qassam Brigades, Hamas's military wing in Gaza) and pinpoint attacks against other targets. Hamas and PIJ vowed to avenge the killing of Jabari.

After Hamas's barrage of rockets on November 13, 2012, Israel's security cabinet met to decide on an operation that would include a broad air attack on Hamas infrastructure in Gaza. In addition, the security cabinet approved targeted killings of key Hamas leaders, hoping to achieve maximum effect on the enemy early in the operation. [...]

The campaign began on the afternoon of November 14 with a series of IAF air strikes on 20 Hamas targets. The IDF conducted additional air and naval strikes on Hamas missile and rocket infrastructure, including (according to the IDF) most of Hamas's long-range missiles and missile launchers and the organization's stock of UASs. In the attack, according to the health ministry in Gaza, ten civilians were killed, including three children and a pregnant woman, and an additional 40 were wounded. Following the initial IAF strikes, Barak announced that they had destroyed the majority of Hamas's longest-range Fajr-5 rockets "within minutes" of the first sorties. Despite this initial blow, Hamas was not defeated. Over the next eight days, IAF airpower was pitted against Hamas' rockets in brief but deadly conflict that ultimately cost six Israelis (including one military) and 167 Palestinians (including at least 30 Hamas and PIJ) militants their lives.

Israel States Its Goals

In a statement on November 14, 2012, then–Defense Minister Barak outlined four major objectives for the operation. First and foremost, Israel wished to restore the deterrence that had been achieved after Cast Lead but eroded since 2011. [...]

Second, Israel wanted to decrease the capability of Hamas and other militant groups to launch rockets at its civilian population. [...]

Third, Israel wanted to minimize the damage to its home front. Israel could not immediately prevent militants from launching rockets at Israel's civilian's population. Israel, however, was equipped with Iron Dome, an active antimissile defense system that could intercept rockets and give the IDF more room to maneuver. [...]

Finally, Israel sought to deliver a blow to Hamas (and other organizations in Gaza) while balancing multiple priorities. The government sought to avoid Israeli casualties, especially in light of the upcoming elections. Israel also wanted to avoid a public dispute with the Obama administration over Gaza, especially because it needed U.S. support for its top priority—the Iranian nuclear program. Further, Israel did not want to strain its relations with Egypt's new Muslim Brotherhood leadership and increase regional turmoil. Finally, especially in light of the Goldstone Report, Israel wanted to avoid collateral damage that could inflame international public opinion. As a result of these constraints, Israel focused on the assassinations of Hamas leaders, starting with Jabari.

[...]

A Campaign Intended to Restore Deterrence—Not Change the Regime

Notably absent from Israel's stated objectives were reoccupying Gaza and destroying the Hamas regime, which Foreign Minister Avigdor Lieberman said were "not on the agenda." For such nonstate actors as Hamas, Israel would continue its strategy of "mowing the grass," whereby "use of force … is not intended to attain impossible political goals, but a strategy of attrition designed primarily to debilitate the enemy capabilities" and create ever longer periods of calm between conflicts along Israel's borders. According to Israeli defense doctrine, the attrition of the enemy that repeatedly "mowing the grass" entailed was part of a longer-term strategy to achieve "cumulative deterrence" over the course of several painful conflicts that would eventually lead to the complete cessation of attacks on Israel.

[...]

Thus, the IDF focused on Hamas military leadership and its "strategic" capabilities early in the conflict. As the Hamas rocket fire continued under air strikes against launchers, the IAF expanded its prosecution of other target sets, including government infrastructure and tunnels used by Hamas to smuggle weapons and other materials. [...] [T]he World Health Organization (WHO) reported that Gaza hospitals were overwhelmed with casualties from Israel's bombings and faced critical shortages of drugs and medical supplies. Quoting health ministry officials in Gaza, the WHO said that 382 people (245 adults and 137 children) had been injured in Israeli air strikes.

On Sunday, in an effort to assassinate a commander of Hamas rocket firing teams, an errant air strike killed 11 civilians, nine representing three generations of the al-Dalu family, including four children, as well as two of the family's neighbors. The IDF said it was the result of a technical error: "either [a] failure to paint the target of the attack on the correct site or one of the munitions [used] in the strike misfired." It was the deadliest single strike of the conflict, and rescue efforts were broadcast live to international audiences. Israeli journalists noted a trend in the Palestinian casualty figures over the previous one or two days, as civilian casualties were increasing while militant casualties were declining. Hamas and other combatants had taken to staying underground in tunnels and bunkers, especially during the day, and were firing rockets quickly or using remote control. [...]

Hamas sought to use the horrifying result of the errant attack to gain international support and discredit Israel—successfully. Following the incident, human rights organizations described it as "an example of blatant targeting of civilians," and said the IDF used "disproportionate" force. Recep Tayyip Erdogan, Turkish prime minister at the time, accused Israel of committing "ethnic cleansing" of Palestinians, and British member of Parliament Gerald Kaufman accused Israel of war crimes. [...]

KEY LESSONS FROM OPERATION PILLAR OF DEFENSE
[...]
Active Missile Defense and Passive Defenses Minimized Israeli Civilian Casualties

During Pillar of Defense, for the first time, Israel had an answer to rocket fire. Iron Dome's successful performance also produced a number of secondary effects. Although Pillar of Defense likely did not last long enough to assess fully the effects on Israeli decisionmaking, it appears that Iron Dome reduced pressure to escalate; for example, by widening air attacks or sending ground troops into Gaza. At the same time, Israel's ability to protect its population, in contrast with the daily images of wounded and dead Palestinians, further opened Israel to accusations from the international community of lack of proportionality. A report by the UNHCR on Pillar of Defense stated that the IDF had "failed in many instances to respect international law," and that it did not "consistently uphold the basic principles of conduct of hostilities, namely, the principles of distinction, proportionality and precautions." [...]

Operation Protective Edge, 2014

On July 8, 2014, Israel launched Operation Protective Edge in response to increased rocket fire by Hamas and the threat to Israeli communities bordering the Gaza Strip from offensive tunnels. The operation began 20 months after the conclusion of Pillar of Defense [....] Operation Protective Edge lasted for 51 days, making it Israel's longest, bloodiest, and most intense military campaign against Hamas since the latter took control of Gaza in 2007. Despite this protracted bloodshed, Protective Edge was fundamentally a limited war: Hamas could not destroy Israel and for reasons that have been alluded to earlier and will be discussed again later, Israel did not actually want to destroy Hamas. [...]

THE ROAD TO WAR

On November 21, 2012, Egypt brokered a cease-fire between Israel and Hamas that concluded Operation Pillar of Defense. The cease-fire included the following agreements:

     1)   Israel should stop all hostilities in the Gaza Strip on land, sea, and air, including incursions and targeting of individuals.

506

2)   All Palestinian factions shall stop all hostilities from the Gaza Strip against Israel, including rocket attacks and all attacks along the border.

3)   The crossings should be opened, facilitating the movement of people and goods; Israel should refrain from restricting residents' movements and from targeting residents in border areas.

Hamas and Israel largely maintained the cease-fire throughout 2013. [I]n the year after Pillar of Defense, the number of Gaza-originated attacks against Israel declined dramatically. Hamas and other militant groups only fired 63 rockets and 11 mortar shells. More important, no Israeli casualties resulted from these attacks. By comparison, in the ten months before Pillar of Defense, 596 rockets and mortars were fired from Gaza. For its part, Israel also mostly halted military operations in Gaza. Between December 2012 and December 2013, Israeli operations killed only nine Palestinians, compared with 79 in the ten months prior to Operation Pillar of Defense.

The cease-fire enabled modest improvements in Gaza's economic situation. Israel extended Gaza's fishing zone from three to six nautical miles and alleviated some of its trade and movement restrictions. January 2013, for example, saw the highest rise in construction aggregate (i.e., gravel) entering the Strip since 2007, before Hamas took over this territory. [...]

Middle East Turmoil Isolates Hamas and Hits Gaza's Economy

In mid-2013, the geostrategic environment in the Middle East changed again, this time to Hamas's disadvantage. Its key foreign ally, Morsi's Muslim Brotherhood–led Egyptian government, was toppled in a coup in July 2013. Egypt's new President el-Sisi saw Hamas as responsible for many of Egypt's security problems, including the rise of militants in the Sinai Peninsula, and took a tougher stance toward the organization than even his predecessor Hosni Mubarak. Determined to seal the border between Egypt and Gaza, el-Sisi closed dozens of tunnels between the Strip and Sinai. Despite some restrictions posed by Morsi's regime, these tunnels had allowed for a flow of consumer goods and fuel, as well as weapons, into Gaza.

And the tunnels were not only a gateway to the outside world; they were also a major source of income for the Hamas regime through the taxes it imposed on tunnel operators. Egypt's tunnel closure activities cost Hamas tens of millions of dollars in losses: half its monthly operating budget. This deficit left Hamas unable to pay the 42,000 civil servants it employed in Gaza (in addition to 20,000 military personnel).

Hamas also lost another key source of revenue when it lost its traditional allies Syria and Iran. In the summer of 2012, Sunni-dominated Hamas backed Sunni rebels fighting the Iranian-backed Shi'ite government of Bashar Assad. [...]

Together, the loss of the tunnel revenues and of Iranian and Syrian support exacerbated the already-severe economic situation in the Strip. Unemployment had been high for years but rose in 2013 to 41 percent of those ages 15 years or over, compared with 26 percent in the West Bank. [...] Growing shortages in fuel exacerbated the humanitarian crisis in Gaza, resulting especially from lack of access to potable water, electricity, and sewage services. [...]

Hamas Goes Underground and Israel Tightens the Blockade

As Hamas felt the economic pinch from its loss of regional supporters and from the Egyptian-Gaza tunnel closures, it shifted its military strategy to rely increasingly on tunnels. [...] After Cast Lead, Hamas's leaders increased its use of tunnels in Gaza as a way of protecting themselves against Israeli airpower and as means of ambushing IDF forces in a future conflict. After Operation Pillar of Defense, Iron Dome proved that it could mitigate the effect of Hamas's rockets, further increasing the appeal of tunnel-borne attacks. Finally, especially as Hamas's smuggling routes were cut off, tunnel strategies had yet another appeal: They could make use of the civilian construction supplies that Israel already allowed into Gaza.

Tunnel activity around Gaza, consequently, increased between Pillar of Defense and Protective Edge. [...] In October 2013, the IDF discovered another such tunnel near Kibbutz Ein HaShlosha. This tunnel, perhaps, best demonstrated Hamas's newfound capabilities. Extending 1.8 km into Gaza, buried 18 meters underneath the surface, and provisioned with electricity and stores to last several months, the IDF estimated that the tunnel required at least 500 tons of concrete, $10 million, and two years to build.

The IDF suspected that Hamas built the Ein HaShlosha tunnel from cement originally intended for civilian construction. As a result, after its discovery, Israel immediately stopped the flow of construction materials into Gaza, arguing that the tunnel constituted a violation of the cease-fire. Hamas, on the other hand, viewed Israel's closure of crossings to construction materials as a further violation of the agreement. Either way, the tightening of the construction blockade dealt another blow to Gaza's already-weakened economy. [...]

Slowly, the cease-fire between Hamas and Israel began to crack. Hamas had established a "Restraining Force" ("Dabat al-Midan") preventing rocket fire at Israel. [...] In January 2014, PIJ launched two rockets toward the western Negev during the funeral of former Israeli Prime Minister Ariel Sharon, which took place at the Sharon family's farm (located 4.3 miles from the border with Gaza) and which was attended by Israeli and world leaders. Just days later, five rockets were fired at residential areas in the city of Ashkelon and were intercepted by Iron Dome. A sixth rocket fell in an open area. Israel responded with targeted killings and warnings that if the violence did not cease, a harsh response would follow. While Hamas reportedly tried to prevent violence, other militant groups sensed that Hamas was weak economically and militarily and tried to exploit the situation. An escalation in violence ensued in the first six months of 2014; however, neither Israel nor Hamas was seeking another war until late June.

Tensions Rise in the West Bank as Hamas and the PA Seek Reconciliation
[...]
Hamas historically used armed confrontation with Israel to renegotiate cease-fire agreements and obtain a better deal. Thus, the escalation in violence in the months before Protective Edge might be explained as a Hamas attempt to emerge from its political isolation and deep economic crisis. At the same time, however, political developments within the Palestinian arena raise the possibility that—at least until June 2014— Hamas had a different strategy in mind to help it improve its position. In April 2014, Hamas and the Fatah-dominated PA signed a reconciliation agreement and a new Palestinian unity government was sworn in on June 2. Hamas saw the agreement as a coping mechanism for its economic troubles: The PA would pay the salaries of Gaza's civil servants. Further, Hamas-PA unity might pressure the international community to lift its sanctions on Hamas. [...]

The heightened tensions in the West Bank and Jerusalem peaked on June 12, 2014, when three Israeli yeshiva (religious school) students, one of them a dual Israeli-U.S. national, were kidnapped while hitchhiking in the West Bank. Their bodies were found on June 30. While the culprits were later identified as Hamas operatives, it remains unclear whether Hamas leadership planned the abduction or whether it was conducted by an independent clan without prior coordination. Either way, both Israel and PA President Mahmoud Abbas blamed Hamas for the abduction. Abbas saw this act as a Hamas attempt to undermine its leadership and canceled the reconciliation agreement.
[...]
Having lost its last potential lifeline—reconciliation with the PA that could have alleviated its economic and political woes— Hamas tried to stoke unrest in the West Bank and inflame Gaza with the aim of provoking Israel into war. [...]

On June 30, the night when the IDF found the bodies of the abducted students, a barrage of rockets was launched from Gaza at Israel, and Israeli warplanes carried out air strikes against 34 Hamas targets in Gaza. On July 2, a group of young Israelis kidnapped and burned to death a Palestinian teenager from East Jerusalem in retaliation for the murder of the three teens. The death triggered riots in East Jerusalem, which quickly escalated to daily rocket fire from Gaza. In response to the attacks, the IAF conducted air strikes in Gaza, killing at least nine Hamas members between July 2 and July 6. On July 7, 68 rockets were fired at Southern Israel, including on the town of Be'er Sheba. Israel responded with attacks against some 50 targets in the Gaza Strip and assassinations of Hamas and PIJ militants.

[…] On July 8, the IDF foiled an attack by five commando Hamas militants that tried to infiltrate Israel by sea near Kibbutz Zikim. That day, Hamas launched rockets— some with a reach not previously seen—at Jerusalem, Tel Aviv, and Haifa. Israel launched Operation Protective Edge on July 8.

Ultimately, according to some Israeli analysts, Israel failed to understand Hamas's intentions and believed that it was still uninterested in full military confrontation before Protective Edge. […]

Arguably, Israel failed to recognize that as Hamas evolved from a pure terrorist organization into more of a hybrid terrorist-state structure, it needed to respond to the concerns of Gaza's residents, if only to maintain its hold on power, and that severe economic downturn would force Hamas to act. […]

Tunnel Fight

As already mentioned, tunnel warfare is not a new phenomenon in Arab-Israeli wars. In the run-up to Protective Edge, the IDF interdicted several Hamas tunnels and knew more existed. And yet, Israel arguably failed to appreciate fully that tunnels were no longer just a one-off tactic, but rather a new operational approach to warfare. An Israeli defense analyst remarked that in his discussions with the Israeli Security Agency […], officials there admitted that they knew there were tunnels in Gaza, but "failed to conceive all these projects as a system." A reserve IDF engineering officer confirmed,

> Israel wasn't surprised by the phenomenon of the tunnels. We knew there were tunnels, though we didn't know where they all were. What was surprising was what the head of Hamas [military

wing Mohammad Deif] did. He took the underground medium and turned it into an operational tool.

By 2014, Hamas had developed an entire tunnel-digging enterprise. Employing as many as 900 full-time personnel at an estimated average cost of $100,000 and taking three months per tunnel, Hamas dug three types of tunnels. "Offensive," or cross-border, tunnels extended into Israel and enabled Hamas to threaten the 20 Israeli towns and villages that lay within 4 km of Gaza border. "Defensive" tunnels linked points inside Gaza and enabled Hamas to maintain its lines of communication during IDF operations. Finally, "smuggling" tunnels into Egypt provided Hamas with between 40 and 75 percent of its revenues. In practice, these three types of tunnels formed a subterranean web inside Gaza.

During Operation Protective Edge, tunnels posed a threefold challenge for the IDF. First, there was the detection problem. The IDF experimented with several different technologies to locate tunnels, but none proved entirely satisfactory. […]

After finding the tunnels, the IDF then needed to clear them. […] [D]uring Protective Edge, conventional forces generally avoided fighting inside tunnels because the IDF often lacked intelligence on what lay inside them, and they negated much of the IDF's technological and firepower edge over Hamas. As one Israeli think-tank analyst commented, "The tunnels are the enemy's domain, and you can never win." For the most part, this assumption proved correct. […]

Finally, once the tunnels had been cleared and mapped, the IDF needed to destroy them. This, too, proved challenging because the tunnel needed to be destroyed beyond repair. […]

AFTERMATH OF THE CONFLICT

Aside from the cessation of hostilities, the August 26 cease-fire allowed Palestinians to farm up to 100 m—rather than 300 m—of the Gaza border and to fish up to 6 (rather than 3) km off the shore. It tabled other issues, such as prisoner swaps and reconstruction, for longer-term negotiations. […]

Protective Edge left a swath of destruction behind it. On the Israeli side, some 66 Israeli soldiers and six civilians died in the conflict. The conflict also exacted a significant economic toll. The Israeli Tax Authority estimated that Protective Edge inflicted almost $55 million in direct damage to private and public infrastructure and another $443 million in indirect damages thanks to economic disruptions caused by the conflict. On the Palestinian side, the UN estimated the number of Palestinian deaths at 2,133, of whom 1,489 were civilians. In contrast, Israeli estimates suggest that, of 1,598 Palestinian fatalities in Operation Protective Edge, 75 percent were combatants. In addition, the UN estimated that 500,000 people—28 percent of Gaza's population—were internally displaced, while some 108,000 people had their homes rendered uninhabitable.

Perhaps the final question is: At the end of the day, who won? It remains unanswered. […]

In interviews conducted almost two years after Protective Edge, however, many IDF officers and outside experts saw the campaign as a small victory. Israel's border with Gaza has been relatively quiet, and they attribute this partially to effective deterrence from Protective Edge. A senior IDF officer at Southern Command remarked,

> The lesson for Hamas is that long wars are not good for them; they are a double-edged sword . . . Hamas leadership knows now, and they knew then, they cannot face the IDF for 55 days and that while Israel as a society moved on, Gaza is left ruined and will remain so for many years.

[…]

A senior Israeli defense correspondent argued that, after Protective Edge, Israel and Hamas have settled on an unwritten *modus vivendi*:

> In a way there is some deterrence between these conflicts. Everyone understands the price. Every day since August 2014 that Hamas hasn't shot rockets and has arrested people who try to do, so that is deterrence. Israel lets trucks go into Gaza every day. Israel is more engaged than anyone else in addressing the humanitarian crisis in Gaza. The Israelis understand that the humanitarian crisis could cause another war. They want to keep the lid on Gaza; this is a strategic calculus.

[…]

Few analysts—and no one interviewed for this report—believe that Operation Protective Edge proved decisive or that Israel has fought its last Gaza war. Both Israel and Hamas worry about their respective security situations, and neither Israel nor Egypt seem likely to loosen the blockade on Gaza. As a result, Gaza's economic plight is unlikely to improve dramatically, and when public pressure mounts sufficiently, Hamas may once again attempt to challenge Israel to achieve a marginally better status quo through fighting another limited war. […] Hamas leader Ismail Haniyeh also recently pledged that Hamas was "digging twice as much as the number of tunnels dug in Vietnam." And so, the question very well may be when—not if—Israel will fight its next Gaza war.
[…]

5.   **Mr. Chomsky** (Professor Emeritus of Linguistics, Massachusetts Institute of Technology) said that many of the world's problems were so intractable, it was hard to imagine how one could even begin to mitigate them. The Israeli-Palestinian conflict, however, was not one of those problems. On the contrary, the general outlines of a diplomatic solution had been clear for at least 40 years. The obstacles to the resolution of the conflict were also quite clear.

6.   The framework for a solution was set out in a draft resolution that Egypt, Jordan and the Syrian Arab Republic had brought before the Security Council in January 1976. The draft, which called for a two-State settlement on the basis of the internationally recognized border, with guarantees for the right of both States to exist in peace and security within secure and recognized borders, had been vetoed by the United States. Since that time, the United States had continued to prevent the Security Council from taking action. The most recent veto had come in February 2011, when it had voted against a draft resolution calling on Israel to halt settlement building, an action that was contrary to official United States policy. In that connection, it should be noted that a veto not only prevented the adoption of resolutions, but also had the effect of deleting them from history. One had to look very hard to find the texts of vetoed drafts.

7.   Although there was an overwhelming international consensus in support of the two-State solution, Israel rejected such a solution and, with the unremitting and decisive support of the United States, had devoted extensive resources to blocking its implementation. One of the primary aims of Israel's efforts had been to establish how the conflict was viewed and interpreted in the United States and within its broad sphere of influence.

8.   The history of Gaza over the past decade illustrated the general character of Israel's policy in that part of the Occupied Palestinian Territory. In August 2014, the latest Israeli aggression against Gaza had ended when Israel and the Palestinian Authority had agreed to a ceasefire. That inevitably had led everyone to wonder what the prospects for the future were. The answer could be found in Israel's response to the succession of ceasefires that had been reached in Gaza over the past decade. As soon as a ceasefire was reached, Israel would disregard it and continue its assault on Gaza, build more settlements and incite violence. On the other hand, Hamas would observe the ceasefire, until some Israeli escalation elicited a response, and that would lead to another exercise of "mowing the lawn", in Israeli parlance, each episode more fierce and destructive than the last. In fact, the successive ceasefires that had been reached essentially reiterated the Agreement on Movement and Access of

November 2005, which had been concluded in the aftermath of the second intifada.

9.   The timing of the Agreement on Movement and Access had been significant, as November 2005 had also marked Israel's so-called disengagement from Gaza. The removal of Israeli settlers from Gaza had been depicted as a noble effort to seek peace and promote development, but the reality was rather different. According to Dov Weisglass, the Israeli official who had been in charge of negotiating and implementing the ceasefire, the goal of the disengagement had been to freeze the peace process, so as to prevent the establishment of a Palestinian State and ensure that diplomacy was removed from the agenda indefinitely. Israel's leading specialists on the occupation, the historian Idith Zertal and diplomatic correspondent Akiva Eldar, the co-authors of *Lords of the Land,* the standard work on the settlement project, had pointed out that, even after the disengagement, Gaza had never been released from Israel's military grip. Israel had left behind scorched earth, devastated services and people with neither a present nor a future. The settlements had been destroyed in an ungenerous move by an unenlightened occupier, which continued to control the territory and kill and harass its inhabitants by means of its formidable military might.

10.   The Oslo Accords had established that Gaza and the West Bank constituted an indivisible territorial unit. For the past 20 years, the United States and Israel had sought to separate Gaza from the West Bank, in violation of the Accords that they had accepted. The major geostrategic aim behind those efforts was to deny Palestine access to the outside world. If Gaza were separated from the West Bank, whatever autonomous entity might emerge in the latter territory would be imprisoned by Israel on one side and a hostile Jordan, ally of Israel, on the other. In addition, Israel's slow and gradual usurpation of the Jordan Valley, which made up approximately one third of the West Bank and contained much of its arable land, would imprison what remained of the territory even more tightly.

11.   In January 2006, the first free election in the Arab world had been held in Palestine. At the conclusion of the carefully monitored elections, Hamas had won the control of the Parliament. Instantly, the United States, along with Israel, had decided to punish the Palestinians for the "crime" that they had committed. A harsh siege had been put into effect and acts of violence had increased. In another familiar practice, the United States had also begun to organize a coup to overthrow the unacceptable Government. The European Union, to its shame and discredit, had gone along with those actions.

12.   A year later, Hamas had committed an even greater crime when it had pre-empted the planned military coup and taken control of Gaza. In the majority of the West, including the United States, that action had been

decried as the takeover of Gaza by force. Although that statement was not false, it was also not completely accurate. Hamas had used force to prevent the violent overthrow of the elected Government. After the Hamas takeover, the attacks on Gaza had increased substantially, until another ceasefire had been reached in January 2008. Once again, the terms of that ceasefire had been essentially the same as those of previous ceasefire agreements, with Hamas observing the ceasefire and Israel constantly breaking it. That pattern had continued until 4 November 2008, when Israeli forces had launched Operation Cast Lead. Hamas had responded by firing rockets at Israel, an action that had been met with a huge reprisal in which many Palestinians had been killed. By the end of December 2008, Hamas had offered to renew the ceasefire, but the Israeli Government had rejected the offer. It should be recalled that Cast Lead had been such a horrible operation that it had provoked a substantial international response and had led the United Nations and non-governmental organizations to establish commissions of inquiry and launch investigations.

13.   In January 2009, the Security Council had adopted resolution 1860 (2009) calling for an immediate ceasefire with the usual terms. However, the ceasefire had broken down completely in November 2012 with the next major episode of "lawn mowing", which, of course, had ended with another ceasefire that included the usual terms. Once again, according to Nathan Thrall, a leading Middle East analyst with the International Crisis Group, Israel had recognized that Hamas had been observing the terms of the ceasefire, and it therefore had little incentive to do the same. Instead, the military attacks on Gaza had increased and more stringent restrictions on imports had been imposed. That state of affairs had continued until April 2014, when Hamas and the Palestinian Authority had signed a unity agreement that had been supported by most of the international community. Israel had been infuriated because unity between the two movements would threaten its long-standing policy of separating Gaza and the West Bank. The prospect of a unified Government also had threatened to undermine Israel's claim that it was not possible to negotiate seriously with an entity that was internally divided. Israel had responded by launching major assaults on the West Bank, primarily targeting Hamas, in which hundreds had been killed.

14.   The Israeli authorities, of course, had offered a pretext for their actions in the West Bank. They had claimed that the assaults had been launched to rescue three Israeli teenagers who had been abducted from a settlement. The truth was that the Israeli authorities had known immediately that the teenagers had been killed. They had also known from the outset that it was unlikely Hamas had been involved, yet they had claimed that they were certain that Hamas had been responsible. The Israeli assaults in the West Bank had ultimately elicited a response from Hamas, and that, in turn, had led to the recently completed Israeli assault, which had been designated Operation Protective Edge.

15.   A ceasefire had been reached on 26 August 2014, only to be followed immediately by Israel's greatest land grab in 30 years. The Israeli authorities had seized almost a thousand acres in the Gush Etzion area, which was near what Israel called Greater Jerusalem. The United States Government had informed Israeli officials that their actions in Gush Etzion had undermined United States efforts to protect Israel at the United Nations. In fact, the United States had delivered that same warning in September 1967, when Israel had first established the illegal colony of Gush Etzion. Little had changed since that time, apart from the scale of the crimes, which had continued with the unremitting support of the United States.

16.   The overwhelming international consensus was that the Israeli-Palestinian conflict would end either with implementation of the two-State solution or the annexation by Israel of the entire West Bank. [...] Although the two-State option was still a feasible solution, the more realistic scenario was that Israel would continue its current policies, with the overt support of the United States, until it had turned the West Bank into a patchwork of illegal settlements and isolated Palestinians cantons. Looking at a map, the casual observer might be led to believe that much of the West Bank was unoccupied. That was not the case, however, as the majority of the unoccupied territory was uninhabitable desert.

17.   While it was not an official policy of Israel to take over the West Bank, it was doing precisely that and in the very same way that had been done for a century, in small steps, so that no one noticed, or so that people could at least pretend not to notice. Using a wide variety of techniques to dispossess Palestinians in the West Bank, Israel had managed to reduce the Arab population of that territory from approximately 300,000 in 1967 to roughly 60,000 today. The Palestinians who remained were virtually imprisoned in their isolated patches of territory, and Israel had no intention of annexing those areas. The analogies that were often made to South Africa were misleading. The South Africa of apartheid had been forced to sustain its black inhabitants because they had been the country's workforce. It had even tried to gain international support for its bantustans. Eventually, the settlements would be absorbed into Israel, thereby increasing the Jewish population of Israel, because there were very few Palestinians left in those areas.

18.   That was the reality that was taking shape before the very eyes of the international community. It was the realistic alternative to a settlement based on the two-State solution, and there was every reason to expect that things would continue as they were, as long as the United States continued its support.
     [...]

Why Mideast Peace Talks Collapsed In 2014 (2017)
NATIONAL PUBLIC RADIO (NPR)

ROBERT SIEGEL, HOST: And if President Trump needs advice about where to start on a new Israeli-Palestinian peace initiative, he may want to look at what went wrong when the Obama administration tried to broker a Middle East peace deal. The Israeli newspaper Haaretz this week reported on what it describes as American memos from early 2014 When then Secretary of State John Kerry was trying to negotiate a peace agreement. The memos detail what President Obama proposed to bridge the differences between Israeli Prime Minister Benjamin Netanyahu and Palestinian President Mahmoud Abbas also known as Abu Mazen.

For the first time, a U.S. president said the Palestinians should have a capital in East Jerusalem. There would be a Palestinian right of return only to Palestine, not to Israel, which would be recognized as a Jewish state, although one that would respect the rights of its non-Jewish minority.

Why did it fail? Well, I asked former U.S. diplomat Martin Indyk, who was a key member of the Kerry team.

MARTIN INDYK: Well, I would say that while we made a massive effort to meet the basic needs of both sides in formulas that the two sides could accept, the bottom line was when we put them to Abu Mazen, he was not prepared to accept them. He was not prepared to answer. Let's put it that way. He didn't say yes or no. […] And so we never had the opportunity to test Prime Minister Netanyahu.

SIEGEL: Netanyahu would not have publicly said what he appears to have agreed to, which was a willingness to negotiate a territorial swap on the West Bank based on the 1967 borders. He seemed to be more flexible behind the scenes than he was in public at that point, wasn't he?

INDYK: Yes, he certainly appears to have been. You have to look at the formula to see that there were certain additional language that would have allowed him to argue for the incorporation of settlement blocks into Israel. But bear in mind that that was a different government, the government that he now has. And I don't think he could say the magic words based on the 1967 lines and keep his current coalition intact.

SIEGEL: So he's still the prime minister, but the parties in his government are a different group today than they were even in 2014. Did you have the impression that if the U.S. could deliver and Netanyahu would agree, did you think that in substance you had something that Mahmoud Abbas can live with, or is he - can he accept that personally, politically?

INDYK: Well, look. It was our judgment call that this met the minimum requirements of both sides, this meaning the document that we were working on. Essentially we really weren't able to test the proposition before the whole thing fell apart. In the end, it seemed they were further apart than they had been at the beginning.

And I think that's a salutary lesson for President Trump because beyond the political problems that both Prime Minister Netanyahu and President Abbas have with their constituencies when it comes to making peace and making the very difficult concessions involved in getting to an agreement, the issues have calcified, and the parties have dug in. And what we thought were bridging proposals that were reasonable and met each side's needs I fear are not acceptable anymore to either side.
[…]

Congress to Palestinians: Drop Dead (2011)
MJ Rosenberg

On Tuesday, Prime Minister Binyamin Netanyahu delivered a speech to Congress that essentially was a series of insults to Palestinians and every insult was met by applause and standing ovations.

In fact, Netanyahu's appearance itself was an insult.
[...]
In his entire term in office he has done nothing but reject every request by the United States that he take some action (like freezing settlements) to promote Israeli-Palestinian negotiations. In the history of Israel, there has been no prime minister as hardline on Palestinian rights and as indifferent to the wishes of the United States as Netanyahu.
[...]
The prime minister unambiguously stated that he had no intention of making peace with the Palestinians.

He began by saying that, in point of fact, there is no occupation, stating, that "in Judea and Samaria [the term Israeli right-wingers use for the West Bank], Israelis are not foreign occupiers" but the native inhabitants. (He cited Abraham and Isaiah from the Bible!)

He said he might consider giving up some of that land but not an inch of Jerusalem. Additionally, he said that Israel would retain most settlements and insist on a military presence in the Jordan Valley (thereby ensuring the any State of Palestine would be locked in on both sides by Israel).

He said that Israel would never negotiate with a Palestinian government that included Hamas, whether democratically elected or not. He declared that not a single Palestinian would be allowed to return to Israel; not even a symbolic return would be acceptable to him.

There is little reason to elaborate. Netanyahu today essentially returned to the policies that Israel pursued before Yitzhak Rabin and Yasir Arafat agreed on mutual recognition and the joint pursuit of peace.

And the worst part is not the appalling things Netanyahu said, but how Congress received them. Even Netanyahu's declaration that there is no Israeli occupation was met with thunderous applause with the Democrats joining the Republicans in ecstatic support. Every Netanyahu statement, no matter how extreme, was met with cheers.

Netanyahu was also applauded wildly when he invoked Palestinian terrorism over and over again, even seeming to lump his former "partner," President Mahmoud Abbas with people who "educate their children to hate, [who] continue to name public squares after terrorists. And worst of all continue to perpetuate the fantasy that Israel will one day be flooded by the descendants of Palestinian refugees."

His bottom line, which Congress fully bought, was that all Palestinians are terrorists who haven't earned a state. And probably never will.

Congress cheered and cheered and when Netanyahu was finished, they climbed over each other to touch the hem of his garment.

It was as if Congress thought that no Palestinians or other Arabs (or Muslims) would be watching. It was as if it believes that it can shout its lungs out for Netanyahu (and thereby secure those campaign contributions from AIPAC), without any consequences to US policy and national interests in the Arab world.

But Congress is wrong. The message it sent to the Middle East today, to the whole world, in fact, was that Palestinians cannot count on the United States to ever play the role of "honest broker" between Israel and the Palestinians. Even if President Obama was inclined to, Congress would stop him. And AIPAC, using the leverage its campaign contributions gives it, would hold Obama's feet to the fire too. As far as Congress is concerned, Palestinians do not exist. They have no rights, to a state least of all.

And that is why Palestinians have no choice but to unilaterally declare a state in the fall. They cannot count on America. As David Ben Gurion understood when he went to the General Assembly to achieve recognition of Israel, a small, powerless people must take its destiny into its own hands.
[…]
And so we can look forward to a unilateral declaration of statehood in September. The Israelis who refuse to negotiate with stateless Palestinians will have no choice but to negotiate with the state whose land it is occupying. And those negotiations, state to state, may produce peace and the "two states for two peoples" that most Palestinians and Israelis aspire to. In any case, it's the only hope.
[…]

Palestine Goes to the UN (2011)
Khaled Elgindy

Mahmoud Abbas, the president of the Palestinian Authority (PA) and chair of the Palestine Liberation Organization (PLO), plans to call on the United Nations in September to recognize a Palestinian state and admit it as a full member of the organization. This strategy marks a dramatic shift in the Palestinians' approach to the conflict with Israel: they are not seeking to revive the moribund peace process; they are seeking to bypass it altogether.

Following the collapse of direct negotiations last fall, Abbas and his Fatah-dominated leadership launched an aggressive diplomatic campaign to secure broad international recognition of a Palestinian state along the 1967 borders as a prelude to applying for formal UN membership this fall. If the Palestinian bid to get full UN membership in September is defeated in the UN Security Council -- a U.S. veto is all but assured -- the PA says it is prepared to take the matter to the General Assembly. [...] The PA [...] is [...] planning to seek a simple majority in the General Assembly, which would allow Palestine to be recognized as a "nonmember state" of the UN, alongside Kosovo, Taiwan, and Vatican City.
[...]
In going to the UN, the Palestinians are seeking not to obtain statehood but to gain full UN membership as an existing state. Since last year, some 120 countries have recognized a "state of Palestine" drawn along the 1967 borders.

[...] In any event, UN membership requires the approval of the Security Council, and the United States will surely veto the Palestinians' bid. [...]

PEACE PROCESSING

This strategy did not come about in a vacuum or overnight. Its roots lie in the belief, long held by ordinary Palestinians and more recently adopted by the Abbas leadership, that two decades of "peace processing" have failed to realize Palestinian national aspirations and have helped prolong and deepen Israel's occupation while weakening Palestinian political institutions. [...]

Chief among the Palestinian people's demands was national reconciliation, which seemed to them a prerequisite to ending the Israeli occupation. Young Palestinians across the West Bank and Gaza took to the streets calling for an end to the political division between Fatah and Hamas, a self-inflicted schism that had become a source of intense collective shame.

(The PA is mainly an administrative body, whereas the PLO, of which Fatah is the dominant faction, is recognized internationally as the legal and diplomatic representative of the Palestinian people -- which is the reason that Hamas' exclusion from the PLO has persistently undermined the PLO's claim that it represents all Palestinians.) With little prospect of a credible negotiation process with Israel and the winds of change blowing at his back, Abbas and Fatah saw no choice but to end their four-year feud with Hamas [....]

GAMBIT OR GAMBLE?

[…] Abbas and Fatah would much rather engage in a credible negotiation process and avoid a power-sharing arrangement with Hamas. Unlike Hamas, whose street credibility is based on resistance, Fatah's credibility derives from the promise of bringing about change through peace negotiations.

Having borne the brunt of repeated failures in the peace process, the PA's primary aim now is to regain some badly needed political leverage, mainly by forcing a shift in the cost-benefit calculations of Israel and the United States. Palestine's admission into the UN would, in Abbas' view, transform the Israeli-Palestinian conflict into a matter of one UN member state violating the sovereign rights of another. That could give the Palestinians access to various international forums and mechanisms, such as the UN's human rights bodies, the International Court of Justice, and even the International Criminal Court, and offer them new avenues to seek redress. […]

Thus, far from negating the possibility of peace negotiations, the Palestinians' UN gambit is a strategy aimed at strengthening their negotiating posture vis-à-vis Israel and the United States while improving the domestic standing of Abbas and his colleagues. Its goal is more to level the playing field than to change the game itself. […]

A GAME OF CHICKEN
[…]
Whether the UN bid is a success, pursuing it has already borne fruit. For the first time in many years, it is the Palestinians, rather than the Americans or the Israelis, who have set the agenda. Obama probably would not have declared that the 1967 lines should define the borders of Israel and Palestine, as he did earlier this year, if the Palestinians had not threatened to go to the UN. The UN bid has also played well back home, helping stanch the PA's hemorrhaging legitimacy, if only temporarily. And the Palestinians have also won strong Arab support, including official backing from the Arab League, Egypt's transitional government, and Saudi Arabia.
[…]

522

When the UN was founded in 1945, its Charter provided for an
International Court of Justice (ICJ) to resolve legal disputes submitted to it
by states and to give advisory opinions on legal questions referred to it by
authorized United Nations organs and specialized agencies. Since July
2002, it has also become possible for states to have recourse to the
Internation Criminal Court (ICC) to complement national legal systems in
matters of individual criminal responsibility. [...] Additionally, if
Palestine's UN bid is successful, Palestine could also avail itself of the
conciliation and arbitration services provided by the Permanent Court of
Arbitration (PCA). In addition to gaining access to the ICJ, the ICC, and
the PCA, a key explanation as to why President Abbas laid particular
emphasis on attaining membership of the UN is that Palestine's admission
would provide compelling evidence from the international community that
Palestine is a state.
[...]

I.   The Various Forms of International Litigation

[...] We know from the publication of the confidential *Palestine Papers*
that the PLO's Negotiation Support Unit (NSU) [...] has in recent years
been considering various international litigation options. [...]

a.   CONTENTIOUS CASES

Under Articles 42 and 48 of the International Law Commission's Articles
on The Responsibility of States for Internationally Wrongful Acts (the
Articles on Responsibility), it is possible for an "injured state" to invoke
the responsibility of another state. This can be done under Article 42 if the
obligation breached is owed to the state individually. Alternatively,
responsibility can also be invoked if the breach is of such character as to
radically change the position of all other states to which the obligation is
owed with respect to the further performance of the obligation. In the case
of Article 48, any state other than the injured state is entitled to invoke the
responsibility of another state if the obligation breached is owed to the
international community as a whole, i.e. an obligation *erga omnes*. An
example of an obligation *erga omnes* is a breach of the right to self-
determination. Any state entitled to invoke the responsibility of another
state can claim cessation of the internationally wrongful act, and seek
assurances and guarantees of non-repetition and reparation. It may
therefore be possible for a third state to invoke Israel's responsibility for
prohibiting the Palestinian people from exercising their right to self-
determination (or for breaching another peremptory norm of international
law if applicable), although it would be necessary to establish a
jurisdictional link.

From HASTINGS INT'L & COMP. L. REV., Vol. 35, No. 1, pp. 129-148   523
Jan. 1, 2012). Reprinted with permission.

So long as the international community does not consider Palestine a state, the prospect of bringing a contentious case against Israel is bleak. [...] [A]ny decision in a contentious case would have no binding force except between the parties and in respect to that particular case. In the event of a decision favorable to Palestine, it would not be surprising if Israel were to refuse to abide by the decision. In such a situation, it would be necessary to apply to the UN Security Council for enforcement of the decision. [...]

b. ARBITRATION

[...] It would also be possible to resort to arbitration if Israel were agreeable, and if the arbitration were related to an issue on which there is a treaty obligation between Israel and another state. In this connection, Israel's peace treaty with Egypt and its peace treaty with Jordan provide that any dispute that cannot be settled between the parties by negotiation is to be resolved by conciliation or submitted to arbitration. [...] Egypt resolved a dispute with Israel at the PCA in 1988 Taba arbitration. Jordan could use the services of the PCA to raise those sections of its peace treaty with Israel on refugees and on Jerusalem if it turns out that Israel is not fully abiding by its obligations. However, Israel would have to agree to arbitration as a means to resolve any dispute that arises from these treaty provisions. The PLO and Israel could have engaged in arbitration on the basis of Article XV of the Declaration of Principles (1993) and Article XXI of the Cairo Agreement (1995) in the event of a dispute arising with respect to these agreements, and in the event that conciliation failed. However, Israel and the PLO have not exercised this right.

c. ADVISORY OPINIONS

[...] The UN Diplomacy memo explains "the United Nations General Assembly and Security Council may request advisory opinions on 'any legal question.'" Other United Nations organs and specialized agencies which have been authorized to seek advisory opinions can only do so with respect to "legal questions arising within the scope of their activities." [...]

II.   The Prospects of Success and the Perils of Failure
[...]
On two occasions, the Palestine question found its way to The Hague. The issue first arose indirectly during a legal dispute between the UN Headquarters and the United States in 1988; it again emerged directly in the case of the wall in 2004. In both cases, the Palestinians emerged victorious. Of course it cannot be assumed that the Palestinians would be as successful in any future cases brought before the ICJ. Success largely depends on the circumstances surrounding the request for the opinion and on the question asked. And indeed *asking the right question* is absolutely crucial to success at the ICJ. [...]

[I]t is necessary for the questions formulated for an advisory opinion to be a "legal question" within the meaning of [...] the ICJ's Statute. [...] [T]he ICJ has repeatedly affirmed "that a question [which] has political aspects does not suffice to deprive it of its character as a legal question," [....] [T]he ICJ can exercise its discretion to refuse to respond to a request for an advisory opinion, although it is rare for the Court to do so [....]

UN membership does not determine statehood. Rather admission to the UN is based on an assumption that the entity seeking membership is already a state. [...]

a. LEGAL ISSUES ARISING FROM PALESTINE'S QUEST TO ACHIEVE STATEHOOD

[...] If Palestine seeks full UN membership, and if its request is either vetoed in the Security Council or fails to pass due to a lack of support, then Palestine may seek to "upgrade" its status in the UN General Assembly. If Palestine decides to pursue the latter option then it may be subject to a legal challenge. This is because the ICJ, in an early opinion, ruled that the admission of a state to membership of the UN [...] could not be effected by a decision of the General Assembly when the Security Council has made no recommendation for admission, by reason of the candidate failing to obtain the requisite majority or due to a negative vote of a permanent member upon a resolution so to recommend. [...]

[T]here may be further grounds to challenge Israeli policy if it continues to populate the settlements with its own citizens, either by expanding existing settlements or constructing new ones, contrary to international law. This is because one of the outcomes of an ICJ opinion to the effect that Palestine is a state is that Israel would be required to withdraw from the territory, and cease its support for settlement activity, because of its infringement of Palestine's sovereignty. [...]

III.   A Comment on the ICC

[...]

According to Article 13 of the ICC Statute, the court may exercise its jurisdiction by one of three ways: First, referral by a state party; second, referral by the Security Council; and third, the Prosecutor may initiate his own investigation. In order for Palestine to refer a situation to the Prosecutor in which one or more crimes within the jurisdiction of the court have been committed, Palestine must be a party to the ICC, and it can only become a party if it is a state. In order for the Prosecutor to initiate his own investigation he needs to be assured that the crimes complained of fall within the jurisdiction of the court. Again, this comes down to whether Palestine was a state when the crimes complained of were alleged to have been committed.

[...]

Resolution 67/19 – Status of Palestine in the UN (2012)

UNITED NATIONS GENERAL ASSEMBLY

The General Assembly,

[…]

Recognizing that full membership is enjoyed by Palestine in the United Nations Educational, Scientific and Cultural Organization, the Economic and Social Commission for Western Asia and the Group of Asia-Pacific States and that Palestine is also a full member of the League of Arab States, the Movement of Non-Aligned Countries, the Organization of Islamic Cooperation and the Group of 77 and China,

Recognizing also that, to date, 132 States Members of the United Nations have accorded recognition to the State of Palestine,

Taking note of the 11 November 2011 report of the Security Council Committee on the Admission of New Members,

Stressing the permanent responsibility of the United Nations towards the question of Palestine until it is satisfactorily resolved in all its aspects,

Reaffirming the principle of universality of membership of the United Nations,

1. *Reaffirms* the right of the Palestinian people to self-determination and to independence in their State of Palestine on the Palestinian territory occupied since 1967;

2. *Decides* to accord to Palestine non-member observer State status in the United Nations, without prejudice to the acquired rights, privileges and role of the Palestine Liberation Organization in the United Nations as the representative of the Palestinian people, in accordance with the relevant resolutions and practice;

3. *Expresses the hope* that the Security Council will consider favourably the application submitted on 23 September 2011 by the State of Palestine for admission to full membership in the United Nations;
[…]

Today, Palestine accepts the jurisdiction of the International Criminal Court—or, put another way, the ICC accepts that Palestine accepts its jurisdiction. This more awkward formulation is more accurate, since what matters is not Palestine's quixotic quest to join The Hague Court, but the ICC's acknowledgement that it can.

Palestinian claims to statehood are nothing new. What has changed is that Palestine is now seeking (and getting) membership in international organizations. But because Palestine still has so few qualities of a real state, this trend promises plenty of turmoil and trouble—for the ICC, for Israel, and for Palestine itself. And it is a reminder that in a world of states, statehood matters. For Palestinians, statehood is a delusion worth having and trouble worth making.

STATE OF PLAY

Palestine has acceded to the Rome Statute, the ICC's founding charter, and issued a declaration accepting the court's jurisdiction, something only a state can do. Palestine first tried to join the ICC in 2009; it was rebuffed after a three-year delay, with the court noting that "competent organs" at the United Nations had not recognized a Palestinian state. That decision was illogical, even cowardly: nothing required the ICC to defer to UN standards, which are not synonymous with statehood. A young court, not wanting to wade into one of the world's oldest conflicts, punted to the UN.

For a time, The Hague's dodge kept the wolf from the docket. But a few months later, in November 2012, the UN General Assembly admitted Palestine as a non-member observer state. By The Hague's own UN-centric logic, Palestine could now join the ICC. When Palestine applied again this January, it was quickly accepted.

Palestine hopes that the court will prosecute Israeli forces operating in the West Bank and in Gaza. Whatever its merits, a case could cause real trouble for the ICC. Israel's chief ally, the United States, has already filed a protest, arguing that Palestine is not a state. The United States is not a party to the court—having signed but never ratified the Rome Statute—but could do much to undermine it, including by supporting disaffected African states that have threatened to abandon the court altogether. The ICC is a weak institution; prosecuting Israel could prove fatal.

There are plenty of complications that could give the court an exit. The Oslo II Accords, signed in 1995, confirmed Israel's "sole criminal jurisdiction" over Israelis in Palestinian territory, so Palestine may in fact have no jurisdiction to grant. There are also questions about what constitutes Palestinian territory, and defining Palestine's borders would mean defining Israel's. Since Israel is not a party to the ICC, the court's prosecutor might decide that a case based only on Palestinian jurisdiction would risk interpretive overreach. Finally, there are the merits of the case themselves: the ICC's prosecutor could conclude that the evidence simply isn't strong enough to pursue.

But not pursuing a case could also imperil the court. The Hague is already under intense criticism for exclusively prosecuting African cases, which is why many of those states are considering withdrawing. Much of the world considers Israel's actions in the 2014 war in Gaza and its occupation of the West Bank as a gross violation of international law. If the court were seen to be avoiding a legitimate case against Israel, this limping institution could become irrelevant.

Whatever the danger to the ICC, the possible trouble for Israel—the prosecution of its forces in Palestine—is even more obvious. The ICC could reason that Palestine never had the power to bargain away its obligation to prosecute international crimes during the Oslo negotiations. And the court could assert that its jurisdiction reaches deep into the Israeli state: Israel considers Jerusalem sovereign territory, but many countries consider it occupied. And if the ICC brought charges against an Israeli soldier or politician, he would have to plan his vacations carefully: 122 other countries, including most of Europe, are parties to the Rome Statute, obligating them to hand over anyone the court indicts.

There are plausible objections to these scenarios, but now that it has jurisdiction in Palestine, the ICC has the ability to decide for itself if an investigation is warranted. Its self-image as a professional court, or its need to prove its relevance, might compel the court to take a complaint against Israel seriously. Either way, the decision is not Israel's. And that, after all, was the point.

INTERNATIONALIZE THIS

Joining the court is part of a larger Palestinian strategy to internationalize its dispute with Israel. Palestine has recently joined a host of multilateral treaties, including the Genocide and Geneva Conventions, the International Covenant on Civil and Political Rights, and the Vienna Conventions—all part of an effort that one senior official in the Palestinian Liberation Organization has called a "diplomatic intifada."

The point of this strategy is to escape the trap of negotiating only with Israel. Israel's leaders formally back a two-state solution, but that position has always been more rhetorical than real. (In the country's recent election, Prime Minister Benjamin Netanyahu opposed a Palestinian state, only to backtrack days later.) Israel benefits tremendously from its asymmetrical relationship with the Palestinians, insisting they acknowledge Israel's right to exist—and its Jewish character—as a prerequisite for talks, while treating Palestinian statehood as something to be bargained for.

The strategy also means bypassing the United States: For all the alienation between U.S. President Barack Obama and Netanyahu, U.S. policy remains reflexively on Israel's side. Although long supporting a two-state solution, administrations of both parties have been uninterested in actually letting Palestinians achieve statehood. [...]

Notionally, such resistance stems from a belief that there is no unilateral shortcut to a negotiated settlement. But this is sophistry and self-dealing: All statehood does is make Israel's preferred deal more difficult. Conditioning statehood has made the likely terms of any deal more favorable to Israel—including no deal, which may be Netanyahu's real preference. That is the asymmetry Israel and its chief ally wish to preserve, which Palestine's new strategy threatens to overturn.

So it's no surprise that trouble has already started for the Palestinians. Israel is withholding $120 million in monthly tax receipts it collects on the behalf of the Palestinian Authority. Washington, meanwhile, is cutting funding to organizations that allow Palestine to join their ranks.

PLAYING PRETEND

Self-servingly punitive as it may be, this pushback makes sense: Palestine's bare claim doesn't make it a state where the conditions for statehood don't exist.

There are two approaches to statehood in international law. The dominant view, enshrined in the 1933 Montevideo Convention, is the so-called declarative theory of statehood: An entity with a territory, population, government, and capacity for relations is a state, whether or not others recognize it. The minority view is called the constitutive theory: recognition makes a state. The more it receives, the more state-like it becomes.

The trouble with Palestine is that it's not much of a state either way. Palestine cannot be a state in declarative terms, since it has never controlled its own finances, borders, seas, or airspace. But it is equally unsatisfying to suppose Palestine's 135 bilateral recognitions make it a state. There's a reason the constitutive model is the minority view: Recognitions can be aspirational, reflecting the desire to see a state that isn't actually there. After all, only one recognition really matters, and Israel's prime minister just made it clear that's not happening.

Hence the new, slightly desperate Palestinian strategy: as Israeli leaders hold their line, take to the international community, where those 135 recognitions can translate into membership in multilateral organizations. Membership gives Palestine some of the powers a state normally exercises, without having to wait for a recalcitrant Israel to grant them.

But membership won't make life better for average Palestinians; ratifying the International Covenant on Civil and Political Rights, for example, won't end the occupation. It could even make things worse: The ICC may never actually put Israelis in legal jeopardy, but it can try Palestine's citizens for their own violations. Standing trial for war crimes is a funny way to prove you're a state, but if Hamas keeps firing rockets at Israel, Palestinians may get their day in court.

The larger question is whether statehood really matters at all. Chasing sovereignty doesn't make Palestinians masters of their own destiny any more than they very much aren't now. Perhaps statehood is just a bundle of functions. Palestine already takes part in the Olympics, the Red Cross; its recent push simply adds other capacities. And some functions are homegrown: Palestinian leaders have been pushing to build domestic institutions to make Palestine a more competent actor—what an earlier generation of Israelis called creating "facts on the ground." Statehood may add up to nothing more than adding up those facts.

The problem is that the actors objecting most vociferously to Palestine's nonsensical push for recognition of statehood it doesn't possess are the same ones actively standing in the way of Palestinians' creating the facts that would make statehood possible. This is why, for all the trouble it will cause, Palestine's push is right, and the United States is wrong to oppose it. Palestine's statehood would either change the balance of forces, or show it hasn't changed. Either way, it matters in the way tilting pointlessly at giant windmills matters. Statehood is either a bundle of practical powers, or a fantasy people genuinely believe in. Or both. Either way, to be a state—to be recognized as a state, in a way that means something—you have to pretend you are one. Even if, like Palestine, you aren't.

Palestinian Initiatives in the International Fora (2022)
Jim Zanotti

The PLO has pursued a number of international initiatives—opposed by
the United States and Israel—that are part of a broader effort to obtain
greater international recognition of Palestinian statehood. Some 139 out of
193 U.N. member states reportedly have formally recognized the state of
Palestine that the PLO declared in 1988. Palestinian leaders also have
taken actions to facilitate an International Criminal Court (ICC)
investigation into possible crimes in the West Bank and Gaza.

U.N.-Related Issues

[…] In September 2011, PLO Chairman Abbas applied for Palestinian
membership in the United Nations. Officially, the application remains
pending in the Security Council's membership committee, whose members
did not achieve consensus during 2011 deliberations. The application for
Palestinian membership would likely face a U.S. veto if it came to a future
vote in the Security Council. In fall 2011, the Palestinians obtained
membership in the U.N. Educational, Scientific and Cultural Organization
(UNESCO). […]

The following are some other significant steps for the PLO in international
fora:

- On November 29, 2012, the U.N. General Assembly adopted
Resolution 67/19. The resolution changed the permanent U.N. observer
status of the PLO […] from an "entity" to a "non-member state."

- In 2016, the Palestinians acceded to the U.N. Framework
Convention on Climate Change (UNFCCC).

- In 2017, the Palestinians obtained membership in Interpol.

- In 2018, the Palestinians applied to join the U.N. Conference on
Trade and Development (UNCTAD) and deposited an instrument of
accession to the Chemical Weapons Convention (CWC) with the U.N.
Secretary General.

International Criminal Court (ICC) Actions

BACKGROUND

The International Criminal Court (ICC) has an open investigation into
possible crimes committed by Israelis and Palestinians in the West Bank
(including East Jerusalem) and the Gaza Strip since June 13, 2014. The
ICC can exercise jurisdiction over alleged genocide, war crimes, and

crimes against humanity ("ICC crimes") that occur on the territory of or are perpetrated by nationals of an entity deemed to be a State

- after the Rome Statute enters into force for a State Party;

- during a period of time in which a nonparty State accepts jurisdiction; or

- pursuant to a U.N. Security Council resolution referring the situation in a State to the ICC.

The following actions by Palestinian leaders have influenced the overall context in which the ICC's actions have taken place:

- In January 2015, Palestinian leaders deposited an instrument of accession for the "State of Palestine" to become party to the Rome Statute of the ICC, after declaring acceptance in December 2014 of ICC jurisdiction over crimes allegedly "committed in the occupied Palestinian territory, including East Jerusalem, since June 13, 2014."

- Later in January 2015, the U.N. Secretary-General, acting as depositary, stated that the Rome Statute would enter into force for the "State of Palestine" on April 1, 2015.

- Later that same month, the ICC Prosecutor opened a preliminary examination into the "situation in Palestine" to determine "whether there is a reasonable basis to proceed with an investigation" against Israelis, Palestinians, or others, having found that the Palestinians had the proper capacity to accept ICC jurisdiction in light of the November 2012 adoption of U.N. General Assembly Resolution 67/19. [...]

- Palestinian leaders provided information to the ICC on alleged Israeli crimes regarding both the summer 2014 Israel-Gaza conflict and settlement activity in the West Bank. In May 2018, Palestinian leaders made a formal referral of the "situation in Palestine" to the Prosecutor.

As referenced above, the State Department cited Palestinian actions relating to the ICC in connection with the 2018 closure of the PLO office in Washington, DC. Various U.S. and Israeli officials have denounced Palestinian efforts that could subject Israelis to ICC investigation or prosecution. Neither the United States nor Israel is a State Party to the Rome Statute.

Palestinian accession and acceptance of jurisdiction grant the ICC Prosecutor authority to investigate all alleged ICC crimes committed after June 13, 2014, by any individual—Israeli, Palestinian, or otherwise—on "occupied Palestinian territory." However, Palestinian actions do not ensure any formal ICC prosecution of alleged ICC crimes. A party to the Rome Statute can refer a situation to the Court and is required to cooperate with the Prosecutor on investigations, but it is the role of the Prosecutor to determine whether to bring charges against and prosecute an individual. In addition, a case is inadmissible before the ICC if it concerns conduct that is the subject of "genuine" legal proceedings (as described in Article 17 of the Statute) brought by a state with jurisdiction, including a state (such as Israel) that is not party to the Statute.

The ICC Prosecutor is required to notify all states with jurisdiction over a potential case, and such states are afforded the opportunity to challenge ICC jurisdiction over a case on inadmissibility grounds.

Investigation of Possible Crimes in West Bank and Gaza

On March 3, 2021, then-ICC Prosecutor Fatou Bensouda announced that she was opening an investigation of possible ICC crimes in the West Bank and Gaza. She had previously sought a ruling from a pre-trial chamber to confirm her determination that the ICC has jurisdiction over the situation generally, and to determine the extent of the Court's territorial jurisdiction specifically. In a 2-1 decision, the chamber ruled in February 2021 that the ICC has jurisdiction in the West Bank and Gaza (including East Jerusalem), based on the Palestinians' status as a State Party to the Rome Statute. Israel had argued that the ICC should not have jurisdiction in those territories because Palestinians do not have sovereign control there.

Broader Impact of ICC Pre-Trial Chamber Ruling?
The ICC pre-trial chamber's February 2021 decision stated that because the ICC exercises jurisdiction over natural persons rather than states, its decision "is strictly limited to the question of jurisdiction set forth in the Prosecutor's Request and does not entail any determination on the border disputes between Palestine and Israel." According to one commentator, Palestinians and other international actors could use the decision to support for Palestinian statehood and territorial claims.

[...]
While Palestinian leaders (from both the PLO/PA and Hamas) welcomed the news of an ICC investigation, leading Israeli political figures roundly denounced it, with then-Prime Minister Benjamin Netanyahu calling the decision to investigate biased and anti-Semitic.

The investigation under the current Prosecutor, Karim Khan, could focus on a number of possible war crimes from Israeli and Palestinian actions, including

- actions by Israel, Hamas, and other Palestinian militant groups during their 2014 and 2021 Gaza conflicts;

- lethal force used by Israeli soldiers in 2018-2019 against some Palestinian protestors in Gaza seeking to breach or approach the administrative boundary with Israel;

- other Israeli actions in and around the West Bank and Gaza, including settlement activity; and

- possible PA (West Bank) and Hamas (Gaza) human rights abuses.

An investigation could take months or years before the Prosecutor makes decisions on bringing specific charges against individuals. As mentioned above, if an ICC investigation produces any case against Israelis or Palestinians concerning conduct that is the subject of "genuine" legal proceedings by a state having jurisdiction, it would be inadmissible. In Bensouda's announcement of the investigation, she said

> As a first step, the Office [of the Prosecutor] is required to notify all States Parties and those States which would normally exercise jurisdiction over the crimes concerned about its investigation. This permits any such State to request the Office to defer to the State's relevant investigation of its own nationals or others within its jurisdiction in relation to Rome Statute crimes referred to in the notification (subject to possible Pre-Trial Chamber review).

[…]

Basic Law: Israel – The Nation State of the Jewish People (2018)
GOVT. OF ISRAEL

Basic Principles	1. (a) The Land of Israel is the historical homeland of the Jewish People, in which the State of Israel was established.
	(b) The State of Israel is the nation state of the Jewish People in which it realizes its natural, cultural, religious and historical right to self-determination.
	(c) The realization of the right to national self-determination in the State of Israel is exclusive to the Jewish People.
The symbols of the State	2. (a) The name of the State is "Israel"
	(b) The State flag is white, with two light-blue stripes close to the edges, and a light-blue Star of David in the centre.
	(c) The State emblem is a seven-branched menorah with olive leaves on both sides, and the word "Israel" beneath it.
	(d) The national anthem is "Hatikvah".
	(e) Details regarding the State symbols shall be prescribed by law.
The capital of the State	3. The complete and united Jerusalem is the capital of Israel.
Language	4. (a) Hebrew is the language of the State.
	(b) Arabic has a special status in the State. Regulation of the use of Arabic in state institutions or in contacts with them shall be prescribed by law.
	(c) Nothing in this article shall compromise the status given to the Arabic language in practice, before this basic-law came into force.

Ingathering of the exiles	5. The State shall be open to Jewish immigration, and the ingathering of the exiles.
The connection to the Jewish People	6. (a) The State shall strive to secure the welfare of members of the Jewish People and of its citizens, who are in straits and in captivity, due to their Jewishness or due to their citizenship.
	(b) The State shall act in the Diaspora, to strengthen the affinity between the State and members of the Jewish People.
	(c) The State shall act to preserve the cultural, historical, and religious heritage of the Jewish People among Jews of the Diaspora.
Jewish settlement	7. The State views the development of Jewish settlement as a national value, and shall act to encourage and promote its establishment and consolidation.
Official calendar	8. The Hebrew calendar is the official calendar of the State, and side by side with it, the Gregorian calendar shall be used as an official calendar. The use of the Hebrew calendar and the Gregorian calendar shall be prescribed by law.
Independence Day and memorial days	9. (a) Independence Day is the official national holiday of the State.
	(b) Memorial Day for the Fallen in Israel's Wars, and the Remembrance Day for the Holocaust and Martyrdom, are official memorial days of the State.
Days of rest and statutory holidays	10. The Sabbath and the Jewish holidays are the established days of rest in the State. Those who are not Jewish have the right to keep days of rest on their days of rest and holidays. Details regarding this matter shall be prescribed by law.
Rigidity	11. This basic-law may not be changed save by means of a basic-law, adopted by a majority of the Knesset Members.

II/ STATEMENT OF FACTS

21. On 6 December 2017, the President of the United States of America unilaterally recognized the Holy City of Jerusalem as the capital of Israel and announced the relocation of the United States Embassy in Israel from Tel Aviv to the Holy City of Jerusalem.

22. On 18 December 2017, due solely to the veto of the United States of America, the concerned party to the present dispute, the Security Council failed to adopt a resolution reiterating that

> "any decisions and actions which purport to have altered, the character, status or demographic composition of the Holy City of Jerusalem have no legal effect, are null and void and must be rescinded in compliance with relevant resolutions of the Security Council".

23. The Security Council's failure to discharge its responsibilities on behalf of all the Member States to maintain international peace and security led the General Assembly to hold an Emergency Special Session, in which it adopted Resolution ES-10/19 and affirmed

> "that any decisions and actions which purport to have altered the character, status or demographic composition of the Holy City of Jerusalem have no legal effect, are null and void and must be rescinded in compliance with relevant resolutions of the Security Council, and in this regard calls upon all States to refrain from the establishment of diplomatic missions in the Holy City of Jerusalem, pursuant to Council resolution 478 (1980)".

and further called upon

> "all States to refrain from the establishment of diplomatic missions in the Holy City of Jerusalem, pursuant to Council resolution 478 (1980)".

24. On 14 May 2018, the United States of America inaugurated its embassy in the Holy City of Jerusalem.
[...]

IV/ LEGAL GROUNDS FOR THE CLAIMS

36. The relocation of the United States embassy in Israel to the Holy City of Jerusalem constitutes a breach of the Vienna Convention on Diplomatic Relations of 18 April 1961. It is undeniable that the Convention was conceived as a tool for the pacification of international relations. [...]

37. Article 3, paragraph 1, of the Convention provides that:

"1. The functions of a diplomatic mission consist, *inter alia,* in:

(a) Representing the sending State in the receiving State;

(b) Protecting in the receiving State the interests of the sending State and of its nationals, within the limits permitted by international law;

(c) Negotiating with the Government of the receiving State;

(d) Ascertaining by all lawful means conditions and developments in the receiving State, and reporting thereon to the Government of the sending State;

(e) Promoting friendly relations between the sending State and the receiving State, and developing their economic, cultural and scientific relations".

[…]

V/ DECISION REQUESTED

51. By the present Application, the State of Palestine therefore requests the Court to declare that the relocation, to the Holy City of Jerusalem, of the United States embassy in Israel is in breach of the Vienna Convention on Diplomatic Relations.

52. The State of Palestine further requests the Court to order the United States of America to withdraw the diplomatic mission from the Holy City of Jerusalem and to conform to the international obligations flowing from the Vienna Convention on Diplomatic Relations.

53. In addition, the State of Palestine asks the Court to order the United States of America to take all necessary steps to comply with its obligations, to refrain from taking any future measures that would violate its obligations and to provide assurances and guarantees of non-repetition of its unlawful conduct.

[…]

Israel's Possible Annexation of the West Bank Areas: FAQs (2020)
Jim Zanotti

Israeli Prime Minister Binyamin Netanyahu has stated his intent for Israel to annex parts of the West Bank in 2020. [...]

While the West Bank has been under Israeli military administration since its capture from Jordan in the 1967 Arab-Israeli War, its status has been different from Israel proper (the territory Israel controlled before the war). Israel's government has a mandate—based on the May 2020 power-sharing agreement between Netanyahu and Defense Minister Benny Gantz—to bring the matter of annexation to a cabinet and/or Knesset vote as early as July 1, 2020, provided that it is done in coordination with the United States. [...]

Possible U.S. support for annexation could be based on elements of President Trump's January 2020 plan for Israeli-Palestinian peace, otherwise known as the *Vision for Peace*. In line with that plan, a U.S.-Israel joint committee, without Palestinian participation, is to identify the areas Israel can annex—primarily Israeli settlements and the Jordan Valley. [...]

Israeli officials reportedly are considering various annexation scenarios, including partial or phased annexation of West Bank areas. Referencing the Trump plan, U.S. officials have said that the United States could be willing to recognize Israeli annexation in the areas mentioned above (comprising up to 30% of the West Bank), if Israel remains willing to negotiate with the Palestinians about a possible Palestinian state in the Gaza Strip and other parts of the West Bank. [...]

While past U.S. Administrations anticipated that some West Bank settlements likely would become part of Israel pursuant to a final-status peace agreement, none had previously approved of unilateral annexation taking place prior to such an agreement. Many experts argue that annexation is contrary to international law and existing Israeli-Palestinian agreements. Trump Administration officials defend their Israeli-Palestinian policies by saying they more accurately reflect reality and provide more detailed proposals than past U.S. and international diplomatic frameworks for resolving the long-standing conflict. [...]

How would annexation compare with past actions affecting the status of territories Israel captured in 1967?

Steps by Israel to unilaterally annex and set the borders of West Bank areas would differ from efforts that Israel has pursued with various Arab parties since the end of the 1967 war under the internationally supported "land-for-peace" concept found in U.N. Security Council Resolution 242 (1967). The idea that Israel would resolve its conflict with Arab states and the

Palestinians via negotiations based on the return of lands captured in war undergirded Israel's peace treaties with Egypt and Jordan. Land-for-peace also formed the foundation of the Oslo agreements of the 1990s that started the Israeli-Palestinian peace process. However, before the Oslo agreements, Israel effectively annexed East Jerusalem and the Golan Heights [....]

By recognizing Israeli annexation, the Trump Administration would appear to support a fixed outcome to the "land" component of the Israeli-Palestinian conflict in the absence of a negotiated "peace" component. Some observers interpret the Administration's stance as a significant break from previous U.S. policy, partly because of the lack of Palestinian input into the Trump plan released in January. While past U.S. Administrations anticipated that some West Bank settlements likely would become part of Israel pursuant to a final-status peace agreement, none had approved of annexation taking place before such an agreement [....] Trump Administration officials defend their positions by saying that they more accurately reflect reality and provide more detailed proposals than past U.S. and international diplomatic frameworks for resolving conflict.
[...]

Israeli willingness to negotiate with Palestinians on two-state solution

U.S. willingness to recognize Israeli sovereignty over areas designated by the mapping committee also apparently depends on Israeli readiness to engage in future final-status negotiations with the PLO. In Ambassador Friedman's May interview, he said that U.S. recognition could come if "the prime minister will agree to negotiate with the Palestinians and invite the Palestinians to meet, to engage in discussions and keep those discussions open, and pursue them in good faith, for four years." For the Palestinians to be eligible for statehood within those four years under the Trump plan's terms—which they have adamantly rejected to date—they would need to meet criteria that arguably present considerable, if not insurmountable, domestic and practical challenges. Such criteria include disarming the Sunni Islamist group Hamas (a U.S.-designated terrorist organization) in Gaza, ending certain international initiatives and financial incentives for violence, and recognizing Israel as "the nation state of the Jewish people."
[...]

What territory might be annexed?

Based on the Trump Administration's *Vision for Peace*, all Israeli settlements and a major section of the Jordan Valley (a strip of land to the west of the Jordan River and Dead Sea between Jordan and the rest of the West Bank) could be subject to annexation. Pending final maps produced by the U.S.-Israel joint committee, the total territory subject to annexation could constitute approximately 30% of the West Bank, or about half of the territory classified as Area C under the 1995 Israel-PLO Interim Agreement. A provision in the Trump plan anticipates that Palestinians

540

living inside contiguous territory annexed by Israel would be subject to Palestinian civil administration and Israeli security jurisdiction. By anticipating that these people could become citizens of a future Palestinian state, the provision suggests that they would not become Israeli citizens. Additionally, the Trump plan says, "The security [aka separation] barrier will be realigned to match the new borders. New, modern and efficient border crossings will be constructed."

Under the Trump plan, Israeli territory up to the equivalent of about 13.5% of West Bank territory could be ceded to a Palestinian state under a negotiated solution, if the Palestinians meet conditions specified in the plan. [...]

SETTLEMENTS

The Trump plan anticipates that 97% of the approximately 425,000 Israeli settlers in the West Bank could be incorporated into contiguous Israeli territory, with the remaining settlers from 15 enclaves able to be incorporated into Israel via access routes, Israeli civilian administration, and security protection. It does not explicitly refer to the situation of Israelis living in unauthorized outposts outside of these specified areas.

Reportedly, more than 100,000 Palestinians live in areas that the Trump plan anticipates could be inside contiguous Israeli territory. As mentioned above, the Trump plan suggests that these Palestinians might remain subject to Palestinian civil administration instead of becoming Israeli citizens. Israeli annexation of these areas could present challenges in applying a Trump plan provision that calls for these Palestinians not to face discrimination, to receive security protection, and to have access to transportation routes as well as Palestinian zoning and planning services where they live.

JORDAN VALLEY

The Jordan Valley is a sparsely populated but relatively water-rich and fertile region of the West Bank. It is the largest land reserve for future development in the territory. It also has strategic value as a buffer zone between Israel's main population centers and Arab states to the east, as well as a means of encircling Palestinian urban centers in the West Bank. Israel's military has maintained a significant presence there since 1967. The Jordan Valley has particular value for a possible future Palestinian state because of its productive agricultural capacity, and because it is the only West Bank area bordering a country (Jordan) other than Israel.

Under the Trump plan's conceptual map, the area of the Jordan Valley subject to Israeli annexation would be somewhat smaller than the area presented by Prime Minister Netanyahu in a September 2019 map. In either case, the Palestinian city of Jericho (approximate population: 40,000) would not be annexed. Additionally, Prime Minister Netanyahu said in May 2020 that no Palestinians living in the Jordan Valley would become Israeli citizens. [...]

How might the Palestinians respond to annexation?

Palestinian leaders in the West Bank have strongly denounced Prime Minister Netanyahu's plans for annexation, characterizing annexation as an abandonment of the Israeli-Palestinian peace process and a violation of international law and existing Israel-PLO agreements. The Palestinians already have taken some actions to curtail cooperation with Israel in anticipation of annexation (as discussed below), and their responses if it actually happens are uncertain. [...]

In May 2020, after the new Israeli government pledged to pursue annexation, PLO Chairman and PA President Mahmoud Abbas gave a speech immediately absolving the Palestinians of "all the agreements and understandings with the American and Israeli governments and of all the commitments based on these understandings and agreements, including the security ones." In his speech, Abbas also reaffirmed the Palestinians' commitment to a just and comprehensive peace with Israel, and a two-state solution, based on negotiations and legitimate international efforts connected with U.N. resolutions and the Arab Peace Initiative. He called for international efforts that could deter Israel from annexation, protect Palestinians, and uphold international law. In June, PA Prime Minister Mohammed Shtayyeh announced that the PLO/PA has submitted a counter-proposal to the Trump plan to the Middle East Quartet (the United Nations, United States, European Union, and Russia). According to Shtayyeh, the proposal calls for the creation of a sovereign, demilitarized Palestinian state with "minor modifications of borders as necessary." As reported in late June, the counter-proposal calls for resuming direct Israeli-Palestinian talks where they left off in 2014, but the PLO/PA would withdraw the proposal if annexation takes place.

In early July, leading figures from Fatah (the faction that controls the PA) and Hamas held joint events approved by President Abbas to announce that the two factions would work together to show "popular resistance" to thwart annexation and the Trump plan. The events did not announce specific initiatives, but Fatah and Hamas leaders said that the form popular resistance might take could depend on Israeli actions, and that all options were open. The leaders admitted that they remain divided on a number of issues, and it is unclear how substantive any Fatah-Hamas cooperation might be, given continuing tensions between the factions and a lack of success with past efforts toward greater unity.

542

PA efforts to warn Israel about possible consequences of annexation have included two seemingly contradictory threads: threatening to take legal and political steps toward statehood, and anticipating a possible end to PA public services for Palestinians in the West Bank and Gaza. In June 2020, Prime Minister Shtayyeh announced that if Israel continues along a course toward annexation, the PA would transition from a temporary authority to a "state on the ground," using armistice lines as borders (a 1949-1967 line for the West Bank, and a 1950-1967 line for Gaza), and declaring East Jerusalem as its capital. PA Civil Affairs Minister Hussein al Sheikh has said that if Israel moves forward with annexation, the PA would consider ending services such as policing, education, and health care, thus seeking to compel Israel to resume the full responsibility over the West Bank that it had before the PA's creation. On June 24, PA President Abbas said that annexation of even a small portion of West Bank territory "will obligate Israel to bear the responsibilities in occupied land as an occupying power according to the Fourth Geneva Convention." Given an apparent disconnect between stronger claims to statehood and a reduction in public services, it is unclear whether the Palestinians might carry out these threats in tandem, or as only one or the other.

In June 2020, PA leaders announced that because they are no longer bound by agreements with Israel, they are refusing to receive transfers of import and export taxes from Israel that account for at least 60% of PA revenue. Suspending revenue transfers could affect the PA's ability to operate, with possible ripple effects for stability and Israel's security, especially if PA workers do not receive salaries. In June, the PA announced that it would suspend salaries for civil servants, and would not provide a monthly transfer of $105 million to Gaza that normally pays for public salaries, utilities, and medical expenses there. [...]

PA SECURITY COORDINATION WITH ISRAEL

The significant reduction in the PA's West Bank security coordination with Israel in anticipation of possible annexation could affect stability in the region. PA-Israel coordination, with its focus on maintaining order in Palestinian urban areas and preventing terrorism, has been an important anchor for U.S.-Israel-PA relations. [...] Israeli authorities also reportedly fear that Hamas could exploit annexation-related tensions to step up its West Bank activities, in addition to whatever it might do in Gaza. In late June, a Hamas military leader said that annexation would be considered a declaration of war against the Palestinians.

After Abbas's May speech, reports have suggested that the PA has halted most forms of security coordination with Israel and the United States, and other civil ties with Israel. On a number of previous occasions, Abbas had threatened to stop coordination but had either not done so or only paused some aspects of it. Senior Israeli officials have been cited as saying that they expect some security coordination with the PA to continue on a clandestine basis, because their PA counterparts have reportedly said that they were not prepared to end it completely. As of June, reports suggest that Israel and the PA security officials continue to share some information indirectly via international organizations.

Some reports suggest that the PA is making efforts to preserve order, though it is uncertain whether those efforts would continue if annexation takes place. Prime Minister Shtayyeh has said that the PA currently intends to prevent chaos and otherwise act in a sovereign capacity in the West Bank. One Israeli media source reported in May that the PA sent messages to Israel saying that despite ending security coordination, it would not allow terror attacks against Israelis or a mass popular uprising.
[…]

Abraham Accords Peace Agreement (2020)

UNITED ARAB EMIRATES AND THE GOVERNMENT OF THE STATE OF ISRAEL

[The Abraham Accords includes a declaration and a series of bilateral agreements involving Israel and Bahrain, UAE, Morocco, and Sudan. Below is the Israel-UAE agreement.].

The Government of the United Arab Emirates and the Government of the State of Israel (hereinafter, the "Parties")

Aspiring to realize the vision of a Middle East region that is stable, peaceful and prosperous, for the benefit of all States and peoples in the region;

Desiring to establish peace, diplomatic and friendly relations, co-operation and full normalization of ties between them and their peoples, in accordance with this Treaty, and to chart together a new path to unlock the vast potential of their countries and of the region;

Reaffirming the "Joint Statement of the United States, the State of Israel, and the United Arab Emirates" (the "Abraham Accords"), dated 13 August 2020;

Believing that the further development of friendly relations meets the interests of lasting peace in the Middle East and that challenges can only be effectively addressed by cooperation and not by conflict;

Determined to ensure lasting peace, stability, security and prosperity for both their States and to develop and enhance their dynamic and innovative economies;

Reaffirming their shared commitment to normalize relations and promote stability through diplomatic engagement, increased economic cooperation and other close coordination;

Reaffirming also their shared belief that the establishment of peace and full normalization between them can help transform the Middle East by spurring economic growth, enhancing technological innovation and forging closer people-to-people relations;

Recognizing that the Arab and Jewish peoples are descendants of a common ancestor, Abraham, and *inspired*, in that spirit, to foster in the Middle East a reality in which Muslims, Jews, Christians and peoples of all faiths, denominations, beliefs and nationalities live in, and are committed to, a spirit of coexistence, mutual understanding and mutual respect;

Recalling the reception held on January 28, 2020, at which President Trump presented his Vision for Peace, and *committing* to continuing their efforts to achieve a just, comprehensive, realistic and enduring solution to the Israeli-Palestinian conflict;

Recalling the Treaties of Peace between the State of Israel and the Arab Republic of Egypt and between the State of Israel and the Hashemite Kingdom of Jordan, and committed to working together to realize a negotiated solution to the Israeli-Palestinian conflict that meets the legitimate needs and aspirations of both peoples, and to advance comprehensive Middle East peace, stability and prosperity;

Emphasizing the belief that the normalization of Israeli and Emirati relations is in the interest of both peoples and contributes to the cause of peace in the Middle East and the world;

Expressing deep appreciation to the United States for its profound contribution to this historic achievement;

Have agreed as follows:

1. **Establishment of Peace, Diplomatic Relations and Normalization:** Peace, diplomatic relations and full normalization of bilateral ties are hereby established between the United Arab Emirates and the State of Israel.

2. **General Principles:** The Parties shall be guided in their relations by the provisions of the Charter of the United Nations and the principles of international law governing relations among States. In particular, they shall recognize and respect each other's sovereignty and right to live in peace and security, develop friendly relations of cooperation between them and their peoples, and settle all disputes between them by peaceful means.

3. **Establishment of Embassies:** The Parties shall exchange resident ambassadors as soon as practicable after the signing of this Treaty, and shall conduct diplomatic and consular relations in accordance with the applicable rules of international law.

4. **Peace and Stability:** The Parties shall attach profound importance to mutual understanding, cooperation and coordination between them in the spheres of peace and stability, as a fundamental pillar of their relations and as a means for enhancing those spheres in the Middle East as a whole. They undertake to take the necessary steps to prevent any terrorist or hostile activities against each other on or from their respective territories, as well as deny any support for such activities abroad or allowing such support on or from their respective territories. Recognizing the new era of peace and friendly relations between them, as well as the centrality of stability to the well-being of their respective peoples and of the region, the

Parties undertake to consider and discuss these matters regularly, and to conclude detailed agreements and arrangements on coordination and cooperation.

5. **Cooperation and Agreements in Other Spheres:** As an integral part of their commitment to peace, prosperity, diplomatic and friendly relations, cooperation and full normalization, the Parties shall work to advance the cause of peace, stability and prosperity throughout the Middle East, and to unlock the great potential of their countries and of the region. For such purposes, the Parties shall conclude bilateral agreements in the following spheres at the earliest practicable date, as well as in other spheres of mutual interest as may be agreed:

- Finance and Investment
- Civil Aviation
- Visas and Consular Services
- Innovation, Trade and Economic Relations
- Healthcare
- Science, Technology and Peaceful Uses of Outer-Space
- Tourism, Culture and Sport
- Energy
- Environment
- Education
- Maritime Arrangements
- Telecommunications and Post
- Agriculture and Food Security
- Water
- Legal Cooperation

Any such agreements concluded before the entry into force of this Treaty shall enter into effect with the entry into force of this Treaty unless otherwise stipulated therein. Agreed principles for cooperation in specific spheres are annexed to this Treaty and form an integral part thereof.

6. **Mutual Understanding and Co-existence:** The Parties undertake to foster mutual understanding, respect, co-existence and a culture of peace between their societies in the spirit of their common ancestor, Abraham, and the new era of peace and friendly relations ushered in by this Treaty, including by cultivating people-to-people programs, interfaith dialogue and cultural, academic, youth, scientific, and other exchanges between their peoples. They shall conclude and implement the necessary visa and consular services agreements and arrangements so as to facilitate efficient and secure travel for their respective nationals to the territory of each other. The Parties shall work together to counter extremism, which promotes hatred and division, and terrorism and its justifications, including by preventing radicalization and recruitment and by combating incitement and discrimination. They shall work towards

establishing a High-Level Joint Forum for Peace and Co-Existence dedicated to advancing these goals.

7.   **Strategic Agenda for the Middle East:** Further to the Abraham Accords, the Parties stand ready to join with the United States to develop and launch a "Strategic Agenda for the Middle East" in order to expand regional diplomatic, trade, stability and other cooperation. They are committed to work together, and with the United States and others, as appropriate, in order to advance the cause of peace, stability and prosperity in the relations between them and for the Middle East as a whole, including by seeking to advance regional security and stability; pursue regional economic opportunities; promote a culture of peace across the region; and consider joint aid and development programs.

8.   **Other Rights and Obligations:** This Treaty does not affect and shall not be interpreted as affecting, in any way, the rights and obligations of the Parties under the Charter of the United Nations. The Parties shall take all necessary measures for the application in their bilateral relations of the provisions of the multilateral conventions of which they are both parties, including the submission of appropriate notification to the depositaries of such conventions.

9.   **Respect for Obligations:** The Parties undertake to fulfill in good faith their obligations under this Treaty, without regard to action or inaction of any other party and independently of any instrument inconsistent with this Treaty. For the purposes of this paragraph each Party represents to the other that in its opinion and interpretation there is no inconsistency between their existing treaty obligations and this Treaty. The Parties undertake not to enter into any obligation in conflict with this Treaty. Subject to Article 103 of the Charter of the United Nations, in the event of a conflict between the obligations of the Parties under the present Treaty and any of their other obligations, the obligations under this Treaty shall be binding and implemented. The Parties further undertake to adopt any legislation or other internal legal procedure necessary in order to implement this Treaty, and to repeal any national legislation or official publications inconsistent with this Treaty.

10.   **Ratification and Entry into Force:** This Treaty shall be ratified by both Parties as soon as practicable in conformity with their respective national procedures and will enter into force following the exchange of instruments of ratification.

11.   **Settlement of Disputes:** Disputes arising out of the application or interpretation of this Treaty shall be resolved by negotiation. Any such dispute which cannot be settled by negotiation may be referred to conciliation or arbitration subject to the agreement of the Parties. [...]

How Israel Still Uses the Second Intifada as a Pretext (2020)
Ali Adam

[Diana Buttu, a Ramallah-based analyst and former adviser to the Palestinian negotiators on Oslo] noted Israel later used the [second Intifada] to issue demands based on "security" needs.

"They started to make loud demands to take the entirety of the Jordan Valley, taking all of Jerusalem, keeping the settlements there. It later turned into building the wall, it later turned into keeping the checkpoints and army bases inside Palestinian land.

"This is why you see the Trump plan the way it is today. The Trump plan is fitting into all of these demands that Israel imposed as a result of the Second Intifada, which Israel sought and wanted."

Abu Yusuf [a senior Palestinian official and member of the Executive Committee of the Palestine Liberation Organization (PLO)] said 20 years after the start of the second Intifada, Israel still rejects Palestinian rights in any form.

"It still expands settlements, demolishes Palestinian homes, and implements its de facto annexation of the Palestinian territories with the support of the Trump administration," Abu Yusuf said.

"In the same way 20 years later, the Palestinian people, despite everything, remain committed to resisting the occupation and to their rights under international law, and will remain so until achieving freedom in a sovereign independent Palestinian state with East Jerusalem as its capital, and solving the refugees' plight in accordance in 194 UN resolution."

Years after the Israeli attacks against Palestinians during the second Intifada, Israel still "commits all kinds of crimes", al-Masri said. "The silence by the international community is what still encourages Israel to commit crimes and flagrant violations of human rights."

Abu Yusuf said the recent challenges – such as US President Donald Trump's so-called Middle East plan, Israeli annexation, and Arab nations' normalisation with Israel – are all intended "to force the Palestinians to accept to live in cantons and Bantustans".

"But as the Palestinians rejected in the Intifada years and the prior Oslo years to accept anything less than ending the occupation, they will continue to do so now and in the future."

From <u>Palestinian Intifada: How Israel Orchestrated a Bloody Takeover,</u>   549
AL JAZEERA MEDIA (Sep. 28, 2020). Used with permission of Newstex, LLC; permission conveyed through Copyright Clearance Center, Inc.

From Hope to Halt: The Abraham Accords and the Palestinian Predicament (2023)
Gregory Aftandilian

At the time of the [Abraham] Accords' signing, the Arab signatories—namely the United Arab Emirates and Bahrain—claimed to their domestic constituencies that better relations with Israel would allow them to advocate on behalf of the Palestinians more effectively. This diplomatic effort, however, has done nothing to advance a genuine peace between Israel and the Palestinians, which remains the core unresolved issue in the Middle East. The fact that movement to expand the Abraham Accords has now slowed down as Israeli-Palestinian violence has increased should give U.S. policymakers pause about pinning their hopes on other Arab countries joining them—particularly Saudi Arabia.

What Netanyahu Wants

It is no secret that Israeli Prime Minister Benjamin Netanyahu has long wanted Israeli-Arab normalization without any Israeli concessions on the Palestinian issue. For many years, this arrangement seemed impossible to establish; in the 2002 Arab Peace Initiative, the Arab League collectively endorsed peace negotiations with Israel only if the Palestinian issue was resolved. However, the entry of Trump to the Oval Office provided the Israeli leader with a cornucopia of gifts, with no expectation that Israel would improve the treatment of the Palestinians.

Under Trump, the United States recognized Jerusalem as Israel's capital and moved the U.S. Embassy to that city, recognized Israeli sovereignty over the Golan Heights, closed the U.S. consulate in East Jerusalem that primarily served the Palestinian community, and proposed a "peace plan" without consulting the Palestinians that envisioned Israel swallowing one-third of the West Bank and dividing the remaining sections into a patchwork of disjointed islands surrounded by Israeli territory. Netanyahu was pleased by Trump's actions, and featured the two leaders side-by-side on large billboards in Israel during his 2019 political campaign. In addition to being beneficial for Israel, the Abraham Accords were a vindication for him personally: by persuading the UAE and Bahrain to sign, he had successfully separated the Palestinian issue from the normalization issue, a longtime personal aspiration.
[…]
The Abraham Accords caused deep anguish in the Palestinian territories, as a clear majority of Palestinians of varying political persuasions saw them as a betrayal of their cause by some Arab states, abetted by the United States. In the eyes of many Palestinians, Arab normalization with Israel is a trump card that should only be played at the end of a genuine peace process. In other words, in the Palestinian view, normalization should be delayed until Palestinian national self-determination is achieved.

Even Jordan, which established diplomatic relations with Israel in 1994, was uneasy about the Abraham Accords. The Jordanian government has had to tread very delicately on this issue, given that 60 percent of Jordanian citizens are of Palestinian descent.

The Consequences of Escalation

However, the advent of Israel's far-right government after Netanyahu's electoral victory in December 2022, has complicated the Abraham Accords. National Security Minister Itamar Ben-Gvir, the far-right Otzma Yehudit legislator who was once convicted of anti-Arab racism, has done exceptional damage to Israel's new Arab relations by marching on the Haram al-Sharif in January 2023 (and again in July 2023), by causing anger not only among Palestinians but also among Muslims across the Middle East. In addition, the building of more settlements in the West Bank, overseen by extremist Finance Minister Bezalel Smotrich, and an uptick in settler violence against the Palestinians has caused similar outrage.

Such acts have led even the UAE to condemn Israeli policies. Since the beginning of the year, Abu Dhabi has sharply criticized Ben Gvir's antics, Israeli settlement building, and the recent raid on a Palestinian refugee camp in Jenin in the northern West Bank. The UAE was joined by many other Arab countries, including Saudi Arabia, in these condemnations [....] [T]he recent developments have tempered the momentum for expanding the Abraham Accords.

Netanyahu's highest objective for the Abraham Accords would be for Saudi Arabia to join, and there has been much speculation that, with Washington's help, such an achievement is within reach. [...]

But lost in all of this speculation is Saudi Arabia's deep sensitivities over the Palestinian issue. As the self-proclaimed leader of the Islamic world, Riyadh simply cannot ignore Israeli provocations in Jerusalem, which hosts the third-holiest site in Islam. Nor can it ignore the plight of the Palestinians. A spokesman for the Saudi Embassy in Washington explicitly stated in June 2023 that the kingdom will not normalize ties with Israel until a Palestinian state is established.

For these reasons, the optimism in 2020 that the Abraham Accords would usher in a new era of Arab-Israeli relations has given way to a more realistic assessment of the Middle East's geopolitics. As it was before the Accords, the Palestinian issue remains the chief stumbling block, and no U.S. entreaties to prospective Arab states to join the Accords can change this reality until a future Israeli government is willing to make significant concessions.

Israel's Acquisition of Territory Through de facto Annexation (2023)

U.N. COMMITTEE ON THE EXERCISE OF THE INALIENABLE RIGHTS OF THE PALESTINIAN PEOPLE

The study draws on five key indicators to assess the *de facto* annexation: (1) the seizure of territory; (2) the treatment of settlements as inseparable from Israel; (3) Israel's application of domestic legislation to occupied Palestine; (4) an intention to keep the territory; and (5) the permanency of the occupation.

1.2.1 Seizure of Palestinian territory

Similar to *de jure* annexation, *de facto* annexation also includes the seizure of territory; in the latter case, however, the intention to annex is implied. In occupied Palestine, the seizure of territory is evidenced through the sweeping appropriations of private and public Palestinian lands for settlement throughout the West Bank, including Jerusalem. These practices include the appropriation of public and private Palestinian lands for the construction of more than 250 settlements and the transfer of 719,452 Israeli Jewish settlers into the West Bank, including East Jerusalem.

Israel engineers every aspect of the settlement enterprise: planning and zoning; appropriating Palestinian lands, including "uncultivated" agricultural lands, as "State lands"; providing water, sanitation and electricity services to the settlements; and authorizing the construction of roads, railway lines and other infrastructure to connect the settlements to each other and to Israel proper. [...] In 1971, the Israeli Military Commander issued Military Order 418, which transferred competence for planning and zoning from the local Palestinian village councils to the Military Commander. [...] Israel also relies on its provisions to systematically deny Palestinians permits for housing construction. [...] By 1992, out of the 70,000 hectares of Palestinian land in Area C, only 12 per cent remained for Palestinian development after Israel appropriated it as "State land". At the same time, Israel has radically altered the demography of the West Bank, transferring in over 500,000 Israeli Jewish settlers to Area C – an irreversible measure with permanent consequences, and indicative of sovereign expression.

In July 2020, Israel came close to implementing the Trump Peace to Prosperity Plan, which would have seen large tracts of the Jordan Valley and settlement blocs formally annexed to Israel. [...]

1.2.2 Treatment of settlements as inseparable from Israel

[...] Undoubtedly, the planning and zoning of Palestinian land for Israeli residential, commercial and agricultural settlement, repurposing it for

Israeli nationals, reflects an incontrovertible exercise of sovereign authority by successive Israeli governments over occupied Palestine. […]

1.2.3 Israel's application of domestic legislation to occupied Palestine

The application of a series of Israeli laws directly to the West Bank is further evidence of annexationist intent. To start, Israel has avoided determining its borders and considers that its law, jurisdiction and administration extend to any area of "Eretz Israel" – a geographical area comprising the entirety of the territory of Mandatory Palestine, including the occupied territory. Although many of the measures implemented by Israel in the West Bank mirror Israeli law, they are introduced under military order, for example the application of Israel's currency to occupied Palestine. However, Israel directly negotiates leases and licensing agreements for the exploitation of Palestinian natural resources with Israeli and international corporations operating in the occupied territory to exploit quarries, water, oil, and mineral resources. […]

Further, the recent absorption of the Civil Administration and parts of Coordination of Government Activities in the Territories (COGAT), from the authority of the Military Commander into the civil competence of the Minister for Finance sitting as the second Defence Minister, are clear indicators of an intention to extend sovereignty over occupied Palestine.

1.2.4 Demonstrating an intention to keep the territory
[…]
Likewise, in 2020, in the aftermath of the Trump Peace to Prosperity Plan to annex the Jordan Valley and other parts of the West Bank to Israel, Prime Minister Netanyahu emphatically restated Israel's annexationist intent: "There is no change to my plan to extend sovereignty ... our sovereignty in Judea and Samaria [is] in full coordination with the United States".

More recently, Israel amended its quasi-constitutional Nation State Law, providing exclusively that "the State of Israel is the nation state of the Jewish People, in which it realizes its natural, cultural, religious and historical right to self-determination". Presciently, Article 7 of the law established that "the State [of Israel] views the development of Jewish settlement as a national value" and commits to "act to encourage and promote its establishment and strengthening". In December 2022, incoming Prime Minister Netanyahu underscored that the government would "promote and develop settlement in all parts of the Land of Israel – in the Negev, the Golan, Judea and Samaria".

<u>1.2.5 Permanency of the occupation as an indicator for *de facto* annexation</u>
[…]
Following the Israeli High Court of Justice decision in the 1979 *Elon Moreh* case, which ruled that Israel could not construct settlements on privately owned Palestinian land, Attorney General Yitzhak Zamir responded with a legal recommendation to create a special ministerial committee to safeguard settlements from legal challenge and to provide land for settlement construction. In 1982, Israeli Supreme Court Justice Meir Shamgar suggested that a military administration of territory could "from the legal point of view, continue indefinitely".

[…] Israel's application of laws directly to the occupied territory, deliberate evasion of international humanitarian law, and prolonged indefinite occupation, indicate that the massive land appropriations for settlements and the Wall, are reflective of colonial practices revealing a settled and permanent annexationist "character, purpose and intention".
[…]

Israel and Hamas 2023 Conflict FAQS (2023)
Jim Zanotti, et al

On October 7, 2023, the Palestinian Sunni Islamist group Hamas (a U.S.-designated foreign terrorist organization, or FTO) led surprise attacks against Israel from the Gaza Strip by land, sea, and air. The assault came on a Jewish holiday [....] The attacks' scope and lethality against Israel have no precedent in the 16 years Hamas has controlled Gaza, and the nature of the violence stunned Israelis. [...]

In response to the attacks, Israel's cabinet formally declared war on Hamas. [...]

Israeli officials have said that they aim to change the status quo in Gaza, and are contemplating a major ground invasion that may seek to end Hamas's rule there. The Israel Defense Forces has said it "calls for" all civilians residing in northern Gaza to evacuate southward. Hamas called on people to remain in place. [...]

Reportedly, more than 1,400 Israelis [...] and about 3,785 Palestinians in Gaza have been killed as of October 19. [...] Militants are also reportedly holding some 200-250 persons hostage in Gaza [....]

Hamas attacks: Why and why now?

Hamas leaders have said that their planning and preparation for the October 2023 attacks took place over several years, suggesting that the group made a strategic decision to prepare itself to be able to carry out attacks and operations that might change the status quo and prevailing assumptions in the group's long confrontation with Israel. The decision to launch the attacks in October 2023 may reflect various Hamas motivating factors, including the following:

- **Disrupting Arab-Israeli normalization efforts** – The October 7 attacks may have been intended to disrupt existing and potential future normalization agreements between Israel and Arab states, including U.S.-backed efforts to promote Saudi-Israeli normalization. Hamas may have assessed that Arab governments' increased willingness to normalize relations with Israel before the establishment of a Palestinian state—and potential PA acquiescence to this trend—provided an opening for Hamas to portray itself as uniquely committed to the Palestinian national cause.

- **Seeking to strengthen its domestic and regional position** – Hamas may have launched the attacks in a bid to bolster its domestic political position vis-à-vis the struggling PA and its president Mahmoud Abbas. Difficult and deteriorating living conditions in Gaza may have increased local political pressure on Hamas, and Hamas leaders may have perceived political opportunity arising from alleged Israeli encroachments on Muslim holy sites in Jerusalem and a pattern of confrontations in 2022 and 2023 between Israelis and Palestinians in the West Bank. A former senior U.S. official has speculated, "Hamas's intention is to get Israel to retaliate massively and have the conflict escalate: a West Bank uprising, Hezbollah attacks, a revolt in Jerusalem."

- **Capitalizing on Israeli domestic turmoil** – Political tensions have risen in 2023 among Israelis, stemming from disputes over proposed judicial reform and other issues. Hamas and its allies may have perceived an opportunity to strike at a time of internal division and distraction within Israel, and perhaps amplify discord among Israelis, by launching the attacks and successfully targeting Israeli military and civilian targets.

- **Using hostages for prisoner releases or other concessions** – Hamas leaders have long highlighted the release of Palestinian prisoners held by Israel as a priority for the group, and may have launched the attacks to use hostages to obtain prisoner releases or other Israeli concessions.

[…]

How did Hamas achieve the element of surprise?

The nature and timing of the attacks from Gaza have prompted questions about whether or not the Israeli or U.S. governments had prior information to suggest such attacks were possible or imminent or, if not, why they might have missed signs or misinterpreted indications. IDF Major General Aharon Haliva, the head of the Military Intelligence Directorate, has stated that his command failed to warn of the attack and that he bears "full responsibility for the failure." Ronen Bar, head of the Israel Security Agency, also has taken personal responsibility for the intelligence failure. […]

Israel's reportedly advanced intelligence capabilities appear to have failed to detect planning and preparation for the October 7 attacks, including Palestinian groups' acquisition or development of munition-carrying drones, personnel-carrying gliders, and thousands of missiles and rockets. Some former Israeli security officials have speculated that Palestinian armed groups have adapted their operations and methods following repeated rounds of conflict with Israel. […]

Hamas figures have suggested that their planning and preparations for the attacks spanned several years, and included a "subterfuge campaign" in which it sought to convey the impression that it was unprepared for or unwilling to engage in a new round of conflict. As one apparent element of this effort, Hamas encouraged Israel to believe that economic incentives it was providing to Gazans were decreasing Hamas's motivation to engage in conflict. Hamas figures also have told the media that they compartmentalized information about their plans and limited dissemination to exclude even senior political leaders. The groups responsible also may have taken other operational security measures to conceal their activities and preparations. Footage released by the attackers indicates that initial attacks were made against Israeli technical observation infrastructure along the Gaza-Israel line of control; the disabling of these sites may have contributed to the attackers' apparent achievement of operational surprise. [...]

What is the role of the Palestinian Authority in this crisis?

After Hamas's attacks on October 7, despite the considerable animus between the Palestinian Authority and Hamas, PA President Mahmoud Abbas said that Palestinians have the right "to defend themselves against the terrorism of settlers and the occupation forces." In a statement released the same day, the PA Ministry of Foreign Affairs blamed Israel for "the destruction of the peace process" and said that "the continuation of the injustice and oppression to which the Palestinian people are exposed is the reason behind this explosive situation." Per some analysts, the Hamas attack has put Abbas in a difficult position, unwilling to embrace his Hamas rivals and their attack on Israel, but also unable to denounce them for fear of alienating West Bank Palestinians. [...]

How has Israel's military responded to the attacks?

COUNTERATTACKS IN GAZA VIA AIR AND ARTILLERY STRIKES

Having formally declared war on Hamas, the Israeli government has mobilized around 360,000 reservists, or between 3% and 4% of Israel's total population. Netanyahu has stated that Israelis should expect prolonged conflict. With operations against attackers inside Israel reportedly concluded as of October 11, thousands of Israeli air and artillery strikes have occurred in the Gaza Strip, and Israeli ground forces are reported to be building a base and massing in adjacent areas.

Israeli strikes in Gaza present a dilemma because several military targets are located in close proximity to civilian residential areas and other facilities like schools and hospitals. President Biden said in a *60 Minutes* interview that Hamas hides "behind the civilians" and puts "their headquarters where civilians are."

Israeli officials have stated that the IDF tries to avoid civilian casualties and provides warnings to civilians before some strikes. In such efforts, the

IDF may be limited by incomplete or imperfect information, Israeli perceptions regarding operational urgency, and constraints on how precisely the IDF can deliver warnings. An unnamed senior Israeli government source has said:

> the "roof knocking" policy, whereby the IDF has previously used text messages, phone calls, or an initial strike on the roof to warn residents of a building that it is about to be struck, is not the system currently applying. In certain circumstances, it will be used, the source says, but today Israel is already evacuating masses of the [Gaza] populace from central terrorist areas and attacking there.

The effectiveness of Israel's strikes in Gaza in destroying or damaging military positions, personnel, and infrastructure is unclear. Israel claims to have killed a number of militant leaders, including some from Hamas's elite Nukhba forces who reportedly helped spearhead the October 7 attacks. Despite Israeli efforts to target rocket launching infrastructure, Hamas and other militants continue to fire rockets into Israel, though these salvos reportedly have not matched the volume and intensity of the initial barrage on October 7. [...]

IRON DOME

According to figures from the IDF, from October 7 through October 16, Hamas, other Gaza-based Palestinian militants, and Hezbollah fired an estimated 6,000 rockets at Israel. Of that amount, roughly 2,000-3,000 were fired within the initial hours of Hamas's surprise attack against Israel in the early morning of October 7. Iron Dome's targeting system and radar are designed to fire its Tamir interceptors only at incoming projectiles that pose threats to the area being protected, and, in previous rounds of Israel-Hamas confrontations, Iron Dome's interception rate has exceeded 90%. Nevertheless, when facing a rocket barrage, even with success rates exceeding 90%, some rockets reach populated areas. [...]

Though Iron Dome apparently continues to successfully intercept incoming rockets at a high rate, some Israelis and some others have questioned whether Israel has become over-reliant on technological solutions both to deter their adversaries and prolong difficult policy dilemmas vis- à-vis the Palestinians. According to one Israeli critic, though Iron Dome undoubtedly has provided Israelis a certain sense of security, it also has led many Israelis to "not feel the urgency, or sufficient enough optimism, to press their leaders to solve the underlying problems causing the long-term crisis facing Gaza."
[...]

558

[…]

On October 9, Israel announced a "complete siege" in Gaza that would apparently cut Gaza's residents off from the flow of food, water, fuel, and electricity. On October 12, Israel's energy minister said that Israel-imposed restrictions on the flow of goods, including fuel, and the cessation of the provision of water and electricity services from Israel to Gaza would remain in place until the release of Israeli hostages from Gaza.

The siege has generated fierce debate between

- those who argue the siege is a necessary element of Israel's efforts to deprive its adversaries of important supplies and sustenance, and demoralize and confuse them in connection with a likely Israeli ground invasion; and

- those who criticize Israeli measures as potentially severely harmful to civilians— including vulnerable populations in hospitals, the elderly, and young children—and assert that the measures breach international law.

Hamas tunnel system

[…] Hamas claimed in 2021 to have built 311 miles worth of tunnels under Gaza (a little less than half the length of the New York City subway system). Israel's intelligence community contends that resources provided by international donors for Gaza relief, recovery, or reconstruction from past conflicts have been diverted by Hamas to build and fortify its tunnels and bunkers.

[…]

According to various media reports, some features of the tunnel system […], include the following:

- A reported rail system that allows militants to transport rockets underground to different launch sites within the territory, frustrating Israeli efforts to destroy Hamas's rocket capacity from the air.

- Storage of weapons and ammunition, food, electricity generators, and other supplies to allow militants refuge and opportunities for tactical surprise against Israeli forces in Gaza for an extended period of time.

- Opportunities for militants to disperse themselves and the hostages they hold, complicating any potential Israeli operation to enter, clear, or destroy tunnels.

Some observers say that the IDF may opt to find ways to "smoke out" militants from the tunnels rather than storm them. Bombing the underground passages is reportedly the most efficient way to destroy tunnels. However, any method that could cause death or severe injury could also affect hostages possibly held inside or Gazan civilians located above or nearby.

[…]

Regional diplomacy and the Abraham Accords

Some observers, including some Biden Administration officials, have speculated that Hamas's decision to perpetrate its October 7 attacks was intended, in part, to disrupt or weaken U.S.- backed efforts to pursue the type of diplomatic normalization efforts between Israel and Arab states that is exemplified by Israel's 2020-2021 Abraham Accords with the United Arab Emirates, Bahrain, Morocco, and Sudan. Specifically, Hamas may have sought to disrupt reported momentum in autumn 2023 for U.S.-brokered efforts toward Saudi-Israeli normalization. While Saudi-Israeli normalization talks may have shaped the immediate context in which Hamas was considering its options, Hamas figures have suggested that their planning and preparations for the attacks spanned several years. Even if potential Saudi-Israeli normalization was not a specific instigating factor, it seems likely that Hamas's attacks were intended to reassert the immediate relevance of Palestinian movements that (1) reject normalization, (2) insist on an end to Israeli control over Palestinian life, and (3) favor direct confrontation and the use of violence over diplomacy.

As of October 13, reports attributed to an unnamed source claimed the kingdom had informed the U.S. government it was putting further normalization talks on hold. […]

The conduct of the ongoing conflict between Israel and Hamas—and any other regional parties that might become involved—will shape the context for future consideration of the viability and likelihood of pro-normalization diplomacy. Even if Israel's military operations end Hamas's political control of Gaza, they do not appear likely to resolve underlying questions regarding the future political status and potential sovereignty of the Palestinians. The nature and consequences of the October 7 Hamas attacks may reduce popular support among some Israelis for any solution to the underlying Israeli-Palestinian conflict that might reduce Israeli control over the West Bank and Gaza, or empower groups that may have been involved with or sympathetic to the attacks. Similarly, negative effects of ongoing Israeli military and security operations on Palestinian civilians may erode confidence among Palestinians and others in the Middle East region that negotiation and compromise offer a viable path to a just solution for the Palestinians, while in the near-term potentially leading Arab governments and international actors to increase pressure on Israel to end or shorten its military operations.

[…]

In the Name of God, the Most Gracious, the Most Merciful.

O children of our Palestinian people, O children of our Ummah. Today you have a rendezvous with a great victory and a dazzling triumph. From the front line of the indomitable and proud Gaza, Operation Al-Aqsa Flood has been launched by Al-Qassam Brigades, the Resistance factions and the children of our Palestinian people. You have seen the grand images of these pious and courageous fighters who drew the stigmata of humiliation, defeat and collapse on the face of the enemy. [...]

What did these defeatists expect, [these Arabs] who have spread the culture of impotence and despair, and wanted the path to normalization [of relations with Israel] to shape this stage with recognition of the enemy? Did they ever imagine they would see such images, such heroic deeds, such sacrifices, such courage, such pride? The perpetrators of these feats are *"men who were sincere in their commitment to God. Some of them have reached their end [martyrdom], and others are still waiting; and they have not varied in any way (in their commitment)."* (Quran, chapter 33, verse 23). These men shaped the gates of the Great Victory, and opened them for our people and our Ummah. These men, who know the Qur'an by heart, fast and pray in adoration of God the Most High and Exalted, have attacked and *"penetrated inside the dwellings"* (Quran, chapter 17, verse 5) in the heart of our territory occupied [by the enemy], around Gaza and further afield: *"Help [from] God and a (promise of) upcoming victory."* (Quran, chapter 61, verse 13). You are most magnificent, O men of faith, O men of Al-Qassam Brigades, O men of Gaza, Gaza of pride and dignity, of courage, heroism and sacrifice. Today, Gaza erases from the Arab-Muslim community the shame of defeat, the shame of acceptance and inaction. You are most grand, O commanders who lead this battle, the battle of the beginning of the Liberation of Al-Quds [Jerusalem], our land, our people and our prisoners held in the jails of the Zionist occupation.

O my brothers and sisters, we warned the world about this fascist government [in Israel], which has let the settlers and usurpers loose to sow corruption in the holy Al-Aqsa Mosque in Al-Quds. We told them, "Don't play with fire". We told them, "Don't cross the red line." But they plugged their ears and closed their eyes [to our warnings]. And because of their arrogance and insolence, in recent days, during their sinister religious festivals, they have invaded Al-Aqsa Mosque. They desecrated and defiled it. They molested our women. They entered with their shoes up to the mihrab and minbar. They imposed on our people what appears to be a ban on movement in the Holy City. They have forbidden prayer in the Sanctuary of Ibrahim.
[...]

We also warned them about the intensifying colonization of the West Bank. This [Israeli] government planned and continues to plan for two million Zionist settlers in the West Bank, with the aim of Judaising it and tipping the demographic balance by adding occupation to the equation, including in the West Bank itself. And all of this is paralleled by continued aggression against our people there. How many times have they attacked Jenin, Tubas, Nablus, Tulkarem, Al-Khalil, Ramallah, Al-Bira, Bethlehem and all the other cities? How many times have they killed our young men, women and children before the eyes of the whole world? They didn't listen. Certainly, there is popular Resistance in the West Bank which has not laid down its arms, and which is returning blow for blow and more, and carrying out heroic operations. Such are our people. But this enemy and this government thought the situation was favorable to them, and persisted in their aggression.

How many times have we warned the world and this enemy that there are prisoners in the jails of the Zionist occupation, more than 6,000 of our brothers, our children, our youth, our heroes, our men and women, some of whom have spent up to 30, 40, even 43 years behind bars? And this enemy persecutes our prisoners on purpose. The sadist Ben-Gvir makes decisions to impose more pressure and persecution on our prisoners. This government and all Israeli officials have turned their backs on any call for indirect negotiations for a prisoner exchange to free our prisoners.

How many times have we warned them about the unjust blockade imposed on the Gaza Strip, which has led to all this human suffering? Gaza, which has been under this blockade for almost 20 years, made worse by four or five wars that have seen tens of thousands martyred and wounded, and destroyed homes; Gaza, which is experiencing this humanitarian crisis in a giant prison that locks up more than 2.2 million of our people and our families. In Gaza, at the heart of this blockade, which is only broken by a little aid, a few authorizations [for imports] to throw sand in the [world's] eyes. They believed that Gaza, its inhabitants and our people would swallow these blatant injustices and keep quiet in the face of this humanitarian crisis, and in the face of everything that is happening in Al-Quds, Al-Aqsa and the West Bank.

How many times have we warned you about what you are committing and perpetrating in the Palestinian territories occupied in 1948, and your attempts to isolate our people there? You have spread death, terror and targeted assassinations among our people there. All the operations to eliminate Palestinian figures, leaders and scholars; even women, children and ordinary citizens within the territories occupied in 1948, are an occupation policy, and one of the actions of the Israeli security services.

How many times have we warned them of the existence of a Palestinian people who, for 75 years, have been living in the diaspora in tents and refugee camps? You don't recognize our people, and you don't recognize our rights. And, unfortunately, many countries in the world have covered up this Israeli policy and this Israeli arrogance.

And when Al-Aqsa Mosque finds itself in imminent danger [...] what has happened, O my brothers? In the last few days, we have seen some absolutely incredible things. And we have confirmed information that this [Israeli] government is preparing to impose its sovereignty and authority over blessed Al-Aqsa Mosque. And we have full information assuring us that it will persist in its aggression, colonization, arrests and blockade, and take advantage of the normalization process achieved with certain Arab countries and governments to give its presence in the region a veneer of legitimacy, at the expense of our people, our rights, our suffering and our sacrifices.

Israel considered that its strategic environment, its power and arrogance, as well as the silence of the Arab and Muslim peoples, and the world's preoccupation with the war between Russia and Ukraine, made the moment propitious for it to carry out this project and put an end to this battle in Al-Quds, Al-Aqsa, the West Bank and elsewhere. But as God the Most High and Exalted has declared, *"You did not think they would leave, and they thought that in truth their strongholds would defend them against God. But God came to them from where they did not expect, and cast terror into their hearts. They demolished their houses with their own hands, as much as with the hands of the believers. Learn from this, O you who are gifted with foresight."* (Quran, chapter 59, verse 2).

Enough is enough! There was no choice but to embark on this strategic course, and complete the cycle of the First and Second Intifadas, revolutions and Resistance, and crown them with the battle for the liberation of our land, our holy places and our prisoners held in the jails of the Zionist occupation. The promise was to be fulfilled at dawn, and we said to them with God Most High, *"Is not the dawn near?"* (Quran, chapter 11, verse 81). That morning saw the sun of victory and glory rise over our people and our Ummah, and over free men and women all over the world. And it was the morning of defeat, humiliation and collapse for our enemy, its colonies, its settlers and its soldiers.

What happened today, O Palestinian people, O children of the Ummah, reveals the greatness of this Resistance, the greatness of our readiness and the credibility of our declarations, the veracity of our promises and Operation Al-Aqsa Flood. What happened today reveals the powerlessness of the enemy. Today, the enemy has had a political, military, intelligence, security and moral defeat inflicted upon it, and we shall crown it, with the grace of God, with a crushing defeat that will expel it from our lands, our holy city of Al-Quds, our Al-Aqsa mosque, and the release of our prisoners from the jails of the Zionist occupation. We had four [Israeli] prisoners, and [they] refused to respond to intermediaries' solicitations, calls or anything else. And the Resistance had declared more than once that the harvest [of Zionist soldiers] would continue, and that the bill would increase. The Resistance and its leaders do not speak in vain. Now, see the extent of your prisoners, see the number who have fallen into the hands of Al-Qassam Brigades and the Resistance.

This is why I declare today to all the Palestinian people: O our people, be at the highest level of readiness. This battle has begun, and will be fought with blood and fire, with glory and arms. The battle has moved to the heart of the Zionist entity, not only with the missiles of the Resistance, but also with the Resistance fighters, the men of Al-Qassam Brigades. That's why I want to stress three things that must be made clear:

1.   Operation Al-Aqsa Flood was launched from Gaza, but it will extend to the West Bank, to Al-Quds and to our people within the territories occupied in 1948, as well as to the Resistance and the Palestinian people abroad.

2.   This battle is not only that of the Palestinian people, or that of Gaza: Gaza is the spearhead of the Resistance and has launched this battle, but since it concerns the entire land of Palestine and Al-Quds and Al-Aqsa, it is the battle of the entire Arab-Muslim community. This is why I call on all the children of this community, wherever they may be in the world, to join in this battle, each in his own way, without delay or turning away, and not to be of those whom God the Most High and Exalted described in these terms: *"But their departure was repugnant to God; He made them indolent. And it was said to them, 'Stay with those who remain behind'."* (Quran, chapter 9, verse 46). Rather, with God's Grace, be among those who, when called, rush to battle, and those who, when their holy places are desecrated, stand up with honor to fight with their lives and with their possessions, and do not lag behind. This is the battle of the Palestinian people and the battle of the Arab-Muslim community. We have unleashed it, and with God's grace it will end in the victory that God has promised His virtuous servants.

3.   Our objective is clear: we want to liberate our land, our holy sites, our Al-Aqsa mosque, our prisoners. We have no hesitation about this. This is the goal that is worthy of this battle, worthy of this heroism, worthy of this courage. Al-Qassam Brigades made the enemy lose its balance in just a few minutes, with this grand and blessed incursion; with this epic presence of men who write history with their blood and their guns; with their footsteps that crush the occupying invaders.

I appeal to our Resistance, to our West Bank, to our people, to our Resistance abroad, to our strategic allies, to all the children of this community: this is your day. We have an appointment with victory, to work together for this grand victory, with the Grace of God the Most High.

In conclusion, to this threatening and irruptive enemy, we say: neither your threats, nor your irruptions, nor your arrogance, have served you so far, and they will be of no use to you in the future. We have only one thing to say to you: get out of our land. Get out of our sight. Get out of our city of Al-Quds and our Al-Aqsa Mosque. We no longer wish to see you on this land. This land is ours, Al-Quds is ours, everything is ours. You are strangers in this pure and blessed land. There is no place or safety for you.

And we say to all countries, including our beloved Arab countries: you must know that this entity which is incapable of protecting itself from our fighters is incapable of providing you with security or protection. All the normalization and recognition processes, all the agreements that have been signed can never put an end to this battle. It is the terrain that will put an end to this battle; it is these heroic fighters who will put an end to it; it is the blood of the pure martyrs and the heroic deeds of this people, its wounded and its prisoners that will put an end to it.
[...]
May God's prayers and greetings be upon our master, Prophet Muhammad, his family and his companions. This is the ultimate jihad, the outcome of which can only be victory or martyrdom. May God's Peace be upon you, and His Mercy and Blessings.

Gaza: No Let Up in Deadly Toll as Rights Chief Demands End to Suffering (2024)
UN NEWS

"Six months into the war, 10,000 Palestinian women in Gaza have been killed, among them an estimated 6,000 mothers, leaving 19,000 children orphaned," said UN Women, in a new report.

"More than one million women and girls in Gaza have almost no food, no access to safe water, latrines, washrooms, or sanitary pads, with disease growing amidst inhumane living conditions."

Echoing those concerns, the UN World Health Organization (WHO) issued a new ceasefire call so that humanitarian relief can be brought into Gaza to help rebuild hospitals including Al Shifa, which has been "**basically destroyed**" after a recent Israeli incursion.
[...]
Little left to salvage

Only a third of Gaza's 36 hospitals remain functional meaning that it is essential to "preserve what is left" of the enclave's health system, Mr. Jasarevic insisted.

But needs remain massive with **more than 76,000 people injured**, according to the local authorities, and several UN agencies have repeatedly warned that amputations and C-section births have gone ahead without anaesthetic.

"Once again **we're calling really for the deconfliction mechanism to be effective**, to be transparent and to be workable," the WHO officer said, referring to the approvals system used by humanitarians in conjunction with the warring parties to try to ensure that aid convoys are not targeted.

Concerns remain over the deconfliction protocol after seven aid workers from the NGO World Central Kitchen were killed in Israeli airstrikes on 1 April.

But "more than half" of planned WHO missions between last October and the end of March "have been either denied or delayed or face other obstacles so they have to be postponed, so we really need that access", Mr. Jasarevic insisted, amid repeated dire warnings from humanitarians about impending famine in Gaza.

No relief for injured

A lack of staff, needles, stitches and other essential medical equipment have meant that "injured children often languish in pain," in hospitals or in makeshift shelters, noted Tess Ingram, UN Children's Fund (UNICEF) Communication specialist.

Speaking from Cairo after her latest mission to northern Gaza where her UN vehicle came under attack, Ms. Ingram told journalists that it was notable just how many youngsters had been injured during intense Israeli bombardment, launched in response to Hamas-led terror attacks in southern Israel on 7 October.

"Imagine for a second being strip-searched naked and questioned for hours, told that you're safe and then you leave; you quickly walk down the street praying that you will be okay. But then you're shot at, your father is killed and a bullet penetrates your naked pelvis causing serious internal and external injuries that are going to require reconstructive surgery. At a field hospital **Younis told me this happened to him. He is 14**."

The UNICEF officer also highlighted how difficult it remains to evacuate desperately injured or sick patients for medical care outside Gaza. **Less than half of all "medivac" requests have been approved** meaning that only around 4,500 people – "most of them children" - have been able to leave Gaza at a rate of less than 20 a day.
[…]
West Bank spiralling

The High Commissioner for Human Rights also expressed deep concern about rising violence and "waves of attacks" in recent days against Palestinians in the West Bank "**by hundreds of Israeli settlers**, often accompanied or supported by Israeli Security Forces (ISF)".

Following the killing of a 14-year-old Israeli boy from a settler family, four Palestinians, including a child, were killed and Palestinian property was destroyed in revenge attacks, Mr. Türk said in a statement.
[…]
Regional 'trigger'
[…]
To date, more than 33,200 people have been killed, according to Gaza's health authority, Ms. Pillay said, with some 40 per cent of schools directly hit in attacks, and 1.7 million people displaced inside the enclave.

"The complete siege imposed on Gaza since October 2023 has resulted in an unimaginable humanitarian catastrophe with famine and starvation now a reality for its residents," said the head of the Independent International Commission of Inquiry on the Occupied Palestinian Territory, including East Jerusalem, and Israel. The destruction of roads and infrastructure has severely compromised the ability of humanitarian actors to bring in aid to the population."

South Africa vs. Israel – with Jason Beckett (2024)
Nadeen Shaker

Last month, South Africa brough charges against Israel for violating the Genocide Convention in the course of its war on Gaza. […] As attempts to end the war have failed in the Security Council, with the U.S. vetoing a resolution for a ceasefire, what power does the ICJ have over changing the course of the war? And what impact could a positive ruling for provisional measures mean?

Today's episode is with Jason Beckett, associate professor of law at the American University in Cairo.

Nadeen Shaker: Let me begin by asking you if you can tell us the story of the term genocide, how it came into legal discourse, and why it's become such a loaded term in international law. Leading up to this case, I know that's a lot to cover, but how is it important in understanding the South Africa versus Israel case that is before the ICJ today?
[…]
JB: So, genocide as a term, came into being in the mid 1940s. It was coined by the Jewish international lawyer called Raphael Lemkin. And the term was coined as a direct response to the Holocaust. In 1948, under the auspices of the UN, there was a convention adopted on the Prevention and Punishment of the Crime of Genocide. And this feeds into a certain mythology about the Holocaust. And I always want to be careful when I'm talking about the Holocaust. I'm not a Holocaust denier. But I do deny the singularity of the Holocaust.

So the word genocide was created in the mid-1940s and it feeds into this mythology that the Holocaust was a break, a rupture, in history. It was a moment of unique evil. But the only thing that was really unique about the Holocaust, was that it took place in Europe, against an arguably white population.

Famously, in its rule over the Congo, Belgium killed about 10 million Congolese natives.

British rule in India killed over 30 million Indian natives. British invasion and indirect rule in China killed another 30 million Chinese natives. The Holocaust wasn't even Germany's first genocide. Germany had previously carried out genocide, I think, in 1908, around 1910, in what is known Namibia, wiping out the Herero people for which they have recently accepted responsibility and initiated a process of restitution. It wasn't the first genocide in Europe. That was the English genocide in Ireland. So, what I want to say is two things. One, obviously, that genocide is horrible. But two, that it's wrong to say that genocide is rare or unique.

568 From Cairo Review of Global Affairs, Podcast Palestine – The War on Gaza (Jan 24, 2024). Reprinted with permission.

So genocide, for me, has this mixed history. And this is true of the law of international law.

That there's an apparent break that we postulate in the 1940s was the creation of the UN and the articulation of modern humanitarian law. And that is framed as a response to the unique event of the Holocaust. So everything starts again in 1945, we reset to be an ethical world.

And then there's the whole other colonial history of international law and the very simple fact that we never talk about, that the UN was created by the colonial empires. It was created by the colonial states, for the colonial states. So there are very, very different continuities that are very much in contrast to the happy narrative of international law.

Now, coming to the South African case, the reason that I say there is no particular connection, is that I don't believe that court cases are determined by law, especially in international law. So I have a fundamental belief that international law is radically indeterminate. You can use it to make any argument.

NS: So whatever meaning [legally conferred to genocide] wouldn't apply because of this indeterminacy?

JB: It applies, but it can be argued either way, that it happened or it didn't happen. So maybe something I should mention about this ICJ case is that South Africa didn't choose the charge of genocide to be spectacular or provocative. The ICJ is an unusual court and in particular, states can only be taken before the ICJ if they have previously agreed to its jurisdiction. There are two ways that a state can agree to the ICJ's jurisdiction. One is a general declaration saying "We accept the jurisdiction of the ICJ in all cases where the other party also accepts the jurisdiction of the ICJ in all cases".

So the other option is that they are a party to a treaty that grants jurisdiction to the ICJ.

NS: The Genocide Convention. [...]

JB: The Genocide Convention is one of the rare treaties that grants automatic jurisdiction to the ICJ. So we can say, without a doubt, despite what I said about the indeterminacy of international law, we can say without a doubt that Israel is committing war crimes.

We can say, without a doubt, that Israel is committing crimes against humanity. But there's no court that has jurisdiction to hear those charges. So the International Criminal Court will investigate those charges but in relation to specific Israeli officials, whereas the ICJ determines the responsibility of Israel, the state.

NS: Okay, and you mentioned something interesting that South Africa didn't mean for genocide, or bringing that claim, to be spectacular. Can you elaborate more?

JB: What I mean, is it was the only treaty that they could use to give the ICJ jurisdiction. They would, from a legal perspective, much rather have pursued a war crimes and crimes against humanity case, because it's an easier case to make.

Genocidal conduct is clearly occurring in Gaza. You know, I read that 26,500 Gazans have been killed and obviously, that's horrible, but I also hate the reporting because I think it's inaccurate. 26,500 Gazans have been recorded dead, it doesn't count the dead in the rubble. It doesn't, probably, count not as dying of disease and starvation. So, the number actually killed in Gaza is probably near 40,000.

We've seen deliberate attacking of civilian property, deliberate attacks on civilian infrastructure like bakeries, water processing plants. We're seeing the denial of water, the denial of fuel, the denial of food, the denial of medical care.

I mean, it is honestly a miracle in my view, the only 40,000 Palestinians have died so far. Everything is in position for a major disease outbreak. The people are starving. They have limited access to water. They're surrounded by sewage. The rains are coming. Much of the water they do have access to isn't actually drinkable, but they have to drink it anyway. Their immune systems are seriously compromised and they're all packed together in one dense, massively overcrowded area that has been designated safe and is still being bombed on a daily basis. So the conduct is clearly genocidal.

But the tricky legal question is whether Israel intends to be genocidal. So it's only genocide if it's done with the specific intent to destroy, in whole or part, a racial, religious or ethnic group. Israel's argument is that they have no intention of destroying the Palestinians or the Gazans. Their only intention is to destroy Hamas. But of course, earlier in the war, closer to the October 7th attacks, the Israeli political and military elite were much less guarded in the statements that they were making.

It's interesting that, particularly since this case was initiated, official Israeli rhetoric has been very much toned down. Although I came across today a quote by Itmar Ben Gvir, who is always good for a quote. He said, "We must continue to subdue, crush and mow down the Nazi enemy in Gaza with all our might." So he's pretty clear, he may not be official, but he's pretty clear that this is a genocide.

Now, I have to say two things that slightly contradict. One is that international law is indeterminate. But two, in this particular instance, it's probably biased towards Palestine. So, because international law is indeterminate, the advocates at the court have two basic tasks. They have to present the judges a plausible legal argument in their favor and they have to give the judges a reason to want to accept the argument.

To me, the South Africa pleading was stronger, but my sympathies lie with the Gazans, so I was always going to be more sympathetic towards the South African pleading. But the Israeli pleading, particularly on the procedural elements, was very competent.

NS: Can you tell us more what do you mean by the procedural elements? How was it stronger?

JB: So Israel argued a number of different things. They argued that the court did not have jurisdiction. They argued that the remedies requested by South Africa were beyond the court's competence or had been turned down in similar cases by the court before.

NS: Which is to neutralize Hamas, so bringing back the argument of self-defense, that this is their right.

JB: Yeah, so for example, self-defense is a good one, that they said, "If you demand a ceasefire, you are denying us our right to self defense and worse than that, you're not telling Hamas to cease fire", because the court has no jurisdiction over Hamas.

NS: Because it's not a state?

JB: Yep. So it's a very technical argument. There is a very technical response, which I wish was articulated more in the media, which is that according to the International Court of Justice, in the case concerning the Israeli apartheid wall, they call it the separation wall, the court ruled that Israel could not act in self-defense in the occupied territories. That as the occupier, they had no right of self defense.

NS: This was brought up in the hearing?

JB: I think it was yes. So if that is true, and as I say that the court has already said that, then Israel actually has no right to self defense in Gaza; we're talking about this whole thing in the wrong framework.

As I said, both sides did their job competently. So it is now entirely down to the politics and/or the legal beliefs of the 17 judges involved. I think it's almost certain that it will be a split decision. There will be a very strong dissent from the losing side.

Let me say one last thing before, which is the thing that contradicts my indeterminacy argument. So the case right now is what's called a "provisional measures case" and this case isn't designed to establish whether Israel has committed genocide or not. What South Africa has to establish is that there is a plausible argument that Israel is committing genocide.

In both the Myanmar, Gambia-Myanmar case, and Ukraine-Russia cases, the Court has held plausibility to be a very low standard. So, if they follow their own prior decisions, and there's no guarantee they will, but if they do, then they ought to find in favor of South Africa.

NS: I thought what you said about, you know, how different cases before approached the plausibility issue differently and sort of held it to a lower standard because you know, the situation was so urgent. One of my questions was: do you think that might happen again? It possibly can, but also, if we returned to the question of judges, and the biases of the ICJ that existed from before, do you think that the nationalities of the judges or other political considerations might influence the outcome?

JB: The short answer is yes. The long answer is that it's more complicated than that.

So if we start from my initial premise, that international law is indeterminate, then international law itself, by definition, cannot determine the decision. So something else determines the decision. But that "something else" is unique to each judge, based on their background, their upbringing, their specific form of legal education, their personal politics, their ethics.

So it is not that I think that judges are direct representatives of their state, but they're still not applying the law, they're still applying their own intuition, and then reverse engineering a legal argument that makes that intuition seem determined by law.

NB: You mentioned something really interesting before. In this rare case, the results of the provisional measures might create a space for international law to move past its colonial origins, which you mentioned earlier and you also mentioned in an interview with the Cairo Review. What would that mean, for international law in general, to be aided by the occasional win for the oppressed. What would you know, a favorable outcome meaning?

JB: Okay, so I think there are a couple of things to say here. One, is that I wouldn't overstate the radicality of a South African victory and two is that I wouldn't overstate the importance of a South African victory. So, as you mentioned, in my analysis, international law is a colonial or neo-colonial enterprise and I don't think that this case challenges that in any way.

On the sixth of October 2023, Israel was a settler-colonial apartheid state and international law didn't care, because it was a well behaved settler colonial apartheid state. On the seventh of October 2023, Israel became a settler-colonial apartheid state that was attacked by the natives. By the eighth of October 2023, Israel was a settler-colonial apartheid state, openly engaged in genocide. Now, that's the change.

The problem is not that they're a settler-colonial apartheid state, it's whether they're a well behaved settler-colonial apartheid state or not. All this case is saying is, "You've transgressed the boundaries of what states are allowed to do". It's not challenging the settler-colonial nature of Israel. The court has no power to decolonize Israel. It's very unlikely, but there's potentially more radicality, oddly, in the international criminal court.

The international criminal court can investigate war crimes, crimes against humanity, and genocide. One of the crimes against humanity that they could choose to investigate, I don't think they will, but they could, is apartheid itself. Now, if Israeli leaders were to be imprisoned for running an apartheid state, that would be a much deeper challenge to the logic of international law. The second problem with the ICJ, and the reason I say that the decision isn't important, is that it won't be enforced.

It won't actually change Israeli conduct. The only question, and it's a very vague, distant hope, is whether it would impact American thinking. America has come out strongly on Israel's side, but they've done it at a factual level, they've done it by saying "These claims are baseless, these claims are meritless". So they aren't saying, "These claims are not important". No one can say a charge of genocide is not important. So if the court then finds that the charge is plausible, then it's harder for the U.S. to say "We want to support Israel, but we're against genocide".

NS: It always comes back to the U.S., doesn't it?

JB: With Israel in particular, yes.

D. Charges

a) HAMAS LEADERS

16. The Prosecutor seeks arrest warrants against three senior Hamas leaders for the war crimes of murder and the crimes against humanity of murder and extermination for the killing of hundreds of civilians on 7 October 2023. He also seeks to charge them with the war crime of taking at least 245 persons hostage. Finally, he seeks to charge them with the war crimes of rape and other forms of sexual violence, torture, cruel treatment, and outrages upon personal dignity and the crimes against humanity of rape and other forms of sexual violence, torture, and other inhumane acts for acts committed against Israeli hostages while they were in captivity. The Panel notes the Prosecutor's statement that his investigations continue, including in relation to evidence of sexual violence on 7 October itself.

17. The suspects are: Yahya Sinwar, the Head of Hamas in the Gaza Strip; Mohammed Diab Ibrahim Al-Masri, known more commonly as Mohammed Deif, the Commander-in-Chief of the *al-Qassam Brigades* of Hamas; and Ismail Haniyeh, the Head of Hamas' Political Bureau.

18. The Prosecutor seeks to charge Sinwar, Deif and Haniyeh as co-perpetrators under article 25(3)(a) of the ICC Statute on the basis of a common plan to attack military bases in Israel, to attack and to kill civilians, and to take and detain hostages. The Prosecutor also states that they are criminally responsible under other modes of liability under article 25(3) and as superiors for failing to take all necessary and reasonable measures within their power to 'prevent or repress' the crimes or to 'submit the matter to the competent authorities for investigation and prosecution' under article 28 of the ICC Statute.

19. After assessing the material provided by the Prosecutor, including statements from survivors and eye-witnesses at the scene of six key attack locations […] video material and statements by the perpetrators, the Panel has concluded that there are reasonable grounds to believe that the three suspects had a common plan that necessarily involved the commission of war crimes and crimes against humanity. The systematic and coordinated nature of the crimes, their scale, statements by the suspects supporting the commission of such crimes, evidence of the sophisticated planning of the attacks and the ideology and past practices of Hamas all support the finding that the common plan was criminal in character.

20. The Panel also considers that there are reasonable grounds to believe that the crimes were committed in the context of a widespread and systematic attack against the civilian population of Israel, pursuant to an organizational policy of Hamas.

21. The Panel additionally concurs with the Prosecutor's view that Sinwar, Deif and Haniyeh made essential contributions to this plan and that they have through their own words and actions admitted to their responsibility. This includes for one or more of the suspects: acknowledging their, and each other's, roles in the attacks, and acknowledging their control over the hostages' detention and release. The Panel also concurs with the Prosecutor's view that Sinwar, Deif and Haniyeh failed to prevent or to punish the commission of the crimes by their subordinates, although it is clear that they could have done so as senior leaders of the military and political arms of Hamas.

b) ISRAELI LEADERS

22. The Prosecutor seeks arrest warrants against Benjamin Netanyahu, the Prime Minister of Israel, and Yoav Gallant, the Israeli Minister of Defense, on the basis that they committed the war crime of 'intentionally using starvation of civilians as a method of warfare' under article 8(2)(b)(xxv) of the ICC Statute. The Prosecutor also seeks to charge the two suspects with various other war crimes and crimes against humanity associated with the use of starvation of civilians as a method of warfare under articles 7 and 8 of the ICC Statute. These include the war crimes of '[w]ilfully causing great suffering, or serious injury to body or health' or cruel treatment, wilful killing or murder, and intentionally directing attacks against the civilian population. The proposed charges also include the crimes against humanity of murder, extermination, other inhumane acts and persecution with respect to deaths and injuries resulting from or associated with the systematic deprivation of objects indispensable to the survival of Palestinian civilians in Gaza. The Panel notes the Prosecutor's statement that other alleged crimes, including in connection with the large-scale bombing campaign in Gaza, are actively being investigated.

23. The Prosecutor seeks to charge Netanyahu and Gallant on the basis that they made an essential contribution to a common plan to use starvation and other acts of violence against the Gazan civilian population as a means to eliminate Hamas and secure the return of hostages as well as to inflict collective punishment on the civilian population of Gaza who they perceived as a threat to Israel. It is also alleged that they had effective authority and control over their subordinates and knew of their subordinates' crimes but did not take necessary action to prevent or repress these crimes, leading to their criminal responsibility as superiors.

24. The war crime of 'intentionally using starvation of civilians as a method of warfare' requires 'depriving [civilians] of objects indispensable to their survival, including wilfully impeding relief supplies as provided for under the Geneva Conventions'. The crime is not limited solely to the deprivation of food, but includes other objects indispensable for the survival of civilians such as water, fuel and medicine.

25. The Panel notes three preliminary points relevant to its analysis. First, as a result of a number of factors, including the imposition by Israel of restrictions on the movement of people and goods from and to Gaza in the aftermath of its 2005 disengagement, Gazans were highly dependent on Israel for the provision of and access to objects indispensable for the survival of the population even before 7 October.

26. Second, although Israeli officials have a right to ensure that aid is not diverted to the benefit of the enemy and to stipulate lawful technical arrangements for its transfer, they cannot impose arbitrary restrictions -- such as restrictions that violate Israel's obligations under international law, including international humanitarian law and international human rights law, or that contravene the principles of necessity and proportionality -- when exercising these rights.

27. Third, parties to an armed conflict must not deliberately impede the delivery of humanitarian relief for civilians, including humanitarian relief provided by third parties. And when a territory is under the belligerent occupation of one party to the conflict, there is also an enhanced active obligation for the occupying power to ensure adequate humanitarian aid for civilians, including by providing such aid itself insofar as this is necessary. In the Panel's view, while it can reasonably be argued that Israel was the occupying power in Gaza even before 7 October 2023, Israel certainly became the occupying power in all of or at least in substantial parts of Gaza after its ground operations in the territory began.

28. With this in mind, and based on a review of material presented by the Prosecutor, the Panel assesses that there are reasonable grounds to believe that Netanyahu and Gallant formed a common plan, together with others, to jointly perpetrate the crime of using starvation of civilians as a method of warfare. The Panel has concluded that the acts through which this war crime was committed include a siege on the Gaza Strip and the closure of border crossings; arbitrary restrictions on entry and distribution of essential supplies; cutting off supplies of electricity and water, and severely restricting food, medicine and fuel supplies. This deprivation of objects indispensable to civilians' survival took place in the context of attacks on facilities that produce food and clean water, attacks against civilians attempting to obtain relief supplies and attacks directed against humanitarian workers and convoys delivering relief supplies, despite the deconfliction and coordination by humanitarian agencies with Israel

Defence Forces. These acts took place with full knowledge of the extent of Gazans' reliance on Israel for essential supplies, and the adverse and inevitable consequences of such acts in terms of human suffering and deaths for the civilian population.

29. The Prosecutor has also sought charges against Netanyahu and Gallant for the war crimes of wilful killing or murder and intentionally directing attacks against the civilian population, as well as the crimes against humanity of extermination or murder and persecution for deaths resulting from the use of starvation and related acts of violence including attacks on civilians gathering to obtain food and on humanitarian workers.

30. In the Panel's view, there are reasonable grounds to believe that the suspects committed these crimes. The Panel also considers that there are reasonable grounds to believe that the crimes were committed in the context of a widespread and systematic attack against the civilian population of Gaza, pursuant to State policy.

31. The Panel's assessment is that there are reasonable grounds to believe that Netanyahu and Gallant are responsible for the killing of civilians who died as a result of starvation, either because the suspects meant these deaths to happen or because they were aware that deaths would occur in the ordinary course of events as a result of their methods of warfare. According to material submitted by the Prosecutor, a large number of Palestinian civilians have already died in these circumstances. In relation to extermination, the number of deaths resulting from starvation is sufficient on its own to support the charge, according to standards set out in international jurisprudence. And this number is, unfortunately, only likely to rise. There are also reasonable grounds to believe that the starvation campaign and associated acts of violence involved the severe deprivation of victims' fundamental rights by reason of their identity as Palestinians. This can be qualified as the crime against humanity of persecution.

32. The Prosecutor has also sought to charge Netanyahu and Gallant with the crime against humanity of other inhumane acts and the war crime of wilfully causing great suffering, or serious injury to body or health, or cruel treatment, with respect to the non-lethal suffering inflicted through starvation of the civilian population of Gaza. The Panel assesses that there are reasonable grounds to believe that the suspects committed these crimes against many thousands of individuals in Gaza.

33. Based on the material it has reviewed, the Panel assesses that there are reasonable grounds to believe that Netanyahu and Gallant made essential contributions to the common plan to use starvation of civilians as a method of warfare and commit other acts of violence against the civilian population. This is evidenced by their own statements and the statements

of other Israeli officials. It is also evidenced by the systematic nature of the crime, and the involvement of the suspects at the apex of the Israeli governmental apparatus, with effective authority and control over their subordinates and leadership positions in the War Cabinet and Security Cabinet, in which all key decisions on the conduct of the war -- including blocking and limiting humanitarian aid -- have been made. The Panel is also of the view that there are reasonable grounds to believe that the suspects can be held responsible as superiors given their knowledge of the crimes and the fact that they took no steps to prevent or repress their subordinates who committed them.

E. Conclusion

34. The Panel unanimously agrees with the Prosecutor that the applications for arrest warrants, and material submitted by the Prosecutor in support of each application, demonstrate reasonable grounds to believe that the Court has jurisdiction over the crimes set out in the applications for arrest warrants, that these crimes were committed and that the suspects are responsible for them.

35. Having closely reviewed the arrest warrant applications, underlying evidence presented in support for the applications and the Prosecutor's process, the Panel is satisfied that the process was fair, rigorous and independent and that the Prosecutor's applications for arrest warrants are grounded in the law and the facts.

36. While this is the Panel's view, the Panel is cognisant that the decision on the issuance of warrants is for the honourable Judges of the Court.

37. Finally, the Panel welcomes the Prosecutor's statement that the investigation of crimes committed in Israel and Palestine is ongoing and that applications are likely to be made in relation to additional charges and/or suspects in the near future. The Panel agrees with the Prosecutor that further investigations are warranted, and hopes that victims and witnesses will choose to come forward to support the ongoing investigations.

PALESTINIAN IDENTITY

Arab Palestine: Phoenix or Phantom? (1970)
Don Peretz

Because many Palestine Arabs are stateless under international law, their importance has frequently been overlooked in the numerous parleys and in the skein of complex international negotiations over the Middle East crisis. The Palestine dispute, as it is euphemistically labeled in the United Nations, has appeared on the annual agenda of the U.N. General Assembly for over twenty years, generally under the guise of assistance to refugees. Neither the principal antagonists nor the major powers officially acknowledge existence of the Palestinians as a nation-party to the dispute.

In a recent interview Israeli Prime Minister Golda Meir emphasized that there is no such thing as either a Palestinian nation or people. Palestine Arabs are considered by the Government of Israel as little different from those of the surrounding Arab states. When queried about creation of a new Arab Palestine on the West Bank, Prime Minister Meir pointed out that it would be too small; only if it were part of Jordan or Israel could the area remain viable. Furthermore, she emphasized, there is no representative body speaking for the so-called Palestinians. Had the Arabs who fled in 1948 not urged Jordan's King Hussein into the June 1967 war the Hashemite Kingdom might well have become the successor state to Palestine. Israel's experience with the already existing fourteen Arab states discourages it from supporting the creation of still another. […]

The reluctance of Israel and the major powers to recognize the Palestinians only inflames the latters' already deep hostility toward the West. Their situation is not unlike that of other self-identified national groups in the Middle East which sought international recognition during this century— such as the Armenians, the Jews and the Kurds.

The national identity of the Palestine Arabs has gone through a cycle of discovery in the 1920s, political failure in the 1930s, near abandonment in the 1940s, disillusionment in the 1950s and '60s, and rebirth, rediscovery and new expectations since 1967.

II

Prior to establishment of the British Mandate at the end of World War I, there was no distinctive Palestinian people, nor political entity. The land and its inhabitants were considered backwater regions of the less

Used with permission of Foreign Affairs, from FOREIGN AFFAIRS, Vol. 48, No. 2 (Jan. 1, 1970); permission conveyed through Copyright Clearance Center, Inc.

developed Ottoman Syrian provinces. Only after establishment of the British Mandate in 1920, and the rise of Jewish nationalism in the country, did a distinctive Palestinian Arab consciousness emerge in response to the challenge of these two forms of European intrusion. In that era Palestinian Arab nationalism, led by a coalition of Muslim landed gentry and upper-middle-class Christian Arab families, resembled nationalist movements then emerging elsewhere in the Arab East. Some 80 percent of its constituency was a politically unsophisticated rural peasantry. There was little if any ideology, and that little was devoid of social content. Major emphasis was on elimination of foreign control and influence-in the case of Palestine, British controls and European Jewish influences. The Palestinian Arab national effort culminated in the abortive rebellion between 1936 and 1939; it failed because of massive use of British armed force and lack of internal cohesion among nationalist leaders. Nevertheless, heroes of this rebellion are still eulogized by the new nationalist organizations; their military failures and inability to form a cohesive political movement are overlooked.

The major revision of Great Britain's policies in Palestine, embodied in the 1939 White Paper, was a great victory for Palestine-Arab nationalism since it made an independent Arab state seem inevitable. Nevertheless, most of the country's Arab leaders slipped into lethargy and paralysis of action which was to last nearly thirty years. By the end of World War II, Jewish nationalism in Palestine was much more dynamic, well organized and politically effective. Both within the country and abroad, Zionists and their supporters surpassed the Palestine-Arab nationalists in militant political activity, finally voiding the White Paper and achieving their goal of statehood. The disjointed and inchoate Palestine-Arab nationalist movement reached its nadir in 1947-48 with defeat and exodus of the Arab population from Jewish-held areas.

Until termination of the Mandate in 1948, both Arab and Jewish residents of the country were identified as British subjects, although they did not hold British citizenship. When Israel was established, its Jewish and some of its Arab inhabitants became citizens of the new state. More than one million Palestine Arabs were left in an international limbo, with no recognized citizenship status, Within the next decade, Palestinians who remained in the Hashemite Kingdom and in those parts of Palestine annexed to it acquired Jordanian citizenship; a small number of Christian Palestinians qualified for Lebanese citizenship, and the others—some 700,000—have remained stateless persons until today. Syria, while refusing citizenship to Palestine refugees, granted them most, but not all, citizenship rights. Lebanon was reluctant to offer citizenship to the large number of Muslim Palestine refugees it harbored for fear they would destroy the delicate balance between the country's Christians and Muslims. Egypt, already one of the world's most overpopulated nations, kept most of the Palestinians under its jurisdiction penned up in the tiny Gaza enclave, which was governed as though it were still a separate country rather than part of the U.A.R.

During the next two decades "Palestinian Arab" became synonymous with "Palestine refugee" in international consciousness. Even in Arab countries and among the Palestinians themselves there was little distinction, and annual debates over the refugees at the United Nations and the activities of UNRWA further blurred any clear difference. The most visible evidence of Palestinian existence was the network of refugee camps where tensions between the inhabitants and natives of host countries forcefully delineated the occupants from other Arabs.

Jordan needed its Palestinians as a population base for the new Hashemite Kingdom, but all the other Arab states encouraged the displaced Arabs to retain their national identity. This was not difficult since few were socially accepted in the host countries and many non-Palestinian Arabs regarded the outsiders as a disruptive and troublesome element. Palestinians therefore maintained their old social structure and family ties, formed their own political groups, intermarried with each other and continued to regard themselves as a distinctive national group. Recognition of this identity was further encouraged by the United Nations through the network of relief, social and particularly educational services provided to Palestine refugees through UNRWA. In the UNRWA schools, where refugee children were educated by Palestinian teachers, a new generation of ardent Palestine patriots was raised. The most zealous proponent of militant activism against the "intruder state" of Israel was this new generation of U.N.-educated youth.

[...]

After the 1967 fiasco, Palestinians were disillusioned with nearly all the established leadership, organizations and governments [....] Wherever there were large concentrations of Palestinians, diverse new groups emerged, led by a younger generation unfettered by the political and social commitments of its elders. The new leadership reflected the transformation of the Palestine Arab community that had occurred during the "lost" generation. Living in or near to urban areas, most Palestinians had lost their peasant skills and outlook, acquiring many of the views and sophistications of town and city. Several hundred thousand were employed in urban trade, commerce, industry and ancillary occupations. More than one hundred thousand had developed skills in the Arabian oil states. In two decades, approximately 50,000 Palestinians attended universities, nearly equaling the number of young professionals trained by Israel during this period. The new generation of Palestinians had all the attributes of a displaced minority group, including great aspirations for upward mobility, political restiveness, and a core of revolutionary-minded young men who aspired to "reestablish the homeland."

Several dozen new Palestinian organizations were created within two years of the 1967 defeat. By far their greatest emphasis was on military or paramilitary activity aimed at Israel. Disillusioned with failures of conventional tactics against Israel and with Arab government fiascos, most of the new groups drew inspiration from guerrilla techniques and activities modeled on those of Algeria, North Viet Nam and Latin American revolutionaries. The objective was no longer that of Arab governments such as the U.A.R. or Jordan—to achieve Israel's withdrawal from the occupied territories and to circumscribe and delimit its frontiers—but to obliterate completely the Jewish state.

In the ebb and flow of inter-Arab politics since 1967, the new Palestinian groups have merged, subdivided, reunited and again fragmented, finally organizing themselves into three or four principal political-military organizations: the Palestine Liberation Organization; Fatah; the Popular Front for the Liberation of Palestine; and Saiqa. […] They differ generally from the pre-1967 groups in their asserted independence from Arab governments, in the growing number of young intellectuals and professionals they have enlisted in their ranks, and in the extent of support they have received from Arabs generally and from Palestinians in particular. […]

The reliability of commando communiqués is highly questionable, but their political effect throughout the Arab East is becoming increasingly obvious. Within the last two years they have created a new identity for the Palestinians. "Refugee" is no longer synonymous with "Palestine Arab." Increasingly, "Palestinian" is identified with the commando warrior rather than with the downtrodden displaced person. This is evident among Arab students, intellectuals, professionals and the man in the street, from Casablanca to Kuwait While much commando activity is exaggerated if not entirely fictitious, there is sufficient substance to their achievements to have created a commando mystique. Posters on university campuses and in government offices and shopping centers; the daily radio bulletins and pronouncements by commando leaders; and the Arabic press-all have created in Arab consciousness the image of a new Palestinian who, unlike the traditional and now aging military leadership, is young, vigorous, intelligent, self-sacrificing, intensely patriotic and single-mindedly dedicated to reestablishment of Arab Palestine. This image pervades even the thinking of commando critics such as Lebanese and Jordanian officials, who recognize that fedayeen terrorism in Israel serves only to weaken their own stability.

Not only Israel but several Arab governments are targets of commando activities. Some leaders of the organizations aim to overthrow any politician who might interfere with their guerrilla strategy against Israel; others have set their sights on total revolution of Arab political life. Among the former are leaders of Fatah and PLO who can cooperate with conservative monarchs or with radical socialists. Within the past year these two less revolutionary-minded groups have been involved in machinations behind the scenes to topple the ruling establishments of Jordan, Lebanon, Saudi Arabia and Libya, In Jordan and Lebanon, commando leaders have sought, with some success, to gain control of strategically located territories for training recruits, or for striking across the Israeli border. The commandos are reported to have taken over fourteen of the fifteen refugee camps in Lebanon and to have free access to most camps in Jordan. This has led to a de facto partition in which King Hussein's government has been forced to acquiesce. Because of the wide support enjoyed by the commandos among Jordan's largely Palestine Arab population, the Hashemite Kingdom has found it impossible to repress them and on occasion it even cooperates in providing covering fire for their movements across the frontier. Consequently Jordan has become the recipient of nearly daily artillery and air strikes, which have leveled towns, disrupted agricultural life in the river valley and threatened both political and economic stability.

In Lebanon, where Palestinians are a small minority but have considerable support among the population, the commandos threaten to end the country's relative isolation from direct military confrontation with Israel. Since the first Arab-Israeli war of 1948 the Lebanese-Israeli border has been more or less free of the military clashes that have periodically erupted between Israel and Syria, Jordan and Egypt. While willing to permit the organizations free movement, fund raising and propaganda activity within its borders, the Lebanese Government has been reluctant to countenance establishment of guerrilla enclaves. The dilemma has torn the government apart, divided the population into pro and anti commandos, and led to threats of both Syrian and Israeli intervention on behalf of or against the Palestinians. But now the commandos are asserting themselves in all areas they deem vital—including the Lebanese frontier. They recognize no right of withdrawal from confrontation with Israel, insisting that every Arab and Arab state has an obligation to join the "War of Liberation."
[…]
III

It is increasingly evident that instead of being a tool of Arab governmental policies, the new Palestine organizations are striving to reverse the pattern of control and to exercise strong influence on those governments which at one time controlled Palestinian destinies. The commandos have in effect become an instrument of pressure for more militant action by governments such as Lebanon, Jordan and the U.A.R. […]

The commando mystique clearly extends to Arab citizens of Israel and those in the occupied territories. A survey conducted in 1968 by Hebrew University sociologists indicated that Arab defeat in the Six Day War increased respect for the state among Israeli Arab schoolchildren but also greatly intensified feelings of hatred toward Israel, deepened Arab consciousness and made more determined than ever before the resolve to wage still another war against the Jewish state. With each passing month of Israeli occupation, the number of young Arab Israeli supporters of the commando movement grows. During the first half of 1969, the number of youths who were apprehended for supporting commando activities was nearly one hundred. While small in relation to the Arab population of Israel, the number exceeds the total of Israeli Arabs arrested for such activities since the state was established twenty years ago.

[…]

The Arab Refugees: A Changing Problem (1963)
Don Peretz

Adults who fled from Palestine suffered a trauma from which few recovered. Loss of homes, jobs and economic security and the complete uprooting of the familiar social structure engendered deep bitterness against all those responsible for the catastrophe; it expressed itself in absolute refusal to coöperate in transplanting their community to new soil. The older generation made known its fierce determination to return home by rejecting permanent housing, employment and all other assistance which would further its relocation. They were, until recently, abetted in their opposition by the host countries. This obstinate refusal to accept rehabilitation aid gave birth to the view in the West that the refugees would more willingly accept rehabilitation assistance if given a "free choice" about their future.

The younger generation is no less bitter about its refugee status, no less resentful toward those responsible, and no less determined to regain its homeland, but its reactions are less self-destructive. The youth realize that only through strength can they attain their ultimate objective, and that strength will be created through self-improvement, not self-destruction. [...]

While economic conditions have improved considerably in Lebanon and Syria since 1948 and obstacles to employment of Palestinians have been removed, the refugees have not been accepted socially and politically. Not only do official attitudes and policies encourage discrimination, but the man in the street regards the Palestinians as a politically unreliable and often dangerous group whose departure from the country he would view with relief. These social pressures intensify the Palestinian's consciousness of being an outsider, already engendered by the schools and the closely knit social system. Thus, even children barely able to talk identify themselves with the Palestinian town of their parents' origin, such as Jaffa, Haifa or Lydda, rather than with Syria or Lebanon.

The Palestinians have thus developed many characteristic complexes and attitudes of a minority: they marry among themselves more frequently than with others; their friends are fellow countrymen more often than Syrians or Lebanese; their vocational objectives are to attain a middle-class status rather than that of a peasant or city worker. Even the sons of former Bedouin tent-dwellers aspire to become lawyers, doctors, teachers, businessmen and government employees, rather than tillers of the soil or craftsmen who work with their hands. They seek to "do well" in life to compensate for their warped childhood. UNRWA, therefore, has little difficulty recruiting candidates for its higher education and advanced vocational training programs. And it is estimated that some 50,000

Used with permission of Foreign Affairs, from FOREIGN AFFAIRS, Vol. 41, No. 3 (Apr. 1, 1963); permission conveyed through Copyright Clearance Center, Inc.

Palestinians have flocked to the Persian Gulf sheikhdoms in the hope of enriching themselves from the oil boom there.

Contrasted with their apparent middle-class social and economic aspirations is the refugees' great attraction to radical political ideologies. Not only in Syria and Lebanon where they are treated as outsiders, but in Gaza and Jordan where Palestinians are in the majority, and where they find little social discrimination, they are politically volatile and easily incited to activism. In times of internal strife it is not unusual to hear Syrians or Lebanese blame the refugees; this is especially true of the merchant middle class, always concerned to maintain stability. While the fear of the Palestinians is often exaggerated, there have been a few instances where they were involved in political movements to overthrow established governments in Lebanon, Syria and Jordan.

Youth has rejected its own and all other Arab political leaders associated with the 1948 disaster. The former Mufti of Jerusalem, Haj Amin al-Husayni, once the acknowledged leader and a folk hero of Palestine Arabs, and all those in any way identified with him, are shadowy relics of a now remote era. Old political conservatives from the landowning class and the religious hierarchy have also lost their allure. In their place, youth seeks more dynamic leaders who espouse the new socialist, republican and democratic slogans. If any individual can be said to represent the sentiments of Palestinian youth it is Egypt's President Nasser. To them he stands for a new, strong, progressive, dynamic Arab society.

Palestinians are in the forefront of the Arab unity movement. Many of them believe that attainment of a single Arab nation offers the only hope of returning to their homeland. The older generation's attachment to Palestine is primarily a nostalgia for their fields and ancestral homesteads. But their children, who never saw those fields and homes, who never lived in that familiar and comfortable environment, have created a fervent national sentiment that never before existed; and their aspirations are supported by the Arab national movement. Regardless of success or failure in economic integration or repatriation, these new Palestinians want to create a new Palestine.
[…]
While economic integration of the refugees would lessen their visibility in the Arab capitals it would not solve the Palestine problem. As is already evident in Lebanon, Syria and the Persian Gulf, economically integrated refugees do not cease to be Palestine nationalists. For ever increasing numbers of refugees the problem is not lack of a place to live or lack of food or insufficient shelter; it is political homelessness.
[…]

The Evolution of Palestine (1996)
Dr. Mahdi Abdul Hadi

The period of the British mandate witnessed the emergence of Palestinian political elites as well as a class of professionals and technocrats, all of whom were loyal to the Arab Movement and worked towards achieving its goals. Their leadership was embodied in the Arab Higher Committee chaired by Hajj Amin Al-Husseini. Historic documents show exactly to what extent the Palestinian National Movement 'copied' the early days of the Arab awakening under the Ottomans. For example, Al-Muntada Al-Adabi[3] was re-established in Jerusalem in January 1918, and An-Nadi Al-Arabi in 1919, with the very same goals of reviving the Arab heritage, history, language and achieving freedom.

Palestinian history, from the early 1920s up to 1948, is dominated by two major dimensions: Arabizing the Palestinian cause versus Palestinizing it. The first trend had the upper hand, but unfortunately led to the first Palestinian catastrophe, *an-nakba*, in 1948, with the *de facto* partition of Palestine and the establishment of a Jewish state in more than 56% of the Palestinian territory.

It should be emphasized here that some historians introduce the evolution of Palestine in connection with the evolution of Zionism, and they record in detail all the Zionist conferences, statements, leaders, contacts and achievements. I believe the evolution of Palestine should be recorded as an integral part of the Arab National Movement. Both, eventually, confronted the challenges of Zionism.

The Palestinian National Movement struggled against the British mandate, the Zionist movement and various Arab regimes to maintain its identity. But the Palestinian National Program was about to be forgotten geographically, demographically, and politically as a result of the potential disappearance of the Palestinians through the process of assimilation into the Jordanian state. The Arab countries, excluding Jordan, refused to absorb Palestinian refugees. They were assisted in this by the Arab League resolutions that banned its states from granting citizenship to Palestinians.

---

[3] "*The establishment of the Literary Club (Al-Muntada Al-Adabi) in Istanbul in 1909*: The club included in its membership Arab students from higher institutions, literary personalities, and members of parliament. It published a magazine, carrying its name, which dealt with the history, language and aspirations of the Arabs, thus making a significant contribution to the national awakening and to the revival of Arab glories. It placed an emphasis on the Arab identity, and was the first Arab organization to revive the Arab flag.

From The PASSIA Seminar On The Foreign Policies of Arab States. 587
© PALESTINIAN ACADEMIC SOCIETY FOR THE STUDY OF INTERNATIONAL AFFAIRS (PASSIA). Reprinted with permission.

The Partition Plan of 29 November 1947 was an international recognition of the right of the Palestinian people to establish an independent Palestinian national state in Palestine. The document also granted the Zionist movement a Jewish state in part of Palestine. The context of the international plan represented a major injustice for Palestinians.

On 10 July 1948 the political committee of the Arab League called for the establishment of a Palestinian temporary civil administration to govern the Palestinian territories controlled by the Arab armies following the 1948 war, but the plan never materialized because of the strong objection of Jordan. On 1 October 1948 the Arab Higher Committee called a national conference in Gaza. The council elected a government, established a national charter, and declared Palestinian independence in Gaza. All Arab League members recognized the Palestinian government in Gaza with the exception of Jordan.

Palestinian leaders in the West Bank held a series of conferences during which they called for unity with Jordan. At a later stage Jordan granted Jordanian citizenship to Palestinians in the West Bank and endorsed the conference resolutions regarding the unity of the two banks of the River Jordan.

The Arab League did not accept Jordan's unification plans and up until the early fifties it could not change the *de facto* unity. It stated, however, that the annexation of the West Bank to Jordan was pending the final settlement of the Palestine Question and the realization of the Palestinians' right to self-determination.

From the early 1950s, the Palestinians gradually became scattered as refugees and displaced persons in the neighboring host Arab countries. Other Palestinians became second-class residents/citizens under Israeli military occupation in the new Jewish state. The Palestinians in Israel were cut off totally from their brothers in the West Bank and Gaza as well as from the Arab World, yet they struggled to maintain their identity, and continued to wait for a solution, and continued to wait for a solution. Those who stayed in the West Bank including Jerusalem became Jordanian citizens and enjoyed full rights in a sovereign independent Arab state. Their political elite shared in the governing of Jordan, i.e., ministers, members of parliament, ambassadors. Meanwhile, those in Gaza maintained their Palestinian identity under Egyptian civil administration.

The famous story by Ghassan Kanafani, *People Under the Sun*, is a true story of how Palestinians struggled for survival, not only in their own homeland but also in neighboring host Arab countries. The story describes the plight of four people, hidden in an empty water tank, as they were driven across the desert between Jordan and Kuwait. They had no formal travel documents, and were attempting to smuggle themselves into Kuwait to find work. While they were dying under the heat of the sun, the four knocked continuously on the wall of the tank, crying, "We are here, we are dying, let us out, let us free." This story reflects the dilemma of the majority of Palestinians during that era. Palestine, for the Palestinian Diaspora, became a story of a house, a shore, a mountain or other treasured memories.

In the early 1960's Palestinians started again to re-organize and to mobilize enthusiastic popular support for the return to Palestine. This reawakening was on two tracks; the national and the Pan-Arab. With the first we witnessed a formation of Fateh organizations in Kuwait, and these later became the cornerstone of the national military resistance movement, whose leaders were received and supported by President Abdul Nasser of Egypt. The second track was an Arab summit decision to establish the PLO in 1964.

Internal Arab politics were unable to deliver a solution on either track, but the second Palestinian catastrophe in 1967 brought the answer. The defeat of Arab armies and the fall of the West Bank and Gaza brought Palestinians, geographically and demographically, under Israeli military control. From 1967 until the early 70's the Palestinian military resistance against Israeli occupation was the major tool that united Palestinians throughout the world in their confrontation with Israel, with the backing and support of the Arab countries. Those under occupation called for steadfastness (*sumud*) and waiting for a solution to come through the PLO military resistance or Arab regimes, or the implementation of UN Security Council Resolution 242 of 1967.

The PLO faced a struggle for power and authority on Jordanian soil and was defeated and forced out of Jordan in the early 1970's. It re-established itself in Lebanon and succeeded in establishing a mini state within the state of Lebanon. The Israeli invasion of Lebanon in 1982, led by Begin-Sharon, put an end to the PLO mini state, and, with no state or military infrastructure, the PLO departed to Tunis. Meanwhile, Palestinians in the Occupied Territories moved from a stage of steadfastness to a new chapter known as the *Intifada*. The philosophy of the *Intifada* was to change the *status quo* and build a new society: "We cannot undo Israel, we have to co-exist with Israel, we cannot wait for a solution to come from outside, we cannot be anything but Palestinians and we have a future to build, based on what we have in the Occupied Palestinian Territories." [....]

The Palestinians: A Profile

7.   Before the outbreak of the Arab-Israeli War of 1948, there were some 1,280,000 Christian and Muslim Arabs living in Palestine; today their numbers have more than doubled to 2,655,000. This rapid increase is reflected in their age distribution, with fully 50 percent of the Palestinians being under 20 years of age and very likely under 15 years.
[...]

The Palestinian Diaspora and Israel

13. To a great extent, the economic status of the various groups of Palestinians and their relative distance from Israel influence their attitudes toward Tel Aviv and the future of Palestinian-Israeli relations. Those individuals who have become integrated into local societies, for example, are anxious to see a peace solution of any kind as soon as possible so that they will not become more deeply involved with the fedayeen movement.

14. On the other hand, the nonintegrated refugees in Lebanon, both in and outside the UNRWA camps, are perhaps the most anti-Israeli of the peoples in the Palestinian Diaspora. Bitter, frustrated, and extremely hostile, they are encouraged by the "Successes" of the fedayeen, who have finally succeeded in focusing world attention upon the plight of the Palestinians. The refugees in Lebanon are convinced that the Palestinians now are the masters of their own destinies rather than the pawns of the various Arab powers. They will not be satisfied with such half-way measures as the establishment of a truncated state in the West Bank area, but seek rather the complete destruction of Israel as it exists today.

15. Although little is known of the attitudes of the refugees in Jordan, it is likely that their view parallel those of their brethren in Lebanon. Those who have been able to begin a new life favor a peaceful solution to the problem, while the inhabitants of the UNRWA camps, having nothing to lose, look for the complete destruction of Israel so they can return to their lost properties.

16. Having spent the past three years under Israeli control and having viewed Tel Aviv's power at first-hand, the Palestinians in the occupied territories are under no illusions regarding either the possible overthrow of the Israeli occupation or the destruction of Israel. This is not to suggest that they have become resigned to a continuation of the status quo. The majority—who if one must pin a label on them, are moderates—seek a Palestinian state that would encompass both the West and East Bank areas of Jordan. [...]

Israel and the Occupied Territories

[...]

18. Meanwhile, in order to conduct the day-to-day administration of the occupied areas while maintaining a low profile, Israel has worked through the already existing Palestinian leadership establishment. Mukhtars (village headmen), notables, lawyers, religious functionaries, judges, former and present government officials are employed rather than imposed Israeli administrators. Even though the Palestinians regard these individuals for the most part as the corrupt, inefficient, and repressive minions of King Husayn's regime, the Israelis have tended to view them as the natural leaders of the West Bank. This in turn has diminished the acceptability of these men, who now are tainted as quislings.

19. Other natural leaders, such as professional men, who might be able to assume the mantle of the present establishment, have not had an opportunity to come forward. The fedayeen have been able to intimidate anyone advocating a solution other than the one they espouse. Israel's military occupation has likewise had a repressive influence on indigenous leadership; those Palestinians who have spoken out strongly against Tel Aviv's policies in the occupied areas are deported by military officials, while others, finding their political situation intolerable, have left of their own volition. [...]

Conclusion

20. Who speaks authoritatively for the Palestinians? At present, no one. They are a large amorphous mass of people many of whose goals and beliefs still have not jelled. The Palestinians at this time do not have a recognized set of leaders, let alone one individual able to command universal attention. The basically negative nature of "Palestinianism," particularly as enunciated by the fedayeen, has contributed in no small measure to this situation. To date, moreover, the Palestinians have largely reacted to rather than initiated events in the area. The fedayeen movement is a reaction primarily to the inability of the armies of the Arab states to challenge the Israelis and regain the lost territories. What political activity there has been among West Bankers since 1967 has been in reaction to Tel Aviv's occupation, and the only goal the people can agree upon is the withdrawal of the Israeli forces. In Lebanon, the refugees' support of the fedayeen is a reaction to their inability to become a part of Lebanese society.

21. The absence of a comprehensive political program has affected "Palestinianism." As a whole, even the fedayeen movement has only articulated a general goal—the destruction of Israel. Although they mouth a wide spectrum of slogans, ranging from Marxist to conservative, few fedayeen have given serious thought to their political goals other than the establishment of a "democratic secular state of Palestine," and even then

they have no real conception of just what such a state would be. Other Palestinians have given even less thought to their future. The West Bankers are obsessed with Israel's occupation of the area and seek only to end it without any clear idea of what their political future should be thereafter.

22. To date, the fedayeen have been the only Palestinian voices heard. Not only have nonfedayeen Palestinians been intimidated by the fedayeen from speaking out and making their views known, but the news media have focused on the commandos as more newsworthy and photogenic. [...]

The Interdependence of Israeli and Palestinian National Identities: The Role of the Other in Existential Conflicts (1999)
Herbert C. Kelman

The psychological core of the Israeli-Palestinian conflict is the perception by both parties that it is a zero-sum conflict, not only with respect to territory but, most importantly, with respect to national identity and national existence (Kelman, 1987). Each "perceives the very existence of the other—the other's status as a nation—to be a threat to its own existence and status as a nation. Each holds the view that only one can be a nation; Either we are a nation or they are. *They* can acquire national identity and rights only at the expense of *our* identity and rights" (p. 354). This zero-sum view flows directly from the fact that the two national movements focus on the same land, which both claim as their national homeland. Under these circumstances, acknowledging the other's nationhood is seen as acceptance of the other's right to establish a national state in that land, which each side perceives as relinquishing or at least jeopardizing its own claims to the land. "The issue of territorial claims touches directly on more fundamental questions of national survival. Israelis and Palestinians both see their nations as highly vulnerable. In their very different ways, both have lived on the edge of national oblivion. The themes of destruction, of physical annihilation, and of nonexistence play a central role in their national self-images" (Kelman, 1987, p. 354).

Over the course of the conflict, each side has been convinced that the ultimate intention of the other is to destroy it—indeed, that its own destruction is inherent in the other's ideology. Israelis have equated the Palestinian movement's goal of liberating Palestine with the intention of liquidating Israel. Palestinians have seen the establishment of Israel in 1948 and the occupation of the West Bank and Gaza in 1967 as steps in the Zionist project of eliminating the Palestinian presence in the land. Even now, as the parties seem to be moving toward a peace agreement based on territorial compromise, they are not convinced that the other has really abandoned the project of destroying them and is genuinely committed to the peaceful coexistence of two independent states in the land they both claim. In Israeli-Palestinian workshops that we held during the final months of the Netanyahu government, when mutual trust of the two sides was at a low point, even moderate Israelis and Palestinians, committed to a compromise solution, expressed serious doubts about the other side's real intentions. At a deep level, the perceived intentions of the other still arouse fears in each group about its own existence. Thus, the zero-sum view of national identity is still in place: "Fulfillment of the other's national identity is experienced as equivalent to destruction of one's own identity".

This zero-sum view of national identity has in effect created a state of negative interdependence between the two identities: Assertion of the group's own identity requires negation of the other group's identity; each group's success in identity building depends on the other's failure in that task. Negative interdependence not only creates obstacles to conflict resolution and ultimate reconciliation but also makes it more difficult and costly for each group to establish its own identity. It is not enough for it to demonstrate, to itself and to the rest of the world, its own legitimacy, authenticity, and cohesiveness as a national group; it has the additional burden of demonstrating the illegitimacy, inauthenticity, and lack of cohesiveness of the other, often in the face of powerful evidence to the contrary. Thus, each group's identity becomes hostage to the identity of the other: Since its own identity thrives to the extent that the other's identity languishes, it must invest great energy in discrediting the other. If interdependence means that two parties depend on each other in the achievement of their respective goals, then Israeli and Palestinian identities have been truly interdependent. However, unlike positive interdependence, which creates the conditions for cooperation, negative interdependence creates the conditions for protracted conflict.

The zero-sum view of national identity and the negative interdependence of the Israeli and Palestinian identities to which it gives rise have, indeed, greatly contributed to the escalation and perpetuation of the conflict over the decades and created obstacles to its resolution. One of the consequences of this zero-sum view and perhaps the prototypical indicator of the negative interdependence of the two identities is the mutual denial of each other's national identity (and hence right to a national state) that has characterized the conflict from the beginning (Kelman, 1978, 1987). Many Palestinians, and Arabs in general, have denied Jewish peoplehood, often arguing that Jews are a religion and therefore not a true nation entitled to a state of its own. They have also denied the authenticity of the Jewish national movement, describing Zionism as a form of settler colonialism, perpetuated by Europeans who had no historical links to the land. Many Israelis. on their part. have denied Palestinians' distinctiveness, describing them as Arabs whose self-definition as Palestinians—and in many cases even residence in the country—were of recent origin. In their view, Palestinian nationalism is an artificial creation without authentic historical roots. Such denials have persisted in the face of evidence that both peoples had demonstrated all the characteristics of nations, including the Israelis' establishment of a successful state and revival of an ancient language and the Palestinians' continuing struggle for nationhood culminating in the *intifada*—the popular uprising in the West Bank and Gaza—in the late 1980s.

A related indicator of negative interdependence has been the systematic effort to delegitimize the other's movement by placing it outside of the bounds of what the world community can tolerate. The most extreme examples of delegitimization of the other have been equation of Zionism with racism and of Palestinian nationalism, as represented by the PLO, with terrorism. These accusations have gone beyond the condemnation of racist policies and practices pursued by Israel or terrorist acts committed by the PLO. They have, in effect, described the Zionist movement as inherently racist and the Palestinian movement as inherently terrorist. Since racism and terrorism are morally unacceptable in human society, these designations make the other's national movement as such illegitimate by definition. Delegitimization in these cases verges on dehumanization in that it excludes the other from the moral community shared by all members of the human family. It announces that these national movements have no right to exist, which comes close to saying that these national groups have no right to exist, or so it sounds to the targets (cf. Kelman, 1987, p. 355).

At the political level, an important indicator of the negative interdependence of the two identities was the two parties' refusal over many years to recognize each other. Recognition was seen as legitimizing the other, and thus throwing one's own legitimacy into question. Palestinians, as a matter of principle, were unwilling to recognize Israel's right to exist. Indeed, for a long time they did not even recognize the fact of Israel's existence; they referred to Israel as the "Zionist entity" and left it off their maps (as did the Arab states). Israelis, as a matter of principle, were unwilling to recognize the Palestinians as a separate nation with a right to self-determination. They referred to them as Arabs rather than Palestinians and at times argued that there are no Palestinians (as in an often-cited statement by former Prime Minister Golda Meir). Once the two parties became interested in negotiating with each other, they began to recognize at least the fact of each other's existence and to move, slowly and hesitantly, toward recognizing each other's right to exist. The dilemma they faced was that each needed and wanted to receive the other's recognition but was reluctant to extend recognition to the other, certainly not with out assured reciprocation. The thorny issue during those years was who would be the first to recognize the other (Kelman, 1982). Clearly, the answer had to be prenegotiated, simultaneous, mutual recognition, as finally happened in the Oslo agreement of September 1993. The long history of systematic nonrecognition makes it clear why the Oslo agreement, despite its many limitations, represented an important turning point in the conflict (Kelman, 1997b. 1998b). The letters of recognition exchanged by Arafat and Rabin constitute a first step in transforming the relationship: in effect, beginning to move from negative to positive interdependence between the two peoples.

The negative interdependence of the two identities has also burdened the parties with the requirement of maintaining the demonic image of the enemy. Affirming the enemy image is a common feature of conflict norms and indicator of group loyalty in deep-rooted conflicts. Advocates of a softer enemy image and of communication with the enemy open themselves up to intense suspicion and often accusations of treason. One reason for the emphasis on keeping the demonic image intact is its contribution to the group cohesion that is deemed necessary to sustain the group in its life-and-death struggle. The point here is not simply that a group needs an enemy in order to maintain cohesion; rather, it is the felt need of groups engaged in an existential conflict to remain united and steadfast in their vigilance and resistance vis-a-vis a dangerous enemy in order to avoid being lulled into complacency and compromise that may threaten their national existence.

Another reason for maintaining the demonic image of the enemy is that it is considered vital as support for the justice of the group's own cause. The zero-sum view of identity in relation to the conflict does not admit of the possibility that both parties may have some justice on their side, that there may be two perspectives on the conflict, each of which is at least partly legitimate. Any legitimacy extended to the enemy is seen to detract from the group's own legitimacy. The resulting rigidity of the enemy image is a serious obstacle to efforts at conflict resolution. Each party is likely to be unaware of the occurrence or possibility of change on the other side, which might make the other more amenable to serious negotiations. For many years, Israelis and Palestinians have tended to dismiss indications of change on the other side, preferring to stay with the comfortable formula that there is no one to talk to in the enemy camp and nothing to talk about. Those who broke the consensus by "prematurely" entering into dialogue with the enemy or advocating such dialogue were often marginalized, discredited, vilified, or assassinated.

Finally, one of the consequences of the negative interdependence of the two identities is the fact that the ideology and symbols that support each side's positive group identity and sense of legitimacy have entirely negative connotations for the other side. What sustains the identity of one threatens the identity of the other. Thus, such objects of Palestinian pride and hope as the PLO, its ideology, its institutions. and its international stature, or the *intifada,* or the concepts of Palestinian unity and Palestinian statehood, have had negative valence for Israelis. Similarly, objects of Israeli pride and hope, such as Zionism, the State of Israel and its institutions, the unification of Jerusalem in 1967, or the Egyptian-Israeli peace treaty of 1979 have had negative valence for Palestinians. Each party, looking at the other's ideology and associated symbols entirely from its own perspective, has tended to perceive them as having no other purpose than to destroy its own national existence. Each has found it difficult to recognize the positive elements in the other's ideology and symbols, representing the other's vision of national renewal and liberation and of a better future for its people (Kelman, 1987). Under the circumstances, the parties were not very well able to develop the kind of empathy for the other that is necessary for negotiating a mutually satisfactory agreement and moving toward reconciliation.

The *intifada* and the Oslo agreement have begun to produce some changes in this pattern. For example, when the Oslo agreement was signed in September 1993 and Palestinians danced in the streets of East Jerusalem in anticipation of achieving an independent state, many Israelis observed, and Israeli newspapers wrote, that it reminded them of November 1947, when Jews in Palestine joyfully celebrated the news that the UN had passed a partition resolution that authorized the establishment of a Jewish state. The ability to identify in this way with the Palestinians' anticipation of statehood represented a remarkable departure from the zero-sum view of national identity. On the other hand, one can cite recent instances demonstrating that, despite significant movement, the old pattern has not disappeared. In 1998, Israel celebrated the 50th anniversary of the establishment of the state. In the same year Palestinians memorialized the 50th anniversary of *al naqba:* the term, meaning "catastrophe" or "disaster," that Palestinians use to describe the Palestinian experience of 1948. Some Israelis saw these memorial events and writings as efforts to attack and spoil the Israeli celebration, inconsistent with the ongoing peace process. Yet even if the Palestinians were in part responding to the Israeli celebration, the fact remains that 1948 *was* a disaster for the Palestinian people and that they had legitimate independent reasons for recalling and mourning these tragic events on their 50th anniversary and reminding the world of them. In principle, Israelis could have acknowledged the Palestinian tragedy and the Palestinians' reasons for commemorating it on the 50th anniversary without abandoning their own narrative or their own anniversary celebration. But insofar as the two identities remain negatively interdependent, assertion of one's own group's identity requires rejection of the other's.

In the Israeli-Palestinian conflict, as in other existential conflicts between identity groups, each group is to a considerable degree defined and shaped by the conflict. Its relationship to the conflict is a central part of the group's self-definition and worldview. This fact in itself often creates a psychological commitment that becomes a barrier to conflict resolution. A change in the conflict relationship may be resisted because it would require major revisions in the way people think and feel about significant aspects of their national and personal lives (Kelman, 1997c, p. 222). An integral part of the dependence of each group's identity on the conflict is the negative interdependence between their identities: The perceived success of one's own group depends on the other group's failure. This interdependence is very costly to the conflicting groups. Each must be concerned not only with establishing and bolstering its own identity, but also with undermining and destroying the other's identity; not only with advancing its own cause, but also with thwarting the other's cause.

Assertion of the group's own identity requires negation of the other. This dynamic presents serious obstacles to conflict resolution. The parties are impaired in their ability to take the other's perspective, which is an essential step in any effort at mutual accommodation. They are likely to be unaware of the occurrence and possibility of change on the other side, which might point to a convergence between their seemingly incompatible interests. They are hampered in their pursuit of integrative, win-win solutions, which would require some willingness to think of ways of benefiting the other. They interact in ways that create self-fulfilling prophecies, leading to escalation and perpetuation of the conflict.

The Other as Source of Negative Identity Elements in the Self

The negative interdependence of the two identities derives from a view of the other's identity as a direct threat to one's own identity. The conflict thus becomes purely a matter of "us against them": Only one can prevail. To assert one's own identity requires negating the identity of the other. There is another, not entirely unrelated way in which the other, in an intense conflict relationship, often becomes a threat to one's own identity: The other—or, to be more precise, the relationship to the other—serves to bring out some of the negative elements of one's own identity. I refer here to elements of their self-view that the parties want to overcome and put behind them or to suppress and deny. Unlike the negative interdependence of the two identities, this dynamic does not place the two identities in direct competition such that each can prevail only at the expense of the other. It does, however. create obstacles to conflict resolution by making it difficult for the parties to communicate and cooperate with each other at a level of equality.

There are two major types of negative identity elements that are often brought to the fore by the relationship to the other in a protracted conflict: the view or one's self as weak and vulnerable, and the view of one's self as violent and unjust.

The successes of the other in achieving power or legitimacy may serve as reminders of one's own group's weaknesses and vulnerabilities, particularly those that the national movement has been designed to overcome. For Palestinians, of course, their own weakness and vulnerability is directly related to Israel's power. The Palestinian disaster of 1948 is a consequence of Israel's victory in its war of independence; the occupation of the West Bank and Gaza is a consequence of Israel's victory in the 1967 war. Israeli statehood and military power, the strength of its institutions and its economy, and its achievements in various domains underline for Palestinians their own impotence, statelessness, and inability to shape events. They are especially sensitive to the success of the Zionist movement in achieving its goals in contrast to the continuing failure of the Palestinian movement to achieve its goals on the ground. Although the Palestinian movement has scaled down its demands to an independent state in a small part of Palestine and achieved international support for these demands, it is not yet assured that a viable sovereign state will emerge from the negotiations mandated by the Oslo accord. The sense of weakness relative to Israel is one of the reasons for the reluctance of many Palestinians to engage in cooperative enterprises with Israelis unless the power imbalance is reduced or at least seriously addressed.

Although Israel has powerful military forces, far superior to those of its neighbors, its population suffers from a pervasive sense of vulnerability. This sense of vulnerability is rooted in the Jewish historical experience, particularly the Holocaust: "a people that, within its recent memory, has come close to annihilation finds it easy to imagine that it may again be subjected to a similar threat" (Kelman, 1992a, p. 34). Indeed, one of the purposes of the Zionist project of establishing a Jewish state was to put an end to the vulnerability of the Jewish people. But instead, the state was established in a hostile environment, amid neighbors who regarded Israelis as unwanted intruders and denied their state's legitimacy. Palestinians have, over the decades, served as constant reminders to Israelis of their lack of acceptance and legitimacy in the region and hence of their continuing vulnerability. The PLO' s success in achieving international support and legitimacy, particularly within the context of the United Nations, has brought home to Israelis their still precarious position in the Middle East—the fact that the process of international recognition of their state is still incomplete. To be considered aliens, outsiders, in their own country is particularly painful since it recalls the outsider status Jews experienced in the diaspora, which the Jewish state was designed to overcome. The very name "Palestinians" is troubling to Israelis because, in choosing that name, Palestinians have identified themselves as the people who belong to Palestine and to whom Palestine belongs, thus implying that Israelis are outsiders and usurpers. Terrorist acts directed at Israelis are perhaps the most concrete reminder to Israelis of their historic vulnerability. The strength of Israeli reaction to such acts exceeds the military threat that they represent; what is significant for Israelis is that they demonstrate the limits of Israel's ability to protect the physical safety of its people.

The second negative element of each group's identity that the relationship to the other brings to the fore is the view of one's self as violent and unjust. The nature of the conflict forces both sides to entertain views of the self that they find unacceptable, but that they cannot entirely avoid because these views reflect the image of the group held by large parts of the outside world. In the case of Israelis, it is the image of occupiers, oppressors. and racists who are responsible for expulsions, bombings, massacres, torture, cover-ups, and undemocratic practices. In the case of

Palestinians, it is the image of violence-prone, uncivilized fanatics and terrorists who target children and other innocent civilians. In both cases, these images are inconsistent with the parties' self-images and the images they wish to project. They see and present themselves as the victims, not the victimizers; as decent and civilized people; as resorting to violence only when deprived of all other options. They blame the other for forcing them into the role of aggressor and deeply resent being relegated to the pariah status of oppressor or terrorist. The other, however, serves as a constant reminder of the fact that, whether they do so reluctantly or not, they are engaged in actions that cast doubt on their decent and peaceful self-images.

The two types of negative identity elements brought to the fore by the relationship to the other are, in essence, the view of the self as victim and of the self as victimizer. In the rhetoric of conflict, these two self-images perform very different functions. Each party claims the status of victim and each denies the role of victimizer. At the level of self-esteem and self-ideal. however, both of these elements of identity are negative and ego-alien. Each group would rather see itself as neither the other's weak and vulnerable victim, nor the other's cruel oppressor or assailant. Yet the conflict relationship forces these negative self-images upon them. Paradoxically, efforts at conflict resolution often bring these images to the fore: They make it necessary to confront them rather than suppress and deny them. Agreeing to a compromise generally means accepting the reality of one's own weakness; one must compromise because one's options are limited in the face of the countervailing pressures that the other is able to apply. Acknowledging the other's rights generally means admitting (at least by implication) that one may have treated the other unjustly in the past. Conflict resolution, particularly if it is to lead to transformation of the relationship and ultimate reconciliation, thus requires some revision of each party's identity, taking ownership of certain negative elements that it had preferred to overlook.

In sum, the fact that the other is a source of some of the negative elements in one's own identity presents obstacles that must be overcome in setting a process of conflict resolution into motion. It exacerbates the effects of the negative interdependence of the two identities by making it more difficult to engage in the kinds of equal-status interactions that can counteract the zero-sum view of identity and promote the development of a transcendent identity in which each side accommodates the claims, narrative, and particularistic identity of the other.
[…]

Defensible Borders to Ensure Israel's Future (2014)
Maj. Gen. (ret.) Uzi Dayan

Israel Has a Natural and Internationally Recognized Right to Defensible
Borders

Israel's fundamental right to defensible borders is grounded in the strategic
and legal circumstances that emerged immediately after the Six-Day War,
in which Israel captured the West Bank of the Jordan, Sinai, and the Golan
Heights. The "Green Line" that was established in the 1949 Armistice
Agreements was defined as a military border between the Israeli and
Jordanian armies, not as a permanent political border. That situation
provided the background for United Nations Security Council Resolution
242 of November 1967, which did not call on the Israel Defense Forces
(IDF) to withdraw completely to the armistice line, instead affirming that
Israel required "secure and recognized boundaries" that were not identical
to the indefensible prewar lines.

Today it is often forgotten how vulnerable Israel was in the past. Before
1967 Israel's "narrow waist" – that is, the distance between the coastal
cities of its central region and the West Bank under Jordanian occupation –
was only about 8 miles (12 km.), not enough for minimal defensive depth
in case of an invasion. Israel is a country about the size of New Jersey with
a territory of only 16,100 square miles (25,900 sq. km.). Israel's small size
alone is not the basis for its claim to defensible borders, but rather the fact
that it has been a repeated victim of aggression caused the international
community to recognize that right in the aftermath of the Six-Day War.

Israel's vulnerability is made all the more acute by the fact that 70 percent
of the country's population, 80 percent of its industrial capacity, and
crucial infrastructure targets [...] are squeezed into that narrow coastal
strip between the Mediterranean Sea and the West Bank. Moreover, the
adjacent hills of the West Bank topographically dominate the low-lying
and exposed coastal plain, affording an attacker clear advantage in terms of
observation, fire, and defensive capability against an Israeli counterattack.

Thus the 1949 armistice lines were indefensible, leading the architects of
Israel's national security doctrine, from Yigal Allon to Moshe Dayan to
Yitzhak Rabin, to adamantly oppose a return to those lines, which they
believed would invite aggression and endanger Israel's future instead of
paving a path to peace.

These Israeli leaders sought new borders that would enable Israel to defend
itself. According to a broad consensus that emerged in the national security

establishment, these would constitute "defensible borders" and Israel would have to insist on them in any future negotiations. In 2004, the United States gave Israel a letter of guarantees that recognized Israel's right to "defensible borders." The document was signed by President George W. Bush and supported by a bipartisan majority of both houses of Congress.

Since that time the need for defensible borders has only grown. [...]

For borders to be defensible, they must provide an answer to four cardinal threats: a conventional attack, rocket and missile fire, terror, and a nonconventional attack.

A conventional attack – Unlike the armed forces of the Arab states that surround Israel, the IDF is composed mainly of reserve units that need about forty-eight hours to fully mobilize and reach the battlefield. Defensible borders are what gives the regular army the optimal topographical conditions for withstanding an offensive by numerically superior ground forces until the reserve mobilization is completed. After that mobilization, defensible borders must also give Israel the necessary operative depth to conduct a defensive battle. If Israel were to lack this defensive depth, its deterrent power would also decline and the temptation to subject it to a surprise attack, one that could rapidly defeat the IDF before the reserves could arrive, would increase.
[...]
It is important to emphasize that when it comes to Israel's security policy, the ability to provide security in case of a massive conventional attack remains the cardinal criterion. Even in the era of rockets and missiles, it is military offensives by ground forces – not aerial strikes and rocket attacks – that ultimately decide the course of wars. As long as ground forces remain the critical element, factors that affect a ground war – such as territorial depth, topography, and the size and nature of forces – will remain essential to Israel's national security.

Rockets and missiles – If terrorist forces were to fire rockets and mortars from the West Bank as they are now doing from Gaza, the entire Israeli home front would be exposed to this threat. The West Bank overlooks Israel's main cities from a distance of a few miles, and rockets, mortars, and antiaircraft missiles must be kept out of this territory. [...]

Short-range rockets are a special challenge for Israel, making the little territory that Israel possesses a vital and irreplaceable defensive barrier. Ironically, longer-range rockets and missiles, including those with more powerful warheads, pose less of a problem than short-range rockets. Whereas longer-range rockets require launchers that can be identified and attacked (even if it is after the launch), short-range rockets are very hard to stop and there is nothing to hit once they are launched, especially if they are fired from the midst of a civilian population and are numerous because of their low cost. For Israel to prevent the deployment of such rockets in places that are close to vital and vulnerable strategic sites, it has to be present on the ground in those places. Even the interception of longer-range missiles and rockets requires the stationing of warning, detection, and interception systems at locations that give them enough time to function.

Terror – Since its establishment, Israel has had to fight terror backed by states throughout the region, and today this threat is more relevant than ever. It is Israel's military presence on the eastern perimeter of the West Bank, in the Jordan Valley and the Judean Desert, that has prevented arms smuggling and the infiltration of hostile forces. It is this presence that has kept global *jihadists* from turning the West Bank into a battlefield like those they have created in Afghanistan, Iraq, Somalia, and Syria. One of the main preconditions for a terror-fighting strategy is to isolate the area of conflict and thwart the influx of hostile forces with their weapons and equipment. As Israel has learned from direct experience in Lebanon and Gaza, the inability to prevent such an influx turns an area into a source of rocket and mortar fire along with other attacks, leading to instability, diplomatic difficulties, and even wars.

The nonconventional threat – Defensible borders remain relevant even at a time of growing concern about nonconventional weapons, and especially nuclear weapons, in the Middle East. Israel is a country so small that it needs to disperse its population, armed forces, and defensive assets (enabling warning and interception) as widely as possible. Otherwise the enemy will try to gain a decisive military advantage by carrying out a first strike without fear of an Israeli counterattack. The greater Israel's geographic vulnerability, the greater the threat to it, both from a conventional attack by Middle Eastern military forces and from nonconventional terror.

The Jordan Valley

In the southern theater (because of the demilitarization of Sinai) and in the northern theater (because Israel has resisted handing over the Golan Heights), Israel has defensible borders.

In the eastern theater there is no substitute for the Jordan Valley; its location and unique topographical features make it the only feasible eastern border for the State of Israel.

Some key facts about the Jordan Valley:

- Israel's width from the Mediterranean Sea to the Jordan River is only 40 miles (64 km.) on average. This provides minimal strategic depth, and taking the risk of further reducing this strategic depth is out of the question.

- The Jordan Valley is only 4.2 to 9 miles (6.8-14.5 km.) wide. The Jordan River lies 1,300 feet (396 m.) below sea level, but it is adjacent to the steep eastern slope of the West Bank's mountain spine –which, at its highest point (Baal Hatzor), stands 3,609 feet (1,011 m.) above sea level. Hence, the Jordan Valley constitutes a physical barrier with a height of 3,000 to 4,600 feet (914-1,402 m.).

- The Jordan Valley is an arid area with a small and sparse Palestinian population.

- For an attacking army to advance westward from the Jordan Valley, it must make its way through only five mountain passages that can be relatively easily defended, even by the limited regular-army force of the IDF.

In light of the Jordan Valley's strategic importance for Israel's security, the IDF has continued – even since the successful peace treaty with Jordan – to carry out routine security measures there with the help of an active security fence, while also deploying brigade-level forces there that can readily be reinforced by the reserves, along with the necessary equipment, in case a ground threat should materialize from the east. The Israeli force in the Jordan Valley is also a tripwire, since an attack on it would trigger a reserve call-up; and in all negotiations with the Palestinians, Israel has also insisted on the right to transport additional forces to the valley via strategic roads.

Why Can't Israel Rely on Early-Warning Capabilities Instead of Having a Physical Presence?

The question keeps coming up from time to time: why can't Israel rely on advanced technological means to warn of an impending attack, so that it could mobilize the reserves in time to contain any potential ground offensive and thus make a forward deployment in the Jordan Valley unnecessary?

The answer is that in 1973 the IDF maintained insufficient forces on the Egyptian and Syrian fronts because it was confident that, in any event, it would get sufficient prior intelligence warning in order to reinforce these fronts in a timely manner. In retrospect, after Egypt and Syria had succeeded in carrying out surprise attacks, this emerged as a critical error.

The Second Lebanon War in 2006 highlighted an additional failure stemming from excessive reliance on advanced technology. Many commanders preferred to remain at the rear of the battlefield, where they thought they could adequately observe the fighting on plasma screens and direct their forces via advanced teleprocessing systems. Such commanders in fact suffered a total failure of command and control over their battlefield troops.

The painful lesson of the Yom Kippur War and the Second Lebanon War is that Israel must not relinquish the Jordan Valley and rely instead on advanced technological systems. The history of warfare indeed shows that technological advantages are eventually eroded and even neutralized and can hardly be relied upon as permanent; over the last century, offense and defense were in constant competition. Israel's advantage in air power in 1967 was altered by 1973 with the introduction of advanced Soviet air-defense systems.

[…] Should cyber-warfare capabilities indeed proliferate in the decades ahead, then Israeli commanders relying on their plasma screens in their rear command centers, in order to wage a military campaign, will have to contend with the prospect that their picture of the battlefield will go blank as their electronic sensors become blinded.

Western analysts predict that the electromagnetic spectrum will become one of the main targets of future weapons, stripping away the advantages in surveillance that military commanders have recently enjoyed.

Finally, if the forces in place are insufficient to protect the state, then the burden of decision-making during a military crisis will fall entirely on the political echelon to mobilize reserves or even consider a pre-emptive strike. In 1973, Israel's political leadership was reluctant to take either step, due to international political considerations. In short, there is no substitute for a deployed and active force in the territory that Israel controls.

Are Israel's Territorial Considerations Still Relevant in the Missile Age?

Moreover, relying on a timely, rapid reserve call-up to reinforce Israel's eastern front will become more and more dangerous. As already noted, historically, Israel's neighbors have had the advantage of larger regular armies, with only a secondary role for their reserves. This feature of the Arab-Israeli military balance is likely to return once the Arab states achieve a modicum of internal stability in the future. Under such conditions, Israel's adversaries will have an interest in retarding an Israeli reserve call-up for as long as possible, thereby retaining their quantitative superiority in the balance of forces for a longer period of time.

Such a slowdown can be achieved by firing missiles at assembly points and equipment-distribution centers. Neighboring hostile entities, then, can be expected to use their large arsenals of ballistic missiles and rockets for just that purpose – to prevent the arrival of sufficient reinforcements to all of Israel's fronts, including the Jordan Valley. Those who assert that the essentials of land warfare, like terrain and strategic depth, are no longer relevant in the age of ballistic missiles are simply wrong. Indeed, the incorporation of ballistic missiles into the battle plans of Israel's adversaries only magnifies the importance of defensible borders, which will allow Israel's standing army to contain an attack for much longer periods of time.

Why Can't Israel Give Up Optimal Defensive Territory and Rely Instead on its Air Power to Stop any Attacking Army?

In any future battlefield the Israel air force initially will be given tasks of greater importance than providing air support for the deployment of ground forces. It will first have to achieve air superiority by destroying enemy anti-aircraft systems and neutralizing ballistic-missile fire at Israeli cities. Hence, the entry of ballistic missiles and rockets into the arena of warfare has only increased the importance of territory and strategic depth for Israel. With the reserve forces' arrival likely to be delayed by rocket fire, the small regular army will need more time to hold off a ground offensive. Moreover, the regular army may well have to operate for a considerable time without massive air support as the air force is busy striking missile and rocket launchers.

For these reasons there is no substitute for the Jordan Valley as an Israeli defensive buffer. […]

The Jordan Valley's critical importance for Israel's security also emerges clearly from the Israeli experience in Gaza. In implementing the Oslo accords in Gaza in 1994, Israel created a security strip between southern Gaza and Egyptian territory.

This narrow strip, no more than 330 feet (or about 100 m.) wide (!) at some crucial points, was known as the Philadelphi Route. Palestinian groups in Gaza made the most of its narrow size by digging tunnels under it to the Egyptian side of the town of Rafah, located in Sinai, and using these passageways to bring rockets and other weapons into Gaza.

Israel fought the tunnels with partial success until 2005, when it withdrew completely from Gaza – including from the Philadelphi Route. After that, arms smuggling grew rapidly and Gaza became a zone for firing rockets of increasing range and destructive capability at Israeli population centers. […] In many regards the Jordan Valley is the Philadelphi Route of the West Bank, forming Israel's security belt. The only way to ensure that any future Palestinian state is demilitarized, as Israel demands, and will not become another Iranian stronghold, is to maintain full Israeli control of the Jordan Valley.

606

Can't Powerful Israel Rely on its Deterrent Capability?

Deterrence is an important component of the balance of forces between states and also of fighting terror. Basically, deterrence entails presenting a threat that leads opponents to avoid aggressive actions by persuading them that such actions will be more harmful than advantageous to them.

States having military power can be deterred from direct attacks and, specifically, from territorial invasions. It would be very difficult, however, to deter a third state, with which Israel did not share a border, from transferring its forces into a Palestinian state if it was invited in.

Over the years, efforts to deter terror organizations have only partly succeeded. Effectively deterring a terror group requires confronting it with a threat that is existential. A punitive operation that lacks the element of an existential threat causes escalation instead of deterrence. Deterrence does not work against terror organizations that control no territory or population, and have no organizational mechanism or logistical infrastructure that can be hit. The proliferation of such groups, along with the growing power of rocket terror, increasingly means that these groups can only be deterred by preventing them from succeeding (known as deterrence by denial).

Therefore, exercising effective deterrence against a military invasion or terror on Israel's eastern front mandates Israeli military control of the Jordan Valley.

Israeli control of the Jordan Valley also has important implications for Jordan's security. If the IDF evacuates the valley, preventing smuggling will mainly become the Jordanian army's responsibility. As soon as Israel withdraws, however, a plethora of regional terror groups that want to infiltrate the West Bank, thereby bolstering Hamas and joining its war on Israel, will exploit the new situation by seeking a springboard in Jordan. The Jordan Valley's attractiveness as an infiltration route will probably also spark the emergence of terror groups within the Kingdom of Jordan itself. That will undoubtedly add to Jordan's security burden and possibly produce greater risks, as occurred in the late 1960s and led King Hussein in 1970 to finally crush the PLO's extensive terror network, which threatened a civil war and the kingdom's collapse.
[...]

What about Alternative Security Arrangements Involving Foreign Forces?

Another idea sometimes raised is that of "alternative security arrangements," meaning a combination of a limited Israeli presence in the Jordan Valley with warning stations in sovereign Palestinian territory and the deployment of foreign (international, UN, or NATO) forces in the area.

Israel must not agree to such "solutions." Israel's national security doctrine is firmly based on self-reliance, and for good reasons beyond the vital importance of its ethos of self-defense.

Israel's security concerns in the Jordan Valley cannot possibly be met if the territory is transferred to the Palestinians and if any sort of foreign forces are stationed there. International observers can only ensure that arrangements are implemented if all sides want to uphold them. No state will accept having its soldiers endanger their lives in place of Israeli soldiers. Indeed, Israel's experience with international forces or monitors under such conditions is hardly encouraging. In Lebanon, UNIFIL has not met Israel's expectations since the 2006 Second Lebanon War with regard to preventing the rearming of Hizbullah. Similarly, European Union observers at the Rafah Crossing in Gaza abandoned their posts in 2006 when they were threatened by rioters, and UN forces on the Golan Heights have similarly fled the dangers of Syria's civil war.

The Israeli deployment in the Jordan Valley enables the continuous information-gathering that can provide rapid warning when necessary, the maintenance of a regular defensive force that operates in the territory and knows it well, defensive depth to ensure that sudden attacks can be contained, control of that defensive depth and the ability to fortify and barricade it at very short notice, and control over assembly areas for reinforcements and the axes for transporting them. Any Israeli deployment that does not meet all these requirements will be insufficient and will fail the test in the hour of need.

Conclusion

Israel has a natural right and a historically proven and internationally recognized need for defensible borders that enable it to defend itself with its own forces.

An analysis of the four main threats (conventional attacks, rocket and missile fire, terror, and nonconventional attacks), and a consideration of how they can be dealt with, demonstrates that neither the 1967 lines nor the security-fence line can serve as a defensible border for Israel, and that only full Israeli sovereignty over all of the Jordan Valley as a security zone running along the Jordan River, serving as a border, can give Israel security.
[...]
Such defensible borders will not only enable Israel to provide its residents with the security they need, but also will ensure that a future peace treaty is sustainable.

The Future of Israel (1967)
I.F. Stone

[…] In the absence of a general settlement, war will recur at regular intervals. The Arabs will thirst for revenge. The Israelis will be tempted again to wage preventive war. The Israeli borders are so precarious, the communications so easily cut, as to be untenable in static defensive warfare. A surprise attack would cut Israel into half a dozen parts. A long war would be suicidal for a community of little more than two million Jews in a sea of 50 million Arabs. Only total mobilization can defend it, and total mobilization is impossible for any extended term in Israel, since it brings the wheels of the economy to a crawl. The strategic and demographic circumstances dictate *blitzkrieg,* and *blitzkrieg* is a dangerous gamble. To be forced to keep that weapon in reserve is ruinous.

It is ruinous financially and it is ruinous morally. It imposes a huge armament burden. It feeds an ever more intense and costly arms race, as each side seeks frantically for newer and more complex weapons. It brings with it a spiral of fear and hate. It creates within Israel the atmosphere of a besieged community, ringed by hostile neighbors, its back to the sea, skeptical, with good reason, of the world community, relying only on her own military strength, turning every man and woman into a soldier, regarding every Arab within her borders distrustfully as a potential Fifth Columnist, and glorying in her military strength. Chauvinism and militarism are the inescapable results. They can turn Israel into an Ishmael. They can create a minuscule Prussia, not the beneficent Zion of which the prophets and Zionists dreamed. The East will not be redeemed by turning it into a new Wild West, where Israel can rely only on a quick draw with a six-shooter.

In justice to Israel, no one can forget the terrible history that has turned the Jewish state into a fighting community. Events still fresh in living memory illustrate how little reliance may be placed on the conscience of mankind. Long before the crematoria were built, in the six years of Nazi rule before World War II, refugees met a cold shoulder. Our State Department, like the British Foreign Office, distinguished itself in those years by its anemic indifference to the oppressed and its covert undertone of admiration for the Axis; our few anti-fascist ambassadors, like Dodd in Berlin and Bowers in Madrid, were treated miserably by the Department. The welcome signs in the civilized world were few, and even now, if events were reversed and Israel were overrun, it could expect little more than a few hand-wringing resolutions. […]

From RAMPARTS MAGAZINE, July 1967, pp. 41-44.

Sec. 201 – Assessment of Israel's Qualitative Military Edge Over Military
Threats
[...]
    (d) Certification. —Section 36 of the Arms Export Control Act (22
U.S.C. 2776) is amended by adding at the end the following:

"(h) Certification Requirement Relating to Israel's Qualitative
Military Edge.—

"(1) In general.—Any certification relating to a
proposed sale or export of defense articles or defense services under
this section to any country in the Middle East other than Israel shall
include a determination that the sale or export of the defense articles
or defense services will not adversely affect Israel's qualitative
military edge over military threats to Israel.

"(2) Qualitative military edge defined.-- In this
subsection, the term 'qualitative military edge' means the ability to
counter and defeat any credible conventional military threat from
any individual state or possible coalition of states or from non-state
actors, while sustaining minimal damages and casualties, through
the use of superior military means, possessed in sufficient quantity,
including weapons, command, control, communication,
intelligence, surveillance, and reconnaissance capabilities that in
their technical characteristics are superior in capability to those of
such other individual or possible coalition of states or non-state
actors.".

[...]

Now, some argue that the spread of militant Islam, especially in these turbulent times -- if you want to slow it down, they argue, Israel must hurry to make concessions, to make territorial compromises. And this theory sounds simple. Basically it goes like this: Leave the territory, and peace will be advanced. The moderates will be strengthened, the radicals will be kept at bay. And don't worry about the pesky details of how Israel will actually defend itself; international troops will do the job.

These people say to me constantly: Just make a sweeping offer, and everything will work out. You know, there's only one problem with that theory. We've tried it and it hasn't worked. In 2000 Israel made a sweeping peace offer that met virtually all of the Palestinian demands. Arafat rejected it. The Palestinians then launched a terror attack that claimed a thousand Israeli lives.

Prime Minister Olmert afterwards made an even more sweeping offer, in 2008. President Abbas didn't even respond to it.

But Israel did more than just make sweeping offers. We actually left territory. We withdrew from Lebanon in 2000 and from every square inch of Gaza in 2005. That didn't calm the Islamic storm, the militant Islamic storm that threatens us. It only brought the storm closer and made it stronger.

Hizbullah and Hamas fired thousands of rockets against our cities from the very territories we vacated. See, when Israel left Lebanon and Gaza, the moderates didn't defeat the radicals, the moderates were devoured by the radicals. And I regret to say that international troops like UNIFIL in Lebanon and EUBAM in Gaza didn't stop the radicals from attacking Israel.

We left Gaza hoping for peace.

We didn't freeze the settlements in Gaza, we uprooted them. We did exactly what the theory says: Get out, go back to the 1967 borders, dismantle the settlements.

And I don't think people remember how far we went to achieve this. We uprooted thousands of people from their homes. We pulled children out of their schools and their kindergartens. We bulldozed synagogues. We even moved loved ones from their graves. And then, having done all that, we gave the keys of Gaza to President Abbas.

Now the theory says it should all work out, and President Abbas and the Palestinian Authority now could build a peaceful state in Gaza. You can remember that the entire world applauded. They applauded our withdrawal as an act of great statesmanship. It was a bold act of peace.

But ladies and gentlemen, we didn't get peace. We got war. We got Iran, which through its proxy Hamas promptly kicked out the Palestinian Authority. The Palestinian Authority collapsed in a day -- in one day.

President Abbas just said on this podium that the Palestinians are armed only with their hopes and dreams. Yeah, hopes, dreams and 10,000 missiles and Grad rockets supplied by Iran, not to mention the river of lethal weapons now flowing into Gaza from the Sinai, from Libya, and from elsewhere.

Thousands of missiles have already rained down on our cities. So you might understand that, given all this, Israelis rightly ask: What's to prevent this from happening again in the West Bank? See, most of our major cities in the south of the country are within a few dozen kilometers from Gaza. But in the center of the country, opposite the West Bank, our cities are a few hundred meters or at most a few kilometers away from the edge of the West Bank.

So I want to ask you. Would any of you bring danger so close to your cities, to your families? Would you act so recklessly with the lives of your citizens? Israelis prepared to have a Palestinian state in the West Bank, but we're not prepared to have another Gaza there. And that's why we need to have real security arrangements, which the Palestinians simply refuse to negotiate with us.

Israelis remember the bitter lessons of Gaza. Many of Israel's critics ignore them. They irresponsibly advise Israel to go down this same perilous path again. Your read what these people say and it's as if nothing happened – just repeating the same advice, the same formulas as though none of this happened.

And these critics continue to press Israel to make far-reaching concessions without first assuring Israel's security. They praise those who unwittingly feed the insatiable crocodile of militant Islam as bold statesmen. They cast as enemies of peace those of us who insist that we must first erect a sturdy barrier to keep the crocodile out, or at the very least jam an iron bar between its gaping jaws.

So in the face of the labels and the libels, Israel must heed better advice. Better a bad press than a good eulogy, and better still would be a fair press whose sense of history extends beyond breakfast, and which recognizes Israel's legitimate security concerns.

612

I believe that in serious peace negotiations, these needs and concerns can be properly addressed, but they will not be addressed without negotiations. And the needs are many, because Israel is such a tiny country. Without Judea and Samaria, the West Bank, Israel is all of 9 miles wide.

[...]

So how do you protect such a tiny country, surrounded by people sworn to its destruction and armed to the teeth by Iran? Obviously you can't defend it from within that narrow space alone. Israel needs greater strategic depth, and that's exactly why Security Council Resolution 242 didn't require Israel to leave all the territories it captured in the Six-Day War. It talked about withdrawal from territories, to secure and defensible boundaries. And to defend itself, Israel must therefore maintain a long-term Israeli military presence in critical strategic areas in the West Bank.

I explained this to President Abbas. He answered that if a Palestinian state was to be a sovereign country, it could never accept such arrangements. Why not? America has had troops in Japan, Germany and South Korea for more than a half a century. Britain has had an air base in Cyprus. France has forces in three independent African nations. None of these states claim that they're not sovereign countries.

And there are many other vital security issues that also must be addressed. Take the issue of airspace. Again, Israel's small dimensions create huge security problems. America can be crossed by jet airplane in six hours. To fly across Israel, it takes three minutes. So is Israel's tiny airspace to be chopped in half and given to a Palestinian state not at peace with Israel?

Our major international airport is a few kilometers away from the West Bank. Without peace, will our planes become targets for antiaircraft missiles placed in the adjacent Palestinian state? And how will we stop the smuggling into the West Bank? It's not merely the West Bank, it's the West Bank mountains. It just dominates the coastal plain where most of Israel's population sits below. How could we prevent the smuggling into these mountains of those missiles that could be fired on our cities?

I bring up these problems because they're not theoretical problems. They're very real. And for Israelis, they're life-and-death matters. All these potential cracks in Israel's security have to be sealed in a peace agreement before a Palestinian state is declared, not afterwards, because if you leave it afterwards, they won't be sealed. And these problems will explode in our face and explode the peace.

The Palestinians should first make peace with Israel and then get their state. But I also want to tell you this. After such a peace agreement is signed, Israel will not be the last country to welcome a Palestinian state as a new member of the United Nations. We will be the first.

[...]

SETTLEMENTS

Israeli Settlements (1983)
CENTRAL INTELLIGENCE AGENCY

Construction of Jewish settlements in the West Bank was started almost immediately following Israel's occupation of the territory in 1967. Israeli spokesmen have justified the program at various times as an expression of the right of Jews to live anywhere in "Eretz Israel"—the Biblical land of Israel once occupied by the Jewish people—and as part of Israel's defense against Arab attack from the east.

Israel's Labor-dominated government sought to establish settlements in the West Bank to solidify Israel's political claim to secure borders. It ruled out an indiscriminate settlement policy so as to allow for the possibility of a peace agreement with Jordan that would include large-scale territorial concessions by Israel. Labor leaders also rejected outright annexation of the territory because they were concerned that absorption of the West Bank's large Arab population would over time compromise the Jewish character of Israel. Settlements thus were limited largely to those areas most likely to be claimed by Israel in peace negotiations.

For the most part, the location of the 32 settlements established by Labor in the West Bank followed the geographic priorities of an unofficial plan formulated by then Minister of Labor Yigal Allon in July 1967. Allon proposed creating a security zone approximately 1 05 km long and 16 to 24 km wide west of the Dead Sea and the Jordan River—which would be treated as Israel's eastern security border. Up to 20 military outposts would be established in the sparsely populated zone to deter the crossing of Jordanian or other Arab forces into the West Bank. In Allan's view, Israel's continued presence in the Jordan Valley would give the military the independent capability to monitor any militarization of the West Bank.

Menachem Begin and his Likud Party—which gained control of the government in 1977—have brought a different philosophy to the development of settlements in the West Bank. Begin and his supporters believe that the Israeli Government should strive to regain the key territories that composed the land of Israel during Biblical times. Just as settlement activity before 1948 helped establish a Jewish claim to what is now Israel, the Likud Party believes a vigorous settlement campaign throughout the West Bank will help ensure Israeli retention of the territory. Begin believes that the potential problems posed by the need to govern the West Bank's large Arab population are secondary considerations that can be managed.

614 From Central Intelligence Agency. Report: West Bank: A Handbook (Sep. 1983).

In the nearly six years it has been in office, the Begin government has made significant progress toward its settlement goals. There are today about 135 Jewish settlements in various stages of completion in the West Bank with a population of about 30,000. In addition, approximately 90,000 Israelis live in areas of East Jerusalem annexed by Israel after the 1967 war. Before Begin took office there were less than 5,000 settlers in the West Bank and only about 50,000 Jewish residents in the annexed areas of East Jerusalem.

At the same time that it has increased the number of settlements in the West Bank, the Begin government has also set out to populate new areas of the territory. Most of the new settlers are moving into those regions of the West Bank where 95 percent of the territory's Arab residents live.

Ariel Sharon, first as Agriculture Minister, then as Defense Minister, has been instrumental in encouraging expansion of the settlement program. Even after relinquishing the defense portfolio, Sharon—as the Cabinet's most outspoken hardliner on Palestinian questions—has continued to reinforce Prime Minister Begin's inclination to stand firm on settlement questions. Sharon's replacement, Defense Minister Arens, also takes a hardline position on West Bank questions. Another key figure has been Matityahu Drobles, director of the Settlement Department of the World Zionist Organization (WZO), whose plan for the West Bank calls for the control of large chunks of land surrounding, and hence isolating, concentrations of Arab population. The settlement pattern is designed to prevent the eventual creation of an independent Palestinian state.

Israel's Legal Case for Settlements

The Israeli Government has maintained throughout that its use of West Bank land is consistent with international law. Two international agreements are technically applicable to Israel's role as an occupying power in the West Bank:

- *The fourth Geneva Convention ... forbids an occupying military power from either taking land in an occupied territory for civilian settlements or financing their establishment, and states that an occupying power shall not deport or transfer parts of its own civilian population into the territory it occupies. Israel signed this convention in 1951.*
- *The Hague Convention (1907) forbids the permanent confiscation of land by an occupying power. It allows, however, an occupying government to use publicly (or state-) owned land temporarily and to use privately*

> *owned land for military purposes if compensation is provided.*
>
> *The Israeli Government argues that the more restrictive Geneva Convention does not apply to its activities in the West Bank because the convention relates only to relations between two sovereign nations. Jordan's occupation of the West Bank was recognized only by Great Britain and Pakistan. Jordan, therefore, has no sovereign claim to the West Bank, says Israel. Israeli actions in the territory—Tel Aviv argues—are only affected by the Hague Convention, which contains fewer specific restrictions on the actions of the occupying power.*

The Israeli Housing Ministry's budget report for fiscal year 1983 confirms the trend toward locating settlements in areas close to the pre-1967 border. This trend will be reinforced by government policies aimed at encouraging investors and builders to undertake most of the homebuilding, with the government providing infrastructure, loans, and grants. Such private-sector development is most likely to take place where there is a profitable market—in bedroom communities within easy commuting distance of Israel's main employment centers. Currently, about 70 percent of all settlement construction in the territory is taking place in five such urban settlements.

Land Acquisition

The manner in which West Bank territory has been requisitioned for Jewish settlements has changed over the years. Prior to 1979 an important method of land seizure was expropriation for "vital and immediate military requirements." In October of that year, however, the Israeli Supreme Court ruled that land expropriated from Arab residents for purported security needs was in fact taken for civilian, political reasons and was therefore illegally acquired. The court declared that the government had not demonstrated the military purpose served by the settlement in question and ordered its removal.

Since this decision, the Begin government has made extensive use of the 19th century Ottoman land code and other devices to redefine areas as state land. Under the Ottoman code anyone who is in need of *mawat* land "can, with the leave of the official, cultivate it on the condition that ultimate ownership shall belong to the Sultan." The Israelis argue that they are now administrators of the laws in effect when the occupation began.

State-owned land forms the bulk of the property available for settlements, although private Israeli companies and individuals can also purchase land from Arab owners. Some state land was owned by agencies of the Jordanian Government or by the Jordanian monarchy before 1967 and is now under Israeli trusteeship. Tel Aviv leases this land to settlements. Much of this land, however, comes from the large tracts that the government, after physical and archival survey, decides are state lands.

Following the government's declaration that an area is state land, local Arab inhabitants have 21 days to challenge such a declaration or to provide documented proof of ownership. Prior Israeli administrations accepted oral testimony, tax records, and other forms of proof, but the Begin government specifies the need for formal deeds. Only about one-third of the West Bank's territory is under secure title. Moreover, deeds issued by Ottoman authorities and British Mandate officials often cannot be located, and land records of the Jordanian Government are incomplete because the Jordanian West Bank land survey of the 1960s was stopped by the 1967 war with only 37 percent of the territory surveyed and documented.

The Israeli Government has not made public the extent of land acquired for settlement, but under the principles it is now following, up to two-thirds of the West Bank's territory would theoretically be available for leasing to settlers. In practice, one-third of the West Bank has already been requisitioned, either for settlements or military purposes.

Types of Settlements
[...]
The settlement organizations first present their proposals for new settlements in the West Bank to the World Zionist Organization. WZO-approved proposals are then presented for Israeli Government approval to the Ministerial Committee on Settlements, which gives the official go-ahead.

West Bank settlements range in size from small agricultural communities to large urban centers planned for thousands of inhabitants. About half are Nahal (Fighting Pioneer Youth) outposts or agricultural communities:

• *Civilian agricultural settlements* are usually kibbutzim or moshavim having only a few hundred settlers. In a kibbutz most property is collectively owned and collectively worked on the principle that members should contribute according to their abilities and receive according to their needs. Members share common dining and social facilities. In a moshav, each family works a separate piece of land. The size of the individual plots is governed by the families' ability to work them; hiring outside labor is discouraged. All moshav members buy their agricultural supplies and market their produce jointly. The moshav shitufi is a combination of the moshav and kibbutz; production is cooperative, but income is divided among the individual members.

617

- *Nahal outposts* are paramilitary settlements established by the Nahal Corps of the Israel Defense Forces (IDF). They are founded with the intention of eventually converting to civilian status, though some fail to become viable and are abandoned. Many Nahal outposts are primarily devoted to agriculture.

- *Regional centers* are settlements that function as market towns for four to six smaller agricultural settlements in the surrounding area.

- *Community settlements* and *urban centers* are the largest Jewish settlements and are the type currently being emphasized by the Begin government. Community settlements are generally planned for eventual populations of 1,000 to 1,500. Urban centers are projected to become complete towns with 20,000 or more inhabitants [....] These settlements are located within easy commuting distance of Jerusalem and Tel Aviv and offer low-cost, desirable housing to Israeli families.

They are preferred by the Begin government because they can be built on public land of little or no agricultural value and because they offer the cheapest and most practical way to increase significantly the Jewish population in the West Bank.

Government Projections

[…] By 1986 the government hopes to have 100,000 settlers in the territory, most of them residing in the new community settlements and urban centers. Adding the Jewish population of East Jerusalem to this figure, there could be upwards of 200,000 Israelis living on West Bank territory by 1986.

Much of this goal apparently is achievable, though perhaps not until the late 1980s because of financial constraints and the limited pool of potential settlers. […] To date, young, middle class Israelis looking for inexpensive housing have shown considerable enthusiasm for the West Bank communities, particularly the Jerusalem suburbs and the new settlements located on the border close to Tel Aviv. The Israeli Government is busy building the infrastructure to handle a significant increase in the territory's population. It is likely that the Jewish population of the West Bank—excluding Jerusalem—will double, if not triple, by the end of the decade.

Tel Aviv hopes that most of the funding for these settlements will come from private sources because it does not have the financial resources for the current, accelerated settlement development. Much of the financing for settlements has been provided by Zionist organizations, and private companies are now heavily involved in developing the new satellite communities. […]

The boundary between Israel and the West Bank has virtually disappeared. There are no border checkpoints and few signs that one is entering occupied territory. Increasingly, Jewish settlements in the West Bank are treated as part of Israel proper. Although land for the settlements is technically only leased from the military government, Tel Aviv has reserved the right to claim sovereignty over the territory in any future negotiations.

Under international law the military government is supposed to exercise authority over all of the occupied territory, but in practice six Jewish regional councils and five local (urban) councils control most of the West Bank lands requisitioned for settlement. These councils answer to the Israeli Ministry of the Interior and not to the military government. Israelis living in the West Bank have their own municipal courts, which are part of the Israeli judicial system. They vote in their own districts in national elections instead of through absentee ballots.

[...]

Security Value of Settlements

One of the primary justifications for building settlements in the West Bank—at least initially— was that their inhabitants would help to detect and delay a possible attack from Jordan. This rationale is still occasionally cited, but several senior Israeli military officers have noted that the settlements would actually be a liability in a conventional conflict because, as happened in the Golan Heights in 1973, the IDF would be diverted to rescuing these civilians at the start of the war. By establishing settlements in the West Bank the Israelis have reduced the area's value as a buffer zone; the settlements themselves are now potential targets within range of the Jordan border.

West Bank settlements possess only rudimentary defenses, designed to defend against isolated terrorist attacks or to delay a larger attacking force until help arrives from the IDF. Most settlement sites are selected on the basis of economic, religious, or land availability considerations and not because of their tactical significance.

[...]

Treatment of Settlements as Inseparable from Israel (2023)

U.N. COMMITTEE ON THE EXERCISE OF THE INALIENABLE RIGHTS OF THE PALESTINIAN PEOPLE

A number of elaborate unofficial master plans for the settlement of the West Bank, including East Jerusalem, underpinned successive Israeli government decisions to construct and expand settlements since 1967—acts of settlement which have continued for over half a century. In 2012, an Independent International Fact-Finding Mission to investigate the implications of the Israeli settlements noted that:

> [d]espite these plans not having been officially approved they have largely been acted upon by successive Israeli Governments. The Mission notes a pattern where plans that were developed regarding the settlements were mirrored in Government policy instruments and implemented on the ground.

These plans include the Allon Plan (1967) drafted by Israeli Defence Minister Yigal Allon, which saw the settlement of Ma'ale Adumim between 1975 and June 1979 under the Labour government. The aim, as outlined by Allon, was to secure the "maximum security and maximum territory for Israel with a minimum number of Arabs". Settlement continued with the establishment of the Inter-Ministerial Committee to Examine the Rate of Development for Jerusalem in 1973, which provided for an outer ring of settlements around Jerusalem, including Mishor Adumim, developed by the Jerusalem Municipality. In 1976, Prime Minister Rabin unofficially approved the Wachman Plan (1976), which provided a template for the construction of settlements in sparsely populated areas strategically encircling the major Palestinian population centres around the West Bank. Following the Likud election in 1977, Ariel Sharon become Chairman of the Inter-Ministerial Settlement Committee, and under the Sharon-Wachman Plan (1977) he proposed "urban, industrial settlements on the ridges" and strategically placed settlements in belts to fragment the Palestinian territory. However, it was the Drobles Plan (1977) that became the Likud government's blueprint for settlement in the 1980s. The plan aimed to connect all existing settlements into one network while breaking Palestinian territorial contiguity. This provided "settlements with immediate territorial unity and overall contiguity with Israel's coastal plain". By 1979, some 43 settlements had been established and 10,000 settlers transferred into the West Bank.

Under the Gush-Drobles (1978) and Sharon (1981) plans, then–Minister of Defence Ariel Sharon advanced the plans for settlement construction along the central mountain ridge and the Green Line, while leaving pockets of densely populated Palestinian centres under Palestinian control. This saw the establishment of a corridor of 10 settlements along the mountain ridge in the West Bank and north of Jerusalem. The Hundred Thousand Plan (1983), published by Israel's Ministry of Agriculture, prepared the way for a total of 100,000 settlers to live in 43 new Israeli settlements, with settlement construction plans forecast up to the year 2010. Guidelines presented by Prime Minister Yitzhak Shamir to the Knesset mirrored provisions of the Hundred Thousand Plan. In 1991, Sharon, now serving as Minister of Construction and Housing, developed the Seven Stars Plan (1991), constructing a new industrialized belt of settlement towns and connecting settlement blocs in outer Jerusalem to settlement blocs in other parts of the West Bank. In 1996 Prime Minister Netanyahu's guidelines for government, similarly, focused squarely on settlement expansion beyond the Green Line. The policy dictated that "[s]ettlement in the Negev, the Galilee, the Golan Heights, the Jordan Valley, and in Judea, Samaria [West Bank] and Gaza is of national importance, to Israel's defense and an expression of Zionist fulfilment".

By 1999, at the end of Prime Minister Netanyahu's first term in office, more than 50 new settlement outposts had been established. Settlement construction continued apace, greenlighted by Prime Minister Ehud Barak's "settlement guidelines" in the years 1999 to 2001, continued under Prime Minister Ariel Sharon's government from 2001 to 2003, and again during Sharon's second term from 2003 to 2006. At the same time, a number of Jerusalem master plans including the *Jerusalem 2000,* and the *Jerusalem 2020 Master Plan* (2004) sought to consolidate Israeli Jewish presence in occupied Jerusalem and radically alter the demographic of the City. The Jerusalem 5800 Master Plan lays out plans for a Greater Jerusalem Metropolitan – an area engulfing major Palestinian cities Bethlehem, Jericho and Ramallah. The plan proposes a new international airport for Jericho, and the connection of settlement roads and rail infrastructure to ferry incoming tourists to developed tourist settlements across the West Bank as the planned mainstay of the Israeli economy. Moreover, the Atarot settlement will be expanded and developed as the main industry hub for Israel.

The first six months of 2023 saw Israel advance record rates of settlement housing units. In April 2023, the incoming Israeli government approved six master plans for settlement construction in the West Bank, including for the establishment of two new settlements. Israel advanced plans for 16,000 settlement units in occupied East Jerusalem and 13,000 settlement units in the West Bank. Only six months into 2023, this total of almost 30,000 proposed new housing units in the Israeli settlements in occupied Palestine is already an annual record for the approval of settlement housing units. [...]

Resolution 465 – Territories Occupied by Israel (1980)
UNITED NATIONS SECURITY COUNCIL

Affirming once more that the Geneva Convention relative to the Protection of Civilian Persons in Time of War, of 12 August 1949, is applicable to the Arab territories occupied by Israel since 1967, including Jerusalem,

Deploring the decision of the Government of Israel officially to support Israeli settlements in the Palestinian and other Arab territories occupied since 1967,

Deeply concerned by the practices of the Israeli authorities in implementing that settlements policy in the occupied Arab territories, including Jerusalem. and its consequences for the local Arab and Palestinian population,

Taking into account the need to consider measures for the impartial protection of private and public land and property, and water resources,
[…]

5. *Determines* that all measures taken by Israel to change the physical character, demographic composition. institutional structure or status of the Palestinian and other Arab territories occupied since 1967, including Jerusalem, or any part thereof have no legal validity and that Israel's policy and practices of settling parts of its population and new immigrants in those territories constitute a flagrant violation of the Geneva Convention relative to the Protection of Civilian Persons in Time of War and also constitute a serious obstruction to achieving a comprehensive, just and lasting peace in the Middle East;

6. *Strongly deplores* the continuation and persistence of Israel in pursuing those policies and practices and calls upon the Government and people of Israel to rescind those measures, to dismantle the existing settlements and in particular to cease, on an urgent basis, the establishment, construction and planning of settlements in the Arab territories occupied since 1967, including Jerusalem;

7. *Calls upon* all States not to provide Israel with any assistance to be used specifically in connexion with settlements in the occupied territories;

8. *Requests* the Commission to continue to examine the situation relating to settlements in the Arab territories occupied since 1967, including Jerusalem, to investigate the reported serious depletion of natural resources, particularly the water resources, with a view to ensuring the protection of those important natural resources of the territories under occupation, and to keep under close scrutiny the implementation of the present resolution;
[…]

622

Address Concerning the Middle East Peace Process (2004)
George W. Bush

The Palestinian people must insist on change and on a leadership that is committed to reform and progress and peace. We will help. But the most difficult work is theirs. The United States is strongly committed, and I am strongly committed, to the security of Israel as a vibrant Jewish state. I reiterate our steadfast commitment to Israel's security and to preserving and strengthening Israel's self-defense capability, including its right to defend itself against terror.

The barrier being erected by Israel as a part of that security effort should, as your government has stated, be a security, rather than political, barrier. It should be temporary rather than permanent, and, therefore, not prejudice any final status issues, including final borders. And its route should take into account, consistent with security needs, its impact on Palestinians not engaged in terrorist activities.

In an exchange of letters today and in a statement I will release later today, I'm repeating to the Prime Minister my commitment to Israel's security. The United States will not prejudice the outcome of final status negotiations. That matter is for the parties. But the realities on the ground and in the region have changed greatly over the last several decades, and any final settlement must take into account those realities and be agreeable to the parties.

The goal of two independent states has repeatedly been recognized in international resolutions and agreements, and it remains the key to resolving this conflict. The United States is strongly committed to Israel's security and well being as a Jewish state. It seems clear that an agreed, just, fair and realistic framework for a solution to the Palestinian refugee issue, as part of any final status agreement, will need to be found through the establishment of a Palestinian state and the settling of Palestinian refugees there, rather than Israel.

As part of a final peace settlement, Israel must have secure and recognized borders which should emerge from negotiations between the parties, in accordance with U.N. Security Council Resolutions 242 and 338. In light of new realities on the ground, including already existing major Israeli population centers, it is unrealistic to expect that the outcome of final status negotiations will be a full and complete return to the armistice lines of 1949. And all previous efforts to negotiate a two-state solution have reached the same conclusion. It is realistic to expect that any final status agreement will only be achieved on the basis of mutually agreed changes that reflect these realities.

[...]

The Rise of Settler Terrorism (2012)
Daniel Byman and Natan Sachs

Late this past June, a group of Israeli settlers in the West Bank defaced and burned a mosque in the small West Bank village of Jabaa. Graffiti sprayed by the vandals warned of a "war" over the planned evacuation, ordered by the Israeli Supreme Court, of a handful of houses illegally built on private Palestinian land near the Israeli settlement of Beit El. The torching of the mosque was the fourth such attack in 18 months and part of a wider trend of routine violence committed by radical settlers against innocent Palestinians, Israeli security personnel, and mainstream settler leaders -- all aimed at intimidating perceived enemies of the settlement project.

[…] [I]n recent years, the settler movement has experienced a profound breakdown in discipline, with extremists now beyond the reach of either Israeli law enforcement or the discipline of settler leaders.

[…] Yet just as radical settlers pose an increasing threat, mainstream Israeli society has become more apathetic than ever about the fate of the Palestinians. Negotiations between Israel and the Palestinians remain deadlocked, and even their meaningful resumption, let alone success, seems unlikely in the near future. The Israeli government thus feels little political or diplomatic pressure to confront the extremists.

But with the peace process frozen, what happens under Israeli control matters more, not less. With Israel likely to govern parts of the West Bank for some time, it can no longer shirk its obligations -- to protect not only its own citizens but Palestinian civilians as well -- by claiming that a two-state solution is on the horizon and that the Palestinians will soon assume full responsibility over themselves. And if Israel wants to preserve the possibility of a negotiated peace, it must address this problem before it is too late. Whenever extremist settlers destroy Palestinian property or deface a mosque, they strengthen Palestinian radicals at the expense of moderates, undermining support for an agreement and delaying a possible accord. Meanwhile, each time Israeli leaders cave in to the demands of radical settlers, it vindicates their tactics and encourages ever more brazen behavior, deepening the government's paralysis. In other words, Israeli violence in the West Bank both undermines the ability of Israel to implement a potential deal with the Palestinians and raises questions about whether it can enforce its own laws at home.

Recently, Israeli leaders have begun to recognize the problem. Following extremist vandalism against the IDF and mainstream settler leaders over the past year, some Israeli generals and government ministers began to label radical settlers as terrorists. […]

THE WILD WEST BANK

[...] According to UN investigations, in 2011, extremist settlers launched almost 300 attacks on Palestinian property, causing over 100 Palestinian casualties and destroying or damaging about 10,000 trees of Palestinian farmers. The UN has also reported that violent incidents against Palestinians have proliferated, rising from 200 attacks in 2009 to over 400 in 2011. The spike in assaults on Palestinians by settlers has come despite the fact that over the same period, Palestinian terrorism fell dramatically.

[...] Yet "terrorism" is defined not only by the act itself but also by its purpose: to produce a psychological effect, terror, as a means of advancing a political agenda. This definition fits the aim of extremist settlers, who often scrawl the Hebrew words for "price tag" at the scene of the crime -- a message to their targets that they will exact a price for any act that they oppose. Such attacks target innocent Palestinians in response to and as a deterrent against Palestinian terrorism and target Palestinians, pro-peace Israelis, and Israeli soldiers alike for supposedly anti-settlement measures taken by the Israeli government. By seeking to frighten a rival population and intimidate a government, the extremists mimic the typical methods of terrorist groups across the globe.

The Israeli government does not support or condone settler violence, but it has failed to adequately combat it. Soldiers have been known to look on as violence occurs, and they sometimes do not aggressively seek the perpetrators after the fact. According to Yesh Din, an Israeli human rights organization, of 781 incidents of settler abuse monitored since 2005, Israeli authorities closed the cases on over 90 percent of them without indictment. And the Israeli newspaper *Haaretz* has reported that the IDF is currently probing 15 cases, all of which took place between September 2000 and December 2011, of Israeli soldiers witnessing clashes between settlers and Palestinians and failing to intervene.

Israel's halfhearted response to settler violence is partly a result of the fundamental anomalies of military rule. Unlike East Jerusalem or the Golan Heights, other territories that Israel conquered in the 1967 war, the West Bank was never annexed by Israel, and Israel applies civil law there only to Israeli citizens. Although the Israeli police have authority over criminal matters among settlers, the military governs most aspects of public life, from security to construction permits. The Palestinian Authority assumed sovereignty over parts of the West Bank following the Oslo accords, but Israel still controls "Area C," which includes all the settlements, four percent of the Palestinian population, and 60 percent of the total land. Within that territory, the IDF faces the extremely difficult task of safeguarding both Israelis and Palestinians. Israeli security forces may have helped drastically reduce Palestinian terrorism, but the military

625

unsurprisingly remains wary of Hamas and other militant organizations and views the defense of Israeli citizens as its main task.

The IDF also faces little pressure from the Israeli public to protect the Palestinians under its rule. Although Israelis cared deeply about the peace process during the Oslo years, suicide bombings, the collapse of the negotiations in 2000, and the carnage of the second intifada that followed left them reeling, indignant, and wary of Palestinian intentions. In the eyes of most Israelis, Palestinian leaders not only failed to negotiate in good faith but also responded to Israeli good faith with a wave of terrorism. Although most Israelis support an agreement in principle and question the wisdom of the settlements, they blame the Palestinians for the continuation of the conflict and remain skeptical about the odds for a deal in the near future. With violence down and peace distant, Israelis have become indifferent to the situation in the West Bank and weary of the Palestinian issue in general, preferring to contain and, if possible, ignore the problem. With the peace camp all but dead and a conservative government in power, right-wing politicians exert a great deal of influence on Israeli policy, particularly regarding the settlements. In recent years, the extreme right wing has made inroads even into Prime Minister Benjamin Netanyahu's own party, the Likud, making any opposition to settlement activity a risk for more mainstream Likud politicians.

When it comes to confronting extremist settlers, then, the Israeli government is politically handicapped. Radical settlers understand why Israel has responded so tepidly to their actions and have sought to exploit this reluctance. And their violence has often successfully altered or deterred government actions that they opposed.

SETTLEMENT OVER STATE

The rise in violence among extremist settlers stems from deep changes in the settler population, particularly its dramatic growth and shifting ideological composition. Israeli civilians began moving into the West Bank and Gaza shortly after the 1967 war, when Israel conquered both territories. Some Jews sought to return to Jewish villages destroyed by Arab armies in the war of 1948, and a few hoped to reestablish a Jewish presence near holy sites such as Hebron, which both Jewish and Muslim tradition hold is the burial place of the patriarch Abraham. The Israeli government also sought to create several small settlements for security reasons: to establish "facts on the ground" that might allow Israel to keep several strategic points in the West Bank as part of a peace accord and might even, some argued, help Israel defend itself against an Arab invasion. In the early 1980s, the settler community was still a relatively small, coherent, and disciplined society of about 24,000. Some settlers were secular, but others subscribed to the ideology of Gush Emunim (Bloc of the Faithful), a religious-political movement that sought to fulfill what it viewed as a divine obligation to settle the complete *Eretz Yisrael* (Land of Israel), the territory Jews regard as having been promised to them by God, which includes the West Bank.

Although Gush Emunim strongly opposed any government policy that curtailed the settlement project, it respected the primacy of the state. For example, in the early 1980s, when the Israeli government evacuated all settlements in the Sinai as part of the peace treaty with Egypt, Gush Emunim protested but did not call on its members to take up arms (although several of its members went on to form the Jewish Underground anyway). For religious-nationalist settlers, the state remained an instrument of providence, carrying out God's mission by upholding Jewish sovereignty and protecting Jewish religious life in the Land of Israel. Adherents of Gush Emunim believed that salvation itself would emerge from the state and thus did not challenge its political authority. The IDF and settler leaders maintained close contact and coordination, with the military relying on the settler leadership to police its own while it focused on preventing Palestinian terrorism.

Since then, the settler movement has changed dramatically. In the past three decades, the number of settlers in the West Bank has grown more than tenfold, to some 300,000. Today, most live in large communities that function as suburbs of Jerusalem or greater Tel Aviv. The inhabitants of these settlements represent all walks of Israeli society, including secular and ultra-Orthodox Jews who do not share the nationalist zeal of Gush Emunim. Many of these Israelis moved to the West Bank primarily for economic, rather than political, reasons: the settlements are subsidized by the government, so living in them is much more affordable than living in cities inside the Green Line. Most policymakers in Israel and the United States do not consider these particular settlements to be insurmountable obstacles to a peace agreement with the Palestinians. In the past, Palestinian leaders have suggested that they might accept land swaps that would allow Israel to keep some of these settlement blocs in exchange for other territory, and many of these settlers would likely consider accepting compensation if they were told to leave their homes in the context of a peace agreement.

Yet over the last several years, the evolution of the settler community has also led to the growth of a small but significant fringe of young extremists, known as the "hilltop youth," who show little, if any, deference to the Israeli government or even to the settler leadership. No matter how strongly Gush Emunim opposed government policy, it always officially avoided vigilante violence. But these young radicals, who largely live in settlements deep in the West Bank and do not affiliate with traditional religious authorities, have embraced it. These settlers -- likely no more than a couple thousand, a small but dangerous minority within the broader community -- are the ones leading the "price tag" attacks against

Palestinian civilians and Israeli soldiers. They have lost faith in the notion that the state, under its current leadership, is key to settling the Land of Israel. Instead, they see it as an obstacle to God's will.

Although the Israeli military has traditionally worked closely with the heads of the settlements to maintain security, this new generation of radicals scoffs at such cooperation, viewing the settler leadership as complicit in the government's crimes. As a result, the settler establishment has little control over the most problematic members of its community. Indeed, extremists have targeted some of the most central figures of the settler movement, including Ze'ev Hever, who heads the construction arm of the settlement enterprise. Hever, once a member of the Jewish Underground, is the person perhaps most responsible for the settlement expansion that has occurred in collaboration with the Israeli government. [...]

This new generation of extremists came out of the trauma of Israel's 2005 withdrawal from the Gaza Strip, known by the settlers as "the expulsion." In late 2003, Israeli Prime Minister Ariel Sharon, once a champion of the settler movement, announced that he planned to dismantle the Israeli settlements in Gaza. Sharon's transformation rocked the settlers. Feeling abandoned, many began to question the authority of the state. Whereas settler leaders could once portray previous actions against various outposts or individuals as tactical maneuvers, they understood that Sharon's "disengagement," as it became known in Israel, represented a fundamental break with their religious mission.

Even so, settler elders and their allies upheld the sanctity of the state and opted for largely nonviolent opposition. They embarked on a public relations campaign, portraying themselves as an oppressed minority and borrowing the color orange from the 2004 Ukrainian revolution to reinforce their image as a peaceful civil movement. Even as it became clear that the settlers' challenge to the disengagement would not succeed, most settler leaders called on Jews in Gaza to avoid violence against Israeli soldiers and refrained from urging soldiers, including settlers in military service, to disobey the evacuation orders. Opposition to the withdrawal, in other words, remained within the bounds of Israeli political discourse and preserved the settler movement's deference to the state.

As the disengagement approached, however, a segment of more radical settlers began speaking out against their leaders' acquiescence. Some rabbis even suggested that divine intervention would prevent the withdrawal at the last minute. But in the summer of 2005, Israel did pull all the settlers, some 8,600 people, out of Gaza and ended its military presence there. The Israeli military forcefully removed families from their homes, demolished villages, and transferred entire communities -- homes, synagogues, cemeteries, and schools -- to Israel proper. Neither the nonviolent

628

resistance of the settler establishment nor divine intervention stayed the government's hand. Radical settlers saw the expulsion as a manifest failure of the old guard's approach. Not only was the state of Israel no longer a vehicle of redemption; it had actively rolled back the most important project of contemporary Jewish religious nationalism: settling the Land of Israel. The settlers felt doubly betrayed by the sense that the government failed to reintegrate them properly into Israel, devoting inadequate resources to their relocation and, in their eyes, essentially neglecting them after the withdrawal ended.

Faced with what the radical settlers saw as a choice between the state and the settlements, they picked the latter. To stave off another disengagement of any kind, they resolved to retaliate against any attempt by the Israeli government to crack down on the movement -- hence the birth of the "price tag" attacks. In this climate, the traditional leadership of the settler movement and the authority of the Israeli government are less relevant than ever.

RADICAL SUCCESS

Settler violence is undoubtedly working. It has made it more difficult for the IDF to govern the West Bank and fractured the settler movement, weakening the influence of the more moderate elements that would accept the legitimacy of the Israeli state even if it committed to another withdrawal. The "price tag" doctrine has thus raised the cost of even token settlement removals. The violence has conditioned Israeli politicians to worry that any pullout, whether as part of a peace agreement or as a unilateral measure, will lead to conflict. That puts the government in a bind. If it ignores the radicals, they will undermine its authority and any Palestinian goodwill that might result from a withdrawal. Confronting them, however, risks public spectacles of armed police dragging conservatively dressed young girls out of their homes, a political disaster for any Israeli government.

The first post-Gaza pullout, the dismantlement of the outpost of Amona in 2006, justified such fears among Israeli politicians. During the demolition of nine uninhabited homes built on land determined to belong to Palestinians, thousands of settlers confronted Israeli security personnel, occupying the homes and nearby areas and attacking the officers with rocks, bottles, and cinder blocks. The riot left 200 people injured, including 80 security officers and two Israeli members of the Knesset [...] who had come to support the settlers.

Although the mission technically succeeded, the violence surrounding it strengthened the perception that any withdrawal, no matter how small, risks opening up deep fissures within Israeli society. The incident left

Israeli leaders wary of future evacuations and eager to retroactively legalize the remaining outposts in the West Bank. In fact, this past June, after the Israeli Supreme Court ordered the government to dismantle several outposts built on private Palestinian land, the Knesset debated a bill that would have circumvented the court and legalized several houses there, a move with profound legal ramifications. Only the direct intervention of Netanyahu killed the bill. In response, demonstrators in Jerusalem burned public property and extremists vandalized the mixed Arab-Jewish village of Neve Shalom, in Israel, with graffiti saying "Death to Arabs."

Besides undermining the rule of law and intimidating Israeli politicians, radical settlers have increasingly come to define the way that Palestinians see Israelis as a whole. After Israel took control of the West Bank and Gaza in 1967, the two communities interacted regularly. Israelis shopped in the West Bank, and hundreds of thousands of Palestinians worked in Israel. But the second intifada stopped Israelis from casually entering Palestinian areas, and in response to Palestinian terrorism, Israel enacted policies that made it harder for Palestinians to work inside the country, culminating in the construction of the security barrier. Today, essentially the only Israelis that Palestinians interact with are soldiers and settlers, whom they see as representative of all Israelis. This means that relations among settlers, Israeli soldiers, and Palestinian civilians are now more important than ever.

By making life miserable for their Palestinian neighbors, the radical settlers strengthen those they most fear: Palestinian terrorists. Hamas portrays itself as a resistance organization that defends the Palestinian people, and it uses the most extreme attacks on Palestinians, such as the 1994 massacre of 29 Palestinian Muslim worshipers in Hebron by Baruch Goldstein, to justify its own terrorism as self-defense. Of course, these claims are a sham: groups such as Hamas would try to kill Israelis in any event. But settler attacks do make Hamas' propaganda more credible among the Palestinian public.

Settler radicalism also discredits those Palestinians who oppose terrorism, such as President Mahmoud Abbas and Prime Minister Salam Fayyad. Their inability to get Israel to stop its own citizens from attacking Palestinians makes them appear feeble and undermines the notion that they can negotiate a fair treaty with Israel. The situation recalls the bitterness Israelis felt when dealing with former Palestinian leader Yasir Arafat as Palestinian suicide bombings continued: either he could stop the violence and chose not to or he was unable to end it, in which case there was little reason to talk. As settler violence increases, the Palestinians will begin to say the same about Israel's leadership.
[...]

Resolution 2334 – Condemning Israeli Settlements (2016)

The Security Council,

[…]

Condemning all measures aimed at altering the demographic composition, character and status of the Palestinian Territory occupied since 1967, including East Jerusalem, including, *inter alia*, the construction and expansion of settlements, transfer of Israeli settlers, confiscation of land, demolition of homes and displacement of Palestinian civilians, in violation of international humanitarian law and relevant resolutions,

Expressing grave concern that continuing Israeli settlement activities are dangerously imperiling the viability of the two-State solution based on the 1967 lines,

[…]

Reiterating its vision of a region where two democratic States, Israel and Palestine, live side by side in peace within secure and recognized borders,

Stressing that the status quo is not sustainable and that significant steps, consistent with the transition contemplated by prior agreements, are urgently needed in order to (i) stabilize the situation and to reverse negative trends on the ground, which are steadily eroding the two-State solution and entrenching a one-State reality, and (ii) to create the conditions for successful final status negotiations and for advancing the two-State solution through those negotiations and on the ground,

1) *Reaffirms* that the establishment by Israel of settlements in the Palestinian territory occupied since 1967, including East Jerusalem, has no legal validity and constitutes a flagrant violation under international law and a major obstacle to the achievement of the two-State solution and a just, lasting and comprehensive peace;

2) *Reiterates* its demand that Israel immediately and completely cease all settlement activities in the occupied Palestinian territory, including East Jerusalem, and that it fully respect all of its legal obligations in this regard;

3) *Underlines* that it will not recognize any changes to the 4 June 1967 lines, including with regard to Jerusalem, other than those agreed by the parties through negotiations;

4) *Stresses* that the cessation of all Israeli settlement activities is essential for salvaging the two-State solution, and calls for affirmative steps to be taken immediately to reverse the negative trends on the ground that are imperilling the two-State solution;

[…]

Israeli Settlement Policies in the Occupied Arab Territories (1980)
Kasuka Mutukwa

"Contrary to Israel's allegation that the Jewish settlements (in occupied territories) constituted a private activity on the part of Israeli citizens, it was clear, from the many official statements on the matter, that it was in fact the policy of the Government. Its aims were the Judaization of Palestine through the annexation of (Arab) lands, the expulsion of the Palestinians, and the containment and isolation of the remaining Palestinian agglomerations."

This quotation documents, in summary form, the underpinnings of Israeli settlement policies in the Occupied Arab territories which have the effect of changing the political and legal status, the demographic composition as well as the geographic nature of the region. This problem has led to a serious crisis in international relations. The fundamental thrust of that policy, which is Government policy, is the colonization of Arab territories which Israel has occupied by force. Yet the acquisition of territory by force is inadmissible in international law and the Geneve Conventions on the protection of civilians and property in war situations.

"Settlements" are a euphemism for twentieth century colonies. The "settlers" are colonists. Taken as a whole, the phenomena of Israeli settlements in Occupied Arab Territories represent a case of colonialism. [...]

The June 1967 Arab-Israeli war was a watershed in Israeli expansionism by force. During that war the Israeli military forces proceeded to occupy the remaining territory of what was mandated Palestine (including East Jerusalem) as well as the Sinai region of Egypt and the Golan Heights of the Syrian Arab Republic. After "conquest", military rule was imposed as Israel sought to consolidate its colonization by annexation. By annexation, we mean an illegal act by which a state asserts its sovereignty over a territory previously outside its Jurisdiction.

The war had serious implications for the land and people in Palestine. In this cut-throat zero sum game, what the Israelis gained, the Arabs lost. Indeed, the masterplan of the Zionist Movement for the establishment of a Greater Israel was fulfilled.

Prior to the 1967 war, of the estimated total population of 2.7 million Palestinians, about 300,000 lived in Israeli territory, one million in the West Bank and 400,000 in Gaza. About half a million Palestinians left their homes during the war, and 1.2 million remained under Israel control. The remaining 1.5 million Palestinians were forced to become refugees, many for the second time, having first fled in the war of 1948.

632 From The First United Nations Seminar on the Question of Palestine: The Inalienable Rights of the Palestinian People. Arusha, Tanzania.

Having occupied Arab territories the Israelis embarked on a systematic and relentless process of dispossessing the Palestinians of their land and other properties. The illegality and coercive methods by which the Israeli authorities expropriated Arab lands, both private and public, for locating settlements is no longer in dispute. Several studies, including in particular, the Report of the Security Council Commission established under resolution 446 (1977) have concluded accordingly:

> "On the basis of the information received, the Commission is convinced that a number of settlements were on privately owned land and not only on public land."

The process of acquiring land for use by Israel in the Occupied Territories is by-and-large based on seizure and confiscation. In Israeli thinking, since the occupied terrorists are its colonies it is assumed that arbitrary measures to confiscate land is a matter of policy. Spokesman of the Government including the Prime Minister have stated publicly that "Israel would never return to the pre-June 1967 frontiers".

Typical in most colonization cases, the process of establishing settlements of colonies in form of migrants from the metropolitan countries follows occupation. In the case of Israel however, one should hasten to point out that Jews from all over the world have been lured to settle in occupied Arab territories. […]

The need to maintain Israel's security has been cited as the rationale for its settlements policy. An appraisal of the policy and its implementation proves to the contrary. First and foremost, it has been demonstrated that the settlements policy is not a haphazard venture rather it is an outgrowth of a careful masterplan with its origins in the Zionist organizations. What was required in the implementation therefore was the opportunity to do so. It is not the occupation of Arab lands which created conditions for the settlements policy.
[…]
It is equally instructive to note that, Israel has had as its priority, the establishment of settlements in the most fertile and/or water endowed zones of the Occupied Arab Territories. Statistics show that about 30 percent of Israel's water supplies come from the occupied territories. The Golan Heights of Syria and the Jordan River Valley are but a few examples of the more fertile regions which are fully exploited by the settlers. […]

Settlements and the Denial of the Palestinian Right to Self-Determination (2023)
U.N. COMMITTEE ON THE EXERCISE OF THE INALIENABLE RIGHTS OF THE PALESTINIAN PEOPLE

Geographically, the territorial components of occupied Palestine—the West Bank, including Jerusalem, and the Gaza Strip—have been fragmented and segregated administratively from each other. Israel exercises full civil and military control over Area C, an area comprising 61 per cent of the West Bank. Area C surrounds and fragments densely populated Palestinian cities and towns into an archipelago of disconnected islands, systematically cutting them off from each other. Israel further entrenches fragmentation by constructing segregating infrastructure such as the Wall, settlements and "bypass roads connecting the settlements to each other and to the Israeli transportation system", and by restricting Palestinian access physically and administratively via "roadblocks, exclusive zoning laws, restricted areas and military no-go zones". Concomitantly, Israel's zoning of Palestinian immoveable property for residential, agricultural, industrial and tourist settlements; nature and archaeological reserves; and military firing zones has seen the appropriation of over 100,000 hectares of private and public Palestinian land and the demolition of over 50,000 Palestinian homes since 1967. Across occupied Palestine, Israel has granted leases and licences for the exploitation of Palestinian quarries, Dead Sea minerals, oil, gas and water resources, acts which may amount to acts of pillage in breach of [...] the Hague Regulations (1907) and [...] the Fourth Geneva Convention (1949).

Israel administers the West Bank (not including East Jerusalem) under military rule, and separately administers Palestinians in occupied East Jerusalem as "permanent residents" (a temporary and revocable status) in territory it has effectively annexed in contravention of international law. Meanwhile, the Gaza Strip is treated as a "hostile entity" where over two million Palestinians, denied their freedom of movement, have been held since 2007 under a military siege and closure of land, sea and air. The economic loss to the Gaza Strip alone between 2007 and 2018 from the continued military closure amounts to $16.7 billion, which has brought the Gaza Strip to the brink of economic collapse. Crucially, Security Council resolution 1860 (2009) stresses "that the Gaza Strip constitutes an integral part of the territory occupied in 1967 and will be a part of the Palestinian state".

Israel's alteration of facts on the ground and erasure of the Palestinian presence are carried out to compromise Palestine's viability as an independent State. For example, Israeli military orders prevent Palestinian symbols from being displayed, in a repression of Palestinian identity. In this vein, Military Order 101 dictates that Palestinians in the occupied

634 From Study: The Legality of the Israeli Occupation of the Occupied Palestinian Territories, Including East Jerusalem. © United Nations. Reprinted with permission.

territory may not "hold, wave, display or affix flags or political symbols, except in accordance with a permit of the military commander". Likewise, Palestinian presence in the occupied territory is gradually eroded as Israel renames Palestinian villages and roads into Hebrew. Further, the Budgets Foundations Law (Amendment No. 40) authorizes Israel's Minister of Finance to reduce public funding to institutions that fail to commemorate "Israel's Independence Day or the day on which the state was established as a day of mourning" and to those institutions that reject "the existence of Israel as a Jewish and democratic state". This essentially aims at defunding Palestinian institutions in Israel and occupied Jerusalem. Meanwhile, Israel's repeated attacks on the sacred Al-Aqsa Mosque, its facilitation of settler access into the Al-Aqsa compound, and its deliberate restrictions on Holy Easter Sunday ceremonies at the Church of the Holy Sepulchre underscore its targeted erasure of Palestinian Muslim and Christian presence from the City.

Since 1967, Israel, through its laws, policies and practices, has radically altered the demography of occupied Palestine, forcibly displacing the protected population, both directly—through house demolitions, residency revocations, and deportations—and indirectly, through the imposition of coercive measures to force transfer. Since 2009, the demolition of 9,509 structures in the West Bank has resulted in the displacement of 13,739 Palestinians. Under the 2004 Jerusalem Local Outline Plan 2000, Israel aimed to achieve a "demographic balance" of 70 per cent Jews and 30 per cent "Arabs" in Jerusalem by the year 2020. Towards this end, since 1997, Israel has revoked the residencies of 14,643 Palestinians, forcing their transfer from Jerusalem. At the same time, Israel systematically denies the right of Palestinian refugees to return to their homes under its Entry into Israel Law (1952) and Law of Return (1950) in addition to restricting entry to foreigners, including for reasons of family unification, under its Entry Procedure (2022). Today, some seven million Palestinian refugees are denied their right of return, including 450,000 Palestinians displaced as refugees during the Naksa arising from the 1967 Six Day War. Accordingly, in 2013, a United Nations Fact-Finding Mission concluded that:

> the right to self-determination of the Palestinian people, including the right to determine how to implement self-determination, the right to have a demographic and territorial presence in the Occupied Palestinian Territory and the right to permanent sovereignty over natural resources, is clearly being violated by Israel through the existence and ongoing expansion of the settlements.

At the same time, Israel interferes with Palestinian democratic processes, closing the PLO headquarters in Jerusalem, arresting Palestinian parliamentarians, and launching military attacks on Palestinian Legislative

Council buildings and Palestinian cultural properties, including the raid, closure and pillage of archives from Orient House in Jerusalem, which was the former PLO headquarters and the potential seat of the capital of an independent Palestinian State. In the meantime, Israel amended its Entry into Israel law to apply a penalty of revocation of Jerusalem residencies for "breach of allegiance [to Israel]", a provision which Israel has applied to Palestinian parliamentarians elected to the Palestinian Legislative Council. [...] In May 2022, the United Nations Commission of Inquiry reported on the continuation of Israel's systematic control over the Palestinian democratic process, including the detention of elected political representatives and members of the Government, the collective punishment of the Palestinian population for the democratic election of Hamas in 2006, and the military attacks on the Palestinian Legislative Council buildings in Gaza in 2009. The Commission of Inquiry concluded that "the cumulative impact of those policies and actions made prospects for political and economic integration between Gaza and the West Bank more remote". Likewise, Israel's systematic repression of civil and political rights across occupied Palestine, including the lethal suppression of demonstrations, the designation of Palestinian human rights organizations as "terror" organizations, mass arrests and raids, and its arbitrary regime of administrative detentions, ensures that the Palestinian people are systematically prevented from mobilizing to exercise collectively their right to self-determination.
[...]

Myth

Israeli settlements are illegal.

FACT

On November 18, 2019, Secretary of State Michael Pompeo expressed
the Trump administration's position that "the establishment
of Israeli civilian settlements in the West Bank is not per se inconsistent
with international law." […]

The idea that these Jewish communities are illegal derives primarily
from UN resolutions and the International Court of Justice (ICJ), an arm of
the UN. The UN does not make legal determinations, only political ones
tainted by the overwhelming anti-Israel majority. The ICJ "does not have
jurisdiction over all disputes between UN member-states," according to the
Congressional Research Service. In fact, "with the exception of 'advisory
opinions,' which are non-binding, the ICJ may only resolve legal disputes
between nations that voluntarily agreed to its jurisdiction."
[…]
Israel does not recognize the court's jurisdiction on the settlement issue.
Like other democracies, Israel has an independent judiciary. As Pompeo
noted, its Supreme Court has "confirmed the legality of certain settlement
activities and has concluded that others cannot be legally sustained."

Legal scholars dispute the ICJ opinion that the settlements violate
international law. Stephen Schwebel, formerly president of the ICJ, notes
that a country acting in self-defense may seize and occupy territory when
necessary to protect itself. Schwebel also observes that a state may require
security measures to ensure its citizens are not menaced again from that
territory as a condition for its withdrawal.

Furthermore, UN Security Council Resolution 242 gives Israel the legal
right to be in the West Bank. According to Eugene Rostow, a former
undersecretary of state for political affairs in the Johnson administration,
"Israel is entitled to administer the territories" it acquired in 1967 until "a
just and lasting peace in the Middle East" is achieved.

The United States has not regarded Israeli settlements as illegal. The oft-
cited exception is the opinion of State Department legal adviser Herbert
Hansell in the Carter administration. He argued that establishing
settlements in the "occupied territories," which included the West Bank,
the Gaza Strip, the Sinai Peninsula, and the Golan Heights, is "inconsistent

with international law." This conformed to the views of President Carter at the time, who was critical of the Israeli settlement policy. [...]

Ronald Reagan rejected Hansell's opinion of settlements. On February 3, 1981, he said, "I disagreed when the previous Administration referred to them as illegal; they're not illegal."

Secretary of State James Baker was asked if the Bush administration regarded the settlements as illegal, and his answer was, "this is not our policy."

The Obama policy has also been mischaracterized. Secretary of State John Kerry and President Barack Obama were very critical of Israel's settlement policy, but Kerry did not call them "illegal"; he said they were "illegitimate." [...] Obama abstained rather than veto the UN Security Council resolution labeling settlements illegal, which was generally interpreted as an endorsement of that view; however, it did not affect U.S. policy since he left office shortly thereafter.

In response to criticism that the Trump administration's decision on the legality of settlements would harm the peace process, which at the time was moribund, Pompeo said the Carter formulation "hasn't advanced the cause of peace."
[...]
Myth*

Settlements are an obstacle to peace.

FACT

Settlements have never been an obstacle to peace.

* From 1949 to 1967, when Jews were forbidden to live on the West Bank, Arab leaders refused to make peace with Israel.

* From 1967 to 1977, the Labor Party established only a few strategic settlements, yet Arab leaders were unwilling to agree to peace with Israel.

* The fact that a Likud government committed to greater settlement activity took power in 1977 did not stop Egypt from signing a peace treaty with Israel or Prime Minister Menachem Begin from removing the Jewish settlements in the Sinai.

- Israel froze settlement building for three months in 1978, hoping the gesture would entice other Arabs to join the Camp David peace process, but none did.

- In 1994, Jordan signed a peace agreement with Israel, and settlements were not an issue.

- Between June 1992 and June 1996, under Labor Party–led governments, the Jewish population in the territories grew by approximately 50%. This rapid growth did not prevent the Palestinians from signing the Oslo accords in September 1993 or the OsloII agreement in September 1995. Those agreements left the question of settlements for final status negotiations and did not put any restrictions on them in the interim.

- In 2000, Prime Minister Ehud Barak offered to dismantle dozens of settlements, but the Palestinians still would not agree to end the conflict.

- In 2005, Israel evacuated all Jewish settlements in the Gaza Strip and four in Northern Samaria, but terror attacks continued.

- In 2008, Prime Minister Ehud Olmert offered to withdraw from approximately 94% of the West Bank, but the deal was rejected.

- In 2010, Prime Minister Benjamin Netanyahu froze settlement construction for ten months, and the Palestinians refused to negotiate until the period was nearly over. After agreeing to talk, they walked out when Netanyahu ended the freeze and had still not returned to negotiations by August 2022.

The settlements do not displace Arabs living in the territories. The media sometimes gives the impression that several hundred Palestinians are forced to leave for every Jew who moves to the West Bank. The truth is that most settlements have been built in uninhabited areas, and even the handful established in or near Arab towns did not force any Palestinians to leave.

[...]

Myth

Settlements violate the Geneva Convention.

FACT

The Fourth Geneva Convention prohibits the forcible transfer of people of one state to the territory of another state that it has occupied due to war. The Convention was never meant to apply to a case like the settlements.

Morris Abram, one of its drafters, said they were concerned with the types of crimes committed by the Nazis, such as the forcible eviction of Jews for purposes of mass extermination.

This is in no way relevant to the settlement issue. Jews are not being forced to go to the West Bank; on the contrary, they are voluntarily moving back to places where they, or their ancestors, once lived before being expelled by others.

The International Court of Justice's opinion about the illegality of settlements was based on a fallacious interpretation of the Fourth Geneva Convention. The ICJ presupposes that Israel is now occupying the land of a sovereign country; however, as former Israeli Ambassador to the UN Dore Gold notes, "there was no recognized sovereign over the West Bank prior to Israel's entry into the area." Jordan had previously occupied the area.

A country cannot occupy territory to which it has sovereign title; hence, the correct term for the area is "disputed territory," which does not confer greater rights to Israel or the Palestinians. The Palestinians never had sovereignty in the West Bank, whereas the Jews did for hundreds of years.

"The Jewish right of settlement in the area is equivalent in every way to the right of the local population to live there," according to Professor Eugene Rostow, former undersecretary of state for political affairs.

Legal scholar Eugene Kontorovich argues that "Israel has the strongest claim to the land" because "international law holds that a new country inherits the borders of the prior geopolitical unit in that territory. Israel was preceded by the League of Nations Mandate for Palestine, whose borders included the West Bank."

Adam Baker, a former legal adviser to Israel's Ministry of Foreign Affairs, adds that the "Oslo Accords instituted an agreed legal regime that overrides any other legal framework, including the 1949 Fourth Geneva Convention."

The effort to apply the Convention to Israel reflects a clear double standard. Kontorovich notes that "the significant migration of settlers into an occupied territory under the auspices of the occupying power is a ubiquitous feature of prolonged territorial control." He adds that no one has ever been prosecuted for violating the Convention and, except for a few sentences in an advisory opinion by the International Court of Justice, "its interpretation has been confined to academic and political statements – entirely within the particular context of Israel."

<u>Myth</u>

Israel must dismantle all the settlements for peace.

FACT

When serious negotiations begin over the final status of the West Bank, battle lines will be drawn over which settlements should be incorporated into Israel and which must be evacuated. In August 2005, Prime Minister Ariel Sharon acknowledged that "not all the settlements of today in Judea and Samaria will remain," while leaked Palestinian negotiating documents indicate the Palestinians were prepared to accept that some settlements would be incorporated into Israel.

In Gaza, Israel intended to withdraw completely; no settlements were viewed as vital to Israel for economic, security, or demographic reasons. The situation in the West Bank is completely different because Jews have strong historical and religious connections to the area stretching back centuries. Moreover, the West Bank is an area with strategic significance because of its proximity to Israel's heartland, and roughly one-quarter of Israel's water resources are located there.

The disengagement from Gaza involved only 21 settlements and approximately 8,500 Jews. Today, nearly 500,000 Jews live in 128 communities on the West Bank. More than 40% of these settlements have fewer than 1,000 citizens, 23% have fewer than 500, and only 13% have more than 5,000. Approximately 71% of the Jews in the West Bank live in five settlement "blocs," four of which are near the 1949 Armistice Line – the "Green Line". […] Another 330,000 live across Green Line in East Jerusalem.

Bloc	No. of Communities	Population	Approximate Area (sq. miles)
Ma'ale Adumim	4	49,720	28 (73 sq. km.)
Modiin Illit	4	91,016	2 (5 sq. km.)
Ariel	11	65,253	47 (122 sq. km.)
Gush Etzion	13	37,433	10 (26 sq. km.)
Givat Ze'ev	5	36,635	3 (8 sq. km.)
Betar Illit*	1	66,723	2 (5 sq. km.)
Total	**38**	**346,780**	**92 (238 sq. km.)**

As the table shows, these are large communities with thousands of residents. Evacuating them would be the equivalent of dismantling major American cities such as Annapolis, Maryland; Olympia, Washington; or Carson City, Nevada.

[…]

Ariel, with a population of more than 20,000, is now the heart of the second most populous bloc of settlements. The city is just 25 miles (40 km.) east of Tel Aviv and 31 miles (50 km.) north of Jerusalem. Ariel and the surrounding communities expanded Israel's narrow waist, which was just 9 miles (15 km.) wide before 1967, and ensures that Israel has a land route to the Jordan Valley in case Israel needs to fight a land war to the east. It is more controversial than the other consensus settlements because it is the furthest from the Green Line, extending approximately 12 miles (19 km.) into the West Bank. Nevertheless, Ariel is expected to be annexed to Israel if a peace agreement is reached.

Most peace plans envision Israel annexing sufficient territory – 4 to 6% – to incorporate 75–80% of the Jews in the West Bank. In exchange, the Palestinian entity would get the same amount of land from Israeli territory (possibly in the Negev adjacent to the Gaza Strip). […]

Myth

Israel plans to annex all the settlements.

FACT

Israel could have annexed the entire West Bank or the settlements at any time since 1967 but has not done so. It is still a possibility, but those are just two options that have been discussed for the disposition of the West Bank. […]

In 2020, the Netanyahu government considered applying Israeli sovereignty to some or all the settlements but decided not to as a condition for the United Arab Emirates and Bahrain to establish diplomatic relations with Israel.

MYTH

Settlements preclude the creation of a contiguous Palestinian state.

FACT

[…] [I]t is possible to create a contiguous Palestinian state in the West Bank even if Israel incorporates the major settlement blocs. The total area of these communities is less than 2% of the West Bank. A kidney-shaped state linked to the Gaza Strip by a secure passage would be contiguous. Some argue that the E1 project linking Ma'ale Adumim to Jerusalem would cut off East Jerusalem, but that is not necessarily true, as Israel has proposed constructing a four-lane underpass to guarantee free passage between the West Bank and the Arab sections of Jerusalem. […]

642

C. Application of the apartheid test to the Occupied Palestinian Territory

35. Since the beginning of the occupation in June 1967, the rule of Israel over the Palestinian territory has been epitomized by two core features. The first is the establishment of designed-to-be irreversible "facts-on-the-ground": the creation of 300 civilian settlements, with 700,000 Jewish settlers, meant to demographically engineer an unlawful sovereignty claim through the annexation of the occupied territory while simultaneously thwarting the Palestinians' right to self-determination. The second is the development of an oppressive system of military rule over the 2.7 million Palestinians in the West Bank, a shrunken and tenuous range of residency rights for the 360,000 Palestinians living in East Jerusalem, and a medieval military blockade of the 2 million Palestinians in Gaza.

36. These two features are deeply intertwined: it is impossible for an acquisitive occupying Power to settle hundreds of thousands of its citizens into occupied territory, create for them attractive living conditions equivalent to the home territory, and expropriate and alienate huge swaths of land and resources for their benefit and security, without also immiserating the indigenous people and triggering their perpetual rebellion. […]

INSTITUTIONALIZED REGIME OF SYSTEMATIC RACIAL OPPRESSION AND DISCRIMINATION

38. At the heart of the settler colonial project of Israel is a comprehensive dual legal and political system that provides comprehensive rights and living conditions for the Jewish Israeli settlers in the West Bank, including East Jerusalem, while imposing upon the Palestinians military rule and control without any of the basic protections of international humanitarian and human rights law. […]

39. Politically and legally, Jewish Israeli settlers enjoy the same fulsome citizenship rights and protections as Israeli Jews living inside the country's borders of 1949. […]

40. In sharp contrast, the 2.7 million Palestinians living in the West Bank enjoy none of the rights, protections and privileges possessed by the Israeli Jewish settlers living among them. They can vote in elections (when they are held) for the Palestinian Authority, but it has exceptionally limited powers. They have no democratic or political rights to hold the occupying Power—which exercises overwhelming control over their lives—accountable. […]

From Report of the Special Rapporteur on the Situation of Human Rights in the Palestinian Territories Occupied Since 1967, U.N. Doc. A/HRC/49/87 (Aug. 12, 2022).

44. In East Jerusalem, the 360,000 Palestinians have a more enhanced social and legal status than Palestinians in the West Bank, but their position is still greatly inferior to the 230,000 Jewish settlers who live among them in Jewish-only settlements. The Jewish settlers are regarded by Israel as residing in sovereign Israeli territory (arising from its two-stage illegal annexation of East Jerusalem in 1967 and 1980) and, as such, they enjoy full citizenship rights, benefits and privileges. Almost all East Jerusalemite Palestinians possess residency status as opposed to Israeli citizenship; while this entitles them to some Israeli social rights (including health insurance), this residency status can be cancelled if they leave Jerusalem for a period of time, a threat that Jewish Israelis do not face. [...]

45. In Gaza, the apparent strategy of Israel is the indefinite warehousing of an unwanted population of 2 million Palestinians, whom it has confined to a narrow strip of land through its comprehensive 15-year-old air, land and sea blockade (with further restrictions by Egypt on the southern border of Gaza). [...]

ESTABLISHED WITH INTENT TO MAINTAIN DOMINATION OF ONE RACIAL GROUP OVER ANOTHER

46. [...] Among recent and current Israeli political leaders, the only debate regarding the Palestinians has come down to tertiary issues: whether the Palestinians will be granted a shrunken statelet with its own postage stamps and a seat at the United Nations or, alternatively, kept in their present state of statelessness. [...]

47. [...] The intention of Israel in building the settlements was never primarily about security or increasing the incentive of neighbouring Arab States to negotiate a final peace agreement, but to ensure that it retained as much of the land as possible. [...]

48. In 2018, the Israeli Knesset enacted the Basic Law: Israel – the Nation State of the Jewish People. While Israel does not have a constitution, it has adopted a series of Basic Laws that have acquired a quasi-constitutional status. The Nation State Law entrenches constitutional inequality and racial-national discrimination into Israeli law by distinguishing the rights of Jewish Israelis from those of Palestinians and other non-Jewish citizens of Israel. Senior American foreign policy scholar David Rothkopf has written in Haaretz that the Nation State Law "creates an apartheid society in which ethnic identity trumps fundamental human rights". The Nation State Law is consistent with the regular proclamation by Israeli political leaders, including Benjamin Netanyahu, that "Israel is the national state, not of all its citizens, but only of the Jewish people". [...]

50. The administration of the occupation by Israel has been replete with a range of inhumane and inhuman acts prohibited by the International Convention on the Suppression and Punishment of the Crime of Apartheid and the Rome Statute. In summary, these acts include the following:

    (a)   Denial of the right to life and liberty. [...]

    (b)   Denial of full participation in all features of a society. [...]

    (c)   Measures that divide the population along racial lines. [...]

    (d)   Exploitation of labour of a racial group. [...]

    (e)   Other inhumane and inhuman acts causing great suffering. Although strictly prohibited under international law, torture continues to be used in practice by Israel against Palestinians in detention. Methods of torture include sleep deprivation, beating and slapping, humiliation, unhygienic conditions and extended shackling in contorted positions. Challenges to the Israeli Supreme Court against its use have been unsuccessful. Beatings by Israeli soldiers of Palestinians during arrests are regularly reported, with little accountability.

IV. Conclusions

[...]

52. [...] Applying each of the three steps of the amalgamated test from the International Convention on the Suppression and Punishment of the Crime of Apartheid and the Rome Statute, the Special Rapporteur has concluded that the political system of entrenched rule in the Occupied Palestinian Territory that endows one racial-national-ethnic group with substantial rights, benefits and privileges while intentionally subjecting another group to live behind walls and checkpoints and under a permanent military rule *sans droits, sans égalité, sans dignité et sans liberté* (without rights, without equality, without dignity and without freedom) satisfies the prevailing evidentiary standard for the existence of apartheid. [...]

Allegation: Israel is an Apartheid State (2021)
ANTI-DEFAMATION LEAGUE

It is not uncommon today to see critics of Israel accusing it of being an apartheid state. Whether such a description is being used to describe Israeli policies towards Palestinians in the West Bank and Gaza Strip, or towards Arab citizens of Israel, the label is inaccurate, offensive, and often used to delegitimize and denigrate Israel as a whole. Moreover, the use of this inaccurate and highly charged label is also counterproductive to resolving issues related to injustices within Israeli society or the complex Israeli-Palestinian conflict.

Apartheid usually refers to the guiding policy of racial segregation in pre-1990s South Africa. Apartheid was a racist, repressive system, by which South Africa's white minority enforced its domination, through a systematic framework of racist legislation, over black and other non-white racial groups who made up more than 90 percent of the country's population.

The accusation of apartheid fundamentally distorts what Israel is.

While there is no doubt that Israel, like every country, has tremendous societal challenges and must do better in dealing with issues of institutionalized bias, discrimination, inequity and racism, choosing to apply the apartheid label would seem to question the legitimacy of the world's only Jewish state and its continued existence.

Within Israel, there are safeguards aimed at ensuring the equal treatment of all citizens, Jewish or Arab, and Israeli laws and democratic institutions, including the independent courts and robust free press, assigned to uphold and speak out for these rights. Representing over 20% of Israel's population, Israeli Arab citizens serve as judges, ambassadors, legislators, journalists, professors, artists and play prominent roles in all aspects of Israeli society. And for the first time, as of June 2021, an Islamist Arab political party is a partner in a governing coalition.

Israeli policies in the West Bank and related to the Gaza Strip, are still subject to dispute and negotiation by both Israelis and Palestinians. They are complicated, and, due to the lack of final agreement, there are indeed policies and restrictions – including limitations on movement and access to certain resources that can impose tremendous hardships on Palestinians. From an Israeli perspective, such policies are justified by security considerations, given the past and ongoing threats posed by Palestinian terrorist organizations targeting Israeli civilians, even within Israel's pre-1967 borders. While Israel's policies and practices can certainly be criticized, it is not factually accurate to say they are akin to a permanent and institutionalized system motivated and designed by racism.

One must also ask what purpose is served by the accusation of apartheid. Is it to challenge and change specific policies? Or is it to demonize the entire state?

In responding to a 2021 Human Rights Watch Report alleging that Israel engages in apartheid policies, longtime experts engaged in Israeli-Palestinian negotiations Daniel C. Kurzer and Aaron David Miller said about the use of this label: "It will do nothing to improve the situation on the ground. It will infantilize Palestinians and Israelis and, rather than facilitate criticism of Israel, it will likely make it that much more difficult to bring about change in two of the constituencies that really matter: the [U.S.] Biden Administration and Israel."

As noted by Justice Richard Goldstone – a former senior South African jurist and critic of Israeli polices: "those who conflate the situations in Israel and the West Bank and liken both to the old South Africa do a disservice to all who hope for justice and peace."

West Bank: Key Information (2020)
Jim Zanotti

Israel's military occupied the West Bank in 1967. Since Israel and the PLO agreed to the 1995 Interim Agreement on the West Bank and Gaza Strip, the West Bank has been subject to the following tiered system of shared control between Israel's military and the PA:

- **Area A – Main Palestinian cities and urban areas.** The PA provides civilian administration and generally controls security, but Israeli military commanders retain authority to intervene. Israeli security prerogatives in this area include conducting raids to arrest wanted Palestinians or to foil alleged terrorist plots.

- **Area B – Less densely-populated Palestinian areas.** The PA administers the area and Israel controls security (sometimes allowing PA security forces to assist).

- **Area C – Remainder of West Bank (including Israeli settlements and some small Palestinian communities).** Israel administers the area and generally controls security (sometimes allowing PA security forces to assist with Palestinian communities), while the PA has responsibility for Palestinian civil affairs that do not relate to property.
[…]

Legal Systems

Various systems of law apply to different groups and territories within the West Bank. The Israeli military has ultimate responsibility for law and order. Unless superseded by Israeli military orders or PA laws, Jordanian law applies in the West Bank because Jordan was the country that controlled the West Bank before Israel captured it in 1967.

Israeli civilian law largely applies to settlers pursuant to military orders. This allows Israeli ministries and agencies to provide services and regulations for the settlements in a number of fields, including health care and education. During the 20th Knesset (2015-2019), some legislation for settlers and settlements directly authorized the government to treat settlements in the same way as Israel proper on a few matters. In 2017, Israel's attorney general required that any bill proposed by the government explicitly address the legislation's applicability or non-applicability to settlements.

Palestinians in the West Bank are generally subject to PA laws and courts on matters that do not relate to property. They remain subject to overarching Israeli military jurisdiction, and can petition Israel's Supreme Court when legal disputes arise under this jurisdiction.

648 From Israel's Possible Annexation of the West Bank Areas: Frequently Asked Questions, CONGRESSIONAL RESEARCH SERVICE (CRS Report No. R46433).

On matters of property, Israeli military orders since 1967 have amended the underlying Jordanian law (based largely on an earlier Ottoman Empire land code) in key aspects, including planning and construction. According to one anti-settlement advocacy group, Area C, where most of the land open for future development lies, has a two-tiered planning system: "a civil and representative planning system for Jewish settlers, and a military system without representation for Palestinians." PA laws apply to planning and construction in Areas A and B.

[…]

REFUGEES

Distribution of the Palestinian Population (1974)
CENTRAL INTELLIGENCE AGENCY

Introduction

1.   A Palestinian is defined here as any Arabic speaking person who lives in or comes from the area known as Palestine under the British Mandate. Today this includes Israel and the Israel-occupied West Bank of Jordan and Gaza Strip. [...] At present they number approximately 2,900,000, about one-half of whom are under Israeli rule.

2.   [...] When Israel was created, its Jewish and some of its Arab inhabitants became citizens of the now state of Israel. The approximately 1,300,000 Palestinian Arabs who fled were left with no recognized citizenship status. Within the next decade, Palestinians who remained in Jordan were granted Jordanian citizenship; the others have remained stateless persons, living in "host" countries on sufferance. Syria, while refusing them citizenship, granted them many citizenship rights; but Palestinians can not vote or own property in Syria. Lebanon was reluctant to offer citizenship to the large number of Moslem Palestine refugees living within its borders for fear they would destroy the balance between the country's Christian and Moslems. Egypt kept most of the Palestinians under its jurisdiction in the tiny Gaza enclave, which it governed as a separate entity.

3.   Almost half of all known Palestinians are UNRWA-registered refugees, living in Jordan, Egypt, Syria, Lebanon, and the Israeli occupied territories of Gaza and the West Bank. Some 510,000 of their number live in UNRWA camps or emergency camps. When they can, the refugees live with relatives rather than in the camps and go to camps for rations, education, and medical facilities.

4.   UNRWA's strict interpretation of the definition of a refugee as one who lost both his home and livelihood in 1948 excluded many Palestinians; thus the UNRWA refugee statistics do not include the self-supporting Palestinians in exile. [...]

5.   More that 400,000 of the Arabs who fled Israel in 1948 did not become UNRWA refugees because they were able to find work elsewhere. Since that time, many more who were initially UNRWA refugees have become self-supporting and so have had their names removed from UNRWA's roles. Authorities estimate that both groups and their offspring total over one million. [...]

650

East Jordan

6.   The NIS estimated that in mid-1972 about 862,000 Palestinians lived on the East Bank of Jordan. Over two-thirds of them are UNRWA-registered refugees, of which 40 percent reside in camps. [...]

Lebanon

7.   Lebanon has 180,000 registered refugees, over half of whom live in UNRWA camps. There are many Palestinians -- mostly Christians -- in Lebanon who are not registered refugees. The NIS estimates their number at 40,000; the Department of State estimates their number between 60,000 and 70,000.

Syria

8.   Syria harbors about 173,000 Palestinians, 50,000 of whom live in refugee camps. UNRWA operates in Syria, but its administration is limited in many cases by the lack of cooperation on the part of the Syrian Government. [...]

Egypt

9.   There are some 33,000 Palestinians in Egypt, most of whom are refugees of the 1948 war. There are about 3,000 registered refugees who fled the Gaza Strip in June 1967. UNRWA does not operate in Egypt, but it gives the Egyptian government money for these registered refugees.

Israeli Occupied Territory

10. In November 1971 the Israelis estimated the number of Palestinians on the West Bank to be about 700,000 of whom about 72,000 to 74,000 lived in East Jerusalem. The American Consul in Jerusalem noted that the Israeli government would certainly not inflate this particular set of statistics and that any inaccuracies are probably on the low side.

11. The Israeli census of 1967 listed 356,000 as the total population of the Gaza Strip. [...] Some transfers of population outside the strip have occurred. By August 8, 1971 about 2,000 refugees had been settled in Sinai, near Al Arish; about 100 others have been moved to near Jenin, on the West Bank.

Israel Proper

12. The 340,000 Palestinians now in Israel are those who remained after the cease-fire in 1948. They have been assimilated into the economy and have acquired Israeli citizenship, with all its rights except the right to

serve in the armed forces. [...]

Saudi Arabia, Kuwait, and Other Countries

13. Arab sources estimate that some 100,000 Palestinians work in Saudi Arabia, Kuwait, and Iraq -- primarily in the oil fields -- and that some 50,000 other Palestinians live elsewhere in the world. These cannot be specifically identified as Palestinians because their passports and citizenship are usually Jordanian.
[...]

Explaining Transfer: Zionist Thinking and the Creation of the Palestinian Refugee Problem (2009)
Benny Morris

The Palestinian refugee problem was born of the 1948 war, the first war between Israel and the Arabs. It was not the product of a preconceived master plan or, indeed, of a governmental policy decision or of a blanket, systematic implementation of a policy of expulsion. The overwhelming majority of the 700,000 Arabs who were displaced from their homes fled as a result of battle or encroaching battle. Most moved to other parts of Palestine (and, in this sense, they were not really refugees at all) rather than to neighbouring countries (the minority, some 300,000, reached and resettled in Lebanon, Syria, and Transjordan). They fled as the shells landed or, they feared, were about to land on their towns and villages. Many were driven by the economic privations of war—unemployment, soaring prices, and lack of food or fuel. Some left because their local leaders, military and political, urged or ordered them to leave, for military or political reasons. Many fled because of an accumulation of reasons. And some were expelled by advancing Israeli troops, primarily out of military calculation.

But these were the immediate causes of departure. Above and beyond them, there was a wider, general, explanatory meta-narrative. Or, rather, two metanarratives. One metanarrative, traditionally trotted out in Zionist propaganda, is that the Arab leadership—the national Palestinian leadership and/or the leaders of the neighbouring Arab states—beyond the particulars of flight from each area or battle, advised or ordered the Palestinians to leave their homes and move out of actual or potential battle zones to clear the path for the invading or about-to-invade Arab armies and perhaps to affix the stigma of expulsion on the Israeli side, as a justification for their invasion (the armies of Jordan, Egypt, Syria, and Iraq invaded Israel/Palestine on 15 May 1948). This narrative has been thoroughly discredited by historians because there is practically no basis for it in the contemporary documentation. The documentation contains no hint of a general Arab order of this sort and, indeed, for May 1948, contains a great deal of evidence from a contrary direction, showing that at least some Arab leaders (King Abdullah of Jordan and Fawzi al Qawuqji, the commander of the Arab Liberation Army, an Arab League volunteer force sent into Palestine to help the Arab militias even before the pan-Arab invasion) tried to persuade Palestinians to stay put or, if already displaced, to return to their homes.

The other metanarrative, that offered in traditional Arab historiography, is that the Zionists from the first, as part of their ideology and programme, sought to transfer or expel the native Arab population of Palestine, and during the first decades of Zionism, organized for it, prepared a master plan, and, in 1947-8, seized the opportunity and systematically implemented it and expelled the Arab inhabitants from the areas earmarked by the United Nations for Jewish statehood and the additional areas that became 'Jewish' in the course of the fighting.

I would like to focus on an element of this second metanarrative, that part dealing with Zionist aforethought and pre-planning, what can be termed 'transfer' thinking—that the Zionists, from the first, intended and planned to expel the Arabs of Palestine. It is certainly true that Zionist leaders, from the 1890s onwards, indeed, beginning with the Zionist movement's prophet and founder, Theodor Herzl, occasionally toyed with the idea of transferring some or all of the Arabs from the area of the Jewish-state-to-be to make way for massive Zionist immigration and settlement. (The movement's leaders anticipated massive waves of immigration as a result of the surge in eastern European anti-semitism, beginning with the pogroms of 1881-4 in the tsarist empire.) For example, in one passage in his diaries, Herzl wrote: 'We must expropriate gently.... We shall try to spirit the penni-less population across the border by procuring employment for it in the transit countries [i.e. the countries of destination], while denying it employment in our country.... The removal of the poor must be carried out discretely and circumspectly.'

But two points are worth making. First, generally, when speaking and writing about transfer, and they did so rarely, partly because the subject was sensitive, Zionist leaders such as Artur Ruppin and Leo Motzkin, and pro-Zionist writers such as Israel Zangwill, talked in terms of a voluntary agreed transfer of the Arabs out of Palestine, with compensation, rather than a coerced expulsion. Second, the idea of transfer was never adopted as part of the Zionist movement's platform, nor as part of the programme or platform of any of the main Zionist parties, not in the nineteenth century and not in the twentieth century. And, in general, the Zionist leaders looked to massive Jewish immigration, primarily from Russia and Europe, as the means of establishing and then assuring a Jewish majority in Palestine or whatever part of it was to be earmarked for Jewish statehood.

But around 1929 and, with even greater frequency, during the late 1930s and early 1940s, Zionist leaders began to talk, in ever-wider, less discreet forums, about the desirability and possibility of transferring Arabs or 'the Arabs'. Both of twentieth-century Zionism's main leaders, David Ben-Gurion, the head of the Yishuv (the Jewish community in Palestine) and Israel's founding Prime Minister, and Chaim Weizmann, the head of the World Zionist Organization and Israel's first President, repeatedly during these years referred approvingly to the idea. But, again, it is worth noting, this talk never translated into the co-option of the idea into official mainstream Zionist ideology or its advocacy in the movement's programme or in that of any of its chief component parties, the socialist Mapai,

Hashomer Hatza'ir, and Ahdut Ha'avoda, the liberal General Zionists and Progressives, or the right-wing Revisionist Movement.

In August 1937 Ben-Gurion told an emergency meeting of the Zionist Congress, the movement's supreme decision-making body: 'We must look carefully at the question of whether transfer is possible, necessary, moral and useful. ... Transfer of populations occurred previously, in the (Jezreel) Valley, in the Sharon and in other places [Ben-Gurion was referring to the small-scale removal of Arab tenant farmers from plots of land bought and settled by the Zionist movement during the previous decades] .... Now a transfer of a completely different scope will have to be carried out. In many parts of the country new settlement will not be possible without transferring the Arab peasantry.... [It] will make possible a comprehensive settlement program. Thankfully, the Arab people have vast empty areas. Jewish power, which grows steadily, will also increase our possibilities to carry out the transfer on a large scale.'

Four years later, in 1941, at a meeting with Ivan Maiskii, the Soviet ambassador in London, Weizmann said 'that if half a million Arabs could be transferred, two million Jews (from Europe) could be put in their place. That, of course, would be a first instalment; what might happen afterwards was a matter for history.'

The explanation for the increase in volume and intensity of pro-transfer pronouncements in the late 1930s and early 1940s is simple, and goes a long way to explaining the Zionist leadership's growing adoption of this idea in the first place. In 1929 the Palestine Arabs mounted their first major bout of violence against the Jewish community in Palestine. Altogether, some 130 Jews were killed—66 of them, incidentally, non-or anti-Zionist, ultra-orthodox yeshiva students and rabbis and their families, murdered by a Muslim mob brandishing clubs, hatchets, and knives in Hebron's Jewish quarter. In 1936 the Palestine Arabs launched a far more comprehensive campaign of violence directed at the British Mandate authorities and the Zionist settlers. The violence, dubbed by the Arabs the Great Arab Revolt, lasted until spring 1939, and claimed many hundreds of lives and entailed widespread destruction of property.

Apart from the ousting of British governance and the establishment of an independent Arab state in all of Palestine, the rebels demanded an immediate cessation of Jewish immigration to Palestine. And through this violence they succeeded in coercing the British—who faced the prospect of a three-front world war and were bent on appeasing the Arabs to achieve tranquillity in the Middle East, strategically vital because of land, sea, and air routes and oil deposits—severely to curtail jewish immigration, a policy that was subsequently embodied in the government's White Paper of May 1939. The White Paper limited Jewish immigration to 75,000 over the following five years, with any further intake of Jewish immigrants dependent on Arab agreement, and promised the country's inhabitants independence within ten years. Given the demographics of 1939, with about one million Arabs and 450,000 Jews, the British were endorsing the emergence of an Arab-majority state.

This British curtailment of Jewish immigration under Arab military duress, at a point when the Jews constituted about 30 per cent of Palestine's population, put paid to the possibility of the achievement of a Jewish majority through immigration. In the longer term, the problem, from the Jewish perspective, was to be compounded by the Holocaust, in which six million Jews were murdered and in which most of Zionism's potential pool of immigrants was annihilated. Thus Arab violence in the late 1930s coupled during the following years with the Holocaust nixed the possibility of the Jews achieving a majority in Palestine by way of immigration.

But this was in the medium term. In the short term, the Arab violence of 1929, and, even more so, of 1936-9, had a further effect: it put the Jewish community on notice that the Arabs would not countenance the emergence of a Jewish state in Palestine and would fight against it tooth and nail; and that an Arab minority included in that Jewish state, even if established only on a small part of Palestine, would be disloyal and rebellious and would destabilize or overthrow that state from within.

This was the conclusion of the British royal commission, headed by Lord Peel, that was established in late 1936 to investigate the causes of the Arab Revolt and to recommend a solution to the Palestine problem. In its thorough, 400-page report, published in July 1937, the commission made two major recommendations: the termination of the Mandate and the partition of the country into two areas, with a Jewish state to be established on less than 20 per cent of the land (the Galilee and the northern and central Coastal Plain) and an Arab state, to be conjoined to Transjordan, to be established on the bulk of the remainder of Palestine. (Some 5-10 per cent of the country, it further recommended, including Jerusalem, Bethlehem, and a corridor to the Mediterranean, should be retained by Britain.) The commission ruled that the Mandate could not continue and that the two peoples, the Arabs and the Jews, could not live in peace in one unitary state (either the Jews would dominate the Arabs or the Arabs would dominate the Jews, and both possibilities were unthinkable). The commission further recommended the removal of most or all of the Arabs from the area of the Jewish-state-to-be (some 300,000 souls) and their transfer to the Arab part of Palestine or out of the country altogether. The transfer was to be achieved voluntarily, but, if that proved impossible, by coercion. The commission reasoned: 'The existence [of this minority inside the Jewish state] clearly constitutes the most serious hindrance to the smooth and successful operation of partition.... If the settlement is to be clean and final, the question of the minorities must be boldly faced and firmly dealt with.' What the commission was saying was that a disloyal, discontented, and large Arab minority inside a future Jewish state, probably aided by the surrounding Arab world, would destabilize that state and, indeed, threaten the viability and longevity of the settlement itself. It was in the interest of the long-term prosperity of both peoples to separate them as completely as possible, determined the commission.

But the Peel Commission was driven to this conclusion not merely by the spectacle of Arab hatred for and violence against the Yishuv and the Arabs' stated unwillingness to live both inside and alongside a Jewish state in a partitioned Palestine. The commission had also been put on notice as regards the Palestinian Arabs' expulsionist mindset and programme. When the chairman of the Arab Higher Committee, Haj Muhammad Amin al Husseini, the cleric who headed the Palestinian national movement until 1948, testified before the Peel Commission, the members asked him: if Palestine is to become an independent, Arab-majority state—as Husseini, who flatly rejected any form of partition or Jewish statehood, was demanding—what would be the status of the 400,000 Jews already resident in the country? Husseini responded: those who were citizens of the Ottoman Palestine up to 1917—fewer than 60,000-70,000, all told—would receive Palestine citizenship. And what would be the fate of the remaining 330,000 Jews currently resident in the country, asked the commissioners. That would be for history to decide, he responded. The commissioners assumed that at the very least Husseini was consigning them to statelessness and, very possibly, to deportation. And, in their report, the commissioners hinted—alluding explicitly to the fate of the Assyrian Christian community in Iraq, hundreds of whom had recently been massacred by Muslims, despite Iraqi government assurances to the West— that the fate of Palestine's Jews under a Muslim Arab majority government might be much worse.

What Husseini implied before the Peel Commission, when he was at his diplomatic best, was what he usually said more explicitly elsewhere: the Jews who had arrived in Palestine after 1917, they and their children, would not be allowed to remain. And, of course, it was not just Husseini. The cry of 'idbah al yahud' (slaughter the Jews) had accompanied each of the bouts of violence, or anti-Jewish pogroms, unleashed by Palestine's Arabs in 1920, 1921, and 1929, and was echoed repeatedly by Arab mobs during the 1936-9 revolt. And it was in response to this violent and expulsionist mindset and ideology that the Zionist leadership increasingly turned to the idea of transfer as a solution to the Yishuv's 'Arab problem'. If this was the enemy and this is what they did and sought, no viable Jewish state could come into existence with a large Arab minority in its midst.

But events in Europe without doubt compounded the Zionist dilemma and further fuelled its new-found interest in transfer. From 1933 on, central and eastern Europe were in the throes of a violent antisemitic upsurge, leading to a progressive deterioration in the condition of European Jewry and a threat to its very existence. It was this that drove the urgency in the mid and late 1930s of the Zionist demand for a state that could serve as a haven for these threatened millions. And it was this that underlay the readiness both to compromise over territory—the Zionist movement had traditionally sought all of Palestine for its Jewish state, but by 1937 it was ready for partition and resigned itself to obtaining only a chunk of Palestine—and the demand that the small area allotted for Jewish statehood at least be clear of Arabs, so that there would be room to accommodate the needy millions and that they would not be threatened by violent, indeed murderous, neighbours within that state. The facts that the Palestinian Arabs, by their violence in 1936-9, had pushed the British into sealing off Palestine as a possible haven for Europe's persecuted Jews and that Husseini during the 1930s had repeatedly made friendly overtures towards the Nazi regime and, indeed, in 1941 had moved to Berlin and for the next four years worked for the Third Reich, recruiting Muslims for the Wehrmacht and calling for an anti-Allied jihad in the Middle East, only compounded the Yishuv's fears of Palestinian intentions and their animosity towards them. In short, Arab expulsionist and annihilationist, or perceived annihilationist, intentions towards Zion's Jews triggered expulsionist Yishuv attitudes towards Palestine's Arabs.

Without doubt, Zionist thinking about transfer in the late 1930s and early 1940s helped pave the way, at least on a psychological plain, for the massive transfer that occurred in 1948, resulting in the creation of the Palestinian refugee problem. But the process was also driven by the events of 1947-8 themselves, with what had occurred in the 1930s as a backdrop. Without doubt, the Holocaust played a part: the Holocaust had demonstrated that massive murderous intentions could and did translate into reality and that the world would not necessarily intervene to stymie the Arabs.

In November 1947 the Palestinian Arabs, followed by the Arab states, rejected the UN General Assembly partition plan (Resolution 181) and launched a war to prevent the emergence of a Jewish state. Indeed, by rejecting the succession of partition-based solutions—from Peel in 1937, and the United Nations in 1947—the Palestinians had turned the Palestine conflict into a zero-sum game. They had said and were saying, consistently, that it was all or nothing: they wanted all of Palestine, and not an inch for the Jews. In November-December 1947 Palestine's Arabs rose up to frustrate the implementation of the UN resolution. They failed. And in May 1948, the Arab states joined the fray, invading the country. Their radio broadcasts were explicit: the goal was to destroy the Yishuv. Or, as the Arab League's Secretary-General, Azzam Pasha, told the British minister in Amman, Alec Kirkbride, on the eve of the pan-Arab invasion: 'It does not matter how many [Jews] there are. We will sweep them into the sea.' This was the message broadcast by the Arab 'street', which the Arab leaders held in awe, and this was the gist of the fatwas issued by the

Muslim religious authorities in the Middle East. As the ulema, the council of theologians, of Cairo's al-Azhar University, perhaps the supreme authority in Sunni Islam, put it in a fatwa on 26 April: 'The liberation of Palestine [is] a religious duty for all Muslims.... The Islamic and Arab governments should without delay take effective and radical measures.' Jihad had been proclaimed and the infidel was to be put to the sword. Even Matiel Mughannam, the Lebanese Christian woman who headed the ARC-affiliated Arab Women's Organization in Palestine, told an interviewer (in January 1948): 'The UN decision has united all Arabs, as they have never been united before, not even against the Crusaders.... [A Jewish state] has no chance to survive now that the "holy war" has been declared. All the Jews will eventually be massacred.'

Quite naturally, with the Holocaust still fresh in their minds, the Yishuv felt mortally threatened; as, indeed, it was. The Jews took the Arabs at their word; the talk of expulsion and worse lay heavily in the air. No decision was taken in 1947-8 by the Yishuv's leadership bodies—the Jewish Agency Executive, the People's Administration, the Provisional Government of Israel, the Haganah/IDF General Staff—to expel 'the Arabs'; expulsion was never adopted as policy (which is why, incidentally, the newborn Jewish state emerged from the 1948 war with almost a fifth of its citizens Arabs). But a mindset of transfer—not a policy but an unsystematic, inchoate will to be rid of the hostile, threatening Arab population in the area of the Jewish state—took hold in the Yishuv and helped propel the large-scale transfer that was reinforced and consolidated by the decision of the Israeli government, taken in summer 1948, not to allow the return of the refugees. Such a return, it was quite logically felt, would necessarily inject a potential large fifth column into the midst of the newborn state. It could not be countenanced. Continued Arab (including Palestinian Arab) hostility toward Israel made sure that Israel would never accept the refugees' 'right of return', as endorsed in UN General Assembly Resolution 194 in December 1948. At the same time, the Arab states refused properly to resettle the refugees in their midst. Together, these assured the persistence of the Palestinian refugee problem down to the present day.

Letter to U.S. President Truman (1949)
Chaim Weizmann

DEAR MR. PRESIDENT: The Government of Israel have communicated to me the text of the Note transmitted to them on your behalf on the 29th May, as well as their reply of June 8th. The matters raised in the Note are of such gravity that I feel impelled to address you personally on the subject. [...]

Now as to the refugee problem. It is a grave issue, but it was not created by us. It was not the birth of Israel which created the Arab refugee problem, as our enemies now proclaim, but the Arab attempt to prevent that birth by armed force. These people are not refugees in the sense in which that term has been sanctified by the martyrdom of millions in Europe—they are part of an aggressor group which failed and which makes no secret of its intention to resume aggression. They left the country last year at the bidding of their leaders and military commanders and as part of the Arab strategic plan. But in spite of all this we are, for humanitarian reasons ready to contribute as far as we can towards a solution of this problem. We have, in fact, done a good deal more under this head than could, for obvious reasons, be published. Your Ambassador has been given details under this head. We have been steadily re-admitting Arab refugees during the last few months. The number of those who have returned exceeds 25,000. We are ready to re-unite Arab families separated by the war, and we are now approaching the various Arab States through the Mixed Armistice Commissions for setting up special machinery to facilitate their return in organised form. We are prepared to re-admit more as part of a peace settlement. There are, however, two overriding considerations which limit what we can do in this sphere: we dare not again endanger our hard-won independence and security and with all the good will in the world, we cannot undertake tasks which are economically beyond our strength.

So many malicious charges have been levelled against us in connection with this Arab refugee question, that I cannot help drawing attention to the basic realities of the situation. We are a small State, nine hundred thousand Jews wedged in between forty million Arabs. We held our own last year by a terrific effort and at very heavy sacrifices, losing some of our finest youth and suffering heavy damage. The Arab States are making no secret of their intention of resuming war whenever they are ready for it. Only two days ago Faris el Khoury, the former Syrian member of the Security Council and Chairman of the Syrian Chamber, declared that the war against us "remains the corner-stone of Arab policy". Not a week passes without our being warned by authoritative Arab spokesmen of the coming "second round". The Arab States are rearming on a big scale, building up modern armament industries of their own and purchasing the most deadly modern weapons. A few weeks ago squadrons of British Vampire jet fighters were flown to the Suez Canal Zone—half an hour's air flight from our frontier—ready for instant delivery when wanted, while Egyptian pilots are being

trained in their use close by. Egypt has ordered British destroyers with 4"
and 6" guns and submarines, while there is hardly any secret about the
French rearming the Syrians. This rearmament, Mr. President, constitutes a
direct threat to the peace of the Middle East and thereby also to the peace
of the World. With this open threat of war hanging over us, can we ignore
the security aspect of the admission of a large Arab population who,
whatever their individual feelings might be, are likely to turn against us if
war restarts?

Apart from the security question, which to my mind is paramount, there is
the economic difficulty. When the United Nations in November 1947
voted in favour of a Jewish State, it was motivated preeminently by the
purpose of solving once and for all the Jewish question in Europe, to get
rid of the concentration camps and of the aftermath of Hitler's holocaust. I
know, Mr. President, that this purpose was uppermost in your mind when
you gave us your staunch and steady support in those critical days. We are
now doing exactly what we were expected to do. We are liquidating one
camp after another and have already brought over many thousands of their
former inmates. Can we be expected at the same time to build up,
alongside this big effort of reconstruction, a new Arab economy to absorb
hundreds of thousands of Arabs? For let there be no mistake about it: the
Arab economic and social structure as it was prior to last year's exodus has
ceased to exist. The Arab refugee question can be solved in a big way only
by a comprehensive effort of reconstruction. The crucial question is: is that
effort to be undertaken in Israel, with all the political, security and
economic stresses and strains arising therefrom, or in the neighbouring
Arab countries where vast fertile areas are available for such resettlement
and where these people can find a home in the congenial surroundings of
an Arab society?

Our policy, as I stated before, is not one of absolute refusal to readmit
Arabs and we may, if real peace is established, be able to do more in this
respect than if the present atmosphere of latent war and hostility continues.
But an all-round solution can only be found as part of a general
development scheme for the benefit of the Middle East as a whole.
Towards such a development scheme Israel is ready to make its
contribution: I hope it will be a significant contribution: I hope it will be a
significant contribution. But to achieve all this there must be negotiation,
agreement and peace. The most vital need at the present hour is for Arabs
and Jews to enter into direct negotiations and hammer out an agreed
settlement. I plead with you, Mr. President, that you may use your unique
influence to induce the Arab States to face the realities of the situation and
to take that decisive step.

With affectionate greetings,
Yours very sincerely,
CH. WEIZMANN

Demographic Aspects of the Arab-Israeli Dispute (1973)
CENTRAL INTELLIGENCE AGENCY

Summary

The dream of the Zionist fathers was to establish a sovereign independent homeland to which Jews in the Diaspora could come and live in peace, free from discrimination. Since Israel was established in 1948, instead of peace with their Arab neighbors the Jews found 25 years of continuing hostility. Today, few Israelis believe that peace is close; indeed, some Israelis wonder if the Arabs ever intend to accept and make peace with the state of Israel. Since the 1967 war a new problem has arisen; i.e., the demographic threat posed by Arabs living inside the cease-fire lines.

The threat stems from Israel's control of about 1.5 million Arabs, those in occupied territories and in the pre-war Israel itself, and from the almost inexorable intertwining of the two areas. In the future, the Arab population is apt to grow more rapidly than the Jewish population. The former is based on the high Arab birth rate, twice that of the Israelis, while Israeli growth is heavily dependent upon immigration, the rate of which is basically downward. [...]

Thus, one of the basic questions facing Tel Aviv is whether Israel will, as some want, be a relatively small primarily Jewish state, or, as others want, be a larger but increasingly mixed Jewish-Arab state. In the absence of a peace settlement with the Arabs, a kind of territorial imperative operates in Tel Aviv. This being so, Jewish control inside the cease-fire lines will come to depend more and more on either denying the Arabs political rights or goading them into leaving.
[...]

Dimensions of a Problem
[...]
In 25 years, the Jewish majority will be faced with a sizable Arab minority; a generation beyond that, the Arab population could equal the Jewish. To maintain Jewish control, Tel Aviv would be forced either to deny political rights to their Arab wards or goad the Arabs into leaving. Few Israeli leaders face up to the problem, and none appear ready to act on the possibility that, in the long term, the fecund Arab population inside the cease-fire lines may pose a greater threat to the Jewish state than the impotent armies ranged outside them.

The question which even now confronts Israeli leaders is whether to maintain a solidly Jewish state by hedging out areas heavily settled by Muslim and Christian Arabs or to extend the state and take in more land and more Arabs. The first alternative projects a relatively small but almost exclusively Jewish state in the Zionist image--a kind of fortified Jewish ghetto in the Middle East--but a state in which there is no question of Jewish control. The second projects a larger solidly bi-national state, with

662

the Israelis clearly dominant--at least in the beginning--but one in which their control will be in time contested and perhaps diluted by their Arab wards.

[...]

Courses of Action

What is Israel to do? Kamal Nasser, one of three Palestinian leaders killed by Israeli commandos in Beirut in April 1973, said in an interview several years ago that he thought Israel was in a worse position that before the June war. The government's sovereignty over more than a million Arabs, he said, would not be compatible with the ideal of a state both Jewish and democratic. Theoretically, Nasser said, Israel has three options:

    -- To exterminate the Palestinians, a course Israel would find "impracticable."

    -- To withdraw to the pre-war lines, as provided (he said) by UN Security Council Resolution 242, a course Israel was not only unwilling but also unable to follow.

    -- To wait for the Jewish state to break down, a process that would be precipitated by a massive revolt of Israeli youth and could be hastened by a significant Arab military success.

Nasser was probably right about Israel's reaction to his first two possibilities, but wrong about the third. The idea of the Jewish state is so deeply imbedded in the national psychology that Tel Aviv would certainly take action if the existence of that state were threatened. Israeli officials are all dedicated to the proposition that Israel must remain a Jewish state, and they will fight to the death to keep it so. [...]

Solution to Palestine Arab Refugee Problem (1952)
Mohamed El-Tabii

What is the solution to the refugee problem?

The Arab leaders who were responsible for the loss of Palestine say that the solution is the return of the refugees to their homes in the heart of Israel.

How can this be achieved?

1.   By Israel's agreeing and submitting to it? This is impossible, because Israel has consistently refused to let the refugees return to their homes, despite UN resolution to that effect. The UN, meanwhile, could do nothing, because Israel is "Truman's spoiled baby" and because the UN is an "obedient tool in the hands of the U.S., which directs it and guides it as it [the U.S.] pleases."

Those Arabs who expect the new Republican administration to turn the White House policy upside down and turn its back on Israel are entertaining false hopes.

The most that the Arabs can hope for is that Eisenhower becomes less hostile to the Arabs and less appeasing to the Zionists, and unlike Truman, "who was a tool in the hands of Zionists," to "free himself from Zionist domination of White House policy."

Neither Israel, then, nor the US, the UN, Great Britain, or the rest who created, aided, and assisted Israel can be expected to accept or support the principle of letting the refugees return to their homes.

2.   Can the refugees be resettled by force, that is, by the Arab states waging a war to wipe Israel off the face of the map?

The Arab states are not ready today to take such a step for several reasons.

There are those who do not wish to antagonize the US; there are those who are subservient to London; there are those who do not wish to offend France; and those who are always ready to contribute promise and empty talk, but who, when the worst happens, refuse to contribute a single soldier for Palestine. The Arab states simple are not prepared and do not desire to wage such a war on Israel at this time.

Perhaps that day will come. All we can do is pray for the end of causes for dispute, for clear hearts, for uniting the purposes of the Arab states, and for

664 From Central Intelligence Agency. Report: Resettling of Refugees (Apr. 9, 1953) (translating & summarizing article published in AKHBAR EL-YOM (Nov. 8, 1952)).

providing them with the means of power for revenge to eradicate Israel and retrieve Palestine for its owners.

But until that day comes, shall the refugees remain dispersed, scattered, and suffering from disease, misery, and hunger?

3. The best solution to the problem is that advocated by the late King Abdullah of Jordan, which calls for resettling the Arab refugees along the borders of Israel.

King Abdullah believed that it is most dangerous for the Arab cause to have the refugees return to their homes in Israel, and the wisest step is to keep these one million Arabs outside Israel. King Abdullah reasoned that their return to Israel would, with the passing of time, make the refugees forget about their Arabism and the cause. They would be crushed by Israeli laws and assimilated into the population of Israel, or, at best, they would be relegated to the category of a "loyal minority" or a "peaceful minority" accepting Israeli rule and cooperating with their "fellow countrymen" the Jews of Israel.

However, if the refugees remain outside Israel, it would be possible for the Arab states bordering Israel to distribute and absorb them. Thus, Israel would be surrounded by a wall of hatred, embitterment, and readiness for revenge.

Then we will say to these refugees, and our children will say to their children: "Look across the borders: There is your country and your father's country. There is Palestine, which the Jews usurped from you. Prepare for the appointed day when you shall attack across the borders, eject the usurpers from your homes, and cleanse your blood of shame of defeat and all that went with it,"

If the UN, which contributes about 30 million dollars annually for relief to the refugees, donates 200-300 million dollars, and if the Arab states, who contribute millions of dollars yearly for relief purposes each make a lump-sum donation, then Jordan and Syria, as well as Lebanon and Egypt, can easily absorb these refugees by reclaiming lands for their resettlement, establishing industries for their employment, providing them with homes, and guaranteeing for them the means of a decent life.

Thus, the refugees can be provided a temporary home, and Arab home, which would safeguard their Arabism and keep alive in them the spirit of vengeance and that of recapturing their usurped land.

That was the opinion of King Abdullah Ibn al-Husayn; and it is the wisest opinion. May God have mercy on his soul and forgive me for some of the things I wrote about him.

An Arab "Refugee" Writes to the U.N. (1956)
Antoine F. Albina

[Mr. Dag Hammarskjold — Secretary General of the U.N.]

Though I am addressing you in my name, I do not doubt a moment that I am expressing the views and belief of Arabs in general and of every Palestinian Arab in particular, Moslem and Christian alike.

I belong to no party and owe allegiance to no one except to my Country and people.— I will not use preambles and avant propos and will go straight to the point, in short clear submissions and plain words.

No peace Mr. Secretary General, can be anticipated in this part of the world, as there can be no peace in the Middle East as long as Justice does not prevail and as long as Might persists to be Right.

The Palestine Arabs ask no favors and want no charity. No amount of dollars and no schemes can make them forget their homeland and desist from their natural, just and legal right to their possessions and the enjoyment of their private property, as words of sympathy lead us nowhere.

What we want is that the United Nations should implement their own resolutions and honor their own pledges. — We want men of good will to right the wrong done the Arabs; we want our appeals for Justice not to fall on deaf ears. — What we ask is that the United Nations should refrain from backing criminals to secure their theft of Palestine as it must be remembered that Israel exists only by virtue of power politics and continues to exist only because it is able to manipulate the machinery of the United Nations.

It is Israel who pleads for peace; it is Israel who has the greatest desire for peace. Yes, it is Israel who wants protection for territory they have stolen and approval of crimes committed against Arabs. It is Israel who wants protection of looted property and ravaged lands of Palestine. — It is the robber, the murdered, who wants to sit down with the victim and settle things amicably, by keeping the loot and enjoying what is not his.

Do you really, Mr. Secretary General, expect the Arabs to fall into this trap and enter in a pact with the thief, the robber and the murderer, surrendering their rights and their property?

Will you, and will Members of the United Nations for once visualize a group of gangsters, thieves and assassins invading your homes, farms, offices, shops, taking away all your belongings, looting, destroying, murdering those most dear to you, then settling down in your place as if it has always been their own. Then imagine someone in authority stating that

666

the thieves and the murderess have come to stay and that you are prevented to make any effort or take steps to recover your own things and throw out the criminal intruder from your own house.

How would you feel about it Mr. Secretary General?

Zionist aggression and many atrocities have driven one million Arabs from their homes and fields. They have taken refuge wherever they could, where very little is to be had.

How would you feel when you see the criminal aggressor enjoying your own home, looking at you from your own window, relaxing in the shade of your garden, gathering the fruit of your trees, sitting behind your desk, sleeping in your bed? How would you feel when you find him to be in possession of sentimental relics and most dear things to your heart while you are left in the open deprived of everything, living on charity and probably starving? How would you feel when after being robbed from everything, the thief shouts loud to all who want to hear him "Let's shake hands and keep the peace and forget about it, not that I have all that is yours"?

These are questions we want you to discuss with your own conscience and to answer to your own self.

This hypothetical suggestion Mr. Secretary General, clearly states the case of the Palestine Arab, now labelled 'Refugee', dispossessed of his home, his land and everything he possessed.

The Western Powers who have created the Israeli State at the expense of innocent Arab victims, seem to believe that one million or two of these Zionist gangsters gathered from various parts of the globe, allied to every underground center, and polluted with destructive doctrines, they seem to believe that these gangsters planted in Palestine are a great safeguard than the legal and rightful Arab owners of the Country and adjoining Arab States. Therefore the Arabs who were faithful allies and the most staunch supporters of the West and would have remained so, were antagonized, cheated and betrayed as if the Western Powers have forgotten that the friendship of both the Arab and Islamic World are of first importance to them and essential to world stability.

Therefore we earnestly ask the United Nations not to lure themselves in vain hopes: We will not sell our Country for any amount of Dollars or other aids and it should be realized that real peace in the Middle East cannot be achieved until there is a Just and Equitable solution of the Palestine Question, until the Palestine Arabs are given the Rights that are most certainly theirs ... their Country, their Properties, their Homes.
[...]

667

The Palestinian Predicament in Lebanon (2000)
Simon Haddad

What to do with the Palestinian refugees has been a core issue in the Arab-Israeli conflict since 1948. And of all the countries hosting Palestinians, Lebanon probably confronts the most sensitive and serious problems.

Lebanese authorities consider Palestinians a threat to the sensitive balance of religious and ethnic communities in their country. So, fearing that the Middle East peace process will try to implant Palestinians in Lebanon against the will of the Lebanese, the government continues to deny the Palestinians basic social and economic rights in order to discourage them from remaining there. As a result, Lebanon hosts the highest percentage of Palestinians living in camps (55 percent or 200,000 people). But then Lebanon's worries stem also from the continued presence of these armed Palestinians in the camps, because they represent a potential for instability, threatening to re-enact the civil war days unless a solution for the Palestinians is found: "If Palestinian refugees in Lebanon were not given the right to return home, they will become a time bomb."

In light of the foregoing, it is important to understand how Lebanese citizens look at the Palestinians resident in their country, and especially the prospect that they might settle permanently there. Toward this end, the author conducted a survey exploring several aspects of this question in late 1999 and early 2000. Survey questions probed the awareness of issues, attitudes, and expectations of likely results. The study has shown that barriers to social integration of Palestinians exist among the native population, although to varying degrees. Christians are manifestly more reluctant to tolerate Palestinians than their Muslim counterparts. Unexpectedly, though, there is a shared consensus on granting the refugees their basic rights, in a clear opposition to the Lebanese government's actual strategy. However, most Lebanese are aware of the ongoing debate over Palestinian settlement in the country, tend to oppose the idea, and call for preventing its imposition. Most Lebanese communities view the Palestinians as a major destabilizing force capable of upsetting the precarious sectarian balance of inter-group relations, and possibly even bringing on a renewed of civil war.

The Predicament

A community of Palestinians numbering about 400,000 lives in Lebanon, representing not less than 10 percent of the country's population. Moreover, conditions in the camps are grim because Palestinians in Lebanon suffer from discriminatory official policies preventing them from improving their living conditions.

Only a small fraction of Palestinians have acquired Lebanese citizenship,

668 From MIDDLE EAST QUARTERLY, Vol. 7, No. 3, pp. 29-40 (Sep. 2000).
Url: https://www.meforum.org/68/the-palestinian-predicament-in-lebanon

with a mere 3,000 naturalized until the 1980s. Although 60,000 were granted citizenship in 1994, the overwhelming majority of Palestinians remain stateless and are treated as foreigners who have no rights of property ownership, investment, or employment—at most, they have privileges granted by a complex and lengthy permit process. Large institutions are essentially closed to Palestinians because these are governed by rules that make allocations in accordance with sectarian affiliation. Moreover, Palestinians continue to be excluded from more than seventy-two professions. Basic Lebanese labor law says that non-Lebanese must obtain work permits for all regular jobs: construction, sanitation, agriculture. A second law restricts the practice of most professions—medicine, engineering, pharmacy—to Lebanese, forcing Palestinians to take jobs that offer low wages, insecurity, and no benefits.
[...]
In the past, high levels of education enabled Palestinians to compete for jobs even though they were disadvantaged as non-nationals. Educational achievement was also a source of collective pride and individual motivation—an interim substitute for a country and a passport. Today, after years of destruction and disruption, Palestinians in Lebanon are facing an educational crisis. While the United Nations Relief and Works Agency (UNRWA) provides Palestinians in Lebanon with primary education, they find it extremely difficult to enter the government secondary schools, which is a prerequisite for access to the university, and they continue to be excluded from public institutions for higher education. The resulting lack of education has jeopardized the economic independence and productivity of Palestinians.

The Lebanese state's reluctance to absorb the refugees means that 150,000 to 200,000 Palestinians live in twelve registered refugee camps intended to accommodate just 50,000 refugees. Restrictions on building and reconstruction in the camps contribute to the insecurity of Palestinians in Lebanon, forcing them to live in building semi- or totally destroyed during the civil war, inasmuch as rebuilding has been strictly and legally controlled.

It bears noting that Palestinians living in other Arab countries, such as Jordan and Syria, are not so marginalized. In Jordan, Palestinians constitute approximately 60 percent of the total population and 95 percent of them hold citizenship. They are a powerful force in the nation's economy and can work in any occupation of their choice; indeed, they have served as generals in the army and prime ministers. Palestinians in Syria are integrated into society at all levels and rarely suffer discrimination in employment, ownership, or political activity. Although they are not eligible for citizenship, they do enjoy a full legal equivalency with local nationals in almost all areas, including employment and governmental services. There are, however, some restrictions on Palestinian property ownership and mobility in Syria, as well as tight controls over political activities. To be sure, in other parts of the Arab world (Iraq and Egypt particularly), Palestinians have been subjected to harsh treatment and restrictions, but their numbers in those countries are much smaller than in Lebanon.

Reluctance for Palestinian Settlement

Why this especially poor situation of the Palestinians resident in Lebanon? One Lebanese writer, Raghid as-Sulh, has listed four reasons for opposing the permanent settlement Palestinians:

* Original Intent: Granting the refugees sanctuary was undertaken as a humane, emergency measure; it was never intended to be permanent.

* Economic: Lebanon is a small country with limited resources, which makes it unable to absorb the Palestinian refugees, especially following the devastation inflicted by the civil war.

* Political and historical: Lebanese see themselves as having paid a much higher price for the Palestinian cause than any other country, for they blame the Palestinians for all the wars and troubles their country has been through. Lebanese feel they cannot be asked to pay more in the form of the consequences incumbent on settling the Palestinians in Lebanon.

* Demographic: Absorbing the Palestinians would alter the country's complex sectarian balance and unsettle the political structures that have been crafted to reflect that balance. Specifically, in a country divided between Muslims and Christians, an influx of Palestinians would dilute the power of the Christians, and particularly the Maronite Christians.

Formally speaking, Lebanese officials reject the prospect of permitting Palestinians to become naturalized Lebanese because this "would constitute a negation of the Palestinian right to return to their homeland." But most Lebanese have other motives for resisting this prospect: they see citizenship for Palestinians upsetting the delicate confessional balance in the country's political structure that is predicated on demographics. Reflecting the complete lack of popular support of Palestinian citizenship, Interior Minister Michel al-Murr recently announced that a new clause has been added to the naturalization draft law to prevent Palestinians from gaining citizenship. At the same time [...] well over a majority of Lebanese believe that Palestinians should be allowed some social and economic rights, such as the right to work.

In sum, the Palestinians' adverse conditions appear to result from a deliberate strategy to discourage Palestinians from remaining in Lebanon. Seeing Palestinians as a threat to the Lebanese people, Beirut has treated them as second-class citizens, denying them basic social and economic rights since 1948 and keeping them apart from the Lebanese population, so as not to be able to assimilate. The authorities constantly repeat the mantra of former prime minister Rafiq al-Hariri, uttered in 1998, that "Lebanon will never, ever integrate Palestinians. They will not receive civic or economic rights or even work permits. Integration would take the Palestinians off the shoulders of the international agency which has supported them since 1948."

[…]

Implications for Arab-Israeli Diplomacy

[…]

The study also shows that, more than any other group, Druze and Sunni respondents are ready to accept settlement. This is noteworthy because settlement has long been seen by many Sunnis—traditionally strong advocates of Arab nationalism—as an admission of final defeat by Israel. Not all of them appear ready to accept the loss of an Arab cause that is linked to the repatriation of the refugees.

For Israel, however, whatever the legal and moral merit of the Arab claims of the "right of return," this will not under any conceivable set of circumstances be realized. No Israeli government will ever accept changing substantially the demographic balance of the Jewish state—since the state's very *raison d'être* is its Jewish character. Former prime minister Shimon Peres has voiced the Israeli position on this point:

> a maximalist claim; if accepted, it would wipe out the national character of the state of Israel, making the Jewish majority into a minority. Consequently, there is no chance it will be accepted, either now or in the future.

[…]

In line with these popular attitudes, Lebanese officials continue to refuse settlement and to insist on repatriation. While Israel has refused even to consider repatriation, Lebanon has made resolving the refugee crisis a precondition for peace. […]

An Imposed Settlement

[…]

U.S. proposals to settle refugees in Arab states have so far proven unworkable. They were met with official rejection in the case of Jordan's King Abdullah: "Everybody wants to solve this problem but it will not be at the expense of Jordan." The Gulf states also rejected the proposals as a potential danger to political stability. As permanent status negotiations resumed, the Palestinian Authority has shown no enthusiasm for taking the Palestinians in Lebanon into a future Palestinian state. Interestingly, like Lebanon, Syria, and Jordan, the Palestinian Authority considers itself one of the countries hosting refugees. Arafat prefers to hold onto the Palestinian right of return in order to keep the pressure on Israel and also because of economic obstacles facing those who want to relocate to the

West Bank and Gaza Strip.

One proposed solution to the refugee problem is emigration to Western countries. In a study involving Palestinian refugees from the Ain Al-Hilwa camp near Sidon, Hilal Khashan found that 98 percent of the respondents wished to emigrate to the West. Probably, that would also be the most popular alternative among the population at large. To date, Canada has offered to host 15,000 Palestinians.

Still, there will continue to be a significant Palestinian presence in Lebanon and some very tentative steps have been taken to address this fact. In October 1992, Lebanese foreign minister Faris Buwayz stated that the permanent settlement of 50,000-100,000 Palestinians in Lebanon should be viewed as acceptable One solution is for a portion of the Palestinian community to have its legal status normalized through extended Palestinian citizenship coupled with permanent residency status. The U.S. green card or the French *carte de sejour* could serve as a model: full civil and economic rights but not political rights (voting, office-holding) thus promoting socioeconomic integration without hampering political stability.

Why Egypt and Other Arab Countries Are Unwilling to Take in Palestinian Refugees from Gaza (2023)

ARAB NEWS

As desperate Palestinians in sealed-off Gaza try to find refuge under Israel's relentless bombardment in retaliation for Hamas' brutal Oct. 7 attack, some ask why neighboring Egypt and Jordan don't take them in.

The two countries, which flank Israel on opposite sides and share borders with Gaza and the occupied West Bank, respectively, have replied with a staunch refusal. [...]

Egyptian President Abdel Fattah El-Sisi made his toughest remarks yet on Wednesday, saying the current war was not just aimed at fighting Hamas, which rules the Gaza Strip, "but also an attempt to push the civilian inhabitants to ... migrate to Egypt." He warned this could wreck peace in the region.

Jordan's King Abdullah II gave a similar message a day earlier, saying, "No refugees in Jordan, no refugees in Egypt."

Their refusal is rooted in fear that Israel wants to force a permanent expulsion of Palestinians into their countries and nullify Palestinian demands for statehood. El-Sisi also said a mass exodus would risk bringing militants into Egypt's Sinai Peninsula, from where they might launch attacks on Israel, endangering the two countries' 40-year-old peace treaty.

Here is a look at what is motivating Egypt's and Jordan's stances.

A history of displacement

Displacement has been a major theme of Palestinian history. In the 1948 war around Israel's creation, an estimated 700,000 Palestinians were expelled or fled from what is now Israel. Palestinians refer to the event as the Nakba, Arabic for "catastrophe."

In the 1967 Mideast war, when Israel seized the West Bank and Gaza Strip, 300,000 more Palestinians fled, mostly into Jordan.

The refugees and their descendants now number nearly 6 million, most living in camps and communities in the West Bank, Gaza, Lebanon, Syria and Jordan. The diaspora has spread further, with many refugees building lives in Gulf Arab countries or the West.

After fighting stopped in the 1948 war, Israel refused to allow refugees to return to their homes. Since then, Israel has rejected Palestinian demands for a return of refugees as part of a peace deal, arguing that it would threaten the country's Jewish majority.

Egypt fears history will repeat itself and a large Palestinian refugee population from Gaza will end up staying for good.

No guarantee of return

That's in part because there's no clear scenario for how this war will end.
[...]
El-Sisi said fighting could last for years if Israel argues it hasn't sufficiently crushed militants. He proposed that Israel house Palestinians in its Negev Desert, which neighbors the Gaza Strip, until it ends its military operations.

"Israel's lack of clarity regarding its intentions in Gaza and the evacuation of the population is in itself problematic," said Riccardo Fabiani, Crisis Group International's North Africa Project Director. "This confusion fuels fears in the neighborhood."

Egypt has pushed for Israel to allow humanitarian aid into Gaza, and Israel said Wednesday that it would, though it didn't say when. According to United Nations, Egypt, which is dealing with a spiraling economic crisis, already hosts some 9 million refugees and migrants, including roughly 300,000 Sudanese who arrived this year after fleeing their country's war.

But Arab countries and many Palestinians also suspect Israel might use this opportunity to force permanent demographic changes to wreck Palestinian demands for statehood in Gaza, the West Bank and east Jerusalem, which was also captured by Israel in 1967.

El-Sisi repeated warnings Wednesday that an exodus from Gaza was intended to "eliminate the Palestinian cause ... the most important cause of our region." He argued that if a demilitarized Palestinian state had been created long ago in negotiations, there would not be war now.

"All historical precedent points to the fact that when Palestinians are forced to leave Palestinian territory, they are not allowed to return back," said H.A. Hellyer, a senior associate fellow at the Carnegie Endowment for International Peace. "Egypt doesn't want to be complicit in ethnic cleansing in Gaza."

Arab countries' fears have only been stoked by the rise under Israeli Prime Minister Benjamin Netanyahu of hard-right parties that talk in positive terms about removing Palestinians. Since the Hamas attack, the rhetoric has become less restrained, with some right-wing politicians and media commentators calling for the military to raze Gaza and drive out its inhabitants. One lawmaker said Israel should carry out a "new Nakba" on Gaza.

674

Worries over Hamas

At the same time, Egypt says a mass exodus from Gaza would bring Hamas or other Palestinian militants onto its soil. That might be destabilizing in Sinai, where Egypt's military fought for years against Islamic militants and at one point accused Hamas of backing them.

Egypt has backed Israel's blockade of Gaza since Hamas took over in the territory in 2007, tightly controlling the entry of materials and the passage of civilians back and forth. It also destroyed the network of tunnels under the border that Hamas and other Palestinians used to smuggle goods into Gaza.

With the Sinai insurgency largely put down, "Cairo does not want to have a new security problem on its hands in this problematic region," Fabiani said.

El-Sisi warned of an even more destabilizing scenario: the wrecking of Egypt and Israel's 1979 peace deal. He said that with the presence of Palestinian militants, Sinai "would become a base for attacks on Israel. Israel would have the right to defend itself ... and would strike Egyptian territory."

"The peace which we have achieved would vanish from our hands," he said, "all for the sake of the idea of eliminating the Palestinian cause."

The Arab World Uses Palestinian Refugees as Pawns Against Israel

(2023)

Zina Rakhamilova

Throughout the entire Israeli-Palestinian conflict, it has been clear that the plight of the Palestinians is being used as a political tool and weapon against Israel. My career has been dedicated to educating the public about the Middle East, highlighting that Palestinian suffering has persisted since Israel's War of Independence. Unlike other displaced groups, Palestinians have remained refugees because no other country has offered them a home.

Since the Six Day War in 1967, the struggle for Palestinian liberation has (supposedly) been at the heart and soul of the Arab world. However, actions speak louder than words, and at a time when Palestinians in Gaza need help the most, leaders of these Arab countries show just how little they care about them. Egypt's and Jordan's unwavering refusal to grant Gazan civilians refuge while Israel wages its war against Hamas is proof that, to Arab leaders, concern for the Palestinians is nothing but empty words.

War is always tragic and, in most cases, leaves populations displaced, as we saw in February 2022 when Russia invaded Ukraine. The United Nations High Commissioner of Refugees (UNHCR) reports that nearly six million Ukrainian refugees were recorded across Europe, while an estimated eight million had been displaced by May 2022. In other words, according to these stats, about one-quarter of Ukraine's population had to flee their homes as a result of the war.

In the case of Israel and the Palestinians in 1948, when Arab dictators and ultra-nationalist Palestinian leaders started the War of Independence, about 750,000 Palestinians were displaced.

In most cases, refugees and displaced persons fall under UNHCR, the UN agency that protects and assists refugees and displaced persons by helping them find solutions after war. Most of the time, UNHCR provides humanitarian assistance to refugees and helps to facilitate voluntary return to their home countries, integrate them into host communities, or resettle them in third countries when return and integration are impossible. An example with my own family happened in 1991, when the Iron Curtain fell in Russia and we were forced to flee as refugees. We immediately were absorbed into Israel, which took in many Jewish Russians who were fleeing Soviet persecution.

Today, the 750,000 (at most) Palestinian refugees from the War of Independence have turned into over 5.9 million refugees. The vast majority of today's Palestinian refugees are now the descendants of Palestinians who were expelled or fled their homes during the War of Independence. While UNHCR exists to mitigate these problems, the reason the Palestinian refugee crisis is growing is that Palestinians do not fall under UNHCR; instead, they are the only refugees in the world to fall under an exclusive UN refugee category.

The United Nations Relief and Works Agency for Palestine Refugees (UNRWA) was established in 1949 and has contributed to the prolonged Palestinian refugee situation. While other refugees under UNHCR adhere to the standard international definition of refugees outlined in the 1951 Refugee Convention, UNRWA's definition of a refugee includes descendants of those displaced in the 1948 Arab-Israeli War. This definition is a huge departure from the standard refugee definition, creating a perpetuation of refugee status for the Palestinians for generations to come.

Why have Palestinians been forced to stay as refugees for 75 years?

This raises a legitimate question, which is "why?" Why on earth would it be advantageous to force the Palestinians to carry on a refugee status for 75 years? The vast majority of Palestinians were not alive in 1948, so what other explanation could there be for perpetuating their suffering and the refusal of Arab countries to take them? The Arab leaders claim to care about Palestinians, yet all their actions prove otherwise. The only legitimate answer is that they want to prolong Palestinian suffering in order to continue the conflict against Israel.

Palestinians are also fed an unrealistic notion of the "Right of Return," a political position that the Palestinian refugees of today will return to the territory that is now Israel proper. In no way is this a realistic notion, and it is used as nothing more than to undermine Israel as a Jewish state. While the Palestinians were offered reparations in several previous peace deals, their leadership has rejected all of them and instead pushed the notion of "right of return." Holding on to this unrealistic expectation and rejecting statehood and liberation multiple times has also contributed to the Palestinian refugee problem.

History repeats itself as Arab leaders have taken the same positions ever since the Six-Day War. Indeed, King Abdullah II of Jordan announced shortly after the October 7 Hamas massacre of Israelis that accepting Palestinian refugees is a "red line" for Jordan. Egyptian Prime Minister Mostafa Madbouly dismissed calls to take in Palestinians from Gaza and said, "We are ready to sacrifice millions of lives to protect our territory from any encroachment."

Twenty-one Arab countries claim to care about Palestinians but none of them are taking in Palestinian refugees.

At a time when Gazans need help the most, Arab leaders demonstrate that they are actively willing to watch millions of them die to prevent them from entering their territory. They want Palestinians to suffer and fail because it continues to excuse any altercations with Israel. Anyone who is ignoring all this and the context in which Hamas murdered, raped, burned, and decapitated civilians when they choose to blame Israel for Palestinian civilian deaths is just a vicious antisemite. Neither do they honestly care about a better and safer future for the Palestinians.

TERRORISM

Debate on Palestine (1939)
U.K. HOUSE OF COMMONS

Mr. Williams [...] Every man and woman in this country who remembers the fate of the Jews and political prisoners in Austria must be filled today with distrust and foreboding. And who can fail to feel his heart go out in sympathy to a proud and brave people who have so suddenly been subjected to these inflictions, whose liberties are curtailed, whose national independence has gone? I repeat that question, which was submitted by the Prime Minister in his Birmingham speech, "Who can fail to feel his heart go out in sympathy ... to those who have so suddenly been subjected to these inflictions, whose liberties are curtailed today, whose national independence have gone?" [....]

Mr. Crossley The force of the hon. Gentleman's final quotation was a little lost because it could equally be applied to the Arabs. They also have been denied for 10 years their legitimate aspirations, but it is at least surprising to hear the Labour party of Great Britain denying to a subject population the right to govern themselves.

Mr. T. Williams What did the hon. Member say they had lost?

Mr. Crossley They have been denied their political aspirations. The hon. Gentleman [...] asked me whether I could say that Arabs and Jews had not lived in certain parts of Palestine in happiness together even during the troubles. It is true that there were a few Jewish colonies which were absolutely unmolested throughout the troubles. What were they? They were the old Jewish prewar settlements, and they were not Zionist settlements at all. That is the significant fact, and the true one. He asked me why Arabs had killed Arabs, and I can only answer that by saying that whenever you get a population engaged in what is really civil strife, that sort of thing occurs. There is the analogy of Ireland. The whole of the Irish people were against us after the War. It is no use denying that. The whole of them to a man in the whole of Southern Ireland, except a very few who are known as the Irish loyalists, were against us. The extremists, undoubtedly, gained control and many Irish moderates at that time were killed. But I hope those unhappy days for Palestine are over. I conceive it as my task today to deploy the Arab case in this Debate just as the hon. Gentleman has deployed the Jewish case. I do not believe that there has ever been a Debate in this House when this House would have been more justified in calling to the Bar an Arab speaker to explain the Arab point of view from the point of view of his own countrymen and his own country. I would have liked to have seen Mr. George Antonius called to the Bar. There are no Arab Members of Parliament. There are no Arab constituents to bring influence upon their Members of Parliament. There is no Arab control of newspapers in this country. It is impossible almost to get a pro-Arab letter in the "Times." There are in the City no Arab financial houses who control large amounts of finance. There is no Arab control of newspaper advertisements in this country. There are no Arab ex-Colonial Secretaries, who one by one can get up and thunder, as they will, at the Government during this Debate, because of the mistakes they themselves have made in the past. Finally, and I want the Colonial Secretary to pay particular attention to this point, tomorrow night there is to be a broadcast. There is to be himself giving the Government point of view. There is to be the hon. Member for the Don Valley (Mr. T. Williams) to advance what is undoubtedly the Zionist point of view although there are many Arab supporters on his benches. There is to be the right hon. Member for Carnarvon Boroughs (Mr. Lloyd George) supporting the Zionist point of view. There will not be a supporter of the Arabs who can advance his point of view. […]

I congratulate the Minister on the presentation of his case today, but if it gives any comfort to hon. Members opposite I may say that I found myself as violently disagreeing with parts of his speech from the Arab point of view as some of them did from the Zionist point of view. There is this to be said about violence in Palestine, that in face of absolute misrepresentation, or lack of representation, the Arabs have had in this House for 20 years, it is a lamentable fact that only violence brought their claims to our attention. I have been consistently and steadily an adviser of moderate methods. The more I advised moderate methods in the past the less I got a hearing. It is a fact that in the first speech I ever made in this House I was interrupted over and over again. I could not put the Arab case across the Floor of the House at that time, when I was practically the only Arab supporter called.
[…]

The Fedayeen: Politics of Spoiling (1972)
CENTRAL INTELLIGENCE AGENCY

1. […] The commandos had been on the defensive since their defeat by the Jordanian army in 1970 and their virtual expulsion from Jordan in 1971. They had lost the support of the public, Palestinians included. Developments in Jordan seriously damaged their capability to operate in the Arab world as well as in Israel, for Egypt and Syria have long imposed strict controls on operations against from their territory. In the wake of Israeli raids against fedayeen areas in Lebanon, the Beirut government has too tightened restrictions on the guerillas. In recent months extremists have gained influence among the fedayeen and more and more guerillas have come to see terrorist operations outside Israel as their only remaining weapon. The new tactics have, in fedayeen eyes, been successful. […]

The Black September Organization

2. The most notable manifestation of the trend toward terrorism has been the Black September Organization -- whose name derives from the date of King Husayn's defeat of the fedayeen in Jordan. Like the bulk of the Palestinian population, Black September feats that a settlement of the Arab-Israeli conflict would involve Arab concessions at the expense of the Palestinians. Black September goes further in believing that, through fostering acts of violence against King Husayn and his government as well as against Israel and its international supporters (principally in the US), tensions can be increased and the chances of negotiations reduced.

3. There is still much we do not know about this group, which practices a high order of security. Its leadership is closely intertwined with that of Fatah. Indeed, it appears that Black September is simply a cover name that allows Fatah -- the largest and heretofore relatively most moderate guerilla organization -- to disclaim responsibility for terrorist operations carried out by its numbers. […]

Israeli Reaction

7. The Israeli government has decided that the emphasis by the fedayeen on spectacular acts of terrorism requires new methods on Israel's part. Mrs. Meir has announced what amounts to a policy of striking at the fedayeen without waiting for prior incident. Tel Aviv has always believed that forceful reaction against guerilla bases located in neighboring Arab states would both discourage the fedayeen and, more important, induce the Arab host governments themselves to move against the commandos. The Israelis see King Husayn's blows against the guerillas in 1970 and 1971 and present Lebanese restrictions on the fedayeen as the fruit of their forceful retaliation. Tel Aviv obviously hopes that anticipatory strikes will have even greater effect.

[...]
<u>Outlook</u>

9.   The terrorists have achieved some of the aims of their recent series of spectacular acts. [...] Also of great importance from Fatah's point of view, the recent wave of terrorism and the major Israeli retaliation it provoked further embittered Arab-Israeli retaliations. It further isolated Jordan, which alone of the Arab governments forthrightly condemned the terrorists. And finally, the fedayeen succeeded in shifting world attention from efforts to promote a settlement of the Arab-Israeli conflict to international efforts to combat terrorism.
[...]
14.   Fedayeen pride in the success of spectacular acts of terrorism will not induce greater cooperation among the rival guerilla groups. Instead, Black September success may spur the Front for the Liberation of Palestine and other splinter groups to step up their own terrorist efforts in order to boost their own prestige. [...] [T]he rise of Black September is proving unsettling. It is strengthening the extremists in Fatah who have long been pressuring Arafat for greater influence. The Black September Organization will almost inevitably play a larger role in making Fatah policy. [...]

15.   Continuing recourse to terror by the fedayeen will breed counter-terror by their opponents. Some Israelis themselves have frequently been tempted to retaliate in kind, particularly when they concluded that regular military operations were not enough reply to terrorists.

16.   *In sum*, despite their defeat in conventional military encounters with Israel and in confrontations with Husayn, the fedayeen have shown that they cannot be counted out of the Middle East equation. They are certainly not likely to make much headway in weakening the Israeli position in the Arab-Israeli conflict. But they still can play -- and are playing -- a spoiling role, in respect of negotiations toward a settlement. For they are able to provoke both the Arab governments, and especially the Israelis, into reactions that further embitter the conflict. And they are able to concentrate the attention of the outside world on themselves rather than on parties to the conflict who are willing to entertain thoughts of compromise.

Terrorism at the Munich Olympic Games: How an Event Five Decades Ago Has a Lasting Impact Today (2019)
Ben McEvoy, et al

What began as the 1972 Munich Olympic Games quickly became a live broadcast of terror that forever changed the world. The organizers had aimed to overcome the dark history of Hitler's 1936 Berlin Olympics, which were coloured by the spectre of Nazi power, by stressing the themes of unity and peace going so far as naming the event the 'Happy Games'.

Despite this message, the Munich Olympic Committee refused to acknowledge two requests by the Palestine Liberation Organization (PLO) to compete in the Olympic Games. This snub inspired the leaders of the Black September Organization, who put forward a plan to use media coverage of the Olympics to draw attention to the plight of the Palestinian people and pressure Israel to set free Palestinian prisoners.

The first live broadcast of terror

Early in the morning of September 5, 1972, eight members of Black September shot their way into the Israeli quarters at the Olympic village. By 5:00 a.m. the terrorists had taken 11 Israelis hostage, killing one and wounding another. By 8:00 a.m. news of the siege had been broadcast by Bavarian radio.

The coverage that ensued was the first time that TV networks broadcast an act of terrorism to an audience of almost 900 million in real-time. Black September demanded a plane to fly the hostages to Egypt. German authorities schemed to ambush the terrorists and rescue the hostages. Initial reports indicated the police had succeeded, but the unprepared rescuers bungled the mission. The remaining nine hostages died horribly at Fürstenfeldbruck airbase just after midnight that same day.

Jim McKay of ABC News got official word of the disaster back in the United States — during primetime no less — and delivered the terrible news.

"They're all gone."

The event left an indelible mark on the souls of millions. For Olympic athletes, their families, their countrymen and an audience of 900 million worldwide, the image of an unknown man in a balaclava became the defining image of the Munich Games. The Munich Olympic crisis became "one of the hottest news stories of the year" dominating the U.S. network evening news of all three networks for days — only to be superseded by the unfolding Watergate Scandal.

It was the first terrorist spectacle to be exposed to the public in such visceral, electrifying detail. And it was this spectacle that set in motion a relationship between the media and terrorists that has had an indelible impact on all of us today.

Media gives terrorists the attention they need to succeed

Terrorists require attention to succeed. American scholar Mark Juergensmeyer calls terrorism "performance violence" and notes "if terrorism is theatre, then terrorists want to perform where there are plenty of spectators in the seats." The success of an attack then is measured not only by the number of casualties and whether demands are met but by how many people witness the act itself.

After Munich, terrorists learned to attract worldwide attention through mainstream television in order to achieve this end. The relationship between terrorism and the media had become crucial to their success — and the media has almost always obliged. So why do they continue to cover terrorism so extensively?

The media makes money on how much engagement their content gets. More viewers mean more advertising or subscriber dollars, which means more profit. It makes sense that the media is eager to report — and even over-report — on terrorist attacks and groups. In 2015, Priceonomics researcher, Nemil Dala, found that "regardless of the reason, currently, terrorism deaths are the single most heavily covered type of death per capita in the first pages of the New York Times compared to every other way a human can die."

Margaret Thatcher famously addressed this concern in 1985. She proposed a voluntary code of conduct among the media to "try to find ways to starve the terrorist and the hijacker of the oxygen of publicity on which they depend."

Larry Grossman, then President of NBC News, believed that NBC should not be held accountable, stating "the job of the press is not to worry about the consequences of its coverage, but to tell the truth... and let the chips fall where they may."

Recent studies have revealed that the media's reporting actually elicits terrorist attacks. One report by scholar Michael Jetter shines a light on CNN, CBS, NBC, and Fox News and shows how a one-minute news segment about a terrorist act caused on average of 1.4 attacks the following week.
[...]

Fatah's Restraint

The supporters of PLO Chairman Yasir Arafat continue to adhere to the PLO's decade long ban on international terrorism, although they still carry out attacks against civilian and military targets in Israel and the occupied territories. Palestinians refer to these attacks as the "armed struggle to liberate the homeland" and do not consider them to be terrorism. Virtually all Arab nations endorse the so-called armed struggle.

Palestinian groups launched more than 50 attacks in Israel or the occupied territories in 1984. Fatah or other pro-Arafat cells inside the occupied territories probably were responsible for at least some of these attacks. In most cases, however, we have been unable to determine the exact perpetrators. Sometimes, several Palestinian groups claim responsibility for the same incident in an effort to demonstrate their dedication to the anti-Zionist cause and their continued capability to operate inside Israeli territory. At times the true perpetrators will not claim responsibility, so as not to reveal their operational infrastructure or prompt Israeli reprisals against their bases outside Israel.
[…]

Syrian-Based PLO Groups

All the anti-Arafat PLO groups are based in Syria or Syrian-controlled territory in Lebanon. From these locations they can infiltrate teams into Israel or the West Bank, either directly or through Jordan, and provide support to terrorist cells already in place. We believe that most of the Palestinian terrorist incidents in Israeli-controlled territory were the work of these radical Palestinians.

The Democratic Front for the Liberation of Palestine (DFLP) claimed credit for two of the most notable attacks. The first was a grenade attack in a Jerusalem store last February that wounded 21. Then, in April, three DFLP terrorists attacked shoppers on a crowded street in Jerusalem with automatic weapons and hand grenades. Forty-eight persons were wounded before the terrorists were overpowered.

Most of the Palestinian attacks against Israel were like the February incident—small bombs or grenades left in places where Israeli civilians congregate. In the last year there was also a resurgence of a type of attack common before the Israeli invasion of Lebanon: Katyusha rockets fired at Israeli border settlements. At least 10 such attacks occurred in the last 12 months. The Popular Front for the Liberation of Palestine (PFLP) and the Popular Struggle Front (PSF) claimed credit for some of them.
[…]

Jonathan Gullis [...] [N]o matter what land borders have been proposed in peace negotiations in the 73 years since the UN partition plan of 1947, the Palestinian leadership has rejected every option. I found myself wondering how that could be the case, when a two-state solution is clearly the only way to reconcile Jewish and Arab aspirations of self-determination in the land. It became apparent that the answer is not especially palatable: over many decades, Palestinian children have grown up in an environment of institutionalised radicalisation.

In schools named after suicide bombers, schoolchildren are taught from the age of six that Israel is a temporary construct that will,

> "disappear as the fog over the sea".

Palestinians are rightly proud of their youth literacy rate, which is among the highest in the world, but it is undermined by the more harmful material within the curriculum, which plays a significant part in indoctrinating the population. Eight-year-olds learn poetry from the following verse:

> "I vow I shall sacrifice my blood, to saturate the land of the generous and will eliminate the usurper from my country, and will annihilate the remnants of the foreigners."

[...]

A report published by the Institute for Monitoring Peace and Cultural Tolerance in School Education in September 2019 found that the most recent Palestinian Authority school textbooks are even more extreme than previous editions. Despite promises from the PA to review and remove unacceptable content, the report concludes that there is a "clear deterioration" in terms of content meeting UNESCO-derived standards for peace and tolerance in school education. After examining 202 textbooks from the current curriculum, IMPACT-se found,

> "a systematic insertion of violence, martyrdom and jihad across all grades and subjects",

where,

> "the possibility of peace with Israel is rejected".

[...]

Peace is not presented as preferred or even possible. Palestinian children are not taught what peace will even look like. Peace agreements and proposals with Israel that previously appeared in Palestinian Authority schoolbooks have been removed. Nine-year-olds are asked to count the number of martyrs in Palestinian uprisings—"If the number of martyrs of the first intifada is 2,026 martyrs, and the number of martyrs of the Al-

Aqsa martyrs intifada is 5,050" and so on. Imagery in a textbook for 16-year-olds implies that Jews control the world. Ten-year-olds are taught that Jews are enemies of Islam and eight-year-olds learn in their textbooks that Jerusalem is a holy city only for Muslims and Christians. Right hon. and hon. Members will no doubt be aware that Jerusalem has been at the core of the Jewish faith and world for more than 3,000 years. Make no mistake: this is antisemitism, and we must condemn it as strongly as we fight antisemitism at home.

[…]

I mentioned that Palestinian schools are named after terrorists—at least 31 at the last count. Five of those schools are named after Dalal Mughrabi, the perpetrator of one of the worst terror attacks in Israel's history, the 1978 coastal road massacre. Mughrabi led the hijacking of a bus and the murder of 38 civilians, including 13 children. She is portrayed as a central female role model for Palestinian girls. In the Arabic language textbook for 10-year-olds, of which I have a copy here, there is a large image of Mughrabi with the accompanying text:

> "Dalal Mughrabi Our Palestinian history is brimming with names of martyrs who have given their lives to the homeland, including the martyr Dalal Mughrabi. Her struggle portrays challenge and heroism, making her memory immortal in our hearts and minds".

[…]

Dr Matthew Offord I congratulate my hon. Friend on the great speech that he is making. Is he aware that in addition to the 31 schools named after terrorists from the Palestinian Authority, three are named after Nazi collaborators? That sends a clear message, not only that killing Israelis is something that children should be encouraged to do, but that they will be honoured for undertaking such a heinous crime.

Jonathan Gullis I am aware of that. Such a blatant attempt to stir up racial hatred and bring up what is a very dark history is despicable and disgusting. As one whose step-grandmother was born in Germany in the 1920s, went through an education system under Nazi rule and has lived with the shame of a nation—as many Germans do, even though they played no part in the atrocities that took place—I absolutely agree that reliving, remembering and reminding the Israeli people of such horrors should never ever be allowed, and that it should be called out for what is.

Nicola Richards The fact that holocaust denial is most prevalent in Gaza and the west bank compared with elsewhere in the world—standing at around 82% of the population—proves that something is going seriously wrong. […]

Jonathan Gullis […] The majority of Palestinians are under the age of 25, and recent polling has shown that they are increasingly moving towards more extreme ideology. It is with sad inevitability that the radical incitement I highlight will be a central contributing factor. The Palestinian leadership have failed to provide a positive vision for the future of their people. Until they ensure that their curriculum promotes peace, the prospects for an agreement with Israel will remain bleak.

Tim Loughton [...] Most alarming is that these propaganda books are available to children as young as six, and that those on the Palestinian side found guilty of terrorism offences against Israelis—not throwing stones at buses; I have been critical about the way such people have been treated by the courts—are as young as 11. These deeply impressionable young people are being indoctrinated by the failed Palestinian Authority, which relies on fear and the poverty of the Palestinians to foment hatred against Israelis and the wider world. That is what this amounts to. [...]

Robert Largan [...] It worries me that they not only glorify terrorism but financially reward it, paying monthly salaries to terrorists and their families to the tune of £260 million in 2018, or 7% of their entire budget. Like him, I desperately want to see peace, but while those payments continue, the prospect is bleak.

Jonathan Gullis My hon. Friend speaks with absolute authority on this subject. It is utterly shameful that money is paid to terrorists who have committed heinous crimes against the people of Israel and foreign nationals in Israel. This problem affects us globally. We absolutely need to ensure that the funding stops, because it does not show any sign of facilitating peace in the future. [...]

[...] There are now more than 320,000 Palestinian refugee children in UNRWA schools in the west bank and Gaza—internationally designated Palestinian territories. Children in those schools are taught that they are refugees from what is now Israel, and that they will one day return, in line with the teachings in their textbook. Does the Minister believe that that is compatible with our stated aim to protect the political and physical viability of a two-state solution? A right of return for 5 million Palestinian refugees will demographically end Israel's existence as a Jewish state. [...]

I shall finish by reflecting on the impact that the Palestinian Authority curriculum has had in recent years on the children whom they are duty-bound to protect. Since September 2015, 87 Israelis and foreign nationals have been killed and more than 1,520 wounded in 210 stabbings, 239 shootings, 77 car rammings and one bus bombing. Palestinian youths under the age of 21 have carried out many of those acts of terrorism. Even screwdrivers have been used as weapons, and perpetrators have included children as young as 11 years old.

It is well known that Palestinian terrorists who kill Israelis receive monthly payments to reward their acts of terrorism, with higher salaries given to those who have killed more Israelis. It should be a matter of great sadness to us all that these children are raised in an environment infected with radical messages, with no hope for peaceful co-existence with Israel. [...]

Robert Courts [...] Like everyone here, I long for nothing more than for peace, and for the Israelis and Palestinians to be able to live together in harmony and make the most of this wonderful land together, but I struggle to see how that will happen when the educational biosphere in which young Palestinians grow up is saturated with antisemitic hatred. My hon. Friend quoted some examples from the IMPACT-se report, which I also have in front of me, and I will quote one or two others. One example that particularly struck me was the teaching in science of Newton's second law:

> "During the first Palestinian uprising, Palestinian youths used slingshots to confront the soldiers of the Zionist Occupation and defend themselves from their treacherous bullets. What is the relationship between the elongation of the slingshot's rubber and the tensile strength affecting it? What are the forces that influence the stone after its release from the slingshot?"

I was particularly struck by that because it normalises violence and legitimises hatred. There is no way that children are likely to grow up with a normal, benevolent attitude to their fellow citizens when science is taught in such a way.

A second example that particularly struck me came from "Arabic Language":

> "Students in grade 9 Arabic study a story describing a firebomb attack on Israeli passengers traveling on a bus, reporting the terror incident as a 'barbecue party'...on one of the buses of the colonial settlement."

Not only is that unacceptable material; it constitutes antisemitic hatred that will prolong and worsen the terrible troubles in that land.
[...]
Alyn Smith [...] The radicalisation of Palestinian children is of course a problem and something we should be concerned about, but if anybody thinks textbooks are the primary reason why Palestinian children are being radicalised, they are not paying attention to the wider context. [...] If we want to see where radicalisation is coming from, it is to be found in the hopeless situation that Palestinian youth and the Palestinian people find themselves in.
[...]

Within Israel—Two Societies (1986)
CENTRAL INTELLIGENCE AGENCY

Nineteen years after the Six-Day War, Israel and the occupied territories are a political and economic entity divided into two societies. One society is relatively rich, armed, and powerful, while the other by comparison is poor, defenseless, and impotent. Is it a potentially explosive combination.

Economic integration is considerable. Tens of thousands of West Bank and Gaza Arabs do the menial chores of the Jewish State. Hours before dawn, convoys of laborers leave Gaza, for example, to build homes, pick fruit, and collect garbage around Tel Aviv. Although it is illegal for Arabs to stay overnight inside Israel proper, thousands do. […]

Israeli occupation has brought some prosperity to the territories—a key factor in their relative quiescence—but the economic crisis in Israel is increasing unemployment in the territories. Cutbacks in oil production by the Gulf states are also eroding opportunities for Arab youth. The economic conjuncture threatens to add fuel to the political confrontation.

Political extremism in the guise of religious fundamentalism and radicalism is growing on both sides. Among Gazans and West Bankers, fundamentalism exerts its hold on the young, especially the generation that has been born under Israeli rule. These radicals are first attending to changing the social mores of Palestinians. The confrontation with Zionism has been deliberately postponed until a new Islamic man is ready.

On the Israeli side, religious extremism is a fast-growing phenomenon manifested in Kahanism and the legislative trend against secularism. An Israeli journalist predicted last year that by the mid-1990s Jerusalem will be divided into an Arab eastern sector, a secular Jewish sector, and an Orthodox Jewish northern sector with deep fault lines between them. Allied to the religious right stands the so-called new Zionism of rightwing extremists like Ariel Sharon and the Tehiya organizations.

Last summer witnessed an unprecedented wave of Arab terrorism against individual Israelis in the border towns on both sides of the pre-1967 lines, where commercial interaction between Jew and Arab is most frequent....

Both the fedayeen and Jewish terror underground will seize on opportunities to create crises. Some Israelis fear mixed cities, especially Jerusalem, could become the Belfasts of the Middle East.

[…] [T]he situation is dynamic. There is little reason to believe that the two societies tied together in Israel can avoid growing violence. […]

690 From Central Intelligence Agency. Report: Near East and South Asia Review (Feb. 14, 1986).

The New Palestinian Revolt (2001)
Chris Hedges

A DAY OF RECKONING

It was not clear who fired first. It may have been the cluster of young
Palestinian men hidden in chest-high undergrowth near the Nezarim
junction in Gaza. It may have been the Israeli soldiers at their outpost.
Within a few seconds it no longer mattered. The crowd of 200 Palestinians,
who had gathered for the daily protest, frantically sought cover. Bullets
cracked and whizzed through the air.
[…]
The empty highway where the Nezarim gunfight took place was littered
with the usual detritus—rocks, smashed bottles, brass bullet casings, trash,
pieces of wood, and lumps of blackened rubber from tires that had been set
afire. The Palestinian police had set up a table a few hundred yards down
the road and had watched the clashes from the shade of a small porch. War
and death have become a form of street theater here, as is common in such
upheavals.

Young men carrying plastic bags filled with gasoline bombs sprinted from
sand pile to sand pile, laid there for this purpose by the Palestinian police
the night before. They worked their way toward a concrete wall around
which they could hurl the bombs at an Israeli military outpost. The bottles,
licked by bright red flame, arched skyward and then crashed, sending up
voluminous clouds of inky black smoke. When the shooting became heavy,
the demonstrators chanted Islamic slogans.

There were several sharp cracks—the signature sound of sniper rifles.
Marwan Shamalekh, 22, a bottle in his hand, collapsed dead in a lump on
the ground. His companions scooped him up, each taking an arm or a leg,
and ran to the back of a waiting ambulance near the Palestinian police. […]

The Palestinians had another martyr, more fuel for the insurrection. The
next morning Shamalekh was carried on a bier through the streets of Gaza,
his body wrapped in a Palestinian flag, a prop to whip up angry, vengeful
crowds. After laying him in a shallow pit in the sandy cemetery at the edge
of the city, groups of young men left to confront the Israelis and exact their
revenge. The cycle continued.

SEEKING MARTYRDOM

Gaza, like Kosovo's capital of Pristina, is a derelict, concrete slum where
car exhaust mingles with the stench of raw sewage. One million
Palestinians—70 percent of whom are either refugees from what is now
Israel or the descendants of refugees—live crammed into this dusty, flat,

Used with permission of Foreign Affairs, from FOREIGN AFFAIRS, Vol.   691
80, No. 1 (Jan. 1, 2001); permission conveyed through Copyright Clearance
Center, Inc.

coastal area twice the size of Washington, D.C. Most are stateless and have never left the Palestinian territories and Israel. Families are piled in boxy, concrete rooms capped with corrugated tin roofs weighed down by rocks. They have little furniture. Water and electricity come sporadically. The population growth rate is one of the highest on the planet—a 3.7 percent annual birthrate compared with 1.7 percent in Israel. Donkey carts crowd the streets and orange garbage bins, donated by the European Union, overflow with pungent heaps of refuse.

Rabah el-Loh, 23, stood one afternoon in front of the grave of his brother, Raid, killed in clashes with Israeli soldiers. The funeral had taken all morning and thousands of angry mourners still milled around the barren cemetery in Gaza.

"Goodbye brother," el-Loh said. "Say hello to the other martyrs."

The walls of Gaza are plastered with poster-sized photographs of "martyrs" shot by the Israelis. Many are pictured holding a weapon in front of the gold-topped al-Aqsa Mosque in Jerusalem. These are in fact studio photos taken long before the current unrest. The gun was a prop and the glittering mosque a carefully chosen backdrop. All that was real in these photos, apparently, was the desire of these young men to fight against Israel and for a Palestinian state—and to die in the process if need be. And now, at least until the pictures fade or peel away, the slain youths will have their heroism recognized.

Raid's decision to become a martyr was a conscious one, his family said, based on his despair at life in the Gaza Strip, hatred toward Israel, and a belief that to not sacrifice himself was to dishonor those who had gone before him.

Only 28,000 Gazan workers receive permits to work in Israel. Nearly all who do are middle-aged men who are considered less of a security threat. The young therefore have nothing to do and nowhere to escape to. They cannot get married because they cannot afford housing. They cannot leave Gaza, even for Israel. Martyrdom is the only route offered to those who want to achieve a measure, however brief, of recognition and glory.

"He spoke only of this, of being a martyr for the last four or five days," said Raid's mother, Fatma. "I asked him not to go. But once his younger brother was wounded he felt that it was his duty. When he left I said, 'God be with you.' I knew he would never come back."

Palestinians like Raid have been nurtured on bitter accounts of abuse, despair, and injustice. Families tell and retell stories of being thrown off their land and of relatives killed or exiled. All can tick off the names of martyrs within their own clan who died for the elusive Palestinian state.

The only framed paper in many Palestinians' homes is a sepia land deed from the time of the British mandate. Some elderly men still keep the keys to houses that have long since vanished. From infancy, Palestinians are inculcated with the virus of nationalism and the burden of revenge. And, as in Bosnia, such resentment seeps into the roots of society for generations until it resurfaces or is finally rectified, often after much bloodletting.

"Tell the man what you want to be," said Hyam Temraz to her two-year-old son, Abed, as she peeped out of the slit of a black veil.

"A martyr," the child answered.

"We were in Jordan when my son Baraa was four," she said. "He saw a Jordanian soldier and ran and hugged him. He asked him if it was he who would liberate Palestine. He has always told me that he would be a martyr and that one day I would dig his grave."

Nezar Rayyan, her husband, is a theology professor at Islamic University in Gaza. […]

Rayyan's grandfather and great-uncle were killed in the 1948 war. His grandmother died shortly after she and her son, Rayyan's father, were forced from their village. His father was passed among relatives and grew up with the bitterness of the dispossessed—a bitterness the father passed on to the son and the son has assiduously passed on to the grandchildren.

"There was not a single night that we did not think and talk about Palestine," Rayyan said, his eyes growing moist. "We were taught that our lives must be devoted to reclaiming our land."

Rayyan spent 12 years in an Israeli jail. His brother-in-law blew himself up in a suicide-bomb attack on an Israeli bus in 1998. One of his brothers had been shot dead by Israelis in street protests five years earlier. Another brother was expelled to Lebanon and several more were wounded in clashes.

Today, his three sons—ages 12, 15, and 16—daily join the youths who throw rocks at Israeli checkpoints. All three, according to their father, strive to be one thing: martyrs for Palestine.

"I pray only that God will choose them," he said.

A few days after I had watched Marwan Shamalekh drop dead at Nezarim, I went to call on his parents. […]

Abdel Razaq Shamalekh, Marwan's father, clutched his nine-year-old son, Bilal, who stared at me vacantly.

"I had to carry Bilal to his bed after I told him his brother had been killed," the father said. "He collapsed. Later I found him leaving the house with a knife he had taken from the kitchen. He told me he was going to Nezarim to kill Israelis."

ECONOMIC WARFARE

Gaza and the West Bank have become the Middle East's version of the South African townships during the apartheid regime. Nearly all the indignities visited on South African blacks—the lack of electoral representation, the dependence on work and travel permits, the curfews, the land confiscations, the arbitrary arrests, and the marginalization from the growing economy—are also part of Israel's relationship with the Palestinians.

On Israeli orders in October, travel between Palestinian towns on the West Bank ended, the borders with Egypt and Jordan were sealed, and all trade with those countries stopped. (Israeli authorities later amended this ruling to allow some agricultural imports into Israel.) All commercial trade between the Palestinian Authority and Israel was also cut off, although Israel did pledge to somewhat ease the restrictions for the Muslim holy month of Ramadan that began in late November. Shortages in food and cooking fuel resulted from a halt in Israeli deliveries of basic goods into Gaza, and some 120,000 Palestinians lost access to their jobs in Israel. In addition, because the Israelis control the principal sources of electricity, fuel, and water, they can choose to compound the shortages by cutting basic services or communications with the outside world. Indeed, Israeli authorities have already threatened to turn off the power because of late payments. Fuel, telephone service, and water could be next. Even the currency is Israeli: in Gaza and the West Bank, Palestinians pay for goods in Israeli shekels.

Arafat has called the economic blockade an act of war, little different from "rockets, planes, and tanks." Indeed, the United Nations estimates that the blockade withholds $3.4 million from the territories each day. Salem Ajluni, an economic specialist in Gaza with the U.N. Educational, Scientific, and Cultural Organization (UNESCO), estimates that the losses could amount to $650 million a year, or about 63 percent of the Palestinian Authority's revenue, excluding foreign donations. (Only contributions from Kuwait and Saudi Arabia enabled the Palestinian Authority to pay the November salaries of its 115,000 employees.) And the losses are bound to climb now that Israel has frozen the transfers of funds that it collects on behalf of the Palestinian Authority—as agreed under the autonomy accords—including sales taxes and customs duties.
[...]
"This is so painful for us," said Samil Aloushas, 20, as he stood bare-chested in the street with a group of friends. "The world has left us

694

powerless. We do not have these tanks, these missiles, and these helicopters. How can we fight back? Yet we must. We must defend Jerusalem from attack. All we have to sacrifice is ourselves. Everyone here is ready to do this. We are a nation now of suicide bombers. This is what the Israelis have done to us."

[…]

THE NOOSE TIGHTENS

Ali Dhair, 54, stood oblivious to the periodic pop of gunfire between Palestinian gunmen and Israeli soldiers just over the hill near the Rafah border crossing. He was mourning his cucumber plants. "Look," he said, pointing to piles of twisted brown stems and roots. "It was too expensive to maintain them."

He was not alone. Piles of withered produce dotted the sandy plots around him. The Israeli decision to close the border made it impossible for farmers like Dhair to export farm products. He and many others are now bankrupt.

Not only have scores of farmers gone bust in the last few weeks, unable to export crates of tomatoes and cucumbers to Israel, the West Bank, Egypt, and Jordan; without basic supplies and money to pay workers, everything from tailor shops to construction firms has ground to a halt. The Israelis, who keep gunships off the coast, have curtailed the range of fishing boats. Tourism to places such as Bethlehem, which hosted half a million visitors last year, has dried up. And Israeli shoppers, who spent $500 million last year in West Bank towns, are no longer traveling into Palestinian areas.

The downward spiral strengthens the radicals. Armed fighters, who like their predecessors in the first intifada are intoxicated by newfound power and authority, have aided the Israeli blockade. They have stopped Palestinian workers from going to their jobs in the industrial park at the Erez checkpoint in Gaza, and the park has already lost about a third of its 3,500 workers. Radical Palestinians have also burned factories in Gaza and the West Bank. One fire forced developers to halt work on a fiber-optic-wired industrial park being set up in the West Bank by Israeli software companies—once touted as the model of how the Israeli and Palestinian economies could be merged. "I am too scared to go to work," said Mohammed al-Kahlout, 28, who is a tailor in the Erez industrial zone. "Two days ago someone was shot and killed. In my workshop only 2 out of 20 people go to work."

As the closure drags on and the nearly 120,000 Palestinians with jobs in Israel stay home, pressure mounts in Israel to bring in foreign guest workers to replace them. Gaza's economy is sustained by its exports of fruits and vegetables and the salaries earned by 28,000 laborers who work in Israel. About 30,000 more are licensed to work from the West Bank. Another 60,000, nearly all from the West Bank, work illegally.

[...]
THE NEW WARRIORS
[...]
Rayad Zaid, 21, is typical of those who have spent most of their lives fighting Israelis. As a child he often missed school to stone Israeli soldiers on patrol. He has been shot in the leg three times and carries a scar on his forehead from a rubber bullet. His father spent 13 years in Israeli jails. He said his mother, an asthmatic, died after inhaling tear gas when he was 11. "I will make any sacrifice for my people and my country," he said in the Jabaliya refugee camp, "and I will strap explosives on my body and blow myself up to attack the Israelis if it is required."
[...]
AN UNWINNABLE WAR?
[...]
Palestinian resistance may prove surprising. Indeed, given the drudgery and poverty of life in the occupied territories, resistance will be for many Palestinians the headiest and most exciting time in their lives. If the attacks and counter-attacks between intifada fighters and the Israeli military grow harsher and the numbers of Palestinian dead mount, the one million Israeli Arabs who do not serve in the army and feel like foreigners on their own land are sure to bring the violence deeper inside Israel.
[...]

Address at Bar-Ilan University (2009)
Benjamin Netanyahu

The right of the Jewish people to a state in the land of Israel does not derive from the catastrophes that have plagued our people. True, for 2000 years the Jewish people suffered expulsions, pogroms, blood libels, and massacres which culminated in a Holocaust—an unprecedented tragedy in the history of nations. There are those who say that if the Holocaust had not occurred, the state of Israel would never have been established. But I say that if the state of Israel would have been established earlier, the Holocaust would not have occurred. This tragic history of powerlessness explains why the Jewish people need a sovereign power of self-defense. But our right to build our sovereign state here, in the land of Israel, arises from one simple fact: Eretz Israel is the birthplace of the Jewish people. [...]

Today In History: IDF Airlifts 14,500 Ethiopian Jews to Israel (2024)
IDF EDITORIAL TEAM

On May 24, 1991, the IDF carried out Operation Solomon, a massive airlift that brought Ethiopian Jews to Israel. After 34 planes and 36 hours, the Israeli Air Force safely carried 14,500 Jews to Israeli soil. The mission remains the largest aerial expedition in Israel's history.

In the 1970's, the Israeli government made the decision to authorize the use of the IDF to enable the immigration of thousands of Jews who were living in Ethiopia, a country that at the time prohibited its citizens from emigrating to Israel. Beginning in 1984, the IDF brought Ethiopian Jews to Israel in three airlift operations, the last of which was Operation Solomon in 1991.

"Operation Solomon truly represents what Zionism is," said Israel's air force commander of the time, Maj. Gen. Avihu Ben-Nun. "It demonstrates the purpose for the State of Israel: to provide a home and shelter for Jews around the world who have suffered and were prosecuted merely for bearing the Jewish religion."

It was a great operation on a global scale. "Never before, did so few pilots transport such a great number of people in such a short time," Maj. Gen. Ben-Nun said.

Turmoil in Ethiopia

In 1991, Ethiopia was experiencing great political instability. The acting government was weak, and the likelihood of it falling to Eritrean rebels was high. Ethiopia's Jews were in danger. On March 7, Uri Lubrani, an Israeli diplomat, reported on the worsening military situation in Ethiopia, and advised the formulation of "an emergency plan, for the protection and evacuation of the Jewish community."

Leading up to the operation, $35 million were raised almost overnight in order to pay the Ethiopian government to allow the Jews to leave.

The Operation Begins

The Israel Air Force allocated six Boeing 707 and 18 Hercules planes capable of carrying 18,000 people. The mission had two stages: a three hour flight to Addis Ababa (using the Boeing 707 plane) and another five hours to Israel, using the Hercules aircraft. [...]

The first Hercules landed in Addis-Ababa around 10:00 AM, and the crew immediately began assembling the command room. "The first control tower in the northern part of the country did not even respond to our call, as the local city was taken over by rebels, hours earlier," recalled Lieut.

698 Used with Permission of ISRAEL DEFENSE FORCES (IDF).

Col. A., who landed the first Boeing in Ethiopia. "There was a lot of traffic over the airport at Addis-Ababa, and we had to wait for 30 minutes before we could land. The airport itself was very organized, and ground services worked very well".

The ground plan involved gathering everyone at the Israeli embassy, and transporting them to the planes using specially designated buses. Each bus was to be escorted by an Israeli soldier, of Ethiopian origin.

In order to accommodate as many people as possible, the seats of the planes were removed and up to 1,200 passengers were able to board a single plane. Those who planned the operation expected that the planes would hold only 760 passengers, but the Ethiopians – many of whom were malnourished – were so light that many more were able to fit.

Almost 20 years later, IDF Chief of the General Staff, Lt. Gen. Benny Gantz, who led the ground operation as commander of the IAF's elite Shaldag commando force, spoke of the mission: "As commander of Shaldag Unit, I had to deal primarily with technical details. Only during the mission did I get a sense of how meaningful it was to be part of this crucial event. It's a turning point in my service which encompasses both my Zionist values and the meaning of our existence in this country."

"I vividly remember those images from Addis Ababa," recalls Maj. B., an IAF pilot at the time. "An incredible number of people walked towards the plane, organized in groups of 200. The doctors and paramedics provided ongoing support." The first Boeing plane took off at noon, followed by the rest. At one time, 27 planes were in the air.

On the Ground

At 5:00 P.M. the first plane landed in Tel Aviv. As the passengers walked out, Prime Minister Itzhak Shamir and other leaders greeted them on the ground in Israel.

The children came out first. "Everyone looked tired and scared", described Anat Tal-Shir, a reporter for the newspaper "Yediot Aharonot." "The people who arrived during Operation Solomon fled their country with nothing but the clothes they were wearing. The children stayed close to their mothers. A young man carried his elderly father on his shoulders. They both bent down and kissed the Israeli soil."

The arrivals were met with cheer and celebration. "We didn't bring any of our clothes; we didn't bring any of our things," said 29 year old Mukat Abag at the time. "But we are very glad to be here." After one of the most complex and emotional operations in IDF history, Ethiopia's Jews had finally landed safely in Israel.

'A' Jewish State vs. 'The' Jewish State (2014)

Michael Oren and David Rothkopf

[Oren and Rothkopf are longtime friends and were college roommates. This is an edited email exchange following Rothkopf's first visit to Israel].

Michael,

You asked me a pretty simple, straightforward question in your email that has been careening around my brain like a stray pinball. It was, "Did Israel live up to your expectations?"

It is hard for me not to have strong reactions to Israel.

My father was raised as a Zionist, going to Jabotinsky-inspired summer camps in Europe before the Nazis ran his family out of Austria. His aunt was blown up on the Patria in Haifa harbor. Of the few relatives who survived the war, a couple made their way to Israel. When I was a little boy, as I suspect was the case with you, I had this sense of Israel as a different kind of "promised land," not something from a biblical text but a place where special people were making special things happen. It was the country that was making the desert green, the country of great characters like Ben-Gurion and Golda Meir and Moshe Dayan. It was a real source of pride to be Jewish and associated with it.

That only grew as Israel was challenged by her neighbors. I recall sitting around a radio in our kitchen to get real-time reports of the Six-Day War. That Israel was the Israel of David standing up against the Goliaths in the neighborhood again, the democracy fighting against tyrants and bullies — the brave few using brains and technology to defeat the brutal millions who wanted them gone. I felt the same way during the Yom Kippur War, the same way through college.

As you and I have discussed, something began to change in the early 1980s when Ariel Sharon led the Israeli army into the camps in Lebanon. The narrative shifted. Israel was no longer David. Economic, political, social, and military successes had made Israel the local heavyweight champion, even if it was fighting well above its weight class. And the people whom Israel was leaving as victims in the conflict within and nearest its borders appeared to be weaker, vulnerable, and often, though certainly not always, innocent. I understood the blurry lines, even intellectually understood the tactical rationale behind the moves made by Israel's leaders. But narratives are more powerful than armies, and this one was shifting in what would turn out to be a tectonic way.

The First Intifada only compounded this. Initially, I did not feel any sympathy for the Palestinians of Yasser Arafat. Even as I entered the Clinton administration in 1993 and got to view some aspects of the regional debate up close, it was clear to me that the other side was not

700 From FOREIGN POLICY MAGAZINE. Reprinted with permission.

sincere in advancing the interests of the Palestinian people — who I have nonetheless always felt have had a strong claim to their own country. But it is hard to deny that the genius of the Intifada was the imagery: boys with rocks and bottles standing up to tanks and fighter planes. No amount of explanation can change the emotional resonance of such images.

Rather than seeking to reclaim the narrative, the high ground — to appear more open, more flexible, more committed to the just path — the Israel of the past decade has become more committed to a stance that often seems discordant with the best impulses and stated ideals behind its modern origins.

Of course, with a tie to the Patria — the ship sunk by Jewish extremists in 1940, killing over 200 people — it's hard not to recall that this dichotomy has always been at the heart of the battle among Israelis to define the nature of your state. Building settlements may have satisfied a political need for Israeli leaders, but it looked insensitive and unconstructive ... because it was and is. As you and I have also discussed, the opportunity has always been there for Israel to take a different course, embrace the idea of a Palestinian state, and lean in to the peace process precisely because you have known that the Palestinians would struggle to follow through. While this may seem cynical, it meant the risks would be low, the return would be high, and if peace resulted all the better. After all, in my view, demographics and economics and common sense all dictate that nothing could do more to secure Israel than the establishment of a flourishing Palestinian state.

This was the context of my visit. I was only there a couple of days, and I couldn't, of course, see much.... But in driving around Israel, in going to meetings, in listening to discussions at the conference I was at, even in looking at the landscape all around, I got a different sense ... one that was entirely unanticipated.

Israel seemed old to me. Not old in the sense of antiquity. It seemed old like the core ideas that had brought it to life not as a country but as an idea and an ideal in my youth seemed so compromised, so battered by "realism" and self-interest, so undercut by political deals, that I couldn't help but wonder if the country had passed its "sell by" date, that its freshness was gone and some of what was good was starting to turn. That sounds harsh, I know, and that's one reason I haven't written anything yet on my reactions. And I know about the thriving, innovative tech companies, and I felt the vibrancy of some of what young Israelis were doing. (The IDF headquarters visit strangely did more on that front than any other part of what I did.... It felt like a cool college campus leavened with the essence of Silicon Valley).

But this impression isn't just a result of my recent visit. I know my views are colored by my sense of frustration with the policies of Prime Minister Bibi Netanyahu and some of his team and by a quarter-century of dealing with these issues and many of the key players involved in them.

I also know it goes deeper than that — some of it personal. Time has passed. Generations have shifted. My father is dead. Those who knew his story firsthand (and those of his murdered relatives) have also died. And the world has changed. What seemed a compelling need for a Jewish state in the wake of World War II or in the midst of protracted European violence against Jews has lost its sense of urgency. Even if worrisome realities continue to underlie the new situation, all that gave the Israel of Leon Uris its sense of logic and justice seems more distant. We can argue against it, we can condemn it, we can try to deny it … but a generational shift has occurred in the United States and, I believe, worldwide. As we once discussed, Barack Obama is the first president of the United States to spend essentially his entire adult life post Israel's intervention into Lebanon in 1982. Even though he is younger than us, he is a middle-aged man. He is the age of the world's other leaders. They are all a generation raised with a very different narrative of Israel.

J Street is not an aberration. J Street is a reaction to that new narrative and to the perceived excesses of AIPAC and the reflexively pro-Israeli community in the U.S. Reflex was my first instinct for supporting Israel. But it is not sustainable if you have a truly Jewish mind … a mind linked to a tradition of "struggling" with even the Highest Power. Ideas and beliefs have to be tested against a reality. Today there are other safe places for Jews in the world, notably America. Today there are other ways for Jews to live and be true to their traditions that don't involve the harsher realities of a garrison state.

There was, when I was a boy, a kind of Israeli dream that grew out of this notion that there was an opportunity to create an ideal modern state in an ancient setting, one suffused with the best thinking as well as the best that could be drawn from traditions of faith. In all candor, I came away from my visit wondering if that dream had died or withered so that those who believed in it faced an urgent and stark choice: rethink it or accept that it will die and with it will go many of the aspirations we had for it when we were much younger (and that I sense you still have for it today).

Something new is needed — a new paradigm, a new narrative. One in which Israel needs to lead alongside a Palestinian state. One in which Israel must be the most committed of all nations to the success of its neighbors. One in which Israel can't rely on its traditional relationship with the United States and must make new ties that are based less on history, that are less reflexive, that demand more adjustment, flexibility, and creativity.

702

I'm not saying I don't think that's possible. Who knows, maybe it is something you can lead with. But it is what has been lingering in my brain since my visit and something I have not articulated elsewhere. But you are smarter and more knowledgeable about much of this than I am … much closer to all of it … and, above all, you made the mistake of asking.

* * *

David,

As so many American Jews of our generation, you have this idealized image of pre-1967 Israel. But we're adults now and adults inhabiting an illusion-less world.

Israel before 1967 was in fact a far less equitable place than it is today. There were hardly any Sephardi Jews, much less Arabs, Africans, and other minorities in government. And the government was controlled by a single party composed almost exclusively of secular and socialist Eastern European Jews. Most of the Arab population (of Israel!) lived under military rule. The Palestinians didn't really exist and for the same reason that Israel appeared pristine — because the Western press so decided. Israel was the darling and the Arabs weren't. Hollywood helped, too, as you noted. But instead of *Exodus* and *Cast a Giant Shadow*, the film industry could have produced *The Gatekeepers* or *5 Broken Cameras* 50 years ago with the same (often unfounded) sense of righteousness it displays today.

You bought into that myth — we all did. But some of us looked deeper. And what we found was extraordinary. We found a society which, in spite of unspeakable pressures, managed to stay democratic, open, creative, self-correcting (frequently to a fault), self-defending, ultra-literate (in Hebrew), and Jewish. It was the only place on the planet in the last 2,000 years where Jews could take responsibility for themselves — for their governance, their protection, their mess — as Jews. And for those reasons some of us fell in love with the place and decided to try to make it better.

Fifty years later, Israel is by almost any metric inestimably better. More open, democratic; less provincial and homogeneous. In contrast to Washington, where people react passively to a weeklong electrical blackout, when the electricity goes off in Israel — for a single day — residents demand an independent investigation and government resignations. Young people, even if they're not religious, get married and have children, giving us the fastest-growing population per capita in the industrialized world. There's universal health care, a citizens' army, and world-class universities charging less than $10,000 for a BA. Since 1989, we've successfully absorbed more than a million immigrants — the equivalent of about 50 million Americans.

Sound good? Well, it isn't entirely. We have rapidly expanding ultra-Orthodox and Arab populations that for totally different reasons reject the secular and democratic Jewish state. The settler population is burgeoning as well, including elements that also balk at Israeli sovereignty. Israel has a wide income gap, an eroding middle class, and a severe housing shortage for young people. We're surrounded by a sea of supremely armed insanity. And we're caught in an impossible situation with the Palestinians, unable to continue occupying them but no less incapable of ending the occupation in a non-existential way.

That is the tragic truth, and since it's the Palestinian issue that torments you most, you have to hear it. What you're really saying, David, is that Israel must take the steps necessary to shift the blame onto the Palestinians. If so, I agree. But a two-state solution is unfortunately unlikely and not because of Israel. We'd make most of the sacrifices — but only because the Palestinians lack the national cohesion necessary to sustain a state structure. Our identity exists entirely independently of theirs; theirs cannot exist without denying ours. Accepting us would sever the one thread that — sometimes — holds them together.

Escaping this dilemma will require creativity and leadership. There are solutions, none of them perfect. There are solutions to the ultra-Orthodox, Arab, and settler issues. Solutions for the income gap, for the beleaguered middle class, and the housing crisis. But there is no solution for the regional madness other than to gird ourselves against it.

But back to your Israel anguish, and it's here where I want to wax unambassadorial. It's time that American Jews see Israel not as a Hollywood or Hebrew school fantasy but what it was and still is: a real country made of bona fide humans, faults and all, albeit humans caught in inhuman circumstances. It's time they stop judging Israelis by the standards of the American Jewish experience and start trying to understand the Israeli experience. Tired after two wars in which the vast majority didn't fight? Try dealing with eight or so, one every few years, together with thousands of rockets raining on your cities, countless bombs blowing up buses and malls and intersections, and an absolutely relentless total threat. Nobody in Israel — not one single person you met, not our friend Lior [Weintraub], not me — hasn't lost loved ones or hasn't been deeply scarred.

Remembering that, you shouldn't be amazed that the country seems tired. You'll be amazed that the country exists at all. You'll be astonished that those young cool kids you saw in the army are still cool and still want to serve.

Of course, Israel must take into account the fact that the president of the United States has no real recollection of the Six-Day War and that J Street reflects generational shifts in American Jewish opinion. We must do our best to adapt to those changes. But doing our best does not mean taking risks that would endanger the lives of hundreds of thousands of Israelis and perhaps the survival of the state. Israel is not about to leave a vacuum in the West Bank to be filled with Hamas or accord with a nuclear-enabled Iran just to gain the favor of politicians with memories of Sabra and Shatila and American Jews too young to remember Entebbe. Nobody takes more seriously than I the viewpoints of American Jews, both the reflexively supportive and those critical of Israel. But we know that the Jewish people survived — barely — the inaction of American Jewry during World War II, and know that in the future we might have to survive in spite of part of that community's alienation.

You are right in expressing your reservations about your ability to reach such sweeping conclusions after a first visit of a mere three days. Your conclusions showed evidence of years reading press reports and foreign-policy journals that have proved off base on just about everything in the Middle East, Israel included. Certainly Israel, no less than the United States, deserves the serious scrutiny born of a serious investment of time and effort. I know you approach this subject out of a place of caring, even love, but I have also noticed that such love leads some American Jews to be more disturbed by the accidental death of a Palestinian civilian at the hands of the IDF than by the killing of an innocent Pakistani by a U.S. drone. Ask yourself if you fall into this category, and, if so, I urge you to revisit your conclusions about Israel.

Israel is a story, a human story, that you once felt a part of. You no longer do, at least not in the same way, and it's easy to explain the change in terms of a radically transformed Israel. But much of American Jewry has also changed — you, in terms of your Jewish identity, have changed — and acknowledging that is a prerequisite for forming your opinions about the Jewish state.

* * *

Michael,

The case for the progress Israel has made is undeniable.

You continue to have your eyes wide open about many of the challenges Israel faces. It's an admirable trait I have admired in the many, many Israelis I have met over the years. This is not a country of people with blinders on — for the most part. Nor is it a place that is afraid of introspection and debate.

But, I do want to offer a bit of a nuance to your nuances, to put the context you offer in a different context. Yes, I may have been influenced by a superficial view of Israel. Yes, I may not have seen as many weaknesses as were there in the past. And, as an American Jew who continues to view living in America as the best possible answer to the depredations and tragedies that befell my ancestors for many generations, I may come at this from a rather different perspective on several levels.

I'm no Zionist. I'm actually pretty deeply opposed to the notion of religion being in any way involved in either the governing of a state or the formation of its national identity. And, also, to compound my own narcissism, I've got a case of that good old-fashioned American narcissism that I have to fight all the time. You know the disorder I'm talking about. The one that makes us (and our senior officials) typically argue for a new Copernican reality that has every country on Earth orbiting the American sun.

But you should also be more sensitive than anyone to the reality that the U.S. relationship with Israel is central to its history and important to its existence. And though I may be a Hollywood-deluded foreigner who doesn't fully appreciate the rich tapestry of Israeli existence, I'm no boob. Despite the steady diet of foreign-policy journals and newspaper articles that I have been fed over the years, I have traveled throughout the Middle East. I have read and written and researched these issues at length. I have viewed them through the lens of being a senior U.S. government official. I stay as current as modern technology allows me to be. Heck, I even read at least one Israeli newspaper. So, if I don't see the merits to current stances or if I feel the narrative has been lost or squandered, it is worth noting.

I should be among the most supportive of Israel. Indeed, I still think I am in many respects. But, as a member of the U.S. policy community (if there is such a thing … a club that deservedly evokes Groucho Marx's line that he wouldn't want to be a member of any club that would admit him), the fact that I feel Israel is increasingly diverging from what I thought it once was should matter. If the well-informed and well-disposed are concerned for the future of the country and troubled by settlements and apparent insensitivity to the fate of a population that is rapidly growing to be the majority population within your borders, then regardless of the flaws in my education or reasoning, it matters.

You may think my view of Israel was naive. It may have been. But it was also the foundation for the historical narrative. Policy, as you know well, is not driven by reason or facts, but by people, prejudices, expediency, habits, and inertia. Changes are hard to engineer. And when views drift from what they were and support wanes, it may well be not just that facts have changed but that narrative themes and emotional underpinnings of a relationship that are based more on perception than reality have shifted to a degree that makes them more important. And that has an impact on relationships. Generational shifts also play a big role in this.

706

I guess what I'm saying is that I think Israel has a real problem with losing the narrative that can't be rationally argued away but needs to be addressed. I'm just a canary in the coal mine.

* * *

David,

It seems I hit a nerve by suggesting that Americans and American Jews can be naive about Israel and its neighborhood. Certainly they have no monopoly over naiveté, as demonstrated by the Israelis who got us into the Lebanon War or who thought peace with Arafat was possible. But the debate is far deeper than who among us is the most misinformed. Rather, the question is whether any country, much less one confronting Israel's complex environment, can ever meet the stratospheric standards set by the U.S. policy community you referenced, particularly those members who belong to that other self-selecting subset: the American Jewish community.

That standard was best summarized by a 90-year-old woman I met at an art exhibition in Washington. She stood on her toes and pointed her finger in my face and said, "I like you but I do not like everything your government does." I smiled and replied, "Do you like everything *your* government does?" Which earned me another finger-wagging. "No. But *your* government must be perfect."

The expectation of perfection extends beyond my earlier mention of whether Palestinian civilian casualties bother you more than those among Afghans or Pakistanis. It defines those in the media — many of them Jewish — who generally overlook policies on the Texas and Arizona borders but who write serially about Israel's allegedly insensitive treatment of African "refugees" crossing its southern border. (In truth, most of those who illegally entered Israel were unmarried men in search of work — i.e., no more refugees than the Mexicans who slip into the United States.) The same journalists who are not losing sleep over America's practice of detaining and then repatriating those Mexicans are singularly disturbed when Israel, which cannot repatriate most of these men to the African states technically at war with us, does not absorb them. America's policies toward the Mexicans are not perfect, and neither is Israel's toward the Africans. But the expectation of perfection pertains overwhelmingly to Israel.

I collected many examples of this during my tenure. Another favorite was the repeated media condemnations of gender segregation on one or two bus lines serving ultra-Orthodox neighborhoods in Jerusalem. The fact that similar buses serve similar communities in New York went overlooked. Is gender segregation ever justified? No, never. But only one country gets labeled anti-feminist, even anti-democratic, because of it.

This brings me back to your letter. You say you oppose a role for religion in the formation of state or national identity. This means you oppose the state and national identity of roughly 40 percent of the nations on Earth, including not only all the Arab and Muslim countries but also Spain, Iceland, Finland, Denmark, Argentina, Norway, and Great Britain. America is "one nation, under God," and its Declaration of Independence credits the Creator as the source of individual rights. Israel's doesn't. In fact, it doesn't mention God at all. So what is it, exactly, that you find so objectionable about a *Jewish* state?

The truth is that the Jewishness of the Jewish state is understood differently by most Israelis and American Jews. When we say "Jewish," we mean people. We mean nation. But for a large number of American Jews, it means religion. Admittedly, we are an anomaly: a nation-state composed of many ethnicities and cultures but bound by a national religion that is observed — or not observed — in many ways. The closest example, I guess, is Japan, minus the ethnic diversity. But do we have to apologize for being *sui generis*? Do American Jews really want us to be Finland?

I think not. But neither do many of them seem to want us to be a real country with sometimes surreal problems, preferring to objectify us in a way truly reminiscent of anti-feminists. If only I had the proverbial nickel for every time I heard of the need for Israeli soul-searching and every time I silently retorted with the wish that American Jews would conduct that same search. Such introspection would answer basic questions like: Do you regard yourself as part of the Jewish people? Do you consider your life inextricably linked to the Jewish story? Do all Jews — American, Israeli, or French for that matter — share a destiny? I can't speak for American Jews, but my guess is that the overwhelming majority of Israelis, religious and secular, would answer all of those questions in the affirmative. A nation-state will do that for you.

Which brings me to your last and, I think, most compelling point, about the narrative that we once had and are steadily losing. Though this observation, too, needs refining. Popular support for Israel in America has inexorably risen, not declined, from 67 percent to 74 percent in the last few years alone (I take no credit). Perhaps this is not your America, but this is an America that votes and wants its Congress voting in support of the state they admire. And yet, I agree that we cannot afford to lose *elite* opinion in the United States. I agree that this is not just a matter of better PR or even enhanced education. Israel must treat the attitudinal and generational shifts you mentioned not as an image problem but as a strategic threat.

Overcoming that threat is much of which my life is about these days. I am thinking about the creative ways through which Israel can break the status quo in the territories, especially if the peace talks fail, and how we can preserve our democratic and Jewish character. I'm probing the means for making Israel more just, more compassionate, and, in the ethical sense, more Jewish. I'm exploring identity issues, some of them quite sensitive, that seek to bridge the gap between a national identity that is indeed Jewish but also Israeli, incorporating Muslims, Christians, and Druze. I am determined to make Israel the nation-state of all of the Jewish people, including Reform, Reconstructionist, and Conservative Jews.

Which brings me back to the definition of Zionism as Jews taking sovereign responsibility for themselves. Syllogistically, if you respect those Jews who do, and consider yourself a Jew, doesn't that make you — denials notwithstanding — a Zionist? In my book it does.

* * *

Michael,

You raise three points that I want to address: One pertains to the expectation that Israel must meet a higher standard than that set for other countries. The next has to do with the issue of whether or not it is legitimate to take issue with the idea of a Jewish state (especially being a Jew). And the final one has to do with the shifting narrative on Israel.

Regarding the first issue, I think you are straying into *reductio ad absurdum* territory. You both define an impossible goal "perfection"– which may have been the standard by which a little old lady had evaluated Israel but is certainly not the expectation of anyone with a grip on reality — and then you list a number of areas in which Americans take exception to Israeli policy and equate them to flaws afflicting the United States and other governments.

Certainly no one who can read a newspaper expects Israel to be perfect. Nor, I believe, do they expect Israel to operate to a higher standard than any other country. Well, let me modify that. *Americans* don't expect Israel to operate to a higher standard than any other ally to whom we provide a great deal of aid and support. If we are to be closely associated with Israel, then by extension we will be judged based on the actions of our ally. So, if this ally strays or missteps, it resonates for us more than it might for other nations. Further, if we not only support such a country but, by virtue of our agreements with that country, are put in a position to defend it, then we have a legitimate interest in whether that country's behavior reflects well on us (important in terms of our regional and global influence). On top of which, we must also be concerned with whether or not this relationship could somehow get us into trouble we're not looking to be in.

Beyond this point is that the core criticism of Israeli behavior is not about how Orthodox women are treated on buses or how Ethiopian immigrants are treated in Israel. It is about how Palestinians are treated both within Israel's borders and within the Palestinian territories as a consequence of Israeli actions. You, better than anyone, are aware of the facts behind these critiques and know that you do not have to be a Jimmy Carter and loosely throw around terms like apartheid to feel that Palestinians are entitled to their own self-determination. Or to know that Israel's needs should not have a greater claim on outcomes in that part of the world than those of Palestinians; that local resources, like water, ought to be shared equitably; or that the rights of Palestinian people to vote, to have their own state, to have claim to their own historical and cultural heritage should be inviolable as it is for any other people. Further, those rights — the very same ones that have been referred to here for centuries as inalienable — do not simply appertain to Palestinians in what we all must hope will soon become a Palestinian state. They also ought to pertain to Palestinians who choose to live in Israel.

For the state of Israel to undervalue or be slow to implement or respect any of these issues of basic rights not only reflects badly on the United States as a sponsor and supporter and ally of Israel, but it reflects badly on Israel as a democracy and as a state that stakes a claim on representing Jews worldwide. (Personally, I find this latter perspective intolerable too. Netanyahu's tendency to sometimes speak for the Jewish people far overreaches any powers offered him either in the Israeli Constitution or by virtue of any other aspect of his position.) Unilaterally determining where borders may lie, where settlements may be built, what rules may be applied to protect Israeli security within the borders of the Palestinian territories are all behaviors that many would-be supporters of Israel — those of us who want to be supportive and feel a kinship and a connection — find difficult to countenance.

As for the question of the separation of church and state, while I acknowledge many states do not share the views outlined in the U.S. Constitution on this point (and indeed, many Americans seem uncomfortable with the concept in practice), I am as clear and resolute on this as any principle I hold.

History is the story of the human catastrophe that results when states promote religious ends or use religious criteria to guide their governance. As we have often seen, the embrace of religion into the identity of a nation, while being sold to the people as something unifying and elevating, is often something else. It is exclusionary. It is about finding a way to achieve cultural and ethnic "purity." It is an idea that should be more anathema to Jews, given our history, than to any other group. I find the response of Zionism to be exactly the wrong one. It suggests we have seen how others have abused religion by intermingling it with governance and national identity and the only protection is to do the same thing ourselves.

The best protection (as the United States has demonstrated) is to institutionalize the concept of tolerance and diversity and to work tirelessly to ensure that the powerful impulses to segregate and divide are quashed. It

710

is not easy. But it has made the United States the most successful experiment in cultural diversity in history — though only after a series of horrific errors, including slavery and the genocide against Native Americans and the devaluing of the role of women, were ultimately remedied. We're not there yet. But in this respect, we are heading in a better direction than most other states. And for very nearly as many Jews as there are in Israel, it is the model we have embraced and chosen as U.S. citizens. Indeed, it is worth noting that the majority of the world's Jews live somewhere other than in Israel, places that have chosen different environments and approaches to governance.

Therefore Israel cannot be *the* Jewish state. It can be *a* Jewish state. But even should its people choose that path, for it to be a moral state, it must be one that guarantees the rights and prerogatives of every citizen equally regardless of religious orientation, gender, ethnicity, etc. It is hard to say Israel does that now.

This brings us back to the narrative. Certainly, there are many Americans who support Israel. Israel has much to recommend it. But from the massacres in Lebanon through the Intifada, to the contentious and willful construction of settlements that should not be built, Israel has undercut its moral high ground. I know there is a group in Israel who say, this is what we must do to be secure. And certainly Israeli toughness and willingness to accept criticism is as much responsible for the success of the country as anything else. From a purely practical perspective, as a country Israel needs political support abroad, but over these past few years it has almost systematically made it harder for those who would be supportive to follow through on that impulse.

You can refer to it as a problem among "elites." It is not. It is a problem among important communities that are essential to the coalition that has provided support for Israel in the past and will be just as important in the future. You know that. It is not just the rise of J Street. It is not just liberals and the Walt-Mearsheimer anti-Israel Lobby Crowd. It is guys like me. You know, guys who grew up in New Jersey who were captivated by the story of a Jewish state that was in a way "ours," who were lifted up by the heroism of the Six-Day War, guys who admired the stories of turning the desert green. You know guys like that, right? You were one.

It's worth asking why those other guys like me, who started in the same place, the next town over, went to the same schools, who have had a similar career trajectory, could still love much of what they saw in Israel, but so often find the choices made by its government to be troubling.

* * *

Dear David,

Before I move on to my vision of Israel, I have to take issue with several aspects of your last letter.

You deny, David, that Americans (and American Jews) apply a double standard to Israel. Rather, the aid granted by Americans *to* Israel — and the enmity that it arouses against America in certain quarters — entitles them to expect better behavior *by* Israel. But that approach itself betrays a double standard. Americans expect no such probity from the Gulf countries, Turkey, and South Korea, which receive vastly more military support from the United States than does Israel. By the way, Turkey and South Korea have defense pacts with the United States; Israel does not.

Like many of those in the "we-aid-you-therefore-we-can-criticize-you" camp, you seem to minimize what the United States receives in return for its assistance. Start with the superbly skilled and motivated armed forces that are more than twice as large as Britain's and France's combined, are situated in the world's most strategic crossroads, and are unerringly loyal to the democratically elected leaders of an unabashedly pro-American country. Add to that the unrivaled intelligence sharing, weapons development, joint maneuvers, ports-of-call and landing rights, munitions prepositioning, and cyber-cooperation. Israel is the one country in the Middle East where a U.S. president can still come and give a speech and be cheered by thousands of young people. America gets all of that as well as the last significant leverage it stills wields in a region that is still vital for U.S. security.

This does not mean that Israelis — and this one, especially — are not profoundly appreciative of American support. And I agree that the aid reflects not only shared strategic interests but also common values. But surely one of those values is respect for our democratically determined policies, even when they sometimes differ from America's.

As for arousing enmity, I have no doubt that America's alliance with Israel fans Middle Eastern rage. But your position evokes the claim made at the height of the Iraq and Afghanistan wars that support for Israel cost America "blood and treasure." Forget the fact that many Israelis — again, this one included — warned the United States to stay out of those wars; Middle Easterners raged against America well before Israel's creation (the first anti-American demonstration took place in Cairo in 1912, after Teddy Roosevelt told Egyptians that nation-building took decades). And they're raging today for reasons utterly unrelated to Israel. Hillary Clinton was pummeled with shoes in Alexandria not because of her supposed love of Zion but because of her alleged preference for the Muslim Brotherhood. America has spurred resentment among Syrians and the governments of the Gulf not because it stands with its allies but because, purportedly, it won't. Polls show that the highest levels of anti-American sentiment in the region were found in Turkey, Egypt, and the areas controlled by the

Palestinian Authority — all technically at peace with Israel and each a recipient of massive American largesse.

Unquestionably, Israel has made tragic errors in its policymaking toward the territories, but that does not mean that it bears the overriding blame you assign it.

Israel does not, for example, deny West Bank Palestinians the right to vote for their own leaders — their own leaders do that. They are unelected leaders, avowedly secular and far from corruption-free, and such governments have not fared well in the Middle East lately. They praise terrorists and teach their children that Israel will eventually disappear. It's worth remembering that Israel has accepted at least three two-state solutions since 1947, each of which was rejected by the Palestinians and almost always with violence. And still, there is greater support for the two-state solution today in Israel than among Palestinians or even Americans. Israel does not, as you imply, impugn the Palestinians' "historical and cultural heritage," though much of it is obsessed with refuting ours. On the contrary, we recognize the Palestinians as a people endowed with the right of self-determination in their homeland — a recognition that they refuse to extend to us. And Palestinian Israelis do not merely, as you say, "choose to live in Israel," but adamantly refuse to live under the Palestinian Authority, which they know will rescind the democratic rights they enjoy in Israel.

Israel's declaration of independence, modeled on America's, guarantees "complete equality of social and political rights to all [of Israel's] inhabitants irrespective of religion, race or sex," as well as "freedom of religion, conscience, language, education and culture." Yes, discrimination does persist in Israel — as it does in America. Your assertion that the United States represents history's "most successful experiment in cultural diversity" might raise eyebrows among America's prison population, by far the world's largest, the majority of which is African-American and Hispanic. But as you note, America is a work in progress, and so is Israel.

More substantively, I was disturbed by your reference to the unequal distribution of water between Israelis and Palestinians and your assertion that Israel is abusively mingling religion and politics as a means of protecting itself from the religious radicalism that has traditionally targeted Jews. The first is a long-exposed Palestinian canard for which EU Parliament President Martin Schulz, after recently repeating it in front of the Knesset, apologized. The second is just wrong. Far more Jews — and more people generally — have been killed by radically secular communist and fascist regimes than by religious ones. The degree to which Judaism is "mingled" with the Jewish state derives from deep cultural and historical affinities, not fear.

Perhaps your own ambivalence about Jewish peoplehood leads you to emphasize that the majority of Jews live outside Israel and that Israel, therefore, can be merely *a* Jewish state but not *the* Jewish State. But most Irish people live outside Ireland today, and that does not make Ireland any less their nation-state. Israel, by contrast, is home to the world's largest Jewish community and, given current demographic trends, will soon host the absolute majority of Jews. But Israel is *the* Jewish state because it, alone, is situated in our ancestral homeland, has provided refuge to Jews from more than 70 countries, has revived the ancient Jewish language, and observes a national Jewish calendar. It is the Jewish state because it will aid you and your family, should you ever need such assistance, because you are Jews. When, in order to become ambassador, I relinquished my U.S. citizenship, an American consul punched a hole in my passport. But no one can punch a hole in the passport linking you as a Jew to Israel because your passport is your membership in the Jewish people and it's irrevocable.

Your perspective on these fundamental points perhaps seems to me to stem from your decision — a decision made by many American Jews — to be more an observer of the Jewish story than an active participant in it. We both made our choices — you're right — and I've chosen to participate. For me, the issue isn't the right to criticize Israeli policies but the duty to influence and implement them. It's about making the real-life and real-time decisions to ensure my country's survival as a democratic and Jewish state and its ability to surmount existential threats.

Early in our correspondence, I remember saying that Zionism, for me, means Jews taking responsibility for themselves. Israel is rife with responsibilities. It's a responsibility rarely assumed by people in history and certainly not by Jews throughout most of the last two millennia. But, as I've emphasized in my earlier letters, it's a burden I consider a blessing.

I harbor no illusions — the responsibilities are enormous. They require us to stop treating the Palestinians as two-dimensional props in a Jewish morality play but as a people with agency and, yes, responsibility. If they prove incapable of fulfilling those responsibilities, then we must separate from them by declaring our own borders that will best guarantee our security and encompass the maximum share of our citizenry. And those borders should bear the imprimatur of the United States. Your last letter dealt at length with what Americans can expect of Israel. In this, a decision sure to encounter protests in the world and evoke bitter opposition at home, Israel can expect the backing of the United States.

But I don't see Israel or Israel's future solely through a Palestine/conflict lens. Israel must work to make itself the nation-state of the Jewish people and not only in theory. It must respect all streams of Judaism and establish national criteria for determining membership in the Jewish people. My vision of Israel remains that of the Jewish state but the Jewish state that embraces all Jews everywhere, irrespective of how they observe, or prefer not to practice, their Judaism.

That state must also embrace its minorities. In the face of unequaled pressures, Israel has preserved their rights — compare it to the treatment of Japanese-Americans during World War II — and enabled many of them, especially the Christians, to flourish. But we have not done nearly enough. Israel must wage an unremitting war against discrimination and embark on a far-reaching campaign to incorporate non-Jewish Israelis into society, including via national service. On the other hand, Israel deserves the loyalty of its minorities. If a British Jew can salute, fight, and even die for a flag that has not one but three crosses on it, and a government linked to the Church of England, then an Arab can salute the Israeli flag and defend the state for which it stands.

Created as a socialist state, Israel must shed the socialist networks and bureaucracy that keep its price of living inordinately and artificially high, that deny a living wage to the middle class and affordable housing to young people. To remain at once militarily strong and an attractive place to live, Israel must be economically competitive in the world and preserve its technological edge. But to remain the Jewish state, Israel cannot dispense with its social safety nets. It cannot abandon the homeless, the immigrants, the children in need.

Consequently, our society may resemble Sweden's more than America's, but Israelis cannot for a second forget that they do not live in Scandinavia. We must continue to spend a large share of our national wealth on defense, and we must maintain a robust citizen's army. We must preserve our right to defend ourselves by ourselves in the manner and time of our choosing, and we must always have the means for doing so. Ideally, we should shoot less, but we should talk lesser still. But we can never outsource our fundamental protection.

Our responsibility — *my* responsibility — is to fulfill the promising vision of Israel that I know you shared. That is the open, tolerant, secure, dynamic, and moral Israel, the Jewish state not only ethnically but ethically. It is an Israel that retains the support of three-quarters of the American public it currently enjoys (an all-time high — those Beltway elites you cite are very much a minority) and builds on it. But that Israel will never look like Bethesda or even Summit, New Jersey. It will be more intense, louder, more rambunctious and flagrantly creative. It will have to make decisions and take measures that will undoubtedly generate controversy. Still, we can exhibit the vitality, the innovation, the pluralism, and the morality that Americans value in themselves.

And on that, I believe in conclusion, we can both emphatically agree.

COUNTERTERRORISM

Israel: Experience in Combating Terrorism (1984)
CENTRAL INTELLIGENCE AGENCY

Israel's response to terrorism has been characterized by a confrontational approach, with the use of force seen as the essential means for dealing with the threat. In aggregate and over time, four important elements have served to keep the threat at a tolerable level:

- Counterterrorist operations were generally conducted within a political framework conceived and approved by the senior security echelon.

- Appropriate decisionmaking foras were established to permit rapid decision on, and implementation of, counterterrorist actions.

- Concepts and doctrine regarding counter-terrorist measures were developed, which were consistent with the confrontational approach adopted by the government.

- Appropriate antiterrorist and counterterrorist forces were organized and employed against the threat.
[...]
The commitment to a reprisal policy is deeply ingrained in the Israeli military establishment. Although Israeli military intelligence officials have consistently warned that such actions have had little deterrent effect on terrorists, the leadership has shown a willingness to take action if Israel's security interests are at stake. In general, the populace has supported former Prime Minister Rabin's view that "the only place to meet the terrorists is on the battlefield."
[...]
Along with setting up decisionmaking procedures was the development of concepts and doctrine. Israel, again over time, moved from a policy of simple "eye for an eye" operations to a fully developed doctrine of retaliation. This held that terrorism could be countered by placing an unacceptably high price (to the Arabs) on such operations. By the mid-1950s, this idea had been supplemented by the concept of coercion or compulsion. Under this doctrine, terrorism was to be dealt with by forcing the Arab states to curb the activities of terrorist organizations operating from within their territory. This concept no longer linked specific terrorist actions to specific instances of retaliations but left Israel free to act when and where it felt more appropriate.

The doctrines of retaliation and coercion were supplemented in the 1960s and 1970s by those of preemption and prevention, under which Israel conducted operations aimed at heading off threatened terrorist operations or disrupting terrorist organizational activity. These

716

concepts gave Israeli decisionmakers readily available and familiar guidelines to deal with terrorism. Furthermore, the concepts of coercion, preemption, and prevention were applicable to other issues relating to the Arab-Israeli conflict. Regardless of outcomes, Israeli decisionmakers perceive these concepts to be reasonable and justifiable responses to the evolving Arab threat.

Rounding out Israel's approach to countering terror was the development of the types of forces required to implement decisions. Israel deploys a formidable array of territorial brigades. These are backed by impressive physical security measures and a population acutely sensitive to the terrorist threat. One measure of the effort is the 40,000 volunteers serving in the Civil Defense, an organization created in 1974 in the wake of several serious incidents.

Since independence, Israel has developed excellent capabilities for counterterrorist operations. Starting in the early 1950s, when not a single IDF unit was capable of offensive operations, the government created elite strike forces capable of conducting an array of counterterrorist operations. This effort included the doctrine of "exhausting the mission." That is, unless the raiding force suffered at least 50 percent casualties, its commander had to explain personally to the Chief of Staff why an operation failed.

By 1956, Israel had in the Paratroop Brigade a highly trained instrument for counterterrorist operations. It was used to raise capabilities of other units, such as the Golani Infantry Brigade. Although other forces have been added, particularly in the Air Force and Navy, these paratroop and infantry units remain the core for counterterrorist operations outside Israel. They have a long tradition of success, and senior officials have shown great confidence in their ability to carry out complex operations.

Despite the sustained and costly effort, Israel's success in countering terrorism has been mixed. At the most general level, the measures taken have prevented terrorism from seriously damaging the fabric of Israeli society. At a somewhat less general level, it appears that Israeli retaliatory, coercive, and preemptive actions have reduced the level of threat. Israeli cross-border counterterrorist actions, particularly some of the larger ones, have had a suppressive effect.

This was demonstrated along all four of its political boundaries. Successively, and largely through the use of extensive force against either the terrorists or host states, the Israelis brought a virtual end to terrorist operations along its borders with Egypt (1956), Jordan (1970), Syria (1974), and Lebanon (1982). While terrorist acts occasionally occur across these borders, the incidents have been reduced to a manageable level. The main terrorist threat now comes from groups or individuals inside Israel or Israeli-occupied territory, or from attacks on

Israeli interests abroad. [...]

The Cost of Combating Terror

The cost of this relative success has been high, whether measured in economic, social, military, or political terms. Economically, counterterrorist measures consume a significant amount of Israel's scarce resources. For example, in 1975 about one percent of the workforce was involved just in guarding schools. For an economy already burdened by the diversion of personnel to reserve duty, this represents a substantial loss. There have also been social costs. Security measures disrupt civilian life, and the acute sensitivity to the terrorist threat probably produces psychological stress. Militarily, countering terrorism represents a major diversion of resources from the primary objective of meeting the conventional threat from the Arab states and historically has caused attrition among Israel's best combat units.

Politically, the costs have perhaps been the greatest. The severity of particular counterterrorist operations, beginning as early as 1953 with the retaliatory raid on Qibia, Jordan, and the attendant collateral damage, has severely tarnished Israel's image abroad. This was compounded by the IDF attacks on West Beirut in the summer of 1982. No matter how expertly conducted from a military perspective, IDF operations against terrorists operating from bases in civilian areas damaged Israel's prestige, the image of its military, and its relations with friendly states.

There were other costs as well. Since Palestinian terrorism and Israeli counterterrorist measures are inextricably linked to the Arab-Israel conflict, specific actions have had a substantial effect on that conflict. This relationship can be seen in the circumstances leading to the 1956 and 1967 wars and the 1982 war in Lebanon.

Another cost, one much more difficult to measure, is the extent to which Israel's confrontational approach for dealing with terrorism, contributed to its perpetuation. Israel's large-scale actions satisfied the Palestinian goal of eliciting a strong Israeli response, bringing attention, and sometimes sympathy, to the terrorist cause. Furthermore, the Israeli approach does not appear to have hampered recruitment of Palestinians willing to die for their cause. It is an unresolved issue whether a more conciliatory policy toward the Arab states and Palestinian people would have been more effective in the long run. There are Israelis who would argue that it would have, although many past and present Israeli leaders are convinced that a confrontational approach makes terrorists more hesitant to conduct operations, and their supporters less ready to provide assistance.
[...]

718

Human shielding involves the use of persons protected by international humanitarian law, such as prisoners of war or civilians, to deter attacks on combatants and military objectives. […]

In great part, the dramatic asymmetry characterizing many of today's conflicts engenders human shielding. Confronted with overwhelming technological superiority, weaker parties have embraced shielding as a "method of warfare" designed to counter attacks against which they cannot effectively defend using the weaponry and forces at their disposal. The tactic presumes that the prospect of killing civilian shields may dissuade an attacker from striking. In a paradigmatic example, Iraq, fearing a Coalition attack to enforce United Nations weapons inspection requirements, openly announced in 1997 that "volunteers" had gathered at strategic locations; President Saddam Hussein "thanked all the sons of the great Iraqi people who headed for the people's palaces, factories and other installations to be a strong shield against the unjust aggression threatening our country."

Operationally, deterrence can manifest itself in one of three ways (or a combination thereof). First, the attacking side may refrain from conducting an attack based on moral concerns about harming those civilians forced to act as shields. Second, the attacker may abandon a planned strike because of possible negative publicity. After all, images of dead and injured civilians transmitted across a globalized media (which often pays little heed to the military rationale of an operation) can make it appear as if the attacker has mounted inhumane operations. In such an environment, even a tactically sound engagement causing casualties risks strategic fallout. This consequence typically constitutes the principle objective of the party employing shields; it seeks to weaken support for the enemy's war effort on the part of the international community, other States (including coalition partners), non-governmental organizations and individuals, while enhancing its own domestic and international backing. Third, at a certain point, the number of civilians likely to be injured or killed during an attack becomes "excessive" relative to its anticipated "military advantage," such that the international humanitarian law proportionality principle bars attack. Such "lawfare" exploits legal norms to impede the enemy's operations (at the tactical, operational or strategic levels of warfare). It includes not only instances in which an intended operation would be prohibited due to the presence of sufficient numbers of civilians, but also those in which the attacker's operations might be *perceived* as unlawful. […]

The Legal Wars: Balancing Targeting and Collateral Damage (2017)
Raphael S, Cohen, et al

In the IDF, legal advisers review targets and make recommendations to commanders on the possible ramifications under international law of their destruction. This task is made more complicated by the fact that Hamas purposely hides in and fires from civilian structures. For example, on July 17, the day the IDF initiated its ground assault into Gaza, UNRWA, which is responsible for caring for Palestinian refugees, announced that it had found 20 rockets stored in one of its schools in the Gaza Strip. It strongly condemned this as "a flagrant violation of the inviolability of its premises under international law" that "endangered civilians, including staff." In another example, Israel argued that its targeting of the residences of Hamas leaders was justified:

> On July 8, the IDF struck a weapons depot and operational planning site located in the residence of Ibrahim al-Shawaf, a senior military commander in the Palestinian Islamic Jihad.... The IDF considered this site a legitimate military target not because al-Shawaf (a member of an organized armed group) lived there, but because the site was used as an operational planning site and because a large number of weapons had been stored there and designated for attacks against Israeli citizens. During the IDF's strike, secondary explosions of the weaponry hidden inside the building further confirmed that it was a disguised weapons depot and thus constituted a military objective.

[...]

Israel faces three challenges in minimizing collateral damage and adhering to the Law of Armed Conflict (LOAC). The first challenge relates to distinguishing between a lawful and unlawful target. This is particularly difficult because the combatants do not necessarily don uniforms. Commanders rely on specific procedures and intelligence to help them determine whether an individual they see on the battle-field is a legitimate target. For example, if an ISR asset sees an individual preparing to launch a rocket, he would be considered a legitimate target for attack.

The second challenge relates to proportionality when it comes to weighing the military value or advantage of a target against the collateral damage that might be caused by attacking it. Proportionality can be seen along a spectrum. At the extreme ends of the spectrum, the calculus may be relatively straightforward. At one end, where the target value is high (e.g., a large stockpile of long-range missiles) and potential for collateral damage is low (e.g., it is located in a shed in a large, empty field), a commander would authorize a strike without much thought. At the other end, where one would gain little military advantage by taking out a target (e.g., a used Qassam rocket launcher) and the strike would cause many civilian casualties (e.g., the launcher is located in a school used for sheltering civilians), a commander would withhold authorization to attack. It is the cases in the middle of the spectrum that are the most vexing and require analytic procedures in real time to help commanders frame the issue and weigh the consequences of action or inaction.

The final challenge involves the precautions the IDF takes to minimize collateral damage through innovative tactics and concepts. This includes various methods of issuing warnings of impending attack to noncombatants and decisions about which platforms and weapons to use to achieve the desired military effect on a target without hurting civilians nearby. Dropping leaflets with specific instructions to civilians, knocking on the roof (sometimes multiple times), and making phone calls to apartments in a targeted building were all warning methods the IDF used in Operation Protective Edge. [...]

In Protective Edge, procedures to incorporate these issues into targeting decisions existed in the IDF command structure for both preplanned and time-sensitive targets. For preplanned targets, the IDF used the following general process:

1. Collect intelligence on the target. [...]

2. Determine the objective(s) in attacking the target. [...]

3. Develop options for carrying out the strike, including precautions to be taken. [...]

4. Elicit professional advice and opinion from relevant units, including legal advisers. [...]

5. Obtain command decision on attacking a target. [...]

All the information for each target was placed on a "target card" that carried through the entire planning process and undergoes reevaluation and revalidation as conditions changed.

Because of their fleeting nature, time-sensitive targets did not receive the same level of deliberation, but lawyers at different levels of the command structure still provided advice—and, in many cases, this advice was binding on the commanders. In addition, "even in the most time-sensitive situations ... IDF regulations emphasize that commanders and soldiers must still comply with the Law of Armed Conflict.... [C]ommanders rely on the training they have received, as well as directives that specify the checks and authorizations required prior to carrying out attacks."
[...]

Lawfare Is Here to Stay

Operation Protective Edge also demonstrates that lawfare will remain a central part of warfare for the foreseeable future. Retired U.S. Air Force Major General and Duke University Law professor Charles Dunlap defines lawfare as "the strategy of using—or misusing—law as a substitute for traditional military means to achieve a warfighting objective." Hamas's practice of placing weapons in populated urban and suburban areas during Operations Cast Lead and Protective Edge is an example of this practice:

> Conducting urban warfare while maintaining traditionally restrictive implementations of the LOAC represents a significant challenge. This is the dilemma Israel has faced in its three conflicts since 2008 with Hamas in Gaza. Israel is extremely conscious that Hamas will use the proximity of civilians to try to confront it with operational dilemmas to employing precision strike systems against legitimate targets. Rockets, mortars, entrances to tunnels, and fighting positions were situated to create collateral damage and noncombatant casualties if attacked by the Israelis. Although this behavior by Hamas represents a violation of the LOAC, it is a strategy that has frequently been employed by the weak against the strong [....]

During these operations, Israel faced a dilemma: attack legitimate targets as a way of stopping fire on Israel and protecting its soldiers but causing civilian casualties and property damage in the process or not attack those targets and accept Israeli casualties and damage. Iron Dome made this issue even more acute when it raised the question: Why did Israel attack rocket launchers and risk civilian lives when it could neutralize the effects of the rockets with Iron Dome?

The IDF tried a number of ways to combat Hamas's attempt to use lawfare. It tried prestrike notifications to civilians in the vicinity of targets via leaflets, telephone calls, and "knocking on the roof" notification. After the Lebanon War, the IDF pushed legal advisers from the regional command level down to the division level and better integrated the legal advisers into the targeting process. The IDF conducted legal reviews and has judge-advocate attorneys at division and higher headquarters. Lawyers reviewed targets for compliance with the law and estimates of collateral damage. Their decisions were binding on operational commanders. [...]

And yet, these efforts to combat lawfare produced mixed results. Indeed, the intense international scrutiny of Shuja'iya, Khuza'a, and Black Friday underscore that all military actions will be under a microscope in the modern age. The Goldstone Report and the UN Independent Commission of Inquiry on the 2014 Gaza Conflict both questioned the legality of IDF operations (as well as those of Hamas). The latter review called into question the sufficiency of many of the efforts the IDF took during its operations in 2014 [....]

As a result, commanders need to understand and adjust to this environment. As a senior Israeli policymaker remarked,

> Israel is a little country and enemies want to do what they can to subjugate Israel to the ICC [International Criminal Court] and delegitimize Israel's ability to defend itself. This is why Israel is cautious. Most people understand what might be the consequences of this. This extends to the level that it disturbs forces, but to what extent depends on the commanders on the ground and decision makers in the headquarters.

The IDF already plans to do more in this area. On the general staff level, the IDF plans to stand up a new lawfare section [....] The purpose of the staff section is to conduct "offensive" lawfare, proactively explaining why an IDF operation is legal in the first place rather than responding to accusations after the fact. According to one retired IDF officer, such a proposal is about five years overdue. And more work remains to be done. An IDF general officer serving on the general staff said,

> Israel is still inexperienced with this and it is against its ethos. Israel thinks when they conduct war, no one should interfere. Israel has a long way to go, but is starting to grow up. They understand this is an issue, and they need to figure out how to do this. In the small HQs, it isn't clear where the lawfare should come into play. In the big headquarters, integrating lawfare works better.

The left-leaning Israeli nongovernmental organization Breaking the Silence agreed and found in their interviews with IDF soldiers after Protective Edge that the rules of engagement "were at times ambiguous, leaving junior officers with much discretion regarding the amount of fire to use, and the acceptable degree of collateral damage that may be caused." For better or worse, lawfare is here to stay, and the IDF— like all Western militaries—will have to wrestle with its implications in any future operation.
[…]

Ringside Seat to Real-Time Radicalization (2023)
Lawrence Pintak

Imagine you are a 12-year-old Palestinian boy in Gaza. You are lying wounded in a hospital. Air strikes periodically rock the building. Your parents are dead. Your one-year-old brother and three-year-old sister have just been zipped together into a body bag. Three siblings are still buried somewhere under your apartment building with six of their cousins and four aunts and uncles who were sheltering in the same apartment with you.

You don't need a PhD in terrorism studies to figure out this kid's likely life path.

Since September 11, 2001 governments around the world—including Israel—have spent tens of millions of dollars on research to identify the triggers for radicalization. Cut through all the other noise and the findings come down to this: If you have been exposed to violence you are significantly more likely to commit violence.

Nearly 4,000 Gazan children have been killed by Israeli bombs in the last month, some 40 percent of the total fatalities. According to Save the Children, that's more than the annual toll in all the world's conflict zones combined since 2019. At least a thousand more children are believed buried beneath the rubble. The rest have been exposed to trauma at a level that even American soldiers who served in Afghanistan, Iraq, or Vietnam can only imagine.

Now think about what the next decade is going to bring.

We're not talking here about the horror of what Hamas inflicted on Israel. That was unspeakable. We are not talking about the trauma that Israelis and Jews around the world are enduring. That is tragic. We are talking about the arc of terrorism and the stark reality that a new cycle of radicalization is being seeded in Gaza, which UNESCO calls a "graveyard for children" and a "living Hell for everyone else."

We can all write the script for this novel. It doesn't take much imagination. A decade ago, a team led by the chair of a NATO research task force had university students role play the personae of a would-be suicide bomber. The results "were eerily similar to accounts of real (failed) suicide bombers." They were driven by secondary trauma, motivated by "revenge and justice," and "[m]ost imagined targeting children or civilians" in order to "inflict the worst and most horrific revenge on their enemies."

Those students were triggered by *imagining* the circumstances that create a terrorist, without ever leaving the comfort of the focus group room. They were motivated by that ideology of revenge in response to perceived injustice and humiliation at the heart of terrorism.

Imagine their real-world counterparts in Gaza today.

A U.S. government study of Palestinian suicide bombers between the ages of 12 and 17 years old found that, "In almost every case, these potential bombers […] have a relative or close friend who was killed, wounded, or jailed during the Israeli occupation." A European Union report published last summer concluded that 91 percent of Palestinian children in the territory suffered from PTSD.

That was all *before* the current conflict.

The 12-year-old in the emergency room is, of course, a fictional composite, but variations of his story are playing out across Gaza, where hospitals are running out of body bags and some dead children will never be identified. Let's say that boy buries his mental trauma and compartmentalizes his anger. What other drivers of radicalization litter his path and those of countless others?

Early experiences of abandonment? Check. Perceived injustice? Check. Experiences of stigmatization? Check. Personal uncertainty? Check. Family dysfunction? Check. Family breakdown? Check. Friendships with radicalized individuals? Check.

"Individuals radicalize through progressive exposure to violent political actions," according to terrorism experts Arie W. Kruglanski, Jocelyn J. Bélanger, and Rohan Gunaratna. It doesn't get much more violent than Gaza today.

Other predictors of radicalization include level of education and professional integration. Parts of Gaza already resemble a post-apocalyptic film set. Hundreds of schools have been damaged or destroyed. It is hard to see any significant portion of this generation of Gazan children ever returning to the classroom — much less having a profession in an economy that barely existed even before the war.

And finally, there is the "deficiency of life skills." UNICEF defines those as "a group of psychosocial competencies and interpersonal skills", from stress management and positive thinking to empathy and resilience. Such skills "help people make informed decisions, solve problems, think critically and creatively, communicate effectively, build healthy relationships, empathize with others, and cope with and manage their lives in a healthy and productive manner." This is pretty much a list of everything a kid growing up in Gaza over the next few years is unlikely to develop.

"Once a 'besieged enclave,' Gaza will be reduced to a 'supercamp' of internally displaced persons," political scientist Nathan J. Brown predicted in a November report on the territory's post-war prospects. "This seems less like the day after a conflict than a long twilight of disintegration and despair."

We don't have to look far to see the cause-and-effect.

Israel's 1982 invasion of Lebanon claimed more than 17,000 Palestinian and Lebanese lives. It resulted in the rise of Hezbollah, the militant organization that killed more Americans than any other group before 9/11 and is today more powerful than Hamas.

The U.S. invasion of Iraq left an estimated 300,000 Iraqis dead. It was responsible for the collapse of Iraqi society and the birth of the Islamic State and a variety of other terror groups.

America's twenty-year occupation of Afghanistan cost 2.3 trillion US dollars and left an estimated 70,000 dead. It produced a revitalized and reenergized Taliban, which is already responsible for a surge in terrorism in neighboring Pakistan.

But, of course, this war will be different…

Just six weeks before Hamas launched its deadly assault in Israel, the UN's Special Coordinator for the Middle East Peace Process warned of an explosion of violence "fueled and exacerbated by a growing sense of despair about the future."

Think of this despair now. History tells us how this latest chapter plays out.

PERSPECTIVES

Address to the World Without Zionism Conference (2005)
Mahmoud Ahmadinejad

We must see what the real story of Palestine is. Is the conflict in Palestine a war between some Jews on the one side and Muslims and non-Jews on the other side? Is it a war between the Jews and other faiths? Is it the war of one country with other countries? Is it the war of one country with the Arab world? Is the conflict only over the limited lands of Palestine? I think the answer to all these questions is negative.

The creation of the regime occupying Al-Qods (Jerusalem) was a heavy move by the globally dominant system and Global Arrogance against the Islamic world. There is a historic battle going on between the Oppressor World and the Islamic world and the roots of this conflict goes back hundreds of years.
[...]
In the past one hundred years, the last trenches of the Islamic world fell and the Oppressor World created the regime occupying Al-Qods as the bridgehead for its domination of the Islamic world. Bridgehead is a military term in warfare. When two divisions or armies are fighting each other, if one side advances and breaks through the front and captures a piece of enemy territory and builds up fortifications and strengthens its hold to make it a base for further territorial expansion, then we call this a bridgehead.

The occupying state (Israel) is the bridgehead of the Oppressor World in the heart of the Islamic world. They have built a base to expand their domination to the entire Islamic world. There is no other *raison d'etre* for this entity without this objective.

The battle that is going on in Palestine today, therefore, is the frontline of the conflict between the Islamic world and the Oppressor World. It is a battle of destiny that will determine the fate of hundreds of years of conflict in Palestine.

Today, the Palestinian nation is fighting the Oppressor World on behalf of the Islamic umma. Thank God, from the day the Palestinian nation moved towards an Islamic struggle with Islamic objectives and an Islamic environment, and made Islam the dominating force in its behavior and orientation, we have been witnessing the progress and successes of the Palestinian nation every day.
[...]
Our dear Imam ordered that the occupying regime in Al-Qods be wiped off the face of the earth. This was a very wise statement. The issue of Palestine

is not one on which we could make a piecemeal compromise. This would mean our defeat. Anyone who would recognize this state [Israel] has put his signature under the defeat of the Islamic world.

[...]

Recently, a new conspiracy has been plotted and is underway. They have been forced to evacuate a corner of Palestine and this was imposed on them by the Palestinian nation. But they want to sell this as the final victory and use the evacuation of Gaza and the creation of a Palestinian state as an excuse to end the Palestinian cause and goal.

Today they are making an evil and deceptive effort to turn the struggle into an internal conflict of the Islamic world. They want to create conflict among Palestinian groups inside Palestine by making them greedy for political positions or high office, so that these groups abandon the decisive issue for Palestine and turn on each other.

With the excuse of having cleared the Gaza Strip to show their good will, they want a group of Muslim nations to recognize this corrupt regime, and I am very hopeful and pray to God that the Palestinian nation and the dear Palestinian groups will be cautious of such sedition.

Today the unity of the front in Palestine on its goals is a pressing necessity. The issue of Palestine is by no means finished. The issue of Palestine will only be resolved when all of Palestine comes under Palestinian rule, when all the refugees return to their homes, and when a popular government chosen by this nation takes the affairs in its hands. Of course, those who have come to this land from far away to plunder this land have no right to participate in the decision-making process for this nation.

I am hopeful that just as the Palestinian nation continued its struggle for the past ten years, it will continue to maintain its awareness and vigilance. This phase is going to be short-lived. If we put it behind us successfully, God willing, it will pave the way for the annihilation of the Zionist regime and it will be a downhill route.

I warn all the leaders in the Islamic world to beware of this conspiracy. If any of them takes a step towards the recognition of this regime, then he will burn in the fire of the Islamic umma (nation) and will have eternal shame stamped on his forehead, regardless of whether he did this under pressure by the dominant powers, or lack of understanding or naiveté or selfishness or worldly incentives.

The issue of Palestine is the issue of the Islamic world. Those who are closeted behind closed doors cannot make decisions on this issue and the Islamic nation does not allow this historical enemy to exist at the heart of the Islamic world.

Peruse campus literature. Watch clips from university protests. [...] And the one common denominator—besides their arrogance—is their abject ignorance. Take their following tired talking points:

"Refugees"

We are told that the Palestinians after more than 75 years of residence in the West Bank and Gaza are "refugees." If that definition were currently true, then, are the 900,000 Jews who were forcibly exiled from Muslim countries in the Middle East, North Africa, and Asia after the 1947, 1956, 1967 wars still "refugees?"

Most fled to Israel. Do they now live in "refugee" camps administrated by the UN? Are they protesting to recover their confiscated homes and wealth in Damascus, Cairo, or Baghdad? Do Jews on Western television dangle their keys to lost homes in Damascus a half-century after they were expelled?

How about the 150,000-200,000 Greek Cypriots who in 1974 were brutally driven out of their ancient homes in Northern Cyprus? Are they today living in "refugee" camps in southern Cyprus? Are Cypriot terrorists blowing themselves up in "occupied" Nicosia to recover what was stolen from them by Turkey?

Turkish president Recep Erdogan lectures the world on Palestinian "refugees," but does he mention Turkey's role in the brutal expulsion of 40 percent of the residents of Cyprus?

Are there campus groups organizing against Turkey on behalf of the displaced Cypriots? After being slaughtered and expelled, are the Cypriots a cause celebre in academia? Do the "refugee" cities of southern Cyprus resemble Jenin or Jericho?

For that matter, how about the 12 million German civilians who between 1945-50 were expelled, and mostly walked back from, East Prussia and parts of Eastern Europe, some with Prussian roots going back a millennium and more. Perhaps 1 million died during the expulsions.

Are any current survivors still "refugees?" If so, are they organizing for war to get back "occupied" "Danzig" and "Königsberg" for Germany? So why does the world damn Israel and romanticize the Palestinians in a way it does not with any other "refugee" group?

"Apartheid"

Israel is said to practice "apartheid," although since 2005-06 Gaza has been autonomous. Mahmoud Abbas runs in his fashion the West Bank. Like the Hamas clique, he held elections one time in 2005, and then after his election, of course, cancelled any free election in the fashion of the one election, one time Middle East. Who forced him to do that? Zionists? Americans?

At any time, Gaza could have taken its vast wealth in annual foreign aid and become completely independent in fuel, food, and energy, without need of any such help form the "Zionist entity."

Gaza could have capitalized on its strategic location, the world's eagerness to help, and the natural beauty of its Mediterranean beaches. Instead, it squandered its income on a labyrinth of terrorist tunnels and rockets. Today, it snidely snickers at any mention of following the Singapore model of prosperity–a former colonial city whose World War II death count vastly surpassed that of the various wars over Gaza.

Are the Israeli Arabs—21 percent of the Israeli population—living under apartheid?

If so, it is a funny sort of oppression when they vote, hold office, form parties, and enjoy more freedom and prosperity than almost anywhere else in the Middle East under Arab autocracies. Are those in sympathy with Hamas fleeing from Israel into Gaza or the West Bank or other Arab countries to live with kindred Muslims under an autocratic and theocratic dictatorship, or do they prefer to stay in the "Zionist entity" under "apartheid?"

Where then is real apartheid?

The Uyghurs in China, fellow Muslims to Middle Easterners, who are ignored by Israel's Islamic enemies, but who reside in China's segregated work camps to the silence of the usually loud UN, EU, and Muslim world?

How about the Muslim Kurds? Are they second- or third-class citizens in Muslim Turkey? And how about the tens of thousands of foreign workers from India, Pakistan, and other Asian countries who labor under the kafala system in the Arab Muslim Gulf countries, and are subject to apartheid protocols that allow them no free will about how they live, travel, or the conditions of their labor?

Are campuses erupting to champion the Uyghurs, the Kurds, or the subjugated workers of the Gulf?

"Disproportionate"

Israel is now damned as "disproportionally" bombing Gaza. The campus subtext is that because Gaza's 7,000-8,000 rockets launched at Israeli civilians have not killed enough Jews, then Israel should not retaliate for October 7 by bombing Hamas targets–shielded by impressed civilians— because it is too effective.
[…]
Does the U.S. lecture Ukraine not to use to the full extent its lethal U.S. imported weaponry since the result is often simply too deadly? After all, perhaps twice as many Russians have been killed, wounded, or are missing than Ukrainian casualties. Should Ukraine have been more "proportionate?" Has President Biden ordered President Zelensky to offer the Russian aggressors a "pause" in the fighting to end the "cycle of violence?"

Or did U.S.-supplied artillery, anti-armor weapons, drones, and missiles "disproportionally" kill too many Russians? Or does the U.S. assume that since Russia attacked Ukraine at a time of peace, it deserves such a "disproportionate" response that alone will lose it the war?
[…]
Civilian Casualties

Campus activists scream that Israel has slaughtered "civilians" and is careless about "collateral damage." They equate retaliating against mass murderers who use civilians to shield them from injury, while warning any Gazans in the region of the targeted response to leave, as the moral equivalent of deliberately butchering civilians in a surprise attack.

So did protestors mass in the second term of Barrack Obama when he focused on Predator drone missions inside Somalia, Pakistan, and Yemen to go after Islamic terrorists who deliberately target civilians?

At the time, the hard-left New York Times found the ensuing "collateral damage" in civilian deaths merely "troubling." No matter—Obama persisted, insisting as he put it, "Let's kill the people who are trying to kill us." Note Obama did not expressly say the terrorists in Pakistan or Yemen were killing Americans, but "trying" to kill Americans. […]

We have no idea how many women, children, and elderly were in the general vicinity of a targeted terrorist in Pakistan or Yemen when an American drone missile struck. Then CIA Director John Brennan later admitted that he had lied under oath (with zero repercussions), when he testified to Congress that there was *no* collateral damage in drone targeted assassinations.

Obama was proud of his preemptive assassination program. Indeed, in lighthearted fashion he joked at the White House Correspondence Dinner about his preference for lethal drone missions [....]

Did the campuses erupt and scream "Not in my name" when their president laughed about his assassination program? After all, Obama had also admitted, "There is no doubt that civilians were killed who shouldn't have been." Did he then stop the targeted killings due to collateral damage—as critics now demand a cease fire from Israel?

"Genocide"

Genocide is now the most popular charge in the general damnation of Israel, a false smear aimed at calling off the Israeli response to Hamas, burrowed beneath civilians in Gaza City.

But how strange a charge! Pro-Hamas demonstrators the world over chant "From the River to the Sea," unambiguously calling for the utter destruction of Israel and its 9 million population. Are the Hamas supporters then "genocidal?"

Is genocide the aim of Hamas that launched over 7,000 rockets into Israeli cities without warning? What is the purpose of the purportedly 120,000 rockets in the hands of Hezbollah if not to target Israeli noncombatants? Is all that a genocidal impulse?

Do Hamas and Hezbollah drop leaflets to civilians, as does Israel, to flee the area of a planned missile attack—or is that against their respective charters?

Hamas leaders in Qatar and Beirut continue to give interviews bragging about their October 7 surprise mass murdering of civilians. They even promise more such missions that likewise will be aimed at beheading, torturing, executing, incinerating, and desecrating the bodies of hundreds of Jewish civilians, perhaps again in the early morning during a holiday and a time of peace.

Is that planned continuation of mass killing genocidal? [...]

Perhaps students at Harvard, Yale, Cornell, and Stanford will protest the real genocide in Darfur where some half-million black African Sudanese have been slaughtered by mostly Muslim Arab Sudanese. Did the Cornell professor who claimed he was "exhilarated" on news of beheaded Jewish babies protest the slaughter of the Sudanese? Did the current campus protestors ever assemble to scream about the Islamists who slaughtered the indigenous Africans of Sudan?

732

Are professors at Stanford organizing to refuse all grants and donations that originate from communist China? Remember, the Chinese communist Party has never apologized for the party's genocidal murder of some 60-80 millions of its own during the Maoist Cultural Revolution, much less its systematic efforts to eliminate the Uyghur Muslim population?

These examples could easily be expanded. But they suffice to remind us that the Middle-East and Western leftist attacks on Israel for responding to the October 7 mass murdering are neither based on any consistent moral logic nor similarly extended to other nations who really do practice apartheid, genocide, and kill without much worry about collateral damage.

So why does the world apply a special standard to Israel?

To the leftist and Islamist, Israel is guilty of being:

1) Jewish;

2) Too prosperous, secure, and free;

3) Sufficiently Western to meet the boilerplate smears of colonialist, imperialist, and blah, blah, blah.

The United Nations (UN) played a pivotal role in the establishment of the Jewish State by passing UN Resolution 181 in 1947, which called for the partition of British Mandate Palestine into two states, one Jewish and one Arab. Following Israel's independence in 1948, the Jewish State became an official member-state of the international body.

At the same time, the international body has a continuing history of a one-sided, hostile approach to Israel. [...] Successive Secretary Generals have acknowledged this is an issue for the institution. Indeed, in a meeting in April 2007, Secretary-General Ban Ki-moon acknowledged to ADL leaders that Israel has been treated poorly at the UN and that, while some progress has been made, this bias still remains an issue. [...] "Unfortunately, because of the [Israeli-Palestinian] conflict, Israel's been weighed down by criticism and suffered from bias—and sometimes even discrimination," Ban said in response to a question about discrimination against Israel at the UN. [...] In his first public address to a Jewish group, Secretary General Antonio Guterres told the World Jewish Congress in April 2017: "As secretary general of the United Nations I consider that the State of Israel needs to be treated as any other state." And in August 2017, he stated that calls for Israel's destruction are a form of modern-day anti-Semitism.
[...]
Israel's Isolation

Since Israel's establishment, Arab member states of the UN have used the General Assembly (GA) as a forum for isolating and chastising Israel. With support from third-world nations, particularly the Non-Aligned Movement, and others, the Arab states have had little difficulty passing harsh anti-Israel resolutions through the GA. Even today, the strength of these groups in the world body allows them to continue rebuking Israel. While anti-Israel resolutions are easily passed in the GA, this is not the case in the Security Council, where resolutions are binding in nature, as the United States has used its veto power to prevent the passage of such resolutions.

In the 1970s, the Arab bloc used its power to establish and authorize funding for several UN committees and divisions of the Secretariat which primarily carry out the anti-Israel agenda. Among these are: The Division for Palestinian Rights of the Secretariat, The Committee to Investigate Israeli Practices in the Territories, and The Committee on the Exercise of the Inalienable Rights of the Palestinian People. Today, these bodies continue to be deeply engaged in promoting programs and initiatives that are harshly critical of Israel.

A low point at the UN was the passage of the Arab and Soviet-sponsored United Nations resolution of November 10, 1975 which declared Zionism a "form of racism and racial discrimination." The highly politicized resolution was aimed at denying Israel its political legitimacy by attacking its moral basis for existence. The resolution was finally repealed on December 16, 1991.

For decades, Israel was the only member state consistently denied admission into a regional group, the organizational structure by which member states can participate on UN bodies and committees. The Arab states continue to prevent Israeli membership in the Asian Regional Group, Israel's natural geopolitical grouping. As a result, Israel long sought entry into the Western and Others Group (WEOG) and in May 2000 was granted admission in New York. In 2013, Israel was invited to join WEOG in Geneva, the seat of several UN bodies and subsidiary organizations.

The Human Rights Council

The UN Human Rights Council (HRC), which replaced the Commission on Human Rights in March 2006, has continued its predecessor's extreme focus on and biased treatment of issues relating to Israel, particularly in comparison with its mild action on pressing international human rights crises. The permanent agenda of the HRC includes a specific item targeting Israel—Agenda Item #7—which is titled: "Human rights situation in Palestine and other occupied Arab territories: Human rights violations and implications of the Israeli occupation of Palestine and other occupied Arab territories and the Right to self-determination of the Palestinian people." Israel is the only country to appear on the HRC's permanent agenda, while other countries such as Iran and Sudan, notorious for their human rights abuses, are included as part of the general debate.

The HRC has appointed a few "Special Rapporteurs" on "the situation of human rights in the Palestinian territories occupied since 1967," whose biased mandate has been evident in their one-sided reports on the Israeli-Palestinian conflict. Two of the most problematic Special Rapporteurs have been John Dugard—who in 2008 justiced Palestinian terrorism as an "inevitable consequence" of Israel's actions—and Richard Falk—who has made a number of outrageous comments about Israel, including endorsing the anti-Israel BDS movement and comparing Israel's treatment of Palestinians to Nazi activity during the Holocaust.
[…]
In 2016, the HRC ratcheted up its hostility to Israel by passing a resolution calling for the creation of a "blacklist" of companies operating in the West Bank, East Jerusalem and Golan Heights. The resolution condemned Israeli settlements, and called on companies not to do business with them. The UN High Commissioner for Human Rights said he planned to publish the list by the end of 2017, despite objections from Israel and the US. As of

2018, the UN has only published a list of countries where the companies are based, but not the names of the companies themselves.

In June 2018, the US announced that it was formally withdrawing from the HRC, citing anti-Israel bias and the body's inclusion of human rights-violating countries as motivating the decision. The UK also announced that it would withdraw if the Council continued its anti-Israel bias.

<u>United Nations Educational, Scientific and Cultural Organization (UNESCO)</u>

In October 2011, UNESCO granted the Palestinians full admission into the organization, the first UN body to do so. In the past few years, a number of problematic resolutions relating to Israel have been adopted by the body, which have include harsh criticism of Israel's handling of holy sites in Jerusalem.

In April 2016, the UNESCO Executive Board adopted a resolution on "Occupied Palestine" which was harshly critical of Israel and which only refers to the Muslim name for the Temple Mount—Al-Aqsa Mosque/Al-Haram al-Sharif—without using the Jewish "Temple Mount", effectively ignoring the Jewish connection to the site.

In October 2016, the Executive Board passed a resolution on Jerusalem which referred to the Temple Mount / Holy Sanctuary solely by its Muslim name and to the Western Wall Plaza in quotation marks, effectively diminishing the 3,000 year Jewish connection to the city.

In July 2017, UNESCO's World Heritage Committee voted to designate the old city of Hebron, including the Tomb of the Patriarchs, as a "World Heritage Site in Danger" and listed the site as part of the State of Palestine.

In 2018, a toned-down compromise UNESCO resolution was reached on an Israel-focused resolution, which Israel welcomed as a positive step. [...]

Much of the news coverage of 7 October 2023 refers to Hamas's attacks on Southern Israel as ground zero with guests or commentators who try and explain the 75-year-old occupation of Palestine being accused by some presenters and columnists as justifying the attacks. Ignoring the context and history, especially the recent history of 'occupied' Gaza which has been under an Israeli blockade since 2005, is favourable to an Israeli narrative which has constantly promoted the attacks on Gaza and in the West Bank as a war between light and darkness. Having pro-Israel voices and talking points regularly as the lead items in news reports, even as the death toll in Gaza grew exponentially, has given prominence to Israeli life over that of Palestinians.

Differences in the use of language has also been a regular feature of coverage. The language used appears to often underplay Palestinian deaths, compared to those of Israelis. Harsh and emotive terms rightly used to describe the attacks on 7 October and in relation to the deaths of Israelis, have seldom been used for Palestinian deaths, where more passive language which omits the perpetrator (Israel) and the action (shot, bombed, killed) is used. Palestinians simply die as some headlines would suggest. Comparisons are made with reporting of similar deaths in Ukraine where readers and viewers are not left with a guessing game as to who caused the death.

Descriptors such as "Hamas-run" in relation to the Gaza Health Ministry are favoured in the Western media possibly as a mechanism to cast doubt and delegitimise claims coming from Gaza, where international media are denied access. And hateful language used to dehumanise Palestinians, Arabs and Muslims has, on occasion, not been challenged.

Claims made by Israeli politicians, journalists and the Israeli Defence Force (IDF) have been amplified and accepted as truth without verification. Some of these have subsequently been proven to be false yet have not been corrected nor have they been challenged when repeated. This despite the history of Israeli falsehoods even before this current war and as recent as denying responsibility for killing Palestinian journalist Shireen Abu Akleh in May 2022. Treating the Israeli military as a credible source that does not warrant scepticism and further verification, has been one the glaring failures of journalists and media outlets.

The insistence on "Israel's rights" often to the exclusion of Palestinian rights, has been used to shut down pro-Palestinian voices or to legitimize Israeli claims. Such claims are often without recourse to the fact that Israel is an occupying power which continues land grabs and killings in the West Bank at the same time as it rains down bombs on Gaza. There has been very little reference to the Israeli and Egyptian blockades of Gaza that have turned the territory into what some have called 'an open-air prison'.

Pro-Palestinian voices and activists have been routinely denounced, misrepresented and targeted by many national media outlets. The right-wing media has been particularly hostile towards pro-Palestinian voices, framing them as supporters of terrorism and antisemites as well as being hostile to British values.
[…]
Palestinian symbols such as the Palestinian flag are used to illustrate stories on antisemitism and the intersection between Palestine and Islamophobia has been exposed with pro-Palestine support framed as dangerous and akin to a terror threat often because of the large Muslim contingent among it. Furthermore, a historic revisionism of Islam being an antisemitic religion is suggested as the driving force behind the opposition to Israel by editors as well as speakers and columnists.

Researchers in the United States of America have labelled this phenomenon as "presumptively antisemitic" where they have shown how "Islamophobic tropes work to fuel and sustain spurious allegations of antisemitism".
[…]
Key Findings

This CfMM analysis has established 20 statistical insights from the TV News and Online news coverage of Israel's war on Gaza. […]

CONTEXT

- 76% of online articles frame the current war as an "Israel-Hamas war"
- Only 24% of news mentioning Israel or Hamas or Gaza mention the word(s) Palestine/Palestinian, which suggests a lack of context about the Israeli-Palestinian issue.
- Al Jazeera English news channel had more mentions of "occupied territories" than all British and American news channels combined
- In one month out of over 98,500 mentions of the term Gaza there were only 28 instances of the words "occupied Gaza" on Broadcast TV channels, 14 of which were on Al Jazeera English.

FRAMING

- Most TV Broadcast channels promoted "Israel's right" to defend itself compared with the rights of the Palestinians by a ratio of 5 to 1.
- The insistence on "Israel's right" was found on 1,482 occasions across broadcast channels. A similar search for the right of Palestinians to resist yielded only 278 results.

738

- CfMM analysis shows that 36% of mentions of the right of Palestinians came from Al Jazeera's English Channel which reports from the perspective of the Global South.
- Right-wing TV channels in Britain had 36% mentions of Israel's right/s" and only 7% of the rights of Palestinians.
- The label of Israel Hamas War is favoured by Western broadcasters and British based broadcasters with almost twice the number of mentions compared with Israel Gaza War.

LANGUAGE [TV BROADCAST]

- Where emotive language is used, Israelis are about 11 times more likely to be referred to as victims of attacks, compared to Palestinians.
- In broadcast TV clips, 2 out of every 3 emotive terms used were for Israeli deaths. Just 1 in 10 were used for Palestinian deaths.
- Over 70% of the term's atrocities, slaughter and massacre were used in reference to the attacks against Israelis.
- Terms used to describe the deaths of Palestinians are sometimes qualified with phrases such as "what they say is a massacre."

LANGUAGE [ONLINE NEWS]

- In online British news outlets emotive terms were found to be four times more prevalent when describing the actions of Hamas against Israeli's compared with descriptions of the killings of Palestinians or civilians in Gaza.
- 68% of emotive terms were used to describe violence towards Israelis on 7 October or on another occasion with 33% found on the Mail Online website alone.

UNVERIFIED CLAIMS

- There were 361 TV news clips where the term "beheaded" AND "babies" were found.
[...]
- Of the 361 mentions there were 52 which showed any sufficient challenge, rebuttal or questioning of the claims.

LACK OF PROMINENCE OF PALESTINIAN VOICES

- CfMM found that TV reporting of Israeli perspectives was references almost three times more (4,311) than Palestinian ones (1,598). In online news it was almost twice as much (2,983 v 1,737).
[...]

Religious Zionism's Rise and Its Implications (2022)
Jim Zanotti

The rise of Religious Zionism has triggered debate about the implications for Israel's democracy, its ability to manage tensions with its Arab citizens and with Palestinians, and its relations with the United States and other countries. The electoral list's two leading figures, Bezalel Smotrich and Ben Gvir, openly support policies to favor Israel's Jewish citizens over its Arab citizens and annex the West Bank. Religious Zionism leaders aspire to cabinet positions giving them greater control over West Bank issues. Additionally, they advocate legislation that would allow the Knesset to override decisions from Israel's High Court of Justice (or Supreme Court). According to the *Wall Street Journal*:

> If the law is passed, lawmakers in Mr. Netanyahu's bloc say they aim to quickly overturn judicial rulings striking down the yearslong detention of African asylum seekers, a law retroactively legalizing illegal Israeli outposts built on private Palestinian land and a law formally excluding ultraorthodox Israelis from the country's mandatory military service....

> Critics of the judicial overhaul say it will undermine Israel's democracy by giving absolute power to the ruling coalition and leave minorities without protection from the will of the majority. Advocates for the changes say they will restore power to elected officials hamstrung by activist judges.

A Netanyahu-led coalition reliant on Religious Zionism and ultra-Orthodox parties may lead to political shifts favoring stricter application of Jewish law in society, including less inclusion of women in state religious councils and some rollback of LGBTQ rights. [...]

Ben Gvir once belonged to Kach, a movement based on the racist ideology of former Knesset member Meir Kahane (1932-1990) that was finally banned from elections in the 1990s. A Kahanist offshoot of Kach (Kahane Chai) was designated as a Foreign Terrorist Organization by the United States from 1997 until 2022 and remains a Specially Designated Global Terrorist entity. Ben Gvir was convicted in 2007 for incitement to racism and supporting terrorism, but says that he has moderated his positions and does not generalize about Arabs. Ben Gvir has been a regular fixture at contentious gatherings of Jews and Arabs in Jerusalem, and Israel's police chief blamed him for provoking major May 2021 Israeli-Palestinian violence there.

Netanyahu may feel some inclination to accommodate demands from Smotrich and Ben Gvir to serve in the cabinet and pass legislation because Religious Zionism might support legal measures that could retroactively bar corruption charges against serving prime ministers. [...]

740 From Congressional Research Service (CRS Report No. R44245).

An Interview with Rabbi Meir Kahane (1981)

THE YESHIVA UNIVERSITY OBSERVER

Rabbi Kahane, founder of the Jewish Defense League and head of its counterpart party in Israel, Kach, was in the States last month on a speaking and fundraising tour primarily to gain support for his party and his bid for the Knesset.

[…]

Kach has the same non-compromising attitude that Kahane is famous for in all his endeavors. The platform of the party is essentially threefold:

1) To define the Jewish people in the Jewish state in *Torah* terms. "Our concept of Torah," Kahane explained, "includes both ritual and nationalism toward Eretz Yisrael. They are two equal feet and without one, the other cannot stand."

2) To support indivisibility of the Land of Israel. Kahane stresses that this is not a matter of military strategy—that that is irrelevant—but in terms of *Halachic* Judaism, one is not allowed to give up land. Even if it is deemed dangerous to retain land, the concept of *Pikuach Nefesh*—the saving of life, is not relevant, because this is a case of *Milchemet Mitzvah*, fighting for the sanctification of G-d's name. And it is a contradiction in terms to say that *Pikuach Nefesh* is relevant in time, of an obligatory war.

3) To reach out to Jews in Israel and convince them of their place as part of a "chosen nation." On this aspect, Kahane says he has attracted a tremendous following, particularly among the *Sephardim* who are generally low on the economic ladder. Kahane explains to them that their poverty is spiritual, not economic. There is however, an economic bonus for them with Kahane. The Israeli government gives tens of billions of pounds to the Arab sector annually, and with Kahane's plan to remove the Arabs from Israel, the government would have additional billions to spend on them.

The idea of "throwing the Arabs out" is perhaps Kach's most controversial policy. Kahane would like to implement a plan that would give the Arabs two choices—leave with compensation or leave without. Kahane sees the Arabs in Israel as both a security problem and a *halachic* one.

"The very fact that they are citizens makes them dangerous because they vote heavily and know exactly what they're doing. They look at the ballot as a potent weapon. From the *halachic* angle, they are not (nor is any non-Jew) allowed to live in Eretz Yisrael unless they have a subordinate status, that of a *Ger Toshav*, which is delineated in the *Halacha*. If the Arab accepts this status, it gives him the initial right to stay in Israel, as long as he's not a threat to security. Yet i[f] a million Arabs 'accept' this status, we don't have to necessarily accept them if they still constitute a danger.

"Right now the Arabs feel time is on their side and are tremendously confident that Jews are afraid, are nervous about world opinion, and they're right.

"(The concept of removal of Arabs) is a difficult concept for the Western Jew to accept, because even the Orthodox Jew is an assimilated Jew— influenced by Western ideals, which take the place of Torah morality."

Kahane condemned the methodology of most Yeshivot in which students are never exposed to these concepts, although they are basic in Judaism.

Kahane himself is a diverse product of Yeshiva of Flatbush, BTA, and a total of 13 years at the Mir Yeshiva (during which time he was a member of Jabotinsky's Betar movement).

Many criticise Kahane with the argument that "*Ein somechin al ha'nes*"— one must not rely on miracles. But the 49-year-old veteran of not relying on secular help has an answer to that.

"We must do as much as we can, annex the West Bank territories, fight with as best weapons as we have, etc., and once we've done all G-d wants from us and must believe that He will help with the rest. *Ein somechin* doesn't mean we need the exact number of planes they have. It means don't sit down and wait for miracles, but give it your best shot with whatever you have.

"As far as the Jew who lives in America and says he is effecting change from here, goes, a Jew who is living here is *desecrating* G-d's name and nothing he will do will help. ·

The perversion of Judaism in the Diaspora is incredible, as well as the hypocrisy. It is the flesh pot, be it the Glatt Kosher flesh pot, that really moves them. Forget the argument that Torah is better in America, or that Jews must stay here to save other Jews. Most of them graduate college and become accountants. How many actually go out to Iowa to save Jewish souls?"

"A holocaust is coming, and there is nothing anyone can do to stop it, except to get out of here and go home."

SECTION IV: WHERE DO WE GO FROM HERE?

The End of the Road (2022)
Khaled Elgindy

There are some fourteen million people currently living under Israeli rule between the Mediterranean Sea and the Jordan River. Half of them, around seven million Israeli Jews living on both sides of the 1967 border or "Green Line", enjoy full citizenship rights. The other half—seven million Palestinians—enjoy no such rights. The bulk of these Palestinians, some 5.2 million, are stateless persons living under various forms of Israeli military rule in the occupied West Bank, East Jerusalem, and the Gaza Strip.

Over the past quarter century, the conventional wisdom in Washington and among the wider international community has held that the solution to this problem could only be achieved through a territorial partition resulting in two independent states, Israel and Palestine, living side by side in peace and security. Pundits and policymakers alike had agreed that the two-state solution would involve establishing an independent Palestinian state based on the 1967 borders encompassing Gaza and virtually all of the West Bank. Such a solution would allow for limited and mutually agreed upon land swaps, including a sovereign Palestinian capital in East Jerusalem, plus the return of an agreed upon number of Palestinian refugees, who will receive some form of compensation.

While such an outcome remains theoretically achievable, a variety of physical as well as political developments, especially since 1993, have all but foreclosed the possibility of a negotiated two-state solution—at least the kind of territorial partition envisioned in previous negotiations—to the Israeli-Palestinian conflict.
[…]
Collapsing Pillars

While the international community continues to uphold the two-state framework, most of the pillars of a negotiated two-state solution have in practical terms either collapsed or are collapsing. The Oslo process has effectively run its course. Numerous rounds of formal negotiations—in 2000-01, 2007-08, 2012, and finally 2013-14—along with an array of protocols, memorandums, commissions of inquiry, peace plans, and other initiatives have failed to produce a conflict-ending agreement or prevent periodic outbreaks of violence. […]

The slow demise of the Oslo process has occurred in parallel with that of its signature achievement: the Palestinian Authority (PA). Once seen as the embryo of a future Palestinian state, the PA is now facing its own inexorable decline thanks to a perfect storm of internal and external threats.

From CAIRO REVIEW OF GLOBAL AFFAIRS, No. 44 (Winter 2022). 743
Reprinted with permission.

Notwithstanding the international community's rhetorical support for a two-state solution, international donor aid to the PA has dropped by more than 85 percent since 2008. The sharp decline in donor aid, exacerbated by the sweeping aid cuts of the Trump era, as well as the loss of tax transfers collected by Israel on the Palestinians' behalf, have put the PA on the brink of financial bankruptcy. Internally, the debilitating fourteen-year division between President Mahmoud Abbas's Fatah faction in the West Bank and Hamas in the Gaza Strip has paralyzed Palestinian institutional politics and eroded the legitimacy of the Palestinian leadership. The division also helped fuel violence and instability, particularly in Gaza.

Keenly aware of his growing weakness and declining legitimacy, Abbas has generally responded by pursuing periodic attempts at reconciliation with Hamas, working to internationalize the conflict through the United Nations and other international bodies, and participating in U.S.-sponsored peace negotiations. Yet, instead of piecing these three approaches together into a comprehensive political strategy, Abbas has opted to pivot back and forth between all three tracks without fully committing to any of them as a means of ensuring his own political survival. Despite momentary boosts to his popularity, Abbas's domestic standing has continued to decline, with polls in recent years consistently showing between two-thirds and three-fourths of Palestinians saying they want Abbas to resign. Abbas's decision to cancel long-delayed national elections at the last minute in the spring of 2021, along with the murder of Nizar Banat—a popular political activist and outspoken critic of Abbas—at the hands of PA security forces, have underscored the increasingly erratic and repressive nature of his leadership.

The failings of the peace process and the PA stand in stark contrast to the enormous success of Israel's ever-expanding settlement enterprise, which now dominates both the physical and political landscape of the West Bank. Since the start of the Oslo process, Israel's settler population has soared from roughly 250 thousand in 1993 to nearly 700 thousand today. Although formal annexation has been taken off the agenda—for the moment at least—de facto annexation in the form of ongoing settlement expansion and the continued fragmentation of Palestinian territory has continued unabated, even as the international community looks on. Moreover, the absence of any meaningful consequences—economic, political, or otherwise—has emboldened Israel's settler movement and other "Greater Israel" proponents in domestic politics and fueled their sense of triumphalism. As a result, settlement projects—such as so-called "doomsday" settlements in Jerusalem, and the wholesale removal of Palestinian communities, including the forced evictions of dozens of Palestinian families from their homes in the East Jerusalem neighborhoods of Sheikh Jarrah and Silwan—which were once seen as redlines, are now moving forward in earnest.

Perhaps the clearest sign of the impending demise of the two-state solution can be seen in the fact that the precarious consensus within Israeli, Palestinian, and American politics that has kept the concept afloat during the last two decades is now collapsing on all sides. The PA leadership, which has staked its political fate on the creation of an independent Palestinian state in the West Bank and Gaza, remains firmly committed to the goal of two states. Even Hamas, which has a long history of violent opposition to the Oslo process and rejects any recognition of Israel, has steadily come under the two-state consensus.

In contrast to the political echelon, however, ordinary Palestinians in the occupied territories, the constituency that historically has been the most supportive of a West Bank/Gaza state, are abandoning the two-state vision in ever greater numbers. This is one of the many growing gaps between the Palestinian public and the political leadership in Ramallah. According to a September 2021 poll, just 36 percent of Palestinians said they still supported a two-state solution—the lowest proportion since the signing of the Oslo agreement in 1993. As Palestinian public opinion shifts against the two-state solution, Palestinian political factions, including the next generation of Fatah leaders, may have no choice but to follow suit.

In Israel, meanwhile, the political consensus around two states has already collapsed. Right-wing parties opposed to Palestinian statehood have dominated the Knesset and successive governments for most of the last two decades and the traditional peace camp has all but disappeared. Current Israeli Prime Minister Naftali Bennett is from the hard-right Yamina Party and, like his long-serving predecessor Benjamin Netanyahu, has explicitly ruled out the possibility of a Palestinian state or even a return to negotiations. While the Jewish Israeli public remains split—with some 41 percent supporting and 48 percent opposing a two-state solution—a majority of Israelis favor retaining the status quo.

A similar trend can be seen in the United States. One of the two major political parties, the Republicans, has formally abandoned the goal of two states. As Israeli politics have shifted further to the right, so too has the Republican Party. Even before Donald Trump's election in 2016, the Republican Party had already officially removed references to a two-state solution from their party platform while declaring that it "reject[s] the false notion that Israel is an occupier". Moreover, once in office, the Trump administration worked to translate this approach into policy.

In addition to recognizing Jerusalem as Israel's capital (thereby overturning 70 years of U.S. policy and international consensus) and eliminating all forms of U.S. aid to the Palestinians, the Trump administration worked to dismantle the basic principles that had undergirded the peace process for more than half a century. This included abandoning UN Security Council Resolution 242, which called for ending

Israel's occupation on the basis of "land for peace," as well as the two-state solution itself. Trump's so-called "Prosperity to Peace" plan, which was released in January 2020 and called for a Palestinian "state" made up of disconnected fragments of territory surrounded and controlled by Israel, was more reminiscent of the Bantustans of apartheid South Africa than anything that might reasonably be called a sovereign state. At the same time, the administration worked to erase the distinction between Israel and the territories it occupied by declaring that it would no longer consider Israeli settlements to be illegal. The Trump White House even went as far as requiring products originating in the settlements to be labeled as "made in Israel".

Moreover, regional trends are working against the two-state solution. While Arab Gulf states have significantly cut financial assistance to the PA—literally divesting from a future Palestinian state—the so-called Abraham Accords (a series of normalization agreements between Israel and various Arab states in late 2020) have further marginalized the Palestinians politically. The normalization deals between Israel and both the United Arab Emirates (UAE) and Bahrain, in addition to nullifying the Arab Peace Initiative of 2002, are key signs that leading Arab states have effectively moved on from a two-state solution and are no longer willing to hold up their bilateral or geopolitical interests waiting for the "unicorn" of a Palestinian state.

The argument put forward by some that normalizing states might leverage their budding relations with Israel in the service of the Palestinians or a two-state solution has amounted to little more than wishful thinking. Neither the UAE nor Bahrain, for example, attempted to intervene during the crisis surrounding the impending eviction of Palestinian families from their homes in East Jerusalem's Sheikh Jarrah neighborhood or during the subsequent fighting in Gaza last May. Also, these Arab states did not attempt to use their influence in response to the recent announcement that Israel plans to build more than three thousand new settlement housing units, (which even earned a rare rebuke from the Biden administration) or to the ongoing threats to the status quo arrangement in relation to the Al-Aqsa Mosque in Jerusalem. On the other hand, UAE officials have had little compunction about doing business with Israeli settlers or investing in Israeli occupation infrastructure like checkpoints.
[…]
Neither One State nor Two

The probable end of the two-state solution does not mean alternative models are any more viable, including the old-new idea of a single state with equal citizenship rights for both Israeli Jews and Arab Palestinians. The idea of a binational state for Arabs and Jews was first seriously broached by the renowned Palestinian-American intellectual Edward Said at the apex of the Oslo process, and it has steadily gained ground among diaspora Palestinians and, more recently, among younger Palestinians in the occupied territories. Unlike the old one-state vision embraced by the PLO prior to 1988, which called for undoing the events of 1948, the contemporary binational vision imagines a more straightforward and egalitarian future based on existing demographic realities in the whole of Israel/Palestine. The appeal of equal citizenship and "one person/one vote" is difficult to deny. The main obstacles to the one-state vision, however, are not moral but political—most notably how to reconcile the competing (and often mutually exclusive) nationalist narratives of Israeli Jews and Palestinian Arabs, as well as the vast power asymmetry between the two groups. While growing numbers of Palestinians are embracing the idea of one state, the vast majority of Israeli Jews—which remains the dominant group on both sides of the Green Line— remains steadfastly opposed to the enfranchisement of millions of Palestinians, which they see as ending the Jewish character of the state.

Even on the Palestinian side, where support for one equal state is strongest, political support for one state has not yet reached a critical mass. Although growing numbers of Palestinians in the occupied territories, particularly the youth, are embracing the idea, there is currently no organized Palestinian political movement, party, or actor pushing for a one-state solution. [...]

There is another set of options that may offer a reasonably equitable solution to the conflict, but which has largely been overlooked by American policymakers, namely the idea of shared sovereignty, or confederation, which envisions the creation of two states but without physical or territorial separation. Under the "two states in one space" model, there would be two states, Israel and Palestine, along the 1967 border with each side having its own parliament and governing bodies but with open borders in which citizens of both states enjoy full freedom of movement, and even residency, in the whole of the land between the river and the sea.

The chief advantage of confederation is in the recognition that neither the Israelis nor the Palestinians are prepared to abandon their own national identities and narratives, and that both groups continue to maintain an attachment to both sides of the 1967 border. Confederation also unlocks the possibility of new solutions to some of the most intractable issues of the conflict. Thus, it would be possible to imagine the return of large numbers of Palestinian refugees to their former homes or villages in Israel without altering Israel's demographic balance. Likewise, certain settler populations might be allowed to remain as residents of a Palestinian state while maintaining their citizenship in Israel, thus reducing the political and financial costs associated with a largescale evacuation by Israel while preserving the contiguity of a Palestinian state. The idea of open borders also helps to avoid many of the practical problems arising from a territorial

division of Jerusalem, particularly in the highly contentious Old City and its surroundings.
[…]
Changing the Status Quo

In the meantime, with no realistic prospect of achieving any of these theoretical solutions in the foreseeable future—either one state, two states, or confederation—we are left with the unequal one-state reality that exists on the ground.

In the past, scholars and diplomats could defer the uncomfortable issues raised by this "separate and unequal" reality by focusing on the peace process and the understanding that Israel's occupation was temporary. However, the obsolescence of the Oslo framework along with the growing understanding that Israel's fifty-four-year occupation is anything but temporary, have forced policymakers and analysts to reconsider how they think about the situation in Israel/Palestine. […]

While the goal of two states for two peoples remains the guiding framework in Washington and the broader international community, the likely foreclosing of the classic two-state model makes it necessary to now look seriously at alternatives like one egalitarian state and various types of confederation, while working to address the gross inequality that exists on the ground today.

Any solution—whether one state, confederation, or even the traditional two-state model—requires a fundamental change to the power dynamics between the Israelis and the Palestinians. There is no solution that does not entail Israel, and specifically Israeli Jews, giving up some degree of power and privilege. The question of which of the three scenarios is most feasible, therefore, may ultimately depend on which one is deemed the least costly for Israeli Jews as the dominant group. However, as long as the status quo remains less costly than any of these other scenarios, Israeli leaders will have no reason to ever make such a choice.

Peace Versus the People (2017)
Khalil Shikaki

In an interview with the *New York Times* in July 2014, former U.S. Middle East envoy Martin Indyk blamed the failure of the Israeli-Palestinian peace process on "distrust" and "skepticism" between the two peoples. He reported what he felt was the most meaningful personal moment in the previous year's round of talks, when Palestinian Director of Intelligence Majid Faraj told his Israeli counterparts across the table, "You just don't see us." "There is so much water under the bridge," Indyk told the *New York Times*. "The difficulties we faced were far more because of the twenty years of distrust that built up." Israeli negotiator Tzipi Livni expressed similar sentiments in a Tel Aviv University conference in January 2014. U.S. Secretary of State John Kerry, in his assessment of the failure of his 2013–14 peace efforts, declared "negotiations did not fail because the gaps were too wide, but because the level of trust was too low" between Palestinians and Israelis.

The roots of distrust stretch far back into the Israeli-Palestinian conflict. Once the peace process started, the belief that the other side could not be trusted to uphold any agreement served as a barrier to peace building. [...]

Distrust between leaders echoes distrust between publics, which contributes further to the stalemate in the peace process. Leaders tend to be reluctant to engage in negotiations or show willingness to accept painful compromises if they believe that their constituencies do not support the required compromises, and that the public shares their assessment that they have no partner on the other side.

In reality, public opinion is more complicated. Public opinion in Palestine and Israel is not an impediment to peace; but at the same time, it is not a force for peace. These are the paradoxical results of Palestinian-Israeli public opinion polls conducted by the Palestinian-Israeli Pulse, a joint survey research project, in June 2016, December 2016, and June 2017. Had Palestinian and Israeli negotiators reached a comprehensive peace agreement at any time during the past two decades, public opinion on both sides would have supported it—just as it would today. Yet, negative attitudes and the mutual perceptions of Israelis and Palestinians during the same period, and today, contribute toward mistrust and sustain conflict.

How can public opinion play such a double role, both pushing toward and hindering peace? Part of the answer lies with small but highly motivated constituencies on both sides: national-religious Israelis and Palestinian Islamists. Both Jewish religious-nationalist and Islamist minorities are potent sources of continued conflict, as both groups tend to eschew compromise toward a two-state solution. Yet most Palestinians are secular nationalists, and not Islamists. Similarly, most Israelis are secular or non-religious traditionalists; only a quarter or so are religious or ultra-religious.

The broader reason public opinion plays a dual role in both supporting and undercutting peace negotiations has more to do with the ambivalence, even hostility, of most Palestinians and Israelis toward each other. Each side believes that the other is not trustworthy, does not want peace, does not support the two-state solution, and entertains deep-seated, if hidden, long-term aspirations to wipe out the other side from existence. The two publics are equally and highly skeptical about the ultimate viability of the two-state solution which, so far, has been the cornerstone of all efforts to peacefully resolve the conflict. This is an alarming trend, as the perception of two-state viability is a critical driver toward a negotiated peace.

The Bad News

Over the past decade, hostility among Palestinians and Israelis toward a two-state solution, the basis of peace negotiations since the late 1980s, has risen. Recent survey results show a drop in support for the two-state solution, during the period between 2006 and June 2017, from 71 percent among the Palestinians to 52 percent today, and a parallel drop in Israeli support from 68 percent to 53 percent. However, the most recent findings reflect a large increase in Palestinian support compared to December 2016 when, right after the election of President Donald Trump, support stood at only 44 percent. It is worth noting that support among Israeli Jews in June 2017 stood at only 47 percent compared to 50 percent six months before.

Most troubling of all, youth lead in the declining level of support for the two-state solution. Palestinians and Israeli Jews between the ages of 18 and 22 are the least supportive of the idea. Among Israeli Jews, only 27 percent, compared to 52 percent among those who are over 50 years old, are still supportive. While among the Palestinians the gap for the same two groups is narrower, 42 percent to 58 percent respectively, the fact that age is such a decisive factor is highly instructive; the future could bring even smaller levels of support among the two peoples. Palestinian youth are shifting toward support for a one-state solution in which Jews and Palestinians are equal. Among Israeli Jewish youth, the shift is much more dramatic, as a plurality of those between the ages of 18 and 22 are now in favor of a one-state solution in which Israel discriminates against Palestinians—i.e. an apartheid state.

Other poll results confirm the trend in declining support for compromise. [...]

Another critical gap opinion polls reveal is the difference in attitudes toward the Israeli occupation of the West Bank, which would represent the bulk of an independent Palestine's territory under any two-state solution.

750

Israelis are content with the status quo of the West Bank's occupation, while Palestinians are highly dissatisfied with it. The more content with the status quo Israelis are, the more likely the Israeli public will continue to gravitate toward rightwing politics and politicians. Most Israelis, including the mainstream political center, remain opposed to the dismantlement of settlements built by Israel in the West Bank, an essential requirement in any peace agreement.

Yet, Palestinians show significant flexibility on the issue most important for Israelis: the maintenance of a Jewish majority in Israel. On the other hand, Palestinian geopolitical divisions between the Palestinian Authority in the West Bank and Hamas in the Gaza Strip, and the inability to transition to a democratic political system and a pluralistic civil society, constitute an impediment to mutual confidence-building with Israeli society. Israelis tend to view Palestinian divisions and the slide to authoritarianism in the Palestinian political system as an impediment to peace. Palestinians, particularly the youth, on the other hand, tend to become more alienated from their own political system and thereby less willing to support their own leadership.

Two-States, One Solution

Despite the bad news, the public preference for diplomacy over armed conflict or maintenance of the status quo remains relatively high. No other concept is more popular than the two-state solution—and though support may be weakening with both publics, incentives designed to increase support for compromise are highly effective. The nature of national leadership is again decisive in swaying public opinion behind a settlement.

Today, about half of Palestinians and half of Israelis prefer reaching a peace agreement as the best means of changing the status quo. Only one-fifth or less on either side favors violence or armed struggle as the preferred means of change. Alternatives to the two-state framework, such as a democratic one-state solution, an apartheid one-state reality (one in which one side is denied equal rights by the other side), and expulsion (one in which one side expels or "transfers" the population of the other side) remain less popular than the two-state solution. The core constituencies for these alternatives—those who would support these, and only these alternatives—are not great. The largest single constituency is the one that supports the two-state solution. Once these two-stators are excluded from the sample and the remaining public is assigned one alternative at a time, the public splits almost equally on each side, between the three alternatives without any one emerging as the most preferred.

A closer examination of the split within the Palestinian side shows that support for the two-state solution is greater than support for any of the alternatives in both the West Bank and the Gaza Strip, among supporters of all factions—including Hamas. A similar examination of the Israeli Jewish side shows that support for the two-state solution is highest only among secular and traditional Jews, but not among the religious (who prefer apartheid over all other options) and the Ultra-Orthodox (who prefer expulsion over all other). When looking at the Israeli political spectrum, support for the two-state solution is highest among those who place themselves on the left and the center but not among those who place themselves on the right. Those who place themselves on the right side of the Israeli political spectrum prefer apartheid over all others.

Survey research shows that support for a comprehensive agreement can be significantly increased, to levels that exceed two-thirds on both sides, if various constituencies are given a stake in its success. For Palestinians, the most effective incentive—the one that has the widest level of persuasion—is the release of Palestinian prisoners as part of the agreement. This incentive alone can increase the support for the comprehensive package to 70 percent. Similarly, access to the Israeli labor market and free movement for the two peoples between the two states are almost as effective. Intangible incentives, when offered to Palestinians, can be equally effective. For example, an Israeli acknowledgment of the historic and religious roots of the Palestinians in historic Palestine or an Israeli recognition of the Arab and Islamic character of the Palestinian state are highly effective. Similarly, an Israeli acknowledgment of responsibility for the creation of the refugee problem and/or an Israeli apology to the refugees for the suffering they had to endure since the Jewish state's founding in 1948 can change the attitudes of a large minority of those opposed to compromise. Finally, leadership can significantly increase the Palestinian public's willingness to accept compromise: the support of Marwan Barghouti, regarded by many as the leader of the Second Intifada and held in prison by Israeli authorities since 2004, for a comprehensive peace package can convince a third of the Palestinians to switch position from opposition to support.

Similarly on the Israeli side, tangible and intangible incentives—including decisive leadership—can increase the level of support for such a comprehensive package that implements the two-state solution from a large minority to two-thirds. Effective tangible incentives include the following: compensation to Israeli Jews whose property was confiscated by Arab countries when they immigrated to Israel after 1948; a defense treaty with the United States; and the normalization of all political, economic, and trade relations with the Arab World. A combination of only two such incentives can increase support among Israeli Jews to more than 60 percent. Intangible incentives such as a Palestinian recognition of Israel as a Jewish state, and an acknowledgment of Jewish historic and religious ties to the land, are also highly effective. Public endorsement of the peace package by leaders, such as Prime Minister Netanyahu, can also be an incentive for support.

752

Time Is Not on Our Side

Decades of conflict, and repeatedly disappointed hopes for a successful peace settlement, bode badly for the future. Both the Israeli and Palestinian publics are becoming more pessimistic with time. Three factors contribute to the decline in support for the implementation of the two-state solution among Palestinians and Israelis: the prevailing perception that the two-state solution is no longer viable; the belief that the other side does not support the two-state solution; and the belief that the support for such a solution is not the shared normative view of their respective societies. [...]
Evidence also shows that support for the two-state solution and the permanent peace package is dependent on how each side perceives the attitude of the other regarding that solution and package: those who believe that a majority on the other side does indeed support that solution and package are likely to support it, and alternatively, those who think a majority on the other side does not support that solution and package are likely to oppose it. Similarly, those Palestinians and Israelis who believe that the majority of their own public is opposed to that solution and package are more likely to oppose it themselves and vice versa. Again, this would suggest the room for maneuver for national leaders, who can effectively communicate with their publics, build trust, and offer meaningful concessions to the opposing side, is relatively wide.

A Public without Peacemakers

But what if Palestinian and Israeli leaders fail to reach a peace agreement at all? Can one count on the two publics to provide a momentum or a push for peace? The verdict from survey research is a definite no: Palestinian and Israeli public opinion is not an independent force for peace. The preceding evidence suggests that despite the continued decline in support for the two-state solution, the two publics remain open to compromise—but such readiness assumes that the framework for an agreement, offering meaningful incentives to both publics, has been worked out by Palestinian and Israeli leaders.

Why is the verdict so certain and so bleak? The answer lies in the reality in which the two sides live, and more importantly in the way they view each other. The first problem lies in one glaring difference between the two publics: Israelis are content with the status quo, and the Palestinians are not. As of June 2017, a joint Palestinian-Israeli survey showed that Jewish settlers are the most satisfied with the status quo and Gazans are the least satisfied. [...] This asymmetry reinforces Palestinian suspicions that the Israelis are not interested in peace.

This heightened threat perception underlines current perceptions of mutual fear. Most Palestinians fear Israelis soldiers and armed settlers, and most

Israeli Jews fear Palestinians. Indeed, most Palestinians believe that Israelis do not want peace and most Israelis entertain a similar belief; only one-third of Israeli Jews, in June 2017, believed that Palestinians want peace. Among Palestinians, 78 percent believe Israel wants to extend its borders from the Jordan River to the Mediterranean and expel the Palestinian population or deny them their civil and political rights. Among Israeli Jews, almost two-thirds believe that Palestinians hold one of two maximalist positions: take over the entire state of Israel from pre-1948 borders, or conquer Israel and destroy much of the Jewish population.

Threat perception and fear are reinforced by a prevailing perception on both sides that the Palestinian-Israeli conflict is characterized by a zero-sum game. In June 2017, most Israeli Jews (53 percent) and almost three-quarters of the Palestinians agreed with the statement that "Nothing can be done that's good for both sides; whatever is good for one side is bad for the other side."

Distrust, like many of the other attributes mentioned in this section, erodes willingness to take risks and make compromise. Not surprisingly given all of the above, an overwhelming majority of Palestinians (87 percent) and Israeli Jews (77 percent) indicated last June that the other side is untrustworthy. Findings show that among those who think the other side is trustworthy, support for painful compromise, as in accepting a permanent peace package, can rise to 56 percent among Israelis and 61 percent among Palestinians. By contrast, distrust diminishes willingness to compromise, reducing it to 27 percent among Israelis and 40 percent among Palestinians. More importantly, the skyrocketing levels of mutual distrust lead to the conclusion that neither side is a force for peace.

By fearing and refusing to trust the other side, Palestinian and Israeli public opinion contributes to the resilience of the conflict. In its role as the carrier of the national narrative, public opinion therefore sustains conflict. Yet, in its ability to choose from among differing priorities and in its search for stability, peace, and economic prosperity, public opinion has the ability to overcome historic, religious, and ideological narratives, but only if leaders show courage and take the initiative.

Alternatives in the Israeli-Palestinian Conflict (2021)
Daniel Egel, et al.

The Israeli-Palestinian conflict has been one of the most enduring political challenges in the post–World War II period. Despite a multitude of high-profile international efforts, the conflict persists. In the place of political progress is an evolving status quo with growing economic and political inequality and increasingly pronounced divisions. As these divisions grow, the prospects for a two-state solution along the lines agreed to in the historic 1993 Oslo Accords look increasingly grim.

Today, the Israeli and Palestinian people are at a critical juncture. For decades, these two peoples have struggled to define the contours of an outcome that is acceptable to both sides. However, there is a growing awareness that if a resolution is not soon reached, it might never be. And although some groups benefit from the political impasse, current trends are heading in a direction that is undesirable to the majority of both Israelis and Palestinians. Expanding settlements in the West Bank threaten the viability of an independent political future for the Palestinians, and demographic trends undermine the prospect for an Israel that is democratic, Jewish, and economically vibrant.

The purpose of this research was to assess whether there were any viable alternatives to the current status quo. […]

Five Alternatives

Our analysis focused on five alternative futures (henceforth, "alternatives") in the Israeli-Palestinian conflict. We selected these five generalized alternatives based on a functional analysis of the range of existing proposals; we believe that these five alternatives capture the range of concepts that have been put forward.

The first of these alternatives is the perpetuation of today's **status quo**. The status quo emerged in the wake of the 1993 Oslo Accords, a set of historic agreements that began a peace process between the Government of Israel and the Palestine Liberation Organization. This status quo has been marked by limited Palestinian autonomy, overriding Israeli security control, and ongoing Israeli settlement expansion. […]

The second alternative is the **two-state solution**, which has been the international community's preferred alternative for decades. The two-state solution usually includes the establishment of an independent Palestinian state alongside the State of Israel, borders based on the pre-1967 borders (often referred to as the "Green Line") with land swaps to compensate for West Bank land transferred to Israel to reduce the uprooting of settlements, transport infrastructure to ensure that Palestinians have freedom of movement within their new state, a resolution to the issue of the status of Jerusalem, and a mutually acceptable way forward for Palestinian refugees.

Some proposals have suggested the establishment of a **confederation**, following a model similar to the European Union. This alternative would establish two (Israel and Palestine) or three (Israel, West Bank, and Gaza) independent and sovereign states that would cooperate on issues of mutual interest by way of a federal government. In addition to differences in the number of sovereign states, a major difference across variations of the confederation is in the types of powers delegated to the federal government. In all variations, most power remains with the individual states, and powers delegated to the federal government are limited to issues that the individual states mutually agree are common to all states (e.g., shared natural resources, economic relations, external threats).

Annexation describes an alternative in which Israel unilaterally would annex some parts of land it captured during the 1967 Arab-Israeli War, increasing the territorial size of Israel. In this alternative, Palestinians would maintain autonomy comparable to the status quo, in which they have authority over local issues and internal security, although the territory in which Palestinians exercise authority would likely be disconnected and dominated by a small number of urban centers. Movement between the much smaller territory of the West Bank and expanded Israel would continue to be limited, as in the status quo. [...]

The **one-state solution** is the final alternative we examined. It envisages a single state encompassing all (or most) of the land between the Jordan River and the Mediterranean Sea. The various proposals for a one-state solution vary in terms of their assumptions about the democratic character of the new state and whether Gaza would be included.

Focus Group Approach

The findings in this report are derived from a series of innovative, structured focus group discussions, designed to provide a nuanced view of the concerns, views, and uncertainty of the populations toward these alternatives. These focus groups were based on the RAND Corporation's Delphi method, a widely used approach for forecasting in complex settings, which generates a blend of well-informed quantitative and qualitative insights on these alternatives. [...]

This research is designed to complement the extensive random-sample polling that has been done on these topics. [...]

Key Findings

Eight key findings emerged from this research.

756

FINDING 1: NONE OF THE ALTERNATIVES ARE ACCEPTABLE TO A MAJORITY OF BOTH ISRAELIS AND PALESTINIANS.

For Israeli Jews, the only alternative judged as "acceptable" by a majority of focus group participants was the status quo. For the other three populations—Israeli Arabs, Gazan Palestinians, and West Bank Palestinians—none of the alternatives were acceptable to a majority of participants.

FINDING 2: THE TWO-STATE SOLUTION IS THE MOST POLITICALLY VIABLE ALTERNATIVE, ALTHOUGH ALL FOUR POPULATIONS VOICED SKEPTICISM TOWARD THIS ALTERNATIVE.

The two-state solution was the preferred alternative for both the Israeli Arabs and West Bank Palestinians and the second-highest-rated alternative for Israeli Jews and Gazan Palestinians. None of the other alternatives had anything close to this breadth of support.

However, focus group participants from all four population groups voiced skepticism toward this alternative. For Israeli Jews, advocates highlighted the political and security benefits of separation while opponents cited security, settlements, Jerusalem, religion, and feasibility as major concerns. Israeli Arabs saw separation as a benefit for both Israelis and Palestinians but stated that the Palestinians were being asked to sacrifice too much for the limited autonomy provided to them. The Palestinians in Gaza and the West Bank were skeptical of both the viability and the benefits of the two-state solution.

FINDING 3: PALESTINIANS STATE THAT THEY WANT THE TWO-STATE SOLUTION, BUT WITH MAJOR MODIFICATIONS.

The two-state solution was the most highly rated alternative among Palestinians overall. However, our focus group discussions revealed that Palestinians will accept the two-state solution only if some of its characteristics are modified. Participants reported that, among other modifications, the new Palestinian state would need to have an army to defend itself and protect its borders and would need to have economic control over its borders. They indicated that these modifications were necessary to achieve "real" independence and self-governance.

These modifications are included, in part, in the confederation alternative that we presented. Under the confederation, Palestinians would have their own separate state and more control over the borders, economic relations, and shared resources. Although Palestinians would not have an army (similar to the two-state solution), they would be permitted to operate with the Israel Defense Forces to secure borders. They would also be equally represented in a shared federal government responsible for jointly adjudicating key areas common to both states (shared resources, economic relations, and external threats), and they would have more freedom to move within and across both states. However, support for the confederation was low because it did not offer the desired separation from Israel.

FINDING 4: THE STATUS QUO IS PREFERRED BY ISRAELI JEWS BUT STRONGLY DISLIKED BY PALESTINIANS.

Support for the continuation of the status quo came from across the Israeli Jewish political spectrum, with focus group participants offering two types of rationales for their support. The first is that the status quo provides for the continuation of a flourishing economy and a relatively stable security situation. Second, Israeli Jewish participants reported that a major benefit of the status quo is that it is relatively risk-free when compared with the other alternatives. Even though many on the center-left preferred the two-state solution in principle and many on the right similarly preferred annexation, representatives from both political groups reported support for the status quo because they feared what might go wrong with the other alternatives.

For Israeli Arabs and Palestinians, there was a keen and strong desire for a change from the status quo and an end to "occupation." Palestinians expressed the urgent need for a change to address their living conditions and, in particular, the poor economic situation, unemployment, lack of education, water shortages, lack of mobility, and lack of independence. Some expressed frustrations aimed at their leaders, but most blame Israel for what they consider the disastrous status quo in which they are living. Although Israeli Arabs were skeptical that change was possible, they similarly emphasized their desire for improved economic and political opportunities that might come with different alternatives.

FINDING 5: THERE IS WIDESPREAD SKEPTICISM THAT ANY ALTERNATIVE WOULD BE FEASIBLE.

Participants in our focus group discussions were highly skeptical that any alternative to the status quo would be viable. There was widespread distrust among Israelis and Palestinians of their own leadership, the leadership of the other side, and the people from the other side. As a consequence, there was great skepticism that a deal could be reached and that either side would abide by the terms of the deal. Furthermore, many Israelis were skeptical about the feasibility of evacuating settlements, particularly in the wake of disengagement from Gaza. In addition, the majority of Israelis and Palestinians in our focus groups indicated that none of the alternatives would end the conflict.

FINDING 6: SEPARATION WAS THE SINGLE MOST IMPORTANT FACTOR IN DETERMINING ACCEPTABILITY.

The desire for "separation"—that is, separation between Israelis and Palestinians—was the most important overall factor in determining support for alternatives. The overwhelming priority in all discussions with Israeli Jews and with Palestinians was the desire to separate from the other and avoid any governance or living arrangement that brought the two groups closer together. Given this lack of trust and animosity, it is not surprising that alternatives such as a confederation or a one-state solution were considered infeasible. Most Israeli Arabs also wanted complete separation from the Palestinians.

Although Palestinians sought political separation, they wanted to retain economic partnerships with Israel that they saw as critical to their livelihoods. However, most Palestinian participants indicated that they did not believe that this political separation could be guaranteed.

FINDING 7: ISRAELI ARABS AND PALESTINIANS INDICATED THAT ALL ALTERNATIVES WERE BIASED IN FAVOR OF ISRAELI JEWS.

There was a consensus among both Israeli Arabs and Palestinians that the status quo and each of the alternatives as presented were biased in favor of Israeli Jews. Palestinians viewed *all* of the alternatives as primarily serving the interests of the Israelis while asking for more compromises from the Palestinians. The consensus among Israeli Arabs was that each of the alternatives, inclusive of the two-state solution, were discriminatory and biased against both Israeli Arabs and Palestinians. They were also skeptical that any of these alternatives were feasible, as Israel would only be willing to accept an alternative that was clearly in its favor.

FINDING 8: A BLEND OF ECONOMIC AND SECURITY GUARANTEES—FOR ISRAELIS AND PALESTINIANS ALIKE—WILL BE NEEDED TO ENABLE A PEACEFUL RESOLUTION TO THE CONFLICT.

Our findings suggest that an "economic peace" strategy is unlikely to be successful unless accompanied by significant security and other guarantees. Economics was only a modestly important issue for Gazan Palestinians and Israeli Arabs but largely a secondary concern for West Bank Palestinians and Israeli Jews. By contrast, security guarantees are likely to be an important factor in making progress. Security was particularly important for the Israeli Arabs and Palestinian populations, reflecting the fact that these populations fear for their security. Thus, though security guarantees for Palestinians are less often discussed than those for Israelis in the context of resolving the conflict, they are likely to be critical.

There was great concern about the economic and security implications of each of the proposals, with a mutual distrust fueling uncertainty about what the other side might do to gain advantage at their cost. Guaranteeing separation, security, and improved economic conditions would strengthen any of the proposals, though these would likely require unprecedented international commitment.

What Can the International Community Do to Support Peace?

Our research suggests that mistrust, broadly defined, is likely the greatest impediment to peace. Therefore, international action and commitments will likely be necessary to bridge the gap and find a peaceful resolution to the conflict. For the Israeli Jews, this will require external incentives to ensure that peace is better than the status quo. But international engagement that builds optimism and enthusiasm for peace among all parties is necessary and must involve security and economic guarantees and a public dialogue to guide and develop thinking about the alternatives and their implications.
[...]

Conclusion

One of our goals was to determine whether there were areas of overlap in opinions and feeling between Israelis and Palestinians that might offer avenues for negotiation, leading the parties closer to peace. Sadly, the data show the opposite. The data highlight the deep distrust and profound animosity of each side for the other. In light of our findings, it is hard to imagine a departure from present trends and where they lead unless and until strong, courageous leadership among Israelis, Palestinians, and the international community articulates a desire for a better future for all.

Excluding Hamas from the 'Day After' in Gaza Would be a Mistake (2023)
Mahjoob Zweiri

When foreign powers decide to eject a certain political player from power and impose an unelected provisional government, they create two problems.

First, the population of the country is denied their voting rights and their right to voice their political opinions. A governing body that does not represent the people ignores their demands and complaints, which leads to precarious outcomes, including internal conflict.

Second, the forced marginalisation of a political party could weaken and silence it, but it could also backfire. The denial of its right to political participation could push its members to reorganise, remobilise and return to the political scene with more hardline approaches or even violence.

The example of Afghanistan is quite telling. In 2001, a US-led coalition invaded the country and dislodged the Taliban government from power. In the subsequent proceedings to form a government, the Taliban was excluded after being presented as an illegitimate actor. What followed was 20 years of political instability and war, which ended with the Taliban coming back to power.

Today, as the international community mulls the fate of Gaza after Israel's war on it ends, it is on its way to repeating its mistakes of the past. Of course, the history and current situation in Gaza are different from Afghanistan's, but there is a similar desire to marginalise a legitimate political actor.

Since Israel announced its war on Gaza, it has repeatedly made clear that it wants to dismantle and eliminate Hamas, for which it has received backing from its ally, the US, and European countries.

The Israeli military has claimed it is after Hamas's fighters and military infrastructure, but over the past 75 days, it has become evident that it is also targeting its political structures, including ministries, institutions that provide civilian services, facilities responsible for basic utilities and so on.

Worse than that, Israel has demonstrated its intentions to devastate the civilian infrastructure of the Gaza Strip and expel as many of its residents as possible.

In a November 17 interview with NPR, Israeli Prime Minister Benjamin Netanyahu refused to say who should take over governing Gaza; he did insist that whoever it is, it "can't be people committed to funding terrorism and inculcating terrorism". He then went on to compare the Israeli invasion of Gaza to the Allies' occupation of Germany and Japan after World War II.

But the comparison Netanyahu drew between Germany, Japan and Gaza is inaccurate. Gaza, as well as the West Bank and East Jerusalem, has been under Israeli occupation since 1967. The Palestinians, unlike the Germans and the Japanese, do not have a state and have the status of an occupied population. As such, under international law, their acts of armed resistance are not equal or comparable to acts of aggression by an independent state with a national army.

Resistance in Palestine under occupation has historically taken numerous forms and has been channelled by various political parties, both on the left and on the right. Yet, Israel has labelled all of them as "terrorist", whether it was the Palestinian Liberation Organization (PLO), the Popular Front for the Liberation of Palestine, the Democratic Front for the Liberation of Palestine, or any other.

If Hamas is dismantled, as Israel seeks to do, another resistance group would take its place. This is due to the fact that the culture of resistance is embedded in the Palestinian society on the religious, political, economic and social levels and it will require much more than the eradication of one party to change that.

That is why, the plans of foreign powers to impose an unelected government on Gaza are likely to backfire. The US specifically has proposed the unification of the West Bank and Gaza under the rule of the Palestinian Authority as a step towards Palestinian statehood.

Such a move would deny the right of the Palestinian people to choose who they want to be governed by. It is important to note that Hamas won the 2006 legislative elections in the occupied Palestinian territories and its government was democratically elected.

Since then, it has become so embedded in the Palestinian society in general, and in Gaza specifically, that its marginalisation in any future Palestinian would create massive societal tensions.

It would also create a political, social and security vacuum that would not spell any good for whoever takes over governance.

How and when the war in Gaza will end and what follows next is still uncertain. But one thing is clear: If Western and regional powers repeat past mistakes of marginalising a major political actor and seek to impose their will on the Palestinian people, they would not get a different outcome than they have had in the past.

Marwan Barghouti Eyes Presidential Run from Behind Israeli Bars (2021)

Lubna Masarwa and Mustafa Abu Sneineh

Palestinian political prisoner and veteran Fatah party leader Marwan Barghouti is reportedly mulling whether to run in the upcoming Palestinian Authority (PA) presidential elections, planned for July, from his prison cell, sources have told Middle East Eye.

If his candidacy becomes official, Barghouti would be the first candidate in the history of the Israeli occupation to run for the highest post of the Palestinian leadership from behind bars.

Barghouti is currently serving five life sentences in an Israeli prison for allegedly plotting attacks on Israeli targets during the Second Intifada.

Fatah officials familiar with talks of a Barghouti election run told MEE that he was considering whether to run for president. Speaking on condition of anonymity, the sources said that negotiations were currently taking place within Fatah, the longstanding ruling party of the PA in the occupied West Bank.

Incumbent PA President Mahmoud Abbas, who has held the position since 2005, was confirmed earlier this month to be running for re-election, Prime Minister Mohammad Shtayyeh told Al Araby News.

Fatah's Internal Tensions

Abbas's term officially expired in June 2009, but no presidential elections have been organised by the PA in 16 years.

Abbas, 85, announced earlier this month that new parliamentary and presidential elections would take place in July, in an effort to heal longstanding political divisions — notably the rift between Fatah and Hamas, the de facto ruling party in the besieged Gaza Strip.

According to MEE's sources, there have been talks on how to compromise Barghouti's political ambitions without creating an internal clash within Fatah, of which Abbas is the chairman.

Options reportedly presented to the imprisoned leader have included him running for the position of head the Palestinian Legislative Council, of which he has been a member since 1996.

Another alternative floated around has been for Barghouti to create his own party and run for president under that banner.

Lubna Masarwa and Mustafa Abu Sneineh, Middle East Eye at www.middleeasteye.org (printed with permission).

Barghouti's family told MEE they could not confirm whether he intended to run, saying that his stance on the issue would become clearer after a planned meeting in Cairo this week between Palestinian political factions to discuss the election.

Barghouti was born in 1958 in the central West Bank village of Kobar. He was the president of the Fatah Youth Movement while he studied history and political science at Birzeit University. He was first arrested by Israeli forces in 1976, three years after he became a Fatah member.

Popular among Palestinians

Barghouti was active during the First Intifada between 1987 and 1993. Israeli authorities arrested him and exiled him to Jordan for seven years, but Barghouti returned to the West Bank in 1994, after the signing of the Oslo Accords. He was elected as an MP in the first Palestinian legislative election of 1996.

He was arrested in the West Bank city of Ramallah in 2002 and sentenced for his alleged role in a series of attacks during the Second Intifada.

In the second PA legislative elections in 2006, Barghouti headed the Fatah list from prison, and helped draft the National Accord Document to set a national basis of agreement for political factions running for election.

Despite being imprisoned for nearly 20 years, Barghouti remains extremely popular among Palestinians. Public opinion polls by the Palestinian Centre for Policy and Survey Research have regularly shown that Barghouti would win presidential elections, whether he runs within Fatah or with a new party.

One of the officials who spoke to MEE estimated that half of current Fatah supporters would side with Barghouti over Abbas, noting that the rivalry between the two veteran leaders could stoke further divisions within the party.

But before jumping to conclusions on Barghouti's candidacy and the possible impact of a vote, the official cautioned, first it needed to be confirmed whether elections would take place at all.

CONTRIBUTORS

Mahmoud Abbas — PLO representative to Oslo Accords. President of Palestinian National Authority (2005-) and Chairman of PLO (2004-).

Elliott Abrams — U.S. Deputy National Security Advisor (2005-2009).

Dean Acheson — U.S. Secretary of State (1949-1953).

Ali Adam — Journalist.

Gregory Aftandilian — Non-resident Fellow at the Arab Center. Senior Pfrofessional Lecturer at American University.

Mahmoud Ahmadinejad —President of Iran (2005-2013).

Antoine F. Albina — Palestinian refugee.

Yasser Arafat — Chairman of PLO (1969-2004) and President of Palestinian National Authority (1994-2004).

Ahmed Abu Artema — Journalist and activist. Palestinian refugee.

Hafez al-Assad — President of Syria (1971-2000).

Ehud Barak —Israeli Prime Minister (1999-2001).

Mitchell Bard — Executive Director of American-Israeli Cooperative Enterprise (AICE). Director of Jewish Virtual Library.

Marwan Barghouti —Member of the Palestinian Legislative Council (1996-). Leader of the Second Intifada.

Joe Barnes — Brussels Correspondent for The Telegraph.

Jason Beckett — Associate Professor at the American University in Cairo.

David Ben-Gurion — Chairman of Jewish Agency Executive Committee (1935-1948). Israeli Minister of Defense (1948-1954, 1955-1963). Israeli Prime Minister (1948-1953 and 1955-1963).

Marwan Bishara — Senior political analyst at Al Jazeera.

Walter J. Boyne — Retired Air Force colonel and former director of the National Air and Space Museum in Washington, DC.

George W. Bush — U.S. President (2001-2009).

Daniel Byman — Professor at the Edmund A. Walsh School of Foreign Service at Georgetown University.

James F. Byrnes — U.S. Secretary of State (1945-1947).

Jimmy Carter — U.S. President (1977-1981).

Henry Cattan — UN delegate for Arab Higher Committee throughout partition proceedings.

Noam Chomsky —Professor at Massachusetts Institute of Technology. Leading critic of American foreign policy

Winston Churchill — U.K. Secretary of State for the Colonies (1921-1922).

Ziyad Clot — Legal advisor to PLO during peace negotiations with Israel (2008).

Raphael S. Cohen — Director of the Strategy and Doctrine Program of RAND Project AIR FORCE

Mohammed Dajani — Fellow at the Washington Institute for Near East Policy.

Major-General Moshe Dayan —IDF Chief of General Staff (1953-1958). Israeli Minister of Defense (1967-74).

Maj. Gen. (ret.) Uzi Dayan — IDF Deputy Chief of the General Staff. National Security Adviser (2000-2002).

William Dodd — U.S. Ambassador to Germany (1933-1937).

Daniel Egel — Director of RAND Economics and National Security Initiative.

Albert Einstein — Scientist. Jewish refugee exiled from Nazi Germany.

Khaled Elgindy — Senior fellow and director of the Program on Palestine and Palestinian-Israeli Affairs at Middle East Institute.

Nabil Fahmy — Egyptian Foreign Minister (2013-2014). Egyptian Ambassador to U.S. (1999-2008). Founded School of Global Affairs and Public Policy at The American University in Cairo.

John Fletcher-Cooke —Counsellor of U.K. Mission to the UN (1948-1951).

Felix Frankfurter — Legal advisor to Zionist delegation at the Paris Peace Conference.

David Fromkin — Professor at Boston University.

Mahatma Gandhi — Indian independence activist. Renowned for nonviolent resistance to British rule.

Lieutenant-General J. B. Glubb — Commander of the Arab Legion, Jordan (1939-1956).

Richard Goldstone — Jurist and ICC prosecutor. Led fact-finding mission for UN Human Rights Council.

Richard Gottheil — Professor at Columbia University.

Dr. Mahdi Abdul Hadi — Founded Palestinian Academic Society for the Study of International Affairs (PASSIA). Special advisor to the Jordanian Ministry of Occupied Land Affairs (1985-86).

Faisal Hanif — Media analyst at Centre for Media Monitoring.

Ismail Haniyeh — Head of Hamas' Political Bureau.

Victor Davis Hanson — Senior Fellow at Stanford University's Hoover Institution. 2007 National Humanities Medal recipient.

Earl G. Harrison — U.S. representative on the Intergovernmental Commission on Refugees following WWII.

Richard Haass —Principal adviser on the Middle East to U.S. President George H.W. Bush (1989-1983). President Emeritus of the Council on Foreign Relations (2003-2023).

Simon Haddad —Professor at The Notre-Dame University

Chris Hedges — New York Times Middle East Bureau Chief (1991-1995).

Loy W. Henderson — U.S. Director of the Office of Near Eastern Affairs (1945-1948).

Theodor Herzl — Founded the Zionist Organization. Considered the father of modern political Zionism.

Michael Herzog — Retired IDF Brigadier General. Chief of Staff to the Minister of Defense (2006-2009).

John H. Hilldring — U.S. Assistant Secretary of State for Occupied Areas (1946-1947).

King Abdullah Ibn Hussein — Son of Husein bin Ali (Grand Emir and Sharif of Mecca and the founder of the Hashemite dynasty). Emir of Transjordan (1921-1946). King of Jordan (1946-1951).

Feisal bin Al-Hussein — Son of Husein bin Ali (Grand Emir and Sharif of Mecca and the founder of the Hashemite dynasty). Represented the Arab delegation at the Paris Peace Conference. King of Syria (1920). King of Iraq (1921-1933).

Haj Amin al-Husseini — Grand Mufti of Jerusalem (1921-37). President of the Supreme Muslim Council (1922-37).

Jalal Al Husseini — Associate research fellow at the French Institute for the Near East.

Martin Indyk — U.S. Ambassador to Israel (2000-2001), and Special Envoy for Israeli-Palestinian negotiations (2013-14).

Herschel V. Johnson — U.S. Chargé in the United Kingdom (1937-1941).

Paul Johnson — Historian and journalist.

Rabbi Meir Kahane — Elected to Knesset in 1984. Founder of Kach movement.

Marvin Kalb — Journalist. Nonresident senior fellow with the Foreign Policy program at The Brookings Institution.

Victor Kattan —Assistant Professor at the University of Nottingham School of Law.

Herbert C. Kelman — Psychologist. Professor at Harvard University.

Robert Kennedy — Correspondent for The Boston Post (1948).

Henry Kissinger — U.S. Secretary of State (1973-77).

Oren Kessler — Political analyst, author, and journalist.

Raphael Krafft — Journalist.

T.E. Lawrence ("Lawrence of Arabia") — Archaeologist and diplomat. Renowned for role in the Arab Revolt during WWI.

Michael Lynk — UNHRC Special Rapporteur (2016-2022).

Malcolm MacDonald — U.K. Secretary of State for the Colonies (1938-40)

Ramsay MacDonald — U.K. Prime Minister (1929-1935).

George Marshall — U.S. Secretary of State (1947-1949).

Lubna Masarwa — Middle East Eye's Palestine and Israel bureau chief in Jerusalem.

Ben McEvoy — Filmmaker.

Golda Meir — Head of Political Department of the Jewish Agency (1946-1949).

Lord Edwin Montagu — U.K. Secretary of State for India (1917-22).

Benny Morris — Professor at Ben-Gurion University of the Hegev.

Leland Morris — U.S. Consul General in Jerusalem (1936).

Kasuka Mutukwa — Minister Counsellor and Deputy Permanent Representative of Zambia to the UN.

Gamal Abdel Nasser — Egyptian President (1956-1970). Egyptian Prime Minister (1954-1962, 1967-1970). UAR President (1968-1970). UAR Prime Minister (1958-1962, 1970-1971).

Donald Neff — Time Magazine Jerusalem Bureau Chief (1975-1978).

Benjamin Netanyahu — Israeli Prime Minister (1996-99, 2009-21, 2022-).

Michael Oren — Israeli Ambassador to the U.S. (2009-2013).

Don Peretz — Professor Emeritus at State University of New York, Binghamton.

Amos Perlmutter —Professor at American University.

Lawrence Pintak — Founding dean of the Edward R. Murrow College of Communication at Washington State University.

Yitzhak Rabin — Israeli Minister of Defense (1984-1990). Israeli Prime Minister (1974-1977, 1992-1995).

Itamar Rabinovich — Israeli Ambassador to the U.S. (1993-1996). Distinguished nonresident fellow with the Foreign Policy program at The Brookings Institution.

Dr. Asad Abdul-Rahman — Member of PLO Executive Committee (1977-2018). Founding member of Popular Front for the Liberation of Palestine (PFLP).

Zina Rakhamilova — Columnist and activist.

Gabrielle Rifkind — Director of Oxford Process.

MJ Rosenberg — Senior Foreign Policy Fellow at Media Matters Action Network.

David Rothkopf — CEO and editor of Foreign Policy (2012-2017).

Barry Rubin — Director of the Global Research in International Affairs (GLORIA) Center.

Natan Sachs — Director of Center for Middle East Policy at the Brookings Institution.

Anwar Sadat — Egyptian President (1970-1981). Egyptian Prime Minister (1973-1974, 1980-1981).

Herbert Samuel — U.K. President of the Local Government Board (1914-1915). U.K. High Commissioner for Palestine (1920-1925).

Abdul Aziz Ibn Saud — King of Saudi Arabia (1932-1953).

Abdullah bin Abdulaziz al-Saud — Crown Prince of Saudi Arabia (1982-2005). King and Prime Minister of Saudi Arabia (2005-2015)

Harold H. Saunders — U.S. Assistant Secretary of State for Near Eastern Affairs (1978-1981).

Michael N. Schmitt — Distinguished Scholar at the Lieber Institute of the United States Military Academy at West Point. Distinguished Scholar in Residence at the US Naval War College.

Nadeen Shaker —Senior Editor at the Cairo Review of Global Affairs.

Ariel Sharon — Israeli Prime Minister (2001-2006).

Khalil Shikaki — Director of the Palestinian Center for Policy and Survey Research (PSR).

Robert Siegel — Radio journalist.

Mustafa Abu Sneineh — Journalist.

Leonard Stein —Political Secretary of the Zionist Organization (1920-1929) and legal advisor to the Jewish Agency for Palestine (1929-1939).

I.F. Stone — Journalist.

Asher Susser — Senior Fellow at the Moshe Dayan Center for Middle Eastern Studies at Tel Aviv University.

Mohamed El-Tabii — Journalist and commentator.

King Hussein bin Talal — King of Jordan (1952-1999).

Aymenn Jawad Al-Tamimi — Research Fellow at the Middle East Forum.

Harry Truman — U.S. President (1945-1953).

Rudolf Vrba — Escaped from Auschwitz-Birkenau concentration camp. Co-author of Vrba-Wetzler report.

Timothy William Waters — Associate Director of the Center for Constitutional Democracy at Indiana University Maurer School of Law.

Dr. Chaim Weizmann — President of the World Zionist Organization (1921-1931, 1935-1946). President of Israel (1949-1952).

Alfred Wetzler — Escaped from Auschwitz-Birkenau concentration camp. Co-author of Vrba-Wetzler report.

Robert Gale Woolbert — Research Associate for the Council on Foreign Relations.

Malcolm X — Civil rights activist. Muslim minister.

Jim Zanotti — Specialist in Middle Eastern Affairs for Congressional Research Service.

Mahjoob Zweiri — Director of the Gulf Studies Center at Qatar University.